Fodor's

THAILAND

D0062146

WELCOME TO THAILAND

Thailand conjures images of white sand beaches and cerulean waters, peaceful temples, and lush mountain jungles. In Bangkok, a 21st-century playground, the scent of spicy street food fills the air, and the Grand Palace recalls the country's traditions. Outside the capital, the wonders of the countryside enchant, whether you are elephant trekking in the northern hills, exploring Ayutthaya's splendid ruins, or diving in the waters of the idyllic southern coast. The unique spirit of the Thai people—this is the "land of smiles," after all—adds warmth to any visit.

TOP REASONS TO GO

★ **Beaches:** Pristine strands and hidden coves bring vacation daydreams alive.

★ **Food:** Rich curries, sour-spicy tom yum soup, and tasty pad Thai are worth savoring.

★ **Architecture:** Resplendent stupas and pagodas evoke the glory of ancient kingdoms.

★ **Spas:** Luxurious retreats offer indulgences such as world-renowned Thai massage.

★ **Trekking:** On foot or by elephant, a trek to visit hill tribes is a memorable experience.

★ **Shopping:** Iconic night markets sell everything from hand-carved crafts to handbags.

Fodor's THAILAND

Publisher: Amanda D'Acierno, *Senior Vice President*

Editorial: Arabella Bowen, *Executive Editorial Director*; Linda Cabasin, *Editorial Director*

Design: Fabrizio La Rocca, *Vice President, Creative Director*; Tina Malaney, *Associate Art Director*; Chie Ushio, *Senior Designer*; Ann McBride, *Production Designer*

Photography: Melanie Marin, *Associate Director of Photography*; Jessica Parkhill and Jennifer Romains, *Researchers*

Maps: Rebecca Baer, *Senior Map Editor*; Henry Colomb and Mark Stroud, Moon Street Cartography; David Lindroth *Cartographers*

Production: Linda Schmidt, *Managing Editor*; Evangelos Vasilakis, *Associate Managing Editor*; Angela L. McLean, *Senior Production Manager*

Sales: Jacqueline Lebow, *Sales Director*

Marketing & Publicity: Heather Dalton, *Marketing Director*; Katherine Fleming, *Senior Publicist*

Business & Operations: Susan Livingston, *Vice President, Strategic Business Planning*; Sue Daulton, *Vice President, Operations*

Fodors.com: Megan Bell, *Executive Director, Revenue & Business Development*; Yasmin Marinaro, *Senior Director, Marketing & Partnerships*

Copyright © 2014 by Fodor's Travel, a division of Random House, Inc.

Writers: Alexia Amurazi, Karen Coates, Sophie Friedman, Dave Stamboulis, Simon Stewart, Robert Tilley, Adrian Vrettos

Editor: Róisín Cameron

Production Editor: Jennifer DePrima

13th Edition

ISBN 978-0-7704-3206-5

ISSN 1064-0993

All details in this book are based on information supplied to us at press time. Always confirm information when it matters, especially if you're making a detour to visit a specific place. Fodor's expressly disclaims any liability, loss, or risk, personal or otherwise, that is incurred as a consequence of the use of any of the contents of this book.

SPECIAL SALES

This book is available at special discounts for bulk purchases for sales promotions or premiums. For more information, e-mail specialmarkets@randomhouse.com

PRINTED IN CHINA

10 9 8 7 6 5 4 3 2 1

CONTENTS

Fodor's Features

MAPS

ABOUT
THIS GUIDE

Fodor's Recommendations

Everything in this guide is worth doing—we don't cover what isn't—but exceptional sights, hotels, and restaurants are recognized with additional accolades. **Fodor's Choice★** indicates our top recommendations; and **Best Bets** call attention to notable hotels and restaurants in various categories. Care to nominate a new place? Visit Fodors.com/contact-us.

Trip Costs

We list prices wherever possible to help you budget well. Hotel and restaurant price categories from $ to $$$$ are noted alongside each recommendation. For hotels, we include the lowest cost of a standard double room in high season. For restaurants, we cite the average price of a main course at dinner or, if dinner isn't served, at lunch. For attractions, we always list adult admission fees; discounts are usually available for children, students, and senior citizens.

Hotels

Our local writers vet every hotel to recommend the best overnights in each price category, from budget to expensive. Unless otherwise specified, you can expect private bath, phone, and TV in your room. For expanded hotel reviews, facilities, and deals visit Fodors.com.

Restaurants

Unless we state otherwise, restaurants are open for lunch and dinner daily. We mention dress code only when there's a specific requirement and reservations only when they're essential or not accepted. To make restaurant reservations, visit Fodors.com.

Credit Cards

The hotels and restaurants in this guide typically accept credit cards. If not, we'll say so.

Top Picks

★ **Fodor's** Choice

Listings

⊠ Address
⊠ Branch address
☎ Telephone
🖷 Fax
⊕ Website
✐ E-mail
🖾 Admission fee
🕙 Open/closed times
Ⓜ Subway
⊹ Directions or Map coordinates

Hotels & Restaurants

🏨 Hotel
🛏 Number of rooms
🍽 Meal plans
✕ Restaurant
🪑 Reservations
👔 Dress code
▭ No credit cards
$ Price

Other

⇨ See also
☞ Take note
⛳ Golf facilities

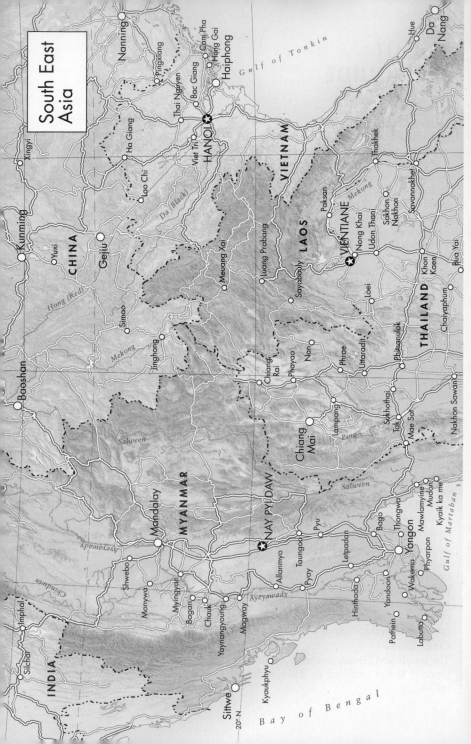

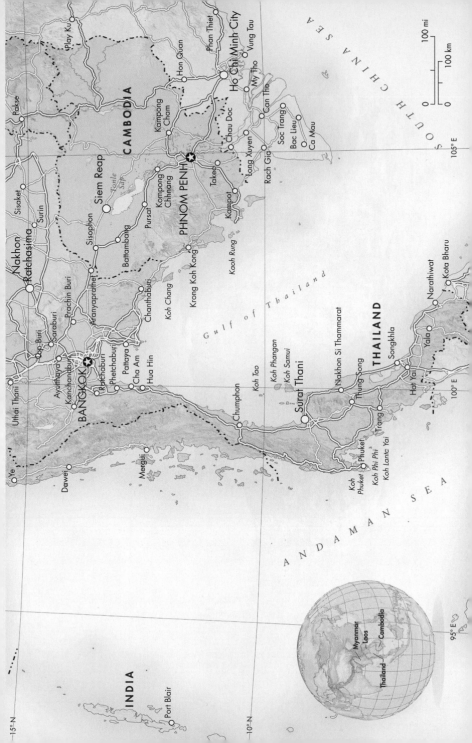

EXPERIENCE THAILAND

WHAT'S
WHERE

The following numbers refer to chapters in the book.

2 Bangkok. In this boom-town of contrasts where old-world charm meets futuristic luxury, you can dine at street stalls or ritzy restaurants, visit the jaw-dropping Grand Palace, and shop at Chatuchak Weekend Market or Pathum-wan's designer malls. At night there are hip mega-clubs and Patpong's famous red lights.

3 Around Bangkok. Petcha-buri has ancient temples and a royal retreat, while Thailand's oldest city, Nakhon Pathom, is home to Phra Pathom Chedi, the world's largest Buddhist structure.

4 The Gulf Coast Beaches. Thailand's two shores have alternating monsoon sea-sons, so there's great beach weather *somewhere* year-round. The Gulf has Pattaya's nightlife and the island trio of Koh Samui (good sailing), Koh Pha Ngan (full-moon revelry), and Koh Tao (diving).

5 Phuket and the Anda-man Coast. Highlights of this spectacular coastal region include Phuket, Phang Nga Bay (James Bond Island), and Krabi, which is a paradise for divers and rock climbers.

6 Chiang Mai. This lovely moat-encircled old city is riddled with temples and markets, and deserves a lingering stop in any tour of the north.

7 Northern Thailand. Chiang Rai is a chilled-out regional center and the gateway to the Golden Triangle, where Laos, Myan-mar (Burma), and Thailand meet. Thailand's first capital, Sukhothai, has carefully restored ruins.

8 Cambodia. No Southeast Asia trip is complete without a visit to the temple ruins of Angkor. The capital, Phnom Penh, is a vibrant city with a thriving food scene. Cross the Tonle Sap (the great lake) to communities living in floating houses, or laze on Cambodia's spectacular coastline.

9 Laos. Photogenic rivers, mountainous countryside, and the dreamy feeling of going back in time are major reasons to make the trip across the border. World Heritage sites Luang Pra-bang and Champasak both have beautiful temples.

10 Myanmar. Bagan's tem-ple ruins rival those of Siem Reap; in nearby Mandalay, the royal palace and Man-dalay Hill offer a rich dose of history. The country's one-time capital, Yangon, is a chaotic, colorful feast for the eyes and the stomach; at quiet Inle Lake, villagers have made their homes on the water.

THAILAND PLANNER

Visitor Information

The website of the Tourism Authority of Thailand (TAT), ⊕ *www.tourismthailand.org*, has details of events, transportation options, destination guides, and more. On the ground, it has branches in many tourist towns, although outside the major cities sporadic opening hours can be frustrating and the information often a little sparse. TAT Call Centre (☎ 1672) offices at Suvarnabhumi Airport are open 24 hours, other city offices open daily 8:30 to 4:30. Check the website for details (⊕ *www.tatcontactcenter.com*). The Tourist Police also have a hotline: ☎ 1155.

National Parks

Thailand has 103 land and marine national parks with many rare species of flora and fauna. The website of the National Park Wildlife and Plant Conservation Department (⊕ *www.dnp.go.th/ index_eng. asp*) is a good resource for getting the lowdown on all facilities (including food and drink vendors), animal-spotting opportunities, notable features like waterfalls, and available cabin rentals or camping areas (you can book accommodation online), plus weather news and updates on which areas are closed.

Travel Agents

Thailand-based travel agents can be useful if you're trying to pack a lot into a short trip. The 24-hour support many agents offer is particularly helpful if things go wrong, such as when internal flights are delayed.

Asian Oasis ☎ *66/8880–97047* ⊕ *www.asian-oasis.com*.
Asian Trails ☎ *66/2626–2000* ⊕ *www.asiantrails.travel*.
Circle of Asia ⊕ *www.circleofasia.com*.
Diethelm Travel ☎ *66/2660–7000* ⊕ *www.diethelmtravel. com*.
Exotissimo ☎ *66/2633–9060 in Bangkok* ⊕ *www. asiantrails.travel*.
Queen Bee ☎ *66/5327–5525* ⊕ *www.queenbeetours. com*.

When to Go

Thailand has three seasons: rainy (June–mid-November), cool (late November–February), and hot (March–May). In central Thailand temperatures average 73°F to 90°F in the rainy season; 68°F to 86°F in the cool season; and 77°F to 95°F in the hot season. The north is a bit cooler, the south a bit hotter.

City sightseeing is okay during the rainy season: downpours lower the temperature, and storms, though fierce, don't last all day. But flooding can make rural areas inaccessible, and it's not a reliable time to plan a trek. The south gets wet by May, but the Gulf islands generally have decent weather until August. Cool-season weather, which is less humid, is perfect for everything: the beaches, Luang Prabang, Angkor Wat, trekking, or exploring Bangkok. But accommodation rates sometimes double, and rooms can be scarce in hot spots like Phuket. The northern nights are chilly in winter—generally in the 50s, but as low as freezing. Pollution in the north can reach dangerous levels toward the end of the dry season in March and April. By April you can find good hotel deals, if you can stand the heat, though some hotels in less touristy areas shut down for the hot season.

1

With Kids

Thais dote on kids, so chances are you'll get extra help and attention when traveling with them, and the experience should be relatively problem-free. Powdered, canned, and pasteurized milk are readily available. Stomach bugs and infections thrive in the tropical climate. Basic cleanliness— washing hands frequently and making sure any cuts are treated with antibacterial ointment and covered—is the best protection against bacteria. Don't let children play with or touch street animals; they may have rabies. Be careful while walking along sidewalks, where open manhole covers and people riding motorbikes can be hazardous.

What It Costs

Despite rapid development, Thailand is still a relatively cheap destination. You'll spend the most getting here: at this writing, round-trip fares start at around $1,000 from the West Coast of the United States and $50 or so more from New York. Traveling within Thailand is a bargain (though becoming less so). You can cross Bangkok in a taxi for $5, while a third-class train to Ayutthaya, 45 miles away, costs $1.50. Budget accommodation runs from as low $4 a night, and even five-star is available at $250. One of the reasons people dine out regularly is the cost: a street-food meal might set you back $1.50, while a blow-out Thai restaurant meal with a beer would be about $15. High-end international dining starts at around $40, though imported wine could easily double that.

Health

Vaccinations aren't required to enter Thailand, but cholera, hepatitis A and B, Japanese encephalitis and tetanus shots are a good idea. The mosquito-borne illness dengue fever is a problem, even in Bangkok, and malaria is present, though not prevalent, in some outlying regions. It's best to drink bottled water. Hospitals and dentists in major cities are of a good standard. They may even accept your health insurance, so carry proof with you (and if you know your insurance doesn't cover you abroad, buy travel insurance before you go, just in case).

Safety

Thailand is generally safe for travelers, but it still pays to take sensible precautions. The political situation has grown unstable in recent years, erupting in violence across Bangkok and Chiang Mai, so be aware of current events. Be careful about accepting food or drinks from strangers, and don't flash money around. Though women generally travel without hassle, it's advisable to avoid walking alone in secluded areas after dark. Pickpockets and con men (and women) patrol some touristy areas. The Royal Thai Police contact number is 191, but better communication will be had with the Tourist Police on their 1155 hotline.

THAILAND TODAY

Today's Thailand . . .

. . . is politically divided. For several years, three major political parties were at violent odds with one another: the TRT, the PPP, and the PAD. In 2005, when Prime Minister Thaksin Shinawatra of the populist Thai Rak Thai (TRT) party was found guilty of tax evasion, the People's Alliance for Democracy (PAD) led demonstrations against him. In 2006 Thaksin was overthrown in a bloodless military coup and fled to London with his wife. A general election in 2007 brought in the People's Power Party (PPP), a civilian government let by Samak Sundaravej. The TRT was banned the same year. But some Thais believed Thaksin still controlled the new government, and PAD demonstrations resumed. In August 2008 demonstrators occupied Government House; in September the government declared a state of emergency and Samak was forced to step down. PPP member Somchai Wongsawat, Thaksin's brother-in-law, replaced Samak but protests continued. In November PAD protesters shut down Bangkok's international airport—a blow to tourism and the economy. The following month the courts removed Somchai from power, ruled that the PPP was guilty of electoral fraud, and ordered the PPP and two affiliated parties to dissolve. In mid-December Abhisit Vejjajiva of the Democrat Party became prime minister. The worst riots in nearly two decades broke out in April and May 2010, when the anti-government "Red Shirts" staged protests across Bangkok. For weeks business and politics remained at a standstill until the military crushed the protests. Hundreds of people were killed and injured as central Bangkok became a war zone. Nothing was resolved. Protesters went home but vowed to continue their fight against the government. In July 2011, Yingluck Shinawatra, the younger sister of Thaksin, led the Pheu Thai Party to victory and became Prime Minister. She has not had a smooth ride. Sporadic protests continue, sometimes erupting into further street violence.

. . . is ethnically diverse. Throughout its history, Thailand has absorbed countless cultural influences, and is home to groups with Chinese, Tibetan, Lao, Khmer, Malaysian, Burmese, and other origins. Migrating tribes from modern-day China, Cambodia, Myanmar, and the Malay Peninsula were the region's earliest inhabitants. Ancient trade routes meant constant contact with merchants traveling

WHAT'S HOT IN THAILAND NOW

Sophisticated Thai architects and designers, historically obsessed with European classical forms, are increasingly turning to their own heritage for inspiration. Hip new hotels and restaurants are now choosing contemporary indigenous fabrics and traditional painted ceramics, not faux Doric columns and Louis XIV furniture.

Young Thais love all things Japanese. Teenagers lounging in Bangkok's Siam Square and other hangouts around the country are filling breaks from school with Japanese comics and tapping their feet to J-Pop, the latest hits from Tokyo. Japanese TV series and accessories are all the rage with the young crowd, as are Thai-language magazines with articles on sushi joints, tea-drinking ceremonies, and the Japanese art of gift-wrapping.

from India, China, and other parts of Southeast Asia. Conflicts and treaties have continued to alter the country's borders—and ethnicity—into the 20th century. Contemporary Thailand's cultural richness comes from its ethnic diversity. Though Buddhism is the predominant religion, Hindu and animist influences abound, and there's a significant Muslim population in the south. Malay is spoken in the southern provinces; Lao and Khmer dialects of Thai are spoken in the northeast; and the hill tribes have their own dialects as well.

. . . is steeped in mysticism. Many Thais believe in astrology and supernatural energy. The animist element of Thai spirituality dictates that everything, from buildings to trees, has a spirit. With so many spirits and forces out there, it's no surprise that appeasing them is a daily consideration. Thais often wear amulets blessed by monks to ward off evil, and they believe that tattoos, often of real or mythical animals or magic spells, bring strength and protect the wearer. Car license plates with lucky numbers (such as multiple nines) sell for thousands of baht; important events, such as weddings, house moves, and even births, are arranged, when possible, to fall on auspicious days, which are either divined by shamans or consist of lucky numbers. Newspapers solemnly report that politicians have consulted their favorite astrologers before making critical policy decisions. Businesses erect shrines to powerful deities outside their premises, sometimes positioned to repel the power of their rivals' shrines.

. . . is fun-loving. Thais are guided by a number of behavior principles. Many, such as *jai yen* (cool heart) and *mai pen rai* (never mind), are rooted in the Buddhist philosophies of detachment, and result in a nonconfrontational demeanor and an easygoing attitude. Perhaps most important of all is *sanuk* (fun). Thais believe that every activity should be fun—work, play, even funerals. Of course, this isn't always practical, but it's a worthy aim. Thais enjoy being together in large parties, making lots of noise, and—as sanuk nearly always involves food—eating. With their emphasis on giving and sharing, these activities also reflect elements of Buddhist teaching; being generous is an act of merit making, a way of storing up points for protection in this life and in future lives.

In a high-end housing craze, developers are building sky-scraping condos in Bangkok and tourist destinations like Phuket and Pattaya. But there's a lot of debate over who will buy all them—rents start at around $300 a month (close to the average Thai salary) and skyrocket from there.

Foreigners, who aren't allowed to buy land but can own condo units, can only fill 49% of the total area of a building, so developers are offering significant discounts to Thais. Still, there may not be enough money around to fill all these pricey new homes, and many pundits were warning of a crash even before the global economic downturn in the fall of 2008.

TRANSPORTATION, THAI STYLE

With reasonably priced internal flights and reliable train and bus service, getting around Thailand can be efficient and straightforward. Taxis are often happy to travel distances of around 160 km (100 miles), and you can hire a car and driver for a fraction of what it would cost back home. But several quirkier modes of transport have true local color (though sometimes not much regard for safety).

Longtail Boat
The slim longtail boat gets its name from the huge V8 car engine that protrudes on an elongated pole from the back of the craft. Catch one of these brightly colored, 40-foot monsters to navigate the river in Bangkok for a bumpy, noisy, and exhilarating ride. When the going gets choppy, passengers huddle behind plastic sheeting. Garlands wrapped around the prow, dedicated to Mae Yanang, the goddess of travel, are also there for your protection.

Motorcycle
In cities there are so many motorcycles skittering between cars it seems every resident must own one. And no wonder: in the gridlocked traffic they're often the only way to get anywhere on time. Consequently, people frequently abandon taxis or cars and hop on motorcycle taxis (called "motorcy"), the drivers of which are notorious for two things: shady dealings and scary driving. Yet it's not uncommon to see entire families piled helmetless on a single vehicle. Women passengers usually ride sidesaddle, with both hands clasped between their knees to preserve modesty—a balancing act of high skill and great faith.

Samlor
The quaint *samlor* (literally meaning "three wheels") is a variation on a rickshaw: the driver pedals a three-wheeled bicycle, pulling an open carriage with room for two in back. It's a slow, quiet, and cheap way to travel short distances, and samlors are still common on the streets of provincial towns. Often, street vendors will attach the carriage to the front of the vehicle instead of the back and use it to display their wares.

Songthaew
Songthaews are converted pickup trucks with two benches in the back and a metal roof. Thais ride songthaews both within a town and between towns. They aren't cheaper than local buses, but they are more frequent and will sometimes drive slightly out of their way to drop you nearer your destination. Just stick out your hand as one passes, negotiate a price, and climb in back. Songthaews are often packed, and if all the seats are taken, Thais will just climb on the back and hang onto the railings. It's a bumpy ride on rural roads; for longer trips, you'll be more comfortable on the bus.

Tuk-Tuk
Although the *tuk-tuk* is practically Thailand's icon, it is in fact a Japanese import. This three-wheeled motorized taxi with open sides is a logical progression from the samlor. It's an atmospheric—that is, fume-filled, hot, and noisy—way to get around city streets, and a more pleasant ride on rural lanes, although you have to hunker down in the seat to actually see much, and you'll definitely feel every bump in the road. Tuk-tuks come in a variety of styles, including bullet-nosed models in Ayutthaya, elongated "hot rods" on the Eastern Gulf, and elevated versions nicknamed "Skylabs" in the northeast.

TOP EXPERIENCES

Beach Life

Thailand's beach culture is world class. The famous Full Moon Parties on Koh Phangan heave with all-night raves; you may be happier lazing under coconut palms with a gentle massage between dips, or having a beach barbecue with fresh seafood on Koh Chang.

Chatuchak Market

There are almost 10,000 stalls at Chatuchak Market, which operates in northern Bangkok each weekend. One of the world's biggest markets, it's great for textiles, jewelry, books, clothes, food, plants, Buddha statues, and pretty much anything else you can think of.

Diving

For unforgettable underwater theater, head to one of Thailand's top dive sites, where facilities range from beginner courses of a few hours to live-aboard boats that stay out several days. Koh Tao, in the Gulf of Thailand, is popular, but the best locations are the Similan and Surin islands, where you meet nomadic island-hopping people known as Sea Gypsies and swim with whale sharks, clownfish, and leatherback turtles.

Muay Thai

With fighters allowed to inflict damage with anything but the head, *muay thai* (Thai boxing) is reputed to be the most brutal of all martial arts. But it's also a fine spectacle of ritual, in which boxers initially perform a *wai kru* (a bow to their trainer) followed by a *ram muay* (literally, "boxing dance") to warm up, seal the ring from evil spirits, and honor their families and gods.

Phuket Vegetarian Festival

In the ninth lunar month, usually October, religious devotees known as *Ma Song* walk on hot coals and drive a variety of metal objects through their bodies. These feats are believed to deflect evil, and are part of a Chinese Buddhist–Taoist period of spiritual cleansing, when adherents abstain from meat, alcohol, and sex.

Songkran Festival

Each April, during Thai New Year celebrations (Songkran), the country becomes a three-day street party of water fights. Participants go armed with cups, buckets, and water guns, and tourist centers like Khao San Road are packed with hordes of drenched merrymakers. Traditionalists complain that it's a far cry from the festival's origins—it began as a genteel bathing ritual to honor elders. For those seeking less raucous revelry, neighboring Cambodia and Laos also celebrate the holiday, in a slightly gentler manner. If you really want quiet, spend the new year in Phnom Penh, which empties as residents head to their home villages for the holiday. Cambodians, too, will sprinkle you with water—and then perhaps invite you home to eat a New Year's feast with the family.

Snorkeling

Some of Thailand's most spectacular scenery lies beneath its crystalline waters. The marine parks of the Similan Islands have made Thailand's diving world famous but there is plenty to see all along the coastline, even with just a snorkel.

Street Food

Rich and poor mingle over bowls of soups and curries at Thailand's street stalls. Many vendors are famous for a particular dish, whether pad thai; the spicy, sour shrimp soup *tom yum goong*; or duck with noodles. It's a wonderful journey of discovery, where you can chomp on seemingly anything, from deep-fried flowers to a mixed bag of insects.

THAILAND TOP ATTRACTIONS

Ancient Sukhothai

(A) Sukhothai is recognized as the first independent kingdom in what would eventually become Thailand. Its 13th-century ascendancy is referred to as the country's golden age: religion was codified; a writing system was introduced; and the arts flourished. The city's impressive ruins are preserved in Sukhothai Historical Park.

Chiang Mai

(B) Chiang Mai was the capital of the ancient kingdom of Lanna, which grew to prominence in the 13th century. Even after it became part of Siam, Lanna was largely independent until the early 20th century, due to its mountainous terrain, and it retains a distinct culture. Chiang Mai was located on historically important trade routes, and still has a varied ethnic population and significant old temples. It's the gateway for jungle and hill-tribe treks.

The Grand Palace

(C) Bangkok's Grand Palace and the adjacent royal temple, Wat Phra Kaew, appear like a fairy-tale castle of golden domes and glittering spires within white fortified walls. They were the centerpieces of the new capital when it was built more than 200 years ago, and they still form Bangkok's most impressive architecture. Wat Phra Kaew contains the Emerald Buddha, Thailand's most revered religious image.

The Ruins of Ayutthaya

(D) Thailand's second capital, destroyed by the Burmese in 1767, Ayutthaya had 2,000 gold temples and a population greater than London in its heyday. The Ayutthaya Historical Park has many Thai- and Khmer-style ruins that evoke the city's lost grandeur.

Khao Sok National Park

(E) One of the most spectacular landscapes in Thailand, remote Khao Sok rewards the effort of the journey with lush

greenery and towering mountain ranges. While the chances of seeing a tiger are remote, there's plenty of other wildlife in Khao Sok National Park, and the chance to soak up this unique jungle atmosphere shouldn't be missed.

Koh Samui

(F) This small island in Thailand's Western Gulf is best appreciated by those who linger over its many charms. Explore the interior by car, indulge in some seriously luxurious spa treatments and revel in the chilled-out nightlife that has made this an enduring favorite of those seeking the quintessential Thai beach vacation.

Wat Po

(G) Wat Po is Bangkok's oldest temple, and is sometimes called the country's first university. It has lessons in history and astrology inscribed on the walls, and people still come here to learn traditional medicine. Of the many buildings and images on site, pride of place goes to the 147-foot-long Reclining Buddha, which shows the Buddha ascending into Nirvana after reaching enlightenment.

Ao Phang Nga

(H) One of the most arresting natural sights in Thailand is formed by the jungle-clad limestone karsts and islands that rise like towers around the waters of Ao Phang Nga, a marine national park close to Phuket. The most famous of the islands is Koh Ping Kan, which was featured in the film *The Man With The Golden Gun,* and is hence better known as James Bond Island.

THAI MASSAGE

Thai massage, once only available at temples or tiny shophouses, has become much more popular in recent years. You'll find masseurs and masseuses at work all over the country—in bustling markets, at boutique spas, and in jungle hideaways.

Today massage is a pleasant and relaxing part of Thai culture, and you may see locals giving casual shoulder, back, and arm massages to their friends. But *nuad paen boran* (ancient massage) is also a branch of traditional Thai medicine. Originally it was taught and performed in Thai temples, which were historically places of physical—as well as spiritual—healing.

Traditional massage combines acupressure, reflexology, yoga, and meditation. Practitioners believe that 10 energy lines, called *sip sen,* link the body's meridian points. Blocked lines may lead to physical or spiritual ailments. Massage is thought to unblock the energy lines, clearing toxins and restoring balance to the body.

Where to Get Massage

Outdoors: At markets, on beaches, and at temple fairs, masseurs and masseuses set up shop alongside street vendors. On the beach you'll lie on a mat; at the market you'll probably be seated in a streetside plastic chair set up for foot massage. Prices vary—a one-hour foot massage might cost as little as B100 at a temple fair or B250 on a popular beach.

Resort and Hotel Spas: For five-star pampering, head to upscale hotels and resorts, whose luxurious, tranquil spas offer an extensive array of massages, including Swedish massage, plus other treatments like tai chi and new-age therapies. Expect to pay at least B2,500 for an hour-long massage at a top Bangkok hotel—a lot by Thai standards, but still less than what you'd pay back home.

Restrooms: In a few clubs and bars (both gay and straight), some visitors are alarmed when men's restroom attendants start massaging their shoulders as they stand at the urinal. If you don't like it, ask them to stop (*mai ow, kup*). Otherwise, a B10 tip is welcome.

Shophouses: These ubiquitous massage parlors offer no-frills service. Expect to share a room with other patrons (curtains separate the cots); if you're getting a foot massage, you may be seated in the shop window. There's often music, TV, or chatter in the background. A two-hour massage costs at least B400. Though many shophouses are legitimate businesses, some offer "extra" sexual services. To avoid embarrassing misunderstandings, steer clear of treatments with suggestive names, like "special" or "full body" massage. You can also ask the concierge at your hotel to recommend a reputable place.

Temples: Some temples still have massage facilities, and massages are often provided to the elderly at no charge. At Wat Po in Bangkok you can receive a massage in an open-air pavilion for B420 an hour.

Urban Spas: A growing phenomenon, urban spas are more upscale than shophouse parlors. They're often located in old Thai houses, with contemporary Asian-style private treatment rooms. You'll have more options here: simple Thai massage is still on the menu (for B1,000 and up per hour), along with body scrubs, facials, and various other treatments.

The Moves

Thai massage is an extremely rigorous, sometimes painful experience, and people with back, neck, or joint problems should not undergo it without seeking medical advice first. But it can also be

very pleasurable. It's okay to ask if you want softer pressure (*bow bow, kup/ka*).

Massage artists primarily work with their hands, but they sometimes use elbows, knees, and feet to perform deep-tissue kneading. They occasionally apply balm to ease muscle aches, but they traditionally don't use oil. They may push and pull your body through a series of often contorted yogic stretching movements. There's normally a set sequence: You start lying on your back and the massage artist will work from your feet through your legs, arms, hands, and fingers. Then you turn over for legs, back, neck, head, and face. At the end the masseur will stretch your back across his or her upturned knees. Some people find that they have better flexibility after a massage, in addition to relief from muscular aches.

Massages are booked by the hour, and aficionados say two hours is best to get the full benefit. In most shophouse parlors the masseuse will first bathe your feet and then give you a pair of pajamas to wear. Spas have shower facilities. You can remove your underwear or not—whatever makes you comfortable.

The standard varies enormously. If you find a masseur or masseuse you like, take his or her name (sometimes they'll have an identifying number as well) and return to that person the next time.

Tipping
Tipping is customary. There aren't hard-and-fast rules about how much to tip, but B50 to B150 at a shophouse, and 10% to 20% in a spa, is about right.

Alternative Massage
Foot massage: This popular treatment is typically an hour-long massage of the feet and lower legs, usually with oil or balm. Foot massage is based on the reflexology

principle that manipulating pressure points in the feet can relieve disorders in other parts of the body.

Oil Massage: Most parlors and spas now offer oil massage, which is a gentler treatment based on Swedish massage and doesn't involve stretching. Masseurs will sometimes use oils with delicious aromas, such as lemongrass or jasmine.

Learn the Art of Massage
Bangkok's Wat Po is an acknowledged instruction center with an almost 200-year pedigree. A five-day, 30-hour course costs B9,500. You can get more information on their website, ⊕ *www.watpomassage. com*. The Thai Massage School in Chiang Mai (⊕ *www.tmcschool.com*) is also good. Many shophouse parlors in both cities now also offer courses (a one-hour session at a Khao San Road shophouse costs about B250).

IF YOU LIKE

Ancient Cities and Ruins

Prior to its current incarnation as a unified modern state, Thailand consisted of a series of smaller kingdoms. While some of these kingdoms were destroyed when neighboring armies invaded, others merely lost influence as they merged with other Siamese cities and remained beautifully intact.

Angkor Wat. Yes, it's actually in Cambodia, not Thailand—but this massive ancient temple and its surrounding complex, built by a succession of Khmer kings between the 9th and 13th century, which has miraculously survived the ravages of time and the Khmer Rouge, is Southeast Asia's most spectacular architectural site.

Ayutthaya. After a number of unsuccessful attempts, the Burmese sacked and brutally destroyed this city, which was the second Siamese capital, in 1767. The redbrick foundations of the Old City and its remaining stupas and wats are now beautiful ruins to explore.

Chiang Mai. The Old City of Chiang Mai has continued to develop so that today its streets include bars and minimarts. Regardless, a stroll through the back alleys, both inside and outside the old walls, reveals centuries-old masterpieces of Thai art and architecture.

Sukhothai. Thailand's first capital, Sukhothai was established in 1238 and saw more than 100 years of prosperity and artistic development known as Thailand's golden age. Sukhothai began to lose its regional influence in the 14th century, ultimately falling under Ayutthaya's control. Its Khmer- and Hindu-influenced sculpture and architecture are relatively unspoiled by the ages.

Beaches

Thailand's clear turquoise waters and soft, white, palm-fringed sands are stunning, and they offer plenty more to do than sunbathing and sunset strolls.

Koh Phi Phi. These six islands have some of the best diving and snorkeling in Thailand. Crowds flock to Maya Bay both for its spectacular scenery and because it's where the movie *The Beach* was filmed; Loh Samah Bay is more secluded.

Koh Samui. The beaches of Samui offer something to suit most travelers' moods: bustling Chaweng Beach, the fishermen's village of Bophut, the scented oils of spa retreats, and the briny aromas of beachfront shacks. Serious divers head for neighboring island Koh Tao.

Nang Cape/Railay Beach. These four connected beaches are only accessible by boat, but it's an easy 15-minute trip from Krabi Town on the mainland. Two of the beaches, Tonsai and East Railay, are rock-climbing centers; West Railay is known for its gorgeous sunsets; and beautiful Phra Nang has a cave with phallic offerings left for a fabled princess.

Phang Nga Bay. This national marine park is an eerily beautiful landscape dotted with limestone islands and karsts that rise like vertical sculptures from the sea. Many people come to kayak, to visit James Bond Island, or explore sea caves with prehistoric rock art.

Similan Islands. These nine islands in the Andaman Sea, part of the Mu Koh Similan National Marine Park, are considered Thailand's best dive sites. Visibility is exceptional, and encounters with whale sharks are not uncommon. The isolation heightens the appeal.

Shopping

The first time you set foot in one of Thailand's ubiquitous markets you'll be absolutely mesmerized by the variety of goods, from hand-carved figurines to polo shirts with the alligator slightly askew. In larger cities, malls sell international brands at prices significantly lower than in Singapore or Hong Kong.

Bangkok's Chinatown. In Bangkok, if you ask where you can buy something, the answer is usually, "Try Chinatown." Anything goes in this labyrinthine quarter, equally flush with gold shops and grubby souvenir stalls.

Bangkok's Shopping Streets. Bangkok's glitziest mega-malls are located on a section of Thanon Rama I and Thanon Ploenchit. A skywalk links the malls, including upscale Siam Paragon, Siam Center, and Central World (which was burned in the 2010 riots but soon reopened with no sign of the turmoil), allowing you to bypass the heat and congestion of the busy streets below. There's a lot more than clothing here, too—great bookshops, fabrics, electronics, Ferraris, iPads. Siam Paragon mall even has an aquarium where you can scuba dive.

Chatuchak Weekend Market. Also called "JJ," this is one of the world's largest markets. Every weekend, thousands of locals and tourists flock to northern Bangkok to navigate the mazes of stalls shopping for pets, clothing, souvenirs, and almost anything else imaginable.

Night Markets. Put on your best bargaining face and hit the streets of Silom, Patpong, Sukhumvit, and Khao San for the best night-market shopping in Bangkok. Most towns, including Chiang Mai, Pattaya, and Hua Hin, have great souvenirs available after dark.

Trekking

Thailand's mountain forests would be good for trekking for their rugged beauty alone, but this terrain is also home to hill tribes—Karen, Hmong, Yao, and others—that maintain their traditional languages and cultures. The more remote the village, the more authentic the experience (and the more challenging the trek).

Chiang Mai. The city is one of two northern centers for both easygoing and adventurous tours to hill tribe villages, some of which accommodate overnight visitors. Elephant rides and bamboo rafting are often included. From here it's easy to get to departure points in Pai and Mae Hong Son.

Chiang Rai. Another northern gem for soft-adventure enthusiasts, Chiang Rai has many tour operators and individual guides. Lahu, Akha, and Lisu villages are all easily accessible from here. There's a growing number of eco-conscious initiatives, and it pays to shop around, both here and in Chiang Mai. Guesthouses can often recommend guides.

Kanchanaburi. Though Kanchanaburi itself is a touristy town, the surrounding area offers some of the most untouched landscape in the country. Parts of Sai Yok National Park, with its Kitti's Hog-nosed Bats (the world's smallest mammal), are easy to reach from Kanchanaburi, as is Erawan Waterfall.

Luang Prabang. Treks in northern Laos transport you back in time. In some villages the only apparent connections to the outside world are discharged Vietnam War–era bombs used as water troughs—and cell phones, solar panels, and micro hydropower systems that generate enough power to run a light bulb or a TV.

WHERE TO STAY BEACHSIDE

Thailand's beaches are so inviting you might be tempted to sleep under the stars. And you can do that if you like, but there are tons of other surfside lodging choices. So even if you're on a budget, there's no need to camp out—or move inland.

Budget Bungalows

Warm weather and beautiful palm-fringed beaches mean you can spend just a few dollars on a room and still be in paradise. **Somewhere Else** on Koh Lanta has funky huts and friendly staff; **Smile Bungalows** on Koh Pha Ngan has great ocean views. At the cheapest places you'll share a bathroom, have cold showers, and sleep to the whirring of a rickety fan (unless the power's out).

Private Houses

Rental houses are much less pricey than resort villas and come in all sorts of styles. A few websites to check are ⊕ *www.thailandretreats.com*; ⊕ *www. worldvacationrentals.net*; and ⊕ *www. raileibeachclub.com*. Newspapers like the *Bangkok Post* and the *Pattaya Mail* often list rentals and agents.

Rangers Huts

Many national parks, including the Surin Islands and Similan Islands, have accommodation in rangers' huts, bookable through the national park authorities (⊕ *www.dnp.go.th*) or Thai Forest Booking (⊕ *www.thaiforestbooking.com*). Prices start at around B300 per person in a very basic hut that sleeps up to 10 people.

Resorts

Eco: At earth-friendly resorts, the emphasis is on using natural materials and preserving resources and land. **Chumphon Cabana Beach Resort** (⊕ *www.cabana. co.th*) uses bacteria to clean wastewater and produce organic fertilizer.

Luxury Living: There's no shortage of exclusive beach resorts, and though these getaways have traditionally been part of large chains, smaller players—some of them independent—are becoming more common. A number of resorts, such as **Pimalai Resort** on Koh Lanta (⊕ *www. pimalai.com*) and **Amanpuri Resort** on Phuket (⊕ *www.amanpuri.com*), are offering villa-type accommodations for those who want resort amenities but more privacy than hotel rooms afford. Spas like **Chiva-Som** in Hua Hin (⊕ *www. chivasom.com*) are luring pop stars and models through their doors.

Thai Style: In Thailand, the term *resort* is often used for any accommodation that's not in an urban area—it doesn't necessarily mean there are extra facilities. That said, some of these lower-key Thai-style resorts are worth checking out. Though they're not as sumptuous as luxury resorts, they're often tastefully executed and come with a moderate price tag. At friendly **Sarikantang** on Koh Pha Ngan (⊕ *www.sarikantang.com*), the priciest bungalows are around $175 in high season; **Black Tip Dive Resort and Watersport Center** on Koh Tao (⊕ *www. blacktipdiving.com*) runs a great diving school.

Stilt Houses

Bungalows and houses built on stilts above the water make romantic, exotic accommodations. Some are custom built for tourist luxury; others are rustic but still breathtaking.

GREAT ITINERARIES

HIGHLIGHTS OF THAILAND: BANGKOK, BEACHES, AND THE NORTH

10 days

To get the most out of your Thailand vacation, decide what you'd particularly like to do—party in the big city, lie on the beach, go trekking, and so on—and arrange your trip around the region best suited for that activity. Every region has so much to offer, you'll barely scratch the surface in two weeks. However, if you don't know where to start, the following itinerary will allow you see three very different areas of the country without requiring too many marathon travel days.

Almost every trip to Thailand begins in Bangkok, which is a good place to linger for a day or two, because some of the country's most astounding sights can be found in and around the Old City. You'll probably be exhausted by the pace in a few days, so head down to the beach, where you can swim in clear seas and sip cocktails on white sands. After relaxing for a few days, you'll be ready for more adventures, so head to Thailand's second city, Chiang Mai. The surrounding countryside is beautiful, and even a short stay will give you a chance to visit centuries-old architecture and the Elephant Conservation Center.

Days 1 and 2: Bangkok

Experience the Old Thailand hiding within this modern megalopolis by beginning your first day with a tour of Bangkok's Old City, with visits to the stunning Grand Palace and Wat Po's Reclining Buddha. Later in the day, hire a longtail boat and spend a couple of hours exploring the canals. On the river you'll catch a glimpse

of how countless city people lived until not long ago, in wooden stilt houses along the water's edge. For a casual evening, head to the backpacker hangout of Khao San Road for a cheap dinner, fun shopping, and bar-hopping. For something fancy, take a ferry to the Oriental Hotel for riverside cocktails and dinner at Le Normandie.

Start Day 2 with the sights and smells of Chinatown, sampling some of the delicious food along the way. Then head north to silk mogul Jim Thompson's House, a fine example of a traditional teak abode, with antiques displayed inside. If you're up for more shopping, the malls near Siam Square are great browsing territory for local and international fashion, jewelry, and accessories. The malls also have a couple of movie theaters and a bowling alley—Siam Paragon even has an aquarium with sharks. Later, grab a meal at Ban Khun Mae, then if you've any energy left, head over to Lumphini Stadium for a Thai boxing match.

Days 3 to 5: The Beaches

Get an early start and head down to the beach regions. Your choices are too numerous to list here, but Koh Samui, Phuket, and Krabi are all good bets if time is short because of the direct daily flights that connect them with Bangkok. Peaceful Khao Lak is only a two-hour drive from the bustle of Phuket, and Koh Chang is just a couple of hours by ferry from Trat Airport. Closer to Bangkok, Koh Samet and Hua Hin are three hours away by road. But if you have at least three days to spare, you can go almost anywhere that piques your interest—just make sure the time spent traveling doesn't overshadow the time spent relaxing.

Samui, Phuket, and Krabi are also good choices because of the variety of activities each offers. Though Samui has traditionally been backpacker terrain, there are now a number of spa retreats on the island. You can also hike to a waterfall, careen down a treetop zip line, or take a side trip to Angthong National Marine Park. Phuket is the country's main diving center, offering trips to many nearby reefs. There's great sailing around Phuket, too. On Krabi you can enjoy a relaxing afternoon and cheap beachside massage at gorgeous Phra Nang Beach; go rock-climbing on limestone cliffs; kayak from bay to bay; and watch the glorious sunset from nearby Railay Beach.

Day 6: Chiang Mai

Though it shouldn't be a terribly taxing day, getting to Chiang Mai requires some travel time, so you should get an early start. Wherever you are, you'll most likely have to make a connecting flight in Bangkok; if you're pinching pennies, this actually works in your favor, because it's cheaper to book two separate flights on a low-cost airline than to book one ticket from a more expensive airline "directly" from one of the beach airports to Chiang Mai—you'll have to stop in Bangkok anyway. If you play your cards right, you should be in Chiang Mai in time to check into your hotel and grab a late lunch. Afterward, stroll around the Old City, and in the evening go shopping at the famous night market.

Day 7: Chiang Mai

Spend the day exploring the city and visiting the dazzling hilltop wat of Doi Suthep. Ring the dozens of bells surrounding the main building for good luck. On the way back to Chiang Mai, drop in at the seven-spired temple called Wat Chedi Yot or check out the pandas at the zoo. Chiang Mai is famous for its massage and cooking schools, so if you're interested in trying a class in either—or just getting a massage—this is the place to do it.

Day 8: Lampang

An easy side trip from Chiang Mai, Lampang has some beautiful wooden-house architecture and a sedate way of getting around, in pony-drawn carriages.

A short ride out of town is northern Thailand's most revered temple, Wat Phra That Lampang Luang, which contains the country's oldest wooden building. At the Elephant Conservation Center, between Chiang Mai and Lampang, you can take elephant rides, watch the pachyderms bathing in the river, and hear them playing in an orchestra. Proceeds go to promoting elephant welfare.

Day 9: Around Chiang Mai

Your last day in the region can be spent in a variety of ways. Shoppers can takes taxis to the nearby Hang Dong district with furniture and art shops as well as handicrafts villages such as Baan Tawai; or to Lamphun, which has some pre-Thai-era temple architecture from the 7th century. Active types can head to Doi Inthanon National Park, where there are great views across the mountains toward Myanmar, plus bird-watching, hiking to waterfalls, and wildlife that includes Asiatic black bears.

Day 10: Bangkok

Head back to Bangkok. If you're not flying home the moment you step off the plane from Chiang Mai, spend your final day in the city doing some last-minute shopping at the city's numerous markets, such as Pratunam, Pahuraht, and the weekend-only Chatuchak. Or just relax in Lumphini Park.

TIPS

Temples and royal buildings, such as Bangkok's Grand Palace, require modest dress (no shorts or tank tops).

Take a taxi to the Grand Palace or an Express Boat to nearby Tha Chang Pier. Wat Po is a 10-minute walk south. Hire a longtail boat to get to the canals and back at Tha Chang Pier. Khao San Road is a short taxi ride from the pier.

Bangkok Airways owns the airport at Koh Samui, and flights there are relatively expensive due to taxes, but if you book online directly from Bangkok Airways, you might get reduced airfare. Nok Air and AirAsia also offer cheap flights to nearby Surat Thani or Nakhon Si Thammarat, from which you can take a ferry to the island.

Late November through April is the best time to explore the Andaman Coast. For the Gulf Coast there's good weather from late November until August.

Hotels in the south are frequently packed during high season and Thai holidays, so book in advance.

A great alternative to heading north to Chiang Mai is to use Bangkok as a base to explore the Central Plains. Sukhothai Historical Park isn't as famous as Ayutthaya, but it is even more spectacular, and it and the surrounding region would make an excellent two- to three-day side trip from Bangkok.

ECOTOURISM IN THAILAND

Though the tourism boom has been great for Thailand's economy, it has had many negative effects on Thai culture and natural resources. These problems, which range from water pollution to sex tourism to the transformation of hill-tribe villages into virtual theme parks, are difficult to rein in. The good news is that a growing number of tour operators and hotel proprietors are addressing these issues, and are therefore worthy of your support.

Planning Your Trip

Though the worldwide eco trend is catching on in Thailand, truly eco-friendly companies are still thin on the ground. Many businesses describe themselves as "eco," so ask some tough questions about what the company does to preserve the environment and help local communities before you book. And as always, don't be afraid to shop around. Your critical eye will help raise standards. Here are a few questions you might ask.

Accommodations: Ask whether the hotel or resort is energy efficient. Does it use alternative power sources? What steps does it take to conserve water and reduce waste? If it's a beach hotel, how does it handle sewage? Does it recycle? Is the building made with any natural or recycled materials? Does it employ members of the local community? Does it contribute any percentage of profits to health, education, or wildlife preservation initiatives?

Elephant Treks: It's important to find out how tour operators treat their elephants. You might ask how many hours a day the elephants work, and whether you'll be riding in the afternoon heat, or resting until it's cooler.

Hill-Tribe Tours and Other Expeditions: How much the operator knows about the village or wilderness area you'll be visiting is often telling, so ask for details. Also, does the operator work with any NGOs or other interest groups to protect the culture and/or the environment?

Resources

The umbrella group **Thailand Community Based Tourism Institute** (⊕ *www.cbt-i.org*) is a good place to start. It provides information about tour agencies and community programs that promote culturally sensitive tourism.

"Voluntourism"—travel that includes an effort to give back to local communities—is a growing trend in Thailand, and a number of organizations are now offering educational travel programs that incorporate some volunteer work. Lots of businesses are offering eco-minded tours. Here are a few reputable resources that will get you started.

The **Educational Travel Center** (⊕ *www.etc.co.th*) organizes cultural exchanges and ecotours, as well as volunteer programs at a variety of destinations.

The **Himmapaan Foundation** (⊕ *himmapaan.com*) is a reforestation initiative near Chiang Mai. Participants work alongside tribespeople and forestry experts to promote biodiversity.

Lost Horizons (⊕ *www.losthorizonsasia.com*) runs several thematic ecotourism trips in Thailand, including jungle treks, kayaking, beach retreats, and animal conservation.

North by North East Tours (⊕ *www.north-by-north-east.com*) works throughout the Mekong region, offering homestays and volunteer work such as building schools, teaching English, and providing medical care in Thailand, Laos and elsewhere along the Mekong.

Wild Asia's Map of Hope (⊕ *www.wildasia.org/main.cfm/RTI/RT_Map_of_Hope*) is a regional map showing the nonprofit group's recommended responsible travel and tour operators.

Animal Rights

Though preserving wildlife habitats is a priority in Thailand's national parks, illegal poaching is still rampant. There's such high demand for tiger products (not only skins, but also teeth, bones, and penises, which are used as charms or in traditional medicines) that tigers are now virtually extinct in Thailand.

Elephants are revered in Thailand, where they have a long history as laborers. But mechanization has made elephants' traditional timber-hauling jobs obsolete, and elephant handlers (*mahouts*) now rely on elephant shows, treks, and other tourism-related business for their livelihood. Unfortunately, these endeavors often lead to mistreatment. Yet if there's no work, handlers can't afford the 550 pounds of food and 60 gallons of water an elephant consumes each day; malnutrition is another problem for Thai elephants. Organizations like **PeunPa** focus on broader issues, including educating village communities on the importance of wildlife conservation and how to combat problems like illegal trafficking of endangered species.

What You Can Do

Whatever kind of trip you're planning, there are a few simple things you can do to ensure that you're part of the solution, not part of the problem.

Don't litter. Sadly, garbage is a common sight on Thailand's once-pristine beaches. Litter is hazardous to marine life. You can help by disposing of your rubbish properly; you can also pay a little extra for

biodegradable glass water bottles. If you plan to travel regularly in the developing world, consider buying a hand-pump water purifier, available at many sporting-goods stores for $20 and up. You can make your own clean water wherever you go, instead of generating a trail of disposable water bottles.

Don't disturb animal and plant life. Whether you're trekking or snorkeling, be as unobtrusive as possible. Don't remove plants or coral for souvenirs, and don't feed fish or other animals, even if your guide says it's okay.

Respect local customs. Though it may seem like a matter of etiquette, demonstrating respect for a culture is part of ecotourism. Thais tend to be exceedingly tolerant of Western behavior, but tourists who are ignorant about basic customs have a negative effect on the communities they encounter. Take a little time to learn about major cultural mores (especially those related to Buddhism). Thais will appreciate your efforts.

BUDDHISM IN THAILAND

Almost 95% of Thailand's population is Buddhist (4% is Muslim, and the remaining 1% is Taoist, Confucianist, Hindu, Christian, and Sikh). Buddhism is considered one of the foundations of Thai nationhood, represented on the flag by two white bars between red bars for the people and a central blue bar for the monarchy. Thai kings are required to be Buddhist: King Rama IV spent 27 years as a forest monk before ascending the throne in 1851. The country has 400,000 monks and novices, many of whom take alms bowls into the street each day to receive food from laypeople.

Origins

Buddhism first showed up in Thailand in the Dvaravati Mon kingdom between the 6th and 9th centuries. The Dvaravati capital of Nakhon Pathom, 55 km (34 miles) west of Bangkok, was the region's first Buddhist center. In the 14th century, Buddhism became the official religion of Sukhothai, the first Thai kingdom. In 1997 it was written into the constitution as the state religion of modern Thailand. There are two main branches of Buddhism in Asia: Theravada, found today in Thailand, Myanmar, Cambodia, Laos, and Sri Lanka; and Mahayana, which spread north from India to China, Korea, Vietnam, and Japan. The Mahayana movement emerged from Theravada, the original teachings of the Buddha, in the 1st century. It's a less austere doctrine than Theravada, which stresses devotion to study and meditation. *(For more on Buddhism ⇨ The Buddha in Thailand.)*

Practice and Rituals

Thai children learn Buddhist teachings (*Dhamma*) in school, and most males will at some time ordain as a *bhikku* (monk). Some only do this for a few days, but many join the monkhood each July for the three-month Rains Retreat (sometimes referred to as Buddhist Lent, when monks are required to remain in their wats for the duration of the rainy season) in July, which is marked by major festivals, such as the Candle Parade, in Nakhon Ratchasima. Joining the monkhood, even for a short time, is such an important event that employers grant time off for the purpose. Women wanting to devote their lives to Buddhism may become white-robed nuns, known as *mae chi*. However, women aren't allowed to be officially ordained in Thailand, though a growing feminist lobby questions their lower status. Although most Thais don't visit temples regularly, wats are the center of community life and sometimes serve as schools, meeting halls, and hospitals. Alongside spiritual guidance and funeral rites, monks provide ceremonies in houses and businesses to bring good fortune, and will even bless vehicles to keep drivers safe from accidents or cell phones to keep them ringing with business. They are also traditional healers, and created many of the herbal remedies that now form the basis for spa treatments.

Modern Concerns

Many commentators fear that modernization is eroding Thailand's traditional Buddhist values, and that material rewards will overshadow the Buddha's teachings. It's true that greater personal wealth has brought consumerism to the middle classes, and young Thais are exposed to Western culture through foreign education, TV, and the Internet. However, Buddhism continues to be a dominant influence on the national psyche.

COUPS & THE KING
THAILAND'S TURBULENT HISTORY
by Karen Coates

Thais share a reverence for their king, Bhumibol Adulyadej, who has been the nation's moral leader and a unifying figure since 1946. Thais are also united by a deep pride in their country, a constitutional monarchy and the only Southeast Asian nation never colonized by Europeans. But this hasn't stopped political turmoil from roiling beneath the surface and erupting.

Though northeastern Thailand has been inhabited for about 2,500 years, it wasn't until 1238 that Thai princes drove the Cambodian Khmers out of central Thailand and established Sukhothai, the first centralized Thai state. There was conflict again in the late 14th century, when the rival state of Ayutthaya conquered Sukhothai. After over 400 years of power, Ayutthaya in turn was defeated by the Burmese in the late 18th century, and the Thais established a new capital in Bangkok.

As European influence in Southeast Asia grew, Thailand alternated between periods of isolation and openness to foreign trade and ideas. Western-style democracy was one idea that took hold in the early 20th century. But since then a pattern has emerged in Thai politics: a prime minister is elected, allegations of corruption surface, the public protests, and the leader is ousted.

King Rama V
(1853–1910)
and family

TIMELINE
4,000–2,000 BC Rice first cultivated in Thailand

1238
Sukhothai kingdom
founded

1350
Ayutthaya kingdom
founded

| 4000 BC | 1200 | 1300 | 1400 |

(top) Pottery found at Ban Chiang; (left) stone face at Bayon in Angkor Thom, Cambodia; (bottom) Khmer elephant-shaped box.

Bronze & Rice

4000–2000 BC

Scientists think that northeastern Thailand was a hotbed for agricultural innovation. In fact, the Mon people from modern-day Myanmar who settled in Ban Chiang may have been Asia's first farmers. Archaeologists have found ancient pottery, bronze rings, spearheads, bracelets, and axes.

Great Migrations

500–1400

Historians believe the Thais' ancestors were the ethnic Tai people of southern China. The Tai migrated south into modern-day Thailand in waves, but the biggest southern push came after the Mongols invaded their kingdom in the 13th century. The fleeing Tai settled in the Mekong River Valley, inventing elaborate agricultural systems to farm rice. Around this time, the Khmers of what is today called Cambodia were extending the Angkor empire west into Thailand.

Sukhothai & the Golden Age

1238–1438

In 1238 chieftains established the first Thai kingdom at Sukhothai in central Thailand, kicking out the Khmer overlords. The Sukhothai kingdom united many Thai settlements and marked the beginning of a prosperous era when, legend has it, the rivers were full of fish, and the paddies were lush with rice. In the late 13th century, King Ramkhamhaeng created a writing system that is the basis of the modern Thai alphabet.

1511
Portuguese arrive

1782|
Capital moves to Bangkok
1767
Ayutthaya falls to Burmese invaders

1500 | 1600 | 1700 | 1800

1

IN FOCUS COUPS & THE KING

(left) Interior of Wat Po, Bangkok; (top) Royal jewelry from Ayutthaya; (bottom) Buddha statue from Ayutthaya.

Ayutthaya Kingdom

1350–1767

King Ramathibodi founded the kingdom of Ayutthaya, 45 miles up the Chao Phraya River from Bangkok, in 1350 and took over Sukhothai 25 years later. The king made Theravada Buddhism the kingdom's official religion and established the Dharmashastra, a legal code with roots in Hindu Indian texts. Ayutthaya, a city of canals and golden temples, became wealthy and prominent.

European Influence

1511–1800s

The Portuguese were the first Europeans to arrive in Thailand, establishing an embassy in Ayutthaya in 1511. But they brought more than ambassadors: The Portuguese also brought the first chilies to the country, making a huge contribution to Thai cuisine.

Over the following centuries of European trade and relations, Thailand's kings charted a sometimes tenuous course of autonomy as their neighbors were colonized by the Portuguese, Dutch, English, and French.

Burmese Invasion & New Beginnings

1767–1809

In 1767 the Burmese sacked Ayutthaya, destroying palaces, temples, artwork, and written records. But within two years, General Phraya Taksin ran out the Burmese and established a new capital at Thonburi, which is today a part of Bangkok. Taksin became king but was forced from power and executed in 1782. After this coup, Buddha Yodfa Chulaloke the Great (known as Rama I) took control. He moved the capital across the river, where he built the Grand Palace in the image of past Thai kingdoms.

(left) King Mongkut
with queen;
(top) *The King and I*;
(bottom) 19th-century
tin coin.

The King and I & Beyond

1851–1931

In 1862, Anna Leonowens, an English schoolteacher, traveled to Bangkok with her son to serve as royal governess to King Mongkut's wives and children. Leonowens's memoirs inspired Margaret Landon's controversial novel *Anna and the King of Siam*, which in turn was the basis for the well-known Broadway musical *The King and I* and the subsequent film.

Thais were deeply offended by the film, which portrays the king as foolish and barbaric; *The King and I* was consequently banned in Thailand. A 1999 remake, *Anna and the King*, followed Leono-wens's version of the story more closely, but Thais, who are extremely devoted to their royal family, still found this version culturally insensitive.

Mongkut (or Rama IV) earned the nickname "Father of Science and Technology" for his efforts to modernize the country. He signed a trade treaty with Great Britain, warding off other colonial powers while opening Thailand to foreign innovation.

After Rama IV's death in 1868, his son Chulalongkorn became king. Also called "Rama the Great," Chulalongkorn is credited with preserving Thailand's independence and abolishing slavery.

Constitutional Era

1932–41

Thailand moved toward Western-style democracy when young intellectuals staged a bloodless coup against King Prajadhipok (Rama VII) in 1931. Thailand's first constitution was signed that year and parliamentary elections were held the next. In the new system—a constitutional monarchy similar to England's—the king is still head of state, but he doesn't have much legal power.

In 1939 the government changed the country's name from Siam to Thailand. The new name refers to the Tai people; Tai also means "free" in Thai.

1939 Siam renamed Thailand | 1942 Alliance formed with Japan
1944 Phibun ousted
1932 First elections held | 1946 Rama IX crowned | 1959–75 Vietnam War
1925 | 1950 | 1975

1

IN FOCUS COUPS & THE KING

(left) Bridge over the River Kwai; (top) U.S. pilot in Vietnam; (bottom) Postage stamp c. 1950 featuring king Bhumibol Adulyadej.

World War II

1941–46

In 1941, Japan helped Thailand win a territorial conflict with France over parts of French Indochina (modern-day Cambodia, Laos, and Vietnam.) Later that year, the Japanese demanded free passage through Thailand so that they could attack Malaya and Burma. In 1942, under the leadership of Phibun, a military general elected prime minister in 1938, Thailand formed an alliance with Japan.

The Japanese conquered Burma and began to construct the Thailand–Burma "Death Railway," so named because over 100,000 Asian forced-laborers and Allied POWs died while working on it. Meanwhile, an underground resistance called Seri Thai gathered strength as Thais turned against the Phibun regime and the Japanese occupation. Phibun was ousted in 1944 and replaced by a government friendly to the Allies.

In 1946 King Rama VIII was murdered. He was succeeded by his brother, the beloved Bhumibol Adulyadej (Rama IX), who is currently the world's longest-serving head of state.

The Vietnam War

1961–75

While publicly staying neutral, the Thai government let the U.S. Air Force use bases throughout Thailand to bomb Laos and Cambodia between 1961 and 1975. Meanwhile, Bangkok and Thailand's beaches became playgrounds to thousands of soldiers on leave. The Westernization of Thai popular culture has roots in the Vietnam era, when restaurants and bars catered to beer- and Coke-drinking Americans.

TIMELINE
1973–81 Violence against students and activists

1997
Asian Financial Crisis

2001
Thaksin
Shinawatra
elected

2006
Thaksin
outsted

1975   1985   1995   2005

(left) Protesters occupying the Government House garden. Bangkok, September 3rd 2008; (top) Banner demanding that ousted P.M. Thaksin Shinawatra and his wife return to Thailand to stand trial; (bottom) Samak Sundaravej.

1973–PRESENT

Unrest

A new democracy movement gained force in 1973, when protesters charged the streets of Bangkok after students were arrested on antigovernment charges. On October 14, protests erupted into bloody street battles, killing dozens. More violent outbreaks occurred on October 6th, 1976, and again in "Black May" of 1992, when a military crackdown resulted in more than 50 deaths.

In 2001, billionaire Thaksin Shinawatra was elected prime minister on a platform of economic growth and rural development. The year after he was elected, he dissolved the liaison between the Muslim southern provinces and the largely Buddhist administration in Bangkok, rekindling bloody unrest after years of quiet. The situation escalated until insurgents attacked a Thai army arsenal in early 2004; at this writing, over 3,500 people have been killed in frequent outbursts of violence in southern Thailand.

Meanwhile, Thaksin and his family were railed with corruption and tax-evasion charges. In September 2006 he was ousted by a junta, which controlled the country until voters approved a new constitution and elected Samak Sundaravej prime minister. Samak took office in early 2008, but in September, after months of protests, the Constitutional Court demanded his resignation because he had accepted money for hosting a televised cooking show (it's illegal for a prime minister to have other income). Parliament quickly elected Somchai Wongsawat, Thaksin's brother-in-law, to replace Samak.

The protests did not end there, since many Thais believed Somchai's government to be aligned with Thaksin's. In late 2008 Somchai was forced to step down, and Parliament voted in Abhisit Vejjajiva, leader of the opposition party. In early 2011 the government conceded that violence in southern Thailand was on the increase. Thailand's long voyage towards democracy is ongoing.

BANGKOK

WELCOME TO BANGKOK

TOP REASONS TO GO

★ **The Canals:** They don't call it "Venice of the East" for nothing. Sure, boat tours are touristy, but the sights, from Khmer wats to bizarre riverside dwellings, are truly unique.

★ **Street Food:** Bangkok may have the best street food in the world. Don't be afraid to try the weird stuff—it's often fresher and better than the food you'd get at a hotel restaurant.

★ **Shopping Bargains:** Forget Hong Kong and Singapore: Bangkok has the same range of high-end designer goods at much lower prices.

★ **Sky-High Sipping:** "Bar with a view" is taken to the extreme when you sip martinis in open-air spaces atop lofty towers.

★ **Temple-Gazing:** From the venerable Wat Po to the little wats that don't make it into the guidebooks, Bangkok's collection of temples is hard to top.

1 The Old City. The Old City is home to opulent temples like Wat Po.

2 Banglamphu. North of the Old City, Banglamphu is mostly residential; it's known for the famous backpacker street Khao San Road, but it has much more to offer than just touristy kicks with fellow foreigners.

3 Dusit. North of Banglamphu is this royal district, where wide avenues are lined by elegant buildings.

Dusit Park is one of the city's most appealing green spaces.

4 Thonburi. Across the river from the Old City is Thonburi, a mostly residential neighborhood, where you can find Wat Arun.

5 Chinatown. East of the Old City is Chinatown, a labyrinth of streets within which you'll find an impressive array of Buddhas for sale, spice boutiques, and open-air fruit and vegetable

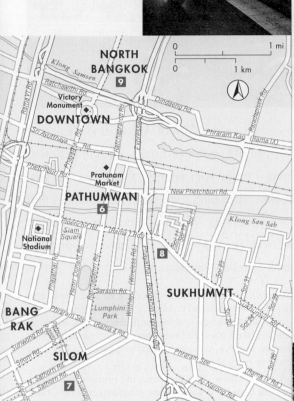

GETTING ORIENTED

Bangkok's endless maze of streets is part of its fascination and its complexity—getting around a labyrinth is never easy. Although the S-curve of the Chao Phraya River can throw you off base, it's actually a good landmark. Most of the popular sights are close to the river, and you can use it to get swiftly from one place to another. Also look at the Skytrain and subway to help you navigate and get around quickly.

markets that are among Bangkok's most vibrant.

6 Pathumwan. This area can be considered Bangkok's "downtown," and is home to the city's greatest collection of shopping malls as well as the popular Pratunam clothing market.

7 Silom and Bang Rak. In this busy area you'll find Lumphini Park, Bangkok's largest park and a pleasantly

green space to escape from the harried pace of the city. With plenty of bars and restaurants, the Silom area also includes the infamous red-light district of Patpong. At the east end of Bang Rak lies the Chao Phraya River, home to some of the city's most opulent hotels.

8 Sukhumvit. Sukhumvit Road is a bustling district filled with high-end restaurants, hotels, and shops, as

well as the red-light areas of Nana and Soi Cowboy.

9 Northern Bangkok. This area includes the Victory Monument and all points north, such as the famous Chatuchak Weekend Market, the northern bus station of Mo Chit, and the budget air terminal at Don Muang.

Updated
by Dave
Stamboulis

Bangkok, also known as the City of Angels and Venice of the East, will hit you like a ton of bricks. It's hot, polluted, and chaotic, and it thrills with energy; there's such a vast array of sightseeing, shopping, and eating possibilities that you'll have little time to rest. When you do find a moment, pamper yourself with spa treatments, skyline-view bars, luxurious hotels, and excellent restaurants.

The city is a mesmerizing blend of old and new, East and West, and dizzying contradictions. Temples and red-light districts, languid canals and permanent gridlock, streetside vendors and chic upscale eateries, all make their home together, all at the same time. Bangkok rarely fails to make an impression, and yes, you might need to go spend a few days on the beach to recover from it all.

Although Bangkok is not known for jaw-dropping tourist attractions, it does have an endless supply of worthwhile pilgrimages. The Grand Palace, Wat Phra Kaew, and the Emerald Buddha are tops on every visitor's itinerary, and lesser-known temples, such as Wat Benjamabophit, the golden stupa of Wat Sakhet, and Wat Suthat, are all worthy of a stop. Besides temples, there are plenty of other interesting niches and touring possibilities to fit just about every interest. Take in a venom extraction and python feeding show at the Queen Saowapha Snake Farm, or go to the nearby Jim Thompson House to learn all about the famed Thai silk industry. If architecture is your forte, there is the Suan Pakkard Palace with its antique teak house collection, and the even more astounding Vimanmek Palace, which contains the world's largest golden teak building. Bangkok's Chinatown merits at least a day on every travel itinerary—be sure to check out the sprawling labyrinthine Flower and Thieves markets.

Thai food is unrivaled for spice, taste, and variation. From multicourse meals to small street vendors, the one constant here is fresh and delicious at every level. You can have superlative roast duck or wonton noodles on a street corner for lunch and then be dining on world-class chef creations in the Oriental or Shangri-La hotels for supper. It doesn't have to be all spicy Thai either, as Bangkok is home to excellent French, Italian, and other world cuisines, and you need a few years just to make a dent in all the options that are available.

PLANNING

WHEN TO GO

Late October to late February is the best time to visit. The city is at its coolest (85°F) and driest. In April the humidity and heat build up to create a sticky stew until the rains begin in late June.

GETTING HERE

Air Travel: Bangkok's Suvarnabhumi International Airport (pronounced "Su-wan-na-poom") is about 30 km (18 miles) southeast of the city. About 25 km (16 miles) north of the city is the former international airport, Don Muang. It offers many domestic flights and has recently become the terminal for budget airline flights. There's a free shuttle service connecting the two airports.

Inexpensive and available around the clock, taxis are the most convenient way to get between downtown and the airport. ■TIP→ Don't forget to have some baht on hand, as you'll need it to pay for your taxi. Get a taxi by heading to one of the taxi counters on Level 1, near Entrances 3, 4, 7, and 8. State your destination to the dispatcher at the counter, who will lead you to your taxi. Allow 30 to 90 minutes to get downtown, depending on traffic. A trip downtown will run about B250 to B300, plus any expressway tolls. ■TIP→ Avoid drivers who insist on a fixed price or refuse to turn on their meters.

The Airport Link rail system is your best option during rush hour. Costing B150, the express train takes 15 minutes to reach Makkasan Terminal, next to the Phetchaburi MRT subway stop. A local train that takes 23 minutes and costs B65 takes you to the Phaya Thai BTS Station, convenient for those staying on the Skytrain line. The entrance to the system is on the airport's lower level.

The Airport Bus Express is also an option, and for one person it costs less than a taxi (for two it's about the same as a taxi). The bus runs from 5 am to midnight. Head to the Airport Bus Counter on Level 1, near Entrance 8. The service, which costs B150, operates four routes; ask at the counter which route to take to reach your hotel. Route AE1 serves the Silom neighborhood. Route AE2 serves Khao San Road and the Old City. Route AE3 serves Sukhumvit, and Route AE4 serves Hua Lumphong, the city's main railway station.

Bus Travel: Bangkok has three major terminals for buses headed to other parts of the country. The Northern Bus Terminal, called Mo Chit, serves Chiang Mai and points north. The Southern Bus Terminal, in Thonburi, is for buses bound for Hua Hin, Koh Samui, Phuket, and points south and west. The Eastern Bus Terminal, called Ekkamai, is for buses headed to Pattaya, Rayong, and Trat provinces. There are also minivans to nearby destinations like Hua Hin, Cha Am, Pattaya, Kanchanaburi, and elsewhere, leaving from Victory Monument.

Bus companies generally sell tickets on a first-come, first-served basis. This is seldom a problem, as the service is so regular that the next bus is sure to depart before long. The air-conditioned orange 999 buses are the most comfortable, along with any services from Nakhon Chai Air. Blue VIP buses, though not quite as luxurious, are the next-best option.

Train Travel: The central train station in Bangkok is Hualamphong, located near Chinatown and accessible by subway. Trains from here leave to all destinations in the country.

GETTING AROUND

Bangkok is large, so remember to pace yourself, and take a break to escape the midday heat. The traffic is unbearable, so do yourself a favor and skip driving in the city.

BOAT TRAVEL

The Chao Phraya River is a great way to bypass the traffic that clogs most of the city. Express boats can get crowded, especially at peak times, but they're still far more pleasant than sitting in the back on a taxi as it navigates bumper-to-bumper traffic.

BUS TRAVEL

For a fare of B8 on non-air-conditioned buses and B12 to B25 on air-conditioned ones, you can travel virtually anywhere in the city. Air-conditioned microbuses charge B25. Most buses operate from 5 am to around 11 pm, but a few routes operate around the clock. You can pick up a route map at most bookstalls for B35, or just to ask locals which bus is headed to your destination.

SKYTRAIN AND SUBWAY TRAVEL

Although the BTS Skytrain covers just a fraction of the capital (it bypasses the Old City and Dusit, for example), it is surprisingly convenient for visitors, with routes above Sukhumvit, Silom, and Phaholyothin roads. ■TIP➜ **If you are traveling between two points along the route, the Skytrain is by far the best way to go.** Rates run between B15 and B40. Like the Skytrain, the MRT subway covers only a small section of the city, but it's a great way to get from the city center out to the train stations. The subway runs daily from 6 am until midnight. Adult fares are B15 to B40. Although the Skytrain and subway are separate entities and use different fare and ticketing systems, the two connect at three points: Sala Daeng Station and Silom Station, Asok Station and Sukhumvit Station, and Mo Chit Station and Chatuchak Station.

TAXI TRAVEL

Taxis can be an economical way to get around, provided you don't hit gridlock. Most taxis have meters, so avoid those that lack one or claim that it is broken. The rate for the first 1 km (½ mile) is B35, with an additional baht for every 55 yards after that; a 5 km (3 miles) journey runs about B60. ■TIP➜ **Ask your concierge to write the name of your destination and its cross streets in Thai.**

HEALTH AND SAFETY

For a city of its size, Bangkok is relatively safe; however, you still need to practice common sense. Don't accept food or drinks from strangers, as there have been reports of people being drugged and robbed. If you plan to enjoy a massage in your hotel room, put your valuables in the safe. Bangkok is no more dangerous for women than any other major city, but it's still best to avoid walking alone at night (take a taxi if you're out late).

⚠ Beware of hustlers who claim that your hotel is overbooked. They'll try to convince you to switch to one that pays them a commission. Also avoid anyone trying to sell you on an overpriced taxi or limo. Proceed to the taxi stand; these taxis will use a meter.

Contact the Tourist Police first in an emergency. For medical attention, Bunrungrad Hospital and Bangkok Nursing Hospital are considered the best.

Emergency Services Ambulance ☎ *1669.* **Fire** ☎ *199.* **Police** ☎ *191.* **Tourist Police** ☎ *1155.*

Hospitals Bangkok Nursing Home Hospital ✉ *9/1 Convent Rd., Silom* ☎ *02/686–2700* ⊕ *www.bnhhospital.com* Ⓜ *Subway: Silom; Skytrain: Sala Daeng.* **Bumrungrad Hospital** ✉ *33 Sukhumvit, Soi 3, Sukhumvit* ☎ *02/667– 1000* ⊕ *www.bumrungrad.com* Ⓜ *Subway: Sukhumvit; Skytrain: Ploenchit.*

MONEY MATTERS
Major banks all exchange foreign currency, and most have easily accessible ATMs that accept foreign bank cards. Currency-exchange offices are common, but don't wait until the last minute. It's distressing to try to find one when you're out of baht.

VISITOR INFORMATION
Tourist Authority of Thailand. The Tourist Authority of Thailand, open daily 8:30 to 4:30, has more colorful brochures than hard information, but it can supply material on national parks and out-of-the-way destinations. A 24-hour hotline provides information on destinations, festivals, and the arts. You can use the hotline to register complaints or request assistance from the Tourist Police. ✉ *1600 New Phetchaburi Rd., Ratchathewi* ☎ *02/250–5500* ⊕ *www.tourismthailand.org* Ⓜ *Subway: Phetchaburi.*

EXPLORING BANGKOK

The Old City is a major destination for travelers, as it's home to opulent temples like Wat Po and Wat Phra Kaew. Across the river is Thonburi, a mostly residential neighborhood, where you can find Wat Arun. At the northern tip of the Old City is Banglamphu, one of Bangkok's older residential neighborhoods. It's best known now for Khao San Road, a backpacker hangout, though the neighborhood has much more to offer, especially when it comes to street food. North of Banglamphu is Dusit, the royal district since the days of Rama V.

East of the Old City is Chinatown, a labyrinth of streets with restaurants, shops, and warehouses. Farther down the Chao Phraya River is bustling Silom Road, one of the city's major commercial districts. Patpong, the city's most famous of several red-light districts, is also here. Bang Rak is home to some of the city's leading hotels: the Mandarin Oriental, the Peninsula, the Royal Orchid Sheraton, and the Shangri-La.

To the north of Rama IV Road is Bangkok's largest green area, Lumphini Park.

Continue north and you reach Sukhumvit Road, once a residential area. More recently, Thong Lor, farther east along Sukhumvit, has become the "in" neighborhood for those want to see and be seen. The Nana and Asok areas of Sukhumvit are now home to the even busier red-light entertainment districts (Nana and Soi Cowboy) than Patpong.

THE OLD CITY

The Old City, which is adjacent to Banglamphu on the north and Thonburi across the Chao Phraya River on the west, is the historic heart of Bangkok where you can find most of the ancient buildings and the major tourist attractions. Because of the city's conscious decision to preserve this historic area, it's the largest part of Bangkok to escape constant transformation. Much of the residential sections look run down, but the whole area is safe, and it's one of the best in the city for a stroll.

The Grand Palace and other major sights are within a short distance of the river and close to where express boats stop. There is a Skytrain station next to a boat pier downriver from the Old City as well, making the Chao Phraya convenient no matter where you're staying.

Of course, the magnificence of the sights, and the ease in reaching them, make them rather crowded. During rainstorms is about the only time you find few people at the sights. ■TIP➜ Arrive at the Grand Palace early in the morning, when the weather is cooler and the crowds are more manageable.

Democracy Monument and October 14 Monument. One of Bangkok's biggest and best-known landmarks, the Democracy Monument was built after the military overthrew the absolute monarchy in 1932 and the country became a constitutional monarchy. Just to the south of the road that circles the Democracy Monument is the October 14 Monument, honoring Thais killed during the student-led uprising against the military government that started on October 14, 1973. Tributes to those killed in October 1976 and May 1992, in other protests against military rule, are also part of the monument. Although mostly written in Thai, it's a sobering sight, especially so close to the Democracy Monument. Traffic is always whizzing about, the gate is often closed, and there seem to be no regular hours, but there

PHONY GUIDES

One downside to the surge of tourism in this area is the presence of phony tour guides, who will most likely approach you by offering tips about undiscovered or off-the-beaten-path places. Some will even tell you that the place you're going to is closed, and that you should join them for a tour instead. Often their "tours" (offered at too-good-to-be-true prices) include a "short" visit to a gem shop for more than a bit of arm-twisting. The situation got bad enough in the mid-1990s that the government stepped in and distributed fliers to passengers on inbound flights warning of these gem scams.

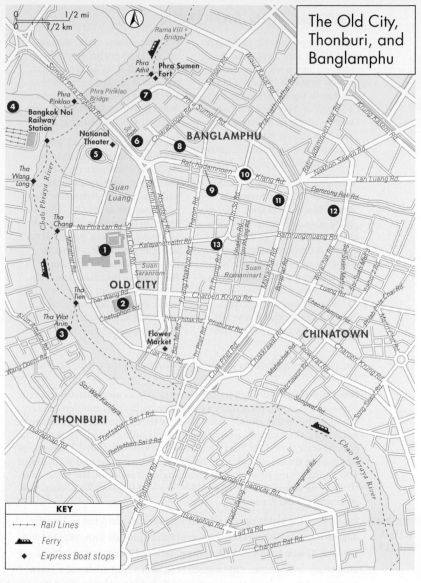

The Old City,
Thonburi, and
Banglamphu

2

TWO DAYS IN BANGKOK

You could spend weeks in Bangkok and not get bored. Especially if you only have a few days, planning around Bangkok's traffic is a must, so look for sights near public transportation or close enough to one another to visit on the same day, and don't assume that taxis will be faster than the Skytrain. You can see a lot in a few days.

Start your first day with the most famous of all Bangkok sights, the Grand Palace. In the same complex is the gorgeously ornate Wat Phra Kaew. Not far south of the Grand Palace is Bangkok's oldest and largest temple, Wat Po, famous for its enormous Reclining Buddha and for being a great place for a traditional Thai massage. Later, head toward Banglamphu to take the river walk from Pinklao Bridge

to Santichaiprakarn Park. That will put you on Phra Athit Road, where you can find many good restaurants and bars. If you feel up for more after that, take a tuk-tuk the short distance to Khao San Road for some shopping and more strolling.

The next day, start out in Chinatown, where you can spend hours browsing the food and spice markets, peeking into temples and shops, and just absorbing the atmosphere. Next, work your way to the Chao Phraya River and take a *klong* (canal) tour, which will give you a glimpse of the fascinating canal life in Bangkok. Then, if it's a weekend head to Kukrit Pramoj Heritage House; if it's a weekday, visit Jim Thompson's House. Take the Skytrain in the evening to Sukhumvit Road, where there are many good restaurants.

are painting exhibitions at times. ⊠ *Ratchdamnoen Rd., at Thanon Din Soi.*

National Gallery. Although it doesn't get nearly as much attention as the National Museum, the gallery's permanent collection (modern and traditional Thai art) is worth taking the time to see; there are also frequent temporary shows from around the country and abroad. To get to the gallery, walk down Na Phra That Road, past the National Theater and toward the river. Go under the bridge, then turn right and walk about 100 yards; it's on your left. The building used to house the royal mint. ⊠ *Chao Fa Rd., Old City* ☎ *02/282–0637* ✉ *B100* ☉ *Wed.–Sun. 9–4.* Ⓜ *Skytrain: Hua Lamphong.*

NEED A BREAK?

Taking in all the sights can be exhausting, especially on a hot and muggy day. Fortunately, two parks by the Grand Palace provide some respite from the heat. **Sanam Luang** is north of the palace and Wat Phra Kaew. Trees offer shade and benches offer a place to sit with a cold drink and a snack from one of the vendors. You can also buy bread if you want to feed the numerous pigeons. **Suan Saranrom**, across from the southeast corner of the palace, is smaller but just as pleasant. It's surrounded by well-kept government buildings. In the late afternoon you can join the free community aerobics sessions.

National Museum. There's no better place to acquaint yourself with Thai history than the National Museum, which also holds one of the world's best collections of Southeast Asian art. Most of the masterpieces from the northern provinces have been transported here, leaving up-country museums looking a little bare. You have a good opportunity to trace Thailand's long history, beginning with the ceramic utensils and bronze ware of the Ban Chiang people (4000–3000 BC). ■TIP➔ There are free guided tours in English on Wednesday and Thursday; they're usually given at 9:30 am. ⊠ *Na Phra That Rd., Old City* ☎ *02/224–1333* ⊠ *B200* ◷ *Wed.–Sun. 9–4.* Ⓜ *Skytrain: Hua Lamphong.*

Wat Po (*Temple of the Reclining Buddha*). The city's largest wat has what is perhaps the most unusual representation of the Buddha in Bangkok. The 150-foot sculpture, covered with gold, is so large it fills an entire viharn. Especially noteworthy are the mammoth statue's 10-foot feet, with the 108 auspicious signs of the Buddha inlaid in mother-of-pearl. Many people ring the bells surrounding the image for good luck.

Behind the viharn holding the Reclining Buddha is Bangkok's oldest open university. A century before Bangkok was established as the capital, a monastery was founded here to teach traditional medicine. Around the walls are marble plaques inscribed with formulas for herbal cures, and stone sculptures squat in various postures demonstrating techniques for relieving pain. The monks still practice ancient cures, and the **massage school** is now famous. A Thai massage (which can actually be painful, though therapeutic) lasts one hour and costs less than B200 (you should also tip B50 to B100) Appointments aren't necessary—you usually won't have to wait long if you just show up. Massage courses of up to 10 days are also available.

At the northeastern quarter of the compound there's a pleasant three-tier temple containing 394 seated Buddhas. Usually a monk sits cross-legged at one side of the altar, making himself available to answer questions (in Thai, of course). On the walls, bas-relief plaques salvaged from Ayutthaya depict stories from the *Ramakien,* a traditional tale of the human incarnation of Vishnu. Around the temple area are four tall chedis decorated with brightly colored porcelain. Each chedi represents one of the first four kings of the Chakri Dynasty. Don't be perturbed by the statues that guard the compound's entrance and poke good-natured fun at *farang* (foreigners). These towering figures, some of whom wear farcical top hats, are supposed to scare away evil spirits—they were modeled after the Europeans who plundered China during the Opium Wars. ⊠ *Chetuphon Rd., Old City* ☎ *02/225–9595* ⊠ *B100* ◷ *Daily 8:30–5.* Ⓜ *Skytrain: Hua Lamphong.*

Wat Rachanada (*Temple of the Metal Castle*). This wat was built to resemble a mythical castle of the gods. According to legend, a wealthy and pious man built a fabulous castle, Loha Prasat, from the design laid down in Hindu mythology for the disciples of the Buddha. Wat Rachanada, meant to duplicate that castle, is the only one of its kind remaining. Outside there are stalls selling amulets that protect you from harm or increase your chances of finding love. These souvenirs tend to be expensive, but that's the price of good fortune. ⊠ *Mahachai Rd.*

TUK-TUKS

Though colorful three-wheeled tuk-tuks are somewhat of a symbol of Bangkok, they're really only a good option when traffic is light—otherwise you can end up sitting in gridlock, sweating, and sucking in car fumes. They're also unmetered and prone to overcharging; unless you are good at bargaining, you may well end up paying more for a tuk-tuk than for a metered taxi. Some tuk-tuk drivers drive like madmen, and an accident in a tuk-tuk can be scary.

⚠ Watch out for unscrupulous tuk-tuk drivers who offer cut-rate tours, then take you directly to jewelry and clothing shops that pay them a commission. If a trip to Bangkok does not seem complete without a tuk-tuk adventure, pay half of what the driver suggests, insist on being taken to your destination, and hold on for dear life.

near Ratchadamnoen Rd., Old City ☎ *02/224–8807* ✉ *Free* ⊙ *Daily 9–5* Ⓜ *Skytrain: Hua Lamphong.*

Wat Saket. A well-known landmark, the towering gold chedi of Wat Saket, also known as the Golden Mount, was once the highest point in the city. King Rama III began construction of this temple, but it wasn't completed until the reign of Rama V. On a clear day the view from the top is magnificent. Every November, at the time of the Loi Krathong festival, the temple hosts a popular fair with food stalls and performances. ⚠ To reach the gilded chedi you must ascend an exhausting 318 steps, so don't attempt the climb on a hot afternoon. ✉ *Chakkaphatdi Phong Rd., Old City* ☎ *02/621–0576* ✉ *B20* ⊙ *Daily 8–5* Ⓜ *Skytrain: Hua Lamphong.*

Wat Suthat and the Giant Swing. Wat Suthat is known for the 19th-century murals in the main chapel, but the numerous statues around the spacious tiled grounds are quite striking, too. There are rows of horse statues along one side of the wat. The Giant Swing (Sao Ching Cha) just outside Wat Suthat (but not part of it) was replaced to great fanfare in late 2006 for the first time in a generation. But it will not be used as it was in ancient times for Brahmanic ceremonies. Apparently, several people were killed in a swing-related accident in the early 20th century, and it has been out of service since. It is in a public area that is free to visit. ✉ *Bamrung Muang Rd., Old City* ☎ *02/222–6935* ✉ *B20* ⊙ *Daily 8–5* Ⓜ *Skytrain: Hua Lamphong.*

BANGLAMPHU

In the northern part of the Old City, Banglamphu offers pleasant strolls, interesting markets, and Khao San Road, one of the world's best-known backpacker hubs. Khao San has become a truly international street, with visitors from dozens of countries populating the scene year-round, and an equally diverse selection of restaurants and street vendors. During high season 10,000 people a day call the area home.

Khao San Road. This thoroughfare, whose name means "Shining Rice," has been the heart of the international backpacking scene for decades.

In the past few years it's made an attempt at trendiness with new out-door bars, a glut of terrible Western restaurants, and hotels sharing the space with the ubiquitous low-budget guesthouses, some of which aren't actually budget anymore. It has become popular with Thais as well, who frequent the bars and watch the farang.

Sunset marks the start of a busy street market. ■ **TIP→ The road is closed to traffic at night, making early evening the best time to stroll or sit back and people-watch.** The frenetic activity can, depending on your perspective, be infectious or overwhelming. During Songkran, the Thai New Year in mid-April, Khao San turns into one huge wet-and-wild water fight. Only join the fun if you don't mind being soaked to the bone.

Phra Athit Road. Take a leisurely stroll along this riverfront walk between the National Museum and Santichaiprakarn Park. The concrete walk-way along the Chao Phraya is cooled by the river breeze and offers views of the life along the water. **Phra Sumen Fort,** one of the two remaining forts of the original 14 built under King Rama I, is in San-tichaiprakarn Park. The park is a fine place to sit and watch the river. Phra Athit Road itself is an interesting street with buildings dating back more than 100 years. It has some good cafés, and at night the street comes alive with little bars and restaurants hosting live music. It's a favorite among university students.

DUSIT

More than any other neighborhood in the city, this area north of Bangl-amphu seems calm and orderly. Its tree-shaded boulevards and elegant buildings truly befit the district that holds Chitlada Palace, the offi-cial residence of the king and queen. The neighborhood's layout was the work of King Rama V, the first of the country's monarchs to visit Europe. He returned with a grand plan to remake his capital after the great cities he had visited. Dusit is a sprawling area, but luckily the major attractions—the Dusit Zoo and the numerous museums on the grounds of the Vimanmek Teak Mansion—are close together.

Chitlada Palace. When in Bangkok, the king resides at this palace across from Dusit Park. Although it's closed to the public, the outside walls are a lovely sight, especially when lighted to celebrate the king's birth-day on December 5. The extensive grounds are also home to a herd of royal white elephants, though it's difficult to see them. ⊠ *Ratchawith Rd. and Rama V Rd., Dusit* Ⓜ *Skytrain: Victory Monument (take a taxi from the station).*

FAMILY **Dusit Zoo.** Komodo dragons and other rarely seen creatures, such as the Sumatran rhinoceros, are on display at this charming little zoo. There are also the usual suspects like giraffes and hippos. (If you've heard about the pandas China gave Thailand, they are in Chiang Mai, not Bangkok.) While adults sip coffee at the cafés, children can ride elephants. ⊠ *Ratchawithi Rd. and Rama V Rd., Dusit* ☎ *02/281–2000* ⊕ *www.dusitzoo.org* 🎟 *B100* ☉ *Daily 8–6* Ⓜ *Skytrain: Victory Monu-ment (take a taxi from the station).*

Vimanmek Palace. The spacious grounds within Dusit Park include 20 buildings you can visit, but the Vimanmek Palace, considered the largest golden teak structure in the world, is truly the highlight. The mansion's original foundation remains on Koh Si Chang two hours south of Bangkok in the Gulf of Thailand, where it was built in 1868. In 1910 King Rama V had the rest of the structure moved to its present location and it served as his residence for five years while the Grand Palace was being fixed up. The building itself is extensive, with more than 80 rooms.

The other 19 buildings include the **Royal Family Museum,** with portraits of the royal family, and the **Royal Carriage Museum,** with carriages and other vehicles used by the country's monarchs through the ages. There are several small air-conditioned restaurants offering a limited menu of Thai food. Admission includes everything on the grounds and the classical Thai dancing shows that take place mid-morning and mid-afternoon (usually 10:30 and 2). English-language tours are available every half hour starting at 9:15. Proper attire is required (no shorts, tank tops, or sandals). ⊠ *Ratchawithi Rd., Dusit* ☎ *02/628–6300* 🚳*B100, free with ticket from the Grand Palace* ⊙ *Daily 9:30–4 (last entry at 3:15)* Ⓜ *Skytrain: Victory Monument (take a taxi from the station).*

Wat Benjamabophit (*Marble Temple*). Built in 1899, this wat is a favorite with photographers because of its open spaces and light, shining marble. Statues of the Buddha line the courtyard, and the magnificent interior has crossbeams of lacquer and gold. But Wat Benjamabophit is more than a splendid temple—the monastery is a seat of learning that appeals to Buddhist monks with intellectual yearnings. ✉ *Nakhon Pathom Rd., Dusit* ☎ *02/280–2273* 🚇 *B20* 🕙 *Daily 8–5:30* Ⓜ *Skytrain: Victory Monument (take a taxi from the station).*

THONBURI

Largely residential, Thonburi is where travelers go to take a ride along the city's ancient waterways. Most of Thonburi beyond the riverbank is of little interest to visitors. Many locals claim it retains more "Thai-ness" than the rest of Bangkok, but you'd have to live here, or visit for a long time, to appreciate that.

Royal Barge Museum. These splendid ceremonial barges are berthed on the Thonburi side of the Chao Phraya River. The boats, carved in the early part of the 19th century, take the form of mythical creatures in the *Ramakien*. The most impressive is the red-and-gold royal vessel called *Suphannahongse* (Golden Swan), used by the king on special occasions. Carved from a single piece of teak, it measures about 150 feet and weighs more than 15 tons. Fifty oarsmen propel it along the river, accompanied by two coxswains, flag wavers, and a rhythm-keeper. The museum is extremely difficult to find, so you may want to join a tour. ⚠ **Steer clear of scam artists offering tours or claiming that the museum is closed.** ✉ *Khlong Bangkok Noi, Thonburi* ☎ *02/424–0004* 🚇 *B100* 🕙 *Daily 9–5.*

Fodor's Choice   **Wat Arun** (*Temple of Dawn*). If this riverside spot is inspiring at sunrise,
★   it's even more marvelous toward dusk, when the setting sun throws amber tones over the entire area. The temple's design is symmetrical, with a square courtyard containing five Khmer-style prangs. The central prang, which reaches 282 feet, is surrounded by four attendant prangs at each of the corners. All five are covered in mosaics made from broken pieces of Chinese porcelain. Energetic visitors can climb the steep steps to the top of the lower level for the view over the Chao Phraya; the less ambitious can linger in the small park by the river, a peaceful spot to gaze across at the city. ✉ *Arun Amarin Rd., Thonburi* ☎ *02/466–3167* 🚇 *B50* 🕙 *Daily 7:30–5:30* Ⓜ *Subway: Hualamphong (then river ferry).*

CHINATOWN

Almost as soon as Bangkok was founded, Chinatown started to form; it's the city's oldest residential neighborhood. Today it's an integral part of the city, bustling with little markets (and a few big ones), teahouses, and restaurants. Like much of the Old City, Chinatown is a great place to explore on foot. Meandering through the maze of alleys, ducking into herb shops and temples along the way, can be a great way to pass an afternoon, though the constant crowd, especially on hot days, does wear on some people.

Continued on page 62

the Grand Palace

Thais regard their royal family with great respect, so it's no surprise that they hold the Grand Palace in high esteem. But the main attraction here is not a royal residence—it's Wat Phra Kaew (Temple of the Emerald Buddha), the home King Rama I built for the country's most revered idol. The temple is a reminder that in a country where everyone bows to the king, even the king bows to the Buddha.

by Lee Middleton

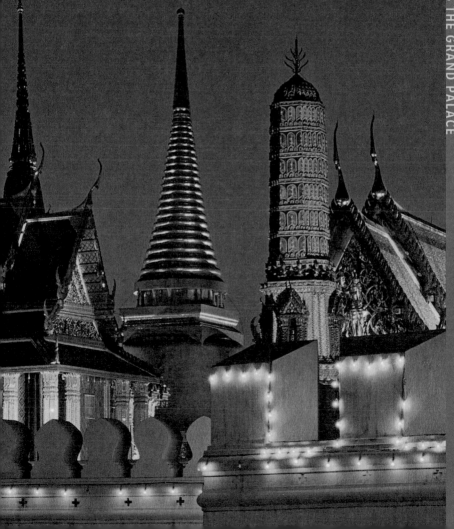

When Rama I was crowned in 1782, he wanted to celebrate the kingdom's renewed power. He moved the capital to Bangkok and set out to exceed the grandeur of Ayutthaya, once one of Asia's finest cities. The result was the dazzling Grand Palace compound, protected by a high white wall over a mile long. Rama I both ruled from and lived in the palace. Indeed, the royal family resided here until 1946, and each king who came to power added to the compound, leaving a mark of his rule and the era. Although the Grand Palace compound still houses the finance ministry, its only other official use is for state occasions and ceremonies like coronations. The current monarch, King Bhumibol (Rama IX), lives in Chitralada Palace which is closed to the public and is in Bangkok's Dusit District, northeast of the palace.

GRAND PALACE COMPOUND

Mural at the Grand Palace.

The palace grounds and Wat Phra Kaew are open to visitors, but many of the buildings in the complex are not. If you arrive by boat, you will land at Chiang Pier (tha Chang). Make your way to the main entrance on Na Phra Lan Road. **Wat Phra Kaew** is the best place to begin your tour. Other highlights are **Phra Thinang Amarin Winichai Mahaisun** (Amarinda Winichai Throne Hall), **Chakri Maha Prasat** (Grand Palace Hall), **Dusit Maha Prasat** (Audience Hall), **Phra Thinang Borom Phiman** (Borom Phiman Mansion), and the **Wat Phra Kaew Museum**.

Phra Thinang
Borom Phiman
5

Wat Phra Kaew **1**

PRASAT PHRA
DHEPBIDORN

HOR PHRA MONTHIAN
DHARMA

PHRA
MONDOP

Shop ◆

PHRA WIHARN
YOD

PHRA SIRATANA
CHEDI

HOR PHRA
NAGA

SALA
SAHADAYA

1 **Wat Phra Kaew.** King Rama I built Wat Phra Kaew— now regarded as Thailand's most sacred temple—in 1785. The main building, called *ubosoth*, houses the Emerald Buddha. The ubosoth has three doors; only the king and queen are allowed to enter through the central door.

2 **Phra Thinang Amarin Winichai Mahaisun.** The only part of Rama I's original residence that's open to visitors is used today for royal events such as the king's birthday celebration. Inside this audience hall are an antique boat-shaped throne from Rama I's reign that's now used to hold Buddha images during ceremonies, and a second throne with a nine-tiered white canopy where the king sits. At the entrance, you'll see gold-topped red poles once used by royal guests to tether their elephants.

MAIN
ENTRANCE

FINANCE
MINISTRY

Na Phra lan Road

Golden
statue.

Wat Phra Kaew.

3 Chakri Maha Prasat. Rama V's residence, built in 1882, is the largest of the palace buildings. The hybrid Thai–European style was a compromise between Rama V, who wanted a neoclassical palace with a domed roof, and his advisors, who thought such a blatantly European design was inappropriate. Rama V agreed to a Thai-style roof; Thais nicknamed the building farang sai chada or "the westerner wearing a Thai hat."

4 Dusit Maha Prasat. Built in 1784, the Audience Hall contains Rama I's original teak and mother-of-pearl throne. Today the hall is where Thais view royal remains, which are placed here temporarily in a golden urn.

5 Phra Thinang Borom Phiman. King Rama V built this French-style palace for his son (the future Rama VI) in 1903. Though later kings did not use the palace much, today visiting dignitaries stay here.

6 Wat Phra Kaew Museum. Stop by after touring the compound to learn about the restoration of the palace and to see the seasonal robes of the Emerald Buddha. Labels are in Thai, but free English tours occur regularly.

PHRA THINANG BUDDHA RATANA STARN

PHRA THINANG SRIDHALA PIROMYA

2

Phra Thinang Amarin Winichai Mahaisun

PHRA THINANG MOONSTARN BAROMART

Inner Palace Area (Closed To Public)

PHRA THINANG SOMUT DEVARAJ UBBAT

PHRA THINANG PHIMAN RATAYA

3

Chakri Maha Prasat

Ticket PHIMANCHAISRI GATE

4 Dusit Maha Prasat

APHONPIMOK PHASAT PAVILION

Wat Phra Kaew Museum

6

SALA LUKHUM

CHANG PIER

Elephants, or *chang*, symbolize independence, power, and luck in Thai culture. Kings once rode them into battle, and the palace even included a department to care for royal elephants. This pier is named for the kings' beasts, which were bathed here. Many elephant statues also grace the complex grounds. Notice how smooth the tops of their heads are—Thais rub the heads of elephants for luck.

Chang Pier

TOURING TIPS

■ Free guided tours of the compound are available in English at 10:00, 10:30, 1:30, and 2:00 daily; personal audio guides are available for B100 plus a passport or credit card as a deposit.

■ The best way to get here is to take the Skytrain to Taksin Station and then board the Chao Phraya River Express boat to Chang Pier. It's a short walk from the pier to the palace entrance. You can also take a taxi to the Grand Palace but you may end up wasting time in traffic or getting ripped off.

■ Admission includes a free (though unimpressive) guidebook and admission to the Vimanmek Palace in Dunsit (☞ above), as long as you go within a week of visiting the compound.

⊠ Sana Chai Rd., Old City

☎ 02/224–1833

🎫 B400, admission includes entrance to Wat Phra Kaew and Vimanemek Teak Mansion for one week.

🕑 Daily 8:30–4:30.

■ Don't listen to men loitering outside the grounds who claim that the compound is closed for a Buddhist holiday or for cleaning, or who offer to show you the "Lucky Buddha" or take you on a special tour. These phony guides will ultimately lead you to a gift shop where they receive a commission.

■ Allow half a day to tour the complex. You'll probably want to spend three hours in Wat Phra Kaew and the other buildings, and another half-hour in the museum.

■ Wat Phra Kaew is actually worth two visits: one on a weekday (when crowds are thinner and you can explore at a leisurely pace) and another on a Sunday or public holiday, when the smell of flowers and incense and the murmur of prayer evoke the spirituality of the place.

The Grand Palace.

WAT PHRA KAEW

As you enter the temple compound, you'll see 20-foot-tall statues of fearsome creatures in battle attire. These are *yakshas*—guardians who protect the Emerald Buddha from evil spirits. Turn right to see the murals depicting the *Ramakien* epic. Inside the main chapel, which is quiet and heavy with the scent of incense, you'll find the Emerald Buddha.

Yaksha.

THE RAMAKIEN

The *Ramakien* is the 2,000-year-old Thai adaptation of the famous Indian epic the *Ramayana*, which dates from around 400 BC. Beginning at the temple's north gate (across from Phra Wihan Yot [the Spired Hall]) and continuing clockwise around the cloister, 178 mural panels illustrate the story, which, like most epics, is about the struggle between good and evil. It begins with the founding of Ayutthaya (City of the Gods) and Lanka (City of the Demons) and focuses on the trials and tribulations of Ayutthaya's Prince Rama: his expulsion from his own kingdom; the abduction of his wife, Sita; and his eventual triumph over the demon Tosakan.

Sita's Abduction

Rama's wife Sita is abducted by the evil demon king, Tosakan, ruler of Lanka. Disguising himself as a deer, Tosakan lures Sita to his palace. A battle ensues, forming a large part of the long and detailed epic, which concludes when Rama rescues Sita.

Section of *Ramakien.*

THE APSONSI

The beautiful gilded figures on the upper terraces of Wat Phra Kaew are *apsonsi*—mythical half-angel, half-lion creatures who guard the temple. According to Thai mythology, apsonsi inhabit the Himavant Forest, which is the realm between earth and the heavens.

Ramakien battle scene.

Aponsi.

THE EMERALD BUDDHA

Thailand's most sacred Buddha image is made of a single piece of jade and is only 31 inches tall. The statue, which historians believe was sculpted in Thailand in the 14th or 15th century, was at one point covered in plaster; in 1434 it was discovered in Chiang Rai as the plaster began to flake.

When the king of nearby Chiang Mai heard about the jade Buddha, he demanded it be brought to him. According to legend, the statue was sent to the king three times, but each time the elephant transporting it veered off to Lampang, 60 miles southeast of Chiang Mai. Finally the king came to the Buddha, building a temple at that spot.

The Buddha was kept at various temples in northern Thailand until Laotian invaders stole it in 1552. It stayed in Laos until the 18th century, when King Rama I captured Vientiane, the capital, reclaimed the statue, and brought it to Bangkok.

Perched in a gilded box high above the altar, the diminutive statue is difficult to see. This doesn't deter Thai Buddhists, who believe that praying before the Emerald Buddha will earn them spiritual merit, helping to ensure a better rebirth in the next life.

The king is the only person allowed to touch the Emerald Buddha. Three times a year, he changes the Buddha's robes in a ceremony to bring good fortune for the coming season. The Buddha's hot season attire includes a gold crown and jewels; in the rainy season, it wears a headdress of gold, enamel, and sapphires; and, in the

Emerald Buddha in hot season outfit.

cool season, it's adorned in a mesh robe of gold beads.

Most Thais make an offering to the Buddha when they visit the temple. Inexpensive offerings, for sale outside the temple, generally include three joss sticks, a candle, and a thin piece of gold leaf stuck on a sheet of paper. At some wats, Thais stick gold leaves on the Buddha, but since that's not possible here, keep it as a souvenir or attach it to another sacred image (some elephant statues have gold leaves on their heads.) Light the candle from others that are already burning on the front alter, then light the incense with your candle.

WHAT'S A WAT?

A *wat* is a Buddhist temple or monastery, typically made up of a collection of shrines and structures in an enclosed courtyard, rather than a single building. Traditionally, monks reside in wats, but Wat Phra Kaew is a ceremonial temple, not a place of Buddhist study, so monks don't live here.

HONORING THE EMERALD BUDDHA

Thais usually follow an offering with three prostrations, or bows, to the Buddha. To prostrate, sit facing the Buddha with your legs folded or your feet tucked under you—then follow the sequence below. After prostrating you can sit in front of the Buddha in prayer or meditation for as long as you like.

1) Hold your hands together in a *wai* (palms together, fingers pointing up) at your heart.

2) Bring the wai up to touch your forehead,

3) Place your palms on the ground and bow your forehead until it's touching the ground between them.

4) Sit up, bring your hands back into a wai in front of your heart, and repeat.

TEMPLE ETIQUETTE

Even if you don't want to make an offering, pray, or prostrate, it's OK to linger in the temple or sit down. Here are a few other things to keep in mind:

■ Appropriate dress—long-sleeved shirts and long pants or skirts—is required. Open-toed shoes must be "closed" by wearing socks. If you've come scantily clad, you can rent a sarong at the palace.

■ Never point—with your hands or your feet—at the Emerald Buddha, other sacred objects, or even another person. If you sit down in the temple, make sure not to accidentally point your feet in the Buddha's direction.

■ When walking around religious monuments, try to move in a clockwise direction. Thais believe that the right side of the body is superior to the left, so it's more respectful to keep your right side closer to sacred objects.

■ Keep your head below the Buddha and anything else sacred. Thais will often bend their knees and lower their heads when walking past a group of older people or monks; it's a gesture of respect even if their heads aren't technically below the monks'.

Offerings.

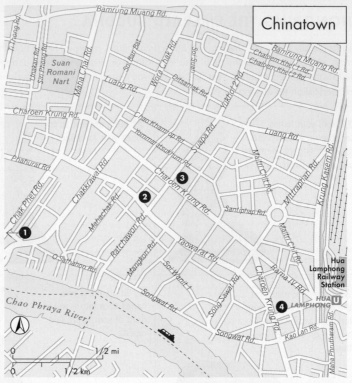

Bustling Yaowarat Road is the main thoroughfare. It's crowded with gold shops and excellent restaurants. Pahurat Road, which is Bangkok's "Little India," is full of textile shops, some quite literally underground. Many of the Indian merchant families on this street have been here for generations.

■ TIP→ Getting to Chinatown is easiest by boat, but you can also start at the Hua Lamphong subway station and head west to the river. The amount of traffic in this area cannot be overemphasized: avoid taking a taxi into the neighborhood if you can help it.

Flower Market (*Pak Khlong Talat*). This street lined with flower shops is busy around the clock, but it's most interesting at night when more deliveries are heading in and out. This is where restaurants, hotels, and individuals come to buy their flowers. Just stroll into the warehouse areas and watch the action. Many vendors only sell flowers in bulk, but others sell small bundles or even individual flowers. As everywhere else where Thais do business, there are plenty of street stalls selling a vast array of food. Though the area is not as busy as the rest of Chinatown, the traffic can still be overbearing. Then again, one can say that about everywhere in Bangkok. ⊠ *Chakraphet Rd. between Pripatt and Yod Fa rds., Chinatown* Ⓜ *Subway: Hua Lamphong.*

SOI BOYS

At many *sois* (side streets) you will find clusters of motorcycle taxis. Their drivers, called "soi boys," will take you anywhere in Bangkok, although they are best for short trips within a neighborhood. Many soi boys know their way around the city better than taxi drivers. Fares are not negotiable—the drivers have set rates to nearby points, usually a bit less than a taxi. Motorcycles can be dangerous; helmets, when available, are often nothing more than a thin piece of plastic without a chinstrap. The risks and discomforts limit their desirability, but motorcycles can be one of the best ways to get around Bangkok, especially if you're in a hurry.

Thieves Market (*Nakorn Kasem*). Once known for its reasonable prices for antiques, the Thieves Market now more closely resembles a flea market. It's not worth a visit on its own, but as you're strolling through Chinatown take a look at this rabbit warren of little shops. Mostly electronic goods are sold, and it really starts slowing down about 5 in the afternoon. For shopping, the Chatuchak weekend market is much better. ⊠ *Yaowarat and Chakraphet rds., Chinatown* Ⓜ *Subway: Hua Lamphong.*

Wat Mangkorn (*Neng Noi Yee*). Unlike most temples in Bangkok, Neng Noi Yee has a glazed ceramic roof topped with fearsome dragons. Although it's a Buddhist shrine, its statues and paintings incorporate elements of Confucianism and Taoism as well. It's open daily from early to very late. It is especially appealing during Chinese New Year, when thousands of Thais visit the temple to burn incense and make merit. ⊠ *Pom Prap Sattru Phai, Chinatown* ☏ *02/222–3975* Ⓜ *Subway: Hua Lamphong.*

Fodor's Choice ★ **Wat Traimit** (*Temple of the Golden Buddha*). The actual temple has little architectural merit, but off to its side is a small chapel containing the world's largest solid-gold Buddha, cast about nine centuries ago in the Sukhothai style. Weighing 5½ tons and standing 10 feet high, the statue is a symbol of strength and power that can inspire even the most jaded person. It's believed that the statue was brought first to Ayutthaya. When the Burmese were about to sack the city, it was covered in plaster. Two centuries later, still in plaster, it was thought to be worth very little; when it was being moved to a new Bangkok temple in the 1950s it slipped from a crane and was simply left in the mud by the workmen. In the morning, a temple monk who had dreamed that the statue was divinely inspired went to see the Buddha image. Through a crack in the plaster he saw a glint of yellow, and soon discovered that the statue was pure gold. There is also an excellent museum that follows the history of the Tha Chinese that is highly worth visiting. ⊠ *Tri Mit Rd., Chinatown* ☏ *02/281–2992* ⊕ *www.wattraimitr-withayaram.com* 🎫 *B40 for statue, B10 for museum* ☉ *Daily 8–4:30* Ⓜ *Subway: Hua Lamphong.*

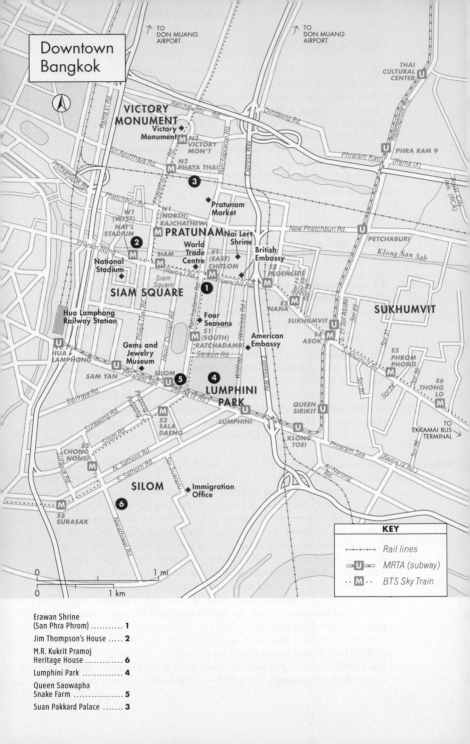

Downtown Bangkok

TO
DON MUANG
AIRPORT

TO
DON MUANG
AIRPORT

THAI
CULTURAL
CENTER

VICTORY
MONUMENT

Ratchawithi Rd.

Dindaeng Rd.

PHRA RAM 9

Victory
Monument

Phraram Kao

(Rama IX)

N3
VICTORY
MON'T

N2
PHAYA THAI

Sri Ayutthaya Rd.

Ratchaprarop Rd.

Express Way

New City
Ave. (RCA)

Phitsanulok Rd.

3

Phetchburi Rd.

Pratunam
Market

New Phetchburi Rd.

PETCHABURI

W1
(WEST)
NAT'L
STADIUM

N1
(NORTH)
RAJCHATHEWI

PRATUNAM

Nai Lert
Shrine

Klong San Sab

Phraram Nung

SIAM

2

World
Trade
Centre

E1
(EAST)
CHITLOM

British
Embassy

National
Stadium

Siam
Square
(Rama I Rd.)

1

Ploenchit Rd.

E2
PLOENCHIT

SUKHUMVIT

SIAM SQUARE

E3
NANA

Sor. 1

Sor. 3

Sor. 5

Hua Lamphong
Railway Station

Ratchadamri Rd.

Four
Seasons

SUKHUMVIT

E4
ASOK

S. 21 Sor Asoke

E5
PHROM
PHONG

HUA
LAMPHONG

Henri Dunant Rd.

S1
(SOUTH)
RATCHADAMRI

American
Embassy

Sukhumvit Rd.

Sor. 23

Gems and
Jewelry
Museum

Phaya Thai Rd.

Wireless Rd.

Sarasin Rd.

Sor. 24

E6
THONG
LO

SAM YAN

Phraram See

SILOM

5

LUMPHINI
PARK

4

QUEEN
SIRIKIT

TO
EKKAMAI BUS
TERMINAL

Siphraya Rd.

(Rama IV Rd.)

Whithau

Express Way

LUMPHINI

Surawong Rd.

S2
SALA
DAENG

Patpong 2

Patpong 1

KLONG
TOEI

Phraram See

(Rama IV Rd.)

CHONG
NONSI

S3

Silom Rd.

N. Sathorn Rd.

Sathorn Tai

At-Narong
Rd.

SILOM

S. Sathorn Rd.

Soi Suanplu

Immigration
Office

Sor. 26

Surasak Rd.

Narathiwat Rd.

S5
SURASAK

KEY

Rail lines

MRTA (subway)

BTS Sky Train

| 0 | | 1 mi |
| 0 | | 1 km |

BANGKOK'S SKYWAYS

The Skytrain transformed the city when it opened on the king's birthday in 1999. It now has more than 30 stations on two lines that intersect at Siam Square. Although the Skytrain bypasses many parts of the city, it is the speediest way to travel when its route coincides with yours. The fare is B15 to B40, depending on how far you plan to travel, and trains run from 5 am to midnight. Trains are still impressively clean and efficient, although they can get tremendously crowded at rush hour.

The sights in downtown Bangkok are spread out, but most are near Skytrain stations. Stations are generally about three minutes apart, so a trip from Chong Nonsi to National Stadium, which is four stations away, will take less than 12 minutes. At three stations—Chatuchak Park, Sukhumvit, and Saladaeng—the Skytrain intersects with the subway, which is convenient for some intercity travel.

PATHUMWAN

Bangkok has many downtowns that blend into each other—even residents have a hard time agreeing on a definitive city center—but Pathumwan is the closest thing to a "downtown" in Central Bangkok. Most of the tourist attractions are around here or in the adjacent neighborhood of Silom

There are numerous markets here, including those in the Pratunam garment district and Panthip Plaza, Thailand's biggest computer center and an overwhelming shopping experience, with five floors of computer stores.

Erawan Shrine (*San Phra Phrom*). Completed in 1956, this is not a particularly old shrine by Bangkok standards, but it's one of the more active ones, with many people stopping by on their way home to pray to Brahma. Thai dancers and a small traditional orchestra perform for a fee to increase the likelihood that your wish will be granted. Its location at one of Bangkok's most congested intersections, next to the Grand Hyatt Erawan and near the Chitlom Skytrain station, detracts a bit from the experience. Even with a traffic jam right outside the gates though, the mix of burning incense, dancers in traditional dress, and many people praying is a memorable sight. Entry is free, but many people leave small donations. A crazed man smashed the main statue in early 2006 and then was beaten to death by people outside the shrine. The statue has since been repaired and is more popular than ever. ⊠ *Ratchadamri and Ploenchit rds., Pathumwan* Ⓜ *Skytrain: Chitlom.*

Fertility Shrine at Nai Lert Park. Hundreds of phalluses from small wooden carvings to big stone sculptures decorated with ribbons make this shrine quite unique. It honors Chao Mae Tuptim, a female fertility spirit. Women visit this shrine when they are trying to conceive, leaving offerings of lotus and jasmine, and if Bangkok gossip is worth anything, the shrine has a good success rate. To get there, go to the Nai Lert Park Hotel and walk to the end of the ground-level garage, where it's on your right. It's free and open 24 hours everyday, but best to visit before dusk. ⊠ *Nai Lert Park Hotel, 2 Wittayu, Pathumwan* Ⓜ *Skytrain: Chitlom.*

Fodor's Choice **Jim Thompson's House.** Formerly an architect in New York City, Jim
★ Thompson ended up in Thailand at the end of World War II, after a stint as an officer of the OSS (an organization that preceded the CIA). After a couple of other business ventures, he moved into silk and is credited with revitalizing Thailand's moribund silk industry. The success of this project alone would have made him a legend, but the house he left behind is also a national treasure. Thompson imported parts of several up-country buildings, some as old as 150 years, to construct his compound of six Thai houses (three are still exactly the same as their originals, including details of the interior layout). With true appreciation and a connoisseur's eye, Thompson then furnished them with what are now priceless pieces of Southeast Asian art. Adding to Thompson's notoriety is his disappearance: in 1967 he went to the Malaysian Cameron Highlands for a quiet holiday and was never heard from again.

The entrance to the house is easy to miss—it's at the end of an unprepossessing lane, leading north off Rama I Road, west of Phayathai Road (the house is on your left). A good landmark is the National Stadium Skytrain station—the house is north of the station, just down the street from it. An informative 30-minute guided tour starts every 15 minutes and is included in the admission fee. ■TIP→ The grounds also include a silk and souvenir shop and a restaurant that's great for a coffee or cold-drink break. ⊠ *Rama I Rd., Soi Kasemsong 2, Pathumwan* ☎ *02/216–7368* ⊕ *www.jimthompsonhouse.com* ☑ *B100* ۞ *Daily 9–5* Ⓜ *Skytrain: National Stadium.*

Siam Square. One of the most popular destinations in the area is glitzy Siam Square, home to Thailand's most prestigious college, Chulalongkorn University. With its neon-covered malls rising several stories, Siam Square is also one of Bangkok's biggest shopping areas. ⊠ *Rama I Road, Pathumwan.*

Suan Pakkard Palace. A collection of antique teak houses, built high on columns, complement undulating lawns and shimmering lotus pools at this compound. Inside the Lacquer Pavilion, which sits serenely at the back of the garden, there's gold-covered paneling with scenes from the life of the Buddha. Academics and historians continue to debate just how old the murals are—whether they're from the reign of King Narai (1656–88) or from the first reign of the current Chakri Dynasty, founded by King Rama I (1782–1809). Other houses display porcelain, stone heads, traditional paintings, and Buddha statues. ⊠ *352–354 Sri Ayutthaya Rd., Pathumwan* ☎ *02/245–4934* ☑ *B100* ۞ *Daily 9–4* Ⓜ *Skytrain: Phaya Thai (10-min walk east of station).*

SILOM AND BANG RAK

The Silom area, with a mix of tall buildings, residential streets, and entertainment areas, is Bangkok's busiest business district. Some of the city's finest hotels and restaurants are in this neighborhood, which retains some charm despite being so developed and chock-full of concrete. Although the entire neighborhood across the Chao Phraya River

CLOSE UP

Roaming the Waterways

Bangkok used to be known as "Venice of the East," but many of the klongs (canals) that once distinguished this area have been paved over. Traveling along the few remaining waterways, however, is one of the city's delights. You'll see houses on stilts, women washing clothes, and kids going for a swim. Traditional wooden canal boats are a fun (although not entirely practical) way to get around town.

Klong Saen Saeb, just north of Petchaburi Road, is the main boat route. The fare is B25, and during rush hour boats pull up to piers at one-minute intervals. Klong boats provide easy access to Jim Thompson's House and are a handy alternative way to get to Khao San Road during rush hour. The last stop is Pan Pha, which is about a 15-minute walk from the eastern end of Khao San Road.

Ferries (sometimes called "river buses") ply the Chao Phraya River. The fare for these express boats is based on how far you travel; the price ranges from B13 to B32. The river can be an efficient way to get around as well as a sightseeing opportunity. Under the Saphan Taksin Skytrain stop, there is a ferry pier where passengers can cross the river to Thonburi for B3. Many hotels run their own boats from the pier at Saphan Taksin. From here you can get to the Grand Palace in about 10 minutes and the other side

of Krungthon Bridge in about 15 minutes. Local line boats travel specific routes from 6 am to 6 pm.

These boats stop at every pier and will take you all the way to Nonthaburi, where you'll find the quaint car-free island of Koh Kret, which has a Mon community and specializes in pottery—a pleasant afternoon trip when the city gets too hot.

A Chao Phraya Tourist Boat day pass is a fun introduction to the river. Passes are a bargain at B150 for the day. One advantage of the tourist boat is that while traveling from place to place there's a running commentary in English about the historic sights along the river. The tourist boat starts at the pier under Saphan Taksin Skytrain station, but you can pick it up at any of the piers where it stops, and you can get on and off as often as you like.

Longtail boats (so called for the extra-long propeller shaft that extends behind the stern) operate like taxis. Boatmen will take you anywhere you want to go for B300 to B500 per hour. It's a great way to see the canals. The best place to hire these boats is at the Central Pier at Sathorn Bridge. For a private longtail trip up the old klongs, a trip to the Royal Barge Museum and the Khoo Wiang Floating Market starts at the Chang Pier near the Grand Palace. Longtails often quit running at 6 pm.

falls under the post code name and number of Bang Rak, locals are more likely to term places that are on Silom Road as Silom, on Sathorn Road as Sathorn, and call the area around the riverside Bang Rak.

Lumphini Park. Two lakes enhance this popular park, one of the biggest in the center of the city. You can watch children feed bread to the turtles or teenagers rowing a boat to more secluded shores. During the dry season (November to February), keep an eye and an ear out for Music in the Park, which starts around 5 pm each Sunday on the

Singha stage; different bands each week play classical and Thai oldies. There are many embassies in the immediate vicinity, and the Bangkok Royal Sports Club is just west of the park. ⊠ *Rama IV Rd., Pathumwan* Ⓜ *Subway: Silom and Lumphini stations; Skytrain: Sala Daeng.*

M. R. Kukrit Pramoj Heritage House. Former Prime Minister Kukrit Pramoj's house reflects his long, influential life. After Thailand became a constitutional monarchy in 1932, he formed the country's first political party and was prime minister in 1974 and 1975. (Perhaps he practiced for that role 12 years earlier, when he appeared with Marlon Brando as a Southeast Asian prime minister in *The Ugly American*.) He died in 1995, and much of his living quarters—five interconnected teak houses—has been preserved. Throughout his life, Kukrit was dedicated to preserving Thai culture, and his house and grounds are monuments to a bygone era; the place is full of Thai and Khmer art and furniture from different periods. The landscaped garden with its Khmer stonework is also a highlight. It took Pramoj 30 years to build the house, so it's no wonder that you can spend the better part of a day wandering around. ⊠ *S. Sathorn Rd., 19 Soi Phra Pinit, Silom* ☎ *02/286–8185* ⊕ *www.kukritshousefund.com* ⊠ *B50* ⊘ *Daily 10–4* Ⓜ *Skytrain: Chong Nonsi (10-min walk from station).*

FAMILY
Fodor'sChoice
★

Queen Saowapha Snake Farm. The Thai Red Cross established this unusual and fascinating snake farm and toxicology research institute in 1923, and it is well worth a visit. Venom from cobras, pit vipers, and some of the other 56 types of deadly snakes found in Thailand is collected and used to make antidotes for snakebite victims. Venom extraction takes place on weekday mornings at 11, while the snake handling show and photo op is at 2:30. A few displays can be viewed any time, but the photo ops are the big draw. ⊠ *1871 Rama IV Rd., Silom* ☎ *02/252–0161, 02/252–0167* ⊕ *www.saovabha.com/en/snakefarm_ service.asp* ⊠ *B200* ⊘ *Weekdays 8:30–4, weekends 9:30–1* Ⓜ *Subway: Silom; Skytrain: Sala Daeng.*

WHERE TO EAT

Thais are passionate about food, and love discovering out-of-the-way shops that prepare unexpectedly tasty dishes. Nowhere is this truer—or more feasible—than in Bangkok. The city's residents always seem to be eating, so the tastes and smells of Thailand's cuisine surround you day and night. That said, Bangkok's restaurant scene is also a minefield, largely because the relationship between price and quality at times seems almost inverse. For every hole-in-the-wall gem serving the best sticky rice, *larb* (meat salad), and *som tam* (the hot-and-sour green-papaya salad that is the ultimate Thai staple) you've ever had, there's an overpriced hotel restaurant serving touristy, toned-down fare. In general, the best Thai food in the city is generally at the most barebones, even run-down restaurants, not at famous, upscale places.

If you want a break from Thai food, plenty of other world cuisines are well represented. Best among them is Chinese, although there's decent Japanese and Korean food as well. The city's ubiquitous noodle shops have their roots in China, as do roast-meat purveyors, whose historical inspiration was Cantonese. Western fare tends to suffer from the distance, although in the past few years, there has been an incredible increase in the number of upscale and trendy western eateries, some of them quite excellent.

As with anything in Bangkok, travel time is a major consideration when choosing a restaurant. If you're short on time or patience, choose a place that's an easy walk from a Skytrain or subway station. ■ **TIP→ Note that the easiest way to reach a riverside eatery is often an express boat on the Chaoe Phraya River.**

Prices in the reviews are the average cost of a main course at dinner or, if dinner is not served, at lunch. Use the coordinate (⊕ B2) at the end of each listing to locate a site on the Where to Eat in Bangkok map.

DINNER CRUISES

Though they're definitely touristy, lunch or dinner cruises on the Chao Phraya River are worth considering. They're a great way to see the city at night, although the food is often subpar. You might even want to skip the dinner, just have drinks, and dine at a real Thai restaurant afterward. Two-hour cruises on modern boats or refurbished rice barges include a buffet or set-menu dinner, and often feature live music and sometimes a traditional dance show. Many companies also offer a less expensive lunch cruise, though the heat can make these a little unpleasant. In general, it's wise to reserve a few days in advance, and reservations are a must for some of the more popular dinner cruises.

$$$$ THAI 🍴 ***Horizon.*** Departing each evening at 7:30, the *Horizon* costs B2,300 per person. Four days a week there's also a bus trip to Ayutthaya with a cruise back for B1,950. It departs at 8 am and returns around 5 pm. [$] *Average main: $77* ✉ *Shangri-La Hotel, Charoen Krung (New Rd.), 89 Soi Wat Suan Plu, Bang Rak* ☎ *02/236–7777* 🌐 *www.shangri-la.com/bangkok/shangrila/dining/restaurants/horizon-cruise.*

$$$$ THAI 🍴 ***Manohra Song.*** The most beautiful dinner boat on the river, the *Manohra Song* offers both lunch and dinner cruises. It's smaller than most of the others, with less space to walk around. A mediocre set-price dinner is B1,990 per person. [$] *Average main: $66* ✉ *Marriott Royal Garden Riverside Hotel, 257/1–3 Charoen Nakhorn, Thonburi* ☎ *02/477–0770* 🌐 *www.manohracruises.com.*

$ THAI 🍴 ***Yok Yor.*** Departing each evening at 8, the *Yok Yor* is a little like a floating restaurant. The boat ride costs B140, and the food is ordered à la carte—which in this case is a plus. [$] *Average main: $5* ✉ *885 Somdet Chao Phraya 17, Klong San* ☎ *02/863–0565* 🌐 *www.yokyor.co.th/english.*

COOKING CLASSES

Culinary tourism is all the rage, and Bangkok is keeping up with the times. A Thai cooking class can be a great way to spend a half day—or longer. You won't be an expert, but you can learn a few fundamentals and some of the history of Thai cuisine. You can also find specialty classes that focus on things like fruit carving (where the first lesson learned is that it's more difficult than it looks) or hot-and-spicy soups. All cooking schools concentrate on practical dishes that students will be

BEST BETS FOR BANGKOK DINING

Fodor's writers and editors have selected their favorite restaurants by price, cuisine, and experience in the lists below. In the first column, the Fodor's Choice properties represent the "best of the best" across price categories. You can also search by area for excellent eats—just peruse our complete reviews on the following pages.

Fodor'sChoice★

Ban Khun Mae, $$, p. 81
Lek Seafood, $$, p. 87
The Local, $$, p. 91
The Mayflower, $$$$, p. 88
Pen, $$$, p. 88
Pochana 55, $, p. 92
Soul Food Mahanakorn, $$, p. 92
Zanotti, $$$$, p. 90
Zuma, $$$$, p. 83

By Price

$

Aw Taw Kaw Market, p. 74
Big C, p. 81
Home Cuisine Islamic, p. 87
Pochana 55, p. 92
Prachak, p. 88
Punjab Sweets, p. 81

$$

Chote Chitr, p. 71
Himali Cha Cha, p. 86

Raan Jay Fai, p. 71
Soul Food Mahanakorn, p. 92
Vientiane Kitchen, p. 93

$$$

Baan Klang Nam, p. 84
Hua Seng Hong, p. 76
The Local, p. 91
Saffron, p. 89

$$$$

Breeze, p. 84
Genji, p. 82
KiSara, p. 82
Mezzaluna, p. 88
Zuma, p. 83

By Cuisine

CHINESE

Hua Seng Hong, $$$, p. 76
Liu, $$$$, p. 82
The Mayflower, $$$$, p. 88
Tang Jai Yoo, $$, p. 81

INDIAN

Hazara, $$$$, p. 90
Himali Cha Cha, $$, p. 86
Punjab Sweets, $, p. 81

JAPANESE

Genji, $$$$, p. 82
KiSara, $$$$, p. 82
Zuma, $$$$, p. 83

THAI

Chote Chitr, $$, p. 71
Lek Seafood, $$, p. 87
Pen, $$$, p. 88
Pochana 55, $, p. 92
Polo Fried Chicken, $, p. 83
Raan Jay Fai, $$, p. 71
Soul Food Mahanakorn, $$, p. 92

WESTERN

Ciao, $$$$, p. 85
Le Normandie, $$$$, p. 87
Prime, $$$$, p. 75

By Experience

CHILD-FRIENDLY

Big C, $, p. 81
Eat Me, $$, p. 85
Hazara, $$$$, p. 90
Polo Fried Chicken, $, p. 83
Raan Jay Fai, $$, p. 71

GREAT VIEW

Breeze, $$$$, p. 84
Mezzaluna, $$$$, p. 88
Sala Rim Naam, $$$$, p. 75
Salathip, $$$$, p. 89
Vertigo, $$$$, p. 89

HOT SPOTS

Breeze, $$$$, p. 84
Liu, $$$$, p. 82

MOST ROMANTIC

Celadon, $$$, p. 85
Saffron, $$$, p. 89
Salathip, $$$$, p. 89
Sala Rim Naam, $$$$, p. 75
Vertigo, $$$$, p. 89

SWANKIEST

Breeze, $$$$, p. 84
KiSara, $$$$, p. 82
The Mayflower, $$$$, p. 88
Mezzaluna, $$$$, p. 88
Prime, $$$$, p. 75

able to make at home, usually with spices that are internationally available, and all revolve around the fun of eating something you cooked (at least partly) yourself. ■ TIP→ Book cooking classes ahead of time, as they fill up fast. Most classes are small enough to allow individual attention and time for questions. Prices vary from B2,000 to more than B10,000.

Blue Elephant Cooking School. The Blue Elephant Cooking School is a long-standing favorite, connected with the restaurant of the same name, but the Thai dishes here are heavily Westernized. However, at about B2,800 per half day, it's cheaper than the others, and the staff is very friendly. ⊠ *233 S. Sathorn Rd., Ket Sathorn* ☎ *02/673–9353* ⊕ *www. blueelephant.com* Ⓜ *Skytrain: Surasak.*

Oriental Cooking School. This is the most established and expensive school (B4,000 for a half day), but far from being stuffy, it's fun and informative, and its dishes tend to be more interesting and authentic than those at other schools. Classes are taught in a beautiful century-old house across the river from the hotel. ⊠ *Mandarin Oriental, 48 Oriental Ave., Bang Rak* ☎ *02/659–9000* ⊕ *www.mandarinoriental.com/bangkok.*

THE OLD CITY

The Old City has every type of restaurant, including a huge proliferation of holes-in-the-wall, many with excellent food.

$$

THAI

✕ **Raan Jay Fai.** "Cult following" would be putting it mildly: it is said that some people come to Thailand just for a serving of the *pad khee mao* (drunken noodles) at this small open-air eatery with cafeteria-style tables, green bare light bulbs, and a culinary wizard presiding over a charcoal-fired wok. The dish, which is all anyone gets here, is a rice noodle preparation with seafood including basil, crabmeat, giant shrimp, and hearts of palm. At around B280, this is a major splurge by Bangkok noodle standards—and the deal of the century for visiting foodies. The lump crabmeat fried with curry powder, though not as wildly popular, is also recommended. ⓢ *Average main: B280* ⊠ *327 Mahachai Rd., Phra Nakhon* ☎ *02/223–9384* ▭ *No credit cards* ☉ *Closed Sat.* ✛ *C3.*

BANGLAMPHU

Touristy Khao San Road is north of the Old City, though the tame Thai food available in this backpacker mecca is nothing to go out of your way for. Don't limit yourself to the listings here, and don't be afraid to sample the street food in the alleyways away from Khao San Road—it often makes for some of your most memorable meals in Bangkok.

$

THAI

✕ **Chote Chitr.** A favorite of legendary Bangkok food writer Bob Halliday, this simple, diminutive restaurant near Wat Suthat specializes in

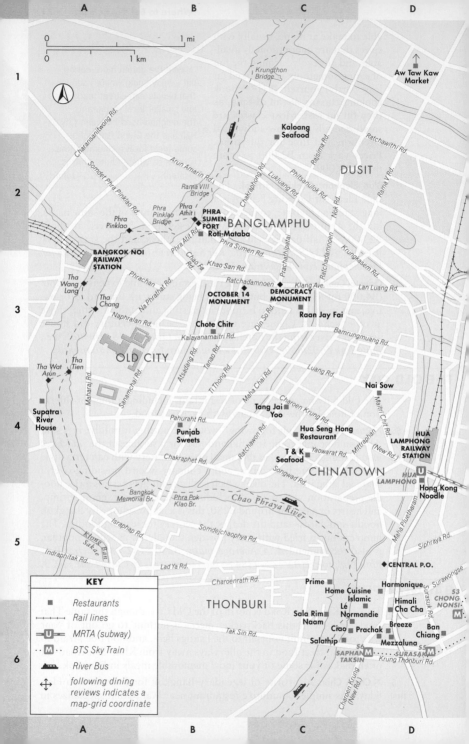

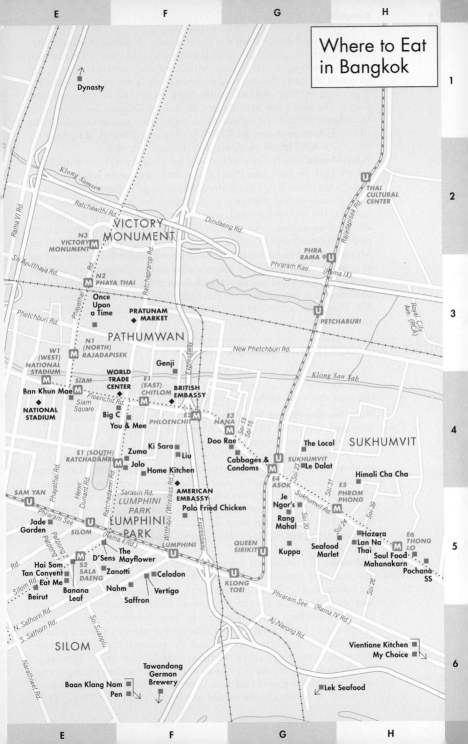

Where to Eat in Bangkok

E · F · G · H

1 · 2 · 3 · 4 · 5 · 6

Dynasty

Klong Samsen

Ratchawithi Rd.

Rama VI Rd.

Sri Ayutthaya Rd.

Phetchburi Rd.

Phayathai Rd.

Dindaeng Rd.

Ratchaprarop Rd.

VICTORY MONUMENT

N3 VICTORY MONUMENT

N2 PHAYA THAI

Once Upon a Time

PRATUNAM MARKET

PATHUMWAN

N1 (NORTH) RAJADAPISEK

W1 (WEST) NATIONAL STADIUM

Genji

WORLD TRADE CENTER

E1 (EAST) CHITLOM

BRITISH EMBASSY

Ban Khun Mae

SIAM

Siam Square

Ploenchit Rd.

NATIONAL STADIUM

Big C

You & Mee

E2 PHLOENCHIT

E3 NANA

Zuma

Ki Sara

Liu

Doo Rae

The Local

SUKHUMVIT

S1 (SOUTH) RATCHADAMRI

Jolo

Home Kitchen

Cabbages & Condoms

Le Dalat

SUKHUMVIT Soi 23

Soi 31

Himali Cha Cha

E5 PHROM PHONG

E4 ASOK

Je Ngor's

Rang Mahal

Sukhumvit Rd.

Soi 39

SAM YAN

Jade Garden

Phraram See

SILOM

Phayathai Rd.

Henri Dunant Rd.

Ratchadamri Rd.

Sarasin Rd.

LUMPHINI PARK

LUMPHINI PARK

Witthayu (Wireless) Rd.

AMERICAN EMBASSY

Polo Fried Chicken

(Rama 4 Rd.)

LUMPHINI

Soi 20

Soi 24

Kuppa

Seafood Marlet

Hazara

Lan Na Thai

Soul Food Mahanakarn

E6 THONG LO

Pochana SS

Hai Som

Tan Convent

Eat Me

Beirut

D'Sens

The Mayflower

S2 SALA DAENG

Zanotti

Banana Leaf

Nahm

Celadon

Vertigo

Saffron

QUEEN SIRIKIT

KLONG TOEI

Phraram See (Rama IV Rd.)

Aj-Narong Rd.

Vientiane Kitchen

My Choice

SILOM

N. Sathorn Rd.

S. Sathorn Rd.

Narathiwat Rd.

Soi Suanplu

Tawandang German Brewery

Baan Klang Nam

Pen

Lek Seafood

THAI CULTURAL CENTER

PHRA RAMA 9

Phraram Kao (Rama IX)

PETCHABURI

Royal City Ave. (RCA)

New Phetchburi Rd.

Klong San Sab

Rajadapisek Rd.

Expressway

recipes handed down from the royal palace. Notable in a constellation of superstar dishes are banana-blossom salad (here it's made with shrimp, chicken, tamarind pulp, chili, and coconut cream); perfectly balanced red curry shrimp; and *makheua yao* (a smoky green eggplant salad with shrimp, shallots, palm sugar, fermented shrimp, and lime juice). The *mee krob* noodles are legendary. Despite declining a bit in authenticity and service due to its popularity, tourists still love this place. [$] *Average main: B180* ✉ *146 Phraeng Phuton, Banglamphu* ☎ *02/221–4082* ▭ *No credit cards* 🕓 *Closed Sun.* ✥ *B3.*

$ INDIAN 🍴 **Roti-Mataba.** Housed in a century-old building across from Santichaiprakarn Park on the Chao Phraya, this little restaurant is where you'll find decent (though not innovative) Indian food in Bangkok. You'll be hard-pressed to find anything on the menu for more than B100. You can hear the *roti* (unleavened, whole-wheat flatbread) filled with your choice of vegetables, chicken, beef, fish, seafood, or just sweetened with thick condensed milk, sizzling near the door. Many curries, including Massaman—a Muslim curry that has a strong peanut flavor—are served at a steam table. Avoid the narrow downstairs dining area, which is unpleasantly hot and usually crowded; there's a more comfortable air-conditioned room upstairs. [$] *Average main: B60* ✉ *136 Phra Athit Rd., Banglamphu* ☎ *02/282–2119* 🌐 *www.roti-mataba.net* ▭ *No credit cards* 🕓 *Closed Mon.* ✥ *B2.*

DUSIT AND NORTHERN BANGKOK

Northern Bangkok is worth dining in only if you happen to be in the neighborhood for sightseeing, or if you really want to get to a part of the river that's off the beaten track.

$ THAI 🍴 **Aw Taw Kaw Market.** Bangkok's best food bargains are found at this legendary spot in the Chatuchak Market. It's noisy, and you'll be inundated with sights and smells in the rows of food stalls; walk around and let your senses take over. The seafood, like raw crab, curried crab, or steamed whole fish with garlic and chili, is especially tasty. Items are dished out in plastic baggies; finding a seat and utensils can be a challenge. The trick is to buy something small at one of the few café-like establishments that offer seats, plates, and cutlery—then open your bags and feast. [$] *Average main: B120* ✉ *Phaholyothin Rd., Chatuchak, Northern Bangkok* ▭ *No credit cards* [M] *Subway: Chatuchak Park; Skytrain: Mo Chit* ✥ *D1.*

$$$$ CHINESE 🍴 **Dynasty.** This restaurant has long been a favorite among government ministers and corporate executives, both for its outstanding Cantonese cuisine and for its 11 private areas, which are perfect for business lunches or romantic dinners. The main dining room is elegant, with crimson carpeting, carved screens, lacquer furniture, and porcelain objets d'art. The Peking duck is among the draws (as are the jellyfish salad and drunken chicken), and the seasonal specialties include everything from hairy crabs (October and November) to Taiwanese eels (March). The service is efficient and friendly without being obtrusive. The restaurant is in Chatuchak, in the north of Bangkok. [$] *Average main: B750* ✉ *Centara Grand at Central Plaza Lad Phrao, 1695*

Phaholyothin Rd., Chatuchak, Northern Bangkok ☎ *02/541–1234* 🌐 *www.centarahotelsresorts.com* ✍ *Reservations essential* [M] *Subway: Phahon Yothin* ✣ *E1.*

$ THAI 🍴 **Kaloang Seafood.** An alley near the National Library leads to this off-the-beaten-track restaurant on the Chao Phraya. Kaloang might not look like much, with its plastic chairs and simple tables on a ramshackle pier, but it's a local favorite and worth the effort—and leap in imagination—for fantastic seafood. Breezes coming off the water keep things comfortably cool most evenings. The generous grilled seafood platter is a bargain, as is the plate of grilled giant river prawns. Try the *yam pla duk foo,* a grilled fish salad that's rather spicy and goes great with a cold beer. Also notable is the *larb goong,* spicy ground shrimp salad with banana blossoms. [$] *Average main: B150* ✉ *2 Sri Ayutthaya Rd., Dusit* ☎ *02/281–9228, 02/282–7581* [M] *Subway: Phahon Yothin* ✣ *C2.*

THONBURI

Thonburi has restaurants boasting unparalleled river views, along with dinner cruises *(⇨ Dinner Cruises, above).*

$$$$ STEAKHOUSE 🍴 **Prime.** Though it's just a toddler in restaurant years, this spot in the Hilton Millennium has already attained the title of best steakhouse in Bangkok. It all begins with the groundbreaking interior architecture, which skillfully blends sweeping river and city views with the restaurant's open kitchen while still managing to feel intimate—an almost alchemical feat. Start with one of the signature martinis, and move on to the Caesar salad prepared tableside and perhaps a magnificent shellfish platter with fresh, briny oysters and lobster tails. Then there is the meat—whether it's Wagyu beef flown in from Australia or USDA Prime, no expense is spared in the kitchen (or on the bill). The grilling is done over an extremely hot open flame. The wine list is one of the best in the city, but everything is überexpensive. [$] *Average main: B750* ✉ *Hilton Millennium Hotel, 123 Charoennakorn Rd., Klong San* ☎ *02/442–2000* 🌐 *www.hilton.com* 🕒 *No lunch* [M] *Skytrain: Krung Thonburi* ✣ *C5.*

$$$$ THAI 🍴 **Sala Rim Naam.** The main reason to come here is to soak up the atmosphere, which includes a classical Thai dancing show. As it gets dark and cools down, the twinkling lights of passing boats set quite a romantic scene at the outdoor tables overlooking the river. The restaurant itself is touristy, with westernized renditions of Thai food. There are set dinners and buffet lunches with plenty of choices. ■ **TIP→ To get here, take the complimentary shuttle boat across the Chao Phraya River from the Oriental Hotel.** [$] *Average main: B2200* ✉ *48 Oriental Ave., Bang Rak* ☎ *02/659–9000* 🌐 *www.mandarinoriental.com* ✍ *Reservations essential* [M] *Skytrain: Saphan Taksin* ✣ *C6.*

$$$ THAI 🍴 **Supatra River House.** Its location on the Chao Phraya River—and across from the Grand Palace—makes this restaurant worth a visit. A free ferry from Maharaj Pier shuttles diners back and forth. In the former home of Khunying Supatra, founder of the city's express boat business, the restaurant has a small museum dedicated to the art she collected. The set menus (B750–B1,200) make for easy ordering; you could also try a la carte options like the steamed sea bass in soy or spicy lemon. There are Thai dancing shows Saturday nights at 7:30. [$] *Average main: B330*

✉ 266 Soi Wat Rakhang, Arunamarin Rd., Thonburi ☎ 02/411–0305, 02/411–0874 🌐 www.supatrariverhouse.net ✍ Reservations essential [M] Subway: Hua Lamphong ✥ A4.*

CHINATOWN

Bangkok's Chinatown is impressive, to say the least, in large part for its food; it draws huge crowds of Thais who spend big bucks on specialties like shark's fin and bird's nest (which you'll see advertised on almost every single restaurant's storefront). Most of the food is Cantonese; many of these restaurants are indistinguishable from what you'd find in Hong Kong. In the middle of Chinatown, just off Yaowarat, there's a massive Indian cloth market known as Pahurat, and unique local Indian restaurants dot the area outside the market. Don't overlook the delicious street food, the noodle and dumpling shops, and the fruit and spice markets.

$ CHINESE 🍴 **Hong Kong Noodle.** This famous noodle shop would be at home in Tokyo or Hong Kong, with its three narrow floors, the top one a no-shoes-allowed tearoom with sofas and floor seating. The second floor has regular table seating and a counter with benches along the window that offer great people-watching on the street below. It's a little more chic than your average noodle stand, and its location near the Hua Lamphong subway station makes it a good place to refuel before exploring the neighborhood or while waiting for your train. As the name implies, you can find plenty of noodle dishes here, but the rice dishes are equally good. [$] *Average main: B90* ✉ *513–514 Rong Muang Rd., at Rama IV, Chinatown* ☎ *02/613–8977* 💳 *No credit cards* [M] *Subway: Hua Lamphong* ✥ *D4.*

$$$ CHINESE 🍴 **Hua Seng Hong Restaurant.** This expensive but worthwhile Chinatown classic takes you straight to Hong Kong with its excellent Cantonese roast meats—try the deliciously fatty duck—and soft, delicious goose-foot-and-abalone stew. Don't pass up the delectable fried pancake with eggs and plump oysters; the dim sum is also impressive. The restaurant is crowded and bustling, and service is authentically brusque. Like many of the neighboring Chinatown restaurants, the place hawks the inexplicably prized shark's fin and bird's nest dishes, but here as elsewhere, they're not worth the sky-high prices—both taste essentially like slightly more resilient glass noodles. [$] *Average main: B350* ✉ *371–373 Yaowarat Rd., Chinatown* ☎ *02/222–0635* 💳 *No credit cards* ✥ *C4.*

$ CHINESE 🍴 **Nai Sow.** Regulars say this Chinese-Thai restaurant, next door to Wat Plaplachai, has the city's best *tom yum goong* (spicy shrimp soup). Chefs may come and go, but the owner somehow manages to keep the recipe to this signature dish a secret. The food here is consistently excellent; try the *naw mai thalay* (sea asparagus in oyster sauce), the *phad kra prao kai moo goong* (spicy chicken, pork, and shrimp with basil leaves), the curried beef, or the sweet-and-sour mushrooms. Simpler options, like fried rice, are also very good. The fried taro is an unusual and delicious dessert. [$] *Average main: B150* ✉ *3/1 Maitrichit Rd., Chinatown* ☎ *02/222–1539* ✍ *Reservations not accepted* [M] *Subway: Hua Lamphong* ✥ *D4.*

Continued on page 81

BANGKOK STREET FOOD

by Robin Goldstein & Alexis Herschkowitsch

In Thailand a good rule of thumb is, the less you pay for food, the better it is. And the food offered by street vendors is very cheap and very good. At any hour, day or night, Thais crowd around sidewalk carts and stalls, slurping noodles or devouring fiery *som tam* (green papaya salad) all for just pennies.

The cooks at street stalls are Thailand's true culinary giants.

If you only eat at upscale restaurants geared to foreigners, you'll miss out on the chili, fish sauce, and bright herbal flavors that define Thai cuisine. Even if you're picky, consider trying simple noodle dishes and skewered meats.

A typical meal costs between B20 and B50 (you pay when you get your food), and most stalls have a few tables and chairs where you can eat.

Street food in Bangkok.

Vendors don't adhere to meal times, nor are different foods served for breakfast, lunch, or dinner, as Thais often eat multiple snacks throughout the day rather than full meals. It's OK to combine foods from more than one cart; vendors won't mind, especially if they're selling something like a curried stew that comes in a plastic bag with no utensils. Find a different stall that offers plates and cutlery, order rice, and add your curry to the mix. Enjoy!

SOM TAM

Thai chefs use contrasting flavors to create balance in their cuisine. The popular green papaya salad is a good example, with dried shrimp, tart lime, salty fish sauce, crunchy peanuts, and long thin slices of green papaya. Pair it with sticky rice for a refreshing treat on a hot day.

SOUR Lime adds a welcome tartness to salads and other dishes, counteracting sweetness.

SPICY Thais like it hot, sometimes using more than 10 fiery chili peppers per dish.

SALTY Instead of salt, Thais often use fish sauce and fermented shrimp paste, which have more nuanced flavors.

BITTER Roasted peanuts add a pleasant bitterness and crunch.

SWEET Palm sugar, a dark brown, natural, aromatic sweetener—will make you wonder why you've been using refined sugar all your life.

STAYING HEALTHY

Sanitary standards in Thailand are far higher than those in many developing countries. By taking a few precautions, you can safely enjoy this wonderful cuisine.

Fruit from Chatusak Market, Bangkok.

■ Avoid tap water. It's the bacteria in the water supply that causes most problems. The water on the table at stalls and restaurants is almost always purified, but stick with bottled water to play it safe.

■ Lots of flies are never a good sign. Enough said.

■ Know your stomach. Freshly cooked, hot food is least likely to contain bacteria. Steer clear of raw foods and fruits that cannot be peeled if you know you're sensitive.

■ Use common sense when selecting a street vendor or a restaurant. Crowds mean high turnover, which translates into fresher food.

WHAT SHOULD I ORDER?

Locals will probably be eating the cart's specialty, so if you're not sure what to order, don't be afraid to point. The following are a few common and delicious dishes you'll find in Bangkok.

Larb.

LARB Another refreshing and flavorful shredded salad, larb (pronounced lahb) consists of ground meat or fish, lime, fish sauce, and a generous helping of aromatic kaffir lime leaves.

PAD Noodles come in many varieties at street carts, and vendors add their own twists. Noodle soups with meat or innards, though traditionally Chinese or Vietnamese, are common in Bangkok, as are *pad khee mao* (drunken noodles) with vegetables, shellfish, or meat, wok-singed and served without broth. If you're in the Old City, stop by Raan Jay Fai (⇨ Ch. 2), an open-air restaurant with legendary *pad khee mao*—decadently big rice noodles with river prawns and basil.

Pad Thai.

TOM YUM This delicious and aromatic water-based soup—flavored with fish sauce, lemongrass, kaffir lime leaves, and vegetables—is a local favorite. *Tom yum goong,* with shrimp, is a popular variation.

YANG Thais love these marinated meat sticks, grilled over charcoal. Pork is usually the tastiest.

Tom yum.

WILL IT BE TOO SPICY?

Because most Thai cooks tone things down for foreigners, the biggest battle can sometimes be getting enough heat in your food. To be sure that your dish is spicy, ask for it *phet phet* (spicy); if you want it mild, request *mai phet* (less spicy). If you get a bite that's too spicy, water won't help—eat a bite of rice or something sweet to counteract the heat.

Food on sale at Damnoen Saduak floating market.

WHAT ARE ALL THE CONDIMENTS FOR?

At some street stalls, particularly soup and noodle shops, you'll be offered an array of seasonings and herbs to add to your dish: chilies marinated in salty fish sauce or soaking in oil; fresh herbs like mint, cilantro, and Thai basil; crunchy bits of toasted rice, peanuts, or fried onions; and lime wedges. Although it's a good idea to taste things you don't recognize so you don't over-flavor your meal, our advice is to pile it on!

Though it has a bad rap, the flavor enhancer MSG is sometimes used at street stalls and restaurants in Thailand. You can ask for food without it *(mai sai phong chu rat)* if it doesn't agree with you. You may also see MSG, a crystal that looks like white sugar, in a little jar on your table, along with sugar, chili paste, and fish sauce.

Two varieties of Thai basil.

YOU WANT ME TO EAT WHAT?

Pan-fried, seasoned insects such as ants, grasshoppers, and cockroaches, are popular snacks in Thailand. A plastic bag full of these crunchy delicacies will cost you about B20 or 50¢. To try your hand at insect-eating, start small. Little guys like ants are the most palatable, since they really just taste like whatever they've been flavored with (lime or chili, for example). Cockroaches have a higher squeamish factor: You have to pull the legs and the wings off the larger ones. And stay away from the silkworm cocoons, which do not taste any better than they sound.

At fruit stalls in Bangkok you may find the durian, a husk-covered fruit famous for its unpleasant smell. In fact the scent, which is a bit like spicy body odor, is so overpowering that some Thai hotels don't let you keep durians in your room. But don't judge the durian by its smell alone: Many love the fruit's pudding-like texture and intense tropical flavor, which is similar to passion fruit. Buy one at a fruit stand, ask the seller to cut it open, and taste its yellow flesh for yourself.

(above) Deep fried bugs (actual size).
(below) Durian.

2

$ INDIAN 🍴 **Punjab Sweets.** This vegetarian south Indian restaurant is always jam-packed with members of the local Indian community enjoying delicately crispy *pani poori* (crispy shells filled with potato and onion) or earthy samosas. The lighting is low, and the place is a bit drab, but the food is top-notch. There's an adjacent restaurant under the same management that serves meat, too. [$] *Average main: B60* ✉ *11/1 Chakraphet Rd., Chinatown* ☎ *02/222–6541, 081/869–3815* [M] *Subway: Hua Lamphong* ✣ *B4.*

$$ THAI 🍴 **T & K Seafood.** Proudly displaying the freshest catches on ice out front, this enormous and popular seafood restaurant begins luring in customers daily at 4:30 pm and serves as late as 1:30 am. Whole fish is always a good option, and generally cheaper than the crustaceans, which are also tasty. The place offers both shark's fin and bird's nest soup, but if you've had either of these once, that's probably enough. Stick with such Thai options as the *pla kapong neung manao* (steamed sea bass) and you can't go wrong. [$] *Average main: B300* ✉ *49–51 Phadungdao Rd., Chinatown* ☎ *02/223–4519* ⏲ *No lunch* [M] *Subway: Hua Lamphong* ✣ *C4.*

$$ CHINESE 🍴 **Tang Jai Yoo.** This open-air ground-floor seafood restaurant, full of festive round tables, is a great Chinatown find. Whole crabs, lobsters, or sea leech come live from tanks inside the restaurant; stewed turtle soup is a fun departure from mainstream Thai cuisine. Roasted pig skin is one of the best terrestrial options. The set menus are the best way to sample a variety of dishes. [$] *Average main: B250* ✉ *85–89 Yaowapanit Rd., Chinatown* ☎ *02/224–2167* 🌐 *www.tangjaiyoo.com* [M] *Subway: Hua Lamphong* ✣ *C4.*

PATHUMWAN

Unimaginably busy Pathumwan, which includes Siam Square, has a little bit of everything, although many of the restaurants cater to the business crowd. These can range from humble lunch stops to power-dining extravaganzas.

$ THAI Fodor's Choice ★ 🍴 **Ban Khun Mae.** This casually upmarket Siam Square restaurant is where the locals go if they want to enjoy skillful, authentic Thai cuisine in an atmosphere that's a couple of notches above that of the simple family restaurants. The room is dark, comfortable, and inviting, filled with big round tables. Start with the sensational *kung sa oug* (a plate of sweet and silky raw shrimp delightfully balanced with chili and garlic), and continue with *pla rad pik* (deep-fried grouper with sweet-and-sour hot sauce). Finish with the unique *tum tim krob* (water-chestnut dumpling in coconut syrup with tapioca). [$] *Average main: B150* ✉ *458/6–9 Siam Sq., Soi 8, Rama I Rd., Pathumwan* ☎ *02/250–1952 up to 13* 🌐 *www.bankhunmae.com* ✣ *E4.*

$ THAI 🍴 **Big C.** The food court on the fifth floor of the Big C shopping mall offers a staggering selection of authentic Thai (and a few Chinese) dishes at rock-bottom prices, with virtually nothing exceeding B80. Service is cafeteria-style: you choose, point, and then bring your tray to one of the tables in the middle of the bustling mall. Before you order, you'll prepay at the cashier station and receive a debit card; your selections are deducted from the balance. B200 should be plenty for two, and you can get a refund on any unspent baht after you're done. Highlights include very spicy chicken with ginger, Cantonese-style honey-roasted pork with crackly skin, and excellent sweetened Thai iced tea with milk. $ *Average main: B60* ✉ *97/11 Ratchadamri Rd., opposite Central World Plaza, Pathumwan* ☎ *02/250–4888* Ⓜ *Skytrain: Chitlom* ✛ *E4.*

$$$$ ✕ **Genji.** Bangkok has plenty of good Japanese restaurants, but many
JAPANESE can be a bit chilly toward newcomers. Genji is the happy exception, and the staff is always pleasant. There's an excellent sushi bar and several small private rooms where you can enjoy succulent grilled eel or a Kobe beef roll with asparagus and fried bean curd. Set menus for lunch and dinner are well conceived, and are a nice change from typical Thai fare. Lunch seats fill up quickly, and dinner sometimes requires a wait. $ *Average main: B750* ✉ *Nai Lert Park Hotel Bangkok, 2 Wittayu (Wireless Rd.), Pathumwan* ☎ *02/253–0123* Ⓜ *Skytrain: Ploenchit* ✛ *F3.*

$ ✕ **Home Kitchen.** A true hole-in-the-wall, this kitchen shines as one of
THAI the best places in the city for authentic local cuisine; it's where many local groups of friends go to celebrate the simple act of eating delicious food. Don't miss the *tom yum goong* (hot-and-sour soup with giant river prawns), which is redolent of lemongrass, Kaffir lime leaves, and galangal; the delicately crispy oyster omelet; the crispy catfish salad with green mango; or the fried whole fish in chili-and-lime sauce. Such classics simply excel here, and you owe it to yourself to try all of them before leaving Bangkok. There is also a larger air-conditioned section of the restaurant just down the street. $ *Average main: B150* ✉ *94 Langsuan Rd., Soi 7, Pathumwan* ☎ *02/253–1888* Ⓜ *Subway: Lumphini* ✛ *F4.*

$$$$ ✕ **JoJo.** Elegant, chic, and delectable, JoJo is all these and more. Start
ITALIAN off a refined dinner with an antipasto featuring burrata cheese, followed by the kitchen's signature dish of squid-ink tagliolini in Boston lobster sauce. For dessert there's a tiramisu martini. There's a huge fine wine selection to accompany the meal. The prices match the fancy surroundings, which are comprised of a romantic candlelight outdoor patio along with an elegant interior dining room, so be prepared to go to town. $ *Average main: $900* ✉ *St. Regis Bangkok, 159 Ratchadamri, Pathumwan* ☎ *02/207–7815* ⊕ *www.stregis.com* ⚭ *Reservations essential* Ⓜ *Skytrain: Ratchadamri* ✛ *F4.*

$$$$ ✕ **KiSara.** This upscale Japanese restaurant serves top-notch sushi, and
JAPANESE the sake selection will please almost anyone. The service is almost uncomfortably deferential, but never pompous. Not surprisingly, the tea is delicious, and the sushi rice is expertly vinegared; you might find yourself ordering it as a side and eating it plain. The prized Matsuzaka beef dish is tasty, with an almost overwhelming surfeit of fat marbled throughout the meat. Dinner prices are sky-high, but set lunches are cheaper. $ *Average main: B800* ✉ *Conrad Hotel, 87 Wittayu (Wireless Rd.), Pathumwan* ☎ *02/690–9233* Ⓜ *Skytrain: Ploenchit* ✛ *F4.*

$$$$ ✕ **Liu.** You'll want to be spotted at this swanky Chinese restaurant,
CHINESE whose concept and design comes from the creator of the equally snazzy Green T. House in Beijing. The interior is dominated by light-color wood, and the overall effect is soothing, especially given the high level of

service you'll receive here. The cuisine, which Liu calls "neoclassic Chinese," is a fusion of different regional styles; they are especially proud of the fried frogs' legs. Reserve well in advance, especially for the always-overbooked dim sum lunches. [$] *Average main: B550* ✉ *Conrad Hotel, 87 Wittayu (Wireless Rd.), Pathumwan* ☎ *02/690–9250, 02/690–9255* ✍ *Reservations essential* [M] *Skytrain: Ploenchit* ✣ *F4.*

$ THAI 🍴 **Once Upon a Time.** Period photos of the royal family, movie stars, and beauty queens cover the pink walls of this restaurant, which is really two old teak houses. The dining rooms are filled with delightful antiques; there are also tables in the garden between the houses. The *mieng khum,* a traditional snack of dried shrimp, dried coconut, peanuts, pineapple, chili pepper, and sweet tamarind sauce rolled together in a green leaf, makes an excellent appetizer. Afterward, move on to the chopped pork with chili sauce, beef fillet with pickled garlic, or whole grouper, served steamed or fried. The restaurant is about 100 yards down Soi 17, across the street from Panthip Plaza, the giant electronics market. [$] *Average main: B150* ✉ *32 Phetchaburi, Soi 17, Ratchathewi* ☎ *02/252–8629, 02/653–7857* [M] *Skytrain: Ratchathewi* ✣ *E3.*

$ THAI 🍴 **Polo Fried Chicken.** After offering only a lunch menu for decades, Polo Fried Chicken finally responded to its unwaning popularity by expanding its hours until 10 pm. The addition of an air-conditioned dining room is another concession to its loyal clientele. Here you'll get world-class fried chicken, flavored with black pepper and plenty of golden-brown garlic; the best way to sample it is with sticky rice and a plate of som tam, all for only B170. The place is a bit hard to find—as you enter Soi Polo (Soi Sanam Khli), it's about 50 yards in on your left. At lunchtime you need to get here before noon to snag a table before the office workers descend. The restaurant will deliver to your hotel (if you're reasonably close to Lumphini Park) for B30. [$] *Average main: B90* ✉ *Wittayu (Wireless Rd.), 137/1–2 Soi Polo (Soi Sanam Khli), Pathumwan (Lumphini)* ☎ *02/251–2772, 02/252–0856* ✍ *Reservations not accepted* 💳 *No credit cards* [M] *Subway: Lumphini* ✣ *F3.*

$$ THAI 🍴 **You & Mee.** Since hotel restaurants in Bangkok are often disappointing, this spot in the Grand Hyatt Erawan is a pleasant surprise: the quality is high, but the prices aren't. The atmosphere is relaxed and casual, with simple colors and largely unadorned tables. Come for the good selection of noodles or the *khao tom* (rice soup). **■ TIP→ There's a khao tom buffet at dinner for B380.** [$] *Average main: B250* ✉ *Grand Hyatt Erawan, 494 Ratchadamri Rd., Pathumwan* ☎ *02/254–1234* [M] *Skytrain: Chitlom* ✣ *F4.*

$$$$ JAPANESE FUSION Fodor's Choice ★ 🍴 **Zuma.** This posh Japanese eatery with branches in London, Hong Kong, Istanbul, Miami, and Dubai has arrived in Bangkok. Looking like an ultrasophisticated Japanese izikaya, the open kitchen serves up some of Bangkok's most innovative Japanese fare, with signature dishes like the dragon maki made with prawn tempura, freshwater eel, avocado, and spicy tempura flakes, or the *buta bara yuzu miso* pork belly skewers with yuzu and miso mustard leading the way. Don't forget to try the outstanding cocktails: the Rhubabu is made with rhubarb-infused vodka, sake, and crushed passion fruit, while the Mandarin Fizz combines Japanese shochu infused with jasmine, gin, apple juice, mandarin

purée, and sorbet, all shaken into a knockout drink. $ *Average main: B450* ✉ *159 Ratchadamri Rd., Pathumwan* ☎ *02/252 4707* ⊕ *www. zumarestaurant.com* Ⓜ *Skytrain: Ratchadamri* ✢ *F4.*

SILOM

Silom has Bangkok's biggest proliferation of restaurants, period. Many of them are in hotels, on the upper floors of skyscrapers, or around Patpong. You can find a vast variety of ethnic cuisines and restaurant styles in this district, from authentic, humble northern Thai to elaborate, wallet-busting preparations of foie gras.

$$$
THAI
✗ **Baan Klang Nam.** This clapboard house is right on the Chao Phraya River, and if you cruise the river at night, you'll probably end up gazing upon it, wishing you were among the crowd dining at one of Bangkok's most romantic spots. Happily, the place is less touristy than other restaurants of this type, most of which are part of big hotels. Spicy fried crab with black pepper, steamed fish with soy sauce, river prawns with glass noodles, and stir-fried crab with curry powder are excellent choices from the seafood-centric menu. The address is in Yannawa, south of Silom. $ *Average main: B390* ✉ *762/7 Bangkok Sq., Rama III Rd., Silom* ☎ *02/682–7180* ⊕ *www.baanklangnam.net* Ⓜ *Skytrain: Chong Nonsi* ✢ *F6.*

$
THAI
✗ **Ban Chiang.** This old wooden house is an oasis in the concrete city; the decor is turn-of-the-20th-century Bangkok, with antique prints and old photographs adorning the walls. The place is popular with the farang set, and your food won't come spicy unless you request it that way. Try the salted prawns or deep-fried grouper with garlic and white pepper, or dried whitefish with mango dip. Finish with banana fritters accompanied by coconut ice cream. $ *Average main: B175* ✉ *Surasak Rd., 14 Soi Srivieng, Bang Rak* ☎ *02/236–7045, 02/266–6994* Ⓜ *Skytrain: Surasak* ✢ *D6.*

$
THAI
✗ **Banana Leaf.** If you need a break from shopping on Silom Road, stop here for delicious and cheap eats. Try the baked crab with glass noodles, grilled black band fish, deep-fried fish with garlic and pepper, or grilled pork with coconut milk dip. The menu also offers 11 equally scrumptious vegetarian selections. There's a B400 minimum to pay by credit card. $ *Average main: B150* ✉ *Silom Complex, Silom Rd., Basement fl., Silom* ☎ *02/231–3124* ⊕ *www.bananaleafthailand.com* Ⓜ *Skytrain: Sala Daeng* ✢ *E5.*

$
LEBANESE
✗ **Beirut Restaurant.** A stone's throw from the hustle and bustle of Patpong, this relaxed neighborhood joint is a good place to enjoy an authentic Lebanese meal. Such Middle Eastern classics as crispy falafel, succulent lamb, and well-prepared salads are well represented. The restaurant also has branches in Thong Lor and Sukhumvit. $ *Average main: B150* ✉ *64 Silom Rd., Silom* ☎ *02/632–7448* ⊕ *www.beirut-restaurant.com* ✉ *No credit cards* ✢ *E5.*

$$$$
MODERN ASIAN
✗ **Breeze.** Practically in the clouds at the State Tower (home of some of the city's priciest restaurants), this ultra-hip eatery is where you'll spot international jet-setters and Bangkok's moneyed set. The shockingly futuristic design will have you thinking it's 2060, an effect that's most

pronounced at night when the dining room glows with purple neon. The kitchen shows off its proficiency with seafood in such dishes as wasabi prawns or wok-fried Maine lobster with champagne. There's a tasting menu (a jaw-dropping 4,300 baht) as well as a la carte options. $ *Average main: B1500* ⊠ *State Tower, 1055 Silom Rd., 52nd fl., Bang Rak* ☎ *02/624–9555* ⚷ *Reservations essential* ⊙ *No lunch* Ⓜ *Skytrain: Saphan Taksin* ✛ *D6.*

$$$ ✕ **Celadon.** Lotus ponds reflect the city's beautiful evening lights at this

THAI   romantic restaurant. The upmarket Thai food is good, with elegant touches that cater to locals as well as foreigners. The extensive menu includes preparations of enormous river prawns, excellent red duck curry, stir-fried morning glory, and a good version of banana-blossom salad. Some of the seafood dishes can be prepared in different styles, but the best choice is usually with chili and basil. Ask for your dishes spicy if you want the more authentic Thai balance of flavors—sometimes the dishes are a bit too sweet. $ *Average main: B390* ⊠ *Sukhothai Hotel, 13/3 S. Sathorn Rd., Silom* ☎ *02/344–8888* ⊕ *www.sukhothai.com* ⊙ *No lunch* Ⓜ *Subway: Lumphini; Skytrain: Sala Daeng* ✛ *F5.*

$$$$ ✕ **Ciao.** The Mandarin Oriental's latest addition to the Bangkok food

ITALIAN   scene, Ciao serves up classical Italian fare in a relaxed riverside setting with pleasant breezes and great views. From bruschetta to foccacia, everything on the menu is made with fine and fresh ingredients, meats and cheeses imported from Italy, and plenty of attention to detail. Entrées include eggplant ravioli or saffron risotto; for more adventurous eaters, there's pigeon breast with coffee sauce. There are plenty of top-notch wines to compliment the elegant food and surroundings. $ *Average main: B600* ⊠ *Mandarin Oriental, 48 Oriental Ave., Bang Rak* ☎ *02/659–9000* ⊕ *www.mandarinoriental.com* ✛ *C6.*

$$$$ ✕ **D'Sens.** Elite chefs and brothers Jacques and Laurent Pourcel, execu-

FRENCH   tive chefs of Le Jardin des Sens in Montpellier, France came to Thailand to start a fine eatery. Granted, they only came to set things up, but they also installed a veteran of their restaurant to stay in Bangkok, and the results are delicious. Skip the dishes with prestige ingredients like foie gras and lobster, and choose instead such subtly prepared dishes as the mussel soup with saffron and orange cream or the delicate roast turbot. The prices and the views from the 22nd floor are both sky-high. Set menus are available at both lunch and dinner. $ *Average main: B3050* ⊠ *Dusit Thani Bangkok Hotel, 946 Rama IV Rd., Silom* ☎ *02/200– 9000* ⊕ *www.dusit.com* ⊙ *Closed Sun. No lunch Sat.* Ⓜ *Subway: Silom; Skytrain: Sala Daeng* ✛ *E5.*

$$$$ ✕ **Eat Me.** This Aussie establishment is both a high-end eatery and a

INTERNATIONAL   swanky art gallery where rotating exhibits provide just the right atmosphere. Some think that the works of art on the walls and on the plates are less of a draw than the young and hip crowd. Dishes like Tasmanian salmon with an espresso mustard emulsion or scallop-and-squid ceviche with watermelon, grapefruit, and tarragon are just a few of the eclectic offerings that lean heavily on seafood. Stop by if you're in the neighborhood to people-watch and see who you can meet. (Hint: It will most likely be an expat.) $ *Average main: B450* ⊠ *Soi Pipat 2, Silom*

The spectacular view from Bangkok's famous Sky Bar, in one of the city's tallest buildings.

☎ 02/238–0931 ⊕ *www.eatmerestaurant.com* ⊘ *No lunch* Ⓜ *Subway: Silom; Skytrain: Sala Daeng* ✛ *E5.*

$ ✕ **Hai Som Tam Convent.** A sure sign of quality, Hai Som Tam Con-
THAI vent is packed with Thais sharing tables filled with northeast favorites like grilled chicken, spicy papaya salad, and savory minced pork. The open-air dining area can be hot, and is often crowded and noisy, but that's part of the fun. The staff doesn't speak much English, so the best way to order is to point to things that look good on neighboring tables. Ⓢ *Average main: B60* ⊠ *Silom Rd., 2/4–5 Soi Convent, Silom* ☎ 02/631–0216 ▭ *No credit cards* ⊘ *Closed Sat.* Ⓜ *Subway: Silom; Skytrain: Sala Daeng* ✛ *E5.*

$ ✕ **Harmonique.** Choose between tables on the terrace or in the dining
THAI rooms of this small house near the river. Inside, Thai antiques, chests scattered with bric-a-brac, and bouquets that seem to tumble out of their vases create relaxing clutter, as though you're dining at a relative's house. The staff is very good at helping indecisive diners choose from the brief menu. The *massaman* (peanut sauce–based curry) pork spare-ribs, the mild crab curry, and the deep-fried fish with lemongrass are all excellent. *Chu-chee* prawns or *larb moo* are slightly more interesting dishes, as is the *hoa mouk*—fish curry in a banana leaf. Over the years the crowd has become increasingly touristy, but there are still Thais who eat here regularly. Ⓢ *Average main: B180* ⊠ *22 Charoen Krung (New Rd.), Soi 34, Silom* ☎ 02/237–8175, 02/630–6270 ⊘ *Closed Sun.* Ⓜ *Skytrain: Saphan Taksin* ✛ *D5.*

$$ ✕ **Himali Cha Cha.** Cha Cha, who cooked for Indian Prime Minister
INDIAN Jawaharlal Nehru, died in 1996, but his recipes live on and are prepared with equal ability by his son Kovit. The tandoori chicken is locally

2

famous, but the daily specials, precisely explained by the staff, are usually too intriguing to pass up. The breads and the mango *lassi* (yogurt drinks) are delicious. The northern Indian cuisine includes garlic naan and cheese naan, served with various dishes—the mutton tandoori is particularly good. The typical Indian-themed decor sets the scene for this oldie but goodie. A branch on Convent Soi in Silom serves similar food in a more spacious dining area. $ *Average main: B270* ⊠ *1229/11 Charoen Krung (New Rd.), Bang Rak* ☎ *02/235–1569, 02/630–6358* Ⓜ *Skytrain: Saphan Taksin* ✣ *D6.*

$ ✕ **Home Cuisine Islamic Restaurant.** It can be a challenge to find a really
INDIAN   good *khao mok gai* (chicken biryani) in Bangkok, but this gem of a restaurant (opposite the French Embassy's parking lot off Charoenkrung Road) comes shining through. Home Cuisine specializes in biryani, and its mutton is perhaps even better than its chicken, and both are served with pickled eggplant and a side dish of sweet yogurt sauce. There are plenty of Thai dishes on the menu, but stick with the biryani. Tell taxi drivers to come in via Soi 40 to get here. It's a 15-minute walk from the Saphan Taksin BTS station. $ *Average main: B120* ⊠ *185 Charoen Krung (New Rd.), Soi 36, Bang Rak* ☎ *02/234–7911* ⊘ *No lunch Sun.* ✣ *D5.*

$$$$ ✕ **Jade Garden.** You won't find a better dim sum brunch than the one
CHINESE   at Jade Garden. The decor is more understated than at many expensive Chinese restaurants, with a remarkable wood-beam ceiling and softly lighted screens. Private dining rooms are available with advance notice. Two good dinner specials are fried Hong Kong noodles and pressed duck with tea leaves. Look for the monthly "special promotion" dish featuring seasonal ingredients. $ *Average main: B500* ⊠ *Montien Hotel, 54 Surawong Rd., Silom* ☎ *02/233–7060* Ⓜ *Subway: Silom; Skytrain: Sala Daeng* ✣ *E5.*

$$$$ ✕ **Le Normandie.** Perched atop the Mandarin Oriental, this legendary
FRENCH   restaurant commands an impressive view of the Chao Phraya. France's most highly esteemed chefs periodically take over the kitchen, often importing ingredients from the old country to use in their creations. Even when no superstar is on the scene, the food is remarkable. The pricey menu (it's hard to get away with spending less than B5,000 on a meal) often includes classic dishes like slow-cooked shoulder of lamb. The best bet is the prix fixe menu for 4,700 baht. $ *Average main: B4600* ⊠ *Mandarin Oriental, 48 Oriental Ave., Bang Rak* ☎ *02/659– 9000* ⊕ *www.mandarinoriental.com* ⚑ *Reservations essential* 🏛 *Jacket required* ⊘ *No lunch Sun.* Ⓜ *Skytrain: Saphan Taksin* ✣ *C6.*

$$ ✕ **Lek Seafood.** This unassuming storefront beneath an overpass is the
THAI   sort of establishment that brings international foodies flocking to Bang-
Fodor's Choice   kok. They come for the spicy crab salad with lemongrass, the catfish
★   with toasted rice salad, or the fried grouper topped with chili sauce—all expertly cooked and perfectly balanced with the five flavors. The interior here is nothing special, with poor lighting and bluish walls, but the lively buzz makes up for it. $ *Average main: B250* ⊠ *156 Narathiwat Ratchanakharin Rd., Soi 3, Bang Rak* ☎ *02/636–6460* ⊘ *No lunch* Ⓜ *Skytrain: Chong Nonsi* ✣ *G6.*

$$$$ CHINESE Fodor's Choice ★ 🍴 **The Mayflower.** Regulars at this top Cantonese restaurant include members of the Thai royal family, heads of state, and business tycoons. These VIPs favor the six opulent private rooms (one-day advance notice required), but the main dining room is equally stylish, with carved wood screens, porcelain vases, and an air of refinement that complements the outstanding food. Delicious Peking duck skin is served without a shred of meat, with roti-like pancakes, plum sauce, and fresh onions. Dim sum options are also stellar, especially the fried taro and pork rolls and the green-tea steam rolls. The wine list is excellent, but pricey. [$] *Average main: B450* ✉ *Dusit Thani Bangkok, 946 Rama IV Rd., Silom* ☎ *02/200–9000* [M] *Subway: Silom; Skytrain: Sala Daeng* ✥ *E5.*

$$$$ MODERN EUROPEAN 🍴 **Mezzaluna.** This blockbuster restaurant soars above the rest of Bangkok in the massive State Tower. A string quartet serenades you and the city's nouveau riche while you dine on innovative European-influenced preparations of caviar, foie gras, lobster, and so on. The food is good, if not great—a different set menu is featured every night—but more importantly, the view is peerless. But don't come unless you're ready to spend: this might be the most expensive restaurant in Bangkok. [$] *Average main: B4800* ✉ *State Tower, 1055 Silom Rd., 65th fl., Bang Rak* ☎ *02/624–9555* 🌐 *www.lebua.com* ✍ *Reservations essential* ⏲ *Closed Mon. No lunch* [M] *Skytrain: Saphan Taksin* ✥ *D6.*

$$$$ THAI Fodor's Choice ★ 🍴 **Nahm.** Master chef David Thompson won accolades for his Thai eatery in London, and his newly opened outpost in Bangkok has been called one of the world's best restaurants. Nahm may be run by a foreigner, but the Thai food here is better than anything else you will find in Bangkok, with all the dishes bursting with flavor and not softened for foreign palates. Standout dishes include the blue swimmer crab with coconut and turmeric curry, frog with chilies and cumin leaves, and grilled southern mussels. Better yet, you can sample all the best dishes by choosing the set menu for 1,700 baht. There's also an extensive wine list with bottles from around the globe to compliment the fantastic food. [$] *Average main: B600* ✉ *Metropolitan Hotel, 27 S. Sathorn Rd., Silom* ☎ *02/625–3333* 🌐 *www.nahm.como.bz* ✍ *Reservations essential* ⏲ *No lunch weekends* ✥ *F5.*

$$$ THAI Fodor's Choice ★ 🍴 **Pen.** This spacious restaurant has little in the way of atmosphere, but it's where the true seafood aficionados go to splurge. Though it's expensive by Thai restaurant standards, it's still a bargain compared to most hotel restaurants. Many dishes are nearly impossible to find outside Thailand: deep-fried parrot fish with shallots, enormous charcoal-grilled river prawns, Chinese-style mantis prawns, delectable mud crabs, and sliced green mango in tamarind sauce. Even though it's a little out of the way in Yannawa, this temple to seafood is not to be missed. [$] *Average main: B390* ✉ *2068/4 Chan Rd., Chong Nonsi, Silom* ☎ *02/287–2907, 02/286–7061* ✥ *F6.*

$ CHIU CHOW 🍴 **Prachak.** This little place with bare walls and tile floor serves superb *pet* (roast duck) and *moo daeng* (red pork), making it a favorite of many locals. The place is famous for its wonton noodle soup, reputed to be the best in Bangkok. It's been in business for more than a century, and wealthy Thai families often send their maids here to bring dinner home. You may want to follow their lead, as the dining room can get crowded.

2

Whether you eat in or take out, get here early—by 6 pm there's often little duck left, and by 8:30 pm the doors are shut tight. Finding Prachak is a bit challenging, as it doesn't have an English sign. It's on busy Charoen Krung, across the street from the big Robinson shopping center near the Shangri-La Hotel. $ *Average main: B90* ⊠ *Bang Rak Market, 1415 Charoen Krung (New Rd.), Bang Rak* ☎ *02/234-3755* ⊕ *www.prachakrestaurant.com* ▬ *No credit cards* Ⓜ *Skytrain: Saphan Taksin* ⊹ *D6.*

$$$ ✕ **Saffron.** The creative modern Thai menu at Saffron is even more
THAI exciting than the stunning views from the 52nd floor of the towering Banyan Tree Hotel. Start with a banana-blossom salad with chicken, which mixes chili paste, dried shrimp paste, and cilantro for brightness. Then move on to the *phad pak kana moo krob* (stir-fried crisp pork belly with kale), a Chinese-influenced gem, or fried crab in Indian curry powder. $ *Average main: B360* ⊠ *Banyan Tree Hotel, 21/100 S. Sathorn Rd., Silom* ☎ *02/679-1200* ⊕ *www.banyantree.com/en/bangkok* Ⓜ *Subway: Lumphini* ⊹ *F5.*

$$$$ ✕ **Salathip.** On a veranda facing the Chao Phraya River, this restaurant's
THAI setting practically guarantees a romantic evening. Be sure to reserve an outside table so you can enjoy the breeze. Although the food may not have as many chilies as some would like, the Thai standards are represented on the menu. Good among those are Phuket lobster dishes and curried river prawns. The set menus feature seven or eight Thai favorites and are worth the splurge of 1,200 baht (or more). The live traditional music makes everything taste even better. $ *Average main: B425* ⊠ *Shangri-La Hotel, Charoen Krung (New Rd.), 89 Soi Wat Suan Plu, Bang Rak* ☎ *02/236-7777* ⌲ *Reservations essential* ◷ *No lunch* Ⓜ *Skytrain: Saphan Taksin* ⊹ *C6.*

$$ ✕ **Tawandang German Brewery.** You can't miss Tawandang—it resembles
ECLECTIC a big barrel. Food may be an afterthought to the 40,000 liters of lager and other beers brewed here each month, but the kitchen turns out decent Thai food, with some German and Chinese fare thrown in for good measure. The taproom (which is really why you should come) is especially boisterous when Bruce Gaston's Fong Nam Band performs its fusion of Thai and Western music. On nights that the band's not playing, local singers warble Thai and Western favorites. Take a taxi from the Skytrain station to this eatery in Yannawa. ■**TIP➔ Tell taxi drivers the restaurant's full name, or you might be taken to a nightclub also called Tawandang.** $ *Average main: B300* ⊠ *462/61 Rama III Rd., Silom* ☎ *02/678-1114* Ⓜ *Skytrain: Chong Nonsi* ⊹ *F6.*

$$$$ ✕ **Vertigo.** You'll dine on top of the world this classy bar, lounge, and
SEAFOOD eatery—it's one of the loftiest open-air restaurants anywhere. Tables are set near the roof's edge for maximum effect; there are also comfy couches and low-lying tables at the adjacent Moon Bar if you prefer to come just for drinks. In spite of its name, the international menu here, which focuses on grilled seafood, is tasty, and the service is friendly. Due to its altitude, the restaurant frequently closes when there are high winds, so you should have a backup plan. It doesn't start serving food until 6:30, but it's nice to come for a sunset drink and take in the stupendous views. $ *Average main: B750* ⊠ *Banyan Tree Hotel, 21/100*

S. Sathorn Rd., Silom ☎ *02/679–1200* 🌐 *www.banyantree.com/en/bangkok* ✍ *Reservations essential* 🕑 *No lunch* [M] *Subway: Lumphini; Skytrain: Sala Daeng* ✣ *F5.*

$$$$ ITALIAN Fodor'sChoice ★ 🍴 **Zanotti.** Everything about this place is top-notch, from the attentive service to the extensive menu focusing on the regional cuisines of Piedmont and Tuscany. You can find anything from pizza and pasta to fish and steak, but the traditional osso buco served with gremolata and saffron risotto is recommended. There's an unusually broad Italian wine list with selections by the bottle, glass, or carafe. The prix-fixe lunches are a bargain. The low ceilings and closely grouped tables give the place some intimacy, but the vibe is more lively than romantic, especially during the lunch and dinner rushes. [$] *Average main: B600* ✉ *21/2 Saladaeng Colonnade Condominium, Silom Rd., Silom* ☎ *02/636–0002, 02/636–0266* 🌐 *www.zanotti-ristorante.com* ✍ *Reservations essential* [M] *Skytrain: Sala Daeng* ✣ *E5.*

SUKHUMVIT

Sukhumvit is Bangkok's hippest area for dining and going out, and consequently many of the restaurants have more style than substance, although there's good food to be had, and the area of Thong Lor has become known as a foodie's paradise in recent times.

$$ THAI 🍴 **Cabbages & Condoms.** Don't be put off by the restaurant's odd name and the wide array of contraceptives for sale. This popular place raises funds for the Population & Community Development Association, Thailand's family-planning program. The food is geared to foreign tastes but is competently prepared; standouts include the deep-fried chicken wrapped in pandanus leaves, the fried fish with mango sauce, and the crispy duck salad. The eatery is comfortable and funky, with fairy lights giving the place a warm glow. [$] *Average main: B250* ✉ *10 Sukhumvit, Soi 12, Sukhumvit* ☎ *02/229–4610* 🌐 *www.cabbagesandcondoms.com* [M] *Subway: Sukhumvit; Skytrain: Asok* ✣ *G4.*

$$ KOREAN 🍴 **Doo Rae.** While there are many authentic Korean restaurants in Sukhumvit Plaza, this unpretentious spot is one of the best. Even though there are three stories of tables, there's often a wait, even at 9 on a weeknight. Barbecue—you cook the meat yourself over a grill at your table—featuring hearty *bulgogi* (thin slices of beef in a tasty marinade) is a good way to go, as are the substantial tofu stews. Drinks include a larger selection of sake and *soju* (a rice-based drink similar to vodka, but with a lower alcohol content) than you'll find elsewhere in the city. [$] *Average main: B300* ✉ *212/15 Sukhumvit Plaza, Soi 12, Sukhumvit* ☎ *02/653–3815* [M] *Subway: Sukhumvit* ✣ *G4.*

$$$$ INDIAN 🍴 **Hazara.** After a long day of sightseeing, the chic atmosphere at this upscale Indian eatery simply can't be beat. Plush couches and beautiful drapes create a cozy feel, and there's a great drink list. Some feel the food itself doesn't hold a candle to the cheap Indian street food you can find elsewhere in the city. It's true that the menu isn't too creative, but there are some interesting options, including delicious tandoori chicken and *dahl* (lentil soup). There's also a large array of vegetarian dishes and different types of naan. [$] *Average main: B450* ✉ *29 Sukhumvit,*

Soi 38, Sukhumvit ☎ *02/713–6048* ⊕ *www.facebars.com* ⊗ *No lunch*
Ⓜ *Skytrain: Thong Lo* ✛ *H5.*

$$
THAI

✕ **Je Ngor's Kitchen.** Stir-fried morning glory is truly glorious at this
eatery, which is absolutely adored by locals. People also swear by the
stir-fried crab in red curry and the deep-fried rock lobster. The decor is
simple but attractive, with warm colors and yellow lanterns. There are
good set menus at lunch. Other branches dot Bangkok, but the Sukhum-
vit location is the biggest. $ *Average main: B250* ⊠ *68/2 Sukhumvit,
Soi 20, Sukhumvit* ☎ *02/258–8008* ⊕ *www.jengor-seafoods.com* Ⓜ *Sky-
train: Phrom Phong* ✛ *G5.*

$$
CAFÉ

✕ **Kuppa.** This light and airy space maintains the aura of its former life
as a warehouse, but it's certainly more chic than shabby these days, with
polished metal and blond wood adding a hip counterpoint to cement
floors. An advantage to such a space is that, unlike many downtown
eateries, each table has plenty of room around it. Kuppa offers traditional Thai fare as well as many international dishes, and it has attracted
a dedicated following because of its coffee (roasted on the premises)
and its impressive desserts. The one drawback is that the portions are
somewhat small for the price. $ *Average main: B240* ⊠ *39 Sukhumvit,
Soi 16, Sukhumvit* ☎ *02/663–0450, 02/258–0194* ⊕ *www.kuppa.co.th*
Ⓜ *Subway: Sukhumvit; Skytrain: Asok* ✛ *G5.*

$$
THAI

✕ **Lan Na Thai.** This hip hangout attracts a cool, mainly international
clientele. The reasonably authentic Thai menu includes the ubiquitous
som tam, steamed freshwater prawns, and duck with Kaffir lime leaf. If
you're feeling adventurous, sea bass wrapped in banana leaf and pork
belly in Chiang Mai–style curry paste are two more exciting options.
Though the beautiful setting (think comfy, plush seating and large tapes-
tries) and toned-down dishes are geared to foreigners, sometimes that's
just what you're in the mood for after a long day of exploring. $ *Aver-
age main: B270* ⊠ *29 Sukhumvit, Soi 38, Sukhumvit* ☎ *02/713–6048*
⊕ *www.facebars.com* ⊗ *No lunch* Ⓜ *Skytrain: Thong Lo* ✛ *H5.*

$$
VIETNAMESE

✕ **Le Dalat.** This classy restaurant, a favorite with Bangkok residents,
consists of several intimate dining rooms in what was once a private
home. Don't pass up the *naem neuang,* a garlicky grilled meatball you
garnish with bits of garlic, ginger, hot chili, star apple, and mango
before wrapping it in a lettuce leaf and popping it in your mouth.
Seafood dishes—which are among the pricier options—include *cha
ca thang long,* Hanoi-style fried fish with dill. $ *Average main: B240*
⊠ *57 Soi Prasarnmitr, Sukhumvit, Soi 23, Sukhumvit* ☎ *02/259–9593*
⊕ *www.ledalatbkk.com* ⌸ *Reservations essential* Ⓜ *Subway: Sukhumvit; Skytrain: Asok* ✛ *G4.*

$$$
THAI
Fodor's Choice
★

✕ **The Local.** A welcome addition to the Sukhumvit scene, this eatery's
emphasis is on fresh traditional fare and hard-to-find regional special-
ties, such as the lemongrass salad with wild betel leaves, or the outstand-
ing *pla ta pien,* a local river fish stewed for 30 hours with sugarcane and
ginger. The owner comes from a long line of food lovers, and the family
has run restaurants for many decades. In addition to the excellent food,
homemade ice cream, and creative cocktails (try a tom yum martini
or a dragonfruit mojito), this restaurant in a century-old house wins
praise for its wood floors, old photos and antiques, and lovely outdoor

terrace. $ *Average main: B360* ✉ *32 Sukhumvit, Soi 23, Sukhumvit* ☎ *02/664–0664* ⊕ *www.thelocalthaicuisine.com* ✢ *G4.*

$

THAI

✕ **My Choice.** Thais with a taste for their grandmothers' traditional recipes have flocked to this restaurant off Sukhumvit Road since the mid-'80s. The *ped aob* (whole roasted duck) is particularly popular. The interior is plain, so when the weather is cool most people prefer to sit outside. $ *Average main: B120* ✉ *5 Sukhumvit, Soi 36, Sukhumvit* ☎ *02/258–6174, 02/259–9470* ⊕ *www.mychoicethaicuisine.com* Ⓜ *Skytrain: Thong Lo* ✢ *H6.*

$

THAI

Fodor's Choice

★

✕ **Pochana 55.** You wouldn't expect much by looking at this nondescript restaurant from the outside, but there is a reason why locals have been packing this place night after night for years. The place started out as a late night khao tom rice soup eatery, and has expanded to having one of the most extensive and tastiest Thai-Chinese menus in town. Just about any dish is a winner, but you will notice that most diners order a plate of *aw suan* (oyster and egg souffle), tom yum soup, and one of the various sizzling beef or fish platters. If you are in town during the rainy season, try the *dok krajon* (literally translated as "little flower") salad made with local vegetables, pork, and spices. $ *Average main: B150* ✉ *1087–1093 Sukhumvit, corner of Soi 55, Thong Lor* ☎ *02/391 2021* ▭ *No credit cards* ☉ *No lunch* ✢ *H5.*

$$$

INDIAN

✕ **Rang Mahal.** Savory food in a pleasant setting with great 26th-floor views of the city brings people back to this upscale Indian restaurant. The *bindi do piaza* (stir-fried onion and okra) is interesting, the *rogunjosh kashmiri* (mutton curry) is a hit, and the homemade naan breads are top-notch. The main dining room has Indian music, which can be loud to some ears, but there are also smaller rooms for a quieter meal. Take a jacket—the air-conditioning can be overpowering—and ask for a window seat for a great view of the city. $ *Average main: B390* ✉ *Rembrandt Hotel, 19 Sukhumvit, Soi 18, Sukhumvit* ☎ *02/261–7100* ♨ *Reservations essential* Ⓜ *Subway: Sukhumvit; Skytrain: Asok* ✢ *G5.*

$$$$

SEAFOOD

✕ **Seafood Market.** Although this place is miles from the ocean, the fish here is so fresh that it feels like the boats must be somewhere nearby. As in a supermarket, you take a small cart and choose from an array of seafood—crabs, prawns, lobsters, clams, oysters, and fish. The waiter then takes your selections to the chef, who cooks it however you like. Typically, your eyes are bigger than your stomach, so select with prudence, not gusto. Unfortunately, the 1,500-seat setting and fluorescent lighting add to the supermarket feel, but it's a fun and unique dining experience. The seafood here is overpriced (plus you pay a charge for the cooking) and the atmosphere is extremely touristy, but the fish is good and the place is always packed. $ *Average main: B450* ✉ *89 Sukhumvit, Soi 24, Sukhumvit* ☎ *02/261–2071* ⊕ *www.seafood.co.th* ♨ *Reservations essential* Ⓜ *Skytrain: Phrom Phong* ✢ *H5.*

$$

THAI

Fodor's Choice

★

✕ **Soul Food Mahanakorn.** Launched by food critic Jarrett Wrisley, this gem of a restaurant and bar is in a converted Chinese shophouse in trendy Thong Lor and is usually packed to the rafters. It's no surprise, as Soul Food Mahanakorn serves some of the best Thai food in the city, ranging from *heng lay* (a curry popular in the north) to *larb pet* (roast duck salad) to an array of fresh vegetables served with several spicy chili sauces. The double-pour drinks here are every bit as good as the food, with concoctions like a Lycheegrass Collins or Lo-So Mojito using local ingredients to compliment the outstanding food. $ *Average main: B240* ✉ *56/10 Sukhumvit, Soi 55, Thong Lor* ☎ *02/714–7708* ⊕ *www. soulfoodmahanakorn.com* ✆ *No lunch* ✛ *H5.*

$$

THAI

✕ **Vientiane Kitchen.** This open-air restaurant, named for the capital of Laos, is set under thatched roofs and has a slightly gritty feel. You can opt for a table or traditional seating on floor mats around a low table. Lao cuisine is similar to northeastern Thai cuisine. Among the Thai-style standards offered here, like traditional grilled chicken, sticky rice, and som tam, are a few riskier dishes like *nam tok muu* (waterfall pork), so named because it's hot enough to makes your eyes run like a waterfall (it's actually toned down quite a bit here). The frog soup and grilled duck beak are actually quite tasty, despite the strange images they conjure up. It's best to go with a group so you can try several dishes. Live Laotian music and dance add to the experience. $ *Average main: B240* ✉ *8 Sukhumvit, Soi 36, Sukhumvit* ☎ *02/258–6171* Ⓜ *Skytrain: Thong Lo* ✛ *H6.*

WHERE TO STAY

Bangkok offers a staggering range of lodging choices, and even some of the best rooms are affordable to travelers on a budget. The city has nearly 500 hotels and guesthouses, and the number is growing. In fact, competition has brought the prices down at many of the city's hotels; unfortunately, the service has suffered at some as a result of cutting corners to lower prices. Still, you'll feel more pampered here than in many other cities.

For first-class lodging, few cities in the world rival Bangkok. In recent years the Mandarin Oriental, Peninsula, Four Seasons, and a handful of others have been repeatedly rated among the best in the world, with new players like the Sofitel So and St. Regis getting major accolades. If there were a similar comparison of the world's boutique hotels, Bangkok's selection would be near the top, too. These high-end hotels are surprisingly affordable, with rates comparable to standard hotels in New York or London. Business hotels also have fine service, excellent restaurants, and amenities like health clubs and spas.

Wherever you stay, remember that prices fluctuate enormously, and that huge discounts are the order of the day. Internet discounts are also widely available, and booking online can often save you up to several thousand baht. ■**TIP➔ Always ask for a better price, even when you are checking in.** Deals may be more difficult to come by during the high season from November through February, but during low season they're plentiful.

Prices in the reviews are the lowest cost of a standard double room in high season. Use the coordinate (✛ B2) at the end of each listing to locate a site on the Where to Stay in Bangkok map.

Hotels are concentrated in four areas: in Silom and Bang Rak (home to many of riverfront hotels); around Siam Square and along Phetchaburi

BEST BETS FOR BANGKOK LODGING

Fodor's offers a listing of quality lodging experiences at every price range, from the city's best budget guesthouse to its most sophisticated luxury hotels. Here, we've compiled our top recommendations by price and experience. The best properties—those that provide a remarkable experience in their price range—are designated with a Fodor's Choice logo.

Fodor's Choice ★

Chakrabongse Villas, $$$$, p. 96
The Conrad, $$$$, p. 100
Hilton Millennium, $$$$, p. 97
Mandarin Oriental, $$$$, p. 102
Peninsula, $$$$, p. 97
Shangri-La, $$$$, p. 102
Sofitel So, $$$$, p. 104
St. Regis, $$$$, p. 101
The Siam Hotel, $$$$, p. 96
Tower Club at Lebua, $$$$, p. 104

By Price

$

La Residence, p. 101
River View Guest House, p. 97

$$

Bangkok Bel-Aire, p. 105

Buddy Lodge, p. 96
Grand China Princess, p. 97
Siam Heritage, p. 102
Triple Two Silom, p. 104

$$$

Swissotel Nai Lert Park, p. 101

$$$$

Mandarin Oriental, p. 102
Sheraton Grande Sukhumvit, p. 106
Sofitel So, p. 104
St. Regis, p. 101
Siam, p. 96
Tower Club at Lebua, p. 104
The W, p. 104

By Experience

BEST FOR KIDS

Anantara Bangkok Riverside, $$$, p. 97
Banyan Tree Bangkok, $$$$, p. 101

Hilton Millennium, $$$$, p. 97
Marriott Courtyard, $$, p. 100

BEST LOCATION

St. Regis, $$$$, p. 101
Shangri-La, $$$$, p. 102
Sheraton Grande Sukhumvit, $$$$, p. 106
Sofitel So, $$$$, p. 104
The W, $$$$, p. 104
Westin Grande Sukhumvit, $$$$, p. 106

BEST POOL

The Conrad, $$$$, p. 100
Hilton Millennium, $$$$, p. 97
Mandarin Oriental, $$$$, p. 102
Swissotel Nai Lert Park, $$$, p. 101
Peninsula, $$$$, p. 97

BEST SPA

Anantara Bangkok Riverside, $$$, p. 97
Four Seasons, $$$$, p. 100
Grand Hyatt Erawan, $$$$, p. 100
Mandarin Oriental, $$$$, p. 102
Metropolitan, $$$$, p. 102

BEST VIEW

Banyan Tree Bangkok, $$$$, p. 101
Grand China Princess, $$, p. 97
Peninsula, $$$$, p. 97
River View Guest House, $, p. 97
Shangri-La, $$$$, p. 102
Sofitel So, $$$$, p. 104
Tower Club at Lebua, $$$$, p. 104

WHERE SHOULD I STAY?

	Neighborhood Vibe	Pros	Cons
North Bangkok	This relatively quiet business and residential neighborhood has plenty of local culture but few tourist attractions.	This is the closest neighborhood to Don Muang, the domestic and low-budget carrier airport—helpful if you have an early flight.	It's a ways from downtown, which means you'll spend a lot on taxis getting to the city center. Public transportation options are limited.
The Old City, Banglamphu, and Dusit	These central neighborhoods are the historic heart of the city. Today they're full of places to stay in all price ranges.	Tons of dining and lodging options here to match any budget; you'll be near many major attractions, like the Grand Palace and Wat Benjamabophit.	May feel chaotic to some, and too touristy to others. Not easily accessible by subway or Skytrain. Not the cheapest part of town.
Chinatown	The utter chaos of Chinatown is not for everybody. You'll be inundated by the sights and sounds—expect a lot of neon.	There are some good hotel deals here, the neighborhood is truly unique, the food scene is great, too, and the street markets are fascinating.	Hectic and not the most tourist-friendly part of town. Limited hotel selection, terrible traffic, and public transportation options are not convenient.
Thonburi	You'll rub elbows with the locals in this mostly residential neighborhood across the river from the Old City.	Tucked away in peaceful seclusion from the noise and chaos of Bangkok; stellar river views.	Everything else is on the other side of the Chao Phraya, so expect to take the ferry a lot and spend more on taxis.
Pathumwan	The neighborhood that makes up Bangkok's "downtown," this sprawling area is full of markets and mega-malls, plus some other attractions.	A shopper's paradise, and relatively convenient to subway and Skytrain. Lots of super-posh hotels; this is the place to stay if you're traveling in style.	Truly horrible traffic—you'll run up quite a taxi tab sitting in gridlock. Most options are pricey, and may be noisy because there's lots of nightlife nearby.
Silom and Bang Rak	Another part of the central area, this neighborhood is the city's biggest business hub and also has the greatest concentration of restaurants. Nightlife is fun, too.	Popular area with travelers, so lots of comfortable restaurants and bars. Convenient subway–Skytrain connection here.	Can be clogged with traffic. Not the most authentic Thai experience, and because it's partially a business district, there's a lot of less-than-charming concrete.
Sukhumvit	This central tourist- and expat-heavy neighborhood is the nightlife area in Bangkok, and you'll find everything from Irish pubs to hostess bars. There's also a good restaurant scene here.	If you want to party, this is the place to be. A wide range of hotels here, from dirt cheap to über-ritzy, and public transit is convenient.	Fast-paced; some areas are noisy well into the night, and you may run into some shady dealings, though there are plenty of classier establishments here as well.

2

Road in Pathumwan; along Sukhumvit Road, which has the greatest number of hotels and an abundance of restaurants and nightlife; and in the Chinatown and the Old City neighborhoods, which have a smaller number of properties, most of which are affordable. Backpackers often head to Khao San Road, also home to some newer, more upmarket guesthouses.

Visit Fodors.com for expanded hotel reviews.

THE OLD CITY

$$$$ B&B/INN Fodor's Choice ★

Chakrabongse Villas. On the banks of the Chao Phraya River in an old part of the city, these traditional Thai houses were originally built up-country and then transported to the grounds of the Chakrabongse House, which was built in 1908. **Pros:** unique hotel experience; beautiful surroundings, large discounts during low season. **Cons:** fills up quickly; feels secluded, extremely expensive. [$] *Rooms from: $350* ✉ *396 Maharaj Rd., Tatien* ☎ *02/222–1290, 02/622–1900* 🌐 *www.thaivillas.com* 🛏 *4 rooms, 3 B&B rooms* 🍴 *Breakfast* [M] *Subway: Hua Lamphong (then river ferry)* ⊕ *A4.*

NEW AIRPORT DIGS

Novotel Suvarnabhumi Airport. The stunning Novotel Suvarnabhumi Airport is the only hotel near the new airport (it's five minutes away via the free shuttle service). **Pros:** no set check-in time; next to airport; lots of amenities: restaurants, spa, and pool. **Cons:** far from town; big and impersonal; plane noise. [$] *Rooms from: $195* ✉ *Moo 1 Nongprue Bang Phli, Samutprakarn* ☎ *02/131–1111* 🌐 *www.novotel.com* 🛏 *612 rooms* 🍴 *No meals.*

$$ HOTEL

Royal Princess Larn Luang. This hotel is ideally located for exploring Dusit, the Old City, and Chinatown, but it's far from Skytrain and subway stations, and the neighborhood is virtually deserted in the evening. **Pros:** beautiful pool area; fair amount of creature comforts, quiet neighborhood. **Cons:** restaurants not outstanding; isolated location. [$] *Rooms from: $107* ✉ *269 Larn Luang Rd., Old City* ☎ *02/281–3088* 🌐 *www.royalprincesslarnluang.com* 🛏 *167 rooms* 🍴 *Breakfast* [M] *Subway: Hua Lamphong* ⊕ *D3.*

$$$$ RESORT Fodor's Choice ★

The Siam Hotel. Old Hollywood meets art deco at this family-owned property on the Chao Phraya River in the regal Dusit neighborhood. **Pros:** everything right on the property; great location, truly classy. **Cons:** very pricey; a long way from public transportation; far from nightlife. [$] *Rooms from: $550* ✉ *3/2 Th. Khao, Vachirapayaabal, Dusit* ☎ *02/621–2296* 🌐 *www.thesiamhotel.com* 🛏 *28 suites, 10 villas, 1 cottage* 🍴 *Breakfast* [M] *Saphan Taksin, then hotel's private boat* ⊕ *C1.*

BANGLAMPHU

$$ HOTEL

Buddy Lodge. This boutique hotel has contributed greatly to the trendiness of Khao San Road. **Pros:** happening location; comfortable rooms; cool clientele. **Cons:** nothing fancy; no subway or Skytrain access; exhorbitant price for Khao San Road. [$] *Rooms from: $93* ✉ *265 Khao*

San Rd., Banglamphu ☎ *02/629–4477* 🌐 *www.buddylodge.com* 🛏 *76 rooms* 🍴 *No meals* ✣ *B3.*

THONBURI

$$$ RESORT **Anantara Bangkok Riverside Resort & Spa.** Getting to the Anantara is a pleasant adventure in itself—free shuttle boats take you across the Chao Phraya River from the Taksin Bridge. **Pros:** resort feel; lots of activities; great service. **Cons:** a hassle to get into the city; may feel too secluded; not all rooms have views. [$] *Rooms from: $150* ✉ *257/1–3 Charoennakorn Rd., Thonburi* ☎ *02/476–0022* 🌐 *www.bangkok-riverside.anantara.com* 🛏 *407 rooms* 🍴 *Breakfast* [M] *Skytrain: Saphan Taksin* ✣ *C6.*

$$$$ HOTEL Fodor's Choice ★ **Hilton Millennium.** Lording over the Chao Phraya River in postmillennial splendor, this flagship Hilton offers some of the city's most cutting-edge design, competing successfully with Bangkok's other long-standing hotel giants. **Pros:** snazzy amenities; cool pool area; reasonable prices. **Cons:** rooms somewhat small; across the river from downtown pursuits. [$] *Rooms from: $258* ✉ *123 Charoennakorn Rd., Thonburi* ☎ *02/442–2000* 🌐 *www3.hilton.com* 🛏 *533 rooms* 🍴 *Breakfast* [M] *Skytrain: Saphan Taksin* ✣ *C5.*

$$$$ HOTEL Fodor's Choice ★ **Peninsula.** The rooms at the Peninsula have plenty of high-tech gadgets, like bedside controls that dim the lights, turn on the sound system, and close the curtains; bathrooms with hands-free phones; and TVs with mist-free screens at the end of the tubs. **Pros:** beautiful pool; exceptional service; awesome views. **Cons:** most attractions are across the river; on-site dining not very good; outrageously expensive for Bangkok. [$] *Rooms from: $533* ✉ *333 Charoen Krung (New Rd.), Thonburi* ☎ *02/861–2888* 🌐 *www.peninsula.com* 🛏 *313 rooms, 67 suites* 🍴 *No meals* [M] *Skytrain: Saphan Taksin* ✣ *C6.*

CHINATOWN

$$ HOTEL **Grand China Princess.** One good reason for staying in Chinatown is the chance to experience the sights and sounds of the city's oldest neighborhood. **Pros:** great city and river views; delicious Chinese food nearby. **Cons:** popular with big groups; not the most tourist-friendly neighborhood. [$] *Rooms from: $100* ✉ *215 Yaowarat Rd., Chinatown* ☎ *02/224–9977* 🌐 *www.grandchina.com* 🛏 *155 rooms, 22 suites* 🍴 *Breakfast* [M] *Subway: Hua Lamphong* ✣ *C4.*

$ HOTEL **River View Guest House.** This family-run hotel is one of the few budget accommodations that overlook the river, and it's the view that sells it. **Pros:** river view; friendly staff; inexpensive rates. **Cons:** not all rooms have air-conditioning; hard to find; feels quite cheap. [$] *Rooms from: $37* ✉ *Songwad Rd., 768 Soi Panurangsri, Chinatown* ☎ *02/234–5429* 🌐 *www.riverviewbkk.com* 🛏 *45 rooms* [M] *Skytrain: Saphan Taksin* ✣ *D5.*

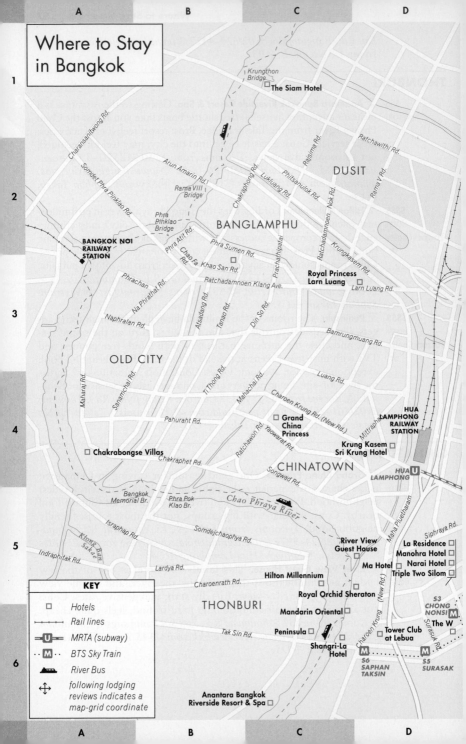

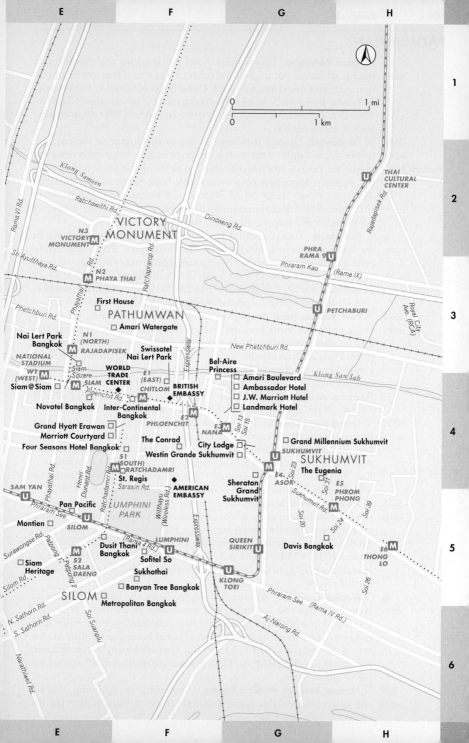

PATHUMWAN

$$ HOTEL **Amari Watergate.** This flagship hotel has spacious and comfortable rooms, all decked out in silks and other rich fabrics. **Pros:** lots of amenities; executive floor; massive pool. **Cons:** huge; feels rather impersonal. [$] *Rooms from: $129* ✉ *847 Phetchburi Rd., Pathumwan* ☎ *02/653–9000* 🌐 *www.amari.com* 🛏 *569 rooms, 26 suites* 🍴 *Breakfast* [M] *Skytrain: Chitlom* ⊕ *E3.*

$$$$ HOTEL Fodor's Choice ★ **The Conrad.** Though this hotel is one of the largest in the city, the service doesn't suffer—the staff is attentive and the beautifully designed rooms are perfect down to the smallest detail. **Pros:** good restaurants; fun nightlife; sprawling pool area. **Cons:** huge hotel; not on the river. [$] *Rooms from: $247* ✉ *87 Wittayu (Wireless Rd.), Pathumwan* ☎ *02/690–9999* 🌐 *www.conradhotels.com* 🛏 *342 rooms, 49 suites* 🍴 *No meals* [M] *Skytrain: Ploenchit* ⊕ *F4.*

$ HOTEL **First House.** Tucked behind the Pratunam Market, this lodging in the bustling garment district is an excellent value. **Pros:** reasonably priced; attractive rooms; comfy furniture. **Cons:** not much natural light in rooms; neighborhood a bit loud. [$] *Rooms from: $67* ✉ *14/20–29 Phetchburi, Soi 19, Pathumwan* ☎ *02/254–0300* 🌐 *www.firsthousebkk.com* 🛏 *100 rooms* 🍴 *Breakfast* [M] *Skytrain: Ratchaprarop* ⊕ *E3.*

$$$$ HOTEL **Four Seasons Hotel Bangkok.** One of Bangkok's leading hotels for many years, the Four Seasons attracts local society for morning coffee and afternoon tea in the formal lobby, where a string quartet often plays. **Pros:** easily accessible location; great pool; magnificent tearoom. **Cons:** decor verges on stuffy; not all rooms have nice views; room rates don't include breakfast. [$] *Rooms from: $345* ✉ *155 Ratchadamri Rd., Pathumwan* ☎ *02/126-8866* 🌐 *www.fourseasons.com/bangkok* 🛏 *354 rooms, 19 suites* 🍴 *No meals* [M] *Skytrain: Rajadamri* ⊕ *F4.*

$$$$ HOTEL **Grand Hyatt Erawan.** This stylish hotel hovers over the auspicious Erawan Shrine. **Pros:** easy access to many points in the city; world-class spa, 10 restaurants. **Cons:** not on the river; expensive rates; breakfast not included in room price. [$] *Rooms from: $383* ✉ *494 Ratchadamri Rd., Pathumwan* ☎ *02/254–1234* 🌐 *www.bangkok.grand.hyatt.com* 🛏 *380 rooms, 44 suites* 🍴 *No meals* [M] *Skytrain: Chitlom* ⊕ *F4.*

$$$$ HOTEL **Inter-Continental Bangkok.** In one of the city's prime business districts, this fine hotel does a good job of catering to its corporate clientele. **Pros:** good location; handy fitness room; executive floor. **Cons:** small pool; many business travelers; high-season rates quite expensive. [$] *Rooms from: $400* ✉ *973 Ploenchit Rd., Pathumwan* ☎ *02/656–0444* 🌐 *www.intercontinental.com* 🛏 *381 rooms, 39 suites* 🍴 *Breakfast* [M] *Skytrain: Chitlom* ⊕ *F4.*

$$ HOTEL **Marriott Courtyard.** Although it doesn't have the luxury of some of Bangkok's high-end lodgings, this reasonably priced hotel does have a young, hip vibe. **Pros:** good value; accommodating to families with children. **Cons:** unexciting room decor; not as luxurious as other Marriotts. [$] *Rooms from: $140* ✉ *155/1 Soi Mahadlekluang 1, Rachadamri Rd., Pathumwan* ☎ *02/690–1888* 🌐 *www.marriott.com* 🛏 *316 rooms* 🍴 *No meals* ⊕ *F4.*

$$$ HOTEL **Novotel Bangkok on Siam Square.** Convenient to shopping, dining, and entertainment, this sprawling hotel is also a short walk from the

Skytrain central station, which puts much of the city within reach. **Pros:** good service; convenient location; cozy rooms. **Cons:** not many in-room amenities; pricey rates. [$] *Rooms from: $154* ✉ *392/44 Siam Sq., Soi 6, Pathumwan* ☎ *02/209–8888* 🌐 *www.novotelbkk.com/novotel-bangkok-on-siam-square* 🛏 *423 rooms* 🍴 *Breakfast* [M] *Skytrain: Siam* ✣ *E4.*

$$$ HOTEL 🏨 **Siam@Siam.** This boutique lodging is definitely the place where the cool kids stay—but that doesn't mean you won't feel welcome if you're traveling with children. **Pros:** great location; super-hip crowd; creative rooms. **Cons:** can be noisy; some rooms have little natural light. [$] *Rooms from: $170* ✉ *865 Rama I Rd., Wang Mai, Pathumwan* ☎ *02/217–3000* 🌐 *www.siamatsiam.com* 🛏 *203 rooms* 🍴 *Breakfast* [M] *Skytrain: Siam* ✣ *E4.*

$$$ HOTEL 🏨 **Swissotel Nai Lert Park.** The best thing about this upscale hotel is the delightful garden, so be sure to ask for a room that looks out on the swaying palm trees surrounding the freeform swimming pool. **Pros:** tropical vegetation; beautiful pool; executive floor. **Cons:** sometimes overrun with groups; not on river. [$] *Rooms from: $133* ✉ *2 Wittayu (Wireless Rd.), Pathumwan* ☎ *02/253–0123* 🌐 *www.swissotel.com/hotels/bangkok-nai-lert-park* 🛏 *299 rooms, 38 suites* [M] *Skytrain: Ploenchit* ✣ *F4.*

$$$$ HOTEL Fodor's Choice ★ 🏨 **St. Regis.** The St. Regis is all about pampering—this was the first hotel in Thailand to offer its guests around-the-clock personal butler service. **Pros:** centrally located; elegant rooms; personal butler service. **Cons:** expensive rates; can be a bit stuffy. [$] *Rooms from: $283* ✉ *159 Ratchadamri, Pathumwan* ☎ *02/207–7777* 🌐 *www.stregis.com/bangkok* 🛏 *227 rooms* 🍴 *No meals* ✣ *F4.*

SILOM

$$$$ HOTEL 🏨 **Banyan Tree Bangkok.** After checking in on the ground floor, you soar up to your room at this 60-story hotel. **Pros:** wonderful views; cozy rooms; feel on top of the world. **Cons:** a bit of a walk to public transportation; expensive rates, especially for Silom area. [$] *Rooms from: $235* ✉ *21/100 S. Sathorn Rd., Silom* ☎ *02/679–1200* 🌐 *www.banyantree.com* 🛏 *327 rooms* 🍴 *Breakfast* [M] *Subway: Lumphini* ✣ *F5.*

$$$$ HOTEL 🏨 **Dusit Thani Bangkok.** This high-rise hotel has a distinctive pyramid shape that makes it immediately identifiable. **Pros:** relaxing retreat; delicious restaurant; a stone's throw from subway and Skytrain stations. **Cons:** small pool; feels past its prime. [$] *Rooms from: $222* ✉ *946 Rama IV Rd., Silom* ☎ *02/200–9000* 🌐 *www.dusit.com* 🛏 *517 rooms, 30 suites* [M] *Subway: Silom; Skytrain: Sala Daeng* ✣ *E5.*

$ HOTEL 🏨 **La Residence.** You'd expect to find this charming little hotel on Paris's Left Bank—the rooms are small but comfortable, and each is individually decorated with an unerring eye for detail. **Pros:** cozy and elegant atmosphere; quiet surroundings; plenty of charm. **Cons:** not as cheap as it was; rooms a bit small. [$] *Rooms from: $60* ✉ *173/8–9 Surawong Rd., Silom* ☎ *02/233–3301* 🌐 *www.laresidencebangkok.com* 🛏 *19 rooms, 7 suites* 🍴 *No meals* [M] *Skytrain: Chong Nonsi* ✣ *D5.*

$$ HOTEL 🏨 **Ma Hotel.** An expansive marble lobby is your first clue that this hotel is head and shoulders above others in its price range. **Pros:** good value;

friendly staff; short walk from river. **Cons:** pool is indoors; popular with tour groups. *Rooms from: $66 ✉ 412 Surawong Rd., Silom ☎ 02/234–5070 up to 88 🌐 www.mahotelbangkok.com 243 rooms 🍽 Breakfast Ⓜ Skytrain: Surasak ⊕ D5.*

$$$$ HOTEL Fodor's Choice ★ **Mandarin Oriental Bangkok.** With a rich history dating back to 1879, the Mandarin Oriental Bangkok is one of the city's most prestigious hotels. **Pros:** excellent staff; butler service in all rooms; outstanding pool. **Cons:** popular for private functions; can be very crowded; charge for Wi-Fi. *Rooms from: $561 ✉ 48 Oriental Ave., Bang Rak ☎ 02/659–9000 🌐 www.mandarinoriental.com/bangkok 358 rooms, 35 suites 🍽 Multiple meal plans Ⓜ Saphan Tak Sin ⊕ C6.*

$$$$ HOTEL **Metropolitan Bangkok.** A crisp, modern aesthetic; a pop-star clientele; and a sexy staff make this one of the city's hippest hotels. **Pros:** very hip; nice city views; free yoga classes. **Cons:** has declined in popularity; not on river; high prices. *Rooms from: $223 ✉ 27 S. Sathorn, Silom ☎ 02/625–3333 🌐 www.comohotels.com/metropolitanbangkok 159 rooms, 12 suites 🍽 Breakfast Ⓜ Subway: Lumphini; Skytrain: Sala Daeng or Chong Nonsi ⊕ E5.*

$$$ HOTEL **Montien.** This hotel, within stumbling distance of Patpong, has been remarkably well maintained since it was built in 1970. **Pros:** regal decor; lots of space; fun and happening neighborhood. **Cons:** not the most modern hotel; popular with tour groups. *Rooms from: $135 ✉ 54 Surawong Rd., Silom ☎ 02/233–7060 🌐 www.montien.com 475 rooms 🍽 Breakfast Ⓜ Subway: Silom; Skytrain: Sala Daeng ⊕ E5.*

$$ HOTEL **Narai Hotel.** Dating back to 1969, this is one of Bangkok's older hotels, but it's well kept up and conveniently located by the business district on Silom Road. **Pros:** fun neighborhood; short walk to river. **Cons:** unexciting pool and decor; a bit of a walk to Skytrain. *Rooms from: $133 ✉ 222 Silom Rd., Silom ☎ 02/237–0100 🌐 www.naraihotel.co.th 475 rooms 🍽 Breakfast Ⓜ Skytrain: Chong Nonsi ⊕ D5.*

$$$ HOTEL **Royal Orchid Sheraton.** Of the luxury hotels along the riverfront, this 28-story palace is most popular with tour groups. **Pros:** nice river views; comfortable beds; good prices for a river hotel. **Cons:** often busy with groups; tired decor; far from public transportation. *Rooms from: $183 ✉ 2 Charoen Krung (New Rd.), Soi 30, Bang Rak ☎ 02/266–0123 🌐 www.starwoodhotels.com/sheraton 726 rooms, 26 suites Ⓜ Skytrain: Saphan Taksin ⊕ D5.*

$$$$ HOTEL Fodor's Choice ★ **Shangri-La Hotel.** Utterly cutting-edge, yet with an extraordinary sense of calm, the Shangri-La has emerged as one of Bangkok's very best hotels, rivaling the more famous Oriental. **Pros:** breathtaking lobby; gorgeous pool and terrace; private balconies available. **Cons:** older wing not as nice; slightly impersonal feel; buffet breakfast costs extra. *Rooms from: $253 ✉ Charoen Krung (New Rd.), 89 Soi Wat Suan Plu, Bang Rak ☎ 02/236–7777 🌐 www.shangri-la.com/bangkok 802 rooms, 52 suites 🍽 No meals Ⓜ Skytrain: Saphan Taksin ⊕ C6.*

$$ HOTEL **Siam Heritage.** The family that runs the Siam Heritage has created a classy boutique hotel with a purpose—to preserve and promote Thai heritage. **Pros:** reasonably priced; family run; cool Thai decor. **Cons:** not on river; rooms and pool a bit small. *Rooms from: $87 ✉ 115/1 Sura-*

Peninsula

Chakrabongse Villas

Hilton Millenium

Conrad

Shangri-La

wong Rd., Silom ☎ *02/353–6101* ⊕ *www.thesiamheritage.com* ⏎ *73 rooms* ⦿*| Breakfast* Ⓜ *Subway: Silom; Skytrain: Sala Daeng* ⊹ *E5.*

$$$$
HOTEL
Fodor's Choice
★

🖼 **Sofitel So Bangkok.** An architectural gem, this elegant hotel is designed around the five elements of water, earth, wood, metal, and fire: the "earth" rooms resemble blue caves, while "water" rooms come with bathtubs overlooking the Bangkok skyline. **Pros:** fantastic location; top-notch service; free computers for in-room use. **Cons:** not all rooms have park views; expensive; can get very busy. Ⓢ*Rooms from: $230* ✉ *2 N. Sathorn Rd., Silom* ☎ *02/624–0000* ⊕ *www.sofitel.com* ⏎ *238 rooms* ⦿*| Breakfast* ⊹ *F5.*

$$$$
HOTEL

🖼 **Sukhothai.** On six landscaped acres near Sathorn Road, the Sukhothai has numerous courtyards that make the hustle and bustle of Bangkok seem worlds away. **Pros:** beautiful decor in suites; spacious grounds; great restaurant. **Cons:** expensive rates; standard rooms not be worth the price. Ⓢ *Rooms from: $267* ✉ *13/3 S. Sathorn Rd., Silom* ☎ *02/344–8888* ⊕ *www.sukhothai.com* ⏎ *210 rooms* ⦿*| No meals* Ⓜ *Subway: Lumphini* ⊹ *F5.*

$$$$
HOTEL
Fodor's Choice
★

🖼 **Tower Club at Lebua.** The Tower Club at Lebua is one of the swankiest places in Bangkok, with a beautiful rooftop bar, great restaurants, and more than a bit of flair. **Pros:** stunning panorama; use of the Tower Lounge; plenty of space in the rooms. **Cons:** sky-high rates; popular with see-and-be-seen crowd; long wait for the elevators. Ⓢ *Rooms from: $560* ✉ *1055 Silom Rd., Silom* ☎ *02/624–9999* ⊕ *www.lebua. com* ⏎ *221 rooms* Ⓜ *Skytrain: Saphan Taksin* ⊹ *D6.*

$$
HOTEL

🖼 **Triple Two Silom.** This trendy hotel is the sister property of the Narai Hotel, with which it shares a swimming pool and fitness center. **Pros:** tasteful decor; friendly and helpful staff. **Cons:** some rooms can be a bit noisy; not a great option for kids. Ⓢ *Rooms from: $125* ✉ *222 Silom Rd., Silom* ☎ *02/627–2222* ⊕ *www.tripletwosilom.com* ⏎ *75 rooms* ⦿*| Breakfast* Ⓜ *Skytrain: Chong Nonsi* ⊹ *D5.*

$$$$
HOTEL

🖼 **The W.** Bangkok's latest high-flying hotel, the W has all sorts of snazzy art and design touches both inside and outside the rooms. **Pros:** great central location; 24-hour pool and fitness center; nice mix of modern and traditional. **Cons:** no views; check-in area can get busy; often occupied with events. Ⓢ *Rooms from: $203* ✉ *106 N. Sathorn Rd., Silom* ☎ *02/344–4000* ⊕ *www.whotels.com/bangkok* ⏎ *407 rooms* ⦿*| Breakfast* ⊹ *D6.*

SUKHUMVIT

$$
HOTEL

🖼 **Amari Boulevard.** This pyramid-shape tower certainly has a dashing profile. **Pros:** interesting architecture; close to Skytrain. **Cons:** uninspired restaurant; slack service; street can get noisy at night. Ⓢ *Rooms from: $96* ✉ *2 Sukhumvit, Soi 5, Sukhumvit* ☎ *02/255–2930* ⊕ *www. amari.com* ⏎ *309 rooms* ⦿*| Breakfast* Ⓜ *Skytrain: Nana* ⊹ *G4.*

$$
HOTEL

🖼 **Ambassador Hotel.** The Ambassador has everything you'd expect, and more: a dozen restaurants, a shopping center with scores of stores, and even a bird sanctuary. **Pros:** lots of activity; relatively cheap. **Cons:** a bit generic; noise from the main drag; staff not the most helpful. Ⓢ *Rooms from: $92* ✉ *171 Sukhumvit, Soi 11–13, Sukhumvit* ☎ *02/254–0444* ⊕ *www.amtel.co.th* ⏎ *740 rooms* ⦿*| Breakfast* Ⓜ *Skytrain: Nana* ⊹ *G4.*

$$ HOTEL [H] **Bel-Aire Bangkok.** This well-managed hotel is steps from clamorous Sukhumvit Road—thankfully, it's on the quiet end of a bustling street, away from the bars. **Pros:** quieter than most in neighborhood; sleek lobby; swimming pool. **Cons:** feels expensive for what it is; often busy with tour groups; mediocre restaurant. [$] *Rooms from: $68* ✉ *16 Sukhumvit, Soi 5, Sukhumvit* ☎ *02/253–4300* 🌐 *www.belairebangkok.com* 🛏 *150 rooms* 🍴 *No meals* [M] *Skytrain: Nana* ✥ *F4.*

$$ HOTEL [H] **City Lodge.** Of the two City Lodges off Sukhumvit (the other is on Soi 9), this one has the superior location. **Pros:** close to transportation; economical rates; super-friendly staff. **Cons:** looks sketchy from the outside; rooms can be noisy. [$] *Rooms from: $73* ✉ *8/1–7 Sukhumvit Soi 19, Sukhumvit* ☎ *02/253–7710* 🌐 *www.oamhotels.com/citylodge9* 🛏 *34 rooms* 🍴 *No meals* [M] *Subway: Sukhumvit; Skytrain: Asok* ✥ *G4.*

$$ HOTEL [H] **Davis Bangkok.** Two hotels in one, the Davis Bangkok has a main building and another one two doors down with a separate lobby and reception area. **Pros:** uniquely decorated rooms; beautiful pool area. **Cons:** not that close to public transit; uninteresting view from rooms. [$] *Rooms from: $103* ✉ *80 Sukhumvit, Soi 24, Sukhumvit* ☎ *02/260–8000* 🌐 *www.davisbangkok.net* 🛏 *247 rooms, 2 villas* 🍴 *Breakfast* [M] *Skytrain: Phrom Phong* ✥ *G5.*

$$$$ B&B/INN [H] **The Eugenia.** Think colonial-era India or Burma, not modern-day Bangkok. **Pros:** classic decor and history; free tuk-tuk shuttle from Sukhumvit; quiet and peaceful. **Cons:** starting to look a bit worn; a long walk from Sukhumvit; surrounding ugly apartments mar the view from swimming pool and courtyard. [$] *Rooms from: $243* ✉ *267 Sukhumvit, Soi 31, Sukhumvit* ☎ *02/259–9011* 🌐 *www.theeugenia.com* 🛏 *12 rooms* 🍴 *Breakfast* ✥ *G4.*

$$$ HOTEL [H] **Grand Millennium Sukhumvit.** It looks like it might have come from the future (think soaring glass and odd angles), so it's no surprise that this upscale lodging also offers cutting-edge technology in its sleek rooms and suites, from LCD TVs with on-demand movies to high-speed Internet access to electronic safes. **Pros:** beautiful modern decor; interesting exterior architecture; crisp service. **Cons:** lots of business travelers; bathrooms lack privacy. [$] *Rooms from: $192* ✉ *30 Sukhumvit, Soi 21, Sukhumvit* ☎ *02/204–4000* 🌐 *www.millenniumhotels.com/th/grandmillenniumsukhumvitbangkok* 🛏 *365 rooms* 🍴 *No meals* [M] *Subway: Sukhumvit; Skytrain: Asok* ✥ *G4.*

$$$$ HOTEL [H] **J.W. Marriott Hotel.** With many restaurants and businesses nearby, the conveniently located Marriot is also around the corner from Nana Plaza, one of the city's biggest red-light districts, which might turn some people off as much as it turns others on. **Pros:** very friendly staff; nice gym; plenty of dining options. **Cons:** not as nice as the Marriott in Thonburi; close to red-light district. [$] *Rooms from: $233* ✉ *4 Sukhumvit, Soi 2, Sukhumvit* ☎ *02/656–7700* 🌐 *www.marriott.com* 🛏 *441 rooms, 39 suites* 🍴 *No meals* [M] *Skytrain: Nana* ✥ *G4.*

$$ HOTEL [H] **Landmark Hotel.** The generous use of polished wood in the reception area may suggest a grand European hotel, but the Landmark prides itself on being thoroughly modern. **Pros:** nicely renovated; modern amenities; attractive discount packages frequently available. **Cons:** may be too formal for families; some rooms a bit noisy. [$] *Rooms from: $132* ✉ *138*

Sukhumvit Rd., Sukhumvit ☎ *02/254–0404* ⊕ *www.landmarkbangkok. com* ⇆ *414 rooms, 39 suites* Ⓜ *Skytrain: Nana* ⊹ *G4.*

$$$$ 🖼 **Sheraton Grande Sukhumvit.** The Sheraton soars 33 floors above the
HOTEL noisy city streets, and the suites on the upper floors get tons of natural light. **Pros:** very close to fun nightlife; near public transportation; impressive views from most rooms. **Cons:** somewhat impersonal due to size; pricey. 💲 *Rooms from: $267* ⊠ *250 Sukhumvit Rd., Sukhumvit* ☎ *02/649–8888* ⊕ *www.sheratongrandesukhumvit.com* ⇆ *420 rooms, 36 suites* ⦿ *No meals* Ⓜ *Subway: Sukhumvit; Skytrain: Asok* ⊹ *G4.*

$$$$ 🖼 **Westin Grande Sukhumvit.** The Westin is fancy-schmancy, with lots of
HOTEL sleek surfaces and neon lighting, and bright and shiny modern decor in the futuristic bathrooms. **Pros:** near Skytrain and subway; nightlife just out the front door; comfortable beds. **Cons:** on-site restaurants not great; feels overpriced compared to other nearby options. 💲 *Rooms from: $259* ⊠ *259 Sukhumvit Rd., Sukhumvit* ☎ *02/207–8000* ⊕ *www. westin.com/bangkok* ⇆ *363 rooms* ⦿ *No meals* Ⓜ *Subway: Sukhumvit; Skytrain: Asok* ⊹ *G4.*

NIGHTLIFE AND THE ARTS

English-language newspapers the *Bangkok Post* and the *Nation* have the latest information on current festivals, exhibitions, and nightlife. Better yet, try picking up a copy of *BK Magazine* for the most recent listings for arts and entertainment. *Bangkok 101* is a monthly magazine with extensive listings and reviews of new hot spots.

NIGHTLIFE

The city that was once notorious for its raunchy sex trade is now entertaining a burgeoning class of professionals hungry for thumping discos, trendy cocktail lounges, and swanky rooftop bars. There are also stricter rules that limit the sale of alcohol and most closing times now hover around 2 am (although nighthawks can probably find a club or two open until 5 or 6 am).

There are a few notable nightlife spots: the area off Sukhumvit Soi 55 (also called Soi Thonglor) is full of bars and nightclubs; Soi Sarasin, across from Lumphini Park, has lots of friendly pubs and cafés frequented by yuppie Thais and expats; and Narathiwat Road, which starts at Surawong, intersects Silom, then runs all the way to Rama III has trendy new bars and restaurants opening every month.

If you want to take a walk on the wild side, Bangkok still has three thriving red light districts: Patpong, Nana Plaza, and Soi Cowboy. Patpong is the largest, most touristy, and includes three streets that run between Surawong and Silom roads. Nana Plaza, at Soi 4, is packed with three floors of hostess bars and is considered the most hard-core in terms sex shows and shock value. Soi Cowboy, off Sukhumvit Road at Soi 21, is a less raunchy and an easier-going version of Patpong, though it's still a red light district and so be prepared.

Even though it may not seem like it, live sex shows are officially banned and prostitution is illegal. The government doesn't always turn a blind eye, so exercise caution and common sense.

NORTHERN BANGKOK

There aren't too many pubs frequented by foreigners around here, but the area around Victory Monument does have the long running Saxophone, along with an excellent smattering of bars and pubs along the nearby Soi Rangnam.

BARS AND PUBS

Saxophone. Popular with locals and expats, Saxophone hosts live R&B, blues, jazz, rock, reggae, and even ska bands seven nights a week. ✉ *3/8 Phayathai Rd., Victory Monument* ☎ *02/246–5472* ⊕ *www.saxophonepub.com* Ⓜ *Skytrain: Victory Monument.*

DANCE CLUBS
BANGLAMPHU

Brown Sugar, one of Bangkok's longest running jazz haunts, tops the list of bars in Banglamphu.

JAZZ BARS

Brown Sugar. A good place to carouse over live jazz, and occasionally blues, is the smoky Brown Sugar. In business for three decades, it has relocated to a bigger space in the Banglamphu area. ✉ *469 Wanchat Junction, Phrasumen Rd., Banglamphu* ☎ *081/805–7759, 085/226–5880* ⊕ *www.brownsugarbangkok.com.*

THONBURI

The best reason to visit Thonburi is to take in the river views at some of the fancier hotel bars.

BARS AND PUBS

Longtail Bar. Though it's not particularly authentic, the Bangkok Marriott Resort & Spa's Longtail Bar distinguishes itself with a tropical feel that is elusive in Bangkok. This place will really make you want to sip a mai tai by the breezy river. You'll have to sail about 30 minutes downriver from the Saphan Taksin Skytrain stop on one of the resort's dedicated boats, not an entirely unpleasant prospect on a nice night. ✉ *Bangkok Marriott Resort & Spa, 257 Charoennakorn Rd., Samrae Thonburi, Thonburi* ☎ *02/476–0022* ⊕ *www.marriott.com.*

Zeta Bar. The crowd here is as swanky as the place itself, a black-and-red showplace with sister locations in London, Sydney, and Kuala Lampur. ✉ *Hilton Millennium, 123 Charoennakorn Rd., Thonburi* ☎ *02/442–2000.*

LADYBOYS

One of the most surprising (and often misunderstood) aspects of Thai culture to first-time visitors is the "ladyboy." These men act, dress, and make themselves up to look—often quite convincingly—like women. Many are found in districts catering to salacious foreign visitors, but this doesn't mean they are sex workers or gay. In fact, many Thais refer to them as a "third sex," Thai men with feminine characteristics and mannerisms, more so than most women. You may hear them referred to as "katoey," but that is a derogatory term—they prefer to be called "ladyboy."

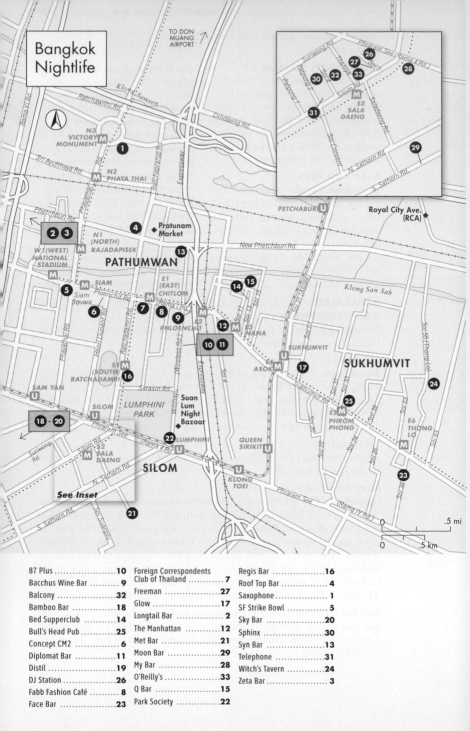

Bangkok Nightlife

TO DON MUANG AIRPORT

PATHUMWAN

The heart of Bangkok has fewer pubs than you'd imagine, but places like the St. Regis offer some great views, and Siam Square is home to thumping dance spots like Concept CM2.

BARS AND PUBS

Bacchus Wine Bar. Wine bars are slowly popping up around the city, and one worth mentioning is Bacchus Wine Bar. Here you'll find four floors of laid-back ambience and a long list of worthy wines. ⊠ *20/6–7 Ruam Rudee, Pathumwan* ☎ *02/650–8986* Ⓜ *Skytrain: Ploenchit.*

Diplomat Bar. Come here for smooth music, a sophisticated crowd, and a splendid selection of Scotch and cigars—cigar makers are sometimes imported from Cuba just to roll at the Diplomat Bar. ⊠ *Conrad Hotel, 87 Wittayu (Wireless Rd.), Pathumwan* ☎ *02/690–9999* ⊕ *www. conradhotels.com* Ⓜ *Skytrain: Ploenchit.*

Regis Bar. On the 12th floor of the prestigious St. Regis Hotel, the Regis Bar overlooks the Royal Bangkok Sports Club. You can watch the horse races while sipping a Siam Mary, the Bangkok version of the Bloody Mary. The bar also continues an age-old St. Regis tradition of champagne sabering, displayed every night just after sunset. ⊠ *St. Regis, 159 Ratchadamri Rd., Pathumwan* ☎ *02/207–7777* ⊕ *www.stregis.com/ bangkok.*

Roof Top Bar. On the 88th floor of Thailand's tallest building, the glass-enclosed Roof Top Bar is one of the highest drinking spots in the city. With lounge singers and neon Heineken signs, it's kitschier than competitors like Vertigo and Skybar. ⊠ *Baiyoke Sky Hotel, 222 Ratchaprarop Rd., Patumwan* ☎ *02/656–3000* ⊕ *www.baiyokehotel.com* Ⓜ *Skytrain: Chitlom.*

SF Strike Bowl. If you're searching for something more than just a typical cocktail bar, look no farther than SF Strike Bowl. One of the city's hottest nightspots, this futuristic bowling alley, lounge, and bar has a sleek style that rivals most nightclubs. A DJ spins house music above the clatter of falling pins. ⊠ *MBK Shopping Center, Phayathai Rd., Pathumwan* ☎ *02/611–7171* Ⓜ *Skytrain: National Stadium.*

DANCE CLUBS

87 Plus. For something sleek, try the 87 Plus, where the dance floor meanders throughout the bar instead of concentrating in front of the DJ booth. The music is thumping, and the crowd is super trendy and very well-to-do. There's live music Tuesday through Sunday. Prices are through the roof. ⊠ *All Seasons Pl., 87 Wittayu (Wireless Rd.), Pathumwan* ☎ *02/690–9999* Ⓜ *Skytrain: Ploenchit.*

Concept CM2. This flashy, energetic club hosts live pop bands every night. Be prepared to pay a steep B550 entrance fee on weekends (B220 on weekdays). ⊠ *Novotel Siam Sq., 392/44 Rama I, Siam Sq., Soi 6, Pathumwan* ☎ *02/209–8888* ⊕ *www.cm2bkk.com* Ⓜ *Skytrain: Siam.*

JAZZ BARS

Foreign Correspondents Club of Thailand. Hosting live jazz on Friday night, the Foreign Correspondents Club of Thailand also sponsors films, lectures, and art exhibits on other nights, and has a pretty nice bar to boot.

It welcomes both members and nonmembers. ✉ *Maneeya Center, 518/5 Ploenchit Rd., Pathumwan* ☎ *02/652–0580* ⊕ *www.fccthai. com* Ⓜ *Skytrain: Chitlom.*

SILOM AND BANG RAK

Many of the best rooftop bars and upscale lounges are in Silom's high-rise towers and in fashionable spots along the Chao Phraya River. Here's where you'll also find the notorious Patpong red light area and the Silom Soi 4 gay bars.

> ### HOT TICKETS
>
> If you plan to hit Bangkok's hottest clubs, namely Q Bar or 87 Plus, it's a good idea to call ahead to be put on the guest list. That said, farang can generally walk right into most establishments, even those that have long velvet-rope queues for Thais.

BARS AND PUBS

Distil. Thai A-listers have made Distil, on the 64th floor of one of Bangkok's tallest buildings, their stomping ground. It's done up in chic black, coffee, and slate tones, and a full-time sommelier is on hand to take care of your wine desires. Make sure to try the place's most famous concoction, the Hangovertini, made famous by the Hollywood film shot here. ✉ *State Tower, 1055 Silom Rd., Silom* ☎ *02/624–9555* Ⓜ *Skytrain: Surasak.*

Met Bar. Done up in sleek red and black, this place is filled with people chilling out on comfortable couches. It used to be *the* place to go out in Bangkok, but those glory days seem to be over. Now it's more akin to a slightly empty club. Still, the decor is fun. ✉ *27 S. Sathorn Rd., Silom* ☎ *02/625–3333* Ⓜ *Subway: Lumphini; Skytrain: Sala Daeng.*

Moon Bar. The appropriately named Moon Bar is perched high atop the Banyan Tree Bangkok, which gives it the best 360-degree panorama in Bangkok. You can lounge around the sofas and low-lying tables with a drink. Come a bit before sunset to get the best seat, and don't forget to pack a camera, the views are staggering. If the weather is clear, do some stargazing with the bar's telescope. If the weather's bad at all, the place will be closed. ✉ *Banyan Tree Bangkok, 21/100 S. Sathorn Rd., Silom* ☎ *02/679–1200* Ⓜ *Subway: Lumphini.*

My Bar. A minimalist lounge, My Bar is ticked away in the Dusit Thani Bangkok Hotel. It serves up signature drinks, hand-rolled Cuban cigars, and the finest single-malt whisky in town. ✉ *Dusit Thani Bangkok Hotel, 946 Rama IV, Silom* ☎ *02/200–9000* Ⓜ *Subway: Lumphini.*

O'Reillys. A convenient location near the gateway to Patpong means that the place is always jumping. If you're a Beatles fan, check out the Betters on Friday night; the band plays starting at 9. ✉ *62/1–4 Silom Rd., Bang Rak* ☎ *02/632–7515* ⊕ *www.oreillyspubbangkok.com/* Ⓜ *Subway: Silom; Skytrain: Sala Daeng.*

Park Society. Sleek and sophisticated, Bangkok's newest rooftop bar has a view that puts it at the top of the pecking order. Park Society (also the name of the adjoining restaurant) looks out over the skyline and has the finest view of the vast expanse of Lumphini Park. Watch the sunset colors while downing a rasberry martini or glass of wine from the globetrotting selection. An upstairs section called Hi So has private

Busy Q Bar in Sukhumvit has international DJs and a spacious outdoor terrace.

cabanas for that special romantic evening. ⊠ *Sofitel So Bangkok, 2 N. Sathorn Rd., Bang Rak* ☎ *02/624–0000* ⊕ *www.sofitel.com.*

Fodor's Choice **Sky Bar.** There's nothing else quite like Sky Bar, on the 63rd floor of one ★ of Bangkok's tallest buildings. Head toward the pyramid-like structure emitting eerie blue light at the far end of the restaurant and check out the head-spinning views. Cocktails include the Hangovertini, now almost as famous as the Hollywood film that spawned it. ⊠ *State Tower, 1055 Silom Rd., Bang Rak* ☎ *02/624–9555* ⊕ *www.lebua.com* Ⓜ *Sky-train: Saphan Taksin.*

GAY BARS

Silom Soi 2 and Silom Soi 4 are the center of Bangkok's gay scene, with every establishment from restaurants to bars to clubs all catering to a gay clientele.

Balcony. Balcony overlooks the crowds along Soi 4, and sometimes the party spills out onto the street. It has a friendly staff and one of the best happy hours on the soi. ⊠ *86–88 Silom, Soi 4, Bang Rak* ☎ *02/235–5891* ⊕ *www.balconypub.com* Ⓜ *Subway: Silom; Skytrain: Sala Daeng.*

DJ Station. On elbow-to-elbow Silom Soi 2, the sleek and modern DJ Station is packed with a young crowd. The cover charge is B100 on weekdays and B200 on weekends. ⊠ *8/6–8 Silom, Soi 2, Bang Rak* ☎ *02/266–4029* ⊕ *www.dj-station.com* Ⓜ *Subway: Silom; Skytrain: Sala Daeng.*

G.O.D. This place, whose name is short for Guys on Display, is famous for its drag show every night at midnight and its balcony where you can watch the dance floor. Most of the action doesn't get going until the wee hours. The cover charge is 300 baht. ⊠ *60/18–21 Silom Rd., Bang Rak* ☎ *02/632–8033* Ⓜ *Subway: Silom; Skytrain: Sala Daeng.*

Sphinx. Sublte Egyptian motifs lend an exotic atmosphere to Sphinx, which has a sleek decor and a sohisticated dinner menu. ⊠ *100 Silom, Soi 4, Bang Rak* ☎ *02/234–7249* ⊕ *www.sphinxbangkok.com* Ⓜ *Skytrain: Sala Daeng.*

Telephone. The most venerable of Bangkok's gay bars, the pub-style Telephone is hopping every night of the week. There are telephones on the table so you can chat up your neighbors. The staff is friendly and knowledgable about the neighborhood. ⊠ *114/1 Silom, Soi 4, Bang Rak* ☎ *02/234–3279* ⊕ *www.telephonepub.com* Ⓜ *Subway: Silom; Skytrain: Sala Daeng.*

JAZZ BARS

Bamboo Bar. For easy-on-the-ears jazz, try the Oriental Hotel's Bamboo Bar. This legendary warering hole features international jazz musicians. ⊠ *Mandarin Oriental, 48 Oriental Ave., Bang Rak* ☎ *02/659–9000* Ⓜ *Skytrain: Saphan Taksin.*

SUKHUMVIT

There's an incredible mix of bars and clubs around Sukhumvit. Lower Sukhumvit (Asok and Nana) is where you'll find the Nana Plaza and Soi Cowboy red-light district. Farther east, the neighborhoods of Thong Lor and Ekkamai are *the* places for wealthy young Thais to party. Expect tables full of whisky-drinking revelers listening to live music. There are also plenty of expat pubs in this area, many of which are also popular with Thais.

BARS AND PUBS

Face Bar. A strong South Asian theme—the bar shares the space with an Indian restaurant called Hazara—makes this a comfortable spot to enjoy a couple of drinks. Seating is on cushy pillows in semiprivate areas. ⊠ *29 Sukhumvit, Soi 38, Sukhumvit* ☎ *02/713–6048* ⊕ *www.facebars.com/en/bangkok/restaurant/bar* Ⓜ *Skytrain: Thing Lo.*

The Manhattan. Sexy and stylish, this lounge is adorned with velvet chairs, low tables, and black-and-white photos of New York. This is the place to enjoy some of the city's finest martinis and such tapas-style dishes as crab cakes and fresh oysters. An elegant choice in the Sukhumvit neighborhood, this place never fails to impress. ⊠ *J. W. Marriott, 4 Sukhumvit, Soi 2, Sukhumvit* ☎ *02/656– 7700* ⊕ *www.marriott.com* Ⓜ *Skytrain: Asok.*

Royal Oak Pub. This very British pub is a good place for serious beer drinkers. There are lots of activities to keep you entertained, including a quiz night on Wednesday and a disco night on the last Friday of the month. There are plenty of different beers, both on tap and in bottles. ⊠ *595/10–11 Sukhumvit, Soi 33, Sukhumvit* ☎ *02/662–1652* ⊕ *www.royaloakthailand.com* Ⓜ *Subway: Sukhumvit; Skytrain: Phrom Phong.*

Syn Bar. With its selection of pretty cocktails, the hip Syn Bar is decorated in cool shades of gray and red. Creative design elements include floating seating. DJs start spinning most nights at 9. ⊠ *Swissotel Nai*

Lert Park, 2 Wittayu (Wireless Rd.), Sukhumvit ☎ *02/253–0123* ⊕ *www.swissotel.com* Ⓜ *Skytrain: Ploenchit.*

DANCE CLUBS

Bed Supperclub. Dress to impress at Bed Supperclub, Bangkok's answer to cool. (There's a dress code for men, so don't expect to get in wearing shorts, tank tops or flip-flops.) The futuristic Jetsons-like bar has been all the rage since its inception, and is where all the see-and-be-seen crowd hangs out. Grab a drink and sprawl out on an enormous bed while listening to a rotating cast of DJs mix hip-hop, house, and a variety of other genres. ✉ *26 Sukhumvit, Soi 11, Sukhumvit* ☎ *02/651–3537* ⊕ *www.bedsupperclub.com* Ⓜ *Skytrain: Nana.*

Glow. An underground club with cutting-edge electronic music, Glow lights up Sukhumvit with an eternally trendy, beautiful crowd dancing to techno. The sound system is out of this world, and it's got the biggest vodka selection in the city. ✉ *96/4–5 Sukhumvit, Soi 23, Sukhumvit* ☎ *02/261–3007* ⊕ *www.glowbkk.com.*

Q Bar. International DJs add a cosmopolitan flair to Q Bar. Upstairs there's a romantic lounge and a huge outdoor terrace. Between the casually hip crowd, the effortlessly energetic scene, and the reasonable door policy (you don't have to be a supermodel, although you won't get in wearing shorts and sneakers), this is perhaps the best nightclub in town. ✉ *34 Sukhumvit, Soi 11, Sukhumvit* ☎ *02/252–3274* ⊕ *www.qbarbangkok.com* Ⓜ *Skytrain: Nana.*

JAZZ BARS

Witch's Tavern. With live music on Friday, Saturday, and Sunday, Witch's Tavern serves up good drinks and hearty English fare. ✉ *306/1 Sukhumvit, Soi 55, Sukhumvit* ☎ *02/391–9791* ⊕ *www.witch-tavern.com* Ⓜ *Skytrain: Thong Lo.*

THE ARTS

A contemporary arts scene is relatively new to Thailand, but the last decade has seen great changes in the fine arts: artists are branching out into all kinds of media, and modern sculpture and artwork can be increasingly found in office buildings, parks, and public spaces.

Bangkok also offers an eclectic range of theater and dance performances, such as traditional khon, and masterful puppet shows. Music options range from piano concertos and symphonies to rock concerts and blues-and-jazz festivals.

OLD CITY

THEATER AND DANCE

National Theatre. Classical dance and drama can usually be seen at the National Theatre on the last Friday and Saturday of each month. ✉ *Na Phra That Rd., Old City* ☎ *02/224–1342* Ⓜ *Skytrain: Hua Lamphong.*

Sala Chalerm Krung Royal Theater. Designed in 1933 by a former student of the Ecole des Beaux-Arts in Paris, the Sala Chalerm Krung Royal Theater's design might be called Thai Deco. The place hosts traditional khon, a masked dance-drama based on tales from the *Ramak-*

Thai Puppetry

For hundreds of years Thailand's puppeteers have entertained both royal courts and village crowds with shadow puppets and marionettes. Historically, the *Ramakien*, Thailand's version of the ancient Indian *Ramayana* epic, provided puppeteers with their subject matter. Today performances are more varied: many stick to the *Ramakien* or other Thai folklore and moral fables; some are contemporary twists on the classic material; and some depart from it entirely. It's an art form that exemplifies Thailand's lively blend of tradition and innovation.

SHADOW PUPPETS

Shadow puppets—carved animal hide stretched between poles—showed up in Thailand during the mid-13th century. Historians believe the art form originated in India more than 1,000 years ago and traveled to Thailand via Indonesia and Malaysia. By the 14th century shadow puppetry had become a leading form of entertaining in Ayutthaya, where it acquired the name *nang yai* or "big skin," which is also what large shadow puppets are called.

Today nang yai troupes perform at village festivals, temple fairs, marriages, and royal ceremonies, as well as in theaters. Puppeteers maneuver colorful, intricately carved leather puppets behind a transparent backlighted screen. A narrator and musicians help tell the story. A classical music ensemble called a *piphat* adds to the charged dramatic atmosphere with rapid-paced *ranat* (xylophone-like instrument), drums, and haunting oboe.

Large puppets (nang yai) are used to form the set at shadow puppet performances, while smaller puppets called *nang thalung* are the characters.

There are some macabre traditions about how shadow puppets should be made, though it's unclear how often, if ever, these customs are followed today. Nang yai are supposed to be made from the hide of a cow or buffalo that has died a violent and accidental death, while nang thalung should be made with the skin from the soles of a dead puppet master's feet, so that the puppets are literally walking in the footsteps of the former artist. Clown characters' lips should be formed from a small piece of skin from the penis of a deceased puppeteer.

Wherever the animal skin comes from these days, it must be carefully prepared. The hide is cured and stretched, then carved (puppet makers use stencils to outline the intricate, lacy designs) and painted. Puppet makers then mount the leather on sticks. You won't see shadow puppets for sale much, though some markets sell greeting cards with paper cut to resemble shadow puppets. You may find authentic shadow puppets at antiques markets.

Though today shadow puppetry is much more common in Thailand's south, the largest shadow-puppet troupe in Thailand, **Nang Yai Wat Khanon Troupe** (⊠ *T. Soifah, Amphur Photharam, Rachburi* ☎ *03/223–3386*), performs in Damnoen Saduak, at Wat Khanon, next to the floating market. Performances, which are on Saturday at 10 am and cost B200, are hour-long versions of *Ramakien* stories performed in Thai.

2

MARIONETTES

Marionettes, born from a blend of shadow puppets and *khon,* a traditional form of Thai dance,

entered the scene at the beginning of the 20th century when Krae Saptawanit, a renowned khon performer, began to make them. Krae's first 2-foot-tall puppet was a miniature version of his own stage persona, with an elaborate costume, a golden mask, and long, curling finger extensions. Soon after, Krae formed a touring troupe of khon puppet performers.

Marionette choreography is highly stylized and symbolic. It takes three experienced puppeteers to manipulate each doll into a series of gymnastic twists and graceful dance moves. Puppeteers dance alongside and behind the puppets, but they remain in shadow; the dramatically lighted and costumed dolls take center stage. As in nang yai, classical Thai music adds to the intense atmosphere and indicates the mood of the story.

The art of puppet making—or *hadtasin*—requires great attention to detail. Marionettes consist of a frame covered with papier-mâché. Most of the frame is made of wood. Parts that must be able to move independently—like the head, neck, and hands—are made of aluminum and wire, which are more malleable. The hand joints require the most attention, since they must be capable of intricate khon movements. Puppet makers must also attach the sticks the puppeteers will use to make the puppets move.

Once the frame is constructed, the puppet maker adds layers of papier-mâché and then paints the top layer, paying particular attention to the face. The puppets wear ornate costumes of silk and gold leaf. According to tradition, the puppet maker must clap three times to create the completed marionette's soul.

At the **Baan Tookkatoon Hookrabok Thai Puppet Museum** (✉ *Soi Vibavhadi 60, Laksi* ☎ *02/579-8101* ⊕ *www.tookkatoon.com* ⊙ *Weekdays 9–5*) you can watch marionette makers at work and purchase puppets. There's also a substantial private collection in the museum, which is a beautiful wooden house. You may even catch an impromptu show. Admission is free, but advance booking is required.

OTHER SHOWS

Chiang Mai is a hot spot for contemporary puppet troupes. **Hobby Hut** (⊕ *www.cmaipuppet.com*) and **Wandering Moon** (⊕ *www. wanderingmoontheatre.com*) are both based here.

In the southern province of Nakhon Si Thammarat, about three hours by bus from Krabi or Surat Thani, national artist and puppeteer Suchart Sapsin's house has been turned into the **Shadow Puppet Museum** (✉ *10/18 Si Thammarat Rd., Soi 3, Nakhon Si Thammarat* ☎ *07/534-6394*) with regular 20-minute performances (B100) in a small theater; a workshop; and a gallery.

Keep an eye out for performances at fringe festivals and temple fairs throughout the country. For information about upcoming shows, check the website of the Tourism Authority of Thailand (⊕ *www.tourismthailand.org*).

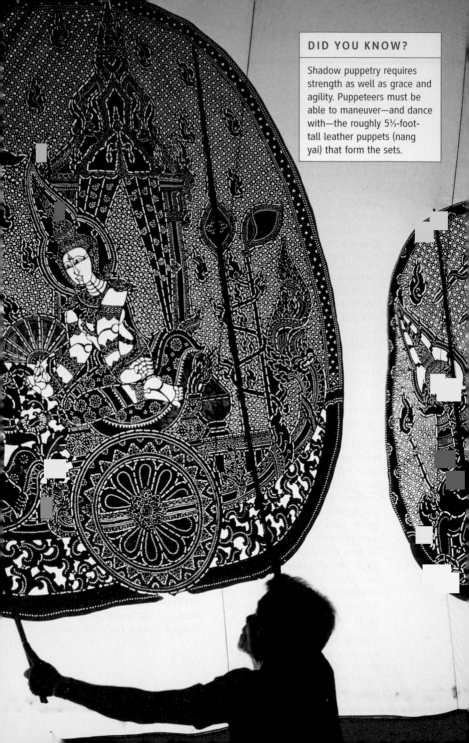

ien. ⊠ *66 Charoen Krung (New Rd.), Old City* ☎ *02/222–0434* ⊕ *www. salachalermkrung.com* Ⓜ *Skytrain: Hua Lamphong.*

THONBURI
THEATER AND DANCE

For Thais, classical dance is more than graceful movements. The dances actually tell tales from the religious epic *Ramakien*. Performances are accompanied by a woodwind called the *piphat,* which sounds like an oboe, as well as a range of percussion instruments. Many restaurants also present classical dance performances.

PATHUMWAN
ART GALLERIES

Four Seasons Hotel Bangkok. The lovely courtyard at the Four Seasons Hotel Bangkok host frequently changing exhibits. It features works in different media, with an emphasis on photos. ⊠ *Four Seasons Hotel Bangkok, 155 Ratchadamri Rd., Pathumwan* ☎ *02/250–1000* ⊕ *www. fourseasons.com/bangkok* Ⓜ *Skytrain: Ratchadamri.*

SILOM
ART GALLERIES

H Gallery. Solo exhibitions from renowned artists are on display Wednesday to Monday from 10 to 6. ⊠ *201 Sathorn, Soi 12, Silom* ☎ *085/021–5508* ⊕ *www.hgallerybkk.com* Ⓜ *Skytrain: Surasak.*

Tang Gallery. This gallery features works by Chinese artists, including contemporary oil and watercolor paintings and ceramic sculptures. ⊠ *919/3 Silom Rd., Silom* ☎ *02/630–1114* Ⓜ *Skytrain: Sala Daeng.*

THEATER AND DANCE

Sala Rim Naam. Across from the Mandarin Oriental, Sala Rim Naam stages a beautiful dance show nightly at 8:15, accompanied by a touristy dinner. ⊠ *Mandarin Oriental, 48 Oriental Ave., Bang Rak* ☎ *02/659–9000* ⊕ *www.mandarinoriental.com/bangkok* Ⓜ *Skytrain: Saphan Taksin.*

Silom Village. This place appeals mostly to foreigners, but it also draws many Thais. The block-size complex, open daily 10 to 10, features performances of classical dance. ⊠ *286 Silom Rd., Silom* ☎ *02/234–4448* ⊕ *www.silomvillage.co.th* Ⓜ *Skytrain: Sala Daeng.*

SUKHUMVIT
ART GALLERIES

Carpediem Gallery. Owned by a vivacious, charismatic Singaporean woman, Carpediem Gallery hosts prominent artists and often features oversize artwork. It's in Yannawa, south of Silom. ⊠ *399 Nanglinchee, Soi 9, Silom* ☎ *089/115–4014* ⊕ *www.carpediemgallery.com* Ⓜ *Skytrain: Thong Lo.*

Tadu Contemporary Art. Tadu Contemporary Art exhibits dynamic, powerful work in a variety of media by an eclectic group of contemporary artists. ⊠ *Thaiyarnyon Building, 8th fl., 2225 Sukhumvit, Soi 87, Phra Khanong* ☎ *02/311 4951.*

Thai boxers strike their opponents with their hands, elbows, knees, and shins.

NORTHERN BANGKOK
THEATER AND DANCE

Siam Niramit. The largest theater in Thailand, the 2,000-seats Siam Niramit is home to *Journey to the Enchanted Kingdom of Siam,* is a brief history of Thailand told in words and music. The 80-minute performance begins at 8 pm nightly. Tickets are B1,500, and with dinner it's B1,850. ✉ *19 Tiamruammit Rd., Huay Kwang* ☎ *02/649–9222* ⊕ *www.siamniramit.com.*

Thailand Cultural Center. The Thailand Cultural Center hosts local and international groups, including opera companies, symphony orchestras, and modern dance and ballet troupes. ✉ *Ratchadaphisek Rd., Huay Kwang* ☎ *02/247–0028* Ⓜ *Subway: Thai Cultural Center.*

SPORTS

Although Thailand has an abundance of outdoor activities, it's often difficult to find any within Bangkok. Due to elevated temperatures, Bangkok residents generally head to the malls on weekends to cool off. Soccer is immensely popular, and the Thai Premier League has matches at several stadiums around town during the season.

Bangkok offers visitors one of the most intense spectator sports in the world, *muay thai* (Thai kickboxing). This is the national sport of Thailand and a quintessential Bangkok experience.

CLOSE UP

Muay Thai, the Sport of Kings

Thais are every bit as passionate about their national sport as Americans are about baseball. Though it's often dismissed as a blood sport, muay thai is one of the world's oldest martial arts, and it was put to noble purposes long before it became a spectator sport.

Muay thai is believed to be more than 2,000 years old. It's been practiced by kings and was used to defend the country. It's so important to Thai culture that until the 1920s muay thai instruction was part of the country's public school curriculum.

Admittedly, some of the sport's brutal reputation is well deserved. There were very few regulations until the 1930s. Before then, there were no rest periods between rounds. Protective gear was unheard of—the exception was a groin protector, an essential item when kicks to the groin were still legal. Boxing gloves were introduced to the sport in the late 1920s. Hand wraps did exist, but some fighters actually dipped their wrapped hands in resin and finely ground glass to inflict more damage on their opponent.

Techniques: Developed with the battlefield in mind, its moves mimic the weapons of ancient combat. Punching combinations, similar to modern-day boxing, turn the fists into spears that jab relentlessly at an opponent. The roundhouse kick—delivered to the thigh, ribs, or head—turns the shinbone into a devastating striking surface. Elbow strikes to the face and strong knees to the abdomen mimic the motion of a battle-ax. Finally, strong front kicks, using the ball of the foot to jab at the abdomen, thigh, or face, mimic an array of weapons.

Rules: Professional bouts have five three-minute rounds, with a two-minute rest period in between each round. Fights are judged using a point system, with judges awarding rounds to each fighter, but not all rounds are given equal weight—the later rounds are more important, as judges view fights as "marathons," with the winner being the fighter who's fared best throughout the entire match. The winner is determined by majority decision. Of course, a fight can also end decisively with a knockout or a technical knockout (wherein a fighter is conscious, but too injured to continue).

Rituals: The "dance" you see before each match is called the *ram muay* or *wai kru* (these terms are often used interchangeably, though the wai kru really refers to the homage paid to the *kru* or trainer). The ram muay serves to honor the fighter's supporters and his god, as well as to help him warm up, relax, and focus. Both fighters walk around the ring with one arm on the top rope to seal out bad spirits, pausing at each corner to say a short prayer. They then kneel in the center of the ring facing the direction of their birthplace and go through a set of specific movements, often incorporating aspects of the *Ramakien*. Fighters wear several good-luck charms, including armbands (*kruang rang*) and a headpiece (*mongkron*). The music you hear during each bout is live. Though it may sound like the tune doesn't change, the musicians actually pay close attention to the fight and they will speed up to match its pace—or to encourage the fighters to match theirs.

MUAY THAI

The national sport of Thailand draws enthusiastic crowds in Bangkok. Unlike some shows you can see in the resort areas down south, which feel touristy, Bangkok has the real thing. Daily matches alternate between the two main stadiums.

Avoid the hawkers outside the stadiums who will try to sell you pricey ringside seats—you'll be able to see all the action very well in the bleachers. The only thing you're getting with the pricier tickets is a little more comfort (a folding chair versus bleacher seating or standing room).

Lumphini Stadium. The Lumphini Stadium has muay thai matches Tuesday, Friday, and Saturday, starting at around 6:30 pm. Tickets range from B1,000 to B2,000. ⊠ *Rama IV Rd., Pathumwan* ☎ *02/251–4303* Ⓜ *Subway: Lumphini.*

Ratchadamnoen Stadium. The sprawling Ratchadamnoen Stadium has muay thai bouts on Monday, Wednesday, Thursday, and Sunday from 6:30 pm to 10 pm. Tickets may be purchased at the gate. ⊠ *Ratchadamnoen Nok Rd., Banglamphu* ☎ *02/281–4205* Ⓜ *Skytrain: Hua Lamphong.*

SHOPPING AND SPAS

Each year more and more tourists are drawn to the Thai capital for its relatively cheap silk, gems, and tailor-made clothes. But there are a slew of other goods worth discovering: quality silverware, fine porcelain, and handmade leather goods—all at prices that put western shops to shame. The already low prices can often be haggled down even further (haggling is mainly reserved for markets, but shopkeepers will let you know if they're willing to discount, especially if you started walking away).

Don't be fooled by a tuk-tuk driver offering to take you to a shop. Shop owners pay drivers a commission to lure in unsuspecting tourists. ⚠ **Avoid getting scammed on big-ticket items like jewelry by patronizing only reputable dealers.**

The city's most popular shopping areas are along Silom Road and Surawong Road, where you can find quality silk; Sukhumvit Road, which is rich in leather goods; Yaowarat Road in Chinatown, where gold trinkets abound; and along Oriental Lane and Charoen Krung (New Road), where there are many antiques shops. The shops around Siam Square and at the World Trade Center attract both Thais and foreigners. Peninsula Plaza, across from the Four Seasons Hotel Bangkok in the embassy district, has upscale shops. If you're knowledgeable about fabric, you can find bargains at the textile merchants who compete along Pahuraht Road in Chinatown and Pratunam Road off Phetchaburi Road. You can even take the raw material to a tailor and have something made.

King Power International Group. If you want the convenience of duty-free shopping, try King Power International Group. You pay for the items at the shop, then pick them up at the airport (or simply take them with you) when you leave. You need your passport and an airline ticket, and you need to make your purchase at least eight hours before leaving the country. There's also a branch at the airport that's open

24 hours. ⊠ *King Power Complex, 8/2 Rangnam Rd., Ratchathewi* ☎ *02/205–8888.*

OLD CITY

Thai antiques and old images of the Buddha require a special export license; check out the Thai Board of Investment's Web site at ⊕ *www. boi.go.th/english* for rules on exporting and applications to do so.

JEWELRY

Thailand is known for its sparkling gems, so it's no surprise that the country exports more colored stones than anywhere in the world. You'll find things you wouldn't find at home, and prices are far lower than in the United States, too. There are countless jewelry stores on Silom and Surawong roads. Scams are common, so it's best to stick with established businesses. ■**TIP→ As usual, deals that seem too good to be true probably are.**

Johny's Gems. If you call first, the long-established firm of Johny's Gems will send a car (a frequent practice among the city's better stores) to take you to the shop near Wat Phra Kaew. There's a massive selection, and you can order custom-design pieces. ⊠ *199 Fuengnakorn Rd., Old City* ☎ *02/224–4065* ☉ *Closed Sun.* Ⓜ *Subway: Hua Lamphong.*

Lin Jewelers. Rest assured that you are getting a genuine piece from Lin Jewelers. The prices are a bit more expensive than average, but so is the quality. ⊠ *Charoen Krung (New Rd.), Soi 38, Old City* ☎ *02/234–2819* Ⓜ *Subway: Hua Lamphong.*

BANGLAMPHU

MARKETS

Khao San Road. In the middle of backpacker central in Banglamphu, Khao San Road has some of the most enjoyable street shopping in the city. If the hip clothes, cheesy souvenirs, used books, and delicious B10 pad thai doesn't make the trip to Khao San worth it, the people-watching will. ⊠ *Between Chakrapong and Tanao rds., Banglamphu* Ⓜ *Subway: Hua Lamphong.*

CHINATOWN

MARKETS

Pahuraht Market. This market near Chinatown is known for its bargain textiles. A man with a microphone announces when items at a particular stall will be sold at half price, and shoppers surge over to bid. It's best to come in the evening, when it's cooler and many street vendors are selling snacks. ⊠ *Near Yaowarat Rd., Sanpanthawong* Ⓜ *Subway: Hua Lamphong.*

Asiatique the Riverfront. In a prime spot along the Chao Phraya River, Asiatique offers plenty of nice eateries, bars, and shops, all housed in 10 old warehouses with retro and industrial themes. You can get here via a free shuttle boat from the Saphan Taksin Pier next to the Skytrain

Bargaining in Bangkok

Even if you've honed your bargaining skills in other countries, you might still come up empty-handed in Thailand. The aggressive techniques that go far in say, Delhi, won't get you very far in Bangkok. One of the highest compliments you can pay for any activity in the Land of Smiles is calling it *sanuk* (fun), and haggling is no exception. Thais love to joke and tease, so approach each bargaining situation playfully. However, be aware that Thais are also sensitive to "losing face," so make sure you remain pleasant and respectful throughout the transaction.

As you enter a market stall, smile and acknowledge the proprietor. When something catches your eye, inquire politely about the price, but don't immediately counter. Keep your voice low—you're more likely to get a deal if it's not announced to the whole shop—then ask for a price just slightly below what you want. Don't get too cavalier with your counteroffer—Thai sellers generally price their wares in a range they view as fair, so asking to cut the initial price in half will most likely be seen as an insult and might end the discussion abruptly. In most cases, the best you can hope for is 20% to 30% discount.

If the price the shopkeeper offers in return is still high, turn your smile up another watt and say something like, "Can you discount more?" If the answer is no, your last recourse is to say thank you and walk away. If you are called back, the price is still negotiable; if you aren't, maybe B500 wasn't such a bad price after all.

—Molly Petersen

station of the same name. ✉ *2194 Charoen Krung Rd. (New Rd.), Bangkor Laem ⊕ www.thaiasiatique.com.*

Soi Sampeng. This street has lots of fabrics—it's Bangkok's best-known and oldest textile center, and is located in the heart of Chinatown off Ratchawong and Yaowarat. ✉ *Soi Sampeng, parallel to Yaowarat Rd., Sanpanthawong* Ⓜ *Subway: Hua Lamphong.*

PATHUMWAN

CLOTHING AND FABRICS

Thai silk gained its reputation only after World War II, when technical innovations made it less expensive. Two fabrics are worth seeking out: mudmee silk, produced in the northeastern part of the country, and Thai cotton, which is soft, durable, and easier on the wallet than silk.

Greyhound. This shop sells casual yet chic street wear. ✉ *Siam Paragon, 991/1 Rama I Rd., 1st fl., Pathumwan* ☎ *02/129–4358* ⊕ *www. greyhound.co.th* Ⓜ *Subway: Silom; Skytrain: Siam.*

Marco Tailor. Many people who visit Bangkok brag about a custom-made suit that was completed in just a day or two, but the finished product often looks like the rush job that it was. If you want an excellent cut, give the tailor the time he needs, which could be up to a week at a reputable place. One of the best custom tailor shops in Bangkok is Marco

Tailor, which sews a suit equal to those on London's Savile Row. It's not cheap, but it's cheaper than what you'd pay in London. ✉ *430/33 Siam Sq., Soi 7, Pathumwan* ☎ *02/252–0689* Ⓜ *Skytrain: Siam.*

Prayer Textile Gallery. Napajaree Suanduenchai studied fashion design in Germany, and more than two decades ago opened the Prayer Textile Gallery in her mother's former dress shop. She makes stunning items in naturally dyed silks and cottons and in antique fabrics from the farthest reaches of Thailand, Laos, and Cambodia. ✉ *Phayathai Rd., near Siam Sq., Pathumwan* ☎ *02/251–7549* Ⓜ *Skytrain: Siam.*

Sretsis. Three Thai sisters, darlings of the local design scene, created Sretsis, a feminine design label that has fashionistas around the world raving. ✉ *Gaysorn Plaza, 999 Ploenchit Rd., 2nd fl., Pathumwan* ☎ *02/656–1125* ⊕ *www.sretsis.com* Ⓜ *Skytrain: Chitlom.*

MARKETS

Pratunam Market. Hundreds of vendors selling inexpensive clothing jam the sidewalk each day at Pratunam Market. It's a popular destination for Indians, who drop by in the evening to sample the dozens of surrounding Indian, Nepali, and Pakistani restaurants. ✉ *Phetchaburi and Ratchaprarop Rds., Pathumwan* Ⓜ *Skytrain: Chitlom.*

SHOPPING CENTERS

Central Chitlom. The flagship store of Thailand's largest department store chain has a good selection of jewelry, clothing, and fabrics, including a Jim Thompson silk shop. ✉ *1027 Ploenchit Rd., Pathumwan* ⊕ *www. central.co.th* Ⓜ *Skytrain: Chitlom.*

Central World. At more than 1 million square meters (about 10,760,000 square feet), this monster claims to be Southeast Asia's biggest mall. It's packed with local and international labels, as well as a multiplex cinema, a hotel, and lots of dining options. ✉ *999/9 Rama I Rd., Patumwan* ⊕ *www.centralworld.co.th* Ⓜ *Subway: Silom; Skytrain: Siam.*

Gaysorn Plaza. This upscale shopping center may outshine all the others with its white marble and chrome fixtures. You'll find all the requisite European labels as well as local designers, such as Fly Now, Senada, and Sretsis. ✉ *999 Ploenchit Rd., Pathumwan* ⊕ *www.gaysorn.com* Ⓜ *Skytrain: Siam.*

MBK Center. An impressive seven stories high, this is one of the busiest malls in the city. It's not as stylish as Siam Centre—the main attractions are cheap clothes and electronics—but there are tons of shops, as well as an IMAX movie theater and a bowling alley. ✉ *Phayathai and Rama I rds., Pathumwan* ⊕ *www.mbk-center.co.th* Ⓜ *Skytrain: Siam, Rajchathewi.*

Pantip Plaza. This mall exists for the computer nerd in everyone. It houses an enormous collection of computer hardware and software (some legal, most not). Shopping here can be overwhelming, but if you know what you're looking for, the bargains are worth it. ■TIP➜ Not all electronics will be compatible with what you have back home, so do your research. ✉ *Phetchaburi Rd., Ratchathewi* ⊕ *www.pantipplaza. com* Ⓜ *Subway: Phetchaburi; Skytrain: Chitlom.*

Siam Centre. This is where Bangkok's young hipsters come for the latest fashion trends. With one-of-a-kind handmade clothing, shoes, and accessories, Siam Centre oozes style, but be forewarned that the clothes are all made to Thai proportions, so they often run small. ⊠ *Phayathai and Rama I rds., Pathumwan* ⊕ *www.siamcenter.co.th* Ⓜ *Skytrain: Siam.*

Siam Discovery. Full of shops selling international labels, Siam Discovery has the added bonus of the most grandiose movie theater in Thailand, the Grand EGV. ⊠ *989 Rama I Rd., Pathumwan* ⊕ *www.siamdiscovery. co.th* Ⓜ *Subway: Silom; Skytrain: Siam.*

Siam Paragon. With 250 stores, including all the big international designers from Porsche to Chanel, Siam Paragon also has a multiplex cinema, tons of restaurants, and an underwater marine park where you can swim with sharks. ⊠ *991/1 Rama I Rd., Pathumwan* ⊕ *www. siamparagon.co.th* Ⓜ *Skytrain: Siam.*

SILOM

CLOTHING AND FABRICS

Jim Thompson Thai Silk Company. This is a prime place for silk by the yard and ready-made clothes. The prices are high, but the staff is knowledgeable. There are numerous other locations throughout the city, such as in the Mandarin Oriental, the Four Seasons, the Peninsula, and Central Chitlom shopping center. ⊠ *9 Surawong Rd., Bang Rak* ☎ *02/632–8100* ⊕ *www.jimthompson.com* Ⓜ *Subway: Silom; Skytrain: Sala Daeng.*

LEATHER

Chaophraya Bootery. Need custom-made cowboy boots? Get some for around $200 at Chaophraya Bootery. There's also a large inventory of ready-made leather shoes, boots, and accessories. ⊠ *141 Sukhumvit, Soi 11, Wattana* ☎ *02/253–5400* Ⓜ *Subway: Silom; Skytrain: Sala Daeng.*

Siam Leather Goods. For shoes and jackets, try Siam Leather Goods. ⊠ *River City Shopping Complex, 23 Charoen Krung (New Rd.), Bang Rak* ☎ *02/237–0077* Ⓜ *Subway: Sam Yan; Skytrain: Saphan Taksin.*

MARKETS

Patpong. Asking a taxi driver to take you to Patpong may prompt a smirk, but for fake Rolex watches, imposter Louis Vuitton handbags, and Western-size clothing there's no better place than this notorious red-light-district street. ⊠ *Silom Rd. at Soi 2, Bang Rak* Ⓜ *Subway: Silom; Skytrain: Sala Daeng.*

PORCELAIN, CERAMICS AND CELADON

Benjarong. This massive ceramics shop has a huge inventory and will make to order dining sets, bowls, and vases. ⊠ *River City Shopping Complex, 23 Charoen Krung (New Rd.), 3rd fl., Bang Rak* ☎ *02/237–0077.*

PRECIOUS METALS

Lin Silvercraft. Among all the knickknacks stacked from floor to ceiling, this shop has some of the most finely crafted silver cutlery in town. ⊠ *3 Charoen Krung (New Rd.), Soi 38, Bang Rak* ☎ *02/235–2108,*

02/234–2391 ⊕ www.linjewelers.com Ⓜ *Subway: Sam Yan; Skytrain: Saphan Taksin.*

Siam Bronze Factory. For quality works in bronze, try Siam Bronze Factory. It's near the Mandarin Oriental. ✉ *1250 Charoen Krung (New Rd.), Bang Rak* ☎ *02/234–9436* Ⓜ *Subway: Sam Yan; Skytrain: Saphan Taksin.*

SUKHUMVIT

CLOTHING AND FABRICS

Naj Collection. The Naj Collection stocks some of the best silk products you will find, from accessories to home decor. It also happens to be housed in a traditional Thai house that serves what might be the tastiest traditional food in Bangkok. ✉ *32–32/1 Sukhumvit, Soi 23, Sukhumvit* ☎ *02/664–0664* ⊕ *www.thelocalthaicuisine.com.*

Raja Fashions. Check out photographs of former heads of state modeling their new suits made by Raja Fashions. Raja has the reputation for tailoring some of the finest men's and women's fashions in Bangkok. ✉ *160/1 Sukhumvit, between sois 6 and 8, Sukhumvit* ☎ *02/253–8379* ⊕ *www.rajasfashions.com* Ⓜ *Subway: Sukhumvit; Skytrain: Nana.*

> ### A UNIQUE SOUVENIR
>
> One of the famous artisanal products of Bangkok is the steel **monk's bowl**, handmade by monks in the area of tiny alleyways around Soi Banbat (near Wat Suthat). The unique bowls, which resonate harmonically when tapped, are made out of eight strips of metal—one for each Buddhist stage—and are traditionally used by the monks to collect donations. At the shop at 14 Soi Banbat (☎ *02/621–2635*) you can purchase one for around B500, which will also buy you a look at the workshop.

JEWELRY

Than Shine. Run by sisters Cho Cho and Mon Mon, Than Shine offers classic and modern designs. ✉ *Imperial Queens Park Hotel, 199 Sukhumvit, Soi 22, Sukhumvit* ☎ *02/261–900* Ⓜ *Subway: Sukhumvit; Skytrain: Thong Lo.*

Uthai's Gems. With top-quality gems, reliable service, and hordes of repeat clients, it's no wonder you need an appointment to peruse the huge inventory at Uthai's Gems. ✉ *28/7 Soi Ruam Rudi, Pathumwan* ☎ *02/253–8582* Ⓜ *Subway: Sukhumvit; Skytrain: Ploenchit.*

MARKETS

Emporium. This glitzy shop has a little sales area on the sixth floor full of beautiful silks, incense, and glassware, all reasonably priced. ✉ *622 Sukhumvit, between Sois 24 and 26, Sukhumvit* ☎ *02/269–1000* ⊕ *www.emporiumthailand.com* Ⓜ *Skytrain: Phrom Phong.*

NORTHERN BANGKOK

MARKETS

Fodor'sChoice ★ **Chatuchak Weekend Market.** You can purchase virtually anything at the sprawling Chatuchak Weekend Market, including silk items in a *mudmee* (tie-dyed before weaving) design that would sell for five times the price in the United States. Strategically placed food vendors mean you don't have to stop shopping to grab a bite. It's open on weekends from 9 am to 7 pm, and the city's (some say the world's) largest market is best in the morning before it gets too crowded and hot. It's easy to reach, across the street from the northern terminus of the Skytrain and near the Northern Bus Terminal. Just follow the crowd.

An afternoon at JJ, as it is known by locals ("ch" is pronounced "jha" in Thai, so phonetically Chatuchak is Jatujak), is not for the faint of heart: up to 200,000 people visit each day, and there are more than 8,000 vendors. But what's a little discomfort when there are such fantastic bargains to be had? Go prepared with bottles of water, comfortable shoes, and make sure to print out a copy of the map of the market from the website. The borders between the market's many sections can be a bit hazy (for example, the animal section—which includes some bizarre pets like squirrels—spills into the silverware section), but you can keep your bearings by remembering that the outer ring of stalls has mainly new clothing and shoes, with some plants, garden supplies, and home decor thrown in for good measure. The next ring of stalls is primarily used (and some new) clothing and shoes plus accessories like jewelry, belts, and bags. Further in are pottery, antiques, furniture, dried goods, and live animals.

Even with a map, it's easy to get turned around in the mind-boggling array of goods, but this is also part of the joy that Chatuchak has to offer—wandering through the maze of vendors and suddenly stumbling upon the beautiful teak table, handmade skirt, or colorful paper lamp you'd been seeking. ✉ *Phaholyothin Rd., Chatuchak* ⊕ *www.chatuchak.org* Ⓜ *Subway: Chatuchak Park; Skytrain: Mo Chit.*

> ### WORD OF MOUTH
>
> "The market was a joy, and far less hot, crowded, and difficult to navigate than I had feared. I had a Nancy Chandler map but did not use it as I found it delightful just to wander around—you guessed it—aimlessly. I spent about three hours in the market. My two "major" purchases were a silk ikat jacket for B480 and a pair of wonderful leather sandals that cost about $20. I wish I had purchased another pair or two of the sandals as the workmanship is excellent and they have an artisanal look that reminds me of the sandals my Mom used to bring back from Capri in the 50s!" —ekscrunchy

SPAS

Venues offering traditional massage are quite common in Bangkok— you can even pamper yourself while sightseeing at Wat Po. The staff at your hotel can recommend reputable therapists. If you have the time,

Bangkok offers massage at every turn—in swanky resort spas, tiny shophouses, and everyplace in between.

pull out all the stops with a two-hour massage. ■TIP➜ Spa treatments at top hotels tend to fill up at least a day in advance, so plan ahead.

PATHUMWAN

COMO Shambhala. The ultimate urban escape, this spa relaxes you instantly with a delicious cup of ginger lemongrass tea. There's a wide range of treatments. The Metropolitan Bath treatments starts with an invigorating salt scrub, followed by a luxurious soak and a relaxing massage. ✉ *Metropolitan Hotel, 27 S. Sathorn, Silom* ☎ *02/625–3355* ⊕ *www.comoshambhala.com* Ⓜ *Subway: Lumphini; Skytrain: Sala Daeng.*

Four Seasons Hotel Bangkok. A relaxing massage with deliciously warm oils is among the many treatments available at the Four Seasons Hotel Bangkok. You can even arrange for a poolside massage. ✉ *155 Ratchadamri Rd., Pathumwan* ☎ *02/250–1000* ⊕ *www.fourseasons.com/ bangkok* Ⓜ *Skytrain: Ratchadamri.*

I. Sawan Spa. This spa's facilities are among the city's most cutting-edge, relaxing, and beautiful. The "residential spa cottages," suites clustered around a courtyard adjacent to the spa, have their own treatment spaces. Reasonably priced spa packages are available. ✉ *Grand Hyatt Erawan, 494 Ratchadamri Rd., Pathumwan* ☎ *02/254–6310* ⊕ *www. bangkok.grand.hyatt.com* Ⓜ *Skytrain: Ratchadamri.*

Seasons Spa. The 11 treatment rooms at the Seasons Spa have views that are among the city's finest. ✉ *Conrad Hotel, 87 Wittayu (Wireless Rd.), Pathumwan* ☎ *02/690–9355* ⊕ *www.conradhotels.com* Ⓜ *Skytrain: Ploenchit.*

SILOM

Mandarin Oriental Spa. A gentle massage in genteel surroundings is what you'll get at Mandarin Oriental Spa. Amid the wood-panel sophistication you can treat yourself to facials, wraps, and massage. The signature treatments run 90 minutes and will leave you feeling exquisitely pampered and begging for more. ⊠ *Mandarin Oriental, 48 Oriental Ave., Bang Rak* ☎ *02/659–9000* ⊕ *www.mandarinoriental.com/bangkok* Ⓜ *Skytrain: Saphan Taksin.*

Ruen Nuad. An inexpensive but excellent option for traditional Thai massage is Ruen Nuad. A 90-minute massage will cost B750. ⊠ *42 Thanon Convent, 2nd fl., Bang Rak* ☎ *02/632–2662.*

SUKHUMVIT

Oasis Spa. The treatments at Oasis Spa take place in a Thai-style house. Among the inventive treatments are a coffee-bean body scrub and detoxifying algae and green-tea body wraps. ⊠ *88 Sukhumvit, Soi 51, Sukhumvit* ☎ *02/662–6171* Ⓜ *Skytrain: Thong Lo.*

Yunomori Onsen Spa. Bangkok's first Japanese hot spring, this traditional bathhouse has first-class spa treatments. There's even real spring water, thousands of gallons of it, trucked up from the famed Raksawarin Hot Springs in Ranong. Choose from among a series of pool, ranging from a toasty hot tub down to a cold plunge pool. There's also a steam room and sauna. ⊠ *Sukhumvit, Soi 26, Sukhumvit* ☎ *02/259–5778* ⊕ *www. yunomorionsen.com.*

AROUND BANGKOK

Trips to Damnoen Saduak floating market, Phetchaburi, Kanchanaburi, and Sangklaburi

WELCOME TO AROUND BANGKOK

TOP REASONS TO GO

★ **Heading into the Wild:** There's a huge expanse of untouched jungle around Kanchanaburi, which is the kickoff point for trekking, elephant riding, and river-rafting adventures.

★ **Floating Markets:** This area has more floating markets than anywhere else in Thailand. The most famous is at Damnoen Saduak—it's the only daily floating market left in the region.

★ **Seeing Old Siam:** History awaits outside Bangkok at a Neolithic site, the remains of a Khmer temple (Muang Singh Historical Park in Kanchanaburi), and in Nakhon Pathom, Thailand's oldest seat of Buddhist learning.

★ **Bridge on the River Kwai:** For a glimpse of more recent history, visit what remains of the "Death Railway" in Kanchanaburi and walk across the bridge made famous by the movie.

★ **River Views in Ayutthaya:** This city, which can be visited as a day trip from Bangkok, combines great river views with an island full of fascinating wats.

1 Day Trips from Bangkok. When most people head south, it's to make for Thailand's famous beaches, but along the way are the floating market at Damnoen Saduak and Muang Boran, a huge park with replicas of the country's landmarks. To the west of Bangkok is Nakhon Pathom, keeper of Thailand's biggest stupa.

2 Phetchaburi. Phetchaburi has many interesting temples and a few royal summer palaces. Three hours south of Bangkok, it makes for a long day trip, so either hire a car and driver to make the trip easier or visit as part of a one- or two-day trip to the coastal resort of Hua Hin.

3 Kanchanaburi and Environs. Kanchanaburi, two hours west of Bangkok, is best known as the site of the famous Bridge on the River Kwai. If you're not in a hurry to get back to Bangkok, you can continue your exploration of stunning Kanchanaburi Province, with day trips to 13th-century Khmer ruins and two national parks containing waterfalls.

Sangklaburi

Khao Laem National Park
Khao Laem Reservoir

Thong Pha Phum

Si Nakharin Reservoir

Sai Yok National Park 323

MYANMAR (BURMA)

4 **Sangklaburi.** Kanchanaburi Province's farthest attraction is the city of Sangklaburi, which is on Myanmar's doorstep. Here Thai, Mon, Karen, and Bangladeshi communities mix, and boats take you to see a village submerged in a reservoir.

5 **Ayutthaya and Environs.** Within easy reach of Bangkok, Ayutthaya is a historically significant ruin, and once one of the country's most important sites. Nearby Bang Pa-In, with its famous Royal Palace, and Lopburi, with its monkey-infested temples, are a bit farther off the beaten track.

GETTING ORIENTED

If you need respite from the heat, noise, and pollution of Bangkok, the surrounding countryside offers many possibilities. There are several sights directly outside the city, easily reached in a few hours by bus, train, or taxi. Kanchanaburi Province can become a mini-vacation all on its own, with Kanchanaburi city being the gateway to a first glimpse of Thailand's wilderness.

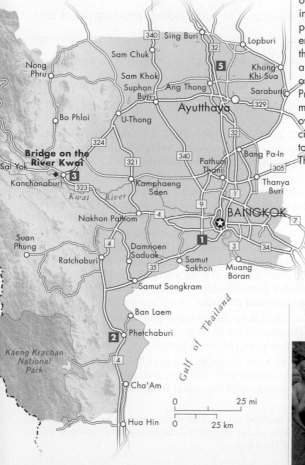

Updated by
Simon Stewart

Escaping the congestion and chaos of Bangkok is quite simple, and a must for anyone who wants a truly memorable Thailand experience. The surrounding provinces and cities make for a comfortably paced day trip, or an easy getaway for a few days. However you spend your time, you're sure to encounter amazing scenery, interesting culture, and unforgettable adventure.

Only 50 km (31 miles) west of Bangkok is a small haven for those seeking enlightenment. The province of Nakhon Pathom has the tallest Buddha monument in the world, Phra Pathom Chedi.

Travel a little farther west and you'll be in Kanchanaburi, with its mixture of tranquil scenery, war museums, and temples. Kanchanburi is most known for the Bridge on the River Kwai, but there's plenty to keep you occupied. If you're an explorer at heart, this is a great starting-off point for visiting national parks, rafting, hiking, and riding elephants.

If you're interested in seeing a more traditional aspect of Thailand, head down to Damnoen Saduak. Here you'll be surrounded by the colors and smells of a market while drifting along in a small, wooden boat. The floating market primarily caters to tourists, so most of the vendors mainly sell souvenirs and produce.

History buffs and Buddhists should travel a bit farther south to the seaport town of Phetchaburi for its wats and palaces. Don't be frightened of the monkeys that roam the streets here.

Don't have time to travel the entire country? The peaceful grounds of Muang Boran, an outdoor park-museum, is roughly shaped like Thailand and displays replicas of important monuments from all parts of the country.

If you're craving seafood served Thai-style, head to Samut Songkram, where you'll be able to eat your fill of clams and other seafood dishes along the Gulf of Thailand.

If you have more time, you might be interested in visiting Sangklaburi, which is close to the Myanmar border. This area is a mixture of Mon, Karen, and Bangladeshi communities, giving it a unique twist. Many people who venture to Sangklaburi go on trekking tours.

PLANNING

WHEN TO GO

On weekends and national holidays (particularly during the mid-April Buddhist New Year water festival), Kanchanaburi and the restaurants at Samut Songkram are packed with Thais. In high season (November to March) the floating market in Damnoen Saduak has more tourists than vendors. The waterfalls of Kanchanaburi Province are at their best during or just after the rainy season (June to November). The fossil shells in Don Hoi Lod in Samut Songkram are best seen in dry season or at low tide in rainy season. See the fireflies in Ampawa between May and October.

GETTING THERE AND AROUND

BUS TRAVEL

Most buses depart from Bangkok's Southern Bus Terminal; tickets are sold on a first-come, first-served basis, but service is so frequent that it's seldom a problem finding an empty seat.

CAR TRAVEL

Distances from Bangkok are short enough to drive, though it's more relaxing to hire a car and driver.

TAXI AND SONGTHAEW TRAVEL

Bangkok's air-conditioned taxis are an often-neglected way of accessing sights outside the city. It can be worth it to use them to explore Nakhon Pathom, Samut Songkram, and Muang Boran. Estimate around B500 per hour, depending on your bargaining skills. Standard rates, implemented by the Ministry of Transport, are displayed in most taxis and should be used as a starting point for any negotiations.

Outside Bangkok, *songthaews* (pickups with wooden benches in the truck bed) are often the closest thing to taxis.

HEALTH AND SAFETY

The region is generally safe, and the towns mentioned in this chapter have hospitals. Take normal precautions and keep valuables on your person at all times when traveling by bus or train. Too-good-to-be-true deals—particularly involving gems—are *always* a rip-off. On a more amusing note, the monkeys of Phetchaburi are cute but cunning, and may relieve you of your possessions, especially food.

MONEY MATTERS

Generally speaking, finding banks and ATMs isn't difficult, especially in towns. Most main bank branches close at 4 pm, with many smaller branches, often located in shopping malls and department stores, remaining open into the evening. Remember that the farther out from civilization you get, the fewer ATMs you'll find. Don't expect to withdraw money outside a national park or in a tribal village. It's probably best if you exchange the money you want before leaving Bangkok.

RESTAURANTS

The areas around Bangkok allow you to sample both regional and non-Thai ethnic foods. Kanchanaburi and Sangklaburi have Mon, Karen, Bangladeshi, and Burmese communities serving their own specialties. A must-try is *laphae to,* a Burmese salad of nuts and fermented tea leaves. In Nakhon Pathom try the excellent rice-based dessert *khao larm.* Phetchaburi is famous for its desserts and for *khao chae,* chilled rice soaked in herb-infused water.

Prices in the reviews are the average cost of a main course at dinner or, if dinner is not served, at lunch.

HOTELS

An overnight stay is essential in Sangklaburi and highly recommended in Kanchanaburi and Petchaburi. Stay in Damnoen Saduak the night before you visit the floating market to avoid an early-morning bus ride.

Luxury accommodations are more common in most provincial towns, but be prepared to stay at a resort on the outskirts if you want to sample the very best. It's best to book ahead on weekends and national holidays in Kanchanaburi.

Prices in the reviews are the lowest cost of a standard double room in high season.

VISITOR AND TOUR INFO

It's easy to get around on your own, but both **Asian Trails** (☎ *02/626–2000* ⊕ *www.asiantrails.net*) and **Diethelm Travel** (☎ *02/660–7000* ⊕ *www.diethelmtravel.com*), in Bangkok, organize trips to the floating markets as well as trekking trips, homestays, and bicycle tours.

DAY TRIPS FROM BANGKOK

MUANG BORAN

20 km (12 miles) southeast of Bangkok.

Muang Boran. Muang Boran (Ancient City) is an outdoor museum with more than 100 replicas and reconstructions of the country's most important architectural sites, monuments, and palaces. The park is shaped like Thailand, and the attractions are placed roughly in their correct geographical position. A "traditional Thai village" on the grounds sells crafts, but the experience is surprisingly untouristy. The park stretches over 320 acres, and takes about four hours to cover by car. Or you can rent a bicycle at the entrance for B50. Small outdoor cafés throughout the grounds serve decent Thai food. ✉ *296/1 Sukhumvit Rd., Bangpoo, Samut Prakan* ☎ *02/709–1648* 🎫 *B500* ☉ *Daily 8–5.*

GETTING HERE AND AROUND

BUS TRAVEL   For buses from Bangkok to Muang Boran (two hours; B30), take the air-conditioned 511, which leaves every half hour from Bangkok's Southern Bus Terminal, to the end of the line at Pak Nam. You can also catch this bus on Sukhumvit Road. Transfer to songthaew 36 (B10), which goes to the entrance of Muang Boran.

CAR TRAVEL   Driving to Muang Boran means a trip through heavy and unpredictable Bangkok traffic. It should take 1½ to 2 hours. Take the Samrong–Samut Prakan expressway and turn left at the Samut Prakan intersection onto Old Sukhumvit Road. Muang Boran is well signposted on the left at Km 33.

SAFETY AND PRECAUTIONS
Safety should not be a concern at Muang Boran. Don't worry about large crowds, because the park is so spacious.

3

DAMNOEN SADUAK

109 km (68 miles) southwest of Bangkok.

The colorful Damnoen Saduak floating market is a true icon of Thai tourism. The image is so evocative that it's become an ad agency favorite. Today the market, which sells mostly produce and other foods, has taken on a bit of the Disneyland effect, as it is often infested with tourists and bears only passing resemblance to the authentic commercial life of this canal-strewn corner of Thailand. On the other hand, even though it feels a bit like a theater production, this is one of the few opportunities to witness a fading Thai tradition. The best way to enjoy the market is to hire a boat; after seeing the market, tour the countryside, take in local temples and gardens, or travel back to Bangkok.

GETTING HERE AND AROUND
Getting to Damnoen Saduak can be tricky. It's probably best to join one of the tours offered at most hotels and guesthouses.

ORM Travel Agency ☎ *026/291–622.*

Siam Travel Center ☎ *662/282–5300.*

BUS TRAVEL   Buses to Damnoen Saduak (two to three hours; B73) leave Bangkok's Southern Bus Terminal every 20 minutes starting at 5 am. From the station in Damnoen Saduak, walk or take a songthaew along the canal for 1½ km (1 mile) to the floating market. Buses also run from Nakhon Pathom and Samut Songkram.

CAR TRAVEL   Take Highway 4 (Phetkasem Road) and turn left at Km 80. Continue for 25 km (16 miles) along the Bang Phae-Damnoen Saduak Road. The drive from Samut Songkram to Damnoen Saduak, along Route 325, is pleasant, particularly if you go via Ampawa. The entire trip takes two hours.

SAFETY AND PRECAUTIONS
The canals are narrow and can get quite crowded. Make sure you keep your hands away from the edge of the boat, since they tend to bump up against each other.

TIMING
There isn't much to do in Damnoen Saduak besides the floating market. Go in the morning, when it isn't so hot, and enjoy another part of Thailand for the rest of the day.

WHERE TO EAT AND STAY
You'll find plenty of food stalls and small street restaurants, as well as fruits and vegetables, along the main road.

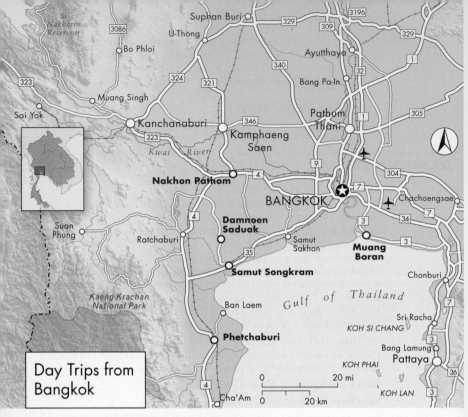

Day Trips from Bangkok

Visit Fodors.com for expanded hotel reviews.

$ **Baan Sukchoke Country Resort.** The small wooden bungalows sur-
RESORT rounding a pond are a bit rickety, but clean and comfortable nonetheless. **Pros:** nice countryside atmosphere. **Cons:** a bit out of town,
aging facilities. $ *Rooms from: $15* ✉ *103 Moo 5* ☎ *032/254301* 🛏 *40
rooms* ▤ *No credit cards.*

$ **Little Bird Hotel.** Convenience is the top selling point of this hotel a
HOTEL 10-minute walk from the boats for the floating market and close to
banks, stores, and cafés. **Pros:** the most convenient hotel to the floating
market; arranges market tours. **Cons:** no hot water. $ *Rooms from: $8*
✉ *Moo 1/8* ☎ *032/254382, 081/587–4519* 🌐 *www.noknoihotel.com*
🛏 *30 rooms* ▤ *No credit cards* 🍽 *No meals.*

SAMUT SONGKRAM

72 km (45 miles) south of Bangkok.

The provincial town of Samut Songkram has little to recommend it, but
it has many nearby attractions that make it an enjoyable day trip from
Bangkok. There are terrific seafood restaurants along the waterfront
at Don Hoi Lod; the area is also a good base for exploring some of the

surrounding villages on the canal network, such as Ampawa, with its small floating market.

GETTING HERE AND AROUND

BUS TRAVEL Buses depart from Bangkok's Southern Bus Terminal for Samut Songkram (1½ hours; B55) every hour from 3 am to 6:30 pm. Bus 996 can drop you off at Ampawa.

CAR TRAVEL Route 35, the main road south to Samut Songkram (one hour), is mainly a two-lane highway that can be slow going if there's heavy traffic. Add an extra half hour to all trip times for possible delays.

SONGTHAEW TRAVEL In town there are frequent songthaews to Don Hoi Lod and Ampawa (10 minutes; B20).

> ### WORD OF MOUTH
>
> "The Floating Market was the next stop. We cruised along the canals, tasting various treats prepared by the floating vendors. The food was excellent—noodle soups, grilled pork and chicken bits on sticks, fried bananas, mango, pomelo, and pineapple. As time passed the canals became clogged with boats packed with tourists. I would recommend arriving here as early as possible to avoid some of the larger tour groups that descend as the morning wears on." —ekscrunchy

SAFETY AND PRECAUTIONS

Ampawa can be crowded, especially during holidays. Keep a careful eye on your possessions. Make sure you keep an eye on the time if you are taking a songthaew from Don Hoi Lod to Ampawa. Drivers stop taking passengers at 5 pm.

TIMING

If you enjoy shopping, Samut Songkram makes a good day trip. It can also be fun to spend the night and see the fireflies, but you probably won't need more than a day and a half to experience the area.

Emergencies Mae Khlong Song Hospital ✉ *198/1 Ratrasit Rd.* ☎ *034/715001.*

EXPLORING SAMUT SONGKRAM

If you want to see both Don Hoi Lod and Ampawa, you'll need a full day. If you don't have a car and want to go on the fireflies tour in Ampawa, you'll have to stay overnight.

Ampawa. The charming village of Ampawa is 10 km (7 miles) by songthaew from Samuk Songkram has a **floating market** similar to (but smaller than) that in Damnoen Saduak on Friday, Saturday, and Sunday evening from 5 to 9. The food market in the street adjacent to the canal starts at around 1 pm. Featured in a Thai movie, popular **fireflies tours** allow you to enjoy both the market and the beautifully insect-lighted trees. The bugs are best seen from May to October and in the waning moon. The hour-long tours usually run every half hour from 6:30 to 9 pm. You can arrange a tour directly at the pier (B650 for a boat) or through your hotel (around B70 per person). Unless you have private transportation, you'll have to spend the night in Ampawa, as the last bus back to Bangkok is in the early evening. ⊕ *www.amphawafloatingmarket.com.*

Don Hoi Lod. On weekends Thai families flock to the village of Don Hoi Lod, about 3 km (2 miles) south of Samut Songkram to eat the clams (try them with garlic and pepper) and other seafood dishes at the tree-shaded restaurants at the mouth of the Mae Khlong River. The village is named after a local clam with a tubular shell, the fossilized remains of which are found on the riverbanks. ■ **TIP→ The best times to view the fossils are March and April, when the water is low.** The rest of the year you can also see the fossils in the early morning and in the evening at low tide.

WHERE TO EAT AND STAY

There are many homestay options in Ampawa for every budget. Call the TAT office in Phetchaburi or Kanchanaburi for more details.

Hotel reviews have been condensed for this book. Please go to Fodors.com for full reviews of each property.

$ SEAFOOD 🍴 **Kunpao.** One of the last in a long row of seafood places in Don Hoi Lod, this restaurant on wooden stilts is usually packed with Thai families who come to enjoy the gentle breeze, the fried sea perch, horseshoe-egg spicy salad, and grilled prawns. The atmosphere is both busy and relaxed. Try to get one of the few sit-on-the-floor tables directly above the water. There's a playground for kids. [$] *Average main: B120* ✉ *1/3 Moo 4, Bangyakang, Don Hoi Lod* ☎ *034/723703.*

$$ HOTEL 🏨 **Thanicha Boutique Resort.** In an old wooden house close to the market, this lovely boutique hotel by the main canal is a perfect weekend escape from Bangkok. **Pros:** nice café and restaurant in front; free Wi-Fi in hotel. **Cons:** busier and more expensive on weekends. [$] *Rooms from: $75* ✉ *261 T. Ampawa A., Ampawa* ☎ *034/725511* 🌐 *www.thanicha.com* 🛏 *24 rooms* 💳 *No credit cards* 🍽 *No meals.*

NAKHON PATHOM

56 km (35 miles) west of Bangkok.

Reputed to be Thailand's oldest city (it's thought to date from 150 BC), Nakhon Pathom was once the center of the Dvaravati kingdom, a 6th- to 11th-century affiliation of Mon city-states. It marks the region's first center of Buddhist learning, established about a millennium ago. It's home to the Buddhist monument Phra Pathom Chedi.

GETTING HERE AND AROUND

BUS TRAVEL Buses depart from Bangkok's Southern Bus Terminal for Nakhon Pathom (one hour; B46) every hour from 5:30 am to 8 pm.

CAR TRAVEL Driving west from Bangkok, allow an hour to get to Nakhon Pathom on Route 4.

TRAIN TRAVEL From Bangkok, 10 trains a day run at regular intervals to Nakhon Pathom (1½ hours; B14 to B20). Some of the Nakhon Pathom trains continue on to Phetchaburi (four hours; B94 to B114) and points farther south. Trains to Kanchanaburi also stop in Nakhon Pathom.

SAFETY AND PRECAUTIONS

Nakhon Pathom is an average Thai province. You shouldn't run into any unusual problems here.

ESSENTIALS

Emergencies Sanam Chan Hospital ✉ *1194 Petchkasem Rd., Nakhon Pathom* ☎ *034/219600.*

Continued on page 144

THAI MARKETS

by Hana Borrowman

For an authentic Thai shopping experience, forget air-conditioned malls and head to the traditional markets, or *talaats*. Take a deep breath and prepare for an intoxicating medley of colors, sounds, smells, and tastes.

Entrepreneurs set up shop wherever there's an open space—roadsides, footbridges, and bustling waterways. You'll find all sorts of intriguing items: caramelized crickets and still-wriggling eels; "potency" potions made from pigs' feet; fierce-looking hand weapons like elegant samurai swords and knife-edged brass knuckles; temple offerings; plastic toys; and clothing.

Markets are an integral part of Thai life. Locals stop by for a meal from their favorite food vendor or to sit at a coffee stall, gossiping or discussing politics. Whole families take part: You might see an old woman bargaining with a customer at a hardware stall while her grandchild sleeps in a makeshift hammock strung up beneath the table.

Damnoen Saduak's floating market.

GREAT FINDS

Low prices make impulse buys almost irresistible. Here are a few things to keep your eyes out for while you shop.

Housewares. You'll find metal "monks' bowls" like those used for alms-collection, cushions, wicker baskets, carved tables, and ornate daybeds. Polished coconut-shell spoons and wooden salad servers are more practical if you're not up for shipping home your wares. Small wooden bowls and utensils start at around B150.

Memorabilia. Toy *tuk-tuks* (three-wheeled cabs) made from old tin cans, sequined elephants sewn onto cushion covers, satin Muay Thai boxer shorts, wooden frogs that croak—all make great and inexpensive souvenirs, and most Thai markets have them in droves.

Jewelry. Throughout the country, hill-tribe women sell beautiful silver and beaded jewelry. Silver bangles start at B250 and chunky silver rings with semiprecious stones like opal and mother-of-pearl are B350 and up. You'll also find "precious" gemstones and crystals, but you're better off making serious purchases at reputable shops in Bangkok.

Silk. Thailand is famous for its bright, beautiful silks. Raw Thai silk has a relatively coarse texture and a matte finish; it's good value, and wonderful for curtains and upholstery. You'll also find bolts of less expensive shimmering satins, and ready-made items like pajamas, purses, and scarves.

Prices vary enormously—depending on quality and weight—from B100 to upwards of B700 a meter. To test for authenticity, hold the fabric up to the light: If it's pure silk, the color changes, but fake silk shines a uniformly whitish tone. You can also ask for a swatch to burn—pure fibers crumble to ash, while synthetics curl or melt.

Clothes. Markets have tons of clothing: the ubiquitous Thai fisherman pants; factory seconds from The Gap; knockoff designer jeans; and, invariably, frilly underwear. But some of Thailand's edgiest designers are touting more modern apparel at markets as well. It's hard to say whether these up-and-comers are following catwalk trends or vice-versa. Bangkok fashion houses like **Sretsis** (feminine dresses; ⊕ www.sretsis.com), **Greyhound** (casual, unisex urbanwear; ⊕ www.greyhound.co.th), and **Issue** (bohemian chic; no Web) are good places to scope out styles beforehand (⇨ *Shopping in Chapter 2*). Prices vary greatly—a cheaply made suit could cost as little as B1,000, while an expertly tailored, high-quality version might be B20,000 or more. But it's difficult to determine quality unless you're experienced.

FLOATING MARKETS

Sunday morning at Damnoen Saduak.

Floating markets date from Bangkok's "Venice of the East" era in the 19th century, when canal-side residents didn't have to go to market—the market came to them. Many waterways have been filled in to create roads, so there are only a handful of floating markets left. These survivors have a nostalgic appeal, with vendors in straw hats peddling produce, flowers, snacks, and crafts against a backdrop of stilt houses and riverbanks.

Thailand's original floating market in Damnoen Saduak (⇨ *above*) is very famous, but it's also crowded and over-priced. Still, you can get a taste of the old river life here, in addition to lots of touristy souvenirs. If you visit, try to stay nearby so that you can arrive near dawn; the market is open from 6 AM till noon, but by 9 it's usually swarming with sightseers.

The Amphawa Floating market near Samut Songkram (⇨ *above*), set on a leafy waterway dotted with temples and traditional Thai homes, is less crowded and more authentic.

LOGISTICS

Many hotels and guesthouses can arrange a longtail boat and an oarsman for you. You can also just head to the pier, though it's a good idea to ask your hotel what going rates are first. Private boats start at around B500 an hour, but oarsmen may try to charge much more. Haggle hard, and don't get in a boat before you've agreed on price and duration. If you join a group of locals in a boat, you'll often pay a set rate per person.

Longtail boat.

SHOPPING KNOW-HOW

Most markets begin to stir around dawn, and morning is the best time to visit—it's not too hot, and most Thais do their marketing early in the day, so you'll get to watch all the local action. Avoid rainy days: The scene loses a lot of its allure when everything's covered in plastic sheets.

Flower market in Bangkok.

SHOPPING TIPS

■ Check prices at less touristy spots—Chinatown, Pratunam Market, and MBK in Bangkok—to get a sense of cost (⇨ *Shopping in Chapter 2*).

■ Keep money and valuables like cell phones tucked away.

■ Avoid tuk-tuk drivers who offer you a shopping tour. They'll pressure you to drop a lot of cash at their friends' stalls.

■ Look for the One Tambon One Product (OTOP) government stamp on market goods. A tambon is a subdistrict—there are over 7,000 in the country, and one handmade, locally sourced product is selected from each.

■ Steer clear of exotic animal products, such as lizard skins, ivory, tortoiseshell, and anything made of tiger. These products may come from endangered animals; if so, it's illegal to leave Thailand with them or bring them into the U.S. If not illegal, they may be counterfeit.

■ Only buy antiques at reputable shops; real Thai antiques cannot be exported without a license, which good shops provide. Most so-called antiques at markets are knockoffs.

■ Thai markets are full of counterfeits—DVDs, computer software, and designer clothes and accessories. In addition to being illegal, these items vary in quality, so examine the products and your conscience carefully before you buy.

Straw hats for sale.

HOW TO BARGAIN

Thais love theatrical bargaining, and it's customary to haggle over nearly everything. Here are some tips for getting a fair price. The most important thing is to have fun!

DO	DON'T
■ Decide about how much you're willing to pay before you start bargaining. ■ Let the vendor set the opening price. This is the standard etiquette; vendors who make you go first may be trying to take you for a ride. Vendors who don't speak English may type their price into a calculator, and you can respond in kind. ■ Come equipped with a few Thai phrases, such as "How much is this?" *(anee tao rai [kaa/krap]?)*, "A discount?" *(Lod mai?)*, and "Expensive!" *(Paeng!)*. ■ Bargain quietly, and if possible, when the vendor is alone. Vendors are unlikely to give big discounts in front of an audience. ■ Be polite, no matter what. Confidence and charming persistence are winning tactics in Thailand—not hostility. ■ Honor your lowest bid if it's accepted.	■ Don't lose your temper or raise your voice. These are big no-no's in the land of smiles. ■ Don't hesitate to aim low. Your opening counteroffer should be around 50% or 60% of the vendor's price, and you can expect to settle for 10% to 30% off the initial price. If you're buying more than one item, shoot for a bigger discount. ■ Don't be afraid to walk away. Often the vendor will call you back with a lower price. ■ Don't get too caught up in negotiating. It's OK to back down if you really want something. ■ Don't bargain for food—prices are fixed.

Woman displaying
Thai silk.

EXPLORING NAKHON PATHOM

Seeing all the sights here will take you a full day, but the bus ride from Bangkok is only an hour, so it's doable as a day trip.

Phra Pathom Chedi. The tallest Buddhist monument in the world, Phra Pathom Chedi tops out at 417 feet, just higher—but less ornate—than the chedi at Shwe Dagon in Myanmar. Erected in the 6th century, the site's first chedi was destroyed in a Burmese attack in 1057. Surrounding the chedi is one of Thailand's most important temples, which contains the ashes of King Rama VI.

The terraces around the temple complex are full of fascinating statuary, including Chinese figures, a large reclining Buddha, and an unusual Buddha seated in a chair. By walking around the inner circle surrounding the chedi, you can see novice monks in their classrooms through arched stone doorways. Traditional dances are sometimes performed in front of the temple, and during Loi Krathong (a festival in November that celebrates the end of the rainy season) a fair is set up in the adjacent park. ⊠ *Khwa T. Praphrathom Chedi Rd., Nakhon Pathom* ⊠ *B50* ☉ *Daily 5 am–6 pm.*

Phra Pathom Chedi National Museum. Next to Phra Pathom Chedi is the Phra Pathom Chedi National Museum, which contains Dvaravati artifacts such as images of the Buddha, stone carvings, and stuccos from the 6th to the 11th century. ⊠ *Khwa T. Praphrathom Chedi Rd.* ⊠ *B30* ☉ *Wed.–Sun. 9–noon and 1–4.*

FAMILY **Sampran Riverside.** Roses are just a part of this complex where herbs, bananas, and various flowers, including orchids and roses, flourish. Within the complex are traditional houses and a performance stage, where shows include dancing, Thai boxing, sword fighting, and even wedding ceremonies (daily at 2:45 pm). ■ **TIP→ The park is popular with Thai families, and has restaurants and a nice hotel with rooms starting at B2,600.** ⊠ *Km 32, Pet Kasem Rd.* ☎ *6634/322544* ⊕ *www. rosegardenriverside.com* ⊠ *B20, B550 with lunch and show* ☉ *Daily 6–6.*

Sanam Chan Palace. Built during King Rama IV's reign, Sanam Chan Palace and the surrounding park are a lovely place to relax. ⊠ *Petchkasem Rd., west of Phra Pathom Chedi* ⊠ *B50.*

WHERE TO EAT

The road from Nakhon Pathom train station has several cafés, and a market where food stalls sell one-plate Thai meals. Similar dining options are at the entrance of the chedi. Keep an eye out for Nakhon Pathom specialties such as *khao larm* (sticky rice, palm sugar, and black beans grilled in hollowed-out bamboo sections) and sweet, pink-flesh pomelo (a large citrus fruit).

PHETCHABURI

132 km (82 miles) south of Bangkok.

This small seaport town with many wats once linked the old Thai capitals of Sukhothai and Ayutthaya with trade routes on the South China

Sea and Indian Ocean. Phetchaburi is famous for *khao chae,* a chilled rice dish with sweetmeats once favored by royals that has become a summer tradition in posh Bangkok hotels. You can find it around the day market on Phanit Charoen Road (look for people eating at stalls from small silver bowls), along with *khanom jeen thotman* (noodles with curried fish cake). The city was also a royal retreat during the reigns of Rama IV and Rama V (1851–1910) and has two palaces open to the public. ⚠ Steer clear of the gangs of monkeys on the streets and around Khao Wang, especially with food in your hands.

GETTING HERE AND AROUND

BIKE TRAVEL A bike or a motorbike at Rabieng Guesthouse (B120 per day for a bike, B200 per day for a motorbike) is a good way to get around town.

BUS TRAVEL Phetchaburi-bound buses depart Bangkok's Southern Bus Terminal (two hours; B126) every 30 minutes from 5 am to 9 pm. The Phetchaburi Bus Station is north of town, near the night market.

CAR TRAVEL If you're driving, take Route 35, the main road south from Bangkok, then continue on Highway 4 to Phetchaburi Province. The trip takes 90 minutes. On the way back to Bangkok, there are two alternatives. Follow signs to Samut Songkram for the shorter trip along Route 35.

TRAIN TRAVEL All trains to southern Thailand stop at Phetchaburi (three hours; B94–B114). The train station is north of Phetchaburi on Rot Fai Road. You can hire motorbikes taxis or tuk-tuks from the train or bus station to get to sights or downtown.

SAFETY AND PRECAUTIONS

The bus lets you off at the side of the road, which can be a little intimidating. Don't worry; there is a motorcycle taxi stand there with a few drivers who will be happy to help you. This area doesn't have many English speakers, so be patient.

ESSENTIALS

Emergencies **Meung Phet Thonburi Hospital** ✉ *150 Phetkasem Rd., Moo 6* ☎ *032/415191.*

EXPLORING PHETCHABURI

Phetchaburi's many wats are within, or easily accessible on foot from, the town center, particularly along Matayawong, Pongsuriya, and Phrasong roads. Two days are sufficient to visit all the sights.

Khao Luang Cave. Studded with stalactites, the Khao Luang Cave is filled with Buddha images, including a 10-meter-long reclining Buddha. Most were put in place by kings Rama IV and Rama V. ■ TIP→ The cave is best appreciated on a clear morning, between 9 and 10, when the sun shines in and reflects off the brass Buddha images. For a donation of B20 or so (to pay for the electricity), the nun will light up the rear of the cave for you. The cave is accessed via a two-minute walk from the parking lot and some steep stairs. Watch out for the monkeys. A large monastery, Wat Tham Klaep, at the bottom of the hill below the cave, is open to the public. ✉ *Off Rot Fai Rd., 5 km (3 miles) north of Phra Nakhon* ☉ *Daily 9–4.*

Phra Nakhon Khiri Historical Park (Khao Wang). On a forested hillside at the edge of Phetchaburi, Phra Nakhon Khiri Historical Park (Khao

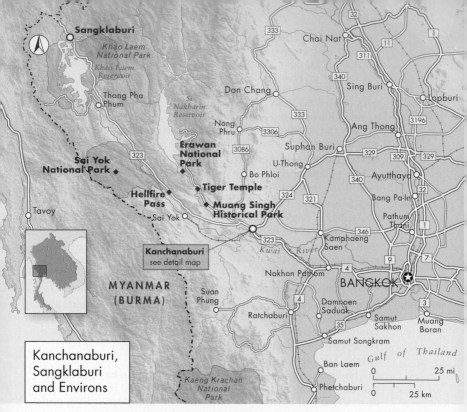

Kanchanaburi, Sangklaburi and Environs

Wang) includes one of King Rama IV's palaces and a series of temples and shrines. Many of these are set high on the hilltop and have good views. Monkeys are a major shoplifting hazard around the gift shops at the foot of the hill. There's a cable car (B50) for those who don't fancy the strenuous walk. ⊠ *Entrance off Phetkasem Rd.* ☎ *032/401006, 032/425600* ☒ *B50* ⊙ *Daily 9–4.*

Phra Ram Ratchaniwet. Built in 1910 as a rainy-season retreat by King Rama V, Phra Ram Ratchaniwet was modeled on a palace of Germany's Kaiser Wilhelm, and consequently has grand European architecture with art-nouveau flourishes. The dining room has ornate ceramic tiles. ⊠ *Ratchadamnoen Rd.* ☎ *032/428083* ☒ *B50* ⊙ *Daily 9–4.*

Wat Mahathat Worawihan. The 800-year-old Khmer-influenced Wat Mahathat Worawihan, on the western side of the Phetchaburi River, is a royal temple. Besides the magnificent architecture, an interesting feature of this wat is a subtle political joke. Look around the base of the Buddha statue outside the main temple. A ring of monkeylike Atlases supports the large Buddha image, but one of the monkeys is not like the others. See if you can find him! ⊠ *Banda-it and Damnoen Kasem rds.* ⊙ *Daily 6–6.*

Wat Yai Suwannaram. Built during the Ayutthaya period by skilled craftsman, Wat Yai Suwannaram has a 300-year-old painting in its main hall, a library on stilts above a fish pond (to deter termites), and an ax mark above one of the temple doors, said to have been left by a Burmese invader. ✉ *Phongsunyia Rd., less than half a mile after crossing the river* ⏲ *Daily 5 am–6 pm.*

WHERE TO EAT AND STAY

Hotel reviews have been condensed for this book. Please go to Fodors.com for full reviews of each property.

$ THAI 🍴 **Rabieng Restaurant.** In a small wooden house by the river, this family-run restaurant offers a wide range of classic Thai dishes, as well as a few Western dishes. American music plays in the background. Attached to Rabieng Guesthouse, it's one of the few places that are open past sunset. Try the spicy banana-blossom salad or the delicious stuffed chicken with pandanus leaves. [$] *Average main: B100* ✉ *1 Shesrain Rd.* ☎ *032/425707* 💳 *No credit cards.*

$ B&B/INN 🏨 **Rabieng Guesthouse.** In a cluster of dark-wood plank buildings, these basic rooms are just big enough for beds. **Pros:** nice restaurant overlooking the river; walking distance to bus terminal. **Cons:** thin walls next to noisey road; shared bathrooms. [$] *Rooms from: $10* ✉ *1 Shesrain Rd.* ☎ *032/425707* 🛏 *10 rooms with shared bath* 💳 *No credit cards* 🍽 *No meals.*

$ HOTEL 🏨 **Royal Diamond Hotel.** About 3 km (2 miles) northwest of town, the Royal Diamond is one of Phetchaburi's few choices for those seeking a hotel instead of a guesthouse. **Pros:** close to Phra Nakhon Khiri Historical Park. **Cons:** out of town. [$] *Rooms from: $30* ✉ *555 Moo 1, Phetkasem Rd., Tambon Rai-Som* ☎ *032/411061 up to 70* 🌐 *www.royaldiamondhotel.com* 🛏 *58 rooms* 🍽 *Breakfast.*

KANCHANABURI AND ENVIRONS

The city of Kanchanaburi is home to interesting and sometimes moving World War II historic sites: the Bridge on the River Kwai (local people actually call it "Kwae") and several war cemeteries. In and around the city are museums, cave temples, tribal villages, and waterfalls. Hiking, rafting and elephant treks are among the main activities. Kanchanaburi is the main access point to the large national parks of western Thailand.

KANCHANABURI

140 km (87 miles) west of Bangkok.

The city is most famous as the location of the **Bridge on the River Kwai**—a piece of the World War II Japanese "Death Railway" and the subject of the 1957 film of the same name starring Alec Guinness and Richard Holden (although it used Thai actors, the film was shot in Sri Lanka).

During World War II the Japanese, with whom Thailand sided, forced about 16,000 prisoners of war and 50,000 to 100,000 civilian slave laborers from neighboring countries to construct the "Death Railway," a supply route through the jungles of Thailand and Myanmar. It's estimated that one person died for every railway tie that was laid. Surefooted visitors can walk across the Bridge on the River Kwai, of which

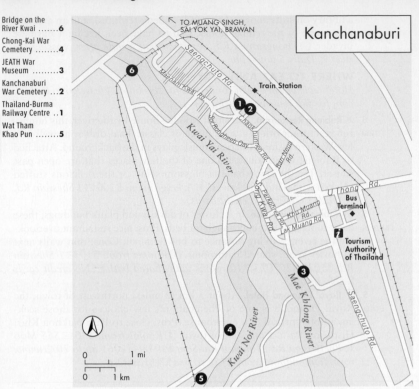

the arched portions are original. In December there's a big fair with a sound-and-light show depicting the Allied bombing of the bridge. Next to the bridge is a plaza with restaurants and souvenir shops.

GETTING HERE AND AROUND

BUS TRAVEL   Air-conditioned buses headed to Kanchanaburi leave from Bangkok's Southern Bus Terminal (two hours; B85) every 20 minutes from 5 am to 10:30 pm. Buses also leave eight times a day from Bangkok's Mo Chit Northern Bus Terminal (three hours; B115).

CAR TRAVEL   Allow two hours to reach Kanchanaburi along Route 4. The first half is on a busy truck route that continues to southern Thailand, but the second half is more pleasant, through agricultural land. The road to Kanchanaburi passes through Nakhon Pathom.

TAXI AND SONGTHAEW TRAVEL   In town, options for getting around include pedicabs and motorcycles with sidecars. Songthaews are better for longer forays out of town and can be flagged down. The few tuk-tuks and taxis are harder to find. Drivers are notorious for hiking up prices for tourists, so bring your best bargaining face.

TRAIN TRAVEL   Two Kanchanaburi-bound trains (three hours; B100) leave every day from Bangkok Noi Railway Station, on the Thonburi side of the Chao Phraya River.

SAFETY AND PRECAUTIONS

It's fun to explore the city on two wheels, but remember that motorbike accidents are the top cause of injuries for tourists in Thailand. Always use a helmet and stay within the speed limit. If you take your own vehicle out of the city, make sure you watch the gas gauge. It can be hard to find a gas station when you need one.

ESSENTIALS

Emergencies Thanakan Hospital ⊠ *20/20 T. Ban Tai, Muang* ☎ *034/622366 up to 75.*

EXPLORING KANCHANABURI

Easy to navigate, Kanchanaburi is laid out along the Mae Khlong and Kwai Yai rivers. Three to four days can easily be spent exploring the town and the surrounding areas. If you're in a rush, you can see the main sights in one or two days by booking package tours.

TOP ATTRACTIONS

JEATH War Museum. A bit more than 2 km (1 mile) downriver from the bridge is the JEATH War Museum (JEATH is an acronym for Japan, England, America, Australia, Thailand, and Holland). The museum, founded in 1977 by a monk from the adjoining Wat Chaichumpol, is housed in a replica of the bamboo huts that were used to hold prisoners of war. On display are railway spikes, aerial photographs, newspaper clippings, and original sketches by ex-prisoners depicting their living conditions. ⊠ *Wat Chaichumpol, Bantai* ☎ *034/515263* 💰 *B40* 🕒 *Daily 8–4:30.*

Thailand-Burma Railway Centre. Next to the Kanchanaburi War Cemetery, the small Thailand-Burma Railway Centre is well designed and packed with informative displays. A walk through the nine chronologically arranged galleries gives a good overview of the railway's history. At the end of the exhibits is a coffee shop on the second floor that has a view of the cemetery. ⊠ *73 Jaokannun Rd.* ☎ *034/512721* ⊕ *www.tbrconline. com* 💰 *B100* 🕒 *Daily 9–5.*

WORTH NOTING

Chong-Kai War Cemetery. On the grounds of a former hospital for prisoners of war, the Chong-Kai War Cemetery is serene and simple, with neatly organized grave markers of the soldiers forced to work on the railway. It's a little out of the way, and therefore rarely visited. To get here, hire a tuk-tuk or moto-taxi for about B60. ⊠ *West side of river, 3 km (2 miles) from town.*

Kanchanaburi War Cemetery. Next to noisy Saengchuto Road, Kanchanaburi War Cemetery has row upon row of neatly laid-out graves: 6,982 Australian, British, and Dutch prisoners of war are laid to rest here. The remains of the American POWs were returned to the United States during the Eisenhower administration. A remembrance ceremony is held every April 25, Australia and New Zealand Army Corps Day. ⊠ *Saengchuto Rd., across from train station.*

Wat Tham Khao Pun. Less than 1 km (½ mile) southwest of the Chong-Kai War Cemetery you'll find Wat Tham Khao Pun, one of the best cave-temples in the area. A guide at the small shrine outside the cave will direct you. Inside, between the stalagmites and stalactites, are Buddhist and Hindu statues and figurines. During WWII the Japanese used the cave complex as a series of storerooms. ✉ *West side of river, 4 km (2½ miles) from town* ⏲ *Daily 9–4.*

WHERE TO EAT

For cheap eats, the Kanchanaburi Night Market opens early in the evening and offers a variety of Thai soups, rice dishes, and satays. The blended frozen fruit drinks are particularly good. The market is on Saengchuto Road, next to the train station.

$ THAI 🍴 **Apple's Restaurant.** This quiet garden restaurant is decked out in wood with lots of local flourishes. The massaman curry is popular with backpackers. Made with heaps of palm sugar, it's a good balm for stomachs struggling with chili overdose. More authentic (hotter) dishes are available on request. Try the whole fish with lemongrass, lime juice, and crushed chili. [$] *Average main: B120* ✉ *153/4 Moo 4, Thamakhan Muang* ☎ *034/512–017, 081/948–4646* 🌐 *www.applenoi-kanchanaburi.com.*

$ THAI 🍴 **Keeree Tara.** With a great view of the River Kwai Bridge from its terraces, this floating restaurant has a sophisticated look. It caters mostly to Thais, so the food can be quite spicy—if you can't handle it, ask them to tone the heat down (say "*mai phet*"). The place serves a wide range of local dishes, but the fish soups and curries are the best choices. [$] *Average main: B150* ✉ *43/1 River Kwai Rd.* ☎ *034/624093* 🌐 *www.keereetara.com.*

$ THAI 🍴 **Mae Nam Restaurant.** The busiest of the floating restaurants at the south end of the River Kwai Yai where it merges with the Kwai Noi, Mae Nam serves Thai seafood standards, including grilled prawns and red curry with snakehead fish (a freshwater relative of the catfish). A singer performs each night. The riverfront serenity is disrupted periodically by the loud music of the disco and karaoke boats that meander past. The restaurant has no English sign, but it's next to the Café de Paradiso. [$] *Average main: B120* ✉ *5/7 Song Kwai Rd.* ☎ *034/512811* 🌐 *www.maenamraft.com.*

$ SEAFOOD 🍴 **River Kwai Floating Restaurant.** Follow the crowds to this open-air restaurant in the shadow of the railway bridge. Fish dishes (fried with pungent spices or lightly grilled), soups, and curries dominate the menu. The local specialty is *yeesok,* a fish caught fresh from the Kwai Yai and Kwai Noi rivers. Another tasty choice is the *tom yum goong,* hot-and-sour shrimp soup. **■ TIP→ The food is toned down for foreigners, so if you want it spicy, tell them so.** [$] *Average main: B120* ✉ *Beside River Kwai Bridge* ☎ *034/512595* 💳 *No credit cards.*

WHERE TO STAY

Visit Fodors.com for expanded hotel reviews.

$ RESORT 🏨 **Apple Retreat and Guesthouse.** At this longtime favorite, choose between guesthouse rooms set around a central courtyard and simple, comfortable rooms in a two-story building on the opposite side of the river. **Pros:** good restaurant; knowledgeable owners; unique tours. **Cons:** can fill quickly in high season; simple decor. $ *Rooms from: $33* ✉ *153/4 Moo 4, Thamakhan Muang* ☎ *034/512017, 081/948–4646* ⊕ *www.applenoi-kanchanaburi.com* ↪ *16 rooms* ⦿*No meals.*

$$
RESORT
🏨 **Felix River Kwai Resort.** Kanchanaburi's first luxury hotel is a bit faded now, but it's still a good value. **Pros:** right by the famous bridge; wonderful tropical garden. **Cons:** you'll have to take a taxi to the city center. $ *Rooms from: $102* ✉ *9/1 Moo 3, Tambon Thamakham* ☎ *034/551000, 02/634–4111 in Bangkok* ⊕ *www.felixriverkwai.co.th* ↪ *255 rooms* ⦿*Breakfast.*

$
RESORT
🏨 **Kasem Island Resort.** On an island in the middle of the Mae Khlong River, this resort has one of the area's most enviable locations. **Pros:** nice view; unique location. **Cons:** isolated. $ *Rooms from: $58* ✉ *44–48 Chaichumpol Rd.* ☎ *081/499–4941, 02/255–3603 in Bangkok* ⊕ *www. kasemisland.com* ↪ *18 bungalows, 15 raft houses* ⦿*Breakfast.*

$$
RESORT
🏨 **Pavilion Rim Kwai Thani Resort.** Wealthy Bangkok residents who want to retreat into the country without giving up creature comforts head to this resort near the Erawan Waterfall. **Pros:** some rooms have great views; huge pool and pretty garden. **Cons:** far from town; a bit outdated. $ *Rooms from: $61* ✉ *79/2 Moo 4, Km 9, Ladya-Erawan Rd., Tambon Wangdong* ☎ *034/513800* ⊕ *www.pavilionhotels.com* ↪ *194 rooms* ⦿*Breakfast.*

$$
RESORT
🏨 **River Kwai Village.** In the jungles of the River Kwai Valley, this resort organizes elephant riding and rafting trips, as well as the usual city excursions. **Pros:** jungle location; river views. **Cons:** vey far from town; no nighttime entertainment. $ *Rooms from: $102* ✉ *72/12 Moo 4, Tambon Thasaso, Sai Yok, Kanchanaburi* ☎ *02/674–5555, 02/251–7828 in Bangkok* ⊕ *www.riverkwaivillage.com* ↪ *191 rooms, 24 raftels* ⦿*No meals.*

$
RESORT
🏨 **Sam's House.** A popular launching pad for treks, Sam's House has a trio of air-conditioned floating rooms that are nice but a bit cramped, as well as less expensive rooms set away from the river. **Pros:** some rooms have nice river views; can arrange tours. **Cons:** more expensive than other "budget" options. $ *Rooms from: $27* ✉ *14/2 River Kwai Rd.* ☎ *034/515956* ⊕ *www.samsguesthouse.com* ↪ *38 rooms* ⊟*No credit cards* ⦿*No meals.*

SPORTS AND THE OUTDOORS
RAFTING
Daylong rafting trips on the Kwai Yai or Mae Khlong rivers let you venture far into the jungle. The mammoth rafts, which resemble houseboats, are often divided into separate sections for eating, sleeping, and sunbathing. ⚠ **Be careful when taking a dip—the currents can sometimes suck a swimmer down.** Rates start at about B450. Longer trips are also available.

TREKKING
Jungle treks of one to four days are possible all over the region. They typically include bamboo rafting, elephant riding, visits to Karen villages, sampling local food, and sometimes a cultural performance. Stick to tour companies with Tourism Authority of Thailand licenses, which will be prominently displayed on the premises.

Good Times Travel. A reputable tour agency with a good track record, Good Times Travel offers all the usual highlights, including national parks, rafting, caves, and Karen village stays. ⊠ *63/1 River Kwai Rd.* ☎ *034/624441* ⊕ *www.good-times-travel.com.*

RSP Jumbo Travel. You can book everything here from day trips to waterfalls to weeklong itineraries that include rafting, elephant riding, and off-road adventures. Some tours include stays at upmarket hotels, so you don't have to give up creature-comforts. ⊠ *3/13 Chao Kun Nen Rd.* ☎ *034/514906* ⊕ *www.jumboriverkwai.com.*

SHOPPING

Blue sapphires from the Bo Phloi mines, 45 km (28 miles) north of Kanchanaburi town, are for sale at many shops and stalls in the plaza near the bridge. The price is determined by the size and color of the stone, and, as usual, your bargaining skills. You'll do best when there are few tourists around and business is slow. Stick to stalls with licenses.

AROUND KANCHANABURI PROVINCE

The third-largest province in Thailand, Kanchanaburi has scenic jungles, rivers, waterfalls, and mountains, especially near Sangklaburi, as you approach the Myanmar border. For centuries it was a favorite invasion route into Siam for the Burmese. Today it is home to Karen and Mon communities, whose villages can be visited.

GETTING HERE AND AROUND

The region is easily accessible by car. Roads 323 and 3199 take you to the main sights. It's also quite easy to travel around by public transportation, although package tours can be helpful if you have limited time. Reaching less-popular sights, such as Muang Singh Historical Park, is complicated if you don't have private transportation. Consider hiring a songthaew (around B750 for half a day). Public buses from Kanchanaburi leave the bus station, or from Saengchuto Road, close to the guesthouse area on River Kwai Road. There's also a private minibus office near the main bus station; minibuses go to many places in the province, but are more expensive than public buses and fill up quickly. Sai Yok Noi National Park is accessible by train.

SAFETY AND PRECAUTIONS

Make sure you pay extra attention if you are driving: stray dogs tend to run out into the street. There aren't many gas stations outside the city.

TIMING

The region surrounding Kanchanaburi is large, and you can easily spend a few days enjoying the sights. A day trip is possible if there's something specific you want to see, but chances are you'll feel rushed.

MUANG SINGH HISTORICAL PARK

45 km (28 miles) northwest of Kanchanaburi.

Ban Khao Museum. This two-room exhibition of 4,000-year-old Neolithic remains is 8 km (5 miles) from Muang Singh Historical Park. Cars and motorcycles are your only options for getting here. ⊠ *323 Ban Khao* ☎ *034/654058* 🎫 *B50* ⊙ *Wed.–Sun. 9–4.*

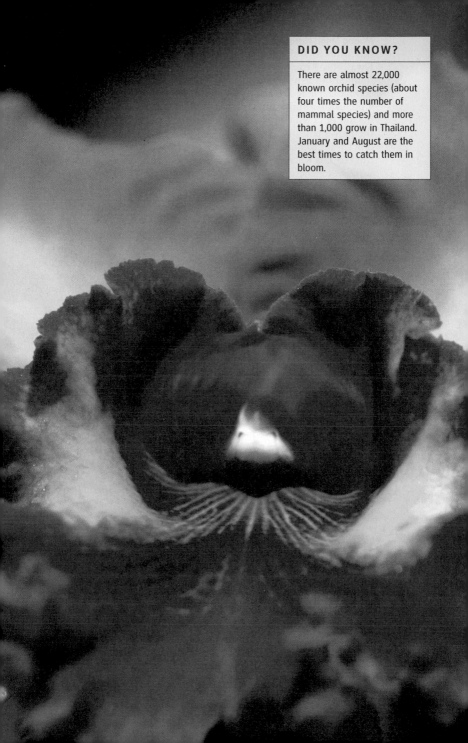

DID YOU KNOW?

There are almost 22,000 known orchid species (about four times the number of mammal species) and more than 1,000 grow in Thailand. January and August are the best times to catch them in bloom.

Muang Singh Historical Park. King Chulalongkorn reportedly discovered this 13th- to 14th-century Khmer settlement while traveling along the Kwai Noi River. The restored remains of the city range from mere foundations to a largely intact, well-preserved monument and building complex. There are also examples of Khmer statues and pottery and a prehistoric burial site. You can navigate the expansive grounds with the aid of taped commentary in English, Thai, or French, available at the park's entrance. Bicycle rentals cost around B20 per hour. If you don't want to make the 45-minute drive from Kanchanaburi, take the train to Tha Kilen Station (one hour; B15); the park is a 1-km (½-mile) walk west. There are lodgings and a small café on the grounds. ⊠ *Tha Kilen* ☎ *034/591122, 034/591334* ☜ *B50* ⊙ *Daily 9–6.*

TIGER TEMPLE
25 km (15 miles) northwest of Kanchanaburi.

Tiger Temple. Also known as Wat Pa Luanta Bua Yannasampanno, Tiger Temple is a forest monastery that houses several kinds of animals on its grounds, most notably tigers. Every day at 3, the 30 or so tigers are brought into a canyon for a photo op that lasts no more than a minute. The rest of the day you can see some of the tigers in their cages, as well as wild boars and water buffaloes.

Controversy surrounds the sight—some locals are concerned about safety (though no injuries have been reported), and many suspect that the tigers have been drugged to make them docile around visitors. Many tour operators claim they'd rather not promote the site, but can't afford to lose customers. ⊠ *Km 21, Rte. 323* ☎ *083/777–8006* ☜ *B600* ⊙ *Daily 9–4.*

ERAWAN NATIONAL PARK
65 km (40 miles) northwest of Kanchanaburi.

Erawan National Park. Some of the most spectacular scenery of Kanchanaburi Province can be found in Erawan National Park. The main attraction is **Erawan Waterfall,** which has seven tiers; the topmost supposedly resembles the mythical three-headed elephant (Erawan) belonging to the Hindu god Indra. You'll need to make a rather steep 2-km (1-mile) hike to get to the top. ⚠ **Comfortable footwear is essential for the two-hour trek, and don't forget to bring water.** You can swim at each level of the waterfall (levels 2 through 5 are the most popular). The first tier has a small café, and there are several others near the visitor center. There are also eight-person bungalows costing B800 to B2,400—the ones nearest the waterfall are quieter.

The park is massive; the waterfall is near the main entrance—so, too, are the visitor center and accommodations. Other highlights of the park include five caves. One of them, **Ta Duang,** has wall paintings, and another, **Ruea,** has prehistoric coffins. The caves are much farther away and are accessed via a different road. About 2 km (1 mile) from the park is Erawan Village; songthaews leave from its market and travel to the park entrance and the caves (B500–B600). Erawan-bound buses (No. 8170) leave Kanchanaburi's bus station every 50 minutes; the trip takes 90 minutes. ⊠ *Erawan National Park* ☎ *034/574222, 034/574234* ⊕ *www.dnp.go.th* ☜ *B200* ⊙ *Daily 8–4:30.*

HELLFIRE PASS
70 km (43 miles) northwest of Kanchanaburi.

Hellfire Pass. The museum at Hellfire Pass is a moving memorial to the Allied prisoners of war who built the River Kwai railway, 12,399 of whom died in the process. Along with a film and exhibits, there's a 4½-km (3-mile) walk along a section of the railway, including the notorious Hellfire Pass, one of the most grueling sections to build. The pass got its name from the fire lanterns that flickered on the mountain walls as the men worked through the night. ■TIP→ Many people do the walk in the early morning, before the museum opens and before it gets too hot. Allow 2½ hours round-trip for the walk. Take plenty of water and snacks; there's a small shack near the museum that sells drinks, but not much food. The pass can be busy on weekends (when an average of 500 people a day visit). Bus No. 8203 (two hours) makes the trip to the museum. The last bus back to Kanchanaburi is at 4 pm. The drive by car is about an hour. ⊠ *Km 66, Rte. 323* ☎ *034/53-1347* ⊕ *www.dva.gov.au* ☎ *Free* ☉ *Daily 9–4.*

SAI YOK NATIONAL PARK
97 km (60 miles) northwest of Kanchanaburi.

Sai Yok National Park. The main attraction in Sai Yok National Park is **Sai Yok Yai waterfall,** which flows into the Kwai Noi River. The waterfall, an easy walk from the visitor center, is single tier and not nearly as spectacular as Erawan's. More unique are the **bat caves,** 2 km (1 mile) past the waterfall. They are the only place you can see the thumb-size Kitti's hog-nosed bat, the world's smallest mammal. Rent flashlights at the visitor center. Other caves worth visiting include Tham Wang Badan and Lawa Cave.

This part of the park has several options for accommodations, all without electricity. The private raft houses on the Kwai Noi River are the more scenic options. Those near the waterfall have inexpensive restaurants that are more pleasant than the food stalls near the visitor center.

Driving here from Bangkok or Kanchanaburi you'll pass **Sai Yok Noi waterfall,** also within the park's boundaries. Despite being taller than Sai Yok Yai, Sai Yok Noi has less water, but there's enough to swim in from June to November, when the area is often packed with Thai families on weekends.

Buses to Sai Yok Yai leave Kanchanaburi every 30 minutes from 6 am to 6:30 pm. If you're headed to Sai Yok Noi, buses leave Kanchanaburi every 30 minutes from 6 am to 5 pm. Either trip takes about two hours. Sai Yok Noi is also 2 km (1 mile) from Nam Tok Station, the terminus of the Death Railway. Trains leave Kanchanaburi each day at 5:52 am and 10:20 am. If you're driving to either waterfall from Bangkok or Kanchanaburi, take Road 323. ⊠ *Park headquarters, Km 97, Rte. 323, Sai Yok, Kanchanaburi* ☎ *034/686024* ⊕ *www.dnp.go.th* ☎ *B200* ☉ *Daily 7–6.*

SANGKLABURI

203 km (126 miles) northwest of Kanchanaburi.

This sleepy town sits on a large lake created by the Khao Laem Dam. There was once a Mon village here, but when the dam was built in 1983 it was almost completely covered by water. (Some parts, including a temple, are still visible beneath the surface.) The sanctuary-seeking Mon, who arrived in the area 50 years ago from Myanmar, were relocated to a village on the shore opposite Sangklaburi.

The Mon village has a temple with Indian and Burmese influences and a bronze-color pyramid chedi that's beautifully illuminated at night. A dry-goods market in the village sells Chinese and Burmese clothes and trinkets, with Mon dishes available at nearby food stalls. Get here by car or boat, or walk across the country's longest wooden bridge.

Due to its proximity to Myanmar's border, Sangklaburi is also home to Karen and Bangladeshi communities, who you'll spot in the town's small night market. Jungle trekking and visits to Karen villages are popular activities for visitors. You can also cross into Myanmar at Three Pagodas Pass with a passport photo and $10 (U.S. currency only—there's an exchange facility at the border), but you can't go any farther than the Myanmar border town of Phayathonzu.

GETTING HERE AND AROUND

BUS TRAVEL Air-conditioned buses from Bangkok's Northern Bus Terminal leave for Sangklaburi four times a day (6½ hours; B330). The last direct Bangkok-bound bus leaves Sangklaburi early in the afternoon. Air-conditioned buses from Kanchanaburi (three hours) leave hourly between 7:30 am and 4:30 pm. Guesthouses are accessible by motorcycle taxi (B10) or songthaew (B60) from the station.

CAR TRAVEL The 2½- to 3-hour drive from Kanchanaburi, on well-paved Route 323, passes fields of pomelo, corn, and banana palms. Myanmar's mist-shrouded mountains are in the distance.

MOTORCYCLE TAXI TRAVEL Motorcycle taxis (B10–B20) are the favored way to get around this sprawling provincial town. For longer trips, ask your hotel to arrange car transport.

SAFETY AND PRECAUTIONS

This can be a long bus ride. Make sure you keep an eye on your belongings.

TIMING

Getting to Sangklaburi can take a while, so plan on spending at least one night.

ESSENTIALS

Emergencies Sangklaburi Hospital ⊠ *Sukhaphiban 2* ☎ *034/595058.*

WHERE TO EAT AND STAY

Six or seven guesthouses are on the lakeside road, all with views of the wooden bridge and the Mon village. The temple's lights shimmer on the water at night. They all have restaurants, and most offer Burmese and Mon food such as *haeng leh curry* (a country dish made of whatever ingredients are on hand, but often including pork) and the coconut-and-noodle dish *kao sawy,* usually made with chicken. Nightlife consists of a karaoke bar and a noodle soup stall at the market that sells beer and local whiskey until 2 am.

Hotel reviews have been condensed for this book. Please go to Fodors. com for full reviews of each property.

$
THAI
✕**Burmese Inn Restaurant.** This terrace restaurant with a view of the wooden bridge across the lake serves local fish dishes and other Thai and Burmese specialties like *laphae to,* a salad of nuts, beans, and fermented tea leaves. It also serves salads and sandwiches, as well as western-style breakfasts. The service is quite laid-back. $ *Average main: B70* ⊠ *Burmese Inn, 52/3 Moo 3, Tambon Nongloo* ☎ *034/595146* ▤ *No credit cards.*

$
B&B/INN
▥**Burmese Inn.** These homey bungalows, run by an Austrian and his Thai wife, sit on a flower-filled hillside above the lake. **Pros:** lots of information on the region. **Cons:** cheapest rooms are tiny, dark, and far from clean—spring for the pricier options. $ *Rooms from: $14* ⊠ *52/3 Moo 3, Tambon Nongloo* ☎ *034/595146, 086/168–1801* ↩ *19 rooms* ▤ *No credit cards* ⃠ *No meals.*

$
B&B/INN
▥**P Guest House.** This cluster of stone bungalows with wooden ceilings sit in a stepped garden leading down to the lake. **Pros:** wooden deck for sunbathing and swimming; all rooms are very clean. **Cons:** no airconditioning in most rooms. $ *Rooms from: $20* ⊠ *81/2 Moo 1, Tambon Nongloo* ☎ *034/595061* ⊕ *www.p-guesthouse.com* ↩ *34 rooms* ▤ *No credit cards* ⃠ *No meals.*

$
B&B/INN
▥**Pornphailin Riverside.** These bungalows sit on the water's edge, but the guesthouse itself is a long walk from town. **Pros:** stunning view of the lake. **Cons:** away from town. $ *Rooms from: $26* ⊠ *60/3 Moo 1, Soi Tonpeung* ☎ *034/595322* ↩ *53 rooms* ⃠ *No meals.*

AYUTTHAYA AND ENVIRONS

Ayutthaya and its environs encompass an important historical journey that traces Thailand's cultural developments from Buddhist art and architecture to modern government and language. Ayutthaya gets the most attention, drawing day-trippers from Bangkok, but a visit to Lopburi, with its Khmer temples and French-influenced Phra Narai Ratchaniwet, lends additional historical context to the museums and ransacked ruins found at Ayutthaya's historical park and the 18th-century Royal Palace in nearby Bang Pa-In.

AYUTTHAYA

72 km (45 miles) north of Bangkok.

Fodor'sChoice
★
Ayutthaya. A UNESCO World Heritage Site, carefully preserved Ayutthaya provides a fascinating snapshot of ancient Siam. Scattered ruins testify to the kingdom's brutal demise at the hands of the Burmese in 1767, while broad thoroughfares preserve a sense of its former greatness. Although the modern town is on the eastern bank of the Pa Sak, most of the temples are on an island. An exception is Wat Yai Chai Mongkol, a short tuk-tuk ride away. ■**TIP**➜ Ayutthaya is best

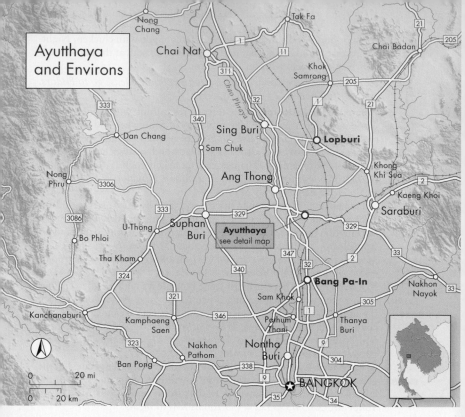

Ayutthaya
and Environs

appreciated in a historical context, and a visit to the Historical Study Center is a must for first-time visitors.

Certain sites are guaranteed to take your breath away—Wat Phra Si Sanphet, Wat Yai Chai Mongkol, Wat Phra Mahathat, and Wat Ratchaburana, to name a few. Aside from the temples, Ayutthaya's friendly guesthouses, welcoming people, and floating restaurants make for a refreshing change from Bangkok.

Ayutthaya was named by King Ramatibodi after a mythical kingdom of the gods portrayed in the pages of the Ramayana legend. The city was completed in 1350 and became both a powerhouse of Southeast Asia and reputedly one of the region's most beautiful royal capitals. It was originally chosen as a capital for its eminently defendable position, lying on an island formed by a bend of the Chao Phraya River, where it meets the Pa Sak and Lopburi rivers. Early residents created the island by digging a curving canal along the northern perimeter, linking the Chao Phraya to the Lopburi River.

However, Ayutthaya quickly changed from being essentially a military base to an important center for the arts, medicine, and technology. Trade routes opened up Siam's first treaty with a Western nation (Portugal, in 1516), and soon afterward the Dutch, English, Japanese and, most influentially, the French, accelerated Ayutthaya's rise to importance in international relations under King Narai the Great. After Narai's death in 1688 the kingdom plunged into internal conflict, and was laid waste by Burmese invading forces in 1767.

GETTING HERE AND AROUND

BOAT TRAVEL River King Cruise runs day trips to Ayutthaya. You'll take an early morning bus (they'll pick you up from most Bangkok hotels at around 6:30 am), stopping at Bang Pa-In Palace, and return to Bangkok by boat at 4 pm. The B1,700 ticket price includes lunch.

BUS TRAVEL Hourly buses to Ayutthaya (1½ hours) leave Bangkok's Mo Chit Northern Bus Terminal between 6 am and 7 pm. Tickets are B50 for the 1½-hour trip.

CAR TRAVEL Driving to Ayutthaya from Bangkok is an easy day trip once you're out of the congestion of the big city. Kanchanaphisek Road, Bangkok's outer ring road, is the best route, costing around B130 in tolls. Following this road will bring you to Bang Pa-In—a good opportunity to visit the Royal Palace before continuing to Ayutthaya.

TAXI AND TUK-TUK TRAVEL All forms of local transport are available from samlors to songthaews, but the brightly colored tuk-tuks are most popular. Tuk-tuks can be hired for an hour for around B300 or the day for around B800 to B1,000, and make easier work of Ayutthaya's historical sites.

TOUR TRAVEL Travel agents and tour companies abound in Ayutthaya. Most hotels and guesthouses also have tour desks.

TRAIN TRAVEL The Northeastern Line, which heads all the way up to Isan, has frequent service from Bangkok to Ayutthaya. Beginning at 4:30 am, trains depart about every 40 minutes from Bangkok's Hua Lamphong Station, arriving in Ayutthaya 80 minutes later.

MONEY MATTERS

ATMs and exchange services are abundant on Naresuan Road in Ayutthaya and in Lopburi on Ratchadamnoen Road.

SAFETY AND PRECAUTIONS

Ayutthaya is safe for foreign visitors, although elementary precautions should be taken. Valuables should be left in your hotel safe or with the management.

TIMING

Ayutthaya can be visited on a day trip from Bangkok, but the city really warrants a longer stay. Besides the temple ruins there are many other attractions—such as boat tips on the Chao Praya River. Ayutthaya is an excellent base for exploring the surrounding region.

ESSENTIALS

Visitor and Tour Information Tourist Authority of Thailand (TAT) ⊠ *Si Sanphet Rd.* ☎ *035/246076* ⊕ *www.tourismthailand.org.* **River King Cruise** ⊠ *Ayutthaya* ☎ *02/673-0966.*

EXPLORING AYUTTHAYA

The temple ruins of Ayutthaya can be toured in a morning or afternoon, although a full day is hardly sufficient to take in their full beauty. Though the island site of the Old City is quite compact, don't be tempted

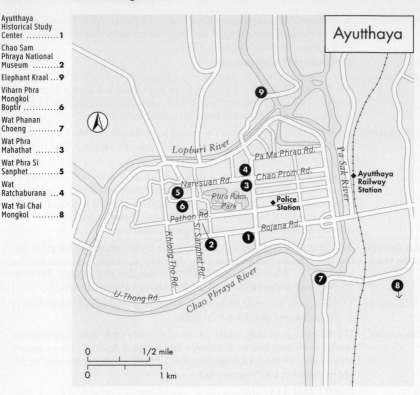

to tour it on foot; hire a tuk-tuk (about B600 for an afternoon) or a three-wheeled bicycle cab (about B500).

TOP ATTRACTIONS

Viharn Phra Mongkol Bopitr. When this temple's roof collapsed in 1767, one of Thailand's biggest and most revered bronze Buddha images was revealed. It lay here uncovered for almost 200 years before a huge modern viharn was built in 1951. Historians have dated the image back to 1538. ⊠ *Off Naresuan Rd.* 🖾 *Free* ⊙ *Weekdays 8–4:30, weekends 8–5:30.*

Wat Phanan Choeng. This bustling temple complex on the banks of the Lopburi River is an interesting diversion from the dormant ruins that dominate Ayutthaya. A short B3 ferry ride across the river sets the scene for its dramatic origins. The temple was built in 1324 (26 years before Ayutthaya's rise to power) by a U-Thong king in atonement for the death of his fiancée. Instead of bringing his bride, a Chinese princess, into the city himself, the king arranged an escort for her. Distraught at what she interpreted to be a lackluster welcome, the princess threw herself into the river (at the site of the current temple) and drowned. ⊠ *East of the Old City* 🖾 *Free* ⊙ *Daily 8–5.*

Wat Phra Si Sanphet. This wat was the largest temple in Ayutthaya, and was where the royal family worshipped. The 14th-century structure lost its 50-foot Buddha in 1767, when the invading Burmese melted it down for its 374 pounds of gold. The trio of chedis survived, and are the best existing examples of Ayutthaya architecture; enshrining the ashes of several kings, they stand as eternal memories of a golden age. If the design looks familiar, it's because Wat Phra Si Sanphet was the model for Wat Phra Keo at the Grand Palace in Bangkok. Beyond the monuments you can find a

grassy field where the Royal Palace once stood. The foundation is all that remains of the palace that was home to 33 kings. ⌧ *Naresuan Rd.* 🎫 *B50* 🕙 *Daily 7–6:30.*

WORTH NOTING

Ayutthaya Historical Study Center. Financed by the Japanese government, this educational center houses fascinating audiovisual displays about Ayutthaya. Models of the city as a rural village, as a port city, as an administrative center, and as a royal capital detail the site's history. ⌧ *Rotchana Rd., between Si San Phet and Chikun rds.* 🕾 *035/245124* 🎫 *B100* 🕙 *Weekdays 9–4:30, weekends 9–5.*

Chao Sam Phraya National Museum. This museum on spacious grounds in the center of the Old City was opened by the King and Queen of Thailand in 1961. Among its many exhibits, including Buddhist sculpture from the Dvaravati, Lopburi, Ayutthayan, and U-Thong periods, is a jewel-encrusted sword with which one Ayutthaya prince killed his brother in an elephant-back duel. ⌧ *Rotchana Rd. at Si San Phet Rd.* 🕾 *035/241587* 🎫 *B150* 🕙 *Wed.–Sun. 9–4.*

Elephant Kraal. Thailand's only intact royal kraal was built to hold and train elephants for martial service; it was last used during King Chulalongkorn's reign in 1903. The restored teak stockade is a gateway to the Royal Elephant Kraal Village, which cares for about 100 elephants. Though it looks like a working village, it's primarily a business—rehabilitating and parenting elephants for work on tours around Ayutthaya and also for TV and film productions (most recently Oliver Stone's *Alexander*). It's free if you just want to take a look, or B200 if you want to take a ride on an elephant. ⌧ *Hwy. 3060, 5 km (3 miles) north of Ayutthaya* 🕾 *035/321982* 🎫 *Free* 🕙 *Daily 8–5.*

Wat Phra Mahathat. Building began on this royal monastery in 1374 and was completed during the reign of King Ramesuan (1388–95). Today tree-shaded, parklike grounds are a pleasant place to linger, and contain what's left of its 140-foot brick prang. The prang collapsed twice between 1610 to 1628, and again in the early 20th century, and today barely reflects its former glory. The stunted ruins and beheaded Buddhas that remain in Wat Phra Mahathat are a result of the Burmese sacking of this once revered temple in 1767. Its partially destroyed Khmer-style

prang is said to contain relics of the Lord Buddha. ✉ *Naresuan Rd. at Chee Kun Rd.* 🎫 *B50* 🕒 *Daily 8–6:30.*

Wat Ratchaburana. Across from Wat Phra Mahathat is Wat Ratchaburana, its Khmer-style prang dominating the skyline. King Borommaracha II (Chao Sam Phraya) built this temple in 1424 to commemorate the death of his two older brothers, whose duel for the throne ironically left their younger brother as king. Their relics, including their swords, were buried in a crypt directly under the base of the prang, which was looted in 1957. Arrests were made, however, and the retrieved treasures can now be seen in the Chao Sam Phraya National Museum. ✉ *Naresuan and Chee Kun rds.* 🎫 *B50* 🕒 *Daily 8:30–4:30.*

Wat Yai Chai Mongkol. The enormous chedi at Wat Yai Chai Mongkol, the largest in Ayutthaya, was constructed by King Naresuan after he defeated the Burmese crown prince during a battle atop elephants in 1593. (A recent painting of the battle is one of the highlights of the temple.) The chedi is now leaning quite a bit, as later enlargements are weighing down the foundation. The complex, dating from 1357, was totally restored in 1982. Linger a while to pay your respects to the huge reclining Buddha, or climb to the top for a spectacular view. ■ **TIP→ The site closes at 5pm, but you can enter after that if the gates are left open, as they often are. The view at sunset is beautiful, and you'll completely escape the crowds.** ✉ *Ayutthaya to Bang Pa-In Rd., about 5 km (3 miles) southeast of the Old City* 🎫 *B20* 🕒 *Daily 8–5.*

WHERE TO EAT

$ THAI 🍴 **Bann KunPra.** Housed in a century-old teak home, this atmospheric old restaurant retains many of its original features, including handsome locally fired floor tiles. Step onto the riverside terrace and you could be in Venice—the waterway throbs with life, with tiny tugs pulling impossibly large barges loaded with rice. The restaurant has its own small jetty, where an excursion boat calls every evening for guests awaiting a dinner cruise. Above the restaurant are a total of 10 guest rooms, all of them with great river views. [$] *Average main: B120* ✉ *48 Moo 3, Huarattanachai U-Thong Rd.* ☎ *035/241978* 🌐 *www.bannkunpra.com.*

$ THAI 🍴 **Pae Krung Kao.** A plump, self-satisfied mynah bird in a cage greets visitors with a smattering of Thai and a song or two as they enter this utterly charming bar and restaurant on the banks of the Pa Sak River. The unusual reception is only one of several surprises—the low-ceilinged rooms are packed with every kind of collectible imaginable, from old bottles to timepieces. Half the restaurant sits on a pontoon floating on the water. The excellent food is uncompromisingly Thai, but you'll have to get a somewhat early start if you don't want to be rushed—the restaurant closes at 8.30 pm (when the mynah bird also turns in for the night). [$] *Average main: B100* ✉ *4 Moo 2, U-Thong Rd.* ☎ *035/241555.*

WHERE TO STAY

Ayutthaya's oldest and most established hotels look impressive from afar—but some aren't the best value, have rooms of questionable or no taste, and lack personal service. Recently, however, several small-scale guesthouses, run by younger entrepreneurs, have opened up along the waterfront, some of them in historic, beautifully restored timber-built homes. They're cheaper than many of the old established hotels and far better value.

If you're a romantic, a stay in Ayutthaya allows you to wander among the ruins at night. Most tourists leave Ayutthaya by 4 pm, so those who stay are treated to genuine Thai hospitality.

Visit Fodors.com for expanded hotel reviews.

$$
HOTEL
☳ **Krungsri River Hotel.** A refreshingly cool and spacious marble-floor lobby distinguishes this luxury hotel. **Pros:** near the train station; river views. **Cons:** no Wi-Fi in rooms. Ⓢ *Rooms from: $70* ⊠ *27/2 Moo 11, Rojana Rd.* ☎ *035/244333* ⊕ *www.krungsririver.com* ↘ *200 rooms* ⅢⓄⅢ *Breakfast.*

$
HOTEL
☳ **Luang Chumni Village.** This warren of six snug teak rooms has rapidly become one of the most popular lodgings in town, so advanced booking is essential. **Pros:** serene atmosphere; lots of polished teak; tropical gardens. **Cons:** some guests may miss an en-suite bathroom. Ⓢ *Rooms from: $41* ⊠ *2/4 Rojana Rd.* ☎ *035/322990* ⊕ *www.luangchumnivillage.com* ↘ *6 rooms* ⅢⓄⅢ *Breakfast.*

$
HOTEL
☳ **U-Thong Inn.** If the grandiose lobby is bordering on gaudy, the clean, tasteful rooms with firm beds and modern bathrooms make up for it. **Pros:** close to tourist sights; clean. **Cons:** gilded lobby. Ⓢ *Rooms from: $48* ⊠ *210 Rojana Rd.* ☎ *035/524–2235* ↘ *77 rooms, 131 suites* ⅢⓄⅢ *Breakfast.*

BANG PA-IN

20 km (12 miles) south of Ayutthaya.

This village, a popular stopping point between Bangkok and Ayutthaya, has a few architectural sites of note: a Thai palace, a European-style temple, and a Chinese pagoda, all grouped around a lake and open fields with bushes trimmed in the shapes of various animals.

BOAT TRAVEL   The Chao Phraya Express Boat Company runs a Sunday excursion from Bangkok to Bang Pa-In Summer Palace. Launches depart at 8 am and arrive in time for lunch. On the return trip you stop at the Bang Sai Folk Arts and Craft Centre before arriving in Bangkok at 5:30 pm. The trip costs B550.

Manohra Cruises operates a three-day, two-night cruise to Ayutthaya and Bang Pa-In on its luxury vessel *Manohra Song,* a converted rice barge described as the "Orient Express of the River" because of the sheer luxury of its accommodation and facilities. Such opulence doesn't come cheap—the cruise costs B200,000. A cooking course on board adds B2,800 to the bill.

BUS TRAVEL   Buses regularly leave from Bangkok's Northern Bus Terminal to Bang Pa-In Bus Station, less than half a mile from the palace. Fares are about B50 for an air-conditioned bus. From Ayutthaya, buses leave from the station on Naresuan Road.

CAR TRAVEL   Once you get out of Bangkok's labyrinthine roads, it's also easy to get to Bang Pa-In by car. Get on Highway 1 (Phahonyothin Road) to Highway 32. It's a 30-minute drive here from Ayutthaya along Highway 32.

SONGTHAEW TRAVEL	Songthaews travel regularly between the bus stations in Bang Pa-In and Ayutthaya.
TAXI TRAVEL	One-way taxi fares from Bangkok to Bang Pa-In should be around B800 (depending on your starting point), but be sure that the driver agrees to this fare before departing, or you may be charged more upon arrival.
TRAIN TRAVEL	Trains from Bangkok's Hua Lamphong Station take an hour to get to Bang Pa-In Station, where you can catch a tuk-tuk or songtheaw to the palace. The train fares are generally less than B70 and vary by class of travel.

SAFETY AND PRECAUTIONS
Bang Pa-In is perfectly safe for visitors.

TIMING
A morning or afternoon is sufficient for strolling around the sights of Bang Pa-In, although if the weather's not too hot you might be tempted to linger longer on the banks of its calm lake.

ESSENTIALS
Boat Info Chao Phraya Express Boat Company ✉ *Maharaj Pier, Maharaj Rd., Bangkok* ☎ *024/458888* ⊕ *www.chaophrayaexpressboat.com.* **Manohra Cruises** ✉ *Marriott Royal Garden Riverside Hotel, 257/1–3 Charoen Nakorn Rd., Bangkok* ☎ *024/760022* ⊕ *www.manohracruises.com.*

Bus Station Ayutthaya Bus Station ✉ *Naresuan Rd.* ☎ *035/335304.*

EXPLORING BANG PA-IN
Most visitors spend about two hours at the palaces and topiary gardens before heading for Ayutthaya. However, there's enough here to warrant a longer stay if you have the time.

Royal Palace. Bang Pa-In's extravagant Royal Palace is set in well-tended gardens. The original structure, built by King Prusat on the banks of the Pa Sak River, was used by the Ayutthaya kings until the Burmese invasion. After being neglected for 80 years, it was rebuilt during the reign of Rama IV and became the favored summer palace of King Rama V until tragedy struck. When the king was delayed in Bangkok, he sent his wife ahead on a boat that capsized. Although she could easily have been rescued, people stood by helplessly because a royal could not be touched by a commoner on pain of death. The king built a pavilion in her memory; be sure to read the touching inscription engraved on the memorial.

King Rama V was interested in the architecture of Europe, and many Western influences are evident here. The most beautiful building, however, is the Aisawan Thippaya, a Thai pavilion that seems to float on a small lake. A series of staggered roofs leads to a central spire. The structure is sometimes dismantled and taken to represent the country at worldwide expositions. China also fascinated the two rulers, and Phra Thinang Warophat Phiman, nicknamed the Peking Palace, is a replica of a Chinese imperial court palace. It was built from materials custom-made in China—a gift from Chinese Thais eager to win the king's favor. It contains a collection of exquisite jade and Ming-period porcelain.

The site's most striking structure, though, is a Buddhist temple built in best British neo-Gothic style, Wat Nivet Thamaprawat, which even has a fine steeple, buttresses, a belfry, and stained-glass windows. ☎ *035/261548* ✉ *B100* ◷ *Tues.– Thurs. and weekends 8–5.*

SHOPPING

Bang Sai Folk Arts and Craft Centre. This center was set up by Queen Sirikit in 1982 to train farming families to make traditional crafts for extra income. Workers regularly demonstrate their technique, and a small souvenir shop offers a chance to buy the fruits of their labors. The center holds an annual fair at the end of January. ✉ *24 km (14½ miles) south of Bang Pa-In* ☎ *035/366252* ✉ *B100* ◷ *Weekdays 9–5, weekends 9–6.*

> ## MONKEY BUSINESS
>
> Lopburi has an unusually large monkey population. They cluster around the monuments, particularly Phra Prang Sam Yot. Each November the Lopburi Inn organizes a monkey banquet, in which a grand buffet is laid out for the monkeys and much of the town's population comes out to watch them feast.

LOPBURI

75 km (47 miles) north of Ayutthaya, 150 km (94 miles) north of Bangkok.

One of Thailand's oldest cities, Lopburi has been inhabited since the 4th century. After the 6th century its influence grew under the Dvaravati rulers, who dominated northern Thailand until the Khmers swept in from the east. From the beginning of the 10th century until the middle of the 13th, when the new Thai kingdom drove them out, the Khmers used Lopburi as their provincial capital. During the Sukhothai and early Ayutthaya periods, the city's importance declined until, in 1664, King Narai made it his second capital to escape the heat and humidity of Ayutthaya. He employed French architects to build his palace; consequently, Lopburi is a strange mixture of Khmer, Thai, and western architecture.

GETTING HERE AND AROUND

BUS TRAVEL   Buses to Lopburi leave Bangkok's Mo Chit Northern Bus Terminal (Mo Chit) about every 20 minutes between 6 am and 7 pm. Tickets for the three-hour journey start at around B146 for air-conditioned buses. Lopburi is an hour and a half from Ayutthaya on the green 607 Bus from Ayutthaya's bus terminal. Lopburi's bus station is about 6 km (3.7 miles) from town, making it necessary to take a tuk-tuk or songthaew into town.

CAR TRAVEL   If you're driving from Bangkok, take Highway 1 (Phahonyothin) north via Salaburi. The trip will take up to two hours.

TRAIN TRAVEL   The Northeastern train line has frequent service from Bangkok. Three morning and two afternoon trains depart for the three-hour trip from Bangkok's Hua Lamphong Station. Trains back to Bangkok run in the early and late afternoon. Advance tickets aren't necessary, and fares for air-conditioned cars on the express train are around B350. Lopburi's station is downtown near the historic sites and lodgings on Na Phra Kan Road.

SAFETY AND PRECAUTIONS
The monkeys are perhaps the greatest security risk in Lopburi, where street crime rarely involves foreign visitors.

TIMING
Lopburi is a day trip from Bangkok or Ayutthaya. Its sights can be covered in a few hours, and there are few comfortable overnight accommodation possibilities.

ESSENTIALS
Hospital Lopburi Hospital ⊠ *206 Phahonyothin Rd., Amphoe Muang* ☎ *036/621537 up to 45.*

Visitor and Tour Information Tourist Authority of Thailand (TAT) ⊠ *Ropwatprathat Rd.* ☎ *036/424089* ⊕ *www.tourismthailand.org* ⊙ *Daily 8:30–4:30.*

EXPLORING LOPBURI

Lopburi is relatively off the beaten track for tourists, who are generally outnumbered by the city's famous monkey population. Some foreigners show up on their way to or from Ayutthaya, but few stay overnight. The rarity of foreigners may explain why locals are so friendly and eager to show you their town—and to practice their English. Samlors are available, but most of Lopburi's attractions are within easy walking distance.

Phra Narai Ratchaniwet. This palace's well-preserved buildings, completed between 1665 and 1677, have been converted into museums. Surrounding the buildings are castellated walls and triumphal archways grand enough to admit an entourage mounted on elephants. The most elaborate structure is the Dusit Mahaprasat Hall, built by King Narai to receive foreign ambassadors. The roof is gone, but you can spot the mixture of architectural styles: the square doors are Thai and the domed arches are Western. North of Phra Narai Ratchaniwet is the restored Wat Sao Thong Thong. ⊠ *Ratchadamneon Rd.* ☎ *036/411458* ▭ *B150* ⊙ *Daily 8:30–4:30.*

Phra Prang Sam Yot. Lopburi's most famous landmark is this Khmer shrine called Phra Prang Sam Yot. The three prangs symbolize the sacred triad of Brahma, Vishnu, and Shiva. King Narai converted the shrine into a Buddhist temple, and a stucco image of the Buddha sits serenely before the central prang. The most memorable aspect of the monument is its hundreds of resident monkeys, including mothers and nursing babies, wizened old males, and aggressive youngsters. ⚠ **Hold tight to your possessions, as the monkeys steal everything from city maps to digital cameras.** Most tourists wind up having a blast with the monkeys. Approach them and stand still for a minute, and you'll soon have monkeys all over your head, shoulders, and just about everywhere else—a perfect photo op. ⊠ *Vichayen Rd.*

Vichayen House. Built for French King Louis XIV's personal representative, De Chaumont, Vichayen House was later occupied by King Narai's infamous Greek minister, Constantine Phaulkon, whose political schemes eventually caused the ouster of all Westerners from Thailand. When King Narai was dying in 1668, his army commander, Phra

Phetracha, seized power and beheaded Phaulkon. ✉ *Vichayen Rd.* ⏲ *Wed.–Sun. 9–noon and 1–4.*

Wat Phra Si Rattana Mahathat. Built by the Khmers, Wat Phra Si Rattana Mahathat underwent so many restorations during the Sukhothai and Ayutthaya periods that it's difficult to discern the three original Khmer prangs—only the central one is intact. Several Sukhothai- and Ayutthaya-style chedis sit within the compound. ✉ *Na Phra Karn Rd.* 🎫 *B40* ⏲ *Daily 6–6.*

WHERE TO EAT AND STAY

Hotel reviews have been condensed for this book. Please go to Fodors.com for full reviews of each property.

$ THAI 🍴 **Bualuang Restaurant.** This is the sort of local restaurant that you shouldn't miss on your travels, a place for trying true regional specialties, including spicy salted soft-shell crab, steamed blue crabs, mussels in a hot pot, and charcoal-grilled cottonfish and snakehead fish. There are also multicourse Chinese-style set menus for six or more people. [$] *Average main: B100* ✉ *46/1 Moo 3* ☎ *036/413009, 036/422669.*

$ THAI 🍴 **White House.** A popular haunt for travelers, the White House offers a standard range of Thai and seafood dishes, including a good crab in yellow curry. An English-language menu makes it easy to know what you're ordering. The location is prime, right next to the night market, and the second-floor terrace is both lively and romantic, as is the tree-shaded garden below. The owner, Mr. Piak, is a good source of information on the area. Make sure to flip through his guest book. [$] *Average main: B80* ✉ *18 Phraya Kumjud Rd.* ☎ *036/413085.*

$$ RESORT 🏨 **Lopburi Inn Resort.** This monkey-theme retreat is the best value in Lopburi, with stylish rooms decorated in a modern Thai style, a good range of facilities including a pleasant pool, and a generous buffet breakfast. **Pros:** pool; Wi-Fi access; gym. **Cons:** far from main sights. [$] *Rooms from: $70* ✉ *17/1–2 Ratchadamnoen Rd.* ☎ *036/614790, 036/420777* 🌐 *www.lopburiinnresort.com* 🛏 *100 rooms* 🍽 *Breakfast.*

$ B&B/INN 🏨 **Noom Guesthouse.** Better value can't be found in Lopburi than at this friendly, comfortable guesthouse in the city center. **Pros:** central location. **Cons:** street noise can be disturbing; on-street parking. [$] *Rooms from: $5* ✉ *15/17 Phayakamjad Rd., City Center* ☎ *036/427693, 089/104–1811* 🌐 *www.noomguesthouse.com* 🛏 *7 rooms* 🍽 *No meals.*

THE GULF COAST BEACHES

WELCOME TO THE GULF COAST BEACHES

TOP REASONS TO GO

★ **Sunset at Hua Hin:** Take a stroll down the wide beaches at Hua Hin for unbeatable views of the setting sun.

★ **Exploring Cha Am:** Phang Nga Bay's maze of islands is ideal for gliding alongside towering cliffs.

★ **Dive at Koh Tao:** A diver's heaven, this small island small has escaped some of the worst excesses of tourist development.

★ **Midnight Revelry:** Join 10,000 others for a beachfront bacchanal during the frequent full-moon parties on the island of Koh Phangan.

★ **Explore Koh Samui:** A drive around the island's dramatic rocky coastline takes you from one eye-popping view to another.

BANGKOK
Chachoengsae
Muang
Boran
Phanat Nikhom
Chonburi
Sri Racha
KOH
PHAI
Bang Lamung
Pattaya
Sattahip
Rayong
KOH
SAMET
Chantaburi
Klaeng
CAMBODIA

EAST GULF COAST

Gulf of Thailand

KOH
CHANG
Mu Koh Chang
Marine Nat'l Park
Khlong Yai
KOH KUT
Kaoh Kong
KAOH
KONG
Trat

GETTING ORIENTED

4

In the miles of sandy beaches in southern Thailand there is pretty much something for everyone, from secluded spots in the marine national parks to loud and gaudy resort towns where the bar scene is a bigger draw than the beach. Thailand's eastern shore faces the Gulf of Thailand—also sometimes referred to as the Gulf of Siam—and includes the well-known destinations of Pattaya, Koh Chang, and Koh Samui, among others.

1 The Eastern Gulf.
Several spots are close enough to Bangkok to be easy weekend trips. Gaudy Pattaya is a wild and crazy place, but it also has a few resorts that are secluded from the insanity. Farther east are some great islands, including longtime escape-from-Bangkok favorite, Koh Samet. Koh Chang has also seen considerable growth in the past few years.

2 The Western Gulf.
Cha-am and Hua Hin fill up with Bangkok escapees on weekends and holidays. The beaches only get better as you continue south along the narrow peninsula; they're all reachable from Surat Thani.

3 Koh Samui. This island is very developed, but still not too crazy, and daily flights from Bangkok make it easy to reach.

Updated by
Simon Stewart

The Gulf Coast beaches are a jewel of Thailand's tourist crown. With the onset of Thailand's tourist boom, the Gulf Coast has captured the imagination of the traveling world with its white crescent sandy beaches, crystal-blue water, and laid-back beach lifestyle. High-class luxury nestles sleekly with laid-back traveler chic to showcase a region that is intriguing and complex, relaxing and frenetic, coupled with a welcome that is as warm as the sun. Thailand's Gulf Coast delivers great value, a large variety of attractions, a reputation for excellent service, and a welcome that is legendary.

You don't have to travel far from Bangkok to find exhilarating beaches. The Eastern Gulf offers several close enough for a weekend getaway. Gaudy Pattaya is a wild and crazy place, but now also has many resorts secluded from the main town, as well as some places for families. Farther south along the coast (which runs west to east all the way to the Cambodian border) are some nice beach resorts and even better islands, including longtime escape-from-Bangkok favorites of Koh Samet, and Koh Chang. Koh Chang—Thailand's second-largest island—has seen considerable growth in the past couple of years, with classy resorts now dominating the more modest budget bungalows.

Back over on the west coast south of Bangkok you first come to Cha-am and Hua Hin on the Gulf of Thailand, the former with bigger and more stand-alone resorts, and the latter with both world-class resorts and medium-range accommodation. These cities, like the beaches to the southeast, can fill up with Bangkok escapees on weekends, but are less busy during the week. The beaches only get better as you head south, with scores worth exploring along the narrow peninsula that stretches to the Malaysian border, all reachable from the town of Surat Thani, about 11 hours by train or a one-hour flight south of Bangkok.

The very developed island of Koh Samui is also along this strip—it's perennially popular, in part because daily flights from Bangkok make it so easy to reach.

PLANNING

WHEN TO GO

December to March is the best time to visit the Eastern Gulf: the seas are mostly calm and the skies mostly clear. Pattaya and Koh Samet are year-round destinations. Many places in Koh Chang and nearby islands used to close down in the rainy season, but the tourist boom has given the region a year-round tourist trade. The big car ferries continue to run on a limited schedule during the rainy season, and most resorts and hotels stay open and offer cheaper rates.

During the low season, flying to Koh Samui is still convenient, and the island and its neighbors are beautiful even with cloudiness and rain. Cha-Am is busy year-round, as is historic Hua Hin.

GETTING HERE AND AROUND

AIR TRAVEL

There are relatively inexpensive daily flights from Bangkok to all of the major beach destinations: Surat Thani, Trat, Koh Samui, and Pattaya. It's generally cheaper to fly to Surat Thani, mostly because the airport is owned by the government. There are some flights from Chiang Mai to the beaches. Thai Airways and Bangkok Airways have regular flights, as do the budget carriers Air Asia and Nok Air. All the airports in this region are small and much easier to deal with than Bangkok's Suvarnabhumi.

BOAT AND FERRY TRAVEL

Boats depart from the mainland to the islands from Chumporn and Surat Thani. There are a number of type of ferry, including high-speed catamarans, regular passenger ferries, and "slow boats," which are car ferries. The main boat operators are Lomprayah, Seatran, Songserm, and Raja.

A note of caution: Don't take the chance of getting on rickety or over-crowded boats. Because of lax safety standards, dangerously crowded boats are all too common. Ensure that life jackets are available and that the crew takes safety seriously. All responsible companies—and there are many—will offer safety briefings and keep safety concerns front and center.

Contacts Lomprayah ☎ *02/629–2569, 02/629–2570 in Bangkok, 077/427765 in Samui, 077/456176 on Koh Tao* ⊕ *www.lomprayah.com.* **Raja Ferry** ☎ *077/471151 in Surat Thani, 077/377452 in Koh Phangan.* **Seatran Ferry & Express** ☎ *02/240–2582 in Bangkok, 077/275060 in Surat Thani, 077/426000 in Koh Samui, 077/238679 in Koh Phangan* ⊕ *www.seatranferry.com.* **Songserm** ☎ *02/280–8073 in Bangkok, 077/377704 in Surat Thani, 077/420157 in Koh Samui* ⊕ *www.songserm-expressboat.com.*

BUS TRAVEL

Buses travel regularly between Bangkok and all major destinations in southern Thailand. There's also good bus service within the south. ⚠ Public buses have a better reputation than private bus companies, on which travelers often report thefts from luggage compartments and other annoyances.

CAR TRAVEL

Eastern Gulf resorts are fairly close to Bangkok, so driving is a possibility. (The worst part is getting out of Bangkok.) It's a long, exhausting drive farther south to Chumphon, Surat Thani, or Krabi. It may be cheaper, safer, and more convenient to hire a car and driver. It's easiest to arrange this while in Bangkok; your hotel can make arrangements.

MOTORCYCLE TRAVEL

Scooters are often seen as a fun way to explore the islands and beaches, but think twice before renting one. Every year hundreds of foreigners are killed or injured in accidents on Pattaya, Samui, and Chang. A small wreck is much worse if you're only wearing shorts and flip-flops. If you've never driven a motorcycle before, this is not the time to learn.

SONGTHAEW, TAXI, AND TUK-TUK TRAVEL

Most areas of the south have everything from samlors to tuk-tuks to songthaews. "Metered" taxis can be found in the larger towns and on Samui. Drivers don't actually run the meters, however, and are unscrupulous bargainers.

TRAIN TRAVEL

One daily train departs Bangkok's Hua Lamphong Station for Sri Racha and Pattaya; there's more frequent service to Hua Hin, Chumphon, and Surat Thani. In general, bus travel is a better way to go in southern Thailand.

HEALTH AND SAFETY

Malaria is very rare but not unheard of in Thailand's southeast. Health authorities have done a great job controlling mosquitoes in and around the southern resorts, but you'll still need a good supply of repellent.

Be careful at the beach, as the sun is stronger than you think. Wear a hat and plenty of sunscreen. Protective clothing while diving or snorkeling is a good idea, as accidentally brushing against or stepping on coral can be painful. Keep an eye out for sea urchins and even more dangerous creatures like jellyfish, especially during the monsoon season. If you are stung, seek medical attention immediately.

Strong undertows often develop during monsoon season, especially along the west coast. Pay attention to posted warnings and listen if locals tell you not to swim.

Condoms are available in southern Thailand; not all brands are equally reliable, so it may be simpler to bring any you'll need.

MONEY MATTERS

Hotel prices in beach areas are generally lower than what you'd pay in Bangkok, but higher than in other parts of the country. There are budget bungalows and guesthouses everywhere, though many aren't air-conditioned. At the other end of the spectrum are upscale resorts that run more than $1,000 a night.

Banks and ATMs are numerous, but it's always a good idea to carry some extra cash. Places on remote islands often don't accept credit cards. Some add a small service charge, typically 3%, when you pay with a credit card.

RESTAURANTS

Restaurants of all sorts are available in the beach regions, from exclusive (and expensive) resort restaurants to wooden shacks that seem like they're about to fall over. On Koh Chang and Koh Samet "dining rooms" are set up each night on the beach. Pattaya, Hua Hin, and Samui have the widest range of restaurants, from fast-food chains to five-star restaurants.

Prices in the reviews are the average cost of a main course at dinner or, if dinner is not served, at lunch.

HOTELS

There's something for everyone in this region, from the height of luxury to simple thatch huts on the beach. Many places combine the two experiences by offering pricey luxury bungalows. Rates fluctuate widely—in holiday periods they can more than double. Always double-check your rate when you book.

Prices in the reviews are the lowest cost of a standard double room in high season.

THE EASTERN GULF

The Eastern Gulf has long been a favorite escape from the heat and humidity of Bangkok. Its proximity to the capital means that weekend trips are possible, which in turn means that the area is overrun with sunseekers during long or holiday weekends. As the capital becomes more and more congested and its residents more affluent with disposable income, the region is growing rapidly. Some of the closer beaches have become so crowded that people now continue down the coast to quieter shores.

Many people go no farther than the coastal city of Pattaya, less than two hours south of Bangkok, which is both a notorious commercial sex hub and a popular weekend beach retreat for Bangkok residents. Pattaya is the most highly developed area in the Eastern Gulf—too much so, it seems, as two consecutive prime ministers have pointed to the area as an example of the evils of unchecked development. For years now the city has been cleaning up its beaches and its act, but it remains an eyesore. But if you're looking for raucous entertainment, this is the spot. That said, there are numerous secluded resorts dotted in and around the city that provide some isolation and a shield from the frenetic, seedy face of Pattaya.

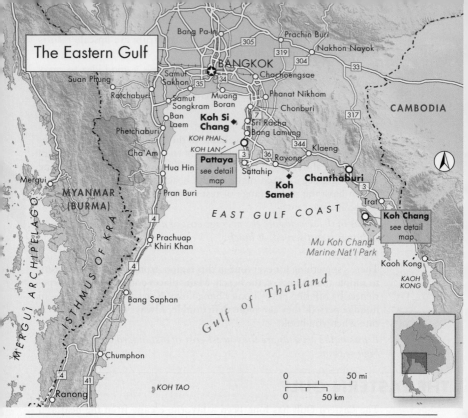

PATTAYA

147 km (88 miles) southeast of Bangkok.

Pattaya proponents like to boast that their city has finally emerged as a legitimate upscale beach destination. This is partly true: recent years have seen the opening of chic restaurants and more family-friendly attractions. Still, Pattaya remains a city as divided as ever between sand and sex—and the emphasis still falls clearly on the latter. ⚠ **If you can't handle encountering live sex shows and smut shops at every turn, then avoid Pattaya. Commercial sex is not just a reality here: it is the lifeblood of the city.**

Pattaya was not always like this. Until the end of the 1950s it was a fishing village sitting on an unspoiled natural harbor. Even after it was discovered by affluent Bangkok residents, it remained rather small and tranquil. Then came the Vietnam War, with thousands of American soldiers stationed at nearby air and naval bases. They piled into Pattaya, and the resort grew with the unrestrained fervor of any boomtown. But the boom eventually went bust. Pattaya was nearly abandoned, but its proximity to Bangkok and the beauty of the natural harbor ensured that it didn't crumble completely.

In the late 1990s, after much talk and government planning, Pattaya started regaining popularity. Two expressways were finished, making the trip from Bangkok even easier. Now that Bangkok's international airport is located on the southeast side of the capital, it is even more convenient to visit Pattaya.

GETTING HERE AND AROUND

Buses to Pattaya leave from Bangkok's Eastern Bus Terminal on Sukhumvit at least every hour daily. The journey takes about an hour and a half, and fares are cheap—usually around B120. You can also drive from Bangkok, and many rental companies vie for your business. One of the cheapest available is Thai Rent a Car. A number of taxi and limousine services are available, including Pattaya4leisure.

Contacts Pattaya4leisure ⊕ *www.pattaya4leisure.com.* **Thai Rent A Car** ☎ *02/737–8888* ⊕ *www.thairentacar.com.*

SAFETY AND PRECAUTIONS

Pattaya is a city built on prostitution, and it has all the trappings that go with the seedy atmosphere generated by the sex trade. Street thefts do happen, and thefts from hotels are not unheard of. Take sensible precautions with valuables, always use hotel safes, and avoid late-night strolls down dark streets. Tourist police are on duty, and in recent years they've been joined by tourist police volunteers, who are expat residents acting as liaisons with the regular police units.

TIMING

Pattaya is best visited during the dry, cooler season. Prices rise November to March, but the city welcomes visitors all year. Most travelers spend a week or two; on the other hand, some find that 24 hours is more than enough.

Visitor and Tour Information Tourism Authority of Thailand ⊠ *382/1 Moo 10, Chaihat Rd.* ☎ *038/427667, 038/428750* ⊕ *www.tourismthailand.org.*

EXPLORING PATTAYA

The curving bay is traced by Beach Road, with palm trees on the beach side and modern resort hotels on the other, is the central part of the city. By the old pier are pedestrian streets where bars, clubs, and open-air cafés proliferate. South of this area is Jomtien, a beach that is somewhat overdeveloped but pleasant enough. The northern part of the bay is the quietest, most easygoing section of Pattaya. Pattaya has a big water-sports industry, with a beach full of jet-skiers, paragliders, and even water-skiers.

Bottle Museum. In this museum, Dutchman Pieter Beg de Leif exhibits more than 300 miniatures—tiny replicas of famous buildings and ships—in bottles. ⊠ *297/1–5 Moo 6, Sukhumvit Rd.* ☎ *038/422957* 💵 *B200* ⊙ *Daily 9–6:30.*

FAMILY **Nong Nooch Village.** If you want to see elephants and monkeys in one trip, head to the small zoo at Nong Nooch Village. Despite its touristy nature—the elephants do silly tricks like driving scooters—this is a pleasant place, particularly if you're traveling with children. Two restaurants serve refreshments that you can enjoy beneath a coconut tree. Hotels arrange transportation for morning and afternoon visits to the zoo, 15 km (9 miles) south of Pattaya. ⊠ *163 Sukhumvit Rd., Bang Saray* ☎ *038/709358* ⊕ *www.nongnoochtropicalgarden.com* ⊠ *B400* ⊙ *Daily 9–5:30; shows at 9:45, 10:30, 3, and 3:30.*

FAMILY **Pattaya Elephant Village.** Children love the Elephant Kraal, where a few dozen pachyderms display their skills in a two-hour show. There are demonstrations of everything from their part in ceremonial rites to their usefulness in construction. Everything is staged, but it's always fun to see elephants at work and at play. It's a bit unsettling to see these gentle giants languishing in the city, but the Elephant Kraal has a good reputation as one of the few places that doesn't mistreat the animals. One-hour elephant rides are available for an extra B1,200 between 8 and 5. For tickets, go to the Tropicana Hotel on Pattaya 2 Road. ⊠ *48/120, Moo 7, Tambol Nong Prue* ☎ *038/249818, 038/249853* ⊕ *www.elephant-village-pattaya.com* ⊠ *B650* ⊙ *Daily 10:30–4; shows at 2:30 pm.*

FAMILY **Ripley's Believe It or Not.** This collection of curiosities from all corners of the world is the same attraction you can find in plenty of touristy areas. There's an extensive collection of authentic items and replicas in categories ranging from peculiar lifestyles to optical illusions. ⊠ *Royal Garden Plaza, 218 Moo 10, Beach Rd.* ☎ *038/710294* ⊕ *www.ripleysthailand.com* ⊠ *B500* ⊙ *Daily 10–10.*

Sanctuary of Truth. The late tycoon Lek Wiriyaphen started building this massive teak structure in 1981—it's still not finished. The aim of the building, which looks like an intricate collection of carvings, was to make a statement about the balance of different cultures, mixing modern and traditional styles. The waterfront setting north of Pattaya is pleasant, too. ⊠ *206/2 Moo 5, Naklua Rd., Banglamung* ☎ *038/367229, 038/367230* ⊕ *www.sanctuaryoftruth.com* ⊠ *B500* ⊙ *Daily 8–6.*

BEACHES

There are a number of beaches in the Pattaya area, including Pattaya Beach and Jomtien Beach. The islands surrounding Pattaya also offer up a few nice beaches, the pick being Koh Lan.

Jomtien Beach. Pattaya Beach's quieter neighbor, Jomtien Beach is less gaudy, less crowded, and a bit cheaper. The white sand and cleaner waters are also draw, as are the cordoned off swimming areas. Large sections of the beach are covered with shaded areas with deck chairs, all selling food and drinks at inflated prices. Water sports play a dominant role here, with Jet Skis, paragliding and speedboats available up and down the beach. Jomtien is also home to a few windsurfing schools. **Amenities:** food and drink. **Best for:** swimming; windsurfing. ⊠ *Jomtien Beach, Pattaya, Chonburi.*

Koh Lan. From Pattaa Bay, speedboats take just 15 minutes to reach the island of Koh Lan. The beaches have white sand and the water is cleaner than Pattaya Beach. It gets busy by midday, so if you want peace and quiet arrive in early morning. The waters are crowded with speedboats and other motorized crafts. Be cautious when swimming—some speedboat operators have been reckless when navigating these waters. There are plenty of food and drink vendors mingling among the shaded deck chairs, although the prices are steep. Ferries leave South Pattaya

Pier daily at 10 am to 6:30 pm and cost B50. Speedboats can be hired for B2,200. **Amenities:** food and drink. **Best for:** partiers; swimming. ✉ *Koh Lan, Pattaya, Chonburi.*

Pattaya Beach. On Pattaya Bay, this beach is slightly murky, but the sand is golden and fine. There are blocks of shaded deckchairs that you can rent by the hour. Food vendors and trinket merchants wander up and down the beach. The bay is usually crowded with small boats, Jet Skis, and other diversions. Parallel to the shore is Pattaya Beach Road, which has a delightful landcaped walkway that separates the beach from the restaurants, shopping malls, and resorts on the opposite side. **Amenties:** food and drink. **Best for:** walking. ✉ *Pattaya Beach Rd., Pattaya, Chonburi.*

WHERE TO EAT

Much of Pattaya feels like Little America, with McDonald's, Burger King, *and* KFC next to each other in the Royal Gardens Plaza mall. But Pattaya has access to just-picked produce and seafood right out of the gulf, so you'll have no trouble finding fresh local fare. Fancier (although not necessarily better) restaurants can be a refuge if you get weary of the noise and crowds at the simple beachside places.

$$$ ITALIAN 🍴 **The Bay.** Giuseppe Zanotti's flashy restaurant represents the hip, modern side of Pattaya. Here you can dine at sleek modern tables overlooking the resort's expansive pool and (you guessed it) the shimmering bay. The menu isn't just luxe (as in a rack of venison with porcini mushrooms and juniper berries), it's also unusually authentic (as in *gnochetti sardi*, or gnocchi as tasty as they make it in Sardinia). [$] *Average main: B300* ✉ *Dusit Resort, 240/2 Pattaya Beach Rd.* ☎ *038/425611* 🌐 *www.dusit.com* ⏲ *Closed Sun.*

$$$ SWISS 🍴 **Bruno's.** This restaurant and wine bar has built up a good reputation among the expat community. The set menus for B370 are a real bargain at lunch, and the dinner menu has plenty of interesting options. The international cuisine here leans toward Swiss recipes, but you can also find a wide range of American staples. The wine list is extensive enough to necessitate a walk-in wine cellar. [$] *Average main: B400* ✉ *306/63 Chateau Dale Plaza, Thappraya Rd.* ☎ *038/364600, 038/364601* 🌐 *www.brunos-pattaya.com.*

$$$$ ECLECTIC 🍴 **Flare.** This is discreet, sophisticated dining at its very best: the decor is chic, the feeling intimate, and the vibe is very romantic. The mainly modern food takes on classic dishes. The central theme is steak and seafood, but there is also plenty of variety. The service is ultra attentive, slick, and professional. The wine collection is considered the eatery's main selling point, and with good reason. For the quality of service and the caliber of the cooking, this restaurant is one of the best in Pattaya. [$] *Average main: B500* ✉ *Pattaya Hilton Hotel, Soi 9, Pattaya Beach Rd.* ☎ *038/253000* 🌐 *www1.hilton.com* ⏲ *No lunch.*

$$$$ ECLECTIC 🍴 **Mantra.** This enormous, ultramodern restaurant is one of the most talked-about eateries in Pattaya. The menu tries to cover too much territory, geographical speaking. There are dishes from Japan to Italy, and at least some of the dishes are finely realized: brick-oven pizza with arugula and four cheeses, for instance, or Wagyu beef sizzled on a lava stone. Oddly enough, just about the only cuisine you won't find here is

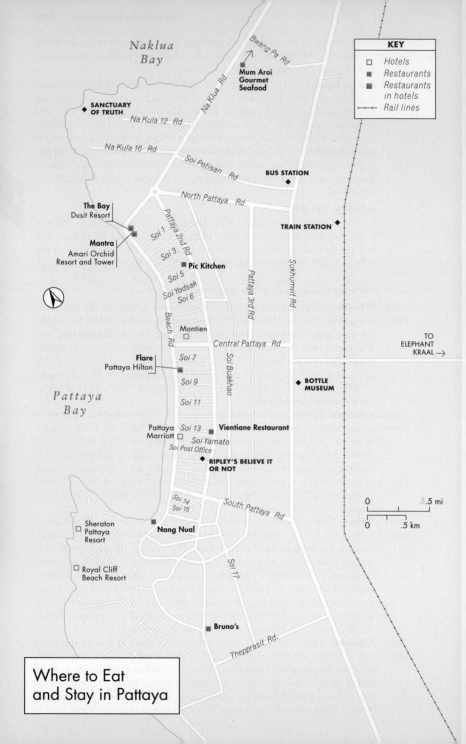

KEY

☐ Hotels
■ Restaurants
■ Restaurants in hotels
⊢⊢⊢ Rail lines

Naklua Bay

Bwang Pa Rd

Mum Aroi Gourmet Seafood

◆ SANCTUARY OF TRUTH

Na Kula 12 Rd

Na Kula Rd

Na Kula 16 Rd

Soi Potisan Rd

BUS STATION ◆

North Pattaya Rd

TRAIN STATION ◆

The Bay
Dusit Resort

Soi 1

Pattaya 2nd Rd

Mantra
Amari Orchid Resort and Tower

Soi 3

Soi 5

■ Pic Kitchen

Pattaya 3rd Rd

Sukhumvit Rd

Soi Yodsak

Soi 6

Beach Rd

☐ Montien

Central Pattaya Rd

TO ELEPHANT KRAAL →

Flare
Pattaya Hilton

Soi 7

Soi Buakhao

◆ BOTTLE MUSEUM

Soi 9

Pattaya Bay

Soi 11

Pattaya Marriott ☐

Soi 13

■ Vientiane Restaurant

Soi Yamato

Soi Post Office

◆ RIPLEY'S BELIEVE IT OR NOT

Soi 14
Soi 15

South Pattaya Rd

Sheraton Pattaya Resort ☐

■ Nang Nual

☐ Royal Cliff Beach Resort

Soi 17

0 ____ .5 mi
0 ____ .5 km

■ Bruno's

Thepprasit Rd.

Where to Eat and Stay in Pattaya

Thai. $ *Average main: B500* ⊠ *Amari Orchid Resort, Pattaya Beach Rd.* ☎ *038/429591* ⊕ *www.mantra-pattaya.com* ⊘ No lunch Mon.–Sat.

$ ✕ **Mum Aroi Gourmet Seafood.** For a different side of Pattaya, head a
SEAFOOD   bit north of the city and seek out this beautiful, romantic seafood restaurant that sits right on the waterfront. The almost exclusively Thai clientele chooses their lobsters, giant tiger prawns, crabs, oysters, and fish from a series of huge tanks, and enjoys them amid shimmering pools, palm trees, and sweeping views of the bay. There is no English-language menu, so you'll have to point to what you want. Prices are reasonable, especially given the upmarket feel of the place. $ *Average main: B150* ⊠ *83/4 Na Klua Rd., near Ananya Beachfront Condominium* ☎ *038/223252.*

$$ ✕ **Nang Nual.** At the southern end of Pattaya Beach Road is one of the
SEAFOOD   city's best places for seafood. A huge array of freshly caught fish is laid out on blocks of ice at the entrance; point to what you want, explain how you'd like it cooked (most people prefer grilled), and ask for some fried rice on the side. A menu filled with photographs of the dishes overcomes the language barrier, and the staff will understand the cooking method as long as you don't make it too complicated. For meat lovers, the huge steaks are a treat. There's a dining room upstairs, but ask for a table on the terrace overlooking the ocean. A newer branch sits across from Jomtien Beach, near the Sigma Resort. $ *Average main: B200* ⊠ *214–10 S. Pattaya Beach Rd.* ☎ *038/428177.*

$$ ✕ **Pic Kitchen.** Actually a series of classic teak pavilions, this upscale
THAI   eatery lets you dine inside or outside, and you can choose from table seating, floor seating, or sofas in the jazz pit. The Thai dishes are consistently good, especially the deep-fried crab claws and spicy eggplant salad, as well as the ubiquitous *som tam* (green-papaya salad). All the food can be prepared mild or spicy; if you're really averse to chilies, try the mild ginger-scented white snapper. $ *Average main: B150* ⊠ *255 Soi 5, 2nd Rd.* ☎ *038/428374* ⊕ *www.pic-kitchen.com.*

$ ✕ **Vientiane Restaurant.** Named after the capital of Laos, this eatery serves
ASIAN   satisfying Lao cuisine, as well as Thai, Chinese, and Western dishes. Those from Thailand's northeastern province of Isan include what is arguably the best som tam in Pattaya. For something with less heat try the *gai yang* (roast chicken) with sticky rice. Dishes are usually very spicy, so be sure to specify if you prefer gentler use of chilies. There's an air-conditioned dining room if it's too hot outside, but if it's a pleasant evening ask for a table on the terrace. The restaurant is near the Marriott Resort. $ *Average main: B100* ⊠ *485/18 2nd Rd.* ☎ *038/411298.*

WHERE TO STAY

Only Bangkok beats Pattaya in number of hotel rooms. For seclusion, you'll have to spend more for the high-end places. ■ TIP➜ Ask hotels about packages and discounts, as they'll save you a chunk of change.

For expanded hotel reviews, visit Fodors.com.

$$ ⛉ **Amari Orchid Resort and Tower.** Step into this modern, open-air
HOTEL   lobby and you'll immediately be transported to a tropical paradise
Fodor's Choice   that's worlds away from the hectic streets of Pattaya. **Pros:** luxurious
★   tower rooms; superb service. **Cons:** not all rooms have great views;

building looks a bit imposing. $ *Rooms from: $92* ⊠ *Pattaya Beach Rd.* ☎ *038/418418* ⊕ *www.amari.com/orchid* ↵ *513 rooms, 14 suites.*

$$$ ❄ **Dusit Resort.** At the northern end of Pattaya Beach, this sprawling hotel has superb views. **Pros:** not too wild and crazy; many rooms have private balconies. **Cons:** expensive rates; feels a bit large and impersonal. $ *Rooms from: $170* ⊠ *240/2 Pattaya Beach Rd.* ☎ *038/425611, 02/636–3333 in Bangkok* ⊕ *www.dusit.com* ↵ *442 rooms, 15 suites* ⏏ *No meals.*

$$ ❄ **Montien.** Although it couldn't be described as plush, this centrally
HOTEL located hotel has a laid-back atmosphere that many people prefer, and all but 17 of its rooms have terraces facing the sea. **Pros:** on a pretty part of the beach; spacious rooms. **Cons:** some complaints about noise; feels a little dated; service may not meet standards. $ *Rooms from: $110* ⊠ *Pattaya 2nd Rd.* ☎ *038/428155, 02/233–7060 in Bangkok* ⊕ *www. montien.com* ↵ *293 rooms, 7 suites* ⏏ *No meals.*

$$$ ❄ **Pattaya Hilton Hotel.** The location doesn't get much better, right in
HOTEL the middle of the beach, close to most things in Pattaya, especially the mall that this hotel looms over. **Pros:** central location; outstanding restaurants. **Cons:** rooms are unimaginatively decorated. $ *Rooms from: $170* ⊠ *333/101 Moo 9, Nong Prue, Banglamung, Pattaya Beach Rd.* ☎ *038/253000* ⊕ *www3.hilton.com* ↵ *302 rooms, 19 suites* ⏏ *No meals.*

$$ ❄ **Pattaya Marriott Resort & Spa.** This traditional-style hotel is a block
HOTEL from the beach. **Pros:** convenient to in-town activity; beautiful garden area. **Cons:** not on beach; a little pricey for what it is. $ *Rooms from: $120* ⊠ *218 Beach Rd.* ☎ *038/412120, 02/477–0767 in Bangkok* ⊕ *www.marriotthotels.com* ↵ *287 rooms, 8 suites* ⏏ *No meals.*

$$$ ❄ **Royal Cliff Beach Resort.** This cluster of four well-kept hotels is noth-
RESORT ing less than an institution in Thailand, known far and wide for its staggering size and its setting, perched high on a bluff overlooking the Gulf. **Pros:** attractive Thai decor; beautiful views. **Cons:** tricky to get to beach; so-so dining; out-of-town location. $ *Rooms from: $140* ⊠ *Jomtien Beach, 353 Phra Tamnak Rd.* ☎ *038/250421, 02/2820999 in Bangkok* ⊕ *www.royalcliff.com* ↵ *966 rooms, 162 suites.*

$$$$ ❄ **Sheraton Pattaya Resort.** This spectacular resort established a new stan-
HOTEL dard not just for Pattaya, but for all of the Eastern Gulf. **Pros:** unbeat-
Fodor's Choice able setting; spectacular spa; feels shiny and new. **Cons:** expensive rates;
★ rooms a bit small for price. $ *Rooms from: $290* ⊠ *437 Phra Tamnak Rd., 1½ km (1 mile) south of town* ☎ *038/259888* ⊕ *www.sheraton. com/pattaya* ↵ *114 rooms, 40 cabanas, 2 villas* ⏏ *No meals.*

NIGHTLIFE

Nightlife in Pattaya centers on the sex trade. Scattered throughout town (though mostly concentrated on Sai Song) are hundreds of beer bars, which are low-key places where hostesses merely want to keep customers buying drinks. The raunchy go-go bars are mostly found on the southern end of town. But Pattaya's, and perhaps Thailand's, most shockingly in-your-face red-light district is on Soi 6, about a block in from the beach. Whether you find it intriguing or sickening, the street is a sight to behold, with hundreds of prostitutes lined up shoulder-to-shoulder at all hours, spilling out of bars and storefronts and catcalling to every male passerby. Gay bars are in the sois between Pattaya Beach Road and Pattaya 2 Road called Pattayaland.

■TIP→ Generally, the only bars in town that are somewhat removed from the commercial sex trade are in pricey hotels.

Below we've listed a few alternatives to the red-light district scene.

Latitude. At this hotel bar you'll get a great view of the sunset over the Gulf of Thailand—through plate-glass windows or, better yet, alfresco—while sipping wines or well-crafted cocktails, perhaps accompanied by tapas. There's also a small library adjacent to the wine bar. ⊠ *Sheraton Pattaya Resort, 437 Phra Tamnak Rd.* ☎ *038/259888* ⊕ *www.sheraton. com/pattaya.*

Mantra. As popular for drinks as it is for food, Mantra is the see-and-be-seen spot for business executives and visiting jet-setters. Don't miss the secluded table surrounded by ornate curtains. ⊠ *Amari Orchid Resort and Tower, Pattaya Beach Rd.* ☎ *038/428–1611* ⊕ *www.amari.com/ orchid.*

Shenanigans. This hotel bar tries hard to conjure up an Irish pub by serving favorite brews like Guinness. There's Irish food, too, at sky-high prices. A few large-screen TVs make this popular with sports fans. ⊠ *Pattaya Marriott Resort & Spa, 399/9 Moo 10* ☎ *038/723939* ⊕ *www.marriotthotels.com.*

Tiffany. To get a glimpse at Pattaya's spicier side, check out one of the city's famous cabaret shows. There are memorable routines at Tiffany, famous all over Thailand. All the beautiful dancers are really young men, but you'd never know it. ⊠ *464 Moo 9, Pattaya 2nd Rd.* ☎ *038/421711* ⊕ *www.tiffany-show.co.th.*

Tony's. For live music, this place sits the heart of the nightlife district. Grab a beer and head to the outdoor terrace. ⊠ *Walking Street Rd.* ☎ *038/425795.*

SPORTS AND THE OUTDOORS

Pattaya Beach is the spot for water sports. Waterskiing starts at B1,500 for 30 minutes, jet skiing is B1,000 for 30 minutes, and parasailing is B500 for 15 minutes. Big inflatable bananas, yet another thing to dodge when you're in the water, hold five people and are towed behind a speedboat. They cost B1,000 or more for 30 minutes. For windsurfing, head to Jomtien Beach. ■TIP→ Beware of a common scam where Jet Ski vendors try to charge you for "damage" to their equipment. Inspect the equipment beforehand and take pictures of any damage.

KOH SAMET

30 minutes by passenger ferry from Ban Phe, which is 223 km (139 miles) southeast of Bangkok.

Koh Samet's beautiful beaches are a hit with Thais and Bangkok expats, especially on weekends. Although newer resort areas beckon, Koh Samet remains popular with laid-back travelers who just want to sunbathe and read on the beach. There are no high-rises, and just one rutted road for songthaews.

Continued on page 190

Thailand's Beaches

Thailand is a beach-lover's paradise, with nearly 2,000 miles of coastline divided between two stunning shores. Whether you're looking for an exclusive resort, a tranquil beach town, an island with great rock-climbing, or a secluded cove, you can find the right atmosphere on the Andaman or the Gulf coast.

by Martin Young

With so many beaches to choose from, deciding where to go can be overwhelming. What time of year you're traveling helps narrow things down, since the two coasts have different monsoon seasons. In general, the Andaman Coast has bigger waves and better water clarity, although the Gulf Coast has some great snorkeling and diving spots too, particularly around the islands. On both coasts there are windy spots ideal for wind- and kitesurfing, and peaceful bays that beckon swimmers and sunbathers.

Sea temperature averages near a luxurious 80 degrees on both coasts, and almost all beaches are sandy; Andaman beaches tend to have more powdery sand, while Gulf sand is a bit grainier. Though the 2004 tsunami devastated some Andaman beaches, affected areas are now thriving again, and you probably won't even see traces of damage. Developed beaches on both coasts offer tons of activities like sailing, fishing, and rock climbing.

Ao Nang beach, Krabi.

Southern Beaches

Kanchanaburi · Kamphaeng Saen · 305 · Nakhon Nayok
319 · 304 · 33
Suan Phung · BANGKOK · Chachoengsae
Ratchaburi · 35 · Samut Sakhon · 34 · Muang Boran · Phanat Nikhom · 317
Samut Songkram · Chonburi · Sri Racha · Bang Lamung · 7
Ban Laem · Phetchaburi · Pattaya · 344 · 3
Cha'Am · *KOH PHAI* · Sattahip · 36 · Rayong · Klaeng · Chantaburi
Hua Hin · **Hua Hin** · *KOH SAMET* · **2** · 3
Pran Buri · **Khao Takiab** · **Haad Sai Kaew** · **1** · Trat
3 · **EAST GULF COAST** · *KOH CHANG*
Prachuap Khiri Khan · **Haad Sai Khao**
Mu Koh Chang Marine Nat'l Park

BURMA (MYANMAR)

Mergui

MERGUI ARCHIPELAGO

ISTHMUS OF KRA

Kaeng Krachan Nat'l Park

Bang Saphan

Gulf of Thailand

4 · **Tung Wa Laen** · Chumphon

WEST GULF COAST

Ranong · **5** · *KOH TAO* · **Sairee**
Angthong Marine Nat'l Park
12 · *KOH PHANGAN* · **Haad Thong Nai Pan** · **Haad Rin**
SURIN ISLANDS
Surat Thani · Don Sak · **13** · *KOH SAMUI* · **Chaweng Mae Nam**
Sichon

SIMILAN ISLANDS
Ban Ta Khun · 44 · 41 · 401 · Tha Sala
Koh Miang · **7** · 402 · Phang Nga · 401 · Nakhon Si Thammarat
Khao Lak · *KOH YAO YAI* · **10** · **Ao Nang** · Krabi · Pak Phanang
KOH PHUKET · **Nai Yang** · **9** · **Koh Poda** · Thung Song · 408
Karon Kata · **8** · Phuket · **11** · **Railay Beach** · 4
KOH PHI PHI · **14** · **6** · 41 · Phatthalung
Maya Bay Loh Samah Bay · **Klong Dao** · *KOH LANTA* · Trang
KOH TA LIBONG · Songkhla

ANDAMAN COAST
KOH TARUTAO
Andaman Sea · *KOH RAWI* · Hat Yai · Pattani
LANGKAWI · Satun · Narathiwat
MALAYSIA

0 — 50 mi
0 — 50 km

TOP SPOTS

(left) Kata beach, Phuket (right) Maya Bay, famous from the Hollywood film *The Beach.*

1 On mountainous **Koh Chang**, hillside meets powdery white sand and calm, clear water at **Haad Sai Khao.**

2 **Koh Samet** is famous for its sugary beaches and crystal-clear water; there's room for everyone on **Haad Sai Kaew,** the island's longest beach.

3 Water sports enthusiasts like **Hua Hin's** wide, sandy beach. Just south, **Khao Takiab's** longer, wider beach is more popular with locals, but gets busy on weekends and holidays.

4 Kitesurfers love long, quiet **Tung Wa Laen** beach for its winds and shallow water.

5 **Koh Tao's** most developed beach, **Sairee**, is *the* place to learn to dive and has gorgeous sunsets.

6 Laid-back **Klong Dao** on **Koh Lanta** has long expanses of palm-fringed white sand and azure water.

7 The clear water around the nine **Similan Islands** is Thailand's best underwater playground. **Koh Miang** has some basic bungalows and tranquil white-sand beaches.

8 On **Phuket**, neighboring beaches **Karon** and **Kata** have killer sunsets, great waves, and plenty of daytime and nighttime activities.

9 **Nai Yang,** a tranquil, curving beach on northern **Phuket**, is a pretty place to relax.

10 **Ao Nang** has a nice strip of shops and restaurants and stunning views of the islands in Phanga Bay from its beach. Boats to **Koh Poda**—a small island with white coral sand, hidden coves, and jaw-dropping views—leave from here.

11 **Railay Beach** peninsula has limestone cliffs, knockout views, and crystal-clear water.

12 Backpackers flock to **Haad Rin** for **Koh Phangan's** famous full-moon parties. To get away from the crowds, head north to **Haad Thong Nai Pan,** a beautiful horseshoe bay on **Phangan's** more remote east coast.

13 **Chaweng, Koh Samui's** busiest beach, has gently sloping white sand, clear water, and vibrant nightlife. On the north coast, less developed **Mae Nam** beach is a natural beauty.

14 On **Koh Phi Phi**, breathtaking **Maya Bay,** where the movie *The Beach* was shot, gets very crowded; small but beautiful **Loh Samah Bay** on the other side of the island is less hectic.

KEY	
	Diving
	Fishing
	Kayaking
	Land Sports
	Sailing
	Snorkeling
	Surfing

IN FOCUS THAILAND'S BEACHES

4

BEACH FINDER

Key: ○ = Available, ● = Exceptional

BEACH	NATURAL BEAUTY	DESERTED	PARTY SCENE	THAI CULTURE	RESORTS	BUNGALOWS	GOLF	SNORKELING/DIVING	SURFING	KITEBOARDING/WINDSURFING	ACCESSIBILITY
EASTERN GULF											
Pattaya	○		●		○	○		○	○	●	●
Koh Samet	●	●			○	○					○
Koh Chang	○		○		○	●		●			○
Koh Si Chang	○	○		○		○					○
WESTERN GULF											
Cha-am	○	○		●	○		○	○	○	○	●
Hua Hin	●	○	●	○	○	○	○	○	○	○	●
Takiab Beach	○	○		○	○	○		●	○	●	●
Koh Samui	●	○	○	○	●	○	○	○	○	○	●
Koh Phangan	●	○	○	○	○	●		○	○	○	○
Koh Tao	●	○	○	○	○	●		●	○	○	○
KOH PHUKET											
Mai Khao Beach	○	●		○	●	○	○	○			●
Nai Yang Beach	○	●		○	●	○	○	○			●
Nai Thon & Layan Beaches	○	●		○	●	○					●
Bang Thao Beach	○	●	○	○	●	○				●	○
Pansea, Surin & Laem Beaches	○	○		○	○	○	○				
Kamala Beach	●	○	○	○	○	○		○			○
Patong	●		●	○	●	●	○	○		○	●
Karon Beach	●	○	○	○	●	●	○	○			●
Kata Beach	○	○	●	○	●	●	○	○	●	○	●
Nai Harn	○	●		●	○	○	○	○			○
Chalong		●		●			○				○
ANDAMAN COAST											
Phang Nga Bay	●		●					●			
Koh Yao	○	●		○	○	○		●			
Khao Lak	●	○		○	○	○	○	●			○
Similan Islands	●	○		○		○		●			
Surin Islands	●	○		○		○		●			
Ao Nang	○		●	○	●	●		●	○		●
Nang Cape/Railay Beach	●	○	●	○	●	●		●			
Koh Phi Phi	●	○	●		●	●		●			
Koh Lanta	○	○	○		●	●	○	○			○

KEY: ○ = Available ● = Exceptional

GOOD TO KNOW

WHAT SHOULD I WEAR?

On most beaches, bikinis, Speedos, and other swimwear are all perfectly OK. But wear *something*—going topless or nude is generally not acceptable. Women should exercise some caution on remote beaches where skimpy attire might attract unwanted attention from locals.

Once you leave the beach, throw on a cover up or a sarong. Unbuttoned shirts are fine, but sitting at a restaurant or walking through town in only your bathing suit is tacky, though you'll see other travelers doing it. Some areas have a Muslim majority, and too much exposed skin is frowned upon.

Beachside dining on Khao Lak.

WHAT TO EXPECT

Eating & Drinking: most popular beaches have a number of bars and restaurants.

Restrooms: few beaches have public facilities, so buy a drink at a restaurant and use theirs.

Rentals & Guides: You can arrange rentals and guides once you arrive. A dive trip costs B2,000 to B3,000 per person; snorkeling gear starts at about B300 a day; a surfboard or a board and kite is B1,000 to B1,500 a day; and a jet-ski rental runs around B500 for 15 minutes.

Hawkers: Vendors selling fruit, drinks, sarongs, and souvenirs can become a nuisance, but a firm "No, thank you" and a smile is the only required response.

Beach chairs: The chairs you'll see at many beaches are for rent; if you plop down in one, someone will usually appear to collect your baht.

WHAT TO WATCH OUT FOR

- **The tropical sun.** Wear strong sunscreen. Drink lots of water. Enough said.

- **Undertows** are a danger, and most beaces lack lifeguards.

- **Jellyfish** are a problem at certain times of year, usually before the rainy season. If you are stung, apply vinegar to the sting—beachside restaurants will probably have some. ("Jellyfish sting" in Thai is *maeng ga-proon fai*, but the locals will probably understand your sign language.)

- **Nefarious characters,** including prostitutes and drug dealers, may approach you, particularly in Patong and Pattaya. As with hawkers, a firm "No, thank you" should send them on their way.

BEACH VOCABULARY

Here are a few words help you decipher Thai beach names.
Ao means "bay."
Haad means "beach."
Koh means "island."
Talay means "sea."

GETTING HERE AND AROUND

Koh Samet is a 30-minute passenger ferry ride (B150) from one of three piers in the small village of Ban Phe, a 90-minute minibus ride east of Pattaya. Ferries to Koh Samet dock at Na Duan on the north shore and An Vong Duan on the eastern shore. The islands' beaches are an easy walk from either village.

EXPLORING KOH SAMET

Kot Samet is a national marine park, so there's a B200 entrance fee. The government has been unable (or unwilling) to control development on the 5-km-long (3-mile-long) island, and although Jet Skis are prohibited in national parks, some find their way to Koh Samet.

BEACHES

Koh Samet's other name is Koh Kaeo Phitsadan (Island with Sand Like Crushed Crystal), so it isn't surprising that its fine sand is in great demand by glassmakers. The smooth water is another attraction. The beaches are a series of little bays, with more than 10 of them running along the east side of the island. The beaches are busier on the northern tip near Na Duan and become less so as you go south, with the exception of An Vong Duan, the second ferry stop.

All the beaches have licensed massage ladies offering one- and two-hour Thai massages, which generally cost B100 an hour (not including tip).

Ao Kiu. On the southern end of Koh Samet, this beautiful and secluded beach has crystal blue waters and fine white sands that give it a picture-postcard feel. If you're looking to relax, Ao Kiu is an ideal choice. **Amenities:** food and drink. **Best For:** solitude. ⊠ *Koh Samet, Chonburi.*

Ao Vong Duan. This beautiful half-moon bay is packed with resorts and restaurants, so you're never far away from food and drink. It's the epicenter of water sports on Koh Samet, with Jet Skis and speedboats operating from the beach. The white sands and crystal blue waters make the beach worth a visit. The beaches of Ao Cho to the north and Ao Thian to the south are both a pleasant five-minute walk away. **Amenities:** food and drink; water sports. **Best For:** walking. ⊠ *Koh Samet, Chonburi.*

Haad Sai Kaew. Located on the northeastern edge of the island, this is the longest beach and also its busiest. Lined by resorts and restaurants, all types of food are steps away. The sand is white and the water is clear, although in the rainy season the seas do get a little rough. There are a few boats operating from the beach, but Haad Sai Kaew is a better place to relax than the crowded beaches of Pattaya. **Amenities:** food and drink; water sports. **Best for:** partiers. ⊠ *Beach Rd., Koh Samet, Chonburi.*

WHERE TO STAY

The island has many bungalows and cottages, with and without electricity. *Although the resorts below have good restaurants, you'll have a more memorable experience at one of the delicious seafood joints that set up along the beach each afternoon.*

For expanded hotel reviews, visit Fodors.com.

$$$$
RESORT
🏨 **Paradee Resort.** The beach here is tops—the resort actually spans beaches on both the east and west coasts of Samet—and it's more

secluded than others. **Pros:** beautiful grounds; lots of privacy. **Cons:** very pricey; may feel isolated; not for families. $ *Rooms from: $350* ✉ *76 Moo 4, Rayong* ☎ *038/644283 up to 88* 🛏 *40 bungalows* 🍴 *No meals.*

$$ RESORT **Samed Cliff Resort.** The rooms at this little cluster of bungalows are simply furnished, but they're clean and comfortable and have the requisite amenities, including hot water and air-conditioning. **Pros:** beachside dining; on scenic stretch of beach. **Cons:** pricey for what it is; not many creature comforts. $ *Rooms from: $70* ✉ *Nanai Beach, Koh Samet* ☎ *016/457115, 02/635–0800 in Bangkok* 🌐 *www.samedcliff.com* 🛏 *38 bungalows.*

$$ RESORT **Vong Deuan Resort.** This resort offers the best bungalows on Ao Vong Duan Beach, and is near much of the island's activity. **Pros:** well located; fun atmosphere. **Cons:** not all bungalows have air-conditioning; pricey for what it is. $ *Rooms from: $70* ✉ *Ao Vong Duan Beach, Koh Samet* ☎ *01/446–1944, 038/651777 in Ban Phe* 🌐 *www.vongdeuan.com* 🛏 *45 bungalows* 🍴 *No meals.*

4

CHANTHABURI

100 km (62 miles) east of Rayong, 180 km (108 miles) east of Pattaya.

Chanthaburi has played a big role in Thai history. It was here that the man who would become King Taksin gathered and prepared his troops to retake Ayutthaya from the Burmese after they sacked the capital of Siam in 1767. The King Taksin Shrine, shaped like a house-size helmet from that era, is on the north end of town.

The French occupied the city from 1893 to 1905, and you can spot some architecture from that era along the river. The French influence is evident in the Cathedral of Immaculate Conception, across the river from the center of town. First built in 1711 by Christian Vietnamese who migrated to the area, the cathedral has been rebuilt four times since, and the present building was completed in the early 1900s when the city was under French control. The best time to visit the church is during the morning market on the grounds, when local foods, fruits, and desserts are sold.

GETTING HERE AND AROUND

Buses make the 90-minute journey from Rayong and Ban Phe. There's also a bus from Bangkok's Eastern Bus Terminal that takes four to five hours.

EXPLORING CHANTHABURI

Most visitors stop here on the way to Koh Chang, attracted by either gem shopping or the fruit season in May and June. The mines are mostly closed, but Chanthaburi is still renowned as a center for gems. On Gem Street, in the center of town, you can see traders sorting through rubies and sapphires and making deals worth hundreds of thousands of baht. The street becomes a gem market on Friday and Saturday.

KOH CHANG

1 hour by ferry from Laem Ngop, which is 15 km (9 miles) southwest of Trat; Trat is 400 km (250 miles) southeast of Bangkok.

The largest and most developed of the 52-island archipelago that became Mu Koh Chang National Park in 1982 is called Koh Chang, or Elephant Island. Most of Koh Chang is mountainous, and there are only a few small beaches. The 30-km-long (18-mile-long) island has only nine villages, a few accessible only by boat. But this little paradise has been the focus of rapid development in the past few years, and the number of resorts is increasing exponentially.

GETTING HERE AND AROUND

To get to Koh Chang you first have to get to Trat, 96 km (60 miles) southeast of Chanthaburi. The easiest way is taking one of Bangkok Airway's daily flights. There are also air-conditioned buses from Bangkok's Eastern and Northern bus terminals; the trip takes a little over five hours and costs about B200.

Boat Travel Take a ferry from one of three piers in Trat (Laem Ngop, Center Point, or Ao Thammachat) to one of two piers on Koh Chang. The trip takes a little more than half an hour, and the fare is roughly B80.

Songthaew Travel Once you're on the island, songthaews are the easiest way to get around. They cost between B30 and B50, or more if you venture toward the eastern part of the island.

SAFETY AND PRECAUTIONS

Koh Chang is becoming a bustling resort island and, unfortunately, with it there are a few annoyances. Crime is still very low, but thieves do strike. Keep your valuables secured and use hotel safes.

During the monsoon season (June to October), take particular care when swimming. Currents can be deceptive. Warning signs have been installed in recent years, but the beaches still lack lifeguards.

TIMING

The best time to visit Koh Chang is during the drier months of November to March. Outside of these months the weather could hinder beach activities.

Visitor and Tour Information Tourism Authority of Thailand. The Tourism Authority of Thailand office has information about the other islands in the archipelago. ⊠ *100 Moo 1, near Laem Ngop pier, Trat* ☎ *039/597255, 039/597259.*

EXPLORING KOH CHANG

Beautiful, albeit somewhat inaccessible rain forest covers a chunk of this territory, making this a great destination if you want more than just sun and sand. But the island is also a good bet for simple beachside relaxation: beaches are picturesque and lack the party scene of Pattaya.

Every beach has something being built or renovated, and those construction sites can ruin your serenity as crews blast electric drills and saws early and late in the day. ■TIP➔ Make sure that there's no major construction project going on near your hotel.

BEACHES

Koh Chang's best beaches are found on the western shore. Haad Sai Khao (White Sand Beach) is the farthest north and the most developed. A few miles south is the more serene Haad Khlong Phrao, a long, curving beach of pale golden sand. Nearby Kai Bae is a mix of sand and pebbles. It has a gentle drop-off, making it safe for weak swimmers. Still farther south is Haad Ta Nam (Lonely Beach), which is perhaps the most picturesque of all. But it's also the smallest one and therefore more crowded. Farther along on the southwest corner of the island is the fishing village Bang Bao, which is also experiencing development, with restaurants, dive shops, and cheap bungalows popping up.

Though the east coast is beautiful, it's mostly rugged rain forest, and beaches are in short supply.

Kai Bae Beach. A mix of pebbles and sand makes Kai Bae Beach less of a draw than nearby beaches, but it has the best, and safest, swimming on Koh Chang. There are a few restaurants in the neighborhood, plus a smattering of resorts. This is a quiet and relaxed beach, still enjoying a sleepy feel. **Amenities:** food and drink. **Best for:** solitude; swimming.

Khlong Phrao Beach. A quieter option that the main beach at Sai Kaew Beach, Khlong Phrao Beach is an arc of golden sand leading down to placid waters. There are a few high-end resorts and a couple of restaurants scattered around the beach. The shallow waters keep boats at bay, but also don't invite much swimming. **Amenities:** food and drink. **Best for:** walking.

Sai Kaew Beach. Koh Chang's busiest beach is the ideal choice for those who like a bustling atmosphere. There are a number of resorts and some great restaurants lining the beach. The beach remains free from deck chair rentals, but a few hawkers ply their wears during the day. The waters are very rough, especially in the rainy season between June and October. There is a severe rip-tide and swimming can be unsafe for extended period. **Amenities:** food and drink. **Best for:** partiers.

WHERE TO EAT

For fresh seafood and skewers of chicken, pork, or beef, neighbors **Mac Resort Hotel** and **Koh Chang Lagoon Resort** excel. Both set up barbecues on the beach just before sunset. Koh Chang Lagoon Resort also offers a reasonable vegetarian selection.

$ ✗ **Cookies.** The best part of Cookies Hotel is its delightful beachfront
ECLECTIC restaurant, where the Thai food is consistently good and inexpensive. The *tom yum talay* (hot-and-sour seafood soup) could be hotter, but is definitely a standout. The banana shakes and banana pancakes alone are worth a visit. The concrete bungalows are basic and somewhat worn, but they're close to the beach and the prices are reasonable, even during high season. $ *Average main: B150* ⊠ *Cookies Hotel, 7/2 Moo 4, Sai Khao Beach* ☎ *039/551107* ⊕ *www.cookieskohchang.com.*

$ ✗ **Magic Resort.** A pleasant breeze cools the open-air dining area at
SEAFOOD this low-key resort, which has good views of the coastline and the high hills surrounding Koh Chang. Sitting over the water, the restaurant is in a rather worn wooden structure, but the tradeoff is the very good seafood—try the crab if you want something spicy. There's also a

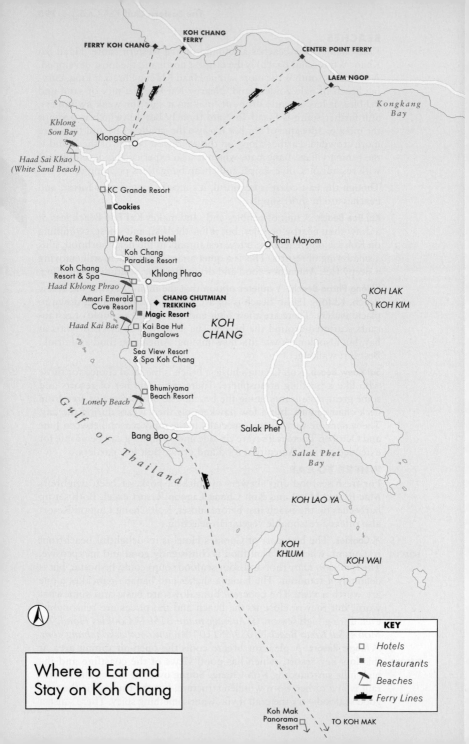

FERRY KOH CHANG

KOH CHANG
FERRY

CENTER POINT FERRY

LAEM NGOP

*Kongkang
Bay*

*Khlong
Son Bay*

Klongson

*Haad Sai Khao
(White Sand Beach)*

☐ KC Grande Resort

■ **Cookies**

☐ Mac Resort Hotel

Koh Chang
Paradise Resort

Koh Chang
Resort & Spa
Haad Khlong Phrao

Khlong Phrao

Than Mayom

KOH LAK

KOH KIM

◆ **CHANG CHUTMIAN
TREKKING**

Amari Emerald
Cove Resort

■ **Magic Resort**

Haad Kai Bae

☐ Kai Bae Hut
Bungalows

*KOH
CHANG*

☐ Sea View Resort
& Spa Koh Chang

☐ Bhumiyama
Beach Resort

Lonely Beach

Gulf of Thailand

Bang Bao

Salak Phet

*Salak Phet
Bay*

KOH LAO YA

*KOH
KHLUM*

KOH WAI

Where to Eat and
Stay on Koh Chang

KEY	
☐	*Hotels*
■	*Restaurants*
⚓	*Beaches*
🚢	*Ferry Lines*

Koh Mak
Panorama
Resort ☐

TO KOH MAK

reasonably priced Western menu. Breakfast is available all day. $ *Average main: B100 ⊠ 34 Moo 4, Khlong Phrao Beach ☎ 039/557074.*

WHERE TO STAY

As the tourism industry grows on Koh Chang, mid-level resorts are becoming more common than expensive upscale establishments. Resorts are also being built on some of the other islands in the marine park, including Koh Mak.

For expanded hotel reviews, visit Fodors.com.

$$
RESORT
Fodor's Choice
★

▦ Amari Emerald Cove Resort. The island's top hotel, the Amari Emerald Cove Resort lives up to its five-star reputation with spacious and tastefully decorated rooms with hardwood floors and private balconies. **Pros:** fancy feeling; high level of service. **Cons:** expensive rates; unexciting dining; a little isolated. $ *Rooms from: $102 ⊠ 88/8 Moo 4, Haad Khlong Phrao ☎ 039/552000, 02/255–3960 in Bangkok ⊕ www.amari.com ➥ 165 rooms ⊙ Breakfast.*

$$
RESORT

▦ Bhumiyama Beach Resort. These two-story bungalows set in a tropical garden have a modern look and a luxurious feel, with white walls and a lot of polished wood. **Pros:** good deal; interesting decor. **Cons:** some rooms lack sea views. $ *Rooms from: $85 ⊠ Tah Nam Beach ☎ 039/558067 up to 69, 02/266–4388 in Bangkok ⊕ www.bhumiyama.com ➥ 43 rooms ⊙ Breakfast.*

$
RESORT

▦ Kai Bae Hut Bungalows. There are many strings of bungalows on Kai Bae Beach, but this property is the most established and reliable. **Pros:** fun people; central location. **Cons:** some rooms far from beach; some bungalows are past their prime. $ *Rooms from: $45 ⊠ 10/3 Moo 4, Kai Bae Beach ☎ 09/936–1149, 039/557128 ⊕ www.kaibaehut.com ➥ 24 bungalows, 30 hotel rooms ⊟ No credit cards ⊙ No meals.*

$$
RESORT

▦ KC Grande Resort. This cluster of bungalows has accommodations ranging from fan-cooled huts to spacious suites with all the amenities. **Pros:** beautiful location; bungalows feel very private. **Cons:** atmosphere may feel stuffy; least expensive rooms not so desirable. $ *Rooms from: $95 ⊠ 1/1 Moo 4, Sai Khao Beach ☎ 039/551199, 02/539–5424 in Bangkok ⊕ www.kckohchang.com ➥ 61 bungalows ⊟ No credit cards ⊙ No meals.*

$
RESORT

▦ Koh Chang Paradise Resort. With all the amenities of a big city hotel, these bungalows are spacious and include private porches where you can enjoy the breeze. **Pros:** cool pool; lovely location. **Cons:** not luxurious; subpar food. $ *Rooms from: $54 ⊠ 39/4 Moo 4, Khlong Phrao Beach ☎ 039/551100, 039/551101 ⊕ www.kohchangparadise.com ➥ 69 bungalows ⊙ Breakfast.*

$$$$
RESORT

▦ Koh Chang Resort & Spa. On the edge of the bay, this self-contained complex was one of the first major lodgings built on Koh Chang. **Pros:** good for couples; nice spa. **Cons:** rooms small and tired; disappointing food. $ *Rooms from: $2700 ⊠ Klong Prao Beach ☎ 039/551082, 02/692–0094 in Bangkok ⊕ www.kohchangresortandspa.com ➥ 145 rooms ⊙ Breakfast.*

$$
RESORT

▦ Mac Resort Hotel. A deluxe room with hot tub and a private balcony overlooking the ocean or one of the bungalows clustered around the beachfront swimming pool is the way to go at the Mac. **Pros:** reasonable rates; generally cool guests. **Cons:** not fancy. $ *Rooms from: $50* ✉ *7/3 Moo 4, Sai Khao Beach* ☎ *039/551124, 01/864–6463* ⊕ *www.mac-resorthotel.com* ⇘ *25 rooms* ⦿| *Breakfast.*

$$
RESORT ⊡ **Sea View Resort & Spa Koh Chang.** At the far end of Kai Bae Beach, this resort and spa are quieter than most. **Pros:** nice beach; beautiful grounds. **Cons:** removed from action; food options limited. $ *Rooms from: $120* ✉ *10/2 Moo 4, Kai Bae Beach* ☎ *039/529022* ⊕ *www. seaviewkohchang.com* ⇘ *74 rooms, 2 suites* ⦿| *Breakfast.*

SPORTS AND THE OUTDOORS
HIKING AND TREKKING

Hiking trips, particularly to some of the island's waterfalls, are popular. It's a good idea to hire a guide if you plan to venture farther than one of the well-traveled routes, as good maps of the mostly jungle terrain are unheard-of.

Ban Kwan Chang. On the northern end of the island, Ban Kwan Chang offers a trekking program supported by the Asian Elephant Foundation, so you can trust that the elephants are treated humanely. Half-day tours (8:30–noon; B900 per person) include a bathing and feeding session and a 90-minute trek into the jungle, as well as transportation from your hotel. There are shorter treks as well. Most hotels can arrange trips for you. ☎ *08/92473161.*

Jungle Way. Both full day and half day are available at Jungle Way. Run by the entertaining and stoic Lek from his guest house of the same name, the tours offer insights into the local environment and way of life. Jungle Way is based in the northern village of Klongson. ✉ *Klong-san* ☎ *09/223–4795.*

SCUBA DIVING AND SNORKELING

Scuba diving, including PADI-certified courses, is readily available. Divers say that the fish are smaller than in other parts of Thailand, but the coral is better. Prices run from B3,500 for an introductory dive to more than B20,000 for dive-master certification. Snorkeling off a boat costs as little as B900 a day. Snorkelers usually just tag along on dive boats, but boat snorkeling excursions are available.

OK Diving. This company offers day dives, scuba courses, and snorkeling excursions ☎ *09/936–7080.*

Ploy Scuba Diving. One of the big names in the business, Ploy Scuba Diving offers a full range of scuba courses and dives for everyone from beginners to dive masters. The main office is on Bang Bao Pier on the south of the island. There are offices on many other beaches, too. ☎ *039/558033* ⊕ *www.ploytalaygroup.com/ployscubadiving.htm.*

Thai Fun. This company runs a 10-hour, 15-island tour of the marine park. The trip includes a buffet lunch, excursions to two or more islands, and two snorkeling stops. The cost is around B1,400. ☎ *06/141–7498.*

Water World Diving. This outfit offers day dives, certification courses, and snorkeling excursions. ✉ *Koh Chang Plaza, Khlong Phrao Beach* ☎ *09/224–1031.*

Koh Mak, an island just south of Koh Chang, is known for its spectacular sunsets.

KOH SI CHANG

40 minutes by ferry from Sri Racha, which is 100 km (62 miles) southeast of Bangkok.

For centuries Koh Si Chang was considered a gateway to Thailand, the spot where huge sailing ships docked and smaller barges loaded goods bound for Bangkok and Ayutthaya. This is still a hardworking port, which means rubbish from the shipping and fishing industries creates a bit of an eyesore. But it's a clean island otherwise.

Koh Si Chang has been a popular retreat for three generations of royalty. In the 19th century King Rama IV noticed that people on this island lived longer than most Thais (to 70 and 80 years). He concluded that this phenomenon had something to do with the island's climate and he started to spend time here. His son, King Rama V, went one step further and built a summer palace on the island, and King Rama VI would spend up to eight or nine months a year here.

GETTING HERE AND AROUND

To get here, first take a B100 bus to Sri Racha, less than three hours by bus from Bangkok's Eastern Terminal. In Sri Racha, catch an hourly ferry to Koh Si Chang. The ride is less than an hour, and it's B50 each way. Transportation around the island is limited to motorcycle taxis, which will take you to most places for B20, and the island's unique "stretch tuk-tuks," which cost about B50 to most spots.

EXPLORING KOH SI CHANG

Koh Si Chang is not known for its beaches—most of the coast is rocky—but it's off the main tourist routes, so it has an easygoing pace that makes it a real escape. It's relatively close to Bangkok, so Thais flood the island on weekends. During the week, however, it's peaceful. All the sights are within easy walking distance, and there aren't many cars around.

Chudhadhuj Palace. Knowing that the island's residents lived longer here than anywhere else in Thailand, King Chulalongkorn (Rama V) built Chudhadhuj Palace, named after Prince Chudhadhuj, who was born on the island on July 5, 1893. The palace was abandoned in 1894 when France blockaded the Gulf of Thailand during a political crisis. Few buildings remain today, but the palace gardens are a great place for a stroll. Vimanmek Mansion was originally started here before being moved to Bangkok in 1901, and its beachside foundation remains. Nearby, an old wooden pier has been restored to its former glory. ✉ *2 km (1 mile) south of town.*

Khao Yai Temple. On the north side of town is Khao Yai Temple, which attracts hordes of weekend visitors from Bangkok. The temple is a real hodge-podge of shrines and stupas that line a 400-step walkway up a steep hillside. It's an arduous climb to the main temple building, but the view of the northern half of the island, the mainland, and the rows of barges and ships is worth the effort. Koh Si Chang has no natural water sources, and you can see from above that nearly every roof on the island has a big jar for collcting water. ✉ *North of town.*

Wat Yai Prik. West of town, Wat Yai Prik is easy to spot as you near the island by boat—it's on the top of a hill and has eight 40-foot reservoirs. The wat often donates drinking water to villagers when they need it. But Yai Prik is as dedicated to the spiritual as it is to the practical. Meditation courses are available, and signs throughout the grounds explain Buddhist principles. Simplicity rules here—though donations are accepted, the monks don't collect money to build ornate temples. ✉ *West of town.*

WHERE TO EAT

One of the main reasons for visiting Koh Si Chang is its seafood, and the island's simple eateries draw flock of fans on weekends. Fine dining hasn't arrived on the island, so you'll be eating just like locals.

$ SEAFOOD 🍴 **Lek Noi.** This place doesn't look like much—it's little more than a shack with plastic chairs and simple wooden tables—but many locals say it's the best place for seafood on the island. It's a little more than a kilometer (½ mile) out of town on the way to Chudhadhuj Palace. [$] *Average main: B80* ✉ *Mekhaamthaew Rd.* 💳 *No credit cards.*

$$ ECLECTIC 🍴 **Pan & David.** The owners are a Thai-American couple, so it's not surprising that their eatery offers a good mix of both types of food. The best dishes are an inventive combination of the two—spaghetti with a spicy seafood sauce is tops. The open-air dining area is cooled by ocean breezes. [$] *Average main: B120* ✉ *167 Moo 3, Mekhaamthaew Rd.* ☎ *038/216629.*

WHERE TO STAY

The island caters to mostly Thai weekend visitors, and therefore has a limited selection of guesthouses and hotels. You need to book ahead for a weekend stay, but getting a room during the week is no problem. *For expanded hotel reviews, visit Fodors.com.*

$ **Rim Talay Resort.** If you want to be lulled to asleep by the sound of
RESORT the surf, stay in one of this trio of boats that have been converted into bungalows. **Pros:** unique concept; cheap rates. **Cons:** rooms could be more comfy. $ *Rooms from: $51* ⊠ *130 Moo 3, Mekhaamthaew Rd.* ☎ *038/216116* 🛏 *20 bungalows* ⊟ *No credit cards.*

$ **Sichang Palace Hotel.** The island's biggest hotel, the Sichang Palace
HOTEL is comfortable enough and has a central location. **Pros:** well located; reliable option. **Cons:** can feel too empty; doesn't have many amenities. $ *Rooms from: $51* ⊠ *81 Atsadang Rd.* ☎ *038/216276 up to 78* ⊕ *www.sichangpalace.com* 🛏 *56 rooms* ⊟ *No credit cards* ❢❢ *No meals.*

THE WESTERN GULF

South of Bangkok lies the Western Gulf coast, hundreds of miles of shoreline where resort towns are the exception rather than the rule. Most towns along the Gulf are either small fishing villages or culturally and historically significant towns like Surat Thani. Some touristy areas have grown up around the smaller villages, but they are considerably less developed than some of their counterparts in the other coastal areas. Thus, the allure of the Western Gulf is its charming towns, spectacular beaches, and not-yet-overgrown tourist destinations.

About three hours south of Bangkok are the laid-back beaches of Cha-am and Hua Hin. Bangkok residents have traveled to Hua Hin since the 1920s, when King Rama VII built a palace here. Where royalty goes, high society inevitably follows, but despite the attention the city received, Hua Hin was spared the pitfalls of rapid development.

Another 483 km (300 miles) south is Surat Thani, the former capital of an ancient Siamese kingdom. As the center of its own civilization, Surat Thani developed its own artistic and architectural style. In modern times it has remained an important commercial and historic Thai city, and the province is home to one of the most pristine tropical forests in Thailand, Khao Sok National Park. However, most travelers know Surat Thani only as a departure point for the islands off its coast, primarily Koh Samui.

CHA-AM

163 km (101 miles) south of Bangkok, 40 km (25 miles) from Petchaburi.

It may not be the most picturesque seaside town, but Cha-am does offer an authentic Thai-style beach experience. The pier is the center of this small, quiet town. Its main street, full of restaurants, bars, guesthouses, and hotels, passes by a tree-lined strip of beach. You can often

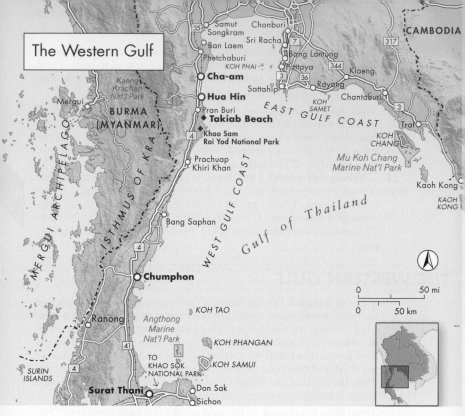

see Bangkok families here—gathered at umbrella-covered tables for all-day meals, stocking up on fresh seafood and beer from wandering vendors. Cha-am retains its sleepy charm, and those searching for peace and quiet may find their niche here.

GETTING HERE AND AROUND

Buses leave Bangkok's Southern Bus Terminal every 30 minutes between 6:30 am and 7 pm; the 2½-hour trip costs around B150. Once you're here, tuk-tuks are the best way to get around.

SAFETY AND PRECAUTIONS

Taking simple precautions with money and valuables should ensure a trouble-free stay. Most guesthouses and hotels have safes, and even if they don't, most are more than happy to take good care of your belongings.

TIMING

Like most of the upper southern Gulf area, Cha-am can be visited all year round, but it's best in the drier, cooler months between November and March. Prices do rise in this traditional high season, especially on weekends, but it's worth visiting during these months for the calmer seas and cooler temperatures.

Cha-am is a small town, and it doesn't really take long to see the highlights. However, if you are after an isolated vacation far from the madding crowds you can quite easily relax here for a week. Spending too long in Cha-am could be difficult for those yearning for western comforts.

Visitor and Tour Information Tourism Authority of Thailand ✉ *Petchkasem Rd.* ☎ *032/471005, 032/471502* 🌐 *www.tourismthailand.org.*

EXPLORING CHA-AM

Around the pier, the beach has fairly dark and dirty sand. Most visitors head to one of the many all-inclusive resorts farther from the town beach, where the sand is prettier and the water better for swimming.

WHERE TO EAT

Fresh seafood is available at small cafés along Ruamchit Beach Road, where there are also stalls selling trays of deep-fried squid, shrimp, and tiny crab for around B25.

$ SEAFOOD 🍴 **Poom Restaurant.** The seafood here is perhaps the best in town, which is obvious from steady stream of locals. Try the charcoal-grilled whole fish, large prawns, crab, and squid—all fresh and accompanied by a delicious chili sauce. The decor is nothing special—the metal-table-and-plastic-chair variety—but there's some outside seating under the trees. The restaurant next door, owned by the same people, has an air-conditioned dining area if you really can't take the heat. [$] *Average main: B120* ✉ *274/1 Ruamchit Rd.* ☎ *032/471036.*

WHERE TO STAY

A steadily improving mix of small hotels and guesthouses for all budgets lines this road, while a string of luxury hotels and resorts runs along the main highway south of town to Hua Hin.

For expanded hotel reviews, visit Fodors.com.

$$$ 🏨 **Dusit Resort and Polo Club.** The spacious lobby serves as a lounge for afternoon tea and evening cocktails, sipped to the soft melodies of traditional Thai music. **Pros:** beachfront setting; traditional architecture; lots of amenities. **Cons:** need a car (or taxi) to get around; some rooms need updating. [$] *Rooms from: $136* ✉ *1349 Petchkasem Rd.* ☎ *032/520009, 02/636–3333 in Bangkok* 🌐 *www.dusit.com* 🛏 *291 rooms, 9 suites* 🍽 *Breakfast.*

$$ RESORT 🏨 **Regent Cha-am.** Taking a swim couldn't be easier than at the Regent Cha-am, which has a quartet of pools spread among the dozens of bungalows facing the beach. **Pros:** pretty layout; fun nightlife. **Cons:** unpredictable availability. [$] *Rooms from: $68* ✉ *849/21 Cha-am Beach* ☎ *032/451240, 02/251–0305 in Bangkok* 🌐 *www.regent-chaam.com* 🛏 *630 rooms, 30 suites* 🍽 *Breakfast.*

$$ 🏨 **Sabaya Jungle Resort.** Whether you're relaxing in your room or chilling out in the common area, you'll feel at home at this attractive, personable resort. **Pros:** nice spa; cool rooms; breathtaking location. **Cons:** not on the beach; unexciting pool. [$] *Rooms from: $54* ✉ *304/7 Nong Chaeng Rd.* ☎ *032/470716, 032/470717* 🌐 *www.sabaya.co.th* 🛏 *16 bungalows* 🍽 *No meals.*

4

HUA HIN

66 km (41 miles) from Cha-am, 189 km (118 miles) south of Bangkok.

The golden sands near the small seaside city of Hua Hin have long attracted Bangkok's rich and famous. The most renowned visitors are the King and Queen of Thailand, who now use the Klai Kangwol Palace north of Hua Hin town as their primary residence. The palace was completed in 1928 by King Rama VII, who gave it the name Klai Kangwol, which means "Far From Worries."

GETTING HERE AND AROUND

The bus is the most convenient way to get here from Bangkok. They depart hourly from the Southern Bus Terminal; the trip takes three hours and costs about B150. Minivans (B200) head here from Bangkok's Khao San Road or Victory Monument and are generally faster than buses, though some operators may try to squeeze in too many passengers.

Bus Contact Hua Hin ✉ *Dechanuchit St.*

SAFETY AND PRECAUTIONS

Hua Hin has witnessed an expat boom in the past five years, and along with high-rise condos there has been an inevitable influx of less desirable elements. Pickpockets have been known to operate in town, and there have been a few thefts from hotel rooms. These incidents are few and far between, however.

Overall, the town is safe, as you would expect for a place that hosts the King and Queen of Thailand, and the police are in full evidence during the day and night. Always engage a registered tuk-tuk driver (easy to spot because they will display their credentials) if you are going some distance.

TIMING

Hua Hin is a year-round destination. Weekends and Thai public holidays are times to avoid, when the Bangkok set floods the city—prices rise and the town's streets become noticeably busier.

EXPLORING HUA HIN

Chatchai Street Market. This long-established market is a favorite with both locals and tourists. In the morning it sells meats and produce, mainly to residents, but after 5 pm you'll find everything from jewelry and clothing to toys and artworks. The evening market also has a selection of interesting eats, including Thai *kanom* (sweets), exotic fruits, barbecue meats, and traditional Thai dishes. ✉ *Dechanuchit St.*

OFF THE
BEATEN
PATH

Khao Sam Roi Yod National Park. You'll pass rice fields, sugar palms, pineapple plantations, and crab farms as you make your way to this park, the gloriously named "300 Peaks" about 63 km (39 miles) south of Hua Hin. The park has two main trails and is a great place to spot wildlife, especially monitor lizards and barking deer. With a little luck you can spot the adorable dusky langur, a type of monkey also known as the spectacled langur because of the white circles around its eyes. About a kilometer (½ mile) from the park's headquarters is Khao Daeng Hill, which is worth a hike up to the viewpoint, especially at sunrise.

Another 16 km (10 miles) from the headquarters is Haad Laem Sala, a white-sand beach. Near the beach is Phraya Nakhon Cave, once visited by King Rama V. The cave has an opening in its roof where sunlight shines through for a beautiful effect. If you don't have a car (or haven't hired one), you'll have to take a bus to the Pranburi District in Prachuab Kiri Khan Province. From here you take a songthaew to the park. ☎ *032/619078* 🌐 *www.dnp.go.th.*

BEACHES

Hua Hin's beach is the nicest of those along this part of the coast, but it's also the most popular. You can get away from the nonstop parade of vendors by booking a relaxing beach massage or by taking a horseback ride to less populated parts of the beach. Water sports can be arranged at various areas along the beach.

Hua Hin Beach. This beach isn't particularly stunning as far as Thai beaches go, but it's popular for its wide boulevard of golden sand and activities ranging from massages to water sports. Vendors hawk food and drink, and a market lines the walk to the beach. The waters can get rough and the sea is anything but clear, but it is possible to swim. There are shaded deck chair areas for relaxing. **Amenities:** food and drink; water sports. **Best for:** walking.

WHERE TO EAT

$$ SEAFOOD 🍴 **Buffalo Bill's at Fisherman's Wharf.** This surf-and-turf restaurant takes pride in using the best of the region's produce and seafood. Try the beer-batter fish-and-chips served in traditional newspaper wrapping. You can start your day with the best eggs Benedict in town or wrap it up with an afternoon beer or cocktails. The Sunday roast gives you a chance to mingle with the expat community. [$] *Average main: B250* ✉ *8 Chomsin Rd.* ☎ *08/07274710* 🌐 *www.buffalobillshuahin.com.*

$ SEAFOOD 🍴 **Koti.** A longtime local favorite for Thai-style seafood, Koti has no-nonsense decor and a packed dining room that attests to the flavor of dishes like *hor mok talay* (steamed seafood curry). A large menu (in English) includes such crowd-pleasers as fried fish with garlic and pepper. [$] *Average main: B120* ✉ *61/1 Petchkasem Rd.* ☎ *032/511252* 💳 *No credit cards* 🕒 *No lunch.*

$$ ASIAN 🍴 **Monsoon Restaurant & Bar.** To wash down dishes such as *luc lac* (sautéed beef) and tom yam goong, Monsoon serves up creative cocktails like the Tonkin Wave (Midori, Creme de Banana, and pineapple juice). There's a full menu of Thai and Vietnamese dishes, including tasty vegetarian options. The daily set menu is popular, as are an array of smaller plates. The restaurant is on the seafront and has an elegant open-air terrace. [$] *Average main: B200* ✉ *62 Naresdamri Rd.* ☎ *032/531062* ✍ *Reservations essential.*

$ SEAFOOD 🍴 **Sang Thai.** Ignore the ramshackle surroundings—for interesting seafood dishes from grilled prawns with bean noodles to fried grouper with chili and tamarind juice, this open-air restaurant down by the wharf can't be beat. It's popular with Thais, which is always a good sign. Don't miss the *kang* (huge prawns). [$] *Average main: B150* ✉ *Naresdamri Rd.* ☎ *032/512144.*

WHERE TO STAY

For expanded hotel reviews, visit Fodors.com.

$$
RESORT

🔲 **Anantara.** Surrounded by a 10-foot-tall terra-cotta wall, this beach resort calls to mind an ancient Thai village. **Pros:** lots of elephants; inspiring setting; many activities. **Cons:** verges on stuffy; expensive rates. $ *Rooms from: $110* ✉ *43/1 Phetkasem Beach Rd.* ☎ *032/520250* ⊕ *www.anantara.com* ⇗ *187 rooms* ۩ *Breakfast.*

$$$$
HOTEL
Fodor's Choice
★

🔲 **Chiva-Som.** Even with the proliferation of spas in Hua Hin, Chiva-Som has not been toppled from its lofty position as one of the best spa resorts in the region—and, possibly, in the world. **Pros:** unique spa program; high level of service; great variety of activities and services. **Cons:** not for partiers; expensive rates. $ *Rooms from: $550* ✉ *73/4 Petchkasem Rd.* ☎ *032/536536* ⊕ *www.chivasom.com* ⇗ *57 rooms* ۩ *No meals.*

$$
RESORT

🔲 **Evason Hideaway and Evason Hua Hin Resort.** These neighboring properties are both set on a quiet beach in Pranburi, about 20 minutes south of Hua Hin. **Pros:** super-comfortable accommodations; access to double the amenities. **Cons:** out of the way; too quiet for some; not-so-great beach. $ *Rooms from: $120* ✉ *9/22 Moo 5 Paknampran, Pranburi* ☎ *032/618200 Hideaway, 032/632111 Resort* ⊕ *www.sixsenses.com* ⇗ *Hideaway: 17 suites, 38 villas. Resort: 185 rooms, 40 villas* ۩ *Breakfast.*

$
B&B/INN

🔲 **Fulay Guesthouse.** On a pier that juts out over the water, this guesthouse is unlike any other in Hua Hin. **Pros:** hard to beat the price; cool location. **Cons:** questionable decor; some rooms lack air-conditioning. $ *Rooms from: $41* ✉ *110/1 Naresdamri Rd.* ☎ *032/513145, 032/513670* ⊕ *www.fulayhuahin.com* ⇗ *14 rooms* ▭ *No credit cards.*

$$$
HOTEL

🔲 **Hilton Hua Hin Resort & Spa.** In the liveliest part of town, the Hilton is perfect for fun-and-sun enthusiasts who want to be close to the action. **Pros:** central location; rooms with great views; high-tech touches. **Cons:** narrow road leading to the hotel. $ *Rooms from: $133* ✉ *33 Naresdamri Rd.* ☎ *032/512888* ⊕ *www.hua-hin.hilton.com* ⇗ *255 rooms, 41 suites* ۩ *Breakfast.*

$
HOTEL

🔲 **Jed Pee Nong.** On one of the main streets leading down to the public entrance to the beach, Jed Pee Nong has bungalows clustered around a swimming pool and standard rooms in a high-rise building. **Pros:** cheap rates; prime location. **Cons:** nothing fancy; lots of nearby foot traffic; lacking in amenities. $ *Rooms from: $51* ✉ *17 Damnernkasem Rd.* ☎ *032/512381* ⊕ *www.jedpeenonghotel-huahin.com* ⇗ *40 rooms* ۩ *No meals.*

$
B&B/INN

🔲 **Pattana Guesthouse.** This pair of beautiful teak-wood houses are hidden down a small alley in the heart of Hua Hin. **Pros:** ideal for budget travelers; cute for what it is. **Cons:** few amenities; no adjacent beach. $ *Rooms from: $12* ✉ *52 Naresdamri Rd.* ☎ *032/513393* ⊕ *www.observergroup.net/pattana.htm* ⇗ *13 rooms* ▭ *No credit cards* ۩ *No meals.*

$$$
HOTEL
Fodor's Choice
★

🔲 **Sofitel Central Hua Hin Resort.** Even if you don't stay at this local landmark, its old-world charm makes it worth a visit. **Pros:** pretty grounds; cool atmosphere. **Cons:** pricey rates; not a party destination. $ *Rooms from: $130* ✉ *1 Damnernkasem Rd.* ☎ *032/512021 up to*

Seven acres of tropical gardens surround Chiva-Som in Hua Hin.

38, 02/541–1125 in Bangkok ⊕ www.centarahotelsresorts.com ⤴ 207 rooms, 30 suites ⏅ No meals.

SPORTS AND THE OUTDOORS
GOLF
Hua Hin Golf Tours. This company can arrange for you to play at any of the 10 or so courses in the area. There's no surcharge added to the greens fees, and free transportation is provided. Rental clubs are available from the pro shop. ☎ 032/530119 ⊕ www.huahingolf.com.

Royal Hua Hin Golf Course. Across the tracks from the quaint wooden railway station is the well-respected Royal Hua Hin Golf Course. You can play for B2300, including a caddie. There's a lounge for refreshments. ✉ Damnernkasem Rd. ☎ 032/512475.

NIGHTLIFE
Hua Hin Brewing Company. Local bands energetically perform Thai and western pop-rock music nightly. Although this isn't a true brewpub (the beers are made in Bangkok), the selection is good, and you can try a sampler of three tasty beers. The outdoor patio offers a full menu and is a prime spot to people-watch. ✉ 33 Naresdamri Rd. ☎ 032/512888.

TAKIAB BEACH

4 km (2½ miles) south of Hua Hin.

GETTING HERE AND AROUND
To get to Takiab, flag down a songthaew (B20) on Petchkasem Road in Hua Hin. You can also hire a horse and trot down the coast.

EXPLORING

Directly to the south of Hua Hin, Khao Takiab is a good alternative for people who wish to avoid Hua Hin's busier scene. Takiab is favored by well-off Thais who prefer Takiab's exclusivity to Hua Hin's touristy atmosphere, and you can find many upscale condos and small luxury hotels here. The beach itself is wide and long, but the water is quite murky and shallow, and not very suitable for swimming.

BEACHES

Khao Takiab Beach. Sunbathing is the ideal activity here, especially during low tide, when the golden, sandy beach is flat and dry (and usually empty). The usual water activities like jet skiing and banana boating are available here, and are more enjoyable than in Hua Hin, as the beach and water are less crowded. The southern part of the beach ends at a big cliff, which has a tall, standing image of the Buddha. You can hike to the top of the hill, where you find a small Buddhist monastery and several restaurants with excellent views. **Amenities:** food and drink; water sports. **Best for:** walking.

WHERE TO EAT AND STAY

For expanded hotel reviews, visit Fodors.com.

$$ THAI 🍴 **Supatra-by-the-Sea.** On the southern end of the beach, this eatery's outdoor seating allows you to dine beneath the tranquil gaze of the standing Buddha on the adjacent hillside. The dining room is exquisitely designed in Lanna style and has water-lily ponds beside several tables. Entrées are mainly seafood, such as prawn soup with a deep-fried green omelet, although other Thai dishes and vegetarian options are included on the extensive menu. The full bar serves inventive cocktails, which may be enjoyed beside the beach. [$] *Average main: B150* ✉ *122/63 Takiab Beach* ☎ *032/536561* 🌐 *www.supatra-bythesea.com.*

$$ HOTEL 🏨 **Kaban Tamor Resort.** The rooms at this stylish resort are tucked inside two-story structures that were designed to resemble seashells, but actually look more like mushrooms. **Pros:** easy beach access; cute rooms. **Cons:** tacky exterior; very oriented to Thai customers. [$] *Rooms from: $85* ✉ *122/43–57 Takiab Beach* ☎ *032/655041* 🌐 *www.kabantamor.com* 🛏 *23 rooms* 🍽 *No meals.*

$$ RESORT 🏨 **Smor Spa Village & Resort.** These accommodations are nearly identical in design to neighboring Kaban Tamor Resort—spacious, single-story, mushroomlike bungalows—but the rooms at Smor have private outdoor hot tubs. **Pros:** pleasant spa; private hot tubs. **Cons:** uninspired decor; beach not always accessible. [$] *Rooms from: $82* ✉ *122/64 Takiab Beach* ☎ *032/536800* 🌐 *www.smorspahuahin.com* 🛏 *14 rooms, 1 suite* 🍽 *No meals.*

CHUMPHON

400 km (240 miles) south of Bangkok, 211 km (131 miles) south of Hua Hin.

Chumphon is regarded as the gateway to the south, because trains and buses connect to Bangkok in the north, to Surat Thani and Phuket to the south, and to Ranong to the southwest. Ferries to Koh Tao dock at Pak

Nam at the mouth of the Chumphon River, 11 km (7 miles) southeast of town. Most of the city's boat services run a free shuttle to the docks.

GETTING HERE AND AROUND

Buses leave regularly from Bangkok's Southern Terminal. The journey takes between six and nine hours; most buses leave at night, so you'll arrive early in the morning, and tickets are between B300 and B600. Though buses are cheaper and more reliable, the *Southern Line* train from Bangkok's Hualamphong Station stops here. In Chumphon proper, tuk-tuks are a ubiquitous and easy way to get around.

SAFETY AND PRECAUTIONS

In recent years there has been an increase in the number of thefts reported on the overnight private buses to and from Bangkok and Chumphon. Never leave valuables in luggage outside of your view.

4

TIMING

You'll soon be on your way, because Chumphon is just a stop along the way to the southern islands and beaches. The best time to visit is in the drier months of November to March.

BEACHES

Thung Wua Laen Beach. Just north of Chumphon there's an excellent beach, Thung Wua Laen. The curving beach is 3 km (2 miles) of white-yellow sand with a horizon dotted by small islands that make up one of the world's strangest bird sanctuaries. Vast flocks of swifts breed here, and their nests are harvested (not without controversy) for the bird's-nest soup served up in Chinese restaurants all over Southeast Asia. It's such a lucrative business that the concessionaires patrol their properties with armed guards. To get here, catch a songthaew on the street across from the bus station. **Amenities:** food and drink. **Best for:** solitude.

WHERE TO STAY

For expanded hotel reviews, visit Fodors.com.

$ 🏨 **Chumphon Cabana Beach Resort.** This friendly resort at the south end
HOTEL of Chumphon's Thong Wua Beach is a great place to stay if you want to make brief visits to Koh Samui and other nearby islands. **Pros:** convenient for island-hopping; eco-friendly vibe. **Cons:** you won't be fawned over; rooms are nothing too special. $ *Rooms from: $56* ✉ *69 Thung Wua Laen Beach* ☎ *077/560245* ⊕ *www.cabana.co.th* 🛏 *73 rooms* ⦿ *No meals.*

SURAT THANI

193 km (120 miles) south of Chumphon, 685 km (425 miles) south of Bangkok.

Surat Thani is where you board the boats bound for Koh Samui. Although it's not a particularly attractive city, don't despair if you have to stay overnight while waiting for your ferry. There are some good restaurants and a handsome hotel.

GETTING HERE AND AROUND

You can get here from Bangkok by bus or train, but flying is the most efficient way to go. Thai Air Asia often has low fares. Buses from Bangkok's Southern Bus Terminal take about 10 hours and cost B400 to B800. There's also an overnight train here from Bangkok's Hua Lamphong Station.

SAFETY AND PRECAUTIONS

The largest annoyance is the propensity of some travel agents to overcharge, however, in most other aspects Surat is a safe town.

TIMING

Surat Thani itself is usually just an overnight stop. However, there are a number of temples, retreats, and national parks that can keep you for few days.

Visitor and Tour Information Tourism Authority of Thailand ⊠ *5 Talat Mai Rd.* ☎ *077/281828* ⊕ *www.tourismthailand.org.*

EXPLORING SURAT THANI

Surat Thani is a regional hub, so there are a few culturally interesting sights that make it a good destination for those who get easily bored on the beach, and Khao Sok National Park is a few hours away.

San Chao Night Market. Every night the sleepy downtown turns into an electrifying street fair centered around the San Chao Night Market, which is illuminated by the lights of numerous food stalls and shop carts. The market is quite popular with Surat locals, as well as with whatever tourists are in town. Choose from any of the delicious seafood meals you see. Looking for a tasty dessert? Across the street from the market you can find Tavorn Roti, which serves delicious traditional roti.

OFF THE BEATEN PATH

Khao Sok National Park. A few hours by bus south of Surat Thani you'll discover a different landscape of tall mountain ranges covered with lush greenery and small streams. Soon you reach Khao Sok National Park, which contains 161,000 acres of the most beautiful forest in Thailand. The park is home to such diverse and rare wildlife as the gaur, banteng, sambar deer, bear, Malayan tapir, macaque, gibbon, serow, mouse deer, and porcupine. It's also one of the few places to see a Raffesia, the world's largest flower, and rare bird species like hornbills. Hiking, boat rides, and night safaris are some of the activities in the park.

Rain is inevitable in Khao Sok, as the weather is influenced by monsoon winds from both the northeast and west—the best and driest time to visit Khao Sok is December to April. Both the national park and some private resorts offer various types of lodging, but don't expect too much. Only very basic accommodation can be found in the park: a privately run, funky-shaped tree house is 1 km (½ mile) before the park's entrance. Visit the local TAT office to stock up on info beforehand. ☎ *077/395154* ⊕ *www.dnp.go.th.*

WHERE TO STAY

For expanded hotel reviews, visit Fodors.com.

$ | **Wang Tai Hotel.** If you find yourself searching for a place to stay in **HOTEL** Surat Thani, this modern high-rise offers everything to prepare you for the onward journey. **Pros:** tasty food; handy location; great views. **Cons:**

the rooms are tatty; doesn't feel particularly Thai. [$] *Rooms from: $34* ✉ *1 Talad Mai Rd.* ☎ *077/283020, 02/253–7947 in Bangkok* 🛏 *230 rooms* 🍴 *Breakfast.*

KOH SAMUI

20 km (12 miles) by boat east of Don Sak.

This is the most popular tourist destination on the Western Gulf coast, which isn't surprising, considering Koh Samui's gorgeous beaches, perfect weather, and sparkling blue, almost turquoise, water. Koh Samui has seen rapid development since the 1990s, and you'll encounter hotels in all price ranges.

Koh Samui is half the size of Phuket, so you could easily drive around it in a day. But Koh Samui is best appreciated by those who take a slower, more casual approach. Most people come for the sun and sea, so they head straight to their hotel and rarely venture beyond the beach where they are staying. Every beach has its own unique character, and with a little exploration you may find the one for you.

GETTING HERE AND AROUND

AIR TRAVEL

Bangkok Airways offers multiple daily flights from Bangkok, and Thai Airways has a morning and an evening flight. At around $200, the hour-long flight is a bit pricier than other flights within Thailand, mainly because the airport is owned by Bangkok Airways and not, as in most cases in Thailand, by the government.

BOAT TRAVEL

From Surat Thani's Donsak Pier, ferries leave every couple of hours for Koh Samui's Na Thon Pier on the west coast; the trip takes roughly two hours. Tour operators in Surat Thani and Koh Samui have information on the ferry schedules, or you can also just head to the pier. Expect to pay around B250 for the trip.

CAR AND TAXI TRAVEL

Budget and Hertz have counters at the Koh Samui airport, and National has its counter in downtown Koh Samui. Thai Rent a Car has a counter near the airport, and the company will deliver your car to you when you land. TA Car Rental is a reputable local company based on Samui.

Taxis don't always meet incoming flights at the airport in Koh Samui, but they can easily be called.

Contacts TA Car Rental ✉ *59/8 Moo 5, Choengmon Beach* ☎ *077/245129* 🌐 *www.samuitacarrent.com.*

SAFETY AND PRECAUTIONS

As in most of Thailand, Samui is a safe place. Crime rarely affects visitors, but there is the odd report of thefts from hotel rooms and late-night robberies. Take sensible precautions, and the risks are minimal.

The greatest safety issue stems from hazardous roads and reckless drivers who know there's little law enforcement to hinder their progress.

DID YOU KNOW?

Koh Samui is the second-most-popular Thai island—only Phuket draws more visitors each year. But it's also the third-largest island geographically, which means that it is possible to escape the crowds.

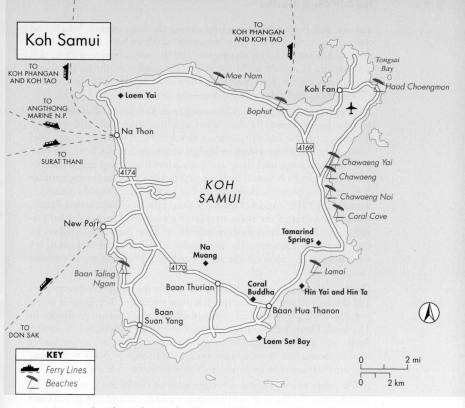

Combine that with visitors with no experience who rent motorcycles and don't bother wearing helmets.

TIMING

Visit anytime, but it's best during the dry, cool months of November to March. It's sometimes dangerous to swim, and intense rain can keep you from exploring or sunbathing.

It's possible to spend a few weeks on the island and still not see everything available. There are also nearby islands and corals to explore.

VISITOR INFORMATION

Contacts Tourism Authority of Thailand ✉ *Na Thon* ☎ *077/421281* ⊕ *www.tourismthailand.org.*

EXPLORING KOH SAMUI

Koh Samui is a delight to explore, and it's one of the few destinations where having a car can come in really handy. A drive along the coastal road will provide one beautiful view after another; the interior of the island isn't as scenic.

Chawaeng Beach, on Koh Samui's east coast, is a fine stretch of glistening white sand divided into two main sections—Chawaeng Yai (yai means "big") and Chawaeng Noi (noi means "little"). Travelers in search of sun and fun flock here, especially during the high season. You'll find the greatest variety of hotels, restaurants, and bars here. During the day the beaches are packed with tourists, and the ocean buzzes with jet skis and banana boats. At night the streets come alive as shops, bars, and restaurants vie for your vacation allowance. But despite the crowds, Chawaeng is no Pattaya or Patong—the mood is very laid-back.

A rocky headland separates Chawaeng from Koh Samui's second-most-popular beach, **Lamai.** Its clear water and long stretch of sand were the first place on the island to attract developers. If you are young and looking for fun, there are more budget accommodations available here than in Chawaeng, and there are quite a few happening clubs. Almost every visitor to Koh Samui makes a pilgrimage to Lamai for yet another reason: at the point marking the end of Lamai Beach stand two rocks, named Hin Yai (Grandmother Rock) and Hin Ta (Grandfather Rock). Erosion has shaped the rocks to resemble weathered and wrinkled private parts. It's nature at its most whimsical. **Laem Set Bay,** a small rocky cape on the southeastern tip of the island, is just south of Lamai. It's a good 3 km (2 miles) off the main road, so it's hard to reach without your own car.

On the west coast of Koh Samui, **Na Thon** is the island's primary port and the spot where ferries arrive from the mainland. Na Thon is home to the island's governmental offices, including the Tourism Authority of Thailand. There are also banks, foreign exchange booths, travel agents, shops, restaurants, and cafés by the ferry pier. There are a few places to rent rooms, but there's really no reason to stay in Na Thon—nicer accommodations can be found a short songthaew ride away.

A few other places on the northern edge of the island are worthy of exploration. On the very northwestern tip of the island you'll find **Laem Yai.** It's also a rather underdeveloped area—for now—that's dotted with a few mega-resorts. But there are also many tiny hole-in-the-wall seaside restaurants with delicious seafood at outrageously low prices. East of Laen Yai is **Mae Nam,** a long, quiet beach, suitable for swimming. Several inexpensive guesthouses and a few luxurious resorts share the 5-km (3-mile) stretch of sand. Mae Nam is also the departure point for boats bound for Koh Phangan and Koh Tao.

A small headland separates Mae Nam from the north shore's other low-key community, **Bophut.** Bophut has a bit of nightlife—central Bophut, known to everyone as Fisherman's Village, has a beachside strip of old houses that have been converted into restaurants, bars, and boutiques. Quaint and romantic, Bophut has a devoted following of return visitors who enjoy its quiet vibe.

On the northeast coast of Samui lies **Choengmon Beach.** A few guesthouses, a handful of luxury resorts, and some restaurants are scattered along the shore of this laid-back beach. The sand is firm and strewn with pebbles and shells, but adequate for sunbathing.

Coral Buddha. About 4 km (2½ miles) from Lamai, at the small Chinese fishing village of Baan Hua Thanon, the road that forks inland toward Na Thon leads to the Coral Buddha, a natural formation carved by years of erosion. ⊠ *Baan Hua Thanon.*

Koh Fan. Off the northeastern tip of Koh Samui is Koh Fan (not to be confused with Koh Fan Noi), a little island with a huge Buddha image covered in moss. The island is best visited at sunset, when the light off the water shows the statue at its best.

Koh Fan Noi. Just offshore at Choengmon Beach is Koh Fan Noi, a little island with a narrow strip of sandy beach. The waters are shallow enough to wade to the island. ✉ *Choengmon Beach.*

OFF THE BEATEN PATH

Mu Koh Angthong National Marine Park. This archipelago of 42 islands covers some 250 square km (90 square miles) and lie 35 km (22 miles) northwest of Koh Samui. The seven main islands are Wua Talap Island (which houses the national park's headquarters), Phaluai Island, Mae Koh Island, Sam Sao Island, Hin Dap Island, Nai Phut Island, and Phai Luak Island. The islands feature limestone mountains, strangely shaped caves, and emerald-green water. Most tourists do a one-day trip, which can be arranged from Koh Samui. Prices vary depending on the tour (some offer kayaking around several islands, others take you out on small speedboats for snorkeling or cave tours). The park is open year-round, although the seas can be rough and the waters less clear during the monsoon season between October and December. ☎ *077/286025, 077/420225* ⊕ *www.dnp.go.th.*

Na Muang. On the inland road to Na Thon lies the village of Baan Thurian, famous for its durian trees. A track to the right climbs up into jungle-clad hills to the island's best waterfall, Na Muang. The 105-foot falls are spectacular—especially just after the rainy season—as they tumble from a limestone cliff into a small pool. You are cooled by the spray and warmed by the sun. For a thrill, swim through the curtain of falling water; you can sit on a ledge at the back to catch your breath. ✉ *Baan Thurian.*

Samui Butterfly Garden. Near Laem Set Bay you'll find the Samui Butterfly Garden, 2 acres of meandering walkways enclosed by nets that take you through kaleidoscopic clouds of butterflies. ✉ *Laem Set Bay* ☎ *077/424020* ⊕ *Apr.–Oct., daily 10–4; Nov.–Mar., daily 9–5* ✉ *B150.*

BEACHES

Bophut Beach. The beach here is quite narrow, but more than wide enough for sunbathing. The water is like glass, making it good for swimming (though it's deep enough to be unsuitable for young children). **Amenities:** food and drink. **Best For:** swimming.

Chawaeng Noi Beach. The smaller and less developed of the beaches adjoining Chawaeng town, quiet and relaxed Chawaeng Noi does not have the charms of its bigger brother, Chawaeng Yai. It lacks the spectacular golden curve of its bigger neighbor, but there are nearby resorts where you can get a snack. **Amenities:** food and drink; water sports. **Best for:** solitude.

Chawaeng Yai Beach. The northern half of this beautiful beach is a hit with with backpackers because it's lined with budget lodgings. The southern half, more popular with the package tourists, is lined with high-end resorts. There's a fair selection of restaurants all along the shore, and the usual water sports are available. The fine sand is a brilliant white and the waters are clear and usually calm. Chawaeng is a

Koh Samui's accessibility and beautiful beaches make it a popular destination year-round.

great swimming beach. **Amenities:** food and drink; water sports. **Best for:** swimming.

Choengmon Beach. On the northeast coast of Samui is the crystal-clear Choengmon Beach, once pitched as Samui's next big thing. There's hardly a boom, but things are changing steadily. It features a wide, sandy shore with an interesting rock formation at one end. There are a few eating options on the beach. **Amenities:** food and drink; water sports. **Best for:** swimming.

Lamai Beach. Lamai Beach lacks the glistening white sand of Chawaeng Beach, but its water is clear and the beach is ideal for swimming. The steeply shelved shoreline might be too much for kids, though. Numerous bars and restaurants lining the beach, emphasizing that Lamai is mostly for young people looking to party. **Amenities:** food and drink; water sports. **Best for:** partiers; swimming.

Mae Nam Beach. Mae Nam Beach lies on the northwestern coast of Samui. Its long, curving beach has coarse, golden sand shaded by tall coconut trees. It's one of the more unspoiled beaches on the island. Quiet both day and night, it has little nightlife and only a scattering of restaurants. The waters are shallow and there are a number of water sports companies in the area. **Amenities:** food and drink; water sports. **Best for:** swimming.

WHERE TO EAT

CHAWAENG

$$$
MEDITERRANEAN
✕ **Betelnut.** Nestled in the Buri Rasa hotel, this restaurant strikes a unique balance between authentic Thai cuisine and western comfort food, with an emphasis on fresh fish. The seared tuna is particularly good. This well-respected eatery has quickly become one of the culinary experiences on Koh Samui. The setting—beachside, with soft lighting—couldn't be more scenic or romantic. $ *Average main: B350* ✉ *Buri Rasa, 11/2 Moo 2, Chawaeng Beach* ☏ *077/413370* ⊕ *www.burirasa. com.*

$$
SEAFOOD
✕ **Captain Kirk.** Okay, so it's one of the more touristy options on Chawaeng, but this place scores with attractive decor and rooftop views. Only about half of the menu is actually Thai food, and this is the half that should keep your attention. Prawns with garlic and pepper rarely disappoint, whereas the French fare—well, what were you expecting? $ *Average main: B250* ✉ *167/42 Moo 2, 2nd fl., Chawaeng* ☏ *081/270–5376* ⊟ *No credit cards.*

$$
SEAFOOD
✕ **Eat Sense.** Despite its manicured grounds, this is not a resort—just a restaurant that serves great Thai food. The dining area has several small fountains and towering palms from which hang giant paper lanterns. Dine on the patio beside the beach or on couches beneath white umbrellas; sip creative cocktails (like the Sabai Sabai Samui, winner of a mixology competition) served in coconut shells; and nosh on exotic seafood creations, such as Phuket lobster with eggplant and Kaffir lime leaves in a green curry paste. For a particular treat, try the locally caught fish, served in all kinds of exotic sauces and styles. Reservations are recommended, particularly during the high season. $ *Average main: B220* ✉ *Near Central Samui Resort, Chawaeng Beach Rd., Chawaeng* ☏ *077/414242* ⊕ *www.eatsensesamui.com.*

$
THAI
✕ **Ninja.** This no-frills dining room is authentic Thai, and popular with locals and foreigners alike. The curries like *massaman* (peanut-based) or *panaeng* (red chili paste and coconut milk) are solid choices, but you really can't go wrong here. Save room for classic desserts, such as *khao niew mamuang* (mango and sticky rice). Ninja's expansive menu includes large color photographs of every dish on the menu, along with phonetic Thai and English captions. $ *Average main: B80* ✉ *Samui Ring Rd., Chawaeng Beach* ⊟ *No credit cards.*

$$$$
THAI
✕ **The Page.** Stick to the fun and interesting cocktails here, not the boring wine list, and you'll soon start to feel as hip as your surroundings. The menu is Thai, with all the favorites like prawns with garlic and pepper, and sea bass with chili and basil. The setting is great, overlooking the beach, and it feels much cooler than most of Chawaeng's hectic scene. And it's always nice to be surrounded by such smart and hip design, such as the lounging figurines that dot the property. $ *Average main: B500* ✉ *14/1 Moo 2, Chawaeng Beach* ☏ *077/422767* ⊕ *www. thelibrary.co.th.*

$$
SEAFOOD
✕ **Tarua Samui Seafood.** We don't know which is better here—the view or the food. High up on a mountain, the restaurant juts out above a rocky beach and turquoise waters. The food is also memorable. The raw shrimp have a silky texture, and the massive grilled prawns with

garlic or curry are delicious. Make sure to check the tank as you walk in; you just might see something you can't resist. $ *Average main: B250* ✉ *210/9 Moo 4, Chawaeng* ☎ *077/960635* ▭ *No credit cards.*

$$$$ ✗ **Zico's.** That disc on your table isn't a coaster! Flip it over to signal that
BRAZILIAN you need a break from the never-ending parade of food that the staff courteously delivers. Hungry again? Flip it back to sample more of the all-you-can-eat barbecue consisting of 15 different skewers of beef, fish, lamb, and shrimp, as well as an ample salad bar. Brazilian samba music sets the scene, but authentic Brazilian dancers steal the show, shaking up the room in skimpy outfits and posing for photos with awestruck diners. $ *Average main: B827* ✉ *38/2 Samui Ring Rd., Chawaeng Beach* ☎ *077/231560* ⊕ *www.zicossamui.com* ⚔ *Reservations essential.*

LAMAI

$$$$ ✗ **The Cliff.** Halfway along the road from Chawaeng to Lamai is the
MEDITERRANEAN Cliff, perched on a big boulder overlooking the sea. You can have lunch or dinner either inside the spartan dining room or out on the scenic terrace. The lunch menu includes sandwiches and hamburgers; dinner features steaks and Mediterranean specialties. The prices are a bit high for the small servings, and the service isn't great, but the Cliff is a nice place to enjoy a drink and check out the view. In the evening, cooler-than-thou staff serve cocktails in the enclosed, air-conditioned club. $ *Average main: B500* ✉ *124/2 Samui Ring Rd., Lamai Beach* ☎ *077/448508* ⊕ *www.thecliffsamui.com* ⚔ *Reservations essential.*

$ ✗ **Mr. Pown Seafood Restaurant.** This place is nothing fancy, but it serves
SEAFOOD up reliable Thai seafood dishes, as well as some German and English fare. Try the red curry in young coconut (a moderately spicy, not quite "red" curry with cauliflower and string beans served inside a coconut) or the catch of the day. The staff is courteous but, it seems, a little jaded by the tourist clientele. There are better restaurants, but not at this price and in this location. $ *Average main: B80* ✉ *Central Lamai Beach* ▭ *No credit cards.*

BAAN TALING NGAM

$$$$ ✗ **Five Islands.** If you want to get away from it all, this is the place.
THAI There's not much in the immediate vicinity except for the beautiful view—the restaurant faces five islands farther out to sea. Fresh oysters with crispy onion, garlic, and chili are a highlight on the Thai menu, as is the section of meals for two to share. Along with your meal you can also book a tour of the islands. $ *Average main: B550* ✉ *Five Islands Resort, Taling Nam* ☎ *077/415359* ⊕ *www.thefiveislands.com.*

MAE NAM

$$ ✗ **Angela's Bakery & Café.** On the main road running through Mae Nam,
CAFÉ Angela's serves salads and sandwiches, both traditional and inventive. The "Hot Bandana" is a tasty vegetarian sandwich baked inside a bread bowl and wrapped in a bandana. Entrées represent Samui's British influence: bangers and mash, fish and chips, and the like. In addition, Angela's sells more than 40 desserts, 20 types of bread, several flavors of muffins, and a variety of imported meats and cheeses, just in case you were looking for some picnic goodies. $ *Average main: B60* ✉ *64/29 Samui Ring Rd., Mae Nam Beach* ☎ *077/427396* ▭ *No credit cards.*

$ ✕ **Bang Po Seafood.** Mere feet away from lapping waves, this shack
SEAFOOD serves up the freshest seafood at the best of prices. The jarringly purple
baby octopus soup and the sour curry with whole fish are two great
options. Price-conscious sushi fans will be in love with the sea-urchin
salad; $3 gets you more *uni* than one person can possibly eat. $ *Average main: B100* ✉ *56/4 Moo 6, Mae Nam Beach* ☎ *077/420010* ▭ *No credit cards.*

$ ✕ **Kohseng.** This two-story seafood restaurant has been feeding Mae
SEAFOOD Nam residents for decades. The interior is quite simple, with lots of
dark wood. Don't be intimidated by the local crowd—menus are in both
Thai and English, though the staff's English is a bit rough around the
edges. The most famous dish, stir-fried crab with black pepper, is highly
recommended. And prices are low, even by Koh Samui standards. $ *Average main: B80* ✉ *95 Soi Kohseng, Mae Nam Beach* ☎ *077/425365* ▭ *No credit cards.*

$ ✕ **Twin Restaurant.** Run by friendly twin sisters, Twin Restaurant serves
THAI both Thai and Western food from breakfast to dinner. Located on the
main road, it's very easy to find. The open-air restaurant is small, with
only nine tables. You can peek into the restaurant's clean kitchen where
the duo prepares tasty, inexpensive dishes like curry soup, and more
extravagant fare, like steaks. $ *Average main: B90* ✉ *237 Samui Ring Rd., Mae Nam Beach* ☎ *077/247037* ▭ *No credit cards.*

$ ✕ **Whan Tok.** Perched on the water, this family-owned joint is filled with
SEAFOOD locals who come for the seafood—the massive prawns are great, and
seafood soups have wonderfully flavorful broths. Finding the place is
half the fun; the sign out front has no writing in English, so if you're
coming by cab, ask someone at your hotel to write down the name in
Thai. The cheap, delicious food is worth the extra effort. $ *Average main: B80* ✉ *37/1 Moo 5, Mae Nam Beach* ☎ *081/597–3171* ▭ *No credit cards.*

BOPHUT

$ ✕ **La Sirene.** For elegant French cooking, try this small bistro on the
FRENCH waterfront. A three-course tasting menu includes such delicacies as
shark with pineapple, along with a salad and dessert. À la carte dishes
include shrimp in cognac sauce and mussels in a white-wine cream
sauce. Various Thai selections are also served up by the owner, who
moved here from Nice. A few tables are in the dining room, but the real
delight is to sit on the deck overlooking the boats moored a few yards
offshore. $ *Average main: B150* ✉ *65/1 Bophut Beach* ☎ *077/425301, 081/797–3499.*

$$ ✕ **Ocean 11.** This restaurant's unapologetically Western menu attracts
SEAFOOD Americans and Europeans. Soft-shell crab on arugula and white snap-
per baked in a banana leaf are a refreshing change of pace. It's all about
the atmosphere here: warm, inviting, and right on the beach. If you're
feeling homesick, drop in for a rack of lamb. $ *Average main: B250* ✉ *23 Moo 4, Bophut* ☎ *077/245134* ⊕ *www.o11s.com* ☉ *Closed Mon.*

$$ ✕ **The Pier.** The place is beautifully dressed up and waiting for tourists.
THAI The interior is sleek and black, ideal for sipping cocktails by moonlight.
Seats out by the water feel more restaurant-like, while the indoor scene
is clubbier. The menu here is part Thai, part international. Of the Thai

dishes, catfish salad, wing bean salad, or crispy soft-shell crab are standouts. Modern music sets a nice background for it all. $ *Average main: B250* ⊠ *50 Moo 1, Bophut* ☎ *077/430681* ⊕ *www.thepier-samui.com.*

$
SEAFOOD
× **Starfish and Coffee.** You won't find any starfish on the menu, but there's a great deal more on offer than just coffee. Fresh seafood is prepared in a variety of ways; fish, crab, squid, prawns, and mussels are cooked with garlic and pepper, chili and basil, and a number of other primarily Thai styles. The interior is a funky fusion of Thai and Chinese styles, and there's always cool music playing. Seating is outdoors by the sea or indoors on rattan chairs or floor pillows. $ *Average main: B80* ⊠ *51/7 Moo 1, Bophut* ☎ *077/427201.*

$$
ECLECTIC
× **Villa Daudet.** One of the newer additions to Bophut's dining scene, this French-Thai-Italian restaurant has a solid, continent-hopping menu. *Moules marinières* (mussels with white wine and garlic) are a good option. Villa Daudet also doubles as a bar, adding a bit to the beach's nightlife scene, which still has nothing on nearby Chawaeng. A cozy interior of warm oranges and paintings by the owner himself makes the place feel slightly more upscale than its neighbors. $ *Average main: B200* ⊠ *33/1 Moo 1, Bophut* ☎ *083/643–6656* ⊘ *Closed Mon.*

HAAD CHOENGMON

$$$
INTERNATIONAL
× **Dining on the Rocks.** Arranged on a series of terraces, these tables all have panoramic sea views—arrive before sunset to get the full effect. In addition to entrées, there are a number of small plates that blend Western and Thai flavors, like the iced tom yum gazpacho with oysters. A set menu is the best way to go if you want to get a sense of the chef's ambition and range. There's often live music in the evenings. $ *Average main: B350* ⊠ *9/10 Bay View Bay, Bophut* ☎ *077/245678* ⊕ *www. sixsenses.com.*

WHERE TO STAY

For expanded hotel reviews, visit Fodors.com.

CHAWAENG

$
B&B/INN
▦ **AKWA guesthouse.** Rooms at Australian proprietor Timothy Schwan's guesthouse have giant pop-art paintings on the walls, chairs in the shape of giant hands, and kitschy lamps. **Pros:** hip feel; fun crowd; stunning design. **Cons:** can be noisy; not ideal for families. $ *Rooms from: $34* ⊠ *28/12 Moo 3, Chawaeng Beach Rd., Chawaeng Beach* ☎ *04/660–0551* ⊕ *www.akwaguesthouse.com* ⇄ *5 rooms* ▬ *No credit cards* ⏐⊙⏐ *No meals.*

$$$
RESORT
▦ **Amari Palm Reef Resort.** This luxurious resort faces a beach where the water's too shallow for swimming—which can be somewhat of an advantage, as it keeps the crowds away. **Pros:** local touches to the rooms; lovely views; on the beach. **Cons:** some rooms are across the road. $ *Rooms from: $130* ⊠ *Samui Ring Rd., Chawaeng Beach* ☎ *077/422015, 02/255–4588 in Bangkok* ⊕ *www.amari.com* ⇄ *179 rooms, 8 suites* ⏐⊙⏐ *Breakfast.*

$$$$
RESORT
▦ **Buri Rasa.** One of the many hotels along this happening stretch of Chawaeng Beach, Buri Rasa manages to blend in well with the party aspect of the scene while still managing to feel like a bit of a relaxing

getaway. **Pros:** chill vibe; fun pool; great design. **Cons:** on party stretch of beach; some foot traffic. $ *Rooms from: $188* ✉ *11/2 Moo 2, Chawaeng Beach* ☎ *077/230222* ⊕ *www.burirasa.com* 📞 *32 rooms* ❖ *Breakfast.*

$$$
RESORT
🏨 **Central Samui Beach Resort.** This spacious resort has more amenities than any other resort on Chawaeng Beach. **Pros:** plenty of activities; good for families. **Cons:** may feel big and impersonal; you pay a lot for what you get. $ *Rooms from: $133* ✉ *38/2 Samui Ring Rd., South Chawaeng Beach* ☎ *077/230500* ⊕ *www.centralhotelsresorts.com* 📞 *199 rooms, 9 suites* ❖ *Breakfast.*

$$$
RESORT
🏨 **Imperial Samui.** A landscaped terrace leads directly down to a private beach at this resort on the less crowded southern end of Chawaeng Noi. **Pros:** great views from the pool terrace; two tasty eateries; lots of beach activities. **Cons:** may be too quiet for some people. $ *Rooms from: $136* ✉ *Chawaeng Noi Beach, Chawaeng Noi Beach, Chawaeng* ☎ *077/422020* ⊕ *www.imperialhotels.com* 📞 *141 rooms, 24 suites* ❖ *Breakfast.*

$$
RESORT
🏨 **Iyara Beach Hotel and Plaza.** A getaway for young urbanites who don't want to give up the luxuries of home, this complex includes a maze of boutiques, including Lacoste and Bossini. **Pros:** good deal; close to lots of activities; luxurious rooms. **Cons:** feels a bit hectic; many rooms lack views. $ *Rooms from: $85* ✉ *90/13–16 Chawaeng Beach, Chawaeng Beach* ☎ *077/231629* ⊕ *www.iyarabeachhotelandplaza.com* 📞 *75 rooms* ❖ *Breakfast.*

$$$$
RESORT
🏨 **The Library.** This place is so fun that it's worth a visit for its amusingly hip decor—check out the white figures reading books on the lawn, inviting you to lounge as well. **Pros:** very stylish; cool, young crowd. **Cons:** pricey; not ideal if you're looking for quiet; not suited to families. $ *Rooms from: $341* ✉ *14/1 Moo 2, Chawaeng Beach* ☎ *077/422767* ⊕ *www.thelibrary.name* 📞 *23 rooms* ❖ *Breakfast.*

$$
RESORT
🏨 **Montien House.** Two rows of charming bungalows line the path leading to the beach at this comfortable little resort. **Pros:** cute rooms; inexpensive for what it offers. **Cons:** lacks pizzazz and many creature comforts. $ *Rooms from: $85* ✉ *5 Moo 2, Chawaeng Beach* ☎ *077/422169* ⊕ *www.montienhouse.com* 📞 *57 rooms, 3 suites* ❖ *Breakfast.*

$$$
RESORT
🏨 **Muang Kulaypan Hotel.** This hotel puts a little more emphasis on design than some of its neighbors. **Pros:** interesting decor; sea views from many rooms. **Cons:** expensive rates; can be noisy; standard rooms lack sea views. $ *Rooms from: $130* ✉ *100 Samui Ring Rd., Chawaeng Beach* ☎ *077/230849, 077/230850* 📞 *41 rooms, 1 suite* ❖ *Breakfast.*

$$$$
RESORT
🏨 **Muang Samui Spa Resort.** At this tranquil resort, a meandering garden path with small bridges and stepping stones crosses a flowing, fish-filled stream. **Pros:** different style; well-kept grounds. **Cons:** feels sprawling; expensive. $ *Rooms from: $200* ✉ *13/1 Moo 2, Chawaeng Beach* ☎ *077/429700, 02/553–1008 in Bangkok* ⊕ *www.muangsamui.com* 📞 *53 suites* ❖ *Breakfast.*

$$$$
RESORT
Fodor's Choice
★
🏨 **Poppies.** Dozens of friendly employees are on hand to attend to your every need at this romantic beachfront resort on the quiet southern end of Chawaeng Beach. **Pros:** snappy service; immediate area not too crazy. **Cons:** a little staid; not cheap. $ *Rooms from: $255* ✉ *Samui Ring*

Rd., South Chawaeng Beach ☎ *077/422419* ⊕ *www.poppiessamui.com* ⟿ *24 rooms* ⊙ *No meals.*

LAMAI

$$
RESORT

⌂ **Aloha Resort.** All the rooms at this oceanfront resort have private terraces or balconies that face in the general direction of the beach. **Pros:** ideal for families; reasonable price. **Cons:** some rooms not so nice. $ *Rooms from: $75* ⊠ *128 Moo 3, Lamai* ☎ *077/424014* ⊕ *www. alohasamui.com* ⟿ *74 rooms* ⊙ *No meals.*

$$
RESORT

⌂ **Lamai-Wanta.** These incredibly spartan rooms are kept immaculately clean—not surprising, considering that the owners are a nurse and doctor couple. **Pros:** cool pool; beautiful beach. **Cons:** blah decor; lacks spunk. $ *Rooms from: $77* ⊠ *Central Lamai Beach, Lamai* ☎ *077/424550* ⊕ *www.lamaiwanta.com* ⟿ *40 rooms, 10 bungalows* ⊙ *Breakfast.*

$$$$
RESORT

⌂ **Pavilion.** This pleasant place offers a little respite from the downtown hustle and bustle. **Pros:** quiet; hot tubs in some rooms. **Cons:** some rooms very pricey; not the most modern hotel. $ *Rooms from: $205* ⊠ *124/24 Lamai Beach, Lamai* ☎ *077/424030* ⊕ *www.pavilionsamui. com* ⟿ *70 rooms* ⊙ *Breakfast.*

$$$$
HOTEL

⌂ **Renaissance Koh Samui Resort & Spa.** At the far northern end of Lamai, the Renaissance sits on its own secluded, private beach (two small beaches to be exact). **Pros:** sprawling grounds; high-end feel. **Cons:** isolated location; pricey rates. $ *Rooms from: $159* ⊠ *208/1 North Lamai Beach, Lamai* ☎ *077/429300* ⊕ *www.renaissancehotels.com/ usmbr* ⟿ *45 rooms, 33 suites* ⊙ *No meals.*

BAAN TALING NGAM

$$$
RESORT

⌂ **Le Royal Meridien Baan Taling Ngam.** The name means "home on a beautiful bank," but that doesn't come close to summing up the stunning location of this luxurious hotel. **Pros:** beautiful views; plenty of activities. **Cons:** can't lounge on beach; somewhat isolated. $ *Rooms from: $137* ⊠ *295 Taling Ngam Beach, Baan Taling Ngam* ☎ *077/429100, 02/653–2201 in Bangkok* ⊕ *www.lemeridien.com* ⟿ *40 rooms, 30 villas* ⊙ *No meals.*

MAE NAM AND LAEM YAI

$
RESORT

⌂ **The Florist.** This guesthouse is quite small, but in a cute and cozy way. **Pros:** good bang for your buck; easy beach access. **Cons:** not as comfy as some mega-chains; staff not so attentive. $ *Rooms from: $43* ⊠ *190 Moo 1, Mae Nam Beach* ☎ *077/425671* ⊕ *www.floristresort.com* ⟿ *32 rooms* ⊙ *Breakfast.*

$$$$
RESORT
Fodor's Choice
★

⌂ **Four Seasons Koh Samui.** This is easily one of the most spectacular hotels in the world. **Pros:** ultimate luxury and relaxation; cool room design. **Cons:** might break the bank; golf carts necessary to get around. $ *Rooms from: $785* ⊠ *219 Moo 5, Laem Yai* ☎ *077/243000* ⊕ *www. fourseasons.com/kohsamui* ⟿ *74 villas* ⊙ *No meals.*

$$$$
RESORT

⌂ **Napasai.** The name means "clear sky," and if you book a beachfront room you can enjoy the view of both the sky *and* the sea from your outdoor terrace, from inside your room, or even from your bathtub. **Pros:** great views; super staff. **Cons:** pricey rates; some rooms not as nice as others. $ *Rooms from: $358* ⊠ *Ban Tai Beach, Mae Nam* ☎ *077/429200* ⊕ *www.napasai.com* ⟿ *69 rooms* ⊙ *No meals.*

$$$$ RESORT [icon] **Santiburi Resort and Spa.** The villas on this beachfront estate make you feel as if you're staying at a billionaire's holiday hideaway; accordingly, this is one of the most expensive lodgings on the island. **Pros:** on a private beach; elegant rooms; tasty eateries. **Cons:** not ideal for families. [$] *Rooms from: $273* ✉ *12/12 Samui Ring Rd., Mae Nam Beach* ☎ *077/425031, 02/636–3333 in Bangkok, 800/223–5652 in U.S.* 🌐 *www.santiburi.com* 🛏 *71 villas and suites* 🍴 *No meals.*

BOPHUT

$$$ RESORT [icon] **Absolute Sanctuary.** If you're looking to detox while on vacation, this is the spot—and if you aren't, well, it probably isn't. **Pros:** prime yoga facilities; unique concept. **Cons:** no fun if you're not detoxing; pricey rates. [$] *Rooms from: $147* ✉ *43 Moo 1, Bophut* ☎ *077/601190* 🌐 *www.absolutesanctuary.com* 🛏 *38 rooms* 🍴 *Breakfast.*

$$$$ RESORT [icon] **Anantara Resort Koh Samui.** Anantara captures the essence of Samui: coconut trees dot the grounds, monkey statues and sculptures decorate the interior, and, of course, there's a beautiful beach. **Pros:** decent dining; pretty place. **Cons:** feels quite big; not for young party crowd. [$] *Rooms from: $201* ✉ *101/3 Samui Ring Rd., Bophut Beach* ☎ *077/428300* 🌐 *www.anantara.com* 🛏 *82 room, 24 suites* 🍴 *Breakfast.*

$$$ RESORT [icon] **Bandara Resort and Spa.** Bandara gets high marks for its location on the nicest stretch of Bophut Beach. **Pros:** ideal location; attentive staff. **Cons:** pool not inviting; unexciting room decor. [$] *Rooms from: $160* ✉ *178/2 Moo 1, Bophut* ☎ *077/245795* 🌐 *www.bandararesort.com* 🛏 *151 rooms* 🍴 *No meals.*

$$$$ RESORT [icon] **Bo Phut Resort and Spa.** Not every beach hotel that claims to be a "resort and spa" measures up, which is why the massages, scrubs, and herbal steam therapies here are such a pleasant surprise. **Pros:** spectacular spa; nice restaurant. **Cons:** a bit overpriced; not the most happening location. [$] *Rooms from: $201* ✉ *12/12 Moo 1, Bophut* ☎ *077/245777* 🌐 *www.bophutresort.com* 🛏 *61 rooms* 🍴 *Breakfast.*

$$$ RESORT [icon] **Punnpreeda.** Although it doesn't quite achieve the effortlessly cool vibe it's striving for, Punnpreeda is still a pleasant place to stay. **Pros:** fun atmosphere; convenient shuttle. **Cons:** not ideal for families; not on Koh Samui's hip strip. [$] *Rooms from: $51* ✉ *199 Moo 1, Bang Rak Beach, Bophut* ☎ *077/246333* 🌐 *www.punnpreeda.com* 🛏 *25 rooms* 🍴 *Breakfast.*

$$$$ RESORT [icon] **Zazen.** A minimalist Japanese style makes this hotel a refreshing change of place, especially if you've been in Thailand for a while. **Pros:** on a nice stretch of beach; great atmosphere. **Cons:** expensive rates; not a party destination. [$] *Rooms from: $210* ✉ *177 Moo 1, Bophut* ☎ *077/425085* 🌐 *www.samuizazen.com* 🛏 *35 rooms* 🍴 *No meals.*

CHOENGMON

$$$ RESORT [icon] **Kandaburi.** Vaguely Balinese in design, this classy boutique hotel makes use of dark woods—often as a stunning contrast against stark white or shimmering gold. **Pros:** aesthetically pleasing; pretty beach. **Cons:** most rooms lack beach views; service is indifferent. [$] *Rooms from: $188* ✉ *20 Moo 2, Choengmon* ☎ *077/428888, 077/414424* 🌐 *www.kandaburi.com* 🛏 *183 rooms* 🍴 *Breakfast.*

$$$ RESORT [icon] **Sala Samui.** Bright, nearly all-white rooms open onto private courtyards on one side and curtain-enclosed bathrooms on the other.

4

Pros: lots of privacy; good dining options. **Cons:** pricey rates; beach views could be better. [$] *Rooms from: $177* ✉ *10/9 Moo 5, Bophut* ☎ *077/245888* 🌐 *www.salasamui.com* ⇨ *69 rooms* 🍴 *Breakfast.*

$$ RESORT 🏨 **Samui Honey Cottages.** The cottages at this small, cozy resort on one of the island's quieter beaches have glass sliding doors and peaked roofs, and bathrooms have showers with glass ceilings. **Pros:** well located; welcoming staff. **Cons:** not that special; no real nightlife. [$] *Rooms from: $75* ✉ *24/34 Choengmon Beach, Choengmon* ☎ *077/245032, 077/279093* 🌐 *www.samuihoney.com* ⇨ *19 bungalows, 1 suite* 🍴 *Breakfast.*

$$$$ RESORT Fodor's Choice ★ 🏨 **Six Senses Hideaway Samui.** From the moment that you're introduced to your private butler, you'll realize that this is not just another high-end resort—you're about to embark on an amazing experience. **Pros:** butler service; delicious restaurant; every whim catered to. **Cons:** expensive rates; difficult to navigate sprawling hotel. [$] *Rooms from: $392* ✉ *9/10 Bay View Bay, Choengmon* ☎ *077/245678* 🌐 *www.sixsenses.com* ⇨ *66 villas* 🍴 *Multiple meal plans.*

$$$$ RESORT 🏨 **Tongsai Bay.** The owners of this splendid all-suites resort managed to build it without sacrificing even one of the tropical trees that give the place a refreshing and natural sense of utter seclusion. **Pros:** beautiful exterior and interior. **Cons:** not the best beach for lounging; staff attentiveness is not the best. [$] *Rooms from: $317* ✉ *84 Tongsai Bay, Choengmon* ☎ *077/245480, 077/245544* 🌐 *www.tongsaibay.co.th* ⇨ *83 suites* 🍴 *Breakfast.*

NIGHTLIFE

You'll find the most nighttime action in central Lamai and on Chaweng's Soi Green Mango—a looping street chockablock with beer bars and nightclubs of all sizes.

Ark Bar. Ark Bar is one of Samui's original nightlife venues on the beach. It throws a free barbecue every Wednesday around sunset. ✉ *Chawaeng Beach Rd., Central Chawaeng* ☎ *077/422047, 077/413798* 🌐 *www.ark-bar.com.*

Bauhaus. The sprawling party spot Bauhaus has foam parties on Monday and Friday night. In the dead center of town there's a boxing ring that features muay thai exhibitions during high season and women boxers on weekends. The ring is surrounded by beer bars packed with highly skilled Connect Four players. ✉ *Lamai Beach Rd., Lamai* ☎ *077/233147.*

The Deck. This multilevel, open-air bar has plenty of spots to chill out or watch the crowds below. ✉ *Soi Green Mango* ☎ *077/230897.*

Islander Pub & Restaurant. With 11 televisions broadcasting Thai, Australian, and Malaysian programs, this popular place holds in-house pool competitions and quiz nights. ✉ *Off Soi Green Mango, Central Chawaeng* ☎ *077/230836.*

POD. Several nightclubs are clustered together on Soi Green Mango, the most popular and stylish of which is POD. This is a huge bar and disco that gets pumping after midnight. The staff is friendly and the drinks are relatively cheap. ⊠ *Soi Green Mango, Chawaeng* ☎ *083/692–7911.*

Q Bar Samui. The hottest place to be is Q Bar Samui, an upscale nightclub from the owners of bars of the same name in Bangkok and Singapore. Sexy bartenders pour premium spirits while international DJs spin. It's high up on the hillside to the north of Chawaeng Lake—take a taxi there and back. ⊠ *47/57 Moo 2, Bophut* ☎ *081/956–2742* ⊕ *www.qbarsamui.com.*

Reggae Pub. A must if you're a reggae fan, this longtime favorite with several bars and dance floors has a nonstop party atmosphere. ⊠ *Chawaeng Lakeside Rd., Chawaeng* ☎ *077/422331.*

SPORTS AND THE OUTDOORS

Although many people come to Samui to chill out on the beach, there are dozens of activities, certainly more than one vacation's worth.

Canopy Adventures. You get a bird's-eye view of the jungle by sailing through the air on a zip line. Canopy Adventures will have you zipping between six tree houses on 330 yards of wire strung across the tree canopies. The company also offers fun expeditions to waterfalls. ☎ *077/414150* ⊕ *www.canopyadventuresthailand.com.*

Samui Namuang Travel & Tour. Elephant treks are available through Samui Namuang Travel & Tour. ☎ *077/418680* ⊕ *www.namuangsafarisamui.com.*

GOLF

Santiburi Samui Country Club. Santiburi Resort has a driving range and an 18-hole course at the Santiburi Samui Country Club, which uses the natural terrain of the Samui mountains to create a challenging multilevel golfing experience. You can play nine holes for half the price. ☎ *077/421700 up to 08 in Samui, 02/664–4270 up to 74 in Bangkok* ⊕ *www.santiburi.com.*

SPAS

It wasn't so long ago that the only chance of being pampered on Koh Samui was by indulging in a beach massage. Happily, things are starting to change. The island has a few top-end spas, as well as several in the luxury hotels.

Tamarind Springs. The island's ultimate spa experience is at Tamarind Springs. Many different treatments are available, from hot oil massages to herbal rubs to the "Over the Top" massage package, which lasts 2½ hours. The spa employs the latest treatment methods, including the use of Tibetan singing bowls. The plunge pools, hot tubs, and tearoom are built harmoniously into Tamarind's boulder-strewn hillside. ⊠ *205/7 Thong Takian, Lamai Beach* ☎ *077/424221* ⊕ *www.tamarindretreat.com.*

SIDE TRIPS FROM KOH SAMUI

KOH PHANGAN

12 km (7 miles) by boat north of Koh Samui.

As Koh Samui developed into an international hot spot, travelers looking for a more laid-back scene headed for Koh Phangan. Decades ago, the few wanderers who arrived here stayed in fishermen's houses or slung hammocks on the beach. Investors bought up beach property with plans for sprawling resorts, but before commercial development marred too much the island, the allure of Koh Tao's crystalline waters starting drawing away a lot of the attention.

While Haad Rin boomed as a result of its world-famous Full Moon Party, most of Koh Phangan's smaller beaches continued to develop, but at a much slower pace. For now, most of Koh Phangan remains a destination for backpackers looking for beautiful beaches with budget accommodation and hippies (old-school and nouveau) searching for chilled-out beaches and alternative retreats.

GETTING HERE AND AROUND

The best way to get here is by ferry from Koh Samui, or from Surat Thani via Koh Samui. Boats depart hourly from Surat Thani's Donsak Pier to Na Thon Pier on Koh Samui; the price includes the hour-long bus ride from Surat Thani's airport to the pier. After the 2½-hour voyage to Samui, passengers must disembark and catch a second boat to Koh Phangan's Thong Sala Pier, a 30-minute journey. Seatran boats depart from Koh Samui for Koh Phangan daily at 8 am and 1:30 pm. Return travel from Koh Phangan to Koh Samui is at 10:30 am and 4:30 pm.

If you take a Songserm ferry instead, you won't have to switch boats on Samui; however, Songserm makes the Surat Thani–Koh Samui–Koh Phangan run only once a day, leaving Surat Thani at 8 am and returning from Koh Phangan at 12:30 pm.

There are a number of ways to travel between Koh Phangan and either Koh Samui or Koh Tao—Lomphrayah and Seatran boats are the best options. Boats to and from Koh Tao take 2 to 2½ hours.

SAFETY AND PRECAUTIONS

Koh Phangan has become famous for its full-moon parties and for numerous other parties associated with the moon's waxing and waning. These events attract as many as 10,000 revelers, and the criminal element knows this. Break-ins have become problematic. Thieves assume that you're probably out partying, so don't leave valuables in your room.

The biggest problem is drugs, which are treated very seriously by Thai authorities. There are all-too-frequent stories of travelers who have arrested, either for purchasing or consuming, so expect harsh treatment if you're caught.

Koh Phangan's beaches are popular with travelers looking for a tranquil getaway.

TIMING

The Full Moon Party, probably the biggest draw to the island, happens 13 times a year on Haad Rin East. If you want some peace and quiet, consult your lunar calendar. At other times the island is a tranquil place.

EXPLORING

Haad Rin Town has many good restaurants, shops, and bars. It's densely built up, and not very quiet, but full of fun. The town is sandwiched between the beaches of Haad Rin West and Haad Rin East, home of the Full Moon Party.

Boats from the mainland drop passengers off at the main pier in Thong Sala. It's an uninteresting town, but there are taxis that can shuttle you around the island.

BEACHES

Even though most beaches are now accessible via songthaew pickup trucks, the island's twisting roads make it easier and safer to beach-hop via boat. Don't attempt to travel around Koh Phangan on a motorbike.

If you want to find the beach that most appeals to you, take a longtail boat around the island—the trip takes a full day and stops in many places along the way, including Haad Rin. Close to Haad Rin are Haad Sarikantang, Haad Yuan, and Haad Thien: good choices for those interested in going to the Full Moon Party, but who want to stay on a nicer, more relaxing beach.

If you aren't here for the Full Moon Party, head up the east coast to quieter Haad Thong Nai Pan, or even farther afield. One of the island's most remote beaches—and the most beautiful—is Haad Kuat, which has gorgeous white sand and simple accommodations. Haad Salad and Haad Yao, on the northwest coast, are similarly remote beaches for those looking for relaxation.

Haad Kuat. This isolated beach is definitely one of the better ones on the island. With a quarter mile of fine white sand, Haad Kuat (Bottle Beach) is a sunbather's paradise. There are a number of restaurants where you can grab a meal. The vibe is decidedly young and funky. Get here by songthaew from Thong Sala Pier, or by longtail boat from nearby Thong Nai Pan. It might be more difficult to reach than other beaches, but it's definitely worth the hassle. **Amenties:** food and drink; water sports. **Best for:** partiers.

Haad Rin. If you are looking for the party, then head to Haad Rin Beach. The beach is divided into two parts, Haad Rin West and Haad Rin East, each with its own personality. Haad Rin West has swimmable water, but you needn't settle for this beach when Haad Rin East is only a short walk away. Haad Rin East is a beautiful beach lined with bungalows and bars, although the water isn't nearly as pristine as at the more remote beaches. Once a month, Haad Rin East gets seriously crowded when throngs of young people gather on the beach for an all-night Full Moon Party. **Amenities:** food and drink. **Best for:** partiers; swimming.

Haad Sarikantang. Not far from Haad Rin Beach, the smaller, quieter beach of Haad Sarikantang is the place to head for if you want to be close to the party but still on a quiet beach. Also known as Leela Beach, Haad Sarikantang has picturesque palms, fine white sand, and clear blue water. There are a number of resorts and restaurants surrounding the beach. **Amenities:** food and drink. **Best for:** swimming.

Haad Thien. This small beach, just north of the party beaches at Haad Rin, is an ideal choice for those wanting a bit of relaxation and smaller crowds. The beach has a smattering of resort hotels and a number of good waterfront restaurants. The sand is a fine yellow and the waters are shallow and clear. **Amenities:** food and drink; water sports. **Best for:** swimming.

Haad Thong Nai Pan. On the northern end of the island, Haad Thong Nai Pan is your ideal escape from the madness of the Full Moon Party. The beach sits on a horseshoe bay and is split into two. The northern part is the most beautiful, with stunning golden sands set around crystal blue waters. The seas are usually calm, but when the monsoon rains sweep in the waters can get a little rough. There are a number of guesthouses and mid-range resorts surrounding the beach. Food and drink are available from the nearby restaurants. **Amenities:** food and drink; water sports. **Best for:** swimming.

Haad Yuan. This small, beautiful beach sits between Haad Rin and Haad Thien. Despite being a 10-minute boat ride from Haad Rin, Haad Yuan is worlds away. Extremely quiet most of the month, Haad Yuan is wide and clean, with fine sand and crystal blue waters. A rocky outcrop at one end of the beach is a good backdrop for photos. The swimming is good here, but the seas can get rough at times. **Amenities:** food and drink. **Best for:** swimming.

WHERE TO EAT
Haad Rin has the most restaurants, but you'll find plenty of simple seafood restaurants on other beaches as well.

$ ✕**Lucky Crab Restaurant.** The extensive menu includes entrées from all
SEAFOOD around the world, as if trying to please all the island's international visitors. But the specialty at the Lucky Crab is, of course, grilled seafood, served with 12 different sauces. Select your fish, select your sauce, and then enjoy the breeze from the ceiling fans while you await your tasty food at this fun and friendly eatery. Also worth trying is the sizzling seafood in a hot pan. $ *Average main: B150* ✉ *94/18 Haad Rin W, Haad Rin* ☎ *077/375125, 077/375498* ▭ *No credit cards.*

$ ✕**Nira's Bakery and Restaurant.** As you walk into the restaurant, you'll
CAFÉ be bombarded by the mouthwatering smell of fresh-baked goods. The owner picked up his baking skills while living and working in Germany, and then opened this funky bakery in the mid-1980s, before the island even had electricity. Traditional homemade lasagna, fresh fruit juices, and gourmet sandwiches are a few of the specialties here. $ *Average main: B80* ✉ *130 Central Haad Rin, Haad Rin* ▭ *No credit cards.*

WHERE TO STAY
For expanded hotel reviews, visit Fodors.com.

HAAD RIN

$$ ⌂**Cocohut Resort.** Cocohut Resort is on Haad Sarikantang, a five-
RESORT minute walk from Haad Rin West. **Pros:** good deal; cute quarters. **Cons:** not so scenic; not the best swimming beach; staff attitude a little brusque. $ *Rooms from: $68* ✉ *130/20 Leela Beach, Haad Sarikantang* ☎ *077/375368* ⊕ *www.cocohut.com* ↘ *76 bungalows, 24 rooms.*

$ ⌂**Phangan Bayshore Resort.** This resort is near the action, but away from
RESORT the crowds. **Pros:** close to the party; good value. **Cons:** some rooms need renovations. $ *Rooms from: $55* ✉ *Haad Rin East, Haad Rin* ☎ *077/375227* ⊕ *www.phanganbayshore.com* ↘ *71 rooms* ⦿ *No meals.*

$$$ ⌂**Phangan Buri Resort and Health Spa.** This is the latest multimillion-
RESORT baht, modern hotel development in Haad Rin. **Pros:** feels new; nice views. **Cons:** a bit generic; room decor could be nicer. $ *Rooms from: $170* ✉ *120/1 Moo 6, Haad Rin Nai Beach* ☎ *077/375481* ⊕ *www. phanganburiresort.net* ↘ *106 rooms* ⦿ *Breakfast.*

$ ⌂**Sarikantang.** On Haad Sarikantang, this small resort is a short walk
RESORT from the festive atmosphere at Haad Rin. **Pros:** lots of ocean views; friendly place. **Cons:** could be more central; cheapest rooms not comfortable. $ *Rooms from: $48* ✉ *129/3 Leela Beach, Haad Sarikantang* ☎ *077/375055, 077/375056* ⊕ *www.sarikantang.com* ↘ *47 rooms* ⦿ *Breakfast.*

$ ⌂**Sea View Haad Rin Resort.** These simple wooden huts directly on the
RESORT beach at the "quieter" northern end of Haad Rin are the best deal in the area—for the best location. **Pros:** good deal; extremely low-key vibe. **Cons:** not near the action; some rooms lack air-conditioning. $ *Rooms from: $17* ✉ *134 Haad Rin Nok Beach, Haad Rin* ☎ *077/375160* ⊕ *www.seaviewsunrise.com* ↘ *40 rooms* ▭ *No credit cards* ⦿ *No meals.*

HAAD YUAN

$ RESORT **Barcelona Resort.** For very few baht you get a private cottage with doors on two walls that fold open to reveal a wraparound deck. **Pros:** low price; fun experience. **Cons:** no air-conditioning; few amenities. [$] *Rooms from: $17* ✉ *Haad Yuan* ☎ *077/375113* *25 rooms* 💳 *No credit cards* 🍴 *No meals.*

HAAD THONG NAI PAN

$ RESORT **Dolphin.** These are the perfect beach bungalows, built entirely of wood with shuttered windows and hammocks slung on the decks. **Pros:** lush grounds; cool crowd. **Cons:** not beachfront; few creature comforts. [$] *Rooms from: $17* ✉ *Haad Tong Nai Pan* ☎ *077/445135* *20 rooms* 💳 *No credit cards* 🍴 *No meals.*

$$ RESORT **Panviman Resort.** The big attractions at this friendly resort are its two restaurants: one is a circular dining area that's open to the ocean breezes; the other is a seaside terrace. **Pros:** good for families; shuttle service. **Cons:** high rates; not near interesting nightlife. [$] *Rooms from: $102* ✉ *22/1 Thong Nai Pan Noi Bay, Haad Thong Nai Pan* ☎ *077/445101, 077/445220* 🌐 *www.panviman.com* *72 rooms, 32 cottages* 🍴 *Breakfast.*

$ RESORT **Star Hut Resort.** A friendly and chilled-out resort on Tong Nai Pan, Star Hut has simple wooden huts with rattan walls, thatch roofs, and wraparound decks ideal for enjoying this beautiful and peaceful remote beach. **Pros:** great vibe; cheap rates. **Cons:** some rooms lack air-conditioning; not all huts beachside. [$] *Rooms from: $17* ✉ *Thong Nai Pan Noi Bay, Haad Thong Nai Pan* ☎ *077/445085* *26 rooms* 🍴 *No meals.*

HAAD KUAT

$ RESORT **Smile Bungalows.** Of the guesthouses on Haad Kuat, this one on the western end of the beach is the best. **Pros:** cool views; fun staff. **Cons:** no air-conditioning; no electricity during the day; lacking amenities. [$] *Rooms from: $15* ✉ *Haad Kuat* ☎ *085/429–4995* 🌐 *www.smilebungalows.com* *25 rooms* 💳 *No credit cards* 🍴 *No meals.*

NIGHTLIFE

Haad Rin East is lined with bars and clubs—music pumps and drinks pour from dusk until dawn, seven days a week, 365 days a year. All this culminates in a huge beach party with tens of thousands of revelers every full moon (or the night after, if the full moon lands on a major Buddhist holiday). Check out 🌐 *www.fullmoonparty-thailand.com* for details.

KOH TAO

47 km (29 miles) by boat north of Koh Phangan.

Just a few decades ago, the tiny island of Koh Tao could have been compared to the one inhabited by Robinson Crusoe: no electricity, no running water, no modern amenities of any kind. Today there are tattoo parlors, discos, and a few 7-Elevens. Dozens of small lodgings offer everything from basic bungalows to luxurious lodgings.

The peace and quiet has disappeared from the main beaches, but the primary reason to come here is still the underwater world. **TIP→ Koh Tao is an excellent place to get your scuba certification.** Many operators don't have pools, so the initial dives must be done in the shallow, crystal-clear ocean water. Advanced divers will appreciate the great visibility, decent amount of coral, and exotic and plentiful marine life.

GETTING HERE AND AROUND

Getting to Koh Tao is easy—it's on the scheduled ferry routes out of Koh Phangan and Koh Samui, and several boats a day make the trip from Chumphon on the mainland. Catamarans take 1½ hours, high-speed Seatran vessels take two hours, and regular ferry service takes six.

Lomprayah Catamaran has 1¾-hour trips between Koh Samui and Koh Tao for B500 twice daily, at 7 am and 5 pm. In addition, speedboats leave at 8:30 am from Bophut Pier on the north side of Koh Samui, taking snorkelers on day trips to the island and its neighbor, Koh Nang Yuan.

Contacts Lomprayah High Speed Catermaran ⊠ *Koh Phangan* ⊕ *www.lomprayah.com.*

SAFETY AND PRECAUTIONS

Koh Tao is safe. It is mainly a diver's destination, the vibe is reasonably relaxed, and there's little crime.

TIMING

Koh Tao is a year-round destination, but is at its best in the drier months between November and March. Diving activities can be disrupted in the wetter months of September and October, so steer clear if you want good visibility.

EXPLORING KOH TAO

At high tide the three small islands of Koh Nang Yuan sit beside each other in an obtuse, triangular pattern, separated by shallow, translucent water. At low tide the receding water exposes two narrow sandbars connecting the outer islands where the bungalows are to the central island, which has a lodge, restaurant, and beach bar. The islands are privately owned by the Koh Nang Yuan Dive Resort, and all visitors who wish to set foot on the island must shell out a B100 fee. Although many visitors opt to pay, many others simply dock offshore to snorkel and dive the gorgeous waters surrounding the islands. The islands are quite close to Koh Tao; you can kayak from Sairee Beach, or hire a longtail to ferry you here (it takes about 15 minutes). ■TIP➔ The islands are quite busy throughout the day, so try to visit early in the morning or late in the afternoon. While you are visiting, take a trip up to the viewpoint on the southern island for some photos to make your friends at home jealous.

BEACHES

Chalok Baan Kao Beach. On the southern shore of Koh Tao, Chalok Baan Kao Beach is the place for peace and quiet. The beach itself does not have the crystal blue seas and golden sands of other beaches in the region, but it has a relaxed vibe and a friendly atmosphere. The waters are reasonable for swimming, and there is a selection of budget accommodations surrounding the beach. **Amenities:** food and drink. **Best for:** solitude; swimming.

Sairee Beach. The island's most popular beach, crescent-shape Sairee Beach has palm trees arching over the aquamarine water as if they are

Divers travel between Koh Tao's islands by longtail boats.

yearning to drink from the sea. Along the thin sliver of golden sand sit rustic, traditional wooden beach huts with bohemian youths lounging in hammocks; novice divers practicing in seaside pools; and European students sipping cocktails at basic beach bars. On the far northern end of the beach a few resorts sit amid manicured landscapes. Sairee Beach faces west, and therefore great for watching the sun set and for kayaking to Koh Nang Yuan. **Amenties:** food and drink; water sports. **Best for:** partiers.

WHERE TO EAT

$$ TAPAS 🍴 **Papa's Tapas.** Warm lighting and relaxing music contribute to the upscale feel of Papa's—the elegance of this restaurant is indicative of Koh Tao's growing popularity and prosperity. Each of the five courses on the set menu is served with a luscious beverage, such as a Japanese plum martini, that complements the food. You can also sample delectable seafood, meat, and vegetarian tapas (like lemon-and-tandoori black tiger prawns or coffee-flavored duck breast with vanilla foam) à la carte. There is also a small hookah lounge where hip patrons lounge on beanbags while puffing on flavored tobaccos and sipping on glasses of absinthe. Reservations are recommended during the high season. [$] *Average main: B120* ✉ *Northern end of beach, next to 7-Eleven, Sairee Beach, Koh Tao* ☎ *077/457020* 💳 *No credit cards.*

WHERE TO STAY

For expanded hotel reviews, visit Fodors.com.

$ RESORT 🏨 **Black Tip Dive Resort and Watersport Center.** Located on Tanote Bay, on Koh Tao's eastern shore, this resort makes a perfect base for snorkeling because of the colorful coral, the interesting fish, and even the small

CLOSE UP

Diving and Snorkeling Responsibly

Decades of visitors' scuba-diving on Thailand's islands and reefs have had far greater negative effects on marine life than any tsunami. All divers needs to be aware of, and consequently minimize, their impact on the environment.

As fascinating as something you see may be, **do not touch anything** if possible, and **never stand on anything other than sand.** Coral is extremely fragile, urchins are as painful as they look, and although sharks may be no threat to divers, you can appreciate the foolishness of grabbing one's tail. Other dangers to both you and the environment are less obvious: eels live within holes in rocks and reef; turtles are reptiles that require air to breathe and even some dive instructors are guilty of "hitching a ride" on them, causing the turtles to expend precious air. Furthermore, **don't feed fish human food**—feeding the fish bread, peas, or even M&Ms may be entertaining, but it rewards more aggressive fish to the detriment of species diversity.

Divers should also **make sure equipment is securely fastened or stored,** so that no items are lost or scrape against coral. Divers should also **maintain level buoyancy** to prevent inadvertent brushes with coral, as well as to save air. Snorkelers who need to remove their masks should pull them down around their necks rather than up on their foreheads. Masks can fall off and quickly sink, and a mask on the forehead is considered a symbol of distress. When snorkeling, you can **minimize underwater pollution by checking your pockets** before jumping into the water. Conscientious divers can clip a stuffsack to their BCDs to pocket random trash they encounter. Lastly, it seems like a no-brainer, but apparently many people need to be reminded: **don't flick cigarette butts into the water.**

Sunscreen is a must anytime you are exposed to Thailand's tropical sun. Snorkeling unprotected is a guaranteed skin disaster (and painful obstacle to the rest of your holiday); however, sunblock, when dissolving into the water from hundreds of visitors each day, is bound to take its toll on the marine environment. You can limit the amount of sunscreen you must slather on by covering your back with a Lycra Rashguard or a short- or long-sleeve shirt while snorkeling.

Follow the credo, "Leave only footprints, take only memories." Try to minimize your impact on this ecosystem in which you are only a visitor.

4

black-tip reef sharks that cruise around at sunset. **Pros:** great for divers; transportation around island easily arranged. **Cons:** far from action; some rooms lack hot water or private bathrooms. [$] *Rooms from: $58* ✉ *40/6 Tanote Bay, Kah Tao* ☎ *077/456867* 🌐 *www.blacktipdiving.com* 🛏 *25 bungalows* 🍴 *No meals.*

$$ RESORT Fodor's Choice ★ 🏨 **Charmchuree Villa.** Whether you opt to stay in one of the uniquely designed tropical villas or in a deluxe room, you'll enjoy a tiny corner of heaven on the private beach at Jansom Bay. **Pros:** private beach; sweeping views. **Cons:** isolated; feels spread out; staff is very lax. [$] *Rooms from: $109* ✉ *30/1 Moo 2, Jansom Bay, Koh Tao* ☎ *077/456393, 077/456394* 🌐 *www.charmchureevilla.com* 🛏 *40 rooms* 🍴 *Breakfast.*

$$$ RESORT 🏨 **Koh Tao Cabana.** On the far northern end of Sairee Beach, this is one of the few boutique resorts on the island. **Pros:** attractive decor; stylish resort. **Cons:** so-so food; some rooms lack easy beach access. [$] *Rooms from: $181* ✉ *16 Moo 1, Baan Hadd Sai Ree, Koh Tao* ☎ *077/456504* 🌐 *www.kohtaocabana.com* ⇨ *33 villas and cottages* 🍴 *Breakfast.*

$$ RESORT 🏨 **Koh Tao Coral Grand Resort.** On the quieter northern end of Sairee Beach, this resort is a great place to get your scuba certification. **Pros:** feels peaceful; lots of amenities. **Cons:** can be noisy; some foot traffic. [$] *Rooms from: $101* ✉ *15/4 Moo 1, Koh Tao* ☎ *077/456431 up to 33* 🌐 *www.kohtaocoral.com* ⇨ *42 rooms* 🍴 *Breakfast.*

PHUKET AND
THE ANDAMAN
COAST

WELCOME TO PHUKET AND THE ANDAMAN COAST

TOP REASONS TO GO

★ **Sunsets at Railay Beach:** The sunsets here are unbeatable, however you choose to view them: floating in a kayak, strolling along the sand, or lounging in a beachfront bungalow.

★ **Kayaking Phang Nga Bay:** Phang Nga Bay's maze of islands is ideal for gliding alongside towering cliffs.

★ **Camping at Koh Similan:** This gorgeous national park has a handful of tents for rent. Hire a longtail boat to do some snorkeling while you're here.

★ **Exploring Koh Phi Phi:** The jewel of Phang Nga Bay cannot be truly appreciated from one beach. Make day trips aboard a longtail boat: Maya Bay is a must-see and quieter Loh Samah Bay is magical.

2 The Andaman Coast.
Krabi has beautiful lime-stone cliffs shooting straight up out of the water that have become popular with rock climbers.

3 Koh Phi Phi. This area suffered severe damage from the 2004 tsunami, but it has by now resumed its status as a prime destina-tion for snorkeling and diving.

1 Koh Phuket. Phuket is the hub of the western coast, with daily flights from Bangkok landing in its air-port and ferries to Koh Phi Phi, Krabi, and the Similan and Surin islands departing from its docks. Though it's got its share of overdevel-opment issues, Phuket has many beautiful beaches.

GETTING ORIENTED

Thailand's western shore fronts the Andaman Sea, where you'll find the islands of Phuket, Koh Phi Phi, Koh Lanta, and various marine parks. The Andaman Coast thrives during dry season, when tourists are drawn here from around the globe to enjoy stunning beaches, dramatic limestone cliffs that rise from the sea, and lush tropical landscapes. The area is also celebrated for restaurants that increas-ingly push the boundaries of Thai cuisine, multifaceted nightlife and shopping, and a huge range of trendy boutique resorts with high-end spa facilities.

5

EATING AND DRINKING WELL IN SOUTHERN THAILAND

Get ready for the south's distinctive flavors. Turmeric, peanuts, and coconut milk are a few ingredients that play larger roles here than they do in the north. And, of course, there's no shortage of delectable fresh seafood.

The freshness of the seafood here cannot be overstated. Spicy seafood salad (pictured above).

Southern Thailand has a larger Muslim population than the rest of the country, and you'll find this halal diversity in southern cuisine, along with Malaysian, Lao, and even Indian influences along the coast. Spiciness is a defining characteristic of southern food, though as in other regions, restaurants that cater to tourists sometimes tone down the chilies (beware: if you ask for something to be very spicy, locals will be glad to challenge you). A meal in the south is all about the experience. Though you'll run into some tourist traps in areas like Phuket, in general you're likely to find the real deal—authentic cuisine at decent prices. It's hard to beat a frosty Chang beer and fresh crab married with a complex curry paste and coconut cream, just steps from the edge of the turquoise Andaman Sea.

SEAFOOD

In the Andaman Coast it's all about abundant seafood varieties. Beachside shacks serve all sorts of aquatic treats, from octopus to crab—and foodies will absolutely love the prices. Imagine a heaping plate of fresh, grilled sea bass for just a few dollars; that same dish stateside would have a couple more zeros attached to it.

GAENG MASSAMAN

A Muslim dish by origin (its name is derived from Musulman, an older version of the word "Muslim"), massaman curry has a distinct flavor that's somewhat reminiscent of Indian cuisine. It's not usually a spicy dish, but peanuts add a big burst of flavor and an even bigger crunch. Coconut milk softens everything, and the result is a soupy and comforting curry. It's made with a variety of meats but rarely fish.

GAENG SOM

Known as sour curry, this dish is usually spicy as well as tart. It's made with fish sauce instead of coconut milk, and the flavor can take some getting used to. It's typically made with fish (*gaeng som pla*) and green vegetables, such as cabbage and beans. Sour curry is runnier than coconut-milk curries—more like a sauce—and tends to acquire a greenish hue from all the vegetables it contains.

KHAO MOK KAI

This simple but delicious chicken-and-rice dish is a Thai version of Indian chicken *biryani,* which means "fried" or "roasted." Chicken—which is usually on the bone—lies under a fragrant mound of rice, which owes its bright yellow color to a liberal amount of turmeric. Though turmeric often shows up in Indian cuisine, this is one of its few cameos in southern Thailand food.

Deep-fried shallots add another element of textural complexity.

BOO PAHT PONG KAREE

Curry-powder crab is not a traditional, soupy curry: whole crab is fried in a mixture of curry powder and other spices. The piquant curry is a perfect counterpoint to the sweet crabmeat. Coconut milk is often used to moisten the mix and moderate the spiciness. You'll find other kinds of seafood prepared this way in the south, but crab is particularly tasty.

PLA

Whole fish such as *garoupa* (grouper) is often on the menu in the south, and is so much more flavorful than fillets. Garlic and chilies are common seasonings, and the skin is usually cooked until it's deliciously crispy. It may be spicy, but whole fish is definitely a treat you don't get too often stateside. You can also find steamed versions and less spicy seasonings like ginger.

Updated by Alexia Amvrazi and Adrian Vrettos

Though it has its share of overdevelopment issues, Phuket has many beautiful beaches and a dazzling variety in restaurants, hotels, activities, and nightlife. Once you leave Phuket, though, the attractions become even more spectacular.

Phuket is the busy hub of the western coast, with daily flights from Bangkok landing in its airport and ferries to scenic but often packed Ko Phi Phi, Krabi, and the dreamy Similan and Surin islands departing daily from its docks. Beyond Phuket, the secrets of this magical coastline begin to reveal itself. Krabi has powdery white sand and magnificent limestone cliffs shooting straight up out of emerald waters that have become popular with all levels of rock-climbing enthusiasts. Railay Beach is especially popular among adventurers who enjoy acrobatics, climbing, and alternative ideologies. Nearby the Phang Nga National Marine Park attracts nature lovers because of its by now world-renowned postcard-perfect locations, such as Koh Phing Kan, known as James Bond Island. Post-tsunami Ko Phi Phi is a prime destination for snorkeling and diving (you may actually see more divers than fish in some waters as it gets incredibly busy in high season), along with being a mainstay of the easygoing backpacker tourist circuit. Koh Lanta has developed its own scene and attracts visitors who like less crowds and more offbeat individuality—as reflected in some of its quirky shops and restaurants; it combines lovely beaches with colorful villages where you will meet interesting locals and expats who differ from those in other parts of the Andaman coast. Ao Nang has become very popular over the years, and numerous resorts have sprung up near its popular beaches and shops to cater to all tastes and budgets.

A note of caution: Don't take the chance of getting on rickety or over-crowded boats. Speedboats can often be hired to travel the ferry routes. Ensure that life jackets are available and that the crew takes safety seriously.

PLANNING

WHEN TO GO

The peak season on the Andaman Coast is November through April. The monsoon season is May through October, during which high seas can make beaches unsafe for swimming (a number of tourist deaths are registered each year in the treacherous monsoon waters) though hotel prices are considerably lower.

GETTING HERE AND AROUND

AIR TRAVEL

There are daily, relatively inexpensive flights from Bangkok to all of the major beach destinations: Surat Thani, Phuket, and Krabi. It is generally less expensive to fly to Phuket and Surat Thani than to other southern airports. There are also some flights from Chiang Mai to the beaches. Thai Airways, Bangkok Airways, and Phuket Air have regular flights, as do the budget carriers Air Asia and Nok Air (⇨ *Air Travel in Travel Smart Thailand*). All the airports in this region are small and much easier to deal with than Bangkok's Suvarnabhumi.

BUS TRAVEL

Buses travel regularly between Bangkok and all major destinations in the Andaman coast. There's also good bus service within the south. Many Bangkok travel agents charge three times the price for bus tickets, and organize a long, exhausting and convoluted trip with various stops to the main bus stations. It's best to visit a Tourism Authority of Thailand office to purchase your tickets, and then get to the bus station under your own steam; you will save both time and money. ⚠ Private buses are less reputable than public buses.

CAR TRAVEL

It's a long and potentially exhausting drive south to Phuket or Krabi (⇨ *Car Travel in Travel Smart Thailand*).

MOTORCYCLE TRAVEL

Cheap and readily available, scooters are probably the easiest hassle free (park anywhere) way to get around and discover all sites and beaches, but think twice before renting one. Accidents are not uncommon on Phuket, Lanta, or Ao Nang, as the Thais tend to speed, some tourists drink and drive, and proper safety equipment is often shunned. If you've never driven a motorcycle before, this is not the time or place to learn. A somewhat safer option could be to hire a tuk-tuk.

SONGTHAEW, TAXI, AND TUK-TUK TRAVEL

Most areas of the south have a variety of motorized taxi services from samlors to tuk-tuks to songthaews. Some "metered" taxis can be found in most of the region now, but they usually don't run their meters, preferring to set a price at the start of the trip. So if you do take one of these make sure to ask for the meter to be on, as it will often be much cheaper.

TRAIN TRAVEL

Bangkok is connected to Sri Racha and Pattaya via one daily train; there are more frequent trains to Hua Hin, Chumphon, and Surat Thani. There are regular express trains to Surat Thani, the closest station to Phuket, which leave Bangkok's Hua Lamphong Station (⇨ *Train Travel in Travel Smart Thailand).* Bus services or flights though are generally considered to be a far better way to get to the Andaman coast.

HEALTH AND SAFETY

Malaria is rare but not unheard of in Thailand's southeast. Health authorities have done a great job controlling mosquitoes around the southern resorts, but you'll still need a good supply of repellent.

Be careful at the beach, as the sun is stronger than you think. Wear a hat and plenty of sunscreen. Protective clothing while diving or snorkeling is a good idea, as accidentally brushing against or stepping on coral can be painful. Keep an eye out for dangerous creatures like jellyfish, especially during the monsoon season, and sea urchins. If you are stung, seek medical attention immediately.

Strong undertows often develop during monsoon season, especially along the west coast. Pay attention to posted warnings and listen if locals tell you not to swim.

Condoms are widely available in southern Thailand; just remember that not all brands are equally reliable.

MONEY MATTERS

Hotel prices in beach areas are generally lower than what you'd pay in Bangkok (Phuket excluded) but higher than in other parts of the country. There are budget bungalows and guesthouses everywhere, though if you haven't booked ahead in high season you may end up in a questionable room with just a humble fan. At the other end of the spectrum are upscale resorts that run more than $1,000-plus a night—though they are some of the most luxurious resorts in the world.

Banks and ATMs are everywhere, and can always be found outside the numerous 7-Eleven stores, but it's still always a good idea to carry some extra cash. Remote islands do not widely accept credit cards, but have many eager currency exchangers. Some places add a small service charge, typically 3%, when you pay with a credit card.

RESTAURANTS

Restaurants of all sorts are available in the beach regions, from exclusive (and usually expensive) resort eateries to wooden shacks that seem like they're about to fall over. Lanta food stalls pop up just before dusk on the beaches, where in the daytime there's only sand and sunbathers. Phuket has a wide range of restaurants, from the fast-food giants of America (with some Thai adaptations on their menus) to beach huts to five-star western-style restaurants, but Ao Nang and Koh Lanta now also have a great many dining spots to choose from.

Prices in the reviews are the average cost of a main course at dinner or, if dinner is not served, at lunch.

HOTELS

There's something for every budget in this region, whether you're looking for the height of luxury or a simple thatch hut on the beach. Many places combine the two experiences by offering pricey luxury bungalows. Rates fluctuate widely—in holiday periods they can more than double. Always double-check your rate when you book.

Prices in the reviews are the lowest cost of a standard double room in high season.

KOH PHUKET

Phuket is one of the region's economic powerhouses—millions of tourists visit the island every year, enjoying the many delights that are offered in this established resort island. Phuket is a modern, vibrant island with more than 6 million annual visitors, a number that is only increasing year-to-year. If you've never been to Phuket, you will likely love it; returning visitors will find a new island that eagerly greets its next wave of tourism.

Koh Phuket is linked to the mainland by a causeway, and the rest of the world by an international airport. Its indented coastline and hilly interior make the island seem larger than its 48-km (30-mile) length and 21-km (13-mile) breadth. Before tourism, Koh Phuket was already making fortunes out of tin mining and rubber plantations. Then backpackers discovered Koh Phuket in the early 1970s. Word quickly spread about its white, sandy beaches and cliff-sheltered coves, its plunging waterfalls and impressive mountains, its cloudless days and fiery sunsets.

This love of Phuket has brought serious problems. Entrepreneurs built massive resorts, first in Patong, then spreading out around the island. Before the tsunami there was no easy way to navigate the island, which was plagued by horrendous traffic and overdevelopment. Some would say Phuket was being loved to death. Now visitors may be taken aback in some parts by ongoing overdevelopment, but there are also places where you can isolate yourself from the rest of the island.

Even though it may seem like every other business here is a tour operator or dive shop or tailor or jeep rental or pub, there's a lot to love about the island. The beaches are still beautiful, and this remains a top destination for snorkeling and diving (with more than 180 registered dive shops). The island offers some of the most exclusive resorts and spas in the world, yet the food, drink, and accommodations are cheap compared to most visitors' home countries (though Phuket is quite expensive by Thai standards). And direct flights to the island make this a convenient getaway.

⚠ When planning your trip, keep in mind that the monsoon season runs from May to October, and swimming on the west side of the coast is not advisable during this time, as the current can be dangerous.

This section starts with Phuket Town, the hub of the island, and is organized counterclockwise from there. It's best to pick one or two choice spots and stick with them. The frazzling travel between destinations can undo any relaxation you enjoyed the previous day.

GETTING HERE AND AROUND
AIR TRAVEL

Although flights to Phuket used to be quite expensive, the emergence of discount airlines has dropped prices dramatically. A flight now costs around B1,500 to B3,000, little more than taking the train and a bus from Bangkok (B500)—but the trip takes just over an hour, rather than a full day. Bangkok Airways and Thai Airways fly between Bangkok and Phuket daily, as do a couple of newer low-cost airlines, including Air Asia and Nok Air. If you're flexible with your dates, you can find some ridiculously cheap fares on Air Asia; book online for the best deals. Keep in mind that planes fill up fast during the high season, and the lowest fares are mostly available if booked weeks or months in advance (⇨ Air Travel in Travel Smart Thailand).

Phuket's airport is at the northern end of the island. All hotels are to the south. Check to see whether yours offers a free shuttle. Taxis meet all incoming flights. Fares are higher than in Bangkok; expect to pay B850 to Patong, Kata, or Karon, or B550 to Phuket Town. On your way back to the airport, you have to book a taxi for a minimum of B600. Many hotels charge B400 to B500 per person for the journey.

There are also frequent minibus and van services to Phuket Town, Patong, Kata, and Karon that cost between B150 and B200. However, it might be worth springing for a cab, as not all van drivers are reputable, and some might try to take you on an extended detour to a friend's shop or restaurant.

BUS TRAVEL

Numerous buses leave from Bangkok's Southern Bus Terminal, generally in the late afternoon and evening. The trip takes from 12 to 14 hours, depending on the bus and road conditions. You'll need to go to either a travel agent or to the bus station to check exact times and purchase tickets in advance, especially for VIP buses. Costs run from B550 for a large 32-seat air-conditioned bus to B1,300 for 24 seat air-conditioned VIP bus. Most long-haul VIP buses travel overnight, but day trips are recommended, as Thailand's highways grow even more dangerous at night.

There are buses from Phuket to almost every major destination in southern Thailand. This includes, but is not limited to: Surat Thani, Krabi, Trang, Hat Yai, Satun, Phang Nga, and the ferry crossing to Koh Samui. You can check departure times at your hotel or the centrally located bus station just east of Montri Road, two blocks north of Phang Nga Road in Phuket Town.

CAR TRAVEL

You can take Highway 4 from Thonburi in Bangkok all the way to the causeway at the north end of Phuket Island, where it turns into Highway 402. It's a long drive, but once you're out of the capital all you have to do is follow the compass due south. Follow Highway 4 to Chumphon, where it jogs west and south and follows the Andaman Sea coast to Phuket Island. Phuket Town is 862 km (517 miles) from Bangkok; bus companies make the trip in 13 to 15 hours.

Though roads on Phuket are badly congested and poorly marked, it can be handy to have a car on the island. All hotels can arrange for car rentals. Look for Avis, Budget, and Hertz at the airport. In town you can find rental cars at various private shops near the Pearl and Metropole hotels, as well as at shops along all the major beaches. Prices will be a little lower than those at the airport, but not by a lot. If you're driving, make sure you pick up at least two or three tourist maps (available at the airport, travel agencies, and most any tourism-related office), as they differ in details.

TAXI, TUK-TUK, AND SONGTHAEW TRAVEL

Taxis are starting to become common on Phuket. Recently there have been a number of metered taxis added to the island's fleet of passenger vehicles. However, these taxis are few in number, and it's often difficult to get the drivers to switch on their meters (as opposed to charging inflated set prices). Tuk-tuks are registered, insured, and plentiful; drivers will be happy to take you to your destination for an absurd price. Be ready to bargain hard or simply walk away. Fares within any one town shouldn't be much more than B50 per trip, but drivers will often demand a flat B100. Keep in mind that you can catch a minivan from the airport to Phuket Town for B100, a distance of 30 km (19 miles).

Motorcycle taxis—you ride on the back, behind the driver—are cheaper than tuk-tuks and taxis, but much more dangerous.

The best and cheapest way of getting between beaches on the island is by songthaew. You catch songthaews in front of the market on Ranong Road or at the bus stops in the beach towns. These are marked on most maps, and locals can help you find them. Prices run from B30 to B50 per trip. They run every half hour from 7 am to 5 pm. If you miss that last songthaew, you may end up spending B400 on a tuk-tuk. ■TIP→ You can sometimes arrange a cut-rate ride on the sly with a hotel taxi driver who's heading your way. If he drives alone, he makes no money. If he takes you for, say, half the normal hotel fare, he gets to keep that, which will probably pay for his dinner.

■TIP→ Some hotels and resorts provide shuttle service to other beaches—check before you shell out your own money for transportation.

TRAIN TRAVEL

Surat Thani, four hours away, is the closest train station to Phuket. From Surat Thani you can take a bus to Phuket. Express trains from Bangkok's Hua Lamphong railway station stop at Surat Thani on their way south. The journey takes 12 hours or so; if you leave Bangkok at 3 pm, you'll arrive at a dark train station in Surat Thani at around 3 am (⇨ *Train Travel in Travel Smart Thailand*).

SAFETY AND PRECAUTIONS

As with any developed resort location, the dangers and annoyances usually involve petty theft. Phuket has its fair share of crime, usually thefts from hotel rooms or pickpockets operating in the entertainment areas. Ensure that your valuables are secured at all times.

Brawls caused by too much liquor and sun can also be a problem. There are many bars and pubs here, and some tend to overindulge. The police do patrol the area, but violence does occasionally break out.

TIMING

Visitors to Phuket can find a new activity every day; you could spend weeks on Phuket and still not do the same thing twice. It has a great tourism infrastructure. Children and families will find plenty to do and see, as will singles and couples. The best time to visit Phuket is during the drier months of November to March, when temperatures and humidity are lower.

VISITOR INFORMATION

As the saying goes, you can't throw a stone in Phuket without hitting a tour operator. Nearly all of them are selling the same package tours and renting the same cars and motorcycles, so feel free to comparison shop and haggle over prices. Common half-day sightseeing tours include visits to Wat Chalong, Rawai Beach, Phromthep Cape, and Khao Rang.

In general, be wary of what tour operators tell you; they are in business to sell you a trip to the beach, not to tell you how to get there on your own. If you feel you have been ripped off, note the offender's name and other info and report him to the local Tourism Authority of Thailand (TAT) office. Also let the manager at your hotel know, so he or she can steer other tourists clear.

ELEPHANT SHOWS

On Phuket there are many opportunities to ride elephants or see them at work. Many were former logging elephants, whose jobs are now to "entertain" tourists. Before forking over your money, examine how the animals are kept and treated, and whether they show signs of abuse, such as sores on their legs from chains. Even well-respected businesses have been accused of mistreating elephants. If you believe chaining an elephant to a concrete slab in a park or putting him on stage in a show is wrong, then don't pay to see or ride him. Better yet, write a letter to the establishment and the Tourism Authority of Thailand.

Contacts Thailand Divers. Day trips by boat, snorkeling and a broad range of diving courses are offered by this well-organized, friendly and highly professional agency. ⊠ *198/12, Rat-U-Thit Rd., Patong Beach, Patong* ☎ *076/292052* ⊕ *www.thailand-divers.com.* **Dive Asia.** Located on Kata Beach, Dive Asia is a certified PADI instructor and operator that's been in business for more than 20 years. ☎ *076/330598* ⊕ *www.diveasia.com.* **John Gray's Sea Canoe.** This outfit is known internationally for ecotourism trips, including awesome canoeing through Phang Nga Bay. Look for their flyers at travel agencies. ☎ *076/254505 to 7* ⊕ *www.seacanoejohngray.com.* **Tourism Authority of Thailand.** The efficient TAT in Phuket Town provides up-to-date maps, CDs, and brochures, as well as thorough information about local excursions. ⊠ *73–75 Phuket Rd., Amphoe Muang, Phuket Town* ☎ *076/212213* ⊕ *www.tourismthailand.org.*

PHUKET TOWN

862 km (539 miles) south of Bangkok.

Though few tourists linger here, Phuket Town, the provincial capital, is one of the more culturally interesting places on the island. About one-third of the island's population lives here, and the town is an intriguing mix of old Sino-Portuguese architecture and the influences of the Chinese, Muslims, and Thais that inhabit it. The old Chinese quarter along Talang Street is especially good for a stroll, as its history has not yet been replaced by modern concrete and tile. And this same area has a variety of antiques shops, art studios, and trendy cafés.

GETTING HERE AND AROUND

Phuket Town is in the center of the island. Taxis, tuk-tuks, motorcycles, and local buses will take you from here to the surrounding beaches and to the airport. Expect to pay approximately B550 to travel from the town to the airport or Patong via taxi—a little more to most other southern beaches and a little less to more northern beaches. The price will depend on your negotiation techniques. The best place to pick up transport is at the bus station in the center of town. Ranong Road also has a songthaew terminal, where minibuses depart for the most popular beaches every half hour. The fare is B30 to B100.

EXPLORING PHUKET TOWN

Phuket Town is a nice place to visit for half a day or so, but there's no need to plan on a long visit. Besides Talang, the major thoroughfares are Ratsada, Phuket, and Ranong roads. Ratsada connects Phuket Road (where you'll find the Tourism Authority of Thailand office) to Ranong Road, where there's an aromatic local market filled with fruits, vegetables, spices, and meats.

TOP ATTRACTIONS

Khao Rang. If you want to get your bearings, there's a fine view of Phuket Town, the island's interior and even the 45-meter-high Big Buddha, from atop Khao Rang, a hill northwest of town. It can be a tricky drive—you'll need to watch carefully for street signs, as many aren't marked or are covered by foliage, but it's worth it if you want to get a fresh perspective. From the town's center, take either Ranong or Thalang Road west and turn north on Kho Sim Bi Road. Follow the winding, ascending forested road. There are a few restaurants and a picnic area once you reach the top, where you can relax and soak in the views.

FAMILY **Phuket Thai Village & Orchid Garden.** About 5 km (3 miles) north of Phuket Town is the Phuket Thai Village & Orchid Garden, offering gardens and cultural shows. A 500-seat amphitheater presents various aspects of southern culture. Here you can see classical dance, shadow puppet shows, muay thai exhibitions, sword fighting, and an "elephants-at-work" show. It is the best place to be introduced to the more traditional aspects of Thai living, which are not so apparent to most who travel to the region nowadays. ⊠ *Thepkasati Rd.* ☎ *076/214860, 076/214861* ⊕ *www.phuketthaivillage.com* ☎ *B400 entry, B600 for show and lunch or dinner* ☉ *Shows at 11–noon and 5:30–6:30* ☉ *Restaurant closes at 10 pm.*

Thalang National Museum. The National Museum, opposite the Heroine's Monument, has an engaging exhibition of the island's culture and history, including its encounter with the Burmese and their defeat by the island's two heroines. ⊠ *12 km (7 miles) north of Phuket Town, Srisoonthorn* ☎ *076/311426* ☎ *B100* ☉ *Daily 9–4 except holidays.*

Wat Chalong. South of Phuket Town, not far from Chalong Bay, you'll find Wat Chalong, the largest and most famous of Phuket's Buddhist temples. It enshrines gilt statues of two revered monks who helped quell an 1876 Chinese rebellion. They're wrapped in brilliant saffron robes. Wats are generally open during daylight hours, and you can show up at 5 pm to see the resident monks pray. You can take a taxi, tuk-tuk, or motorcycle here from town.

WORTH NOTING

Heroines Monument. Several miles north of Phuket Town, dominating a major crossroads, is the Heroines Monument, a tribute to a pair of women who rallied the locals and repelled Burmese invaders in 1785. At the time, Phuket was without a leader after the governor's death and the Burmese tried to capitalize on this moment of weakness. The governor's wife and her sister persuaded all the town women to dress as men and pretend to bear arms against the Burmese. They didn't really fight, but the Burmese believed them to be a powerful army, so they retreated. The people of Phuket hold these two women in great esteem. Some stories differ, however, having the two women actually fighting. ✉ *12 km (7 miles) north of Phuket Town.*

WHERE TO EAT

$ CAFÉ 🍴 **Chino Café Gallery.** Coffee lovers will immediately yearn for a cup upon entering, as the air carries the smell of freshly ground espresso. The loveliest aspect of this café is its natural wood decor, which gives it a new-age trendy aesthetic. The café gallery also sells nice souvenirs, notebooks and postcards made with natural materials. [$] *Average main: $115* ✉ *4 Talang Rd., Taladyai Muang* ☎ *081/979–6190* 🌐 *www.facebook.com/ChinoCafeGallery* 💳 *No credit cards.*

$ THAI **Fodor's Choice** ★ 🍴 **Kopitiam by Wilai.** The walls of this unique restaurant-café in the heart of the architecturally quaint Sino-Portuguese district are lined with vintage black-and-white images of Phuket, which pretty much reflect the kind of food served up here—old school Thai/Chinese fare. Signiture dishes are inspired by secret recipes of owner Wiwan's mother (who owns the also popular Wilai restaurant nearby) and grandmother, and often include Chinese medicinal ingredients from her uncle's herbal shop next door. Try *bak kut teh,* a pungent shiitake mushroom and pork soup, and *mee sua pad,* noodles with seafood and spices, as well as the crispy noodle and egg salad. Iced teas like Butterfly Pea Flower and lime are especially good for cooling your insides on a hot day, while a variety of smoothies and good coffee made in a cloth bag are also worth a try. ■ **TIP→ For a delicious snack, buy some of the creamy homemade pepper cookies or crunchy caramel peanuts to take with you.** [$] *Average main: B145* ✉ *18 Thalang Rd.* ☎ *083/606–9776* 🕘 *11 am–10 pm* 🕘 *Closed Sun.*

$ INDIAN 🍴 **Khanasutra, A Taste of India.** This restaurant's name is not making false promises—the Sikh owner and Indian chef turn out flavorful, authentic Indian cuisine. The fish tikka is recommended. Part of the unique decor is a bedouin-style tent, where you can enjoy a few cocktails after dinner. The staff, or more accurately the owner, makes the dining experience a memorable one. [$] *Average main: B270* ✉ *18–20 Takua Pa Rd., Tambol Thalad Nuea* ☎ *081/894–0794, 076/256192* 💳 *No credit cards* 🕘 *Closed Tues. Sun. dinner only. Closed daily 3–6.*

$ CAFÉ 🍴 **Kopi de Phuket.** For a good cup of coffee, try this artsy store, which sells funky designer souvenirs and serves traditional Thai food and international snacks, sandwiches, desserts, and shakes. It's across from the Honda Shop/Nai Yao Restaurant. It opens daily at 9:30. [$] *Average*

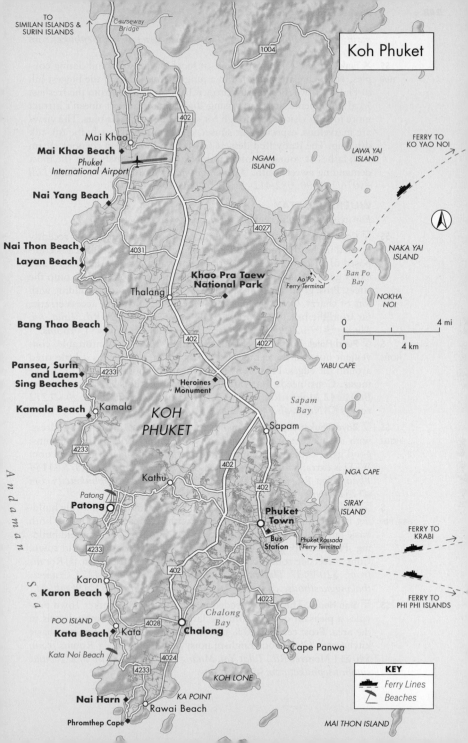

Koh Phuket

TO SIMILAN ISLANDS & SURIN ISLANDS

Causeway Bridge

1004

FERRY TO KO YAO NOI

Mai Khao

Mai Khao Beach
Phuket International Airport

NGAM ISLAND

LAWA YAI ISLAND

Nai Yang Beach

402

4027

Nai Thon Beach
Layan Beach

4031

NAKA YAI ISLAND

Khao Pra Taew National Park

Thalang

Ao Po Ferry Terminal

Ban Po Bay

NOKHA NOI

Bang Thao Beach

402

4027

0   4 mi
0   4 km

YABU CAPE

Pansea, Surin and Laem Sing Beaches

4233

Heroines Monument

Sapam Bay

Kamala Beach   Kamala

KOH PHUKET

Sapam

4233

NGA CAPE

Kathu

402

SIRAY ISLAND

Patong
Patong

402

Phuket Town

Bus Station

Phuket Rassada Ferry Terminal

FERRY TO KRABI

Karon

Karon Beach

402

4023

Chalong Bay

FERRY TO PHI PHI ISLANDS

POO ISLAND

Kata Beach   Kata

4028

Chalong

Kata Noi Beach

4024

KOH LONE

Cape Panwa

4233

Nai Harn

KA POINT

Rawai Beach

Phromthep Cape

MAI THON ISLAND

A n d a m a n   S e a

KEY

🚢 *Ferry Lines*
⚓ *Beaches*

main: B143 ✉ *Phuket Rd.* ☎ *076/212225* 🌐 *www.kopidephuket.com* 💳 *No credit cards.*

$$ THAI 🍴 **Tunk-ka Cafe.** A favorite haunt of local businessfolk and dating couples, Tunk-ka Cafe is nestled in a jungle setting atop of the biggest hill of Phuket Town. Serving up proper Thai food made from the freshest local ingredients, it is surprising that this restaurant doesn't attract more foreign visitors, although for some that may be a plus. The views are marvelous, especially at sunset, and more than justify the tuk-tuk drive up. The Ruby Red dessert (red water chestnut in coconut cream with lashes of young coconut and jack fruit) will satisfy even the most demanding sweet tooth. [$] *Average main: B180* ✉ *Top of Rang Hill* ☎ *076/211500, 082/412–2131* 🕒 *Daily 10–10.*

WHERE TO STAY

For expanded hotel reviews, visit Fodors.com.

$$ B&B/INN 🏨 **Casa Blanca.** The best among a string of boutique B&Bs recently opened in the charming Sino-Portuguese district, Casa Blanca is composed of 17 tasteful rooms with cream walls and wooden floors, and either garden courtyard views or a small balcony looking out onto the street. **Pros:** good location; small swimming pool; historic building with lots of charm. **Cons:** breakfast not included; hot water access erratic; far from the beach. [$] *Rooms from: $85* ✉ *26 Phuket Rd., Talat Yai, Muang* ☎ *076/219019* 🌐 *www.casablancaphuket.com* 🛏 *17 rooms.*

$ HOTEL 🏨 **Pearl Hotel.** For a less expensive option, this is a comfortable, convenient hotel in the center of Phuket Town, though it's a little tired around the edges. **Pros:** convenient location; shuttle service; great live music. **Cons:** needs renovation; basic; can be noisy. [$] *Rooms from: B60* ✉ *42 Montri Rd.* ☎ *076/211044* 🌐 *www.pearlhotel.co.th* 🛏 *212 rooms* 🍽 *No meals.*

$$ HOTEL 🏨 **Royal Phuket City Hotel.** This is arguably Phuket Town's best address, with rooms that are spacious and contemporary. **Pros:** large rooms; good gym; conference center. **Cons:** some rooms lack views; in-room Wi-Fi is extra; a little short on personality. [$] *Rooms from: $75* ✉ *154 Phang Nga Rd., Phuket* ☎ *076/233333* 🌐 *www.royalphuketcity.com* 🛏 *251 rooms.*

$ B&B/INN 🏨 **Thalang 37 Guesthouse.** This inexpensive guesthouse in a lovely building is becoming ever more popular with backpackers, offering both basic fan-cooled rooms and some air-conditioned ones in an old building. **Pros:** cheap; good views from roof, good location in old town. **Cons:** streetside rooms can be noisy; clean but a little worn. [$] *Rooms from: $20* ✉ *37 Thalang Rd., Thalad Yai* ☎ *076/214225* 🌐 *www.thalangguesthouse.com* 🛏 *13 rooms* 💳 *No credit cards* 🍽 *Breakfast.*

$$ 🏨 **Sino House.** This much-needed recent addition to Phuket Town provides a pleasant option from the larger, often less charming hotels in the area. **Pros:** central; 50% discount for the spa for all guests; basic kitchenette. **Cons:** poor English; noisy a/c; dull views. [$] *Rooms from: $40* ✉ *1 Montree Rd., Talat Yai, Muang* ☎ *076/232494 up to 5* 🌐 *www.sinohousephuket.com* 🛏 *57 rooms.*

KHAO PRA TAEW NATIONAL PARK

19 km (12 miles) north of Phuket Town.

GETTING HERE AND AROUND

You can take a taxi, tuk-tuk, or motorcycle here from any of the island's beaches or from Phuket Town. The cost depends on distance—a taxi from Phuket Town would be about B400, a tuk-tuk a little more. If you're driving, take Highway 4027, watch the signs, and turn west toward Bang Pae Waterfall and the Gibbon Rehabilitation Center.

EXPLORING KHAO PRA TAEW NATIONAL PARK

Thailand's islands have several national parks, and this one is home to Phuket's last remaining virgin forest and populations of endangered animals. The park has two easily accessible waterfalls. The Gibbon Center, which works to protect the primates and educate visitors about them, is part of the park (⇨ *The Gibbon Rehabilitation Project*).

You'll have to pay the standard foreigner's fee to enter the park: B200 (Thais pay B40). To access **Tonsai Waterfall** on the other side of the park, follow the signs and turn east off Highway 402. Here you can find two trails (600 meters and 2 km [1 mile]), through rich tropical evergreen forest. Expect buckets of rain in the monsoon season. Gibbons, civets, macaques, mouse deer, wild boar, lemurs, and loris live in the park, but spotting one would be a rare and impressive feat.

The park advertises the good deeds of the Gibbon Center, and indeed it's a worthy cause. (What they don't tell you is that the center, which sits near the parking lot at Bang Pae, receives none of your entrance fee.) After visiting the center, follow the paved trail along the waterfall. It's a relatively easy hike, quite lush in the rainy season. Both park entrances have bathrooms, parking lots, and food stalls. If you plan to visit both waterfalls, make sure you get entrance tickets at your first stop—they're good for both sites.

MAI KHAO BEACH

37 km (23 miles) northwest of Phuket Town.

Mai Khao Beach. This is Phuket's northernmost beach, still a haven for Leatherback turtles that lay their eggs here between November and February. It's an increasingly rare event, but one new nest was found less than two weeks after the tsunami hit. You can pop to the Marriott Resort for a bite at their beach club, or visit the next-door Sirinath Marine National Park (established to protect the turtles) here. Mai Khao connects with Nai Yang Beach to form Phuket's longest stretch of sand, and is ideal for long walks or a jog. ⚠ Dangerous to swim during the monsoons. **Amenities:** food and drink. **Best for:** solitude; sunset; walking.

WHERE TO STAY

For expanded hotel reviews, visit Fodors.com.

CLOSE UP

The Gibbon Rehabilitation Project

Just inside Khao Pra Taew National Park, between a hillside jungle and a gurgling stream, dozens of gibbons swing from branch to branch, filling the forest with boisterous hooting.

It seems like a happy sign of jungle life, but something is wrong with this picture. These animals are not roaming around free; instead, they live in cages near the park entrance as part of the Gibbon Rehabilitation Project. Most of these small apes were poached from jungles around Thailand and kept as pets or zoo and bar amusements. They were forced to perform shows, do tricks, drink beer, or get their pictures taken with tourists before they were rescued by this project. As a branch of the Wild Animal Rescue Foundation of Thailand, the center aims to rehabilitate the gibbons in their natural habitat, with the intention of releasing the animals into the wild (though some animals that were abused will never be able to live freely again).

The center holds more than 60 gibbons. They're kept in large cages, away from visitors. The idea is to purge them of their familiarity with people, although visitors can hear them in the distance and glimpse their playful leaps through the trees. All gibbons are named, and their life stories are posted at the center for tourists to read: Lamut and Pai Mei were working as tourist attractions at Patong Beach before their rescue. A baby, called Bam-Bam, was found in a cardboard box at a roadside. Saul, a young blonde male, is missing a patch of fur, which researchers think could be the result of bullets that grazed him when his mother was shot.

When new gibbons arrive at the center they get a complete medical checkup, including tests for HIV, hepatitis, and tuberculosis. It costs $700 a year to treat, feed, and house each animal, and although the center sits within the national park, it receives none of the $5 entrance fee. In fact, the center receives no funding from the Thai government—it survives on donations alone. For B1,500, the price of a good night out in Patong, visitors can "adopt" a gibbon for a year. If you're unable to make it out to the center, the website of the Gibbon Rehabilitation Project (🌐 *www.gibbonproject.org*) has information on how to adopt a gibbon or make a donation.

—Karen Coates

$$$$ RESORT Fodor's Choice ★ **J. W. Marriott Resort & Spa.** Wow: this secluded resort offers the longest stretch of sand on the island and has spotlessly clean, luxurious rooms with impeccable classic Thai design. **Pros:** great long and quiet beach; Thai-style rooms; a wide range of amenities. **Cons:** may be too isolated for some; surf sometimes too rough for swimming. [$] *Rooms from: $300* ✉ *231 Moo 3, Mai Khao* ☎ *076/338000* 🌐 *www.marriott.com/HKTJW* ⇆ *265 rooms.*

NAI YANG BEACH

34 km (20 miles) northwest of Phuket Town.

Nai Yang Beach. Really a continuation south of Mai Khao, Nai Yang Beach makes a long stretch of sand good for a jog or swimming in the dry season. Casuarina trees line the gently curving shore offering shade. It's a far quieter beach than most, with a strip of trees and a small string of beachside restaurants and bars, tour guides, tailors, and shops. Fishing boats anchor nearby, making for picture-perfect sunrises and sunsets. **Amenities:** food and drink. **Best for:** snorkling; swimming; sunsets; sunrises. ✉ *Nai Yang Beach Rd., near airport.*

WORD OF MOUTH

"The J. W. Marriott is a beautiful property. Great pools, very lush landscaping, and lots to do. With dozens of torches lit up at night, it is very impressive. Yet, it is isolated and may be best enjoyed with kids. If you are traveling during a school vacation the hotel will be packed with younguns. Most spots are 15+ minutes away. We took taxis for dinner most every night. We had some very good meals and prices were much less then eating at the hotel. Yet, in truth, we much prefer being closer to stores and restaurants."

—tengohambre

GETTING HERE AND AROUND

Nai Yang Beach is accessible from Highway 4027, the main road running through the island. Taxis, tuk-tuks, and motorcycles will take you to and from other parts of the island. ■ **TIP→ Transport is often difficult to find on the road through Nai Yang Beach.** Your hotel may be able to help arrange transportation.

WHERE TO STAY

You can find tasty, fresh seafood at Nai Yang's beachside restaurants.

For expanded hotel reviews, visit Fodors.com.

$$$$ HOTEL FAMILY 🏨 **Indigo Pearl.** Phuket's tin mining history is the inspiration for the Indigo Pearl, and the resort features interesting collectibles from the Na-Rarong family mines, with a design-conscious decor that blends funky postindustrial (concrete features strongly) with a hint of Thai rustic luxury. **Pros:** great breakfast; unique decor; good spa. **Cons:** staff can be unhelpful; some rooms affected by noise from nearby beach bar; lots of mosquitos. [$] *Rooms from: $315* ✉ *Nai Yang Beach and National Park* ☎ *076/327006, 076/327015* 🌐 *www.indigo-pearl.com* 🛏 *177 rooms.*

NAI THON AND LAYAN BEACHES

30 km (18½ miles) northwest of Phuket Town.

Nai Thon and Layan Beaches. A few miles north of Bang Thao Bay, follow a smaller highway off the main routes (4030 and 4031) along a scenic coastline reminiscent of California's Pacific Coast Highway. These beaches are good for swimming and snorkeling in the dry season. Layan is a wildlife hotspot, as the lake behind the beach attracts lots of wild fowl. Nai Thon is 1 km (½ mile) long and still has few accommodations. **Amenities:** food and drink. **Best for:** snorkeling; swimming; walking.

GETTING HERE AND AROUND

Nai Thon and Layan beaches are easily accessible from all parts of Phuket Island. Taxis, tuk-tuks, and motorcycles will gladly ferry you to and from these quiet beaches.

WHERE TO STAY

For expanded hotel reviews, visit Fodors.com.

$$$$ RESORT 🏨 **Bundarika Villa.** On a quiet, isolated beach, Bundarika has the ideal environment for relaxation; accordingly, the resort has a special focus on wellness for both body and mind. **Pros:** focus on wellness; quiet location; friendly and efficient staff. **Cons:** not suitable for families; pricey in the high season; beach isn't great. [$] *Rooms from: $250* ✉ *89 Moo 6, Layan Beach* ☎ *076/317200 up to 02* 🌐 *www.bundarika.com* 🛏 *20 villas.*

$$$$ RESORT 🏨 **The Pavilions.** Many resorts claim that they're set up so that you never have to leave your villa, but Pavilions really means it. **Pros:** fabulous views from the bar; great amenities; real sense of privacy. **Cons:** a bit isolated; no children under 14 policy. [$] *Rooms from: $350* ✉ *31/1 Moo 6, Cherngtalay, Thalang* ☎ *076/317600, 091/621–4841 in Bangkok* 🌐 *www.pavilions-resorts.com* 🛏 *30 villas.*

$$$$ RESORT 🏨 **Trisara.** Opulence is the standard at the Trisara resort; rooms feature a variety of Thai wooden art pieces, silk throw pillows on the divans, and 32-inch plasma TVs hidden in the walls. **Pros:** beautiful Thai decor; golf course; subtle and professional service. **Cons:** often fully booked; pricey. [$] *Rooms from: $650* ✉ *60/1 Moo 6, Srisoonthorn Rd., Cherngtalay* ☎ *076/310100, 076/310355* 🌐 *www.trisara.com* 🛏 *42 rooms.*

BANG THAO BEACH

22 km (14 miles) northwest of Phuket Town.

GETTING HERE AND AROUND

Bang Thao Beach is accessible from Highway 4027. Taxis, tuk-tuks, and motorcycles can all take you to and from the beach. Getting away from the beach is sometimes a little difficult, but if you wait on the beach road a taxi or another form of transport will materialize eventually. If you get stuck, ask for help at one of the resorts. There's a free shuttle service between the resorts along the shore.

EXPLORING BANG THAO BEACH

Once the site of a tin mine, Bang Thao Beach (a resort area collectively called Laguna Phuket) now glistens with the more precious metals worn by its affluent visitors. Due to the ingenuity of Ho Kwon Ping and his family, this area was built nearly 20 years ago in a spot so damaged from mining that most thought it beyond repair. Now it's recovered enough to support an array of accommodations, eateries, and golf courses set around the lagoons.

The Laguna Beach Resort has been instrumental in showcasing this part of Phuket and has picked up an enviable international reputation. It holds a famous international triathlon each year, and also hosts many other events throughout the year. However, as anywhere on the island, some of the older resorts are showing signs of age and tropical weather damage, despite frequent renovations.

Bang Thao Beach. The beach itself is a long stretch (4 miles) of white sand, with vendors offering a variety of sports equipment rental, inexpensive seafood, beach massages, and cocktails. The beach is good for swimming in the hot season, the lagoon for kayaking anytime. The atmosphere is relaxed, making this a beach well suited to young families. **Amenities:** food and drink; showers; toilets; water sports. **Best for:** sunset; swimming; walking. ✉ *Bang Thao, Soi Ao Bangtao, Cherngtalay.*

WHERE TO EAT

$ INTERNATIONAL 🍴 **Am & Lee's Restaurant.** The British and Thai owners both influence the menu here, with traditional Thai foods being just as tasty as the British pub food-inspired pies, jacket potatoes, stews and sandwiches. The restaurant, which is part of the Baan Puri complex, is especially popular for its friendly service and hearty breakfasts. [$] *Average main: $120* ✉ *69/34 Moo 3, Bang Thao Beach, Phuket* ☎ *081/787–9767* 🌐 *www.am-lee.com.*

$ SEAFOOD 🍴 **Seafood.** The friendly ladies at this popular street-side shanty serve made-to-order seafood, noodles, and stir-fry. Every meal comes with a bowl of aromatic cardamom soup, which can be a great tonic. During the day there are beach deliveries available if you find you don't want to move from your particular spot in the sun. It's safe for foreign bellies, but if you're wary of street food or spicy food, you probably won't be comfortable here. [$] *Average main: B65* ✉ *About 5 km (3 miles) east of resort. Look for small sign on left side of road that reads "Seafood." If you reach a mosque, you've gone too far* 💳 *No credit cards.*

WHERE TO STAY

For expanded hotel reviews, visit Fodors.com.

$$$$ RESORT 🏨 **Allamanda Laguna Phuket.** Unlike the other four resorts in the area, this all-suites Best Western property sits on the lagoon instead of the beach, and therefore offers lower rates; you definitely get more bang for your buck here. **Pros:** good choice of rooms with different amenities; shuttle boat service; relaxing ambience. **Cons:** away from the beach; not ideal for families; can get busy. [$] *Rooms from: $260* ✉ *29 Moo 4, Srisoonthorn Rd., Cherngtalay* ☎ *076/362700* 🌐 *www.allamanda.com* 🛏 *131 suites* 🍽 *No meals.*

$$ RESORT FAMILY 🏨 **Andaman Bangtao Bay Resort.** Don't expect opulence, but this small, friendly, and beautifully situated resort offers clean, comfortable rooms only 20 meters from the beach, with nice en-suite bathrooms, air-conditioning, and satellite TV, details of traditional Thai decor and beachfront patios. **Pros:** nice location; friendly service; good restaurant. **Cons:** beach is not that great; pool very small; a little pricey for what you get. [$] *Rooms from: $60* ✉ *82/9 Moo 3, Bang Thao Beach, Cherngtalay* ☎ *076/270246, 081/599–7889* 🛏 *8 rooms* 🍽 *Breakfast.*

$$$$ RESORT FAMILY Fodor's Choice ★ 🏨 **Banyan Tree Phuket.** Of the quintet of resorts on Laguna Beach, this is the most exclusive—and expensive. **Pros:** peaceful setting; great spa; children's programs. **Cons:** pricey; resort is huge. [$] *Rooms from: $500* ✉ *33 Moo 4, Srisoonthorn Rd., Cherngtalay, Amphur Talang* ☎ *076/372400* 🌐 *www.banyantree.com* 🛏 *123 villas* 🍽 *No meals.*

5

$$$ RESORT FAMILY

[H] **Sunwing Resort and Spa.** Families keep coming back to this resort, as it really has it all for kids of every age, keeping them busy with numerous facilities and well-organized daily activities, baby-sitting services, discos and shows. **Pros:** safe, fun environment for kids; two restaurants have varied, interesting menus; resort shop sells all the essentials. **Cons:** somewhat remote from shops or restaurants; poolside can be chaotic. [$] *Rooms from: $250* ✉ *22 Moo 2 Chuergtalay, Thalang* ☎ *076/314263* 🌐 *www.sunwingphuket.com* ⇨ *283 rooms* 🍴 *Breakfast.*

PANSEA, SURIN, AND LAEM SING BEACHES

21 km (12 miles) northwest of Phuket Town.

GETTING HERE AND AROUND

The beaches are accessible from Highway 4027. Taxis, tuk-tuks, and motorcycles can all take you to and from the beach. A taxi to or from Phuket Town should cost approximately B550 to B700; expect to pay a little more for a tuk-tuk.

EXPLORING PANSEA, SURIN, AND LAEM SING BEACHES

South of Bang Thao is a jagged shoreline with little inlets. Once secluded, these areas are developing quickly with villas, restaurants, high-end resorts, cheap backpacker hotels, and what is becoming the usual Phuket beach development.

Surin Beach is about 550 yards of sand, where you can get a beer and pretty much anything else that you want. There's a public parking lot above the beach, which is literally a garbage dump in the off-season. Construction is ongoing here, though post-tsunami developments have been more measured than in the pre-tsunami years.

Head north a bit and things change. On the spit of land separating these beaches from Bang Thao sit two of the island's most luxurious resorts, though you may never find them without careful sleuthing. An overgrown sign points the way up a small road to the chedi; no sign marks the Amanpuri resort beyond that, from where tiny Pansea beach is accessible.

Laem Sing Beach. This lovely little beach is off the beaten path but well worth the 10-minute trek down a rocky track. This minor inconvenience means that in contrast to the majority of Phuket's beaches, this is quiet and uncluttered. It's just off the winding coastal road between Kamala and Surin. Luckily there are a couple of food stalls, so you don't need to haul refreshments down with you. **Amenities:** food and drink; toilets; parking (B30/$1) **Best for:** solitude; swimming. ✉ *Laem Sing Beach, just off road from Kamala-Surin.*

Surin Beach. This is a peaceful, long stretch of sandy beach that gets busy on weekends as it is popular with local Thais and expatriates. There are grassy areas shaded by pine trees that make good spots to take refuge from the midday sun. ⚠ **Best avoided during the rainy season as the seas can get rough and there are some strong, dangerous curents.** Tasty treats can be bought from local vendors working the beach. **Amenities:** food and drink; toilets. **Best for:** swimming; walking; snorkeling.

✉ *Surin Beach* ✤ *Go through Kamala and continue past Laem Singh Beach. Take sharp left turn down to beach when you reach the three-way junction. It's a 25-min drive north from Patong.*

WHERE TO EAT AND STAY

There are many little restaurants with cheap and tasty Thai and western food along the shore, and just sitting on the beach will bring many offers of beachside food delivery. Menus will be thrust on you and orders delivered to your beach towel in just minutes.

For expanded hotel reviews, visit Fodors.com.

$$$$
RESORT
Fodor's Choice
★

Amanpuri Resort. You'd be hard-pressed to find a more sparklingly dignified hotel in Thailand—nor one quite as expensive (the nightly rate for the largest of the villas is more than $8,000!). **Pros:** private beach; great sunsets; multi-award-winning. **Cons:** staff may not speak much English; service can be apathetic at times. $ *Rooms from: $1000* ✉ *Pansea Beach, Phuket* ☏ *076/324333* ⊕ *www.amanpuri.com* ⇝*40 pavilions, 31 villas* �’⊙❘ *Breakfast.*

$$
B&B/INN

Surin Bay Inn. For cheaper accommodations near Surin Beach (only a few minutes' walk away), try this small hotel. **Pros:** nice restaurant; great rooms for moderate price. **Cons:** not on beach; no elevator; only top-floor rooms have good views. $ *Rooms from: $80* ✉ *106/11 Surin Beach, Surin Beach* ☏ *076/271601* ⊕ *www.surinbayinn.com* ⇝*12 rooms* ❘⊙❘ *Breakfast.*

$$$$
RESORT

The Surin Phuket. Almost completely concealed by a grove of coconut palms, this resort has more than 100 thatch-roof cottages overlooking a quiet beach. **Pros:** great location; private beach. **Cons:** layout a little confusing; long walk (uphill) from the beach to top villas; isolated. $ *Rooms from: $320* ✉ *118 Moo 3, Cherngtalay, Phuket* ☏ *076/621580 up to 82* ⊕ *www.thesurinphuket.com* ⇝*103 chalets* ❘⊙❘ *No meals.*

KAMALA BEACH

18 km (11 miles) west of Phuket Town.

Unlike the more upscale enclaves to the north, Kamala Beach has some reasonably priced accommodations that attract longer stay visitors as is a good launch pad for the rest of the island, as it retains its calm and quiet. The area, a curving strip of coral sand embraced by coconut palms south of Bang Thao, suffered some of the worst destruction on Phuket during the 2004 tsunami and for those interested there are still many local taxi drivers and shop owners who can give personal accounts.

GETTING HERE AND AROUND

You can get here from Phuket Town or Patong Beach—a taxi will cost about B3,500.

EXPLORING KAMALA BEACH

Kamala Beach is quieter and less touristy than neighboring Patong, and attracts a more laid-back crowd. The beach is quite small, but has a distinct feel to it with mangrove trees and blue water.

Kamala Beach. This beach is unremarkable but endearing, particularly to pensioners who return here year after year for the beach's more reserved ambience. Kamala can get cramped during the day and offers numerous accommodation and dining options, but if you're staying, don't expect a lively nightlife. **Amenities:** food and drink. **Best for:** swimming.

WHERE TO STAY

For expanded hotel reviews, visit Fodors.com.

$ B&B/INN 🏨 **PapaCrab Boutique Guesthouse.** This small, friendly, family-run boutique guesthouse is in a quiet spot near the town. **Pros:** excellent price for what is offered; good service; just off the beach. **Cons:** views not great; patchy Wi-Fi; no landline in rooms. [$] *Rooms from: $70* ✉ *93/5 Moo 3, Kamala Beach, Kamala Beach, Kamala Beach* ☎ *084/744–0482* 🌐 *phuketpapacrab.com* 🛏 *10 rooms.*

PATONG

13 km (8 miles) west of Phuket Town.

You'd hardly believe it today, but Patong was once the island's most remote beach, completely cut off by the surrounding mountains and only accessible by boat. In 1959 a highway linked Patong with Phuket Town, and the tranquil beachfront was bought up by developers who knew the beautiful beach wouldn't stay a secret for long. Today, the cat is definitely out of the bag: Patong is a thriving, thronged beach resort community frequented by both Bangkokians, down for a weekend of fun in the sun and international visitors. Patong is a great place for new visitors to Thailand looking for a nice beach with characteristic Thai experiences, like muay thai, street shopping, and authentic Thai food, as well as familiar facilities, like Starbucks, sushi bars, and chain hotels.

GETTING HERE AND AROUND

Every street, hotel, and shop in Patong seems to have a ready team of taxis, tuk-tuks, and motorcycles whose drivers are all more than happy to ferry you around. Just pick your vehicle of choice and bargain hard. Tuk-tuks to Phuket Town should cost approximately B500; to Karon will be B200; and to Kamala is around B300. It can be a little frustrating to get to the beach during morning rush hour, because the road from Phuket Town is often congested.

EXPLORING PATONG

The beach was hit hard by the 2004 tsunami, and anything close to the water was destroyed. The area has fully recovered, however, and as a result of posttsunami redevelopment Patong's beach road has undergone a beautification that includes a mosaic-inlaid sidewalk. You can now stroll along several miles of boutiques, western restaurants and bars, ice-cream parlors, and upscale nightlife venues, interspersed with traditional Thai market stalls selling food, cheap T-shirts, and knock-off goods. Patong has something for travelers of any age or demeanor. Unlike the more upscale enclaves to the north, Kamala Beach has some reasonably priced accommodations that attract longer stay visitors. It's a good launch pad for the rest of the island, as it retains its calm and quiet. The area, a curving strip of coral sand embraced by coconut

The 2004 tsunami hit Patong's beach hard, but today the area is rebuilt and hopping.

palms south of Bang Thao, suffered some of the worst destruction on Phuket during the 2004 tsunami and for those interested there are still many local taxi drivers and shop owners who can give personal accounts.

Patong Beach. Patong Beach itself, which used to be cluttered with beach umbrellas, now has some room for both sunbathing and playing soccer or Frisbee on the beach. Every conceivable beach activity from wakeboarding to jet skiing to parasailing is available. Patong became so popular because of its picture perfect paradisiacal nature, and now its popularity has caused some degradation of the environment, particularly noticeable when the monsoon rains wash the grime off the street and onto the beach. **Amenities:** food and drink; showers; toilets; watersports. **Best for:** partiers; walking; swimming; sunsets. ✉ *Patong Beach, Thaweewong Rd., Phuket.*

WHERE TO EAT

$$$ THAI 🍴 **Baan Rim Pa.** On a large terrace that clings to a cliff at the north end of Patong Beach, this restaurant has some tables set back from the edge, but you'll then miss the gorgeous ocean views. The food is among the best Phuket has to offer. Well-thought-out set menus make ordering simpler for those unfamiliar with Thai food. They've turned down the heat on many favorites, so you may be disappointed if you like spicier fare. The restaurant has a piano bar open Tuesday through Sunday. [$] *Average main: B1450* ✉ *223 Prabaramee Rd., Kalim Beach, Patong* ☎ *076/340789* 🌐 *www.baanrimpa.com* ✍ *Reservations essential.*

$$$$ ITALIAN 🍴 **Da Maurizio.** An Italian bar-ristorante is the last in the trio of Patong's cliff restaurants. Dining is just above a secluded beach. Try pizza,

fettuccine, ravioli, and other Italian traditions, or opt for fresh seafood baked in a wood-burning oven. The restaurant prides itself on its use of exclusively organic ingredients. $ *Average main: B1000* ⊠ *223/2 Kalim Rd., Patong* ☎ *076/344079* ⊕ *www.baanrimpa. com/italian-restaurant* ☖ *Reservations essential.*

$

INTERNATIONAL

✕ **Sam's Steaks & Grill.** In the Holiday Inn Resort, this stylish restaurant serves prime cuts of imported beef prepared with notable French flair. The lively, popular restaurant serves elegantly presented, delectable meals in a calming ambience, away from the madding crowds on Patong's busy streets. $ *Average main: B15* ⊠ *52 Thaweewong Rd.* ☎ *076/370200.*

WHERE TO STAY

For expanded hotel reviews, visit Fodors.com.

$$

HOTEL

📷 **FunDee Boutique Hotel.** In the heart of Patong and close to all the action, the boutique FunDee is a good budget option for this bustling locale. The rooms are large and clean with hints of art-deco styling and the service is superior to what one would expect for this category of hotel. **Pros:** central but quiet location; Wi-Fi; good service. **Cons:** bit of a trek to the beach (10 minutes); only one elevator; no views. $ *Rooms from: $65* ⊠ *232/3–4 Phung Muang Sai Gor Rd., Patong Kathu* ☎ *076/366780* ⊕ *www.fundee.co.th* ⇆ *36 rooms.*

$$$$

RESORT

FAMILY

📷 **Holiday Inn.** This is no ordinary Holiday Inn: this stylish, modern hotel exudes the kind of sophistication that most people would never imagine possible from a Holiday Inn or from Patong in general. **Pros:** central location; children's programs; next to beach. **Cons:** family atmosphere not ideal for everyone; large complex. $ *Rooms from: $190* ⊠ *52 Thaweewong Rd., Patong Beach* ☎ *076/349991 up to 2, 076/370200* ⊕ *www.phuket.holiday-inn.com* ⇆ *405 rooms* ⎮⊚⎮ *Breakfast.*

$$$$

RESORT

📷 **Impiana Resort Patong.** This hotel's chief attraction is its unbeatable location, right in the middle of the city yet facing the beach. **Pros:** great beachfront spa; good restaurant and bar; best location in Patong. **Cons:** busy beach road traffic; check for rooms with a view; beach fills up. $ *Rooms from: $260* ⊠ *41 Taweewong Rd.* ☎ *076/340138* ⊕ *phukethotels.impiana.com.my* ⇆ *68 rooms* ⎮⊚⎮ *No meals.*

$$

RESORT

📷 **Salathai Resort.** A little away from the rough and tumble of Bangla Rd. but only a three-minute stroll from the beach, Salathai Resort boasts a great location and is a solid midrange option in Patong. **Pros:** friendly and efficient staff; nice pool; quiet location for Patong. **Cons:** ground floor rooms lack privacy; no elevator; a little dated. $ *Rooms*

*from: $120 ✉ 10/4 Sawatdirak Rd. ☎ 076/296631 up to 4 ⊕ www.
phuketsalathai.com ⇆ 41 rooms ¶⊙¶ Breakfast.*

NIGHTLIFE

The vast majority of tourists only venture as far as Bang La Road, a
walking street that is more of a carnival atmosphere than something dis-
turbingly sleazy. Children pose for photos with flamboyant and friendly
transvestites; honeymooning couples people-watch from numerous beer
bars along the traffic-free promenade; and everyone else simply strolls
the strip, some stopping to dance or play Connect Four, Jenga, or a
curiously popular nail-hammering game with friendly Thai hostesses.

The Boat Bar Disco & Cabaret. With numerous male staff, two dance
performances every night, and live DJ sessions, this gay-friendly bar
attracts huge crowds for fun, late-night parties. ✉ 125/20 Rath-U-Thit
Rd., Paradise Complex ☎ 076/342206 ⊕ www.boatbar.com.

Thaweewong Rd. Patong has a reputation for its happening nightlife,
and the seedy side of it is easily avoidable. Some of the more tasteful
nightlife venues are on **Thaweewong Road**, including Saxophone, a
relative of the legendary same-named Bangkok jazz and blues bar, and
the neighboring Rock City, which plays hard rock, metallica and other
rock genres. Both bars host live music events every night.

Whitebox Restaurant & Bar. Let's face it, in Patong it can be difficult to
come by a sophisticated spot to enjoy a drink. Whitebox, designed in
a white, contemporary minimalist style, is a restaurant serving fusion
Thai-European food that generally looks better than it tastes, but its
rooftop bar, offering creative cocktails and tapas paired with open sea
views, fits the bill. ✉ 245/7 Prabaramee Rd. ☎ 076/346271.

There are also regularly scheduled muay thai fights at the arena on the
corner of Bang La and Rat-U-Thit Songroipee roads.

KARON BEACH

20 km (12 miles) southwest of Phuket Town.

Just south of Patong lie Karon Beach and its smaller northern counterpart, Karon Noi. Bunches of hotels, restaurants, tailors, dive operators,
and gift shops have sprung up along the main beach Strip to serve the
influx of tourists, though Karon is also home to a small community of
local artists, who live and work in a cluster of huts and galleries.

GETTING HERE AND AROUND

Taxis, tuk-tuks, and motorcycles take you to and from Karon Beach. A
taxi costs about B150 for the 5-km (3-mile) ride to Patong; a tuk-tuk
is about B200.

EXPLORING KARON BEACH

Getting your bearings is easy in Karon. There's a small village just off
the traffic circle to your left as you enter town from Patong. For the
glut of resorts, continue your journey down the beach road. You can
also find quality restaurants bars and cheerful shops, as well as the
beautiful long beach

FAMILY **Dino Park Mini Golf.** The Flintstones-style buildings along the road in central Karon village belong to Dino Park Mini Golf. Street-side are a dinosaur-theme bar and restaurant, but the real fun is inside: 18 holes of miniature golf, featuring a swamp, a lava cave, and a real live Tyrannosaurus Rex (well, the kids will think so!). Afterward, grab a bite at the restaurant and get your orders taken by Fred and Wilma. ✉ *Karon Beach* ☎ *076/330625* 🌐 *www.dinopark.com* 🎫 *B300* 🕑 *Daily 10 am–midnight.*

Karon Beach. It's impossible not to be tempted by this long stretch of white sand and good dry-season swimming (it's great for running year-round). You will find that the beach is more open than most in Phuket—there are no trees covering the beach and precious little shade. The beach is also strewn with a few rocks; however, on the whole, it is a beautiful, clean, and open space that will appeal to those looking to get away from the more frantic pace of Patong. **Amenities:** food and drink; water sports; showers. **Best for:** snorkeling; sunset; swimming; walking.

WHERE TO EAT

$ THAI 🍴 **Lucky Tom's.** At first glance, Lucky Tom's looks like any other ordinary local restaurant in Phuket, but don't judge a book by its cover; there is great seafood and more to be had in this low-key, family-run roadside eatery. Great-value traditional Thai meals keep loyal customers coming back for more. [$] *Average main: $180* ✉ *90 Taina Rd., off Kata Rd., Kata Center, Kata Beach* ☎ *076/330240* 🌐 *luckytoms-phuket.com* 💳 *No credit cards* 🕑 *Daily 8 am–11 pm.*

$$$ ECLECTIC 🍴 **On the Rock.** Built, you guessed it, on a rock overlooking Karon Beach, this restaurant has great views of the water. Seafood is the specialty, but well-made Italian and traditional Thai dishes are also on the menu. It's part of the Marina Cottage hotel. ■ **TIP→ Book a couple days in advance to ensure you get a beachside table.** [$] *Average main: B350* ✉ *47 Karon Rd., south end of Karon Beach* ☎ *076/330625, 076/330493 up to 5* 🌐 *www.marinaphuket.com/restaurants.html* ✍ *Reservations essential.*

WHERE TO STAY

A sprawling Meridien resort is wedged into Karon Noi. If none of the following options tickles your fancy, there are literally dozens upon dozens of others.

For expanded hotel reviews, visit Fodors.com.

$ B&B/INN 🏨 **Fantasy Hill Bungalows.** Standing on a hill between the two beach areas, these well-situated accommodations are great value. **Pros:** garden courtyard; balconies; good location. **Cons:** few amenities; not all rooms have a/c; breakfast is extra. [$] *Rooms from: $33* ✉ *8/1 Karon Rd., Karon Beach, Phuket* ☎ *076/330106* ✉ *fantasyhill@hotmail.com* 🛏 *18 rooms, 6 bungalows* 💳 *No credit cards.*

$$ HOTEL 🏨 **In On the Beach.** This place way at the north end of Karon is literally on the beach. **Pros:** beach location; quiet; nice swimming pool. **Cons:** slightly removed from center of town; ground floor rooms lack some privacy; noisy a/c. [$] *Rooms from: $115* ✉ *Moo 1, Patak Rd.* ☎ *076/398220 to 4* 🌐 *www.karon-inonthebeach.com* 🛏 *30 rooms* 🍽 *Breakfast.*

A Festival for Health and Purity

Phuket's most important festival is its annual Vegetarian Festival, held in late September or early October. Though no one knows the precise details of the event's origins, the most common story is that it started in 1825, when a traveling Chinese opera group fell ill. The Taoist group feared that their illnesses were the result of their failure to pay proper respects to the nine Emperor Gods. After sticking to a strict vegetarian diet to honor these gods, they quickly recovered. This made quite an impression on the local villagers, and the island has celebrated a nine-day festival for good health ever since. Devotees, who wear white, abstain from eating meat, drinking alcohol, and having sex. Along with detoxing the body, the festival is meant to renew the soul—not killing animals for food is supposed to calm and purify the spirit.

The festival involves numerous temple ceremonies, parades, and fireworks. But what most fascinates visitors are the grisly body-piercing rituals. Some devotees become mediums for warrior spirits, going into trances and mutilating their bodies to ward off demons and bring the whole community good luck. These mediums pierce their bodies (tongues and cheeks are popular choices) with all sorts of things from spears to sharpened branches to florescent light bulbs. Supposedly, the presence of the spirits within them keeps them from feeling any pain.

The events are centered on the island's five Chinese temples. Processions are held daily from morning until mid-afternoon. The Tourism Authority of Thailand office in Phuket Town can provide a list of all activities and their locations. Note that you might want to invest in earplugs—it's believed that the louder the fireworks, the more evil spirits they'll scare away.

$$$ RESORT **Le Meridien.** Between Patong and Karon Beach, this sprawling resort has more bars, cafés, and restaurants than in many small towns. **Pros:** large swimming pool; excellent activities; private beach. **Cons:** too big for some; not all rooms have a view. [$] *Rooms from: $250* ✉ *29 Soi Karon Nui, Karon, Muang, Phuket* ☎ *076/370100* 🌐 *www.lemeridienphuketbeachresort.com* *470 rooms* 🍴 *No meals.*

$$$ RESORT **Marina Phuket Resort.** This surprisingly quiet option has its cottages sprawling over a lush hillside that separates Karon from Kata Beach. **Pros:** good location; private beach; free airport shuttle. **Cons:** some rooms lack amenities; pool closes after sunset; no hotel loungers on beach. [$] *Rooms from: $300* ✉ *47 Karon Rd.* ☎ *076/330493 up to 5, 076/330625* 🌐 *www.marinaphuket.com* *89 rooms* 🍴 *No meals.*

$$$ RESORT FAMILY **Moevenpick Resort and Spa.** Live Thai music greets you as you enter an expansive lobby lavishly decorated with Thai art. **Pros:** beachfront location; amazing facilities; close to Karon Town. **Cons:** slight package-tour feel; old structure; large complex. [$] *Rooms from: $300* ✉ *509 Patak Rd., Karon Beach* ☎ *076/396139* 🌐 *www.moevenpick-hotels.com* *175 rooms 159 suites.*

$$$ RESORT FAMILY **Phuket Orchid Resort.** This resort is slightly inland, but the beach is a short walk away, and the lack of a beachfront brings the rates down considerably. **Pros:** interesting design influences including Khmer and Chinese; great pool; budget. **Cons:** not on beach; slightly confused kitschy decor; only partly renovated. [$] *Rooms from: $120* ✉ *34 Luang Pohchuan Rd., Karon Muang, Phuket* ☎ *076/396519* 🌐 *www.katagroup.com* *525 rooms* 🍴 *No meals.*

KATA BEACH

22 km (13 miles) southwest of Phuket Town.

Popular for its stunning white-sand beach with turquoise waters, and especially appealing to families for its serene ambiance, Kata Beach is made up of its southern part, where numerous resorts are located, and its central part, which is a stone's throw from Karon to the north. There's plenty to see and do, if taking in the beautiful landscapes is not enough for you.

GETTING HERE AND AROUND

Taxis, tuk-tuks, and motorcycles all vie for your attention to take you to and from Kata Beach. Expect to pay B400 into Phuket Town or B300 into Patong by taxi, and about B50 more for a tuk-tuk.

EXPLORING KATA BEACH

Walking around Kata is easy—just follow the beach road from north to south. Kata Yai is the main beach and located near the main shopping street of Thai Na. To the south, Kata Noi is almost exclusively taken up with the long and expensive Kata Thani Phuket Beach Resort. This is a public beach (as all beaches in Thailand are), so be sure to exercise your beach rights and soak up some sun on delightfully quiet Kata Noi if you're in the area.

FAMILY **Kata Beach.** Of the three most popular beaches on the west coast of Phuket, this is the calmest of the lot. A shady sidewalk runs the length of the beach. Club Med dominates a large hunk of the beachfront, keeping the development frenzy to the southern end. There's also a committed group of regulars here who surf the small local breaks. This is one of the calmer beach scenes in Phuket, and so is especially good for families. **Amenities:** food and drink; water sports. **Best for:** sunset; surfing; swimming; windsurfing. ✉ *Pakbang Rd., Laem Sai, Kata Beach.*

WORD OF MOUTH

"Kata Beach on Phuket is my idea of an idyllic beach and you will find plenty of nice little boutique hotels within your price range [in October]. For a big night out, Karon and Patong beaches are a quick taxi ride away and offer plenty of wild and crazy options. Kata itself is nice and relaxed by day and has plenty of little bars and restaurants." —shanek

5

WHERE TO STAY

For expanded hotel reviews, visit Fodors.com.

$$$$ RESORT FAMILY 🏨 **Katathani Phuket Beach Resort.** This long, sprawling lodge fronts most of the Kata Noi beach. **Pros:** peaceful beach location; six swimming pools and another four for children; spacious well-kept grounds. **Cons:** large and rather impersonal touch; the food is average; in room Wi-Fi extra charge. [$] *Rooms from: $220* ✉ *14 Kata Noi Rd., Karon, Muang, Phuket* ☎ *076/330124 up to 6* 🌐 *www.katathani.com* 🛏 *479 rooms* 🍴 *No meals.*

$$$ RESORT 🏨 **Sawasdee Village.** The resort, a few minutes' walk from Kata beach, is sprawled out in a spacious garden with four large swimming pools, lush greenery and beautiful stone-carved fountains is a complex of villas and rooms designed and decorated in a Thai -Moroccan style. **Pros:** for extra comfort choose a villa; attentive staff; good dining. **Cons:** 10 minutes from Kata Beach; rooms on the small side; mosquitoes. [$] *Rooms from: $180* ✉ *38 Katekwan Rd., Kata Beach* ☎ *076/330870, 076/330871* 🌐 *www.phuketsawasdee.com* 🛏 *40 rooms.*

$$ HOTEL 🏨 **Villareal Heights.** Owners Phil and Jo have transformed Villareal Heights from a good boutique hotel into an exceptional one, mainly because of the enthusiastic service. **Pros:** great management; top activity advice; nice views from higher floors. **Cons:** pool shared with hotel next door; location a little out of the way; no elevator. [$] *Rooms from: $100* ✉ *214/14 Patak Rd., Suksan Pl., Tambon Karon, Kata Beach* ☎ *086/032–0263* 🌐 *www.villareal-heights.com* 🛏 *19 rooms.*

NAI HARN

18 km (11 miles) southwest of Phuket Town.

Less busy than other nearby beaches and more popular among locals, Nai Harn offers a small but interesting choice of accommodations and nearby attractions, such as Nai Harn lake and viewpoints such as the Phromthem Cape, as well as simple but authentic restaurants.

GETTING HERE AND AROUND

This is the southernmost beach on Phuket. You can get here from Phuket Town or along the coastal road through Kata, Karon, and Patong. Taxis, tuk-tuks, and motocycles will all take you to and from

Nai Harn; a taxi to or from Phuket Town should be about B550, and it costs B800 to get to the airport.

EXPLORING NAI HARN

Nai Harn. South of Kata Beach the road cuts inland across the hills before it drops into yet another beautiful bay, Nai Harn. On the north side of the bay is the gleaming white Royal Meridien Phuket Yacht Club. On the south side is a nice little beach, removed for now from the tailors and cheap restaurants that have sprung up at the entrance to the Royal Meridien.

Phromthep Cape. From the top of the cliff at Phromthep Cape, the southernmost point on Koh Phuket, you're treated to a fantastic, panoramic view of Nai Harn Bay, the coastline, and a few outlying islands. At sunset you can share the view with swarms of others who pour forth from tour buses to view the same sight. If you're driving, arrive early if you want a parking spot. There's a lighthouse atop the point.

WHERE TO EAT

$$ THAI

🍴 **Phromthep Cape Restaurant.** Although it doesn't look like much from the Phromthep Cape parking lot, views from the tables out back are hard to beat. Just slightly down the hill from the lighthouse, this place enjoys unobstructed perspectives of the cape and coastline. Plus, you get lower prices and better views than at most other places on the island that play up their panoramas. The restaurant serves Thai food specializing in fresh seafood and some western fare. [$] *Average main: $180* ✉ *94/6 Moo 6, Rawai Beach, Nai Harn* ☎ *076/288656, 076/288084* 🌐 *www.phuketdir.com/phromthepcaperest.*

WHERE TO STAY

For expanded hotel reviews, visit Fodors.com.

$$$$ HOTEL

🏨 **The Royal Phuket Yacht Club Hotel.** This place used to be home to the annual King's Cup Regatta—now the only yachts here exist as decorative carvings on the walls, but the place is still every inch a luxury destination. **Pros:** modern Thai furnishings; great views; on a lovely beach. **Cons:** isolated location; needs some modernizing. [$] *Rooms from: $250* ✉ *Nai Harn Beach, Phuket 23/3 Moo 1, Vises Rd., Nai Harn* ☎ *076/380200* 🌐 *www.theroyalphuketyachtclub.com* 🛏 *64 rooms, 25 suites.*

CHALONG

11 km (7 miles) south of Phuket Town.

The waters in horseshoe-shape Chalong Bay are usually calm, as the entrance is guarded by Koh Lone and Koh Hae. It's not a scenic stop in itself—it's more of a working port than a beach. The reason to come is to see Wat Chalong. From the jetty you can charter boats or book one-day or half-day trips to Koh Hae, Koh Lone, and other nearby islands for snorkeling, diving, parasailing, and other activities (B750–B1,600). Waterfront businesses survived the tsunami just fine.

GETTING HERE AND AROUND

Chalong Bay is an easy 11-km (7-mile) ride from Phuket Town. Taxis, tuk-tuks, and motorcycles will all take you here.

EXPLORING

Ao Chalong is a wide-open bay that is most frequently used as a jumping off point for surrounding islands. Head for the pier where you can catch ferries to nearby islands. One road takes you from the northern end to the southern end of the bay.

Wat Chalong. Not far from Chalong Bay you can find Wat Chalong, the largest and most famous of Phuket's Buddhist temples. It enshrines gilt statues of two revered monks who helped quell an 1876 Chinese rebellion. They're wrapped in brilliant saffron robes. Wats are generally open during daylight hours, and you can show up at 5 pm to see the resident monks pray.

WHERE TO EAT

$ CAFÉ 🍴 **Sentai Coffee and Restaurant.** With a cozy living room feel, and decor including vintage items such as an antique gramophone and a sewing machine, good freshly ground coffee and delicious desserts, Sentai is the ideal place for an afternoon stopover to recharge your batteries. If you want more than sugar and caffeine, order a traditional Thai dish or a recipe closer to home from their food menu. [$] *Average main: B150* ✉ *36/9 Moo 9, Choafa Rd.* ☎ *081/797–8327.*

$$ ECLECTIC 🍴 **Vset.** For fine dining, look no further: award-winning chef Ronnie Macuja has created a menu based on simplicity and exquisite style, serving picture-perfect and flavorsome western fusion food. The decor is contemporary and welcoming, and the location pleasant. The cognac-flamed lobster bisque with micro greens is a great way to start your feast, followed by an interesting rendition of the catch of the day or the equally popular steak with mushroom cappucino. [$] *Average main: B345* ✉ *By Chalong Pier* ☎ *076/381159.*

THE ANDAMAN COAST

The Andaman Coast stretches from Ranong Province, bordering Myanmar (Burma) to the north, to Satun Province, flanking Malaysia to the south. Along this shore are hundreds of islands and thousands of beaches. Because of their proximity to Phuket, Phang Nga and Krabi provinces are the two most appealing destinations on the Andaman Coast.

Cleanup after the 2004 tsunami was undertaken almost immediately, and thanks to the popularity of this region and the inherent economic value of these beautiful beaches and islands, reconstruction proceeded rapidly. In some instances (Khao Lak, for example) resorts built just before the tsunami were to be rebuilt exactly as they had been. Today there are few signs of the destruction apart from the newish tsunami warning system with corresponding signs. There are a few memorials around the region that are worth visiting, though memories of the tragedy are fading.

5

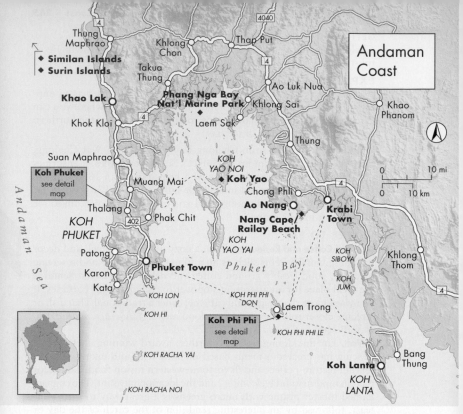

Phang Nga Bay National Park is Phang Nga's most heralded attraction, drawing thousands of day-trippers from Phuket. There are dozens of little islands to explore, as well as offshore caves and startling karst formations rising out of the sea. Most visitors make an obligatory stop at Phing Kan Island, made famous by the James Bond movie *The Man with the Golden Gun*.

The Similan and Surin islands national parks are well known to scuba divers for their crystalline waters and abundant marine life. You can camp or stay in a national park bungalow on either of the islands; no commercial lodging is available in either park. Many divers opt to stay on live-aboard ships departing from Phuket or Khao Lak.

Prior to the tsunami, Khao Lak, the departure point for boats to the Similans, was an up-and-coming beach "town" in its own right. Khao Lak Lamru National Park attracted nature lovers, while the beaches along this coast drew beachgoers who wanted a vibe more tranquil than Phuket has to offer. Although most resorts were destroyed, the "town" was spared and Khao Lak is back to business as usual in 2012. Travelers looking for even greater seclusion head to the Koh Yao Islands, which have cultural tours and homestays that provide insight into southern Thai lifestyles.

DID YOU KNOW?

The limestone formations off Railay Beach—called karsts—are the result of a collision between mainland Asia and India about 30 million years ago, which forced limestone deposits to rise from the ocean floor.

Krabi Province lies to the east of Phuket. Its capital, Krabi Town, sits on the northeastern shore of Phuket Bay. Once a favorite harbor for smugglers bringing in alcohol and tobacco from Malaysia, the town has been transformed into a gateway to the nearby islands. Ao Nang, a short distance from Krabi Town, has evolved into a quaint beach town. Ao Nang and nearby Noppharat Thara exist simply to cater to tourists, with restaurants and shopping for every taste. Ao Nang is a more convenient base of operations than Krabi Town for exploring nearby islands and beaches. Longtail boats and ferries depart from Ao Nang for Koh Phi Phi, Koh Lanta, Nang Cape, and the multitude of smaller islands in eastern Phang Nga Bay.

The islands of Koh Phi Phi were once idyllic retreats, with secret silver-sand coves, unspoiled stretches of shoreline, and limestone cliffs dropping precipitously into the sea. After it was portrayed in the film *The Beach* (2000), Phi Phi became a hot (overcrowded) property. Koh Phi Phi was hit hard by the tsunami, but the beaches are still stunning. Luxury resorts have spread themselves across the sands here and a multitude of restaurants, bars, and smaller guesthouses fill the demand for lodging. Many of the budget accommodations that sprang up right after the tsunami have upgraded their facilities (and their prices) in a hit-and-miss process of renewal—some have achieved grandeur, or class, others are tacky and overpriced for what they offer. It appears that unchecked development has arrived. The buildings are creeping higher each year, and the resorts have generally become more high-end; but beware, the terms "resort" and "deluxe" are used liberally, so do not rely too much on impressions created by artful photographs in websites.

Farther south, more adventurous travelers are discovering the relative serenity of Krabi's "hidden" gem, Koh Lanta. It's one of the largest islands in Thailand, with beautiful beaches, accommodations for budget travelers, and a few activities such as elephant-trekking in the jungle.

PHANG NGA BAY NATIONAL MARINE PARK

Fodor's Choice　　*100 km (62 miles) north of Phuket, 93 km (56 miles) northwest of*
★　　*Krabi.*

GETTING HERE AND AROUND

Many travel agencies in Phuket offer half-day tours of the area, and this is the way most travelers see the park. Another option is to take a bus heading north from Phuket Town (B120) to one of two inlets near the town of Phang Nga, where you can hire a longtail boat and explore at your own pace, but unless you speak Thai or are intrepid, this is likely to be more of a hassle than it's worth. At the western inlet, you can rent a boat for about B1,800 for two hours. The second inlet sees fewer foreign tourists, so the prices are better—about B1,200 for three hours. The bay can also be explored via tour boat, speedboat, or sea canoe. Most tourists don't arrive from Phuket until 11 am, so if you get into the bay earlier, you can explore it in solitude. To get an early start, you may want to stay overnight in the area. Be sure to take time to appreciate the sunsets, which are particularly beautiful on the island of **Koh Mak.**

SAFETY AND PRECAUTIONS

Be careful to protect yourself from the sun (there are not many convenient shops selling sunscreen). Take precautions to keep your valuables dry and safe when exploring the stunning beaches and coves. The crime rate is low, and the locals are extremely hospitable and friendly, even by Thai standards.

TIMING

Travelers head here for the sand and beach life, aside from which there isn't too much to do. If you just want to lie on the beach, stay for a week or two.

EXPLORING PHANG NGA BAY NATIONAL MARINE PARK

From stunning monoliths that rise from the sea to the secluded, crystal-clear bays, Phang Nga Bay is a must-see for any nature lover. The only way to visit is by boat. Tours (B1,000 to B2,000) can be arranged through your hotel or resort if you're staying in the area.

There are several key sights around Phang Nga Bay. The island of **Koh Panyi** has a Muslim fishing village consisting of houses built on stilts. Restaurants are no bargain, tripling their prices for tourists. Beautiful **Koh Phing Kan,** now known locally as James Bond Island, is well worth a visit. The island of **Koh Tapu** resembles a nail driven into the sea. **Kao Kien** has overhanging cliffs covered with primitive paintings of elephants, fish, and crabs. Many are thought to be at least 3,500 years old.

James Bond Island. Named for tourist purposes after the 1974 Bond film *The Man With The Golden Gun* starring Roger Moore as 007, and traditionally known as Koh Phing Kan, this natural attraction has unfortunately fallen victim to greedy tour operators and merchants, losing the beauty that made it famous. Visiting this island (with a stopover often not longer than half an hour) usually involves a day-trip that involves stop-overs to the equally jaded Koh Panyi island known for its charming Muslim gypsy fishing village, a lunch break and other stops such as the Monkey Caves. The water in this zone is visibly polluted, the landscape can easily be beat by a multitude of other stunning landscapes around Thailand's south and the throng of other tourists can be as buzzy for some as unbearable for others.

Tham Lot Cave. Tham Lot is a large limestone stalactite-studded cave that has an opening large enough for boats to pass through. It can be explored by canoe or an inflatable boat, floating along seawater to enjoy the sight of impressive stalactites and stalagmites, some as long as 100 meters. No guide required. ⊠ *Tarnboke Koranee National Park, Ao Luk District.*

Fodor's Choice ★ **Wat Tham Cave.** The Buddha Cave, or fully named in Thai as Wat Tham Suwan Khuha, is a large impressive cavern with a temple gate, filled with a broad and beautiful variety of Buddha statues placed in various spots, inspiring tourists to stop and relax wherever feels right to them. It's mostly known for its giant gold statue of the reclining Buddha, before which a stage is set where faithful visitors can light incense and pray under his gaze. Before or after your uphill walk through the cave, you may get to meet the many gray monkeys jumping down from the top of the hill and ropey trees to be fed, so have some peanuts, bananas, or coconut handy if you want to interact with them. There are several tourist stalls around selling snacks and other items such as jewelry and souvenirs. ✉ *6 miles outside Phang Nga.*

WHERE TO STAY

For expanded hotel reviews, visit Fodors.com.

$$$$ RESORT Fodor's Choice ★ **Aleenta Resort and Spa Phan-Nga.** Stylish design, a romantic atmosphere, and a beautiful beach contribute to the Aleenta experience. **Pros:** great sunset views from some suites; quiet, relaxing location. **Cons:** fills up early in high season; not all rooms have sea views. [$] *Rooms from: $183* ✉ *33 Moo 5, Khokkloy, Phang Nga* ☎ *066/2514–8112* 🌐 *www.aleenta.com* ⇨ *15 suites and villas.*

$$ RESORT FAMILY **Andaman Princess Resort and Spa.** The centerpiece here is an enormous pool with a long bridge over it, surrounded by endless manicured lawns. **Pros:** leisurely atmosphere; nice restaurant; prime location. **Cons:** needs renovation; a bit pricey for what you get. [$] *Rooms from: $100* ☎ *076/592222 up to 9* 🌐 *www.andamanprincessresort.com* ⇨ *82 rooms.*

$ B&B/INN **Ao Phang Nga National Park.** In addition to the camping grounds (where you can rent tents), the park has a few well-built bungalows within its grounds. **Pros:** excellent location; good base for exploring the area; decent service. **Cons:** some rooms are basic; lack of amenities; often booked up. [$] *Rooms from: $4* ✉ *80 Ban Tha Dan, Koh Panyi* ☎ *025/620760 for reservations* ⇨ *15 bungalows* 💳 *No credit cards.*

$$$ RESORT FAMILY **Golden Buddha Beach Resort.** This eco resort has its own stunning 10 km (6.2 mile) beach where the endangered giant leatherback turtle nests, beautiful beachfront and beachback homes, a spa offering a relaxing range of treatments, yoga classes (it's a prime yoga retreat destination), and a desert island feel. **Pros:** wonderful beach; helpful, friendly staff; ideal for nature lovers. **Cons:** no kitchen in-house; remote; no a/c. [$] *Rooms from: $170* ✉ *131 Moo 2, Ko Phra Thong,* ☎ *081/919–5228* 🌐 *www.goldenbuddharesort.com* ⇨ *25 homes.*

KOH YAO

30 mins by boat from Bangrong Pier, Phuket, or 45 mins by boat from Chaofa Pier, Krabi.

GETTING HERE AND AROUND

Public ferry is the easiest, most scenic, and cheapest, way to get to and from Koh Yao Noi. Most of the tourist developments can be found on Koh Yao Noi. Ferries from Bangrong Pier to the north of Phuket leave regularly throughout the day and cost B150 per person. You can also travel from Chaofa Pier in Krabi for B160.

EXPLORING KOH YAO

Koh Yao Yai and Koh Yao Noi are the two large islands in the center of Phang Nga Bay. Both are quiet, peaceful places, fringed with sandy beaches and clear water. Most inhabitants still make their living by traditional means such as fishing, rubber tapping, and batik-painting. Considering their size and proximity to Phuket and Krabi, it's surprising how little development these islands have seen. During the 1990s many tourists began to discover the islands and the impact was, unsurprisingly, negative. So to reduce the impact on the land and their culture the villagers residing on Koh Yao organized the "Koh Yao Noi Ecotourism Club" to regulate growth on the islands. They've certainly been successful—they even picked up an award for tourism development sponsored by Conservation International and *National Geographic Traveler.*

A visit to Koh Yao will allow you to experience the local culture and customs while exploring the beauty of the islands (kayaks and mountain bikes are popular transportation options). The Ecotourism Club provides homestays if you really want the full experience of the islands; otherwise, most resorts provide day tours or information for self-guided exploration.

WHERE TO STAY

For expanded hotel reviews, visit Fodors.com.

$ B&B/INN **Koh Yao Homestay.** Lodgings are organized by a community of Koh Yao residents who invite tourists to experience their way of life. **Pros:** up-close cultural experience; ecotourism at its best; well organized. **Cons:** homestay accommodations don't suit everyone; usually very basic. [$] *Rooms from: B30* ✉ *Baan Laem Sai, Koh Yao Noi, Phang Nga* ☎ *089/970–3384* 🌐 *www.kohyaohomestay.com* 💳 *No credit cards.*

$$$$ RESORT Fodor's Choice ★ **Koyao Island Resort.** This resort has one of the best views among beach resorts in Thailand; from east-facing Haad Pa Sai you can take in a panoramic vista of a string of magnificent islands. **Pros:** captivating views of nearby islands; attentive service; many activities. **Cons:** not family-oriented; open-air can make you more mosquito-accessible; beach itself could be better. [$] *Rooms from: $230* ✉ *24/2 Koh Yao Noi, Phang Nga* ☎ *076/597474 up to 76* 🌐 *www.koyao.com* 🛏 *15 villas.*

KHAO LAK

80 km (50 miles) north of Phuket.

Few resorts here escaped total destruction in the 2004 tsunami. The scale and extent of the damage also makes Khao Lak the region's greatest success story—by 2006, Khao Lak was, amazingly, back on its feet. Today, aside from a few abandoned buildings, there is no physical evidence of the devastation that occurred.

GETTING HERE AND AROUND

VIP and first-class buses leave for Khao Lak from Bangkok's Southern Bus Terminal each evening around 6 or 7 pm. The journey takes at least 12 hours. There's also regular bus service here from other beach areas. The journey to Phuket takes about two hours and costs around B200 (by taxi expect to pay anywhere between B1,600 and B2,000). There's no direct bus from Phuket to Khao Lak, but you can take a local bus bound for Ranong, Surat Thani, or Kuraburi and ask to get dropped off in Khao Lak.

The usual array of motorcycles, songthaews, and taxis will shuttle you around the area.

EXPLORING KHAO LAK

Khao Lak Lamru National Marine Park. Rolling green hills and abundant wildlife are primary attractions. The park grounds cover more than 325 square km (125 square miles) from the sea to the mountains, including a secluded sandy beach and several waterfalls. The park preserves some pristine tropical evergreen forest that is often supplanted in the south by fruit and rubber trees. Wildlife includes wild pigs, barking deer, macaques, and reticulated pythons. Walking trails lead to waterfalls with swimmable pools. Three rudimentary cabins are available for overnight stays, as are tent rentals for visitors who do not have their own. The park headquarters, on the road from Khao Lak Beach to Khao Lak town, provides information about exploring or staying in the park. ☎ 025/794842, 025/578–0529 *National Park Division in Bangkok* ⊕ *www.dnp.go.th.*

Khao Lak Beach. Khao Lak Beach proper lies to the south of the national park, while most resorts and dive operators purporting to hail from "Khao Lak" actually line the coasts of Nang Thong, Bang Niang, Khuk Khak, and Bang Sak beaches to the north. As a result of Khao Lak's (once again) booming popularity, many properties are beginning to stay open more during the low season; however, Khao Lak is best visited near or during the high and dry season (November to May) when you can be sure that all businesses are in full operation. **Amenities:** food and drink; showers; toilets; water sports. **Best for:** sunset; swimming; walking; surfing. ⊠ *Thanon Phet Kasem, Khao Lak.*

WHERE TO EAT

$ ✕ **Hill Tribes Restaurant.** Allow your tastebuds to celebrate this loving
THAI tribute to northern Thai cuisine. The chefs here specialize in seafood and fish dishes made according to traditional recipes from the northern hill tribes folk, and provides a pleasant change from southern fare. Try the tempura of banana flowers, the sizzling seafood hotplate or the prawns fried with herbs in a red whisky sauce, and don't miss out on the mouthwatering sticky rice with coconut cream and ripe mango for dessert. $ *Average main: $145* ⊠ *Phetchkasem Rd. 13/22, Khao Lak* ☎ 086/283–0933 ⊕ *www.hilltribe-restaurant.com* ▭ *No credit cards* ⊙ *Daily 1 pm–10 pm.*

$ ✕ **Smile.** Showing a special awareness to diners with food allergies and
THAI diabetes and offering a menu especially designed for vegetarians and
FAMILY vegans, this successful restaurant serves delicious Thai curries, a wonderful choice of appetizers, salads and stir-fries made with an interesting French twist. $ *Average main: B200* ⊠ *29/31 Phetkasem Rd., Phangnga, Khao Lak* ☎ 083/391–2600 ▭ *No credit cards.*

$ ✕ **Smoh Ruer Restaurant.** A few minutes' tuk-tuk ride north from the busy
THAI part of town, Smoh Ruer is a high-end (in food, not price) local eatery occasionally chanced upon by a few lucky travelers. There's nothing chancey about the food, however. Prepared in the local Khao Lak style, dishes include a mightily spicy wild boar red curry, perfectly cooked prawns fried in sesame oil on a bed of rice noodles and celery, and the mellow egg-fried morning glory in oyster sause. $ *Average main: B1600* ⊠ *12/2 M.6 T. Khukkak, Khao Lak* ☎ 089/288–9889, 089/875–9018 ▭ *No credit cards* ⊙ *Daily 10–10.*

WHERE TO STAY

For expanded hotel reviews, visit Fodors.com.

$$$ RESORT
Baan Krating. Occupying a wonderful spot on a cliff above a beach, this boutique resort boasts a beautiful view and a path down to the shore that travels within Khao Lak Lamru National Park. Within the resort itself, a quiet, natural atmosphere prevails. **Pros:** relaxed atmosphere; captivating views; clean rooms. **Cons:** spartan accommodations; slightly worn; a bit of a trek to beach. [$] *Rooms from: $120* ✉ *28 Khao Lak, Takuapa, Phang Nga* ☎ *076/485188 up to 9* 🌐 *www.baankrating.com* 🛏 *24 cottages.*

$$$$ RESORT FAMILY
Khao Lak Seaview Resort and Spa. Seaview Resort's octagnol villas with high ceilings, four-poster beds, and whirlpool tubs epitomize the luxury available to its guests. **Pros:** tiered pool; luxurious feel; friendly staff. **Cons:** not the best views; somewhat costly; beach not ideal. [$] *Rooms from: $260* ✉ *18/1 Moo 7, Petchkasem Rd., Khuk Khak* ☎ *076/429800* 🌐 *www.khaolak-seaviewresort.com* 🛏 *197 rooms* 💳 *No credit cards.*

$$$ RESORT Fodor's Choice ★
La Flora. La Flora is a lovely, service-oriented boutique resort where rooms are fashionably decorated in modern Asian aesthetic, and most have balconies or daybeds. **Pros:** tasteful, spacious rooms; stunning villas; lovely beach with deep waters. **Cons:** families may find it a little isolated; dining is not outstanding; rooftop bar understaffed. [$] *Rooms from: $220* ✉ *59/1 Moo 5, Khuk Khak, Phang Nga* ☎ *076/428000, 026/798828* 🌐 *www.lafloraresort.com* 🛏 *125 rooms, 13 villas.*

$$$$ RESORT FAMILY
Le Meridien Khao Lak Beach & Spa Resort. Le Meridien is on an isolated 12-km (7-mile) stretch of beach to the north of Khao Lak town. **Pros:** fun for kids; nice spa facilities; luxurious elegance. **Cons:** service is slack; not for romantic getaways; slightly commercial feel. [$] *Rooms from: $450* ✉ *9/9 Moo 1, Tambol Khuk Khak, Amphur Takua Pa, Phang Nga* ☎ *076/427500* 🌐 *www.starwoodhotels.com* 🛏 *243 rooms.*

$$$$ RESORT
Mukdara Beach Resort. This sumptuous resort has been designed in classical Thai style, with a great deal of emphasis on wood and traditional craftsmanship. **Pros:** villas on beach; tasteful Thai furnishings; luxurious. **Cons:** large resort, so not intimate; layout of some rooms is odd. [$] *Rooms from: $200* ✉ *26/14 Moo 7, Thanon Khuk Khak, Takuapa, Phang Nga* ☎ *076/429999* 🌐 *www.mukdarabeach.com* 🛏 *70 rooms, 64 villas, 7 suites.*

$$ RESORT
Nang Thong Bay Resort. The majority of rooms here are surprisingly inexpensive cottages that face the beach and are surrounded by well-maintained gardens. **Pros:** good value; well-located; new pool. **Cons:** disappointing restaurant; service a little amiss. [$] *Rooms from: $70* ✉ *Khao Lak, Takuapa, Phang Nga* ☎ *076/485088, 076/485088* 🌐 *www.nangthongbayresort.de/enangthongbayresort.htm* 🛏 *82 rooms.*

$$$$ RESORT
The Sarojin. This exquisite boutique resort's smaller size makes it more intimate and exclusive than nearby megaresorts. **Pros:** intimate and exclusive; cooking classes; unique aesthetics. **Cons:** price a bit higher than at comparable resorts. [$] *Rooms from: $400* ✉ *60 Moo 2, Khuk Khak, Takuapa, Phang Nga* ☎ *076/427900 up t 7* 🌐 *www.sarojin.com* 🛏 *56 rooms.*

5

SIMILAN ISLANDS

70 km (45 miles) or 1½ hours by boat from Thaplamu Pier.

GETTING HERE AND AROUND

BOAT TRAVEL   Speedboats to Similan National Park leave from Thap Lamu Pier in the Tai Muang District just south of Khao Lak beach at 8:30 am when the park is open to the public (November to May). Once you reach Koh Similan, motorboats will take you to other islands for between B250 and B600 depending on distance.

You can also take a private tour boat from Thap Lamu Pier for around B2,000 per person. The tour boat departs from Thap Lamu at 8 am daily and returns at 2 pm. Direct tickets, booked through the national parks, cost B2,000; however, private tours are a better value.

EXPLORING THE SIMILIAN ISLANDS

Fodor'sChoice   The Mu Koh Similan National Marine Park consists of the nine Similan
★   Islands, as well as Koh Tachai and Koh Bon, which are farther north. The diving around the Similan Islands is world class, with visibility of up to 120 feet; abundant blue, green, and purple coral; and rare marine life, such as the whale shark, the world's largest fish. In addition to sparkling, crystal-clear water, the Similan Islands also have ultrafine, powdery white-sand beaches and lush tropical forests. The National Park Service allows visitors to stay on the beaches of Koh Miang (Island 4) and Koh Similan (Island 8). ■TIP→ **If you plan to dive, contact a dive operator in Phuket or Khao Lak; there are no dive shops on the islands, though snorkeling gear is available for rent from the ranger stations.**

Koh Miang. Koh Miang, where the park headquarters is located, has bungalows with 24-hour electricity and even some with air-conditioning; some bungalows have ocean views as well. Beachside camping is also available on Koh Miang (the park rents out roomy tents, large enough to stand in, which have two camping cots). Koh Similan has no bungalows, but has the same large tents for rent as well as an area for visitors to set up their own tents. If you choose to visit the island to stay at the park, expect to pay B2,000 to B2,500 for a round-trip boat transfer. Once on the island, you can hire a longtail boat to explore the other islands. ■TIP→ **The park is extremely popular with Thais, so book well in advance if you're planning a visit during a Thai holiday. The islands are more enjoyable, and more explorable, if visited midweek.** The park entrance fee is B200 per visit. Note that the islands are normally closed to visitors from mid-May until early November. ☎ *076/595045 for campsite reservations, 02/562–0760 for bungalow reservations* ⊕ *www.dnp.go.th.*

Jack's Similan. Tour groups, such as Jack's Similan, have their own smaller tents set up in this area and rent them out for the same fee charged by the national park. There are also overnight packages, which include tours of the islands, camping, and food. ⊠ *79/36 Moo 5, Tablamu* ☎ *076/443205* ⊕ *www.jacksimilan.com*

Tropical forest meets powdery white sand on the Similan Islands.

SURIN ISLANDS

60 km (37 miles) or 2 hours by boat from Kuraburi Pier.

GETTING HERE AND AROUND

Khuraburi Pier, north of Khao Lak beach, is the departure point for boats to the Surin Islands, and can be reached by any bus going to or from Ranong (about B200 from Phuket or Krabi). Songthaews will take you to the pier, approximately 9 km (5½ miles) out of town. Expect to pay B1,000 and up for boat trips to the various islands. Negotiating prices is not really an option here. An easier option is to book a trip through your resort. They will arrange your transportation to Khuraburi and your boat ticket.

EXPLORING THE SURIN ISLANDS

Mu Koh Surin National Marine Park is a remote island paradise practically unknown to anyone other than adventurous scuba divers and Thais. Five islands make up the national park, each with sea turtles, varieties of sharks, and plentiful coral. If you get tired of sun and sea, there are several hiking trails that lead to waterfalls and a sea gypsy village.

The 2004 tsunami hit the Surin islands quite hard, damaging shallow reefs and destroying all park structures. Coral at snorkeling sites in shallow water received considerable damage, but most dive sites were protected by their deeper water and were generally unaffected. The visibility and diversity of marine life is spectacular, and this is arguably the most unspoiled Thai island retreat, owing to its remote location and low number of visitors. Note that the park is normally closed during the rainy season (June to November).

WHERE TO STAY

Koh Surin Nua. There are 10 recently built, comfortable fan-cooled wooden huts on Koh Surin Nua (B2,000), and tent camping is allowed at a site that has decent facilities, including toilets and showers. You may bring your own tent and camp for B80, or rent one that sleeps two from the national park for B450. ■TIP➔ Book your hut at least 10 days ahead. ☎ *02/562–0760 for inquiries and bungalow reservations, 076/491378 ⊕ www.dnp.go.th.*

KRABI

814 km (506 miles) south of Bangkok, 180 km (117 miles) southeast of Phuket, 43 km (27 miles) by boat east of Koh Phi Phi.

Krabi is a major travel hub in southern Thailand. Travelers often breeze through without stopping to enjoy the atmosphere, which is a shame, because Krabi is a friendly town with great food and charming people. Locals are determined to keep Phuket-style development at bay, and so far they are succeeding.

GETTING HERE AND AROUND

AIR TRAVEL   Flying is the easiest way to get here from Bangkok. Thai Airways, Bangkok Airways, and Air Asia all have daily flights to Krabi International Airport. One-way prices from Bangkok range from B1,000 to B3,500; the flight takes about an hour.

The airport is a 20-minute ride from Krabi Town, and there are taxis (B300) and minibuses (B150) waiting outside the airport. These vehicles can also take you to other nearby (and not-so-nearby) beach areas. Minivans don't leave until they're full, which can happen quickly or after a long wait. Your best bet is to check in with the minivans first to make sure you get a seat if one is about to depart—if not, you can opt for a taxi. Another, more recent transport addition, is the regular bus service to and from Krabi Town. The bus departs hourly (B100) from 6 am and runs throughout the day until 10 pm.

BUS AND   Buses from Bangkok to Krabi leave from Bangkok's Southern Bus Ter-
SONGTHAEW   minal and take at least 12 hours. VIP and first-class buses leave once
TRAVEL   every evening around 6 or 7 pm. Public buses leave Krabi for Bangkok at 8 am and 4 and 5:30 pm. First-class buses travel between Phuket and Krabi (a three-hour journey) every hour. Getting around town or to Ao Nang is best done by songthaew. You can find songthaews at the corner of Maharat Soi 4 and Pruksa Uthit Road.

Bus and boat combination tickets are available from Krabi to Koh Samui and Koh Phangan.

There are a few bus terminals in Krabi, but if you don't arrive at the pier, songthaews can take you there; if you've purchased a combination ticket, this transfer is included.

CAR TRAVEL   The airport has Avis, National, and Budget rental counters. Prices start at about B1,500 per day; for a little more, you can also rent a four-wheel-drive jeep in town.

SAFETY AND PRECAUTIONS

Krabi is a sleepy, laid-back town with little crime and few annoyances, but taking routine precautions with your valuables is always a good idea. People drive annoyingly fast, so take care when crossing the road, especially at the major junctions.

TIMING

Traditionally, Krabi has served as a staging point for onward travel, but the town is slowly becoming a tourist destination in its own right. Attractions and amenities are open year-round. There is enough to keep visitors here for a few days, and day trips to nearby islands can keep you occupied for a great deal longer.

VISITOR INFORMATION

Krabi has its own small Tourism Authority of Thailand (TAT) offices, where you can pick up maps and brochures, as well as information about local excursions. Tour operators and your hotel's tour desk are also good sources of information.

Contacts Krabi Tourist Information Center ✉ *Uttarakit Rd.* ☎ *075/622163.*

5

EXPLORING KRABI

There are a few good restaurants in town, and there's excellent seafood at the night market (try the fish cakes with sweet chili sauce), which also sells clothes, accessories and souvenirs.

Wat Tham Sua. Just 3 km (2 miles, or 10 minutes drive) from Krabi Town is Wat Tham Sua, with its giant Buddha statue and scenic surrounding landscapes. Built in 1976 as a monastery and meditation retreat, Wat Tham Sua is both respected by the local population and popular with tourists. Locals come to participate in Buddhist rituals, while most tourists to climb the 1,277 steps to panoramic views of the cliffs, Krabi Town, Krabi River, and the Panom Benja mountain range. There's also a cave with many chambers, which can be fun to explore, though it's not terribly attractive. A really large tree grows outside the entrance. The wat is between Krabi Town and the airport. ✉ *Tambon Muang Chum, 4 km (2½ miles) after Wachiralongkorn Dam.*

OFF THE BEATEN PATH

Than Bokkharani National Park. Between Krabi and Phang Nga is this forested park, which has several emerald-green ponds surrounded by tropical foliage, including wild gardenia and apocynaceae. The pools are filled with refreshing cool water, fed by a mountain spring 4 km (2½ miles) away. The largest pond is 130 feet by 100 feet, deep and suitable for swimming. The pools are best visited in the dry season, as they get quite murky when it rains. ✉ *From Krabi take Hwy. 4 to Ao Luek, then turn onto Rte. 4039* ☎ *075/681071* 🎫 *B200.*

WHERE TO EAT

$$ INTERNATIONAL

🍴 **Carnivore Steak and Grill.** As the name suggests, meat lovers can find high-quality imported cuts served with delicious sauces and sides this well-known restaurant. Fish lovers can also be satisfied here, with fresh lobster bisque, perfectly grilled tuna steak or white snapper in butter and garlic cream sauce. The efficient service adds to the lively atmosphere. [$] *Average main: B143* ✉ *127 Moo 3* ☎ *075/661061* ✍ *Reservations essential.*

$ ✕ **Chao Fa Pier Street Food Stalls.** Looking for local quality food at a low
THAI   price? This strip of street-side food stalls serves everything from simple
fried rice and papaya salad to more sophisticated southern delicacies
such as *kanom jeen* (rice noodles topped with whatever sauces and
vegetables you want). Open from nightfall until midnight, these stalls
provide an excellent opportunity to discover some exotic and enjoyable
Thai foods. Walk along the street and enjoy the carnival atmosphere,
the local stall-holders are more than happy to let you try the assorted
delicacies before deciding what to buy. This is one of the highlights of
Krabi Town, and the street enjoys a nationwide reputation. $ *Average
main: B57* ✉ *Chao Fa Pier, Khong Kha Rd.* 🖦 *No credit cards.*

$ ✕ **Frog and Catfish.** At the Frog and Catfish you can try some regional
SEAFOOD   specialties that are not that easy to come across. Located in the small
village of Din Daeang Noi, the restaurant serves great seafood (try the
fresh crab spring rolls) as well as delicious curries. The owner is always
happy to share his knowledge about the region to travelers hungry for
new perspectives. $ *Average main: $175* ✉ *76 Moo 6, Din Daeng Noi*
☎ *084/773–0301* ☉ *Daily 10–10.*

$$ ✕ **Marina Villa.** Opened in 2011, this restaurant sits on the banks of
SEAFOOD   Krabi River on a picturesque marina and specializes in thoughtfully
Fodor's Choice   presented Thai seafood dishes. It's a local favorite for the well-to-do
★   Krabi locals. The attentive staff wear different colored uniforms each
day, influenced by flowery Hawaiian fashion. The space itself is mod-
ern and dimly lighted with blues and greens, but weather permitting,
tables by the river are the way to go. Signature dishes include the spicy
green curry with crab, grilled white snapper stuffed with lemongrass
and pandanus leaves, and the large, juicy mussels with garlic and chili.
Most meals are accompanied by whisky or beer on the rocks, Thai
style. $ *Average main: B300* ✉ *Next to yacht club, Krabi Marina*
☎ *075/611635, 086/276–8556* ⚓ *Reservations essential.*

$ ✕ **Relax Coffee and Restaurant.** The menu at this streetside café includes
CAFÉ   more than 10 different breakfast platters; a number of sandwiches,
such as chicken satay, served on homemade freshly baked brown bread,
baguette, or ciabatta; many Thai dishes, including 10 different bar-
racuda plates; and, not surprisingly, a huge variety of coffee drinks,
like raspberry latte frappés. It's in the heart of the hotel district and
caters mainly to the foreigners. $ *Average main: B100* ✉ *7/4 Chaofa
Rd.* ☎ *075/611570* 🖦 *No credit cards* ☉ *Closed 2nd and 4th Fri. of
each month.*

$ ✕ **Ruen Pae.** This massive floating restaurant aboard a large, flat barge
SEAFOOD   serves Thai standards, with an emphasis on seafood dishes. It's at
the Chao Fa Pier beside the night market. The restaurant is popular
with locals and tourists alike, get there early on Friday and Satur-
day evenings. $ *Average main: B100* ✉ *Ut-tarkit Rd.* ☎ *076/611956,
075/611148* 🖦 *No credit cards* ☉ *Tues.–Sun. 11–9*

WHERE TO STAY
For expanded hotel reviews, visit Fodors.com.

$ 🏠 **Hometel.** A solid budget choice, this little family-run hotel is a great
HOTEL   base for those using Krabi as a stepping stone to the tropical islands
beyond. **Pros:** central; speedy free Wi-Fi; good restaurant. **Cons:** book

well in advance; not enough natural light in the rooms; some rooms are small. [$] *Rooms from: $17* ✉ *7 Soi 10 Maharaj Rd., Pak Nam* ☎ *075/622301* 🛏 *10 rooms.*

$$ RESORT **Krabi Maritime Park and Spa Resort.** Featuring a mangrove forest, a sprawling lagoon, a large swimming pool, and views of Krabi's signature limestone cliffs, this resort extends over 25 acres. **Pros:** impressive views over the mangroves and forest; decorative touches in the rooms and lobby; lovely gardens. **Cons:** Staff inattentive at times; needs a makeover; free Wi-Fi only in lobby. [$] *Rooms from: $90* ✉ *1 Thungfa Rd.* ☎ *075/620028 up to 35* 🌐 *www.maritimeparkandspa.com* 🛏 *221 rooms.*

$ HOTEL **Krabi River Hotel.** Not to everyone's taste because it's so basic, the Krabi River Hotel is at the marina (earmarked for major development), and is a good budget option for Krabi. **Pros:** pleasant riverside location; some rooms have lovely views; free Wi-Fi. **Cons:** off the main drag; rooms at the back are small and have no views; breakfast not included. [$] *Rooms from: $27* ✉ *73/1 Kongkha Rd.* ☎ *075/612321* 🌐 *www.krabiriverhotel.com* 🛏 *20 rooms* 🍴 *No meals.*

NIGHTLIFE

The Rooftop Bar. On the top of Hello KR Mansion, this bar offers drinks, live DJ sessions, occasional fireshows and beautiful alfresco views, especially at sunset. ✉ *52/1 Chao Fa Rd.* ☎ *084/3852316.*

EN ROUTE **Shell Cemetery** is a pleasant beach park between Ao Nang and Krabi Town. It has a small information center explaining how snails from tens of millions of years ago were preserved for us to wonder about today. The fossils are probably not that interesting to most people, but the beach here is pleasant for a dip (although sunbathing in skimpy suits would be inappropriate, as many Thai families picnic on the hill above). Also, the view from the hill is quite nice, and if you're cruising on a motorbike, this is a fine place to get some shade in between destinations.

AO NANG

20 km (12 miles) from Krabi Town.

In the daytime, Ao Nang is busy with visitors flowing to and from beaches. In the evening, storefronts light up the sidewalk and open-air restaurants provide excellent places to kick back with a beer and watch the crowd go by. For a more romantic atmosphere, head to the half dozen seafood restaurants atop a pier extending from the bend in Liab Chai Haad Road in between Ao Nang and Noppharat Thara beaches.

GETTING HERE AND AROUND

Buses from Bangkok headed to Krabi stop here. If you fly into Krabi, it takes about 45 minutes to Ao Nang in a taxi. Songthaews travel between Ao Nang and Krabi Town regularly. The fare shouldn't be more than B80; you can find them on the main road, displaying Krabi–Ao Nang signs. A taxi from the airport will cost you considerably more, usually the minimum fare is B650.

EXPLORING AO NANG

During the day, longtail boats depart from Ao Nang for the more spectacular beaches and waters of Hong, Poda, Gai, Lanta, and the Phi Phi islands, as well as nearby Railay Beach. Less adventurous types can find nicer sand and better water for swimming on the far eastern end of the beach or at Noppharat Thara Beach National Park to the west.

BEACHES

Klong Muang. Farther north are the beaches of Klong Muang and **Tubkaak,** isolated beautiful stretches of sand with amazing views of the limestone karst islands on the horizon. The beaches are largely occupied by upmarket resorts such as the Sheraton and The Tubkaak. **Amenities:** water sports; food and drink; toilet. **Best for:** solitude; sunset; walking.

Laem Son Beach. A narrow river pier delineates the western edge of Noppharat Thara National Park. Here you can catch boats departing from the pier to Railay, Phi Phi, and Lanta, or simply cross to the other side and enjoy the unspoiled natural beauty of Laem Son Beach. There are a few cheap beach-side bungalows to stay at. **Amenities:** none. **Best for:** solitude; sunset; walking; swimming.

Noppharat Thara Beach. Noppharat Thara Beach is a 15-minute walk from central Ao Nang. Since the renovated walking path was extended from Ao Nang in 2004, a mishmash of development followed (even though it's supposedly part of the national park). The beach is still pleasant but many of the trees have been uprooted to make way for resorts. **Amenities:** food and drink. **Best for:** swimming; walking. ⊠ *96 Moo 3, Nopphara Thara.*

WHERE TO EAT

$ ✕**Ao Nang Cuisine.** The tender chicken satay (curry chicken skewers), an otherwise ordinary dish, is skillfully prepared at this traditional restaurant, with a side of spicy peanut sauce. More elaborate Thai dishes are available for tourists who are tired of street-side barbecue seafood. Excellent value for both quantity and quality. $ *Average main: B86* ⊠ *245/4 Liab Chai Haad Rd.* ☎ *075/695399.*

THAI

$ ✕**Krua Thara.** There are two positive signs at this restaurant before you even try the food—locals hanging out, and the fish and seafood that will end up on your plate are on display in tanks in all their variety. You'll find every kind of fresh catch prepared using lots of local herbs and spices at this friendly, colorful place. $ *Average main: B115* ⊠ *82 Moo 5, Nopparat Thara Rd.* ☎ *075/637361* ⊟ *No credit cards.*

SEAFOOD

$ ✕**Lae Lay Grill.** The seafood here is perfectly cooked and artfully presented, but what makes Lae Lay Grill more special is its location. The restaurant is on a terrace on a hill overlooking Ao Nang and the sea, which makes it a highly romantic spot from sunset on, but also lovely during the day. They will pick you up from your hotel and bring you here

SEAFOOD

by van. $ *Average main: B175* ⊠ *89 Moo 3, Ao Nang* ☎ *075/661588* ⊕ *laelaygrill.com* ⊟ *No credit cards.*

WHERE TO STAY

For expanded hotel reviews, visit Fodors.com.

$$
HOTEL
▒ **Alis Hotel and Spa.** Whitewashed walls and red ceramic tile floors contribute to the Morrocan design at Alis Hotel. **Pros:** polite, helpful staff; good facilities for the price. **Cons:** whitewash needs to be reapplied; staff can be apathetic. $ *Rooms from: $92* ⊠ *125 Moo 3, Ao Nang* ☎ *075/638000, 02/801-0760 in Bangkok* ⊕ *www.alisthailand. com* ⬟ *34 rooms* ⊚ *Breakfast.*

$$$
RESORT
▒ **Best Western Anyavee Ao Nang Resort & Spa.** The resort is a cluster of four-story buildings in Thai design, including northern-style peaked roofs. **Pros:** good selection of facilities; great location for nature lovers. **Cons:** a bit removed from beach; exterior needs some renovation. $ *Rooms from: $130* ⊠ *31/3 Liab Chai Haad Rd., Ao Nang* ☎ *075/695051 up to 54* ⊕ *www.anyavee.com* ⬟ *71 rooms.*

$$$
RESORT
▒ **The Cliff.** You can get a great view of the cliff that inspired the hotel's name as soon as you step into the lobby. **Pros:** atmospheric design; stunning location; good Wi-Fi connection. **Cons:** *lots* of mosquitos and other small creatures; not on beach; some rooms are very stuffy. $ *Rooms from: $100* ⊠ *85/2 Liab Chai Haad Rd., Ao Nang* ☎ *075/638117 up to 18* ⊕ *www.thecliffkrabi.com* ⬟ *20 rooms, 1 suite.*

$
B&B/INN
▒ **Emerald Bungalow.** On isolated Laem Son Beach, this family-run resort offers genuine Thai hospitality. **Pros:** close to national park; relaxed atmosphere; decent restaurant. **Cons:** a bit pricey for basic lodgings; too remote for some. $ *Rooms from: $80* ⊠ *Noppharat Thara Beach* ☎ *081/892-1072, 081/956-2566* ⊕ *www.the-emerald-bungalow-resortkrabi.com* ⬟ *36 rooms* ⊟ *No credit cards.*

$
HOTEL
▒ **J Mansion.** Top-floor rooms peek out over surrounding buildings for a nice view of the sea. **Pros:** large rooms; good views from top floor; friendly staff. **Cons:** slow Internet connection; very basic. $ *Rooms from: $40* ⊠ *23/3 Moo 2, Ao Nang Beach* ☎ *075/637878* ⊕ *www. jmansionaonang.com/accommodation.htm* ⬟ *21 rooms.*

$$$
RESORT
FAMILY
▒ **Sheraton Krabi Beach Resort.** The Sheraton Krabi is built around an expansive mangrove forest, and there's a wide, sandy beach on the premises. **Pros:** beachfront location; great amenities; stylish. **Cons:** may disappoint beach purists—water isn't crystal-clear; Wi-Fi connection only in reception area; a little worn in places. $ *Rooms from: $280* ⊠ *155 Klong Muang Beach, Nongtalay* ☎ *075/628000* ⊕ *www. sheraton.com* ⬟ *246 rooms, 6 suites.*

$$$
HOTEL
▒ **The Small, Krabi.** This sleek boutique hotel stands quietly in one of the busier parts of Ao Nang, offering proximity to shopping, dining, drinking and swimming at the Noppharatthara and Ao Nang beaches on either side. **Pros:** cleanliness and attention to detail; great location; short walk to beach. **Cons:** staff somewhat slack and hard to communicate with; no big pool; TVs in bathroom not to everyone's taste. $ *Rooms from: B120* ⊠ *167 Moo 3 Tambon Aonang Amphur Muang* ☎ *075/661590* ⊕ *www.thesmallhotelgroup.com/krabi/* ⬟ *38 rooms.*

$$$$
RESORT
▒ **The Tubkaak Boutique Resort.** Each of the elegant wooden buildings here resembles a *kor lae*, a traditional southern Thai fishing boat. **Pros:**

relaxed environment; beach location; great pool area. **Cons:** disappointing restaurant; rooms are small; decor not up to price level. [$] *Rooms from: $420* ✉ *123 Taab Kaak Beach, Nongtalay* ☎ *075/628400* 🌐 *www.tubkaakresort.com* ⇆ *44 rooms, 2 suites.*

NIGHTLIFE

Encore Café. Five to seven nights a week, prominent local and expat musicians play rock, reggae, blues, jazz, funk, folk, and fusion western-Thai tunes. Hidden back behind the main road in central Ao Nang, this is one of the few places to hear quality music while knocking back some beers and eating Thai and western pub grub. ✉ *245/23 Liab Chai Haad Rd., Nang Beach, Ao Nang* ☎ *075/637107.*

Friends Suki. A great bar that invites you to wind down after a long day sipping a refreshing cocktail or two, in the company of expats who can offer insider tips on the town and surrounding areas. ✉ *Moo 2, Rd. 4203* ☎ *075/695751.*

The Last Fisherman's. The last—and most scenic—social spot on the end of Ao Nang beach is where you should have your frosty drink just before sunset; although it's open for lunch as well. If you're peckish, in the early afternoon or at night, a plain surf 'n' turf, barbecue buffet, salads and gooey desserts are on the menu. ✉ *266 Moo 2* ☎ *075/637968.*

NANG CAPE/RAILAY BEACH

15 mins by longtail boat east of Ao Nang.

Careful not to strain your neck admiring the sky-scraping cliffs as your longtail boat delivers you to Nang Cape, four interconnected beaches collectively referred to as Railay Beach; the isolated beaches of Tonsai, Phra Nang, East Railay, and West Railay, only accessible by boat, are sandy oases surrounded by impressive verdant, vertical cliffs. The sand on these beaches is talcum powder white and soft, the water is crystalline and the crowd is an offbeat blend of bohemian travelers and fitness-enthusiasts

GETTING HERE AND AROUND

Longtails will ferry you here from Ao Nang. Prices vary depending on time of day and which beach you're headed to, but expect to pay around B100 or B120 each way. Prices can rise dramatically in the evening, so leave early to save money.

EXPLORING NANG CAPE/RAILAY BEACH

Nang Cape/Railay Beach. The four beaches that make up Railay Beach are connected by walking paths and each has its own attractions. Tonsai Beach, with a pebble-strewn shore and shallow, rocky water, caters to budget travelers and rock climbers. West Railay has powdery white sand, shallow but swimmable water, gorgeous sunset views, and many kayaks for hire. East Railay, a mangrove-lined shore unsuitable for beach or water activities, draws rock-climbing enthusiasts, as well as younger travelers looking for late-night drinks and loud music. Phra Nang Beach, one of the nicest beaches in all Krabi, is ideal for swimming, sunbathing, and rock-climbing. **Amenities:** food and drink; bathrooms; water sports. **Best for:** sunset; swimming; snorkeling.

Railay Beach's dramatic limestone formations attract rock climbers; there are courses and routes for novices.

SPORTS AND THE OUTDOORS
ROCK-CLIMBING
Climbers discovered the cliffs around Nang Cape in the late 1980s. The mostly vertical cliffs rising up out of the sea were, and certainly are, a dream come true for hard-core climbers. Today anyone daring enough can learn to scale the face of a rock (and to jump off it) in one of the most beautiful destinations in the world. There are 500 to 600 established climbing routes. Notable feats include the Tonsai Beach overhang and Thaiwand Wall, where climbers must use lanterns to pass through a cave and then rappel down from the top. Beginners can learn some skills through half-day or full-day courses for fixed rates of B1,200 or B2,000, respectively. Most climbing organizations are found on East Railay. Slightly less adventurous, or more spendthrift, types can try the free climb to "the lagoon." The lagoon itself isn't all that impressive, but the view from the top is spectacular. The trailhead for the fairly arduous climb up the occasionally near-vertical mud, rock, vine, and fixed-rope ascent is along the path to Phra Nang Beach, immediately across from the gazebo. Watch out for monkeys!

Cliffs Man. One of the more reputable rock climbing schools. ☎ *075/ 621768, 012/304619.*

Tex Rock Climbing. Half-day to three-day climbing courses can be arranged here. ☎ *075/631509.*

King Climbers. All the guides here are accredited by the ACGA and have a minimum of five years' climbing experience. ☎ *075/637125* ⊕ *www. railay.com.*

WHERE TO EAT

$ ✕ **Utopia International Delights.** Utopia offers a change of culinary style
INDIAN at Railay, serving tasty Indian food like butter chicken or chicken tikka masala, crispy samosas and refreshing yogurt lassis, in a friendly outdoor setting. The owners are sensitive to people with nut allergies and make sure what you order matches your spice tolerance. $ *Average main: B140* ⊠ *Ban Ao Nang* 🕾 *085/8836170* ▭ *No credit cards.*

WHERE TO STAY

There are plenty of bars and restaurants along the beaches. Most restaurants serve standard Thai and western fare—no gourmet renditions *yet.* As you move away from the beach, you'll find less expensive and more atmospheric places, including some climber hangouts where trainings and socializing with fellow climbers take place.

For expanded hotel reviews, visit Fodors.com.

$$$$ 📷 **Bhu Nga Thani Resort and Spa.** Located on the quieter Railay East
RESORT Beach, the lovely infinity pool and a popular spa makes this a good option for those staying at Railay, though East Beach faces out onto a mangrove swamp, and there is better swimming to be had at Ton Sai or West beach. **Pros:** most rooms have ocean views; bars and restaurants nearby; resort arranges excursions. **Cons:** 10-minute walk from boat drop; not on a swimming beach; food can be hit-and-miss. $ *Rooms from: $200* ⊠ *Railay East Beach, 479 Moo 2, Ao Nang* 🕾 *075/819451 up to 4* ⊕ *www.bhungathani.com* ⤳ *60 rooms.*

$$$ 📷 **Koh Jum Lodge.** On the island of Koh Jum, in Phang Nga Bay between
B&B/INN Krabi, Phi Phi, and Koh Lanta, Koh Jum Lodge has rooms in 20 wooden cottages designed in traditional Thai architectural style. **Pros:** traditional Thai design; helpful management and staff; stunning sunset over the Phi Phi Islands. **Cons:** a bit isolated from resort towns; difficult to access in off-peak season; food and drinks pricey. $ *Rooms from: $150* ⊠ *286 Moo 3, Koh Siboya, Nua Klong, Krabi* 🕾 *075/618275, 089/921–1621* ⊕ *www.kohjumlodge.com* ⤳ *20 bungalows.*

$ 📷 **Railay Garden View.** Among the best of the less-expensive options
B&B/INN on Railay, this place offers clean bungalows in a garden setting, and a great location near the beach. **Pros:** complimentary breakfast; good restaurant; free Wi-Fi. **Cons:** keep an eye on your belongings; no sea view; noise from longtail boats can get tiring. $ *Rooms from: $50* ⊠ *147 M. 5, Saithai district* 🕾 *085/888–5143, 084/295–1112* ⤳ *10 rooms* 🍴 *Breakfast.*

$$$ 📷 **Railay Bay Resort and Spa.** Great Thai food ($$) and a beachside
RESORT patio and bar from which you can watch the sunset are a few good reasons to visit Railay Bay Resort and Spa. **Pros:** alluring views; central location; decent food. **Cons:** staff may not speak great English; pricey spa; patchy Wi-Fi. $ *Rooms from: $190* ⊠ *145 Moo 2, Railay West Beach, Krabi* 🕾 *075/622998 up to 9* ⊕ *www.railaybayresort. com* ⤳ *140 rooms, 10 suites.*

$ 📷 **Railay Highland Resort.** From practically everywhere you stand in this
B&B/INN no-frills resort, you can enjoy overwhelming vistas of the bay and climber-covered limestone cliffs. **Pros:** inexpensive; stunning views; good food. **Cons:** no advance booking; lacking facilities; as the name suggests, an

uphill trek to get there. $ *Rooms from: $23* ✉ *Moo 1, Railay East Beach, Krabi* ☎ *075/621731* ⇌ *20 bungalows* ▭ *No credit cards.*

$$
HOTEL

🔲 **Railay Princess Resort and Spa.** Thai-style lamps and silk throw pillows on the beds and sofas are colorful touches at this quiet retreat midway between East and West Railay beaches. **Pros:** quiet location; good value; tasteful details. **Cons:** not on beach; furniture looks cheap. $ *Rooms from: B100* ✉ *145/1 Moo 2, Railay Beach, Ao Nang* ☎ *075/819401 to 03, 075/819407 to 09* ⊕ *www.krabi-railayprincess.com* ⇌ *59 rooms.*

$$$
RENTAL
FAMILY
Fodor'sChoice
★

🔲 **Railei Beach Club.** Each of the 24 privately owned homes here is individually named and designed, giving each its own unique character. **Pros:** great selection of accommodations and prices; good location; sunsets. **Cons:** fills up early in high season; some staff can be aloof; bring your own beach towels. $ *Rooms from: $110* ✉ *Railay West Beach, 200 Moo 2, Railay* ☎ *086/685–9359* ⊕ *www.raileibeachclub. com* ⇌ *24 houses.*

$$$$
RESORT

🔲 **Rayavadee Premier Resort.** Scattered across 26 landscaped acres, this magnificent resort is set in coconut groves with white-sand beaches on three sides. **Pros:** great dining variety; intricate room design; plenty of facilities. **Cons:** notably nonecological use of wood; beach very busy during the day; during low tide boat access is challenging. $ *Rooms from: $800* ✉ *214 Moo 2, Tambol Ao Nang, Amphur Muang, Krabi* ☎ *075/620740 up to 3* ⊕ *www.rayavadee.com* ⇌ *98 rooms, 5 suites.*

$$$
HOTEL
Fodor'sChoice
★

🔲 **Thanyapura Sports Hotel and Mind Center.** Absolutely unique in its concept and style, Thanyapura is a paradise for sporty people of all ages and levels as well as professional atheletes (including Olympic Gold Medallists), who regularly come here from around the world to train in a pristine, relaxing environment with pacifying mountain views. **Pros:** highly professional staff; unbeatable sports facilities; excellent spa. **Cons:** remote location; quiet from 10 pm; a bit of a mishmash of hotel and sports resort. $ *Rooms from: $170* ✉ *120/1 Moo 7 Thepkasattri Rd., Thepkasattri, Thalang, Phuket* ☎ *076/336000* ⊕ *www.thanyapura. com* ⇌ *77 rooms at sports hotel, 38 rooms at retreat* ⦾ *Breakfast.*

KOH LANTA

70 km (42 miles) south of Krabi Town.

GETTING HERE AND AROUND

Krabi's airport is about two hours from Koh Lanta by taxi (B2,300–B3,000) or minibus (B350). Minibuses depart from Krabi Town and Ao Nang, not the airport. There's no direct bus service from Bangkok to Koh Lanta; you'll have to take the bus to Trang or Krabi and then continue on in a minivan (songthaews will take you from the bus station to the minivans bound for Koh Lanta). There are two short (15 minutes) Ro-Ro ferries crossings between the mainland and Lanta catering specifically to those coming by car or bus. There's one direct passenger ferry every morning from Krabi at 11:30 am; it costs B400.

One main road runs along the island that will take you to all major resorts. Pickup trucks masquerading as taxis and motorcycles with sidecars will take you wherever you want to go. Negotiate hard for good fares; prices start at about B60 for a short ride of 1 km (½ mile).

CLOSE UP

The Tsunami

With the exception of those around Similan Islands 1, 2, and 3 (closed prior to the tsunami), all dive sites in Thailand are open to divers, some indisputably beautiful. Especially around the Similan and Surin islands, there are many dive spots that remain world class.

THE POSTTSUNAMI RECOVERY

Both of Thailand's coasts had been experiencing a tourism boom for years—with many places facing the consequences of overdevelopment—when the tsunami hit the Andaman Coast on December 26, 2004. Several beaches on Phuket, the beach area of Khao Lak, and much of Koh Phi Phi were devastated by the waves, and although many areas on the Andaman Coast were unaffected by the tsunami, tourism on that shore came to a near standstill in the months following the disaster.

More than 12 years later, the situation is considerably different. Phuket's affected beaches have been completely redeveloped, including much improved beachfront sidewalks, street lighting, restaurants, bars, and cafés on par with western beach destinations. Phi Phi Island was rebuilt a bit more slowly, but now development has surpassed pretsunami levels. Most development along Tonsai and Loh Dalam initially focused on upgrading salvageable budget accommodations to nicer, midrange standards to fill the void left as the largest resorts planned their reconstruction. The middle and high-end resorts have now reentered the market, and Phi Phi is once again booming, with plenty of bars and restaurants. Khao Lak also has more hotels, restaurants, and activities than it did before 2004. These days the tsunami's lasting effects are not visible to the naked eye, but many Andaman Coast locals lost friends and family, and their lives have been irrevocably altered.

Overdevelopment is an issue, as it was before the disaster. Once adventurous travelers find a new, secluded, undeveloped beach and start talking about it, rapid development follows at a frightening pace. In many spots this development hasn't been regulated or monitored properly, and the country is now pulling in the tourist dollars at the expense of the environment. It's a cycle that's hard to stop. Redevelopment in the tsunami areas began quite slowly, while developers and local businesses awaited government regulations. In some instances, the planning paid off (Phi Phi now has much-needed waste-water treatment facilities), but as most areas waited for regulations that never arrived, no-holds-barred development quickly followed.

SAFETY AND PRECAUTIONS

Lanta is one of Thailand's quieter islands, not because it lacks a tourism infrastructure but because the traditional way of life is strong here. The majority of inhabitants are Muslim, and this guides much of the island's development. The girly bars, the loud late-night discos, and the hectic frenzy of a drinking culture are largely absent. This means that there's a low crime rate, even for Thailand, though precautions should still be taken.

TIMING

Lanta is traditionally a seasonal island. Many hotels and restaurants close in the low season. Between May and October things are quiet. The best time to come here is in the dry, cooler season, between November and April, when it really comes to life.

You can spend weeks on Lanta, if you love the sun and sea. There is still a great deal to do away from the beach, but people primarily come here to soak up the rays.

EXPLORING KOH LANTA

Long beaches, crystal-clear water, and a laid-back natural environment are Koh Lanta's main attractions. Although "discovered" by international travelers in early 2000, Koh Lanta remains fairly quiet. Early development resulted in the construction of hundreds of budget bungalows and several swanky resorts along the west coast of Lanta Yai (Lanta Noi's coast is less suitable for development); however, as one of the largest islands in Thailand, Lanta was able to absorb the "boom" and therefore remains relatively uncluttered. In addition, Lanta is approximately 70 km (44 miles) south of Krabi Town, far enough outside established tourist circuits that visitor arrivals have increased a little more slowly than at other Krabi and Phang Nga beaches and islands.

5

Ironically, before the tsunami it was hard to imagine how Koh Lanta could be any more beautiful, but afterward the water was bluer and more sparkling, the sand whiter and softer. Though the huge decrease in visitor arrivals to the island initially caused its share of economic hardship, it wasn't long before word of Koh Lanta's renewal spread and lucky travelers again found their way to its shores.

Most smaller resorts are closed during the low season (May through October). However, some do open in late October and remain open until mid-May—during these (slightly) off times, the weather is still generally good, and you can find that the rates are much lower and the beaches much less crowded.

BEACHES

Klong Dao Beach and Phra Ae Beach, both on Lanta Yai's west coast, are the most developed. If you head south, you'll reach calmer Klong Nin Beach and southern Lanta's quiet, scenic coves. Southern Lanta beaches consist of several widely dispersed small coves and beaches ending at Klong Chak National Park. Immediately south of Klong Nin the road suddenly becomes well paved (much smoother than the road from Long Beach to Klong Nin), making the southern beaches accessible by road as well as by taxi boat. The nicest of the southern beaches is Bakantiang Beach, a beautiful one to visit on the way to the national park.

Bakantiang (Kantiang) Beach. The last beach before the national park on the southeren tip of Koh Lanta, the cresent-shape Kantiang beach is small but truely stunning. The fine white sands are favored by travelers in the know, or expat residents who want to get away from the busier beaches. The village that backs the beach is the friendliest on the island and there are a few food stalls and roadside cafés that serve up some of the tastiest food on Koh Lanta. **Amenities:** food and drink; toilets;

showers. **Best For:** sunset; swimming; snorkeling. ⊠ *Last stop on main road heading south, before National Park.*

FAMILY **Klong Dao Beach.** Klong Dao Beach is a 2-km-long (1-mile-long) beach on the northern coast of Lanta Yai, the larger of the two islands that comprise Koh Lanta. Most resorts along Klong Dao are larger facilities catering to families and couples looking for a quiet environment. The water is shallow but swimmable, and at low tide the firm, exposed sand is ideal for long jogs on the beach. **Amenities:** food and drink; toilets. **Best for:** sunset; swimming; walking. ⊠ *To the right of Lanta's main road, 1st beach after port town Saladan.*

Klong Nin Beach. Klong Nin Beach, approximately 30 minutes south of Long Beach by car or boat, is one of the larger, nicer beaches toward the southern end of Lanta Yai. Klong Nin is less developed and more tranquil than Long Beach. A typical day on Klong Nin can be a long walk on the silky soft sand interrupted by occasional dips in the sea, a spectacular sunset, a seaside massage, and a candlelight barbecue beneath a canopy of stars. Central Klong Nin, near Otto Bar, is the best for swimming, as rocks punctuate the rest of the shoreline. Kayaks are available from some resorts, and longtail boat taxis are for hire along the sea. Most resorts here rent motorbikes as well, as the road to the south is much smoother than the road from Long Beach. **Amenities:** food and drink; toilets. **Best for:** sunset; swimming; walking; solitude. ⊠ *To right of Lanta's main road from Saladan, after intersection for Old Town and Southern Lanta.*

Phra Ae Beach. Long and wide, Phra Ae Beach (aka Long Beach) is Lanta Yai's main tourist destination. The sand is soft and fine, perfect for both sunbathing and long walks. The water is less shallow than at other Lanta beaches, and therefore more suitable for diving in and having a swim. However, kayaks, catamarans, and other water activities, while available, are not as ubiquitous as on other islands. Although most lodging consists of simple budget resorts, the beachfront does have several three- and four-star accommodations. Along the beach and on the main road are many restaurants, bars, Internet cafés, and dive operators. **Amenities:** food and drink; showers; toilets; water sports. **Best For:** sunset; swimming; walking. ⊠ *2nd beach to right of Lanta's main road from port town Saladan.*

SPORTS AND THE OUTDOORS

Diving, snorkeling, hiking, and elephant trekking are a few activities available on Koh Lanta and the nearby islands. Diving and snorkeling around Koh Lanta can be arranged through dive and tour operators, though most people choose to book through their own resort. Popular nearby dive sites are **Koh Ha** and **Koh Rok**, off Koh Lanta. If you would like to enjoy Koh Lanta from another viewpoint, elephant trekking is available near Phra Ae (Long) Beach. A boat trip to the famous **Emerald Cave** on **Koh Muk** is a worthwhile experience; it's easiest to inquire at your resort about day-trip options.

WHERE TO EAT

$ THAI 🍴 **Caoutchouk.** At the end of a small dirt road, this café-restaurant, run by its French owner and his chef partner, is in a wooden traditional house with high ceilings from which colorful Chinese lanterns hang, swaying in the sea breeze. You can sit inside or choose to relax on the scenic wraparound terrace at the water's edge, taking in beautiful views of the horizon. The chef is a Thai Sea Gypsy whose highly sophisticated culinary vision and style differs in subtle but also pronounced ways to the standard southern fare. He has a love of fresh products, particularly fish, and lovingly cooks what is in season or accessible that day, so don't expect a menu. ■ **TIP→ As it is off the beaten track and less busy in the evenings, the restaurant only stays open if they receive reservations.** [$] *Average main: B145* ✉ *Moo 1, Old Town* ☎ *075/697060, 084/629–0704* ▭ *No credit cards* ⏲ *Daily 11–8.*

$ THAI 🍴 **Phad Thai Rock n' Roll.** Everything is in the name at this tiny roadside eatery, where you can try fresh, authentic and delicious Phad Thai made with shrimp, chicken, vegetables or all of the above, by the talented rock musician-owner. Meet musicians, sip a delicious, healthy and creative smoothie and watch the world go by. ■ **TIP→ Ask the owner when his next gig is. His band, Why Not, attracts huge crowds of locals, expats and tourists alike and guarantees a rocking night out.** [$] *Average main: B70* ✉ *92 Moo 5, Kantiang Bay* ☎ *080/784–8729* 🌐 *www.facebook.com/phadthairock77* ▭ *No credit cards.*

$ 🍴 **Shanti Shanti.** This large beach hut stands on the sand looking out to the ocean, and serves crepes with homemade French jam, cocktails, ice cream and coffees to accompany the lovely view, as well as having a small shop selling clothes and accessories. Owner Fafa is a young French artist (his works decorate the café, and are on sale) who traveled broadly in India before settling in Koh Lanta, where he creates decorative pieces made from things he finds in his natural environment. He also makes edible art in the form of his fantastic ice cream. Cross your fingers that the day you visit he will have made his by now well known and loved Chai, sweet basil, Provence lavender or Kerala cinnamon flavored ice cream, or Indonesian chocolate sherbert. [$] *Average main: B150* ✉ *Klong Nin, Old Town* ☎ *083/748–9527* ▭ *No credit cards* ⏲ *Closed Tues.*

KLONG DAO

$ INTERNATIONAL 🍴 **Dieck's Deli.** Not extraordinary, but the light meals and selection of imported deli foods here may satisfy the cravings of Americans and Europeans who have been traveling for a while, including a decent variety of cheeses, sausages, hams, salami, homemade honey, sourdough bread and jam. [$] *Average main: $86* ✉ *295/5–7 Moo 3, Klong Dao* 🌐 *www.dieckdeli.com* ⏲ *Daily 8–5.*

$ EUROPEAN 🍴 **Fat Monkey (Ling Uan).** Two kitchens, and two cuisines—Thai and western. Fat Monkey serves an extensive range of Thai dishes but is best known and loved for its large, juicy burgers. In a refreshing, pretty garden, this popular venue is great for kicking back after a long day of adventure tours and enjoying a tasty meal and an ice-cream cocktail in a fun and friendly atmosphere. [$] *Average main: B200* ✉ *Center of*

5

Klong Dao Beach, Klong Dao Rd., Saladan ☎ *087/886–5017* 💳 *No credit cards* 🕒 *Closed Mon.*

$ THAI 🍴 **Picasso Restaurant.** This quirky beachfront restaurant at the Chaba Guesthouse serves traditional Thai fare—well cooked and featuring some less-common traditional dishes, such as pumpkin soup with pineapple—as well as friendly service. Proprietor and artist Khun Toi creates pastel-color oil paintings and surreal sculptures incorporating shells and driftwood from Klong Dao Beach. The guesthouse offers clean, comfortable bungalows. [$] *Average main: $100* ✉ *Klong Dao Beach, Lanta Yai* ☎ *075/684118, 099/738–7710* 💳 *No credit cards.*

$ THAI Fodor'sChoice ★ 🍴 **Time for Lime.** Time for Lime is a large, open-air kitchen/restaurant right off the beach, where you can learn to cook fresh, seasonal and creative Thai food (with Chinese, Malaysian, and Indian twists), under fun, expert instruction. Their excellent classes include a valuable theoretical introduction to Thai food and a five-hour option, during which you will prepare, and learn to beautifully present, your own feast. Each night the restaurant serves a different three-course set menu, and reclining chairs are placed on the recessed sandbar while music plays and wonderful cocktails (try the chili margarita) are served. Time For Lime also offers basic yet comfortable bungalows. **■ TIP→ All proceeds from Time For Lime go to the owner Junie's extremely worthy cause: the Lanta Animal Welfare, which has already offered much-needed help to the many strays on the island.** Take time to visit and volunteer! Find out more: 🌐 *www.lantaanimalwelfare.com.* [$] *Average main: B200* ✉ *72/2 Klong Dao Beach, Lanta Yai, Saladan* ☎ *075/684590, 089/967–5017* 🌐 *www.timeforlime.net* 🕒 *Restaurant: closed Nov.–Apr. No classes: Sun.–Fri. May–mid-Oct.; Mon. mid-Oct.–Apr.*

PHRA AE

$ THAI Fodor'sChoice ★ 🍴 **Cook Kai.** From the outside, this place appears to be a standard, wooden Thai beach restaurant, but the creative cooking elevates it out of the ordinary. Sizzling "hotpan" dishes of seafood in coconut cream, stir-fried morning glory and sweet-and-sour shrimp are succulent. Specials, such as duck curry served in a hollowed-out pineapple, change daily and augment the already extensive menu. [$] *Average main: B115* ✉ *Moo 6, Klong Nin Beach* ☎ *081/606–3015* 🌐 *www.cook-kai.com* 💳 *No credit cards.*

$ THAI 🍴 **Lap Royet.** Thai street food is a class of its own, and you will find it absolutely everywhere you turn, though some eateries are definitely more refined than others. This extremely casual roadside restaurant serves 100% authentic, basic and cheap food that locals seem to relish. Try the Isaan (northeastern) catfish larb, the zingy som tam or the fat noodles cooked in a thick pork broth, and sticky BBQ chicken. [$] *Average main: B50* ✉ *Toward northern end of Klong Dao Beach, Klong Dao Rd.* ☎ *No phone* 💳 *No credit cards.*

$ THAI 🍴 **The Red Snapper.** Serving Thai and European fusion food in an atmospheric garden setting, with a compact menu that creative chef Ed Qarré renews every six weeks, it comes as no surprise that Red Snapper has become one of the island's most happening restaurants. If you're hungry order one of their large platters, or opt for a wonderful selection of tapas dishes if your palate is yearning for adventure; while the eponymous red snapper is always succulent and fresh. Cocktails too are innovative; try the Thaipiroska for a locally inspired alcoholic kick. [$] *Average main: B250* ✉ *Phrae Ae Beach* ☎ *078/856965* 🌐 *www.redsnapper-lanta.com* ✍ *Reservations essential* 💳 *No credit cards.*

$$ THAI **🍴 Tides.** This high-profile restaurant in Layana Resort and Spa welcomes outside visitors for a romantic and sophisticated dinner. Set on a polished seafront terrace, Tides serves specials of the day such as grilled giant prawns, as well as more traditional Thai dishes like green curry, and a selection of international classics with a sophisticated spin. Their sommelier has extensive knowledge of the restaurant's wine list and will take time to find the perfect combination for your meal. Start out your night at sunset, by sinking into one of the resort's giant beanbags set on the beach right in front of the restaurant, and order a Coco Loco cocktail and kaffir-lime toasted peanuts, before moving to the dining area for an elegant meal. [$] *Average main: B250* ✉ *272 Moo 3, Saladan, Phra Ae Beach* ☎ *075/607100* 🌐 *www.layanaresort.com.*

KLONG NIN

$ INTERNATIONAL Fodor's Choice ★ **🍴 Otto Bar & Grill.** One of the most popular old-time bars in Koh Lanta, mostly owing to its vibrant owner Otto, a been-there, done-that, mature rocker-hippie whose *joie de vivre* remains charmingly intact. The bar and grill stands right on the beach and is open all day, serving delicious cocktails made with exotic fruits, and a variety of BBQ meats (burgers have a following) and salads, made by its Britsh chef. Otto also has a few basic bungalows backed away from the beach. [$] *Average main: B130* ✉ *Klong Nin Beach* ☎ *No phone* 🌐 *ottolanta.com.*

$ INTERNATIONAL **🍴 Roi Thai.** With tables facing out to the horizon, and fresh, flavorsome seafood and fish BBQs, this is an idyllic beach dinner location. The simple yet charming restaurant prides itself on its fresh ingredients, quality meats, and authentic dishes prepared without the addition of MSG or other flavor enhancers (that are unfortunately used all too often in Thailand today). The food certainly attracts a loyal clientele, although the waitstaff can be slow. **■ TIP→ You can take a cooking class organized by Roi Thai, which also teaches the traditional art of fruit and vegetable carving.** [$] *Average main: B100* ✉ *75/1 Moo 6, Klong Nin Beach* ☎ *083/636–0470* 💳 *No credit cards.*

SOUTHERN LANTA

$ AMERICAN FAMILY **🍴 Drunken Sailors Coffeeshop.** Drunken Sailors is a friendly, laid-back meeting point for tech-savvy travellers (free Wi-Fi), young families, trendy locals, and expats. The Thai-American owners effortlessly create a sense of ease; beanbags and hammocks that are occupied throughout the day attest to this. Playful and homey dishes inspired by the U.S., Thailand, and India make up the menu; try the tuna wasabi sub, or the veggie samosas in puff pastry, or go for one of their burgers. **■ TIP→ Round the back, Drunken Sailors have a shop selling original Thai-chic clothes, accessories, and funky jewelry made by a young local artist.** [$] *Average main: B86* ✉ *Kantiang Bay* ☎ *075/665076* 🌐 *www.facebook.com/DrunkenSailors* 💳 *No credit cards.*

$ THAI FAMILY **🍴 Same Same But Different.** Relax on the beach all day and dip in and out of this upbeat beach-chic restaurant for tasty snacks and drinks, especially refreshing as tables are strewn across the sand and well shaded by large umbrellas. The beamed, wooden circular area with a bamboo roof, a leafy waterfall shrine to Ganesh and a totem pole wearing a sun-faded straw wig make a quirky backdrop to southern Thai dishes made with modern European flair, including grilled prawns or fried chicken, complex curries and more. Same Same also has a new cocktail/smoothie bar and a shop selling home decor items and clothes. **■ TIP→ You will hear the Tinglish (Thai English) phrase Same Same But Different throughout your travels in the country. It actually means "similar but not the same." T-shirts sporting this phrase are sold everywhere.** [$] *Average main: B150* ✉ *85 Moo 5, Bakantiang Beach, Lanta Yai* ☎ *091/787–8670.*

WHERE TO STAY

For expanded hotel reviews, visit Fodors.com.

KLONG DAO

$$$$ RESORT 🏨 **Costa Lanta.** The coolest thing about Costa Lanta is the room design; each room at this trendy boutique resort is a convertible box, so if you're too hot you can open up the "walls" and allow the breeze to blow through. **Pros:** quiet, green location; art-deco design; innovative housing. **Cons:** not great value; not on best beach. [$] *Rooms from: $275* ✉ *212 Klong Dao Beach, Lanta Yai* ☎ *075/618092, 075/668186* 🌐 *www.costalanta.com* 🛏 *22 rooms.*

$ B&B/INN FAMILY 🏨 **Southern Lanta.** With a fun-slide plunging into a big pool and several two-bedroom villas (each with large multibed rooms), Southern Lanta is understandably popular with families. **Pros:** family-friendly; good location; pleasant restaurant. **Cons:** needs redecoration; pool crowds easily; limited views. [$] *Rooms from: $75* ✉ *105 Klong Dao Beach, Lanta Yai* ☎ *075/684175 up to 77* 🌐 *www.southernlanta.com* 🛏 *100 bungalows.*

$$$$ RESORT 🏨 **Twin Lotus Resort and Spa.** Twin Lotus is as much an architectural and interior-design exhibition as it is a sophisticated and tranquil retreat. **Pros:** quality dining; appealing in-room facilities; stunning location. **Cons:** may be too quiet for families; service can be slack. [$] *Rooms from: $300* ✉ *199 Moo 1, Klong Dao Beach, Koh Lanta Yai* ☎ *075/560–7000, 02/361–1946 up to 9 in Bangkok* 🌐 *www.twinlotusresort.com* 🛏 *81 rooms.*

PHRA AE

$ HOTEL 🏨 **Best House.** The Best House lobby, an inviting high-ceilinged room with comfortable chairs, white tile floors and wooden beams, offers a good sense of what you can expect from the accommodations. The rooms are spacious and comfortable, the closest thing to "normal" western hotel rooms on an island of bungalows and upscale spa-resorts. The place isn't on the beach, but it's very close to it. All rooms are equally nice, but air-conditioned rooms have the added luxury of hot water, which is unavailable in cheaper fan rooms. **Pros:** inexpensive; near the beach; friendly service. **Cons:** rooms basic; no pool; no in-room amenities. ✉ *5/1 Moo 3, Phra Ae Beach, Lanta Yai* ☎ *075/684560, 084/464–1500* 🌐 *www.besthouselantaguesthouse.com* 🛏 *30 rooms* 💳 *No credit cards* 🕒 *Closed Apr.–Oct.*

$$$ RESORT 🏨 **Lanta Sand Resort and Spa.** Large ponds with water lilies and spraying fountains cover the grounds of Lanta Sand Resort and Spa. **Pros:** spacious rooms; romantic; near beach. **Cons:** far from any town; noisy a/c

in some rooms; prices too high for what's on offer. $ *Rooms from: $320* ✉ *279 Moo 3, Phra Ae Beach, Lanta Yai* ☎ *075/684633, 089/724–2682* ⊕ *www.lantasand.com* ⤴ *78 rooms.*

$$$$
RESORT
Fodor'sChoice
★

🛏 **Layana Resort and Spa.** Guests repeatedly return to the Layana for a real sense of pampering, understated luxury and a relaxed, peaceful environment. **Pros:** varied breakfast buffet includes healthy juice bar; many activities organized in-house; lovely beach. **Cons:** strictly no children; some bungalows lack sea views; not for party animals. $ *Rooms from: $420* ✉ *272 Moo 3, Saladan, Phra Ae Beach, Koh Lanta* ☎ *075/607100, 02/713–2313 in Bangkok* ⊕ *www.layanaresort. com* ⤴ *50 rooms.*

$
B&B/INN
FAMILY

🛏 **Somewhere Else.** If you like your huts to be of progressive design, go Somewhere Else—the six octagonal rooms in the front of the clearing are particularly cool. **Pros:** very friendly and helpful staff; wonderful beach location; nice restaurant. **Cons:** no hot water; no TV. $ *Rooms from: B20* ✉ *253 Moo 3, Phra Ae Beach, Lanta Yai* ☎ *091/536–0858, 089/731–1312* ⤴ *16 rooms* ▭ *No credit cards* ☾ *Closed June–Sept.*

KLONG NIN

$$
B&B/INN

🛏 **Lanta Miami Bungalows.** The affordable, beach-side bungalows at the Lanta Miami are clean, spacious, and with big beds, and have nicely sized, tiled bathrooms. **Pros:** great location; comfortable; nice pool. **Cons:** some rooms lack amenities; staff can be unaccommodating; rooms without sea views are a bit stuffy. $ *Rooms from: $80* ✉ *13 Moo 6, Klong Nin Beach, Lanta Yai* ☎ *075/662559* ⤴ *26 rooms* ▭ *No credit cards* ☾ *Closed June–Sept.*

$$
RESORT

🛏 **Lanta Paradise Resort.** It's a short walk along the beach to the best swimming spot, but the sand gets so hot you'll be glad to have the pool outside your room. **Pros:** prime location; impressive western food at restaurant; nice views. **Cons:** not the best value; very basic rooms; lack of amenities. $ *Rooms from: $100* ✉ *67 Moo 6, Klong Nin Beach, Lanta Yai* ☎ *075/662569, 089/473–3279* ⊕ *www.lantaparadisebeachresort. com* ⤴ *34 rooms* ▭ *No credit cards* ☾ *Closed June–Sept.*

$$$$
RESORT
FAMILY

🛏 **Rawi Warin Resort and Spa.** This enormous, lively resort with luxuriously outfitted rooms and high-tech amenities, stretches gracefully across an entire hillside along the road from Klong Khong Beach to Klong Nin. **Pros:** many amenities; helpful staff; family-friendly. **Cons:** not great value; beach is rocky; activities are limited. $ *Rooms from: $175* ✉ *139 Moo 8, Lanta Yai Island, Krabi* ☎ *026/643490 up to 48, 02/434–5526 in Bangkok* ⊕ *www.rawiwarin.com* ⤴ *185 rooms.*

SOUTHERN LANTA

$$
HOTEL

🛏 **Mango House.** In the laid-back and increasingly trendy Old Town, or Sri Raya, Mango House is a home away from home, with three seafront suites and three villas, all in Chinese-style wooden houses that stand on stilts over the water. **Pros:** welcoming atmosphere; comfortable rooms; a great base for exploring the Old Town. **Cons:** private property next to rooms is shabby; no a/c. $ *Rooms from: $60* ✉ *45 Sriraya Rd., Moo 2, Old Town* ☎ *089/948–6836* ⊕ *www.mangohouses.com* ⤴ *6 rooms.*

$$
B&B/INN

🛏 **Narima Resort.** With almost all of its bungalows overlooking a refreshing view of Koh Ha, and with relaxing balconies where you can sway in a hammock or kick back in a palm-straw rocking chair, Narima definitely generates a sense of calm. **Pros:** spanning views; pleasant hosts; professional dive school. **Cons:** rocky beach; bathrooms are rough around the edges; restaurant could be better. $ *Rooms from: $120* ✉ *98 M. 5 Klong Nin Beach, Lanta Yai* ☎ *075/662668, 075/662670* ⊕ *www.narima-lanta.com* ⇆ *32 rooms.*

$$$$
RESORT
FAMILY
Fodor's Choice
★

🛏 **Pimalai Resort and Spa.** Pimalai is a paradisal world unto itself, and true to its mantra of "peace, serenity and solitude," which explains why royalty and celebrities regularly favor it. **Pros:** beautiful location and architecture; friendly, helpful management and staff; uniquely luxurious ambience. **Cons:** prices also exclusive; fills up fast. $ *Rooms from: $1400* ✉ *99 Moo 5, Bakantiang Beach, Lanta Yai* ☎ *075/607999* ⊕ *www.pimalai.com* ⇆ *72 rooms, 7 suites, 40 private villas.*

NIGHTLIFE

Bob Bar. A living tribute to reggae, colorful owner Bob welcomes his adoring clientele in this laid back, popular bar with a big smile, cold beer and friendly banter. ✉ *Klong Dao, Ban Koh Lanta.*

The Frog Wine Cellar. In Saladan port town near the pier, this wine bar with an atmospheric garden setting offers a nice change of scene for those interested in sampling wines and accompanying appetizers. They have labels from 12 countries. ✉ *295/19 Moo 3, Klong Dao Beach* ⊕ *www.thefroglanta.com* ☾ *Daily 5–10.*

Funky Monkey. Designed to look like the inside of a jungle, this roadside bar-club is the venue for live gigs that get locals, expats and tourists dancing together until the late hours. Outside benches offer respite from blaring music and a place to snack from nearby street food stalls. Not as fun on nights when there isn't a live performance. ✉ *Klong Dao Rd.*

KOH PHI PHI

48 km (30 miles) or 90 mins by boat southeast of Phuket Town, 42 km (26 miles) or 2 hours by boat southwest of Krabi.

GETTING HERE AND AROUND

Ferries depart from Ratsada Pier on Phuket five times daily and reach Phi Phi Don two hours later. PP Cruiser also takes two hours to reach Phi Phi Don, but departs from Phuket's Makham Pier. A one-way ticket is B560. Ferries traveling to Phuket from Ao Nang or Koh Lanta stop at Koh Phi Phi in the high season (November to April) as well. From Krabi boats depart four times each day and again cost B560

EXPLORING KOH PHI PHI

The Phi Phi Islands consist of six islands. The largest, Phi Phi Don, is shaped like a butterfly: The "wings," covered by limestone mountains, are connected by a flat 2-km (1-mile) narrow body featuring two opposing sandy beaches. Phi Phi Don is the only inhabited island.

A posttsunami rebuilding program has left the island looking remarkably developed. If you were unaware that such a catastrophe had taken place, you would think it was a beautiful island under a lot of development, rather than one that was destroyed and has been rebuilt. There's quite a bit of construction these days, as resorts as well as budget accommodations update and renovate their facilities. The popularity of the Phi Phi Islands stems from the outstanding scuba diving; leopard sharks, turtles, and sea horses are some species still frequenting popular reefs. The tsunami actually had surprisingly little effect on the dive sites here, with 75% of coral reefs sustaining low to no impact. The best dive sites were relatively unaffected, and those hardest hit were not good snorkeling sites to begin with.

Since the tsunami, farther-flung beaches on Phi Phi Don have been getting the attention that they deserve. Before Tonsai Beach was rebuilt, visitors who were forced to look elsewhere for lodging discovered the magic of sandy and swimmable Laem Tong Beach and beautiful, peaceful Long Beach.

BEACHES

Laem Tong Beach. Accessible by boat only, Laem Tong Beach is more secluded than some of the other Phi Phi beaches. The tourquise waters are warm and the beach is bordered by jungle. All this gives Laem Tong more of a tropical island paradise feel than other busier Phi Phi beaches. Perfect for couples who want an intimate and romantic location. ■TIP➜ Local fishermen can bring you here and take you to other nearby destinations on their longtail boats for less money than organized trips. **Amenities:** food and drink; toilets. **Best for:** swimming; sunrise; snorkeling. ⊠ *Northern Phi Phi.*

Loh Dalum Beach. On the other side of the Phi Phi Don Island from Tonsai Village, Loh Dalum has all the hallmarks of a tropical paradise, clear emerald waters, views onto the beautiful bay, white sandy beach. However it is touristy, busy and noisy an unfortunate symptom of Phi Phi's popularity. Beach bars put on spectacular fire shows at night and the partying lasts well into the early hours. Swimming is best at high tide. **Amenities:** food and drink; showers; toilets; watersports. **Best For:** partiers; swimming. ⊠ *Koh Phi Phi Don.*

Long Beach. Being a few minutes' longtail boat ride from Tonsai affords visitors to Long Beach a calmer and more relaxing experience away from the madding crowds. The white sands are almost silky underfoot and there are gorgeous views of Phi Phi Leh. Day trippers often only stay for a dip and lunch, so the rest of the time its pretty peaceful. **Amenities:** food and drink; toilets. **Best for:** snorkeling; swimming.

Tonsai Beach. This is not a place for the fainthearted, it is crowded, noisy, and not the cleanest. The best time to visit is in the early morning when most of the young revellers are sleeping off the excesses of the previous night. **Amenities:** toilets; showers; water sports. **Best for:** partiers.

OFF THE BEATEN PATH

Phi Phi Lae. A popular day trip from Phi Phi Don is a visit to nearby Phi Phi Lae via longtail or speedboat. The first stop is Viking Cave, a vast cavern of limestone pillars covered with crude drawings. Most boats continue on for an afternoon in **Maya Bay,** aka "The Beach." If you don't mind thronging crowds (the snorkelers practically outnumber the fish), Maya Bay is a spectacular site. If you get a really early jump on everyone, cruise into a secluded bay and leave first tracks along the powdery sand beach; otherwise, head to secluded **Loh Samah Bay,** on the opposite side of the island. Loh Samah Bay may, in fact, be

5

DID YOU KNOW?

Koh Phi Phi is actually six islands, though only the largest, Phi Phi Don, is inhabited. Phi Phi Leh is home to the famous Maya Bay; the other islands are really just large limestone outcroppings.

CLOSE UP

Tsunami Memorials

On the eastern end of Loh Dalam Beach is the Phi Phi Tsunami Memorial Park, a tiny garden with a small plaque listing some of the names of those who lost their lives in the 2004 tsunami. Several benches have been dedicated to the memory of others lost in the disaster. The memorial is a little sad, because it seems so small in relation to the devastation that claimed 5,395 lives. Regardless, it is a nice little park, and looking out across the beach and sea, one cannot help but be moved.

Another memorial, this one underwater, is 66 feet deep, off the coast of Monkey Beach. The granite memorial consists of three pyramid-shape plaques arranged in the shape of an equilateral triangle; the plaques are the exact number of centimeters apart as the number of victims taken by the sea. The bases of the pyramids contain philosophical quotations, and the three markers symbolize the elements of land, water, and air in which humans must learn to live in balance. In the center of the triangle rests a single granite stand that describes the tsunami's occurrence. In addition, 2,874 (the number of missing persons) centimeters from the memorial is a traditional Thai sala made from tsunami debris. It is the first underwater memorial monument on earth.

the better option. Though smaller, it is as beautiful as Maya Bay but receives less attention.

Bamboo Island. Alternatively, you can take a 45-minute trip by longtail boat to circular Bamboo Island, with a superb beach around it. The underwater colors of the fish and the coral are brilliant. The island is uninhabited, but you can spend a night under the stars if you're adventuresome. You can also hike up to a series of viewpoints toward the 1,030-foot peak on the east side of the island. The trailhead is near Tonsai Bay; ask your hotel for directions.

WHERE TO EAT

$ SEAFOOD **🍴 Chao Koh Restaurant.** As you stroll Tonsai's walking path, you'll surely notice the catch of the day on display in front of Chao Koh Restaurant (opposite the Chao Koh Resort). Kingfish, swordfish, and barracuda, grilled with garlic and butter, white wine, or marsala sauce, and served with rice or a baked potato, is a mere B250. Clams, crabs, shrimp, Phuket lobster, and live rock lobsters are priced by weight. Chao Koh also serves a variety of Thai salads, appetizers, noodles, and curry dishes, but seafood is their specialty. This restaurant is popular with day-trippers, and often fills up with boatloads of people herded in by their guides. [$] *Average main: B230* ✉ *Tongsai Bay* ☎ *075/620800* 💳 *No credit cards.*

$ ITALIAN **🍴 Ciao Bella.** It's hardly a local haunt in Napoli or Rome, but for Phi Phi, this offers a tasty rendition of basic Italian cuisine to be enjoyed in a candle-lighted seaside ambience under the moon. Their pizza and focaccia comes from a wood-fired oven, and inventive pasta dishes and classic appetizers such as bruschetta, caprese salad, and prosciuttto di

Parma round out the menu. $ *Average main: B145* ✉ *9 Koh Phi Phi Muu* ☎ *081/894–1246* ▭ *No credit cards.*

$

MIDDLE EASTERN

✕ **Hippies Restaurant and Bar.** On the eastern end of Tonsai Beach, Hippies serves excellent Middle Eastern food, such as falafel and *motobel* (eggplant puree with olive oil). The staff at both the restaurant and seaside bar are friendly. Once the sun sets, this is the most happening beach bar in Tonsai, with people dancing on the sand, a large projector screening music concerts, and regular fire shows. $ *Average main: B175* ✉ *Tonsai Beach* ☎ *081/090–4779* ▭ *No credit cards.*

$

THAI

✕ **Pearl Restaurant.** In the heart of Tonsai Village, this restaurant admirably manages to exist under the radar as a no-frills restaurant in a sea of glitzy bars and high-end eateries. Nothing fancy here, just authentic Thai food prepared and served by genuinely friendly Thai people. Most impressive of all are the views, sea breeeze and laid-back beach atmosphere. They also serve breakfast and a few western dishes. $ *Average main: B200* ✉ *Next to Cosmic Restaurant, Tonsai Village* ☎ *071/645716* ▭ *No credit cards.*

$

CAFÉ

✕ **Phi Phi Bakery.** Craving fresh-baked donuts, Danish, croissants, mouthwatering eggs Benedict, porridge, or real coffee rather than the vile instant stuff? Check out the family-run Phi Phi Bakery, which serves American, Continental, and Thai breakfast and brunch specials and freshly baked pastries (the cinnamon buns are especially good). They also serve Thai and western standards for lunch and dinner. $ *Average main: B150* ✉ *97 Moo 7, Tonsai Village* ☎ *075/601017* ▭ *No credit cards.*

$

SEAFOOD

✕ **Thai Cuisine.** Fresh seafood is not hard to come by on Phi Phi, but even so, Thai Cuisine's selection of white shark, barracuda, swordfish, lobster, and crab has people lining up outside to get a table. In addition to finely cooked fish, Thai Cuisine makes great fried rice. Look for the restaurant with all rattan walls and ceiling across from Phi Phi Bakery in the middle of Tonsai's beach road, near the pier. The food is excellent, although the service is shoddy at times. $ *Average main: B145* ✉ *Central Tonsai Beach, Koh Phi Phi* ☎ *075/631565* ▭ *No credit cards.*

WHERE TO STAY

For expanded hotel reviews, visit Fodors.com.

$$

B&B/INN

🏠 **Chao Koh Phi Phi Lodge.** This B&B a collection of basic but comfortable bungalows near Tonsai Bay. **Pros:** budget accommodation; short walk from the beach; nice pool. **Cons:** bungalows have gaudy exteriors; very basic standards; somewhat pricey for what you get. $ *Rooms from: $50* ✉ *Tongsai Bay* ☎ *075/620800* ⊕ *www.chaokohphiphi.com* ⇲ *44 bungalows* ❘○❘ *Breakfast.*

$$$

RESORT

Fodor's Choice

★

🏠 **Holiday Inn Resort.** On more than 50 acres of tropical gardens along a beach with only three other resorts, which has gorgeous blue water with a sandy sea floor, where you can swim and snorkel year-round—this Holiday Inn couldn't have a better location. **Pros:** secluded, private beach; attentive staff. **Cons:** set away from the main part of Koh Phi Phi. $ *Rooms from: $150* ✉ *Cape Laemtong* ☎ *075/627300* ⊕ *www. phiphi-palmbeach.com* ⇲ *130 bungalows.*

$$ RESORT FAMILY **Outrigger Phi Phi Island Resort and Spa.** At Outrigger Phi Phi you'll find breezily spacious, thatch-roofed bungalows with sharp, bright, contemporary interiors. **Pros:** lovely location; great pool; good restaurants. **Cons:** a little remote; how you get there depends on the tide; staff can be a little lax. [$] *Rooms from: $250* ✉ *49 Moo 8* ☎ *075/628900* 🛏 *144 bungalows, 12 villas.*

$$ RESORT **Paradise Resort.** Despite having undergone renovations and pushing up its prices, this place continues to offer great value for money. **Pros:** budget rooms in idyllic location; clean rooms; great beach massage service. **Cons:** some rooms lack a/c; Wi-Fi at extra charge; may be too quiet for some. [$] *Rooms from: $70* ✉ *Long Beach* ☎ *091/968–3982 up to 9* 🌐 *www.paradiseresort.co.th* 🛏 *25 rooms* 💳 *No credit cards.*

$$$ RESORT **Phi Phi Erawan Palm Resort.** Erawan Palm is a small, comfortable resort in the middle on Laem Tong Beach, next to the sea gypsy village. **Pros:** relaxed resort feel; interesting museum; nice location. **Cons:** boat ride away from main village; decor shows some age. [$] *Rooms from: $160* ✉ *Moo 8, Laem Tong Beach* ☎ *075/627500* 🌐 *www.pperawanpalms.com* 🛏 *18 cottages.*

$$ HOTEL **Phi Phi Hotel.** It's easy to find this hotel—it's the big eyesore directly in front of the pier. **Pros:** central location, nice beach; great views from top-floor rooms. **Cons:** tacky exterior; cleaning not up to scratch; Wi-Fi is extra. [$] *Rooms from: $80* ✉ *129 Moo 7, Tonsai Beach, Koh Phi Phi* ☎ *075/611233, 075/620599* 🛏 *86 rooms* 🍴 *Breakfast.*

$$ RESORT **Phi Phi Natural Resort.** Beautiful sunrise views from the seaside bungalows are this resort's biggest draw. **Pros:** daily boat service to Phuket and Krabi; lovely views at moderate prices. **Cons:** lacks amenities compared to other resorts in price range; remote; can get too busy. [$] *Rooms from: $100* ✉ *53 Moo 8, Laem Tong BeachLaem Tong Beach* ☎ *075/613000* 🌐 *www.phiphinatural.com* 🛏 *70 rooms.*

$$ RESORT **Phi Phi Villa Resort.** Large thatch-covered huts in a natural setting give Phi Phi Villa a relaxing island feeling quite different from bustling Tonsai Bay, a short walk away. **Pros:** budget prices; close to the action; yoga. **Cons:** noise from nearby bars; rocky beach not great for swimming. [$] *Rooms from: $110* ✉ *Tonsai Bay* ☎ *075/601100* 🌐 *www.phiphivillaresort.com* 🛏 *55 bungalows.*

$$$ RESORT **Zeavola.** Zeavola takes its name from a flower, the name of which translates in Thai to "love of the sea." **Pros:** stunning beach location; tasteful design; private. **Cons:** doubled service charge on food; service can be slack. [$] *Rooms from: $180* ✉ *11 Moo 8, Laem Tong, Koh Phi Phi* ☎ *075/627000* 🌐 *www.zeavola.com* 🛏 *52 villas* 🍴 *Breakfast.*

NIGHTLIFE

Many people come to Phi Phi for two reasons only: to go to Maya Bay during the day, and to party in Tonsai Bay at night. As a result, a large number of bars were constructed, primarily out of concrete, most of which were strong enough to survive the impact from the waves. Once you head down the side streets away from the beach there are mazes of bars and clubs competing in stereo wars, filled with young travelers eager to drink and dance the night away. If you like Khao San Road in Bangkok, you will love Tonsai Bay at night. The most popular of these bars, located near the 7-Eleven in the center of "town," are **Tiger**

Bar and **Reggae Bar.** Along the path running parallel to the sea there are several popular bars, notably **Apache Bar,** which has an impressive "katoey" (drag cabaret) show, and farther to the east are fire shows at the popular beach spots **Hippies Bar** and **Carpe Diem.**

Slinky Beach Bar. If you're young, restless, and like to party all night, Slinky is for you. It gathers the wild crowd and regularly hosts theme parties and fire shows. It doesn't get more rowdy and crowded than this on Koh Phi Phi. ⊠ *Loh Dalum Bay.*

Sunflower Bar. More remote beaches around the island have more subdued nightlife, primarily centered on resort restaurants and bars. One of the best of these is Sunflower Bar, which is on the eastern end of Loh Dalum Beach, next to the Tsunami Memorial Park. Constructed almost entirely of driftwood or old wooden bungalows, this laid-back beach bar is a great place to enjoy scenic sea views and listen to local reggae bands jamming beneath the stars. ⊠ *Loh Dalum Bay.*

CHIANG MAI

6

WELCOME TO CHIANG MAI

TOP REASONS TO GO

★ **History:** Chiang Mai's historical heritage is described in two excellent museums and displayed in the architecture of its Old City.

★ **Temples and Monastery Gardens:** The Old City alone has more than 30 ancient temples, where monks are happy to sit with visitors and explain the principles of Buddhism and their cloistered life.

★ **Ethnic Eating:** Chiang Mai's restaurants serve the full range of northern Thai cuisine from menus that usually stretch to more than 100 individual dishes, most of them costing no more than two dollars.

★ **Views for Miles:** Chiang Mai allows easy access to spectacular mountain scenery, criss-crossed by trekking trails that lead to remote hill tribe villages where visitors are welcome guests. The mountainous region north of Chiang Mai also offers a dazzling selection of leisure activities, from elephant riding to white-water rafting and rock climbing.

1 The Old City. The Old City is enclosed by its 800-year-old moat, a tree-shaded stretch of water where locals stroll, lingering at the many markets en route. Much of the wall that once encircled the city has been restored, and the most important of its five original gates, called Pratou Tha Phae, fronts a broad square where markets and festivals are constantly in full swing. Most of Chiang Mai's principal attractions, including its oldest temples, are here.

2 Beyond the Old City. The shortage of available land in the Old City's "square mile" means that most of Chiang Mai's hotels,

GETTING ORIENTED

Modern Chiang Mai is expanding on all sides, but it remains a relatively compact city. First-time visitors are recommended to find accommodations in the Old City, a square mile of busy roads and quiet lanes bounded by ruined walls and a moat, reminders of the eight centuries it served as a citadel and bulwark against invasion from Burma. Most of Chiang Mai's attractions lie within this square mile and are easily accessible on foot. A stroll through the back streets and lanes—known as *sois*—is one of the top pleasures of a visit. Beyond the Old City a couple of suburbs are developing into tourist destinations of their own. Two ring roads, complete with underpasses, keep traffic flowing around the city center.

6

guesthouses, restaurants, and commercial premises are located in the areas beyond the enclosing moat. Some of the city's liveliest nightspots are beyond the walls, and deserve some attention.

3 Greater Chiang Mai.
Two ring roads and a "Super Highway" allow easy access to the rapidly growing residential suburbs and to the mountains that rise east, west, and north of the city. Day trips to the mountains

(including Thailand's highest peak, Doi Inthanon, or the city's "guardian mountain," Doi Suthep) can include an action-packed program of elephant riding, whitewater rafting, and brief jungle hikes and still leave time for a leisurely evening back in Chiang Mai.

Updated by
Robert Tilley

Cosmopolitan Chiang Mai, Thailand's second city, is regarded by many as its rightful, historic capital. It's a fascinating and successful mix of old and new, where 1,000-year-old temples and quiet monastery gardens exist side by side with glittering new hotels and shopping malls. Simple Thai outlets selling local fare rub shoulders with sophisticated restaurants that would merit inclusion in the good-food guides of any U.S. or European metropolis.

The city is enjoying boom times and expanding at a giddy rate, with the latest "entertainment area" zoned beyond its outer ring roads and further ambitious plans afoot: it wants to develop beyond its role as a provincial city to become a gateway to Myanmar, Laos, and western China. Since the late 1990s, luxury hotels have been shooting up, attracting more business and leisure travelers, and the city is bidding to become the site of the World Expo fair in 2020. And although the country's main highway, Highway 1, bypasses Chiang Mai as it runs between Bangkok and Chiang Rai, officials have made sure the city is at the center of a spider's web of highways reaching out in all four directions of the compass, with no major city or town more than a day's drive away. As one local magazine put it, "Chiang Mai is on the fast track to the future"—quite literally since plans have been approved to build a high-speed rail link with Bangkok within the next 10 years, reducing the current 696-km (430-mile), 12-hour journey to less than four hours.

First impressions of modern Chiang Mai can be disappointing. The immaculately maintained railroad station and the chaotic bus terminal are in shabby districts, and the drive into the city center is far from spectacular. First-time visitors ask why they can't see the mountains that figure so prominently in the travel brochures. But once you cross the Ping River, Chiang Mai begins to take shape. Enter the Old City, and Chiang Mai's brooding mountain, Doi Suthep, is now in view—except when shrouded in the month of March, when heavy air pollution is caused by farmers burning their fields for the planting season. ■TIP➜ The

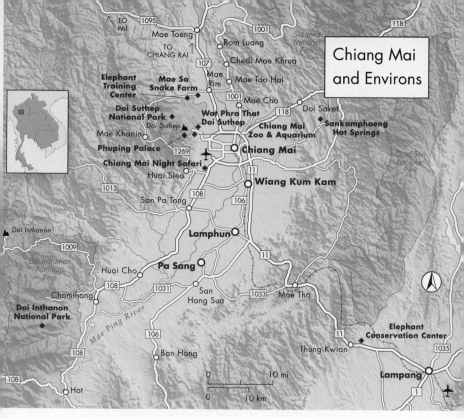

pollution, in fact, is becoming so bad that those with breathing problems are advised to avoid the city in March.

In the heart of the Old City, buildings with more than three-stories high have been banned, and guesthouses and restaurants vie with each other for the most florid decoration. Many of the streets and sois have been paved with flat, red cobblestones. Strolling these narrow lanes, lingering in the quiet cloisters of a temple, sipping hill tribe coffee at a wayside stall, and fingering local fabrics in one of the many boutiques are among the chief pleasures of a visit to Chiang Mai. And whenever you visit, there's bound to be a festival in progress.

PLANNING

WHEN TO GO

Most visitors come to Chiang Mai for only a few days—hardly time enough to take in all its attractions and enjoy all the city has to offer. At least a week's stay is recommended; Chiang Mai's temples alone demand a couple of days' attention, while the surrounding upland countryside is packed with attractions worthy of a day trip. The best time to visit is in the winter months, the dry season between November and February, when days are pleasantly sunny and evenings refreshingly cool. From March to June the weather can be uncomfortably hot, and from July to October the monsoon rains sweep the city. Heavy pollution means March is best avoided.

FESTIVALS AND ANNUAL EVENTS

April sees the city's main holiday, Songkran, or the "water festival," which can offer a refreshing opportunity to cool off in the scorching heat. While Songkran is the hedonistic celebration of the Thai New Year, Loy Kratong in November is a quieter occasion, a combination of thanksgiving and prayers for future prosperity, when small boat-like receptacles (*kratong*) are launched into Chiang Mai's River Ping, surrounding lakes and even ponds. Try to time your stay to coincide with the festive, simultaneous release of thousands of hot-air lanterns into the night sky above Chiang Mai, usually around the middle of November, a truly awesome sight. Awesome, too, is the city's annual flower festival in February, where you're bound to encounter exotic shrubs and flowers you've never seen before, many of them decorating the huge floats that wind their way through the city in one of its most spectacular processions.

GETTING HERE AND AROUND

AIR TRAVEL

Thai Airways has 10 daily flights to Chiang Mai from Bangkok (1 hour 10 minutes) and two direct flights daily from Phuket (1 hour 50 minutes). Bangkok Airways has six flights daily from Bangkok to Chiang Mai. In peak season flights are heavily booked. Four budget airlines, operating from Bangkok's original international airport, Don Muang, offer flights for as little as $70: One Two Go, Orient Thai Airlines, Thai Air Asia, and Nok Air.

Chiang Mai International Airport is about 10 minutes south of downtown and a B100 taxi ride. Songthaews run to the city center for around B50.

Airports and TransfersBangkok Airways ☎ *053/276176, 053/281519.* **Chiang Mai International Airport** ☎ *053/270222.* **Thai Airways** ☎ *053/920999, 053/920920.*

BUS TRAVEL

VIP buses ply the route between Bangkok's Northern Bus Terminal and Chiang Mai, stopping at Lampang on the way. For around B400 to B600 you get a comfortable 10- to 12-hour ride in a modern bus with reclining seats, blankets and pillows, TV, onboard refreshments, and lunch or dinner at a motorway stop. You can take cheaper buses, but the faster service is well worth a few extra baht.

Chiang Mai's Arcade Bus Terminal serves Bangkok, Chiang Rai, Mae Hong Son, and destinations within Chiang Rai Province. Chiang Phuak Bus Terminal serves Lamphun, Chiang Dao, Tha Ton, and destinations within Chiang Mai Province.

CAR TRAVEL

The well-paved roads around Chiang Mai are no problem for most drivers—even the mountainous Mae Sa route north of Chiang Mai is perfectly drivable. However, Thai drivers are notoriously reckless and accidents are frequent. Two major car-rental agencies in Chiang Mai are

Avis and Hertz; Budget has a good range of four-wheel-drive vehicles. Many hotels have motorcycle rentals.

Avoid driving in the city during rush hours, which start as early as 7 in the morning and 3 in the afternoon, and pay special attention to no-parking restrictions (usually 9 am to noon and 3 pm to 6 pm). Parking is prohibited on many streets on alternate days, but the explanatory signs are mostly in Thai. Your best bet is to note on which side of the street vehicles are parking. Chiang Mai's traffic police are merciless, and clamp and tow away vehicles parked illegally. Parking lots are numerous and charge as little as B20 for all-day parking.

A car and driver are the most convenient way to visit the hard-to-find temples outside the city. Car-rental agencies also handle car-and-driver hires.

TAXI, TUK-TUK, AND SONGTHAEW TRAVEL

Metered taxis, which can be flagged down on the street, are being introduced gradually in Chiang Mai, replacing the noisier, dirtier songthaews. The basic taxi charge is B30; you'll pay around B50 for a ride across the Old City. Tuk-tuks are generally cheaper than taxis, but you are expected to bargain—offer B20 or so less than the driver demands. The songthaews that trundle around the city on fixed routes are the cheapest form of transport—just B20 if your destination is on the driver's route. If he has to make a detour, you'll be charged an extra B20 or so. Settle on the fare before you get in. If your Thai is limited, just hold up the relevant number of fingers. If you hold up three and your gesture evokes the same response from the driver, you'll be paying B30. A reliable 24-hour taxi company is Smile Family Taxi Service (☎ *090–5790*).

TRAIN TRAVEL

The State Railway links Chiang Mai to Bangkok and points south. As the uninteresting trip from Bangkok takes about 13 hours, overnight sleepers are the best choice. The overnight trains are invariably well maintained, with clean sheets on rows of two-tier bunks. ■ TIP➔ Spending a few extra baht for a first-class compartment is strongly recommended. In second class you may be kept awake by partying passengers. If you're traveling alone, however, you might find yourself sharing the two-berth compartment with a Thai who speaks no English and snores. Trains for the north depart from Bangkok's Hualamphong Railway Station and arrive in the Chiang Mai Railway Station. First-class fares from Bangkok to Chiang Mai range from B1,300 for a sleeper to B600 or B800 for a day train (➪ *Train Travel in Travel Smart Thailand*).

SAFETY AND PRECAUTIONS

Incidents of street crime involving foreign visitors are rare, and when they do occur they are energetically investigated by the police. Nevertheless, the usual elementary precautions should be taken when walking the city streets, and particularly the sois, at night. Leave your valuables in your hotel (either in a room safe or with the proprietor). If you leave your passport in the hotel, make sure to carry a copy—it's an offense not to carry some form of identification. Women are advised to carry handbags on the side of the sidewalk that's farthest from the street.

VISITOR INFORMATION

Contacts **Tourist Authority of Thailand (Chiang Mai)** ✉ *105/1 Chiang Mai–Lamphun Rd.* ☎ *053/248604, 053/241466* ⊕ *www.tourismthailand.org.*

TOURS AND CLASSES

Every other storefront in Chiang Mai seems to be a tour agency, and not all of them are professionally run. Pick up a list of agencies approved by the Tourism Authority of Thailand before choosing one; the Chiang Mai branch is in a small building on the eastern bank of the Mae Ping River, opposite the New Bridge, open daily 8:30 to 4:30.

Prices vary quite a bit, so shop around, and carefully examine the offerings. Each hotel also has its own travel desk with ties to a tour operator. The prices are often higher, as the hotel adds its own surcharge. If spending time in monasteries makes you wonder about the lives of the monks, or if you find yourself so enthralled by delicious dishes that you want to learn how to prepare them, you're in luck. Chiang Mai has hundreds of schools offering classes in anything from aromatherapy to Zen Buddhism. The city also has dozens of cooking classes—some in the kitchens of guesthouses, others fully accredited schools—teaching the basics of Thai cuisine. Courses cost B800 to B1,000 a day. *Cooking courses are listed in this chapter under Shopping.* Alternative medicine, cooking, and massage are the other most popular courses, but by no means the most exotic. In three weeks at the Thailand's Elephant Conservation Center near Lampang you can train to become a fully qualified mahout.

American University Alumni. The American University Alumni has been offering Thai language courses for more than 20 years. Charges vary according to the duration of the course and the number of pupils. ✉ *73 Ratchadamnoen Rd.* ☎ *053/278407, 053/277951* ⊕ *auathailand.org/chiangmai.*

Best Tuk Tuk Tours. A Thailand-born American, Paul Collins, operates Chiang Mai's only foreign-owned tuk-tuk service, Best Tuk Tuk Tours. Paul is fluent in Thai, and is a knowledgeable guide to the sights in and around Chiang Mai. ☎ *084/948–3315, 085/048406* ⊕ *www.besttuktuktours@yahoo.com.*

Chiangmai Cattleya Tour & Travel Services ✉ *Hillside Plaza 4, 50/53 Huay Kaew Rd.* ☎ *053/223991* ⊕ *www.chiangmaitour.com.*

Chiangmai Tic Travel. Chiangmai Tic Travel arranges custom tours of Northern Thailand ranging from day trips to weeklong holidays, and also has its own elephant park, north of Chiang Mai. ✉ *147/1 Ratchadamnoen Rd.* ☎ *053/814174* ⊕ *www.chiangmaitic.com.*

Chiang Mai Adventure Tour. Tours of Chiang Mai and the North lasting up to one week are offered by the friendly coffee-shop travel agency Chiang Mai Adventure Tour. ✉ *131 Ratchadamnoen Rd.* ☎ *053/277810* ⊕ *www.chiangmai-adventure-tour.com.*

Corner Stone International. Corner Stone International has both group and individual Thai language instruction. ✉ *17/2 Sirimongkalajarn Rd.* ☎ *089/191–9611* ⊕ *www.learnthai.com.*

Nathlada Boonthueng. TAT-registered Nathlada Boonthueng, who works from her home, is an English-speaking guide with a deep knowledge of the region and one of the best local independent operators. She's known as Timmy. ☎ *081/531–6884* ⊕ *www.chiangmaidestination.com.*

Northern Trek and Travel. Two-day treks to remote hill-tribe villages are facilitated by this agency. The B1,200 fee includes overnight accommodation and all meals. ⊠ *Tha Pae Rd., 251 Soi 5* ☎ *053/903849.*

Pu-Chlee Travel. Puwana Mekara (Tony for short) and Thanchanok Wongkhajorn (also known as Ann) run the friendly, efficient Pu-Chlee travel service in the heart of the Old City. Both are fluent in English and are highly qualified. ☎ *083/764–6644.*

Top North. Top North arranges various one-day mountain tours and multiday trekking tours to hill tribe villages. ⊠ *41 Moon Muang Rd.* ☎ *053/279–6235* ⊕ *www.topnorthtourchiangmai.com.*

World Travel Service. Founded in 1947, World Travel Service is Thailand's oldest travel agency. From its central office in Bangkok, it organizes tours of Chiang Mai and Northern Thailand lasting from one to seven days. ⊠ *100/16 Huay Kaew Rd.* ☎ *053/217850, 02/233–5900 up to 9* ⊕ *www.wts-thailand.com.*

6

EXPLORING CHIANG MAI

The compact Old City can be explored easily on foot or by bicycle. The system of one-way streets can be confusing for newcomers, but the plan keeps traffic moving quite effectively around the moat, which is crossed by bridges at regular intervals. The moated "one square mile" of the Old City contains 38 of Chiang Mai's temples, including its oldest and most historic, so there's enough here to keep the most dedicated student of Buddhist architecture and culture occupied. The so-called Lanna style of architecture—stepped eaves, dark teak, and gleaming white stucco construction—has been adopted by the owners of the increasing number of "boutique" hotels arising throughout the Old City, where high-rise buildings are banned.

THE OLD CITY

Covering roughly 2½ square km (1 square mile), the patchwork of winding lanes that make up Chiang Mai's Old City is bounded by remains of the original city wall and a wide, water-filled moat. Start any tour of the Old City at the Thapae Gate, which leads through the ancient city walls into the oldest part of Chiang Mai. Heading west on Ratchadamnoen Road and turning north on Ratchaphakhinai Road brings you to the first of the area's major sights, Wat Chiang Man, the oldest temple in Chiang Mai. Backtracking down Ratchaphakhinai Road and heading west on Ratchadamnoen Road brings you to Wat Chedi Luang and Wat Phra Singh. Several other worthwhile temples are outside the city walls. To the east is the serene Wat Chaimongkol. It's an easy walk from the Tha Pae Gate if the sun isn't too strong. You'll

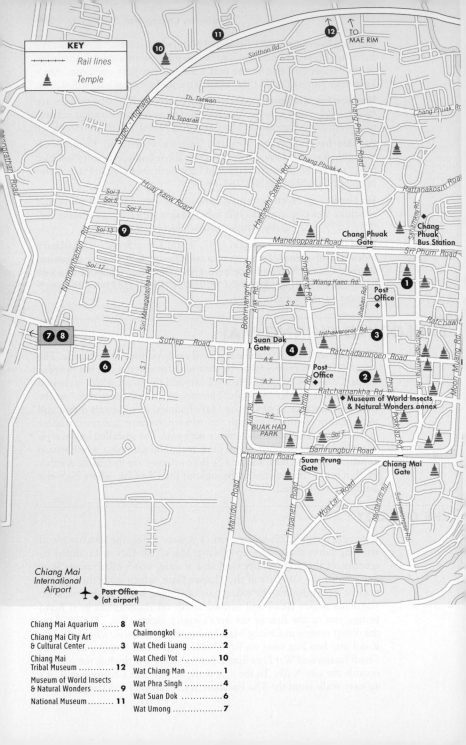

KEY

╂╂╂ Rail lines

🔺 Temple

Kaoprathan Road

Super Highway

Sirithon Rd.

Th. Taewan

Th. Teparak

Chang Phuak Rd

Chang Phuak, Rd

Rattanakosin Road

TO MAE RIM ⑪ ⑫

⑩

Huay Kaew Road

Soi 3
Soi 5
Soi 7
Soi 13 ⑨
Soi 17

Nimmanhemin Rd

Sri Mahagatadan Rd

Suthep Road

S.1

Chang Phuak 4

Hadsadhi Sawtee Rd.

Maneeopparat Road

Chang Phuak Gate

Chang Phuak Bus Station

Sri Phum Road

Wiang Kaeo Rd.

Boonruangrit Road

Arak Rd.

Singharat Rd.

Inthawarorot Rd.

Ratchadamnoen Road

Jhaban Rd.

Post Office

①

S 2

Suan Dok Gate

④

A 6

A 7

③

Ratchawit

Ratchaphakhina Rd

Moon Muang Rd

Post Office

Ratchamankha Rd.

②

Museum of World Insects & Natural Wonders annex

⑦ ⑧

④

Arak Rd.

Samlan Rd.

S 6

BUAK HAD PARK

Soi 7

Bamrungburi Road

Pokkao Rd.

⑥

Changtoh Road

Suan Prung Gate

Chiang Mai Gate

Mahidol Road

Thipanett Road

Wua Lai Road

Nantaam Rd.

Suthewongse Rd.

Chiang Mai International Airport

✈ Post Office (at airport)

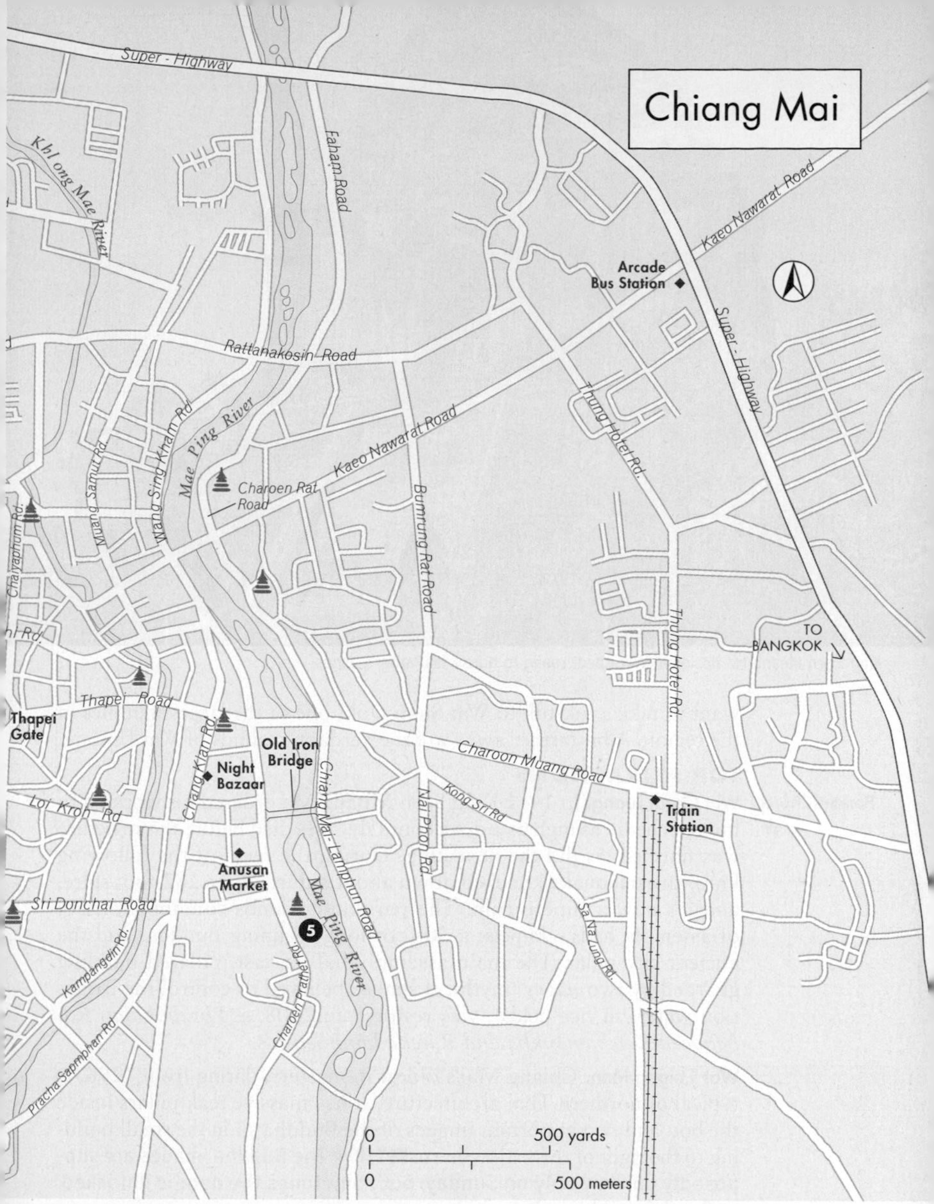
Chiang Mai
Super - Highway
Khl ong Mae River
Faham Road
Kaeo Nawarat Road
Arcade
Bus Station
Rattanakosin Road
Thung Hotel Rd.
Mae Ping River
Wang Sing Kham Rd
Muang Samut Rd.
Charoen Rat
Road
Bumrung Rat Road
Chaiyaphum Rd.
TO
BANGKOK
Thapei Road
Thapei
Gate
Old Iron
Bridge
Night
Bazaar
Chang Klan Rd.
Charoon Muang Road
Kong Sri Rd
Nai Phon Rd.
Train
Station
Loi Kroh Rd
Chiang Mai - Lamphun Road
Anusan
Market
Sri Donchai Road
Sa Na Lung Rd.
Kampangdin Rd.
Charoen Prathet Rd.
Pracha Sapmphan Rd
0
500 yards
0
500 meters

King Saen Muang Ma designed Wat Chedi Luang to house his father's ashes.

want to take a tuk-tuk to Wat Suan Dok, one of the largest temples in the region. A bit farther away are the verdant grounds of Wat Umong.

TOP ATTRACTIONS

Fodor's Choice ★ Wat Chedi Luang. In 1411 King Saen Muang Ma ordered his workers to build a chedi "as high as a dove could fly." He died before the structure was finished, as did the next king. During the reign of the following king, an earthquake knocked down about a third of the 282-foot spire, and it's now a superb ruin. The parklike grounds contain a variety of assembly halls, chapels, a 30-foot-long reclining Buddha, and the ancient city pillar. The main assembly hall, a vast, pillared building guarded by two *nagas* (mythical snakes believed to control the irrigation waters in rice fields), was restored in 2008. ⊠ *Phrapokklao Rd. between Ratchamankha and Ratchadamnoen rds.*

Wat Chiang Man. Chiang Mai's oldest monastery, dating from 1296, is typical of northern Thai architecture. It has massive teak pillars inside the bot, and two important images of the Buddha sit in the small building to the right of the main viharn. ■TIP→ **The Buddha images are supposedly on view only on Sunday, but sometimes the door is unlocked.** ⊠ *Ratchaphakhinat Rd.*

Fodor's Choice ★ Wat Phra Singh. In the western section of the Old City stands Chiang Mai's principal monastery, Wat Phra Singh, which was extensively renovated in 2006. The beautifully decorated wat contains the Phra Singh Buddha, with a serene and benevolent expression that is enhanced by the light filtering in through the tall windows. Note the temple's facades of splendidly carved wood, the elegant teak beams and posts, and the masonry. Don't be surprised if a student monk approaches you to practice his English. ⊠ *Phra Singh Rd. and Singharat Rd.*

WORTH NOTING

Chiang Mai City Art & Cultural Center. The handsome city museum is housed in a colonnaded palace that was the official administrative headquarters of the last local ruler, Chao (Prince) Inthawichayanon. Around its quiet central courtyard are 15 rooms with exhibits documenting the history of Chiang Mai. ■**TIP→** In another small, shady courtyard is a delightful café. The palace was built in 1924 in the exact center of the city, site of the ancient city pillar that now stands in the compound of nearby Wat Chedi Luang. In front of the museum sit statues of the three kings who founded Chiang Mai. ⊠ *Phrapokklao Rd.* ☎ *053/217793, 053/219833* ⊕ *www.chiangmaicitymuseum.org* ⊠ *B90* ☉ *Tues.–Sun. 8:30–5.*

TEMPLE KNOW-HOW

Most temple complexes open about 6 am and don't close until 6 or 8 pm, although the hours can be irregular and the doors may be locked for no reason. If that's the case, approach any monk and explain that you'd like to visit. He'll normally open up the temple. There's no admission charge, except Wat Phra That Doi Suthep (B40) and the *wiharn* (assembly hall) of Wat Phra Singh (B20), but leave some change in one of the collection boxes. (By making a donation you're also "making merit" and easing your journey to the hereafter.) In some temples caged birds are for sale—you're expected to set them free, another means of making merit.

FAMILY **Museum of World Insects & Natural Wonders.** Save a visit to this offbeat museum for a rainy day. Children love its oddball display of creepy-crawlies, which include enormous centipedes, beetles, moths, gaudy butterflies, and the world's largest collection of individual mosquito species. The collection has grown so much that a second, smaller museum has opened in the Old City, in Ratchadamnoen Road. ⊠ *Nimmanhemin Rd., 72 Soi 13* ☎ *053/211891* ⊕ *www.insectmuseumthailand.multiply. com* ⊠ *B200* ☉ *Daily 8:30–4:30.*

BEYOND THE OLD CITY

Outside the borders of the Old City, Chiang Mai expands into urban sprawl; although there are several worthy sights and a handful of identifiable areas, which have preserved or developed some individual style. Shopaholics have to venture outside the enclosing moat and make for the famous Night Market or Nimmanhemin Road, the preserve of Chiang Mai's "tuppies" (Thai Upwardly Mobile Professional People) both a 10-minute tuk-tuk ride away from the city center. Chiang Mai's best and liveliest nighttime scene is to be found on the other side of the city in the Riverside quarter bordering the Ping River.

TOP ATTRACTIONS

FAMILY **Chiang Mai Aquarium.** Asia's biggest aquarium opened in Chiang Mai in 2008. The vast project, on a 4-acre plot next to the city's zoo, features a walk-through underwater tunnel more than 160 yards long. About 8,000 aquatic creatures, embracing 250 species, stock the aquarium.

Monk Chat

If you're like most people, a visit to Chiang Mai's numerous temples is likely to leave you full of unanswered questions. Head to Wat Suan Dok or Wat Chedi Luang, where help is at hand. The monks and novice monks who reside in the two temples eagerly welcome foreign visitors for chats about the history of their temples, the Buddhist faith, and Thai history and culture. Their enthusiasm isn't totally altruistic—they're keen to practice their English.

The talkative monks at Wat Suan Dok are all students of a religious university attached to the temple. Their "monk chat" takes place 5:30 to 7:30 pm on Monday, Wednesday, and Friday. Their counterparts at Wat Chedi Luang can be approached Monday to Saturday, noon to 6:30, as they relax under the trees of their parklike compound. They urge foreign visitors to converse with them about Lanna culture, life in a monastery, or, as one monk put it, "anything at all."

Several varieties of sharks, including the Great White, swim around visitors as they make their way through the viewing tunnel. More daring visitors can don masks and snorkels and join the big fish in the water (B700). There's also a daily water ballet performance by a stunning mermaid. ⊠ *Chiang Mai Zoo, 100 Huay Kaew Rd.* ☎ *053/893111* ⊕ *www. chiangmaiaquarium.com* 🖃 *B500* ⊙ *Daily 9–9.*

Chiang Mai Tribal Museum. The varied collection at this museum, more than 1,000 pieces of traditional crafts from the hill tribes living in the region, is one of the finest in the country and includes farming implements, hunting traps, weapons, colorful embroidery, and musical instruments. The museum is in Ratchangkla Park, off the road to Mae Rim, about 1 km (½ mile) from the National Museum. ⊠ *Ratchangkla Park, Chotana Rd.* ☎ *053/210872* 🖃 *Free* ⊙ *Daily 9–4.*

National Museum. This northern Thai–style building contains many statues of Lord Buddha, including a bust that measures 10 feet high. There's also a huge Buddha footprint of wood with mother-of-pearl inlay. The exhibits have been skillfully arranged into topics such as the early history of the Lanna region, the founding of Chiang Mai, and the development of city's distinctive art forms. The centerpiece of one display is a regal bed covered with mosquito netting that was used by an early prince of Chiang Mai. ⊠ *Super Hwy. (Chiang Mai–Lampang Rd.)* ☎ *053/221308* ⊕ *www.thailandmuseum.com* 🖃 *B30* ⊙ *Wed.–Sun. 9–4.*

Night Market. Sandwiched between the Old City and the riverside, the Night Market (or, more accurately, the "Night Bazaar,") opens for business every night from about 6 pm. More than 200 stalls line a half-mile section of Changklan Road, from Ta Phae Road to the junction with Sri Donchai Road. This is Chiang Mai's leading entertainment zone, where night owls love to prowl. The night market itself sells fake brands and knick-knacks, and may be too tacky and commercial for many visitors, but Loi Kroh Road, which bisects it, is home to some of Chiang Mai's best restaurants. They share space with bars where girls-for-hire outnumber customers, and the city's leading arena, where foreign men get routinely beaten up by challenging Thai kick-boxers. ⊠ *Changklan Rd. from Ta Phae Rd. to Sri Donchai Rd.*

Nimmanhemin Road. Chiang Mai's version of Bangkok's glittering Sukhumvit area, Nimmanhemin Road is a mile-long strip just west of the Old City that connects two of Chiang Mai's main thoroughfares, Huay Khao and Suthep Roads, and is also accessible via the Super Highway. Lined by bars, restaurants, discos (Warm Up is the most famous), art galleries and chic boutiques, it's usually packed with students from the nearby university. Spend some extra time exploring the narrow lanes that lead off the main drag; a vast and continuing development program has spilled over into this jumble of side streets, where more bars, cafés, restaurants and discotheques jostle for space. ⊠ *Nimmanhemin Rd.*

Riverside. Chinese traders originally settled this area, a mile south of the Old City, and some of their well-preserved homes and commercial premises now house smart restaurants, a few attractive guesthouses, galleries, boutiques and antique shops. This stretch of the Ping River has given its name to its most well-known restaurant and music bar, The Riverside. Its popularity has spawned a row of upbeat restaurants offering live music and fine river views to a predominantly young, enthusiastic Thai clientele. This is where to venture to see Thais at play.

Wat Chaimongkol. Although rarely visited, this small temple is well worth the journey. Its little chedi contains holy relics, but its real beauty lies in the serenity of the grounds. Outside the Old City near the Mae Ping River, it has only 18 monks in residence. ⊠ *Charoen Prathet Rd.*

Wat Chedi Yot. Wat Photharam Maha Viharn is more commonly known as Wat Chedi Yot, or Seven-Spired Monastery. Built in 1455, it's a copy of the Mahabodhi temple in Bodh Gaya, India, where the Buddha is said to have achieved enlightenment. The seven intricately carved spires represent the seven weeks that he subsequently spent there. The sides of the chedi have striking bas-relief sculptures of celestial figures, most of them in poor repair but one bearing a face of hauntingly contemporary beauty. The temple is just off the highway that circles Chiang Mai, but its green lawns and shady corners are strangely still and peaceful. ⊠ *Super Highway, between Huay Kaew and Chang Puak rds.*

Wat Suan Dok. To the west of the Old City is one of the largest of Chiang Mai's temples, Wat Suan Dok. It's said to have been built on the site where bones of Lord Buddha were found. Some of these relics are believed to be inside the chedi; others were transported to Wat Phra That Doi Suthep. At the back of the viharn is the bot housing Phra Chao Kao, a superb bronze Buddha figure cast in 1504. Chiang Mai aristocrats are buried in stupas in the graveyard. ⊠ *Suthep Rd.*

Wat Umong. The most unusual temple in Chiang Mai is Wat Umong, dating from 1296. According to local lore, a monk named Jam liked

6

to go wandering in the forest. This irritated King Ku Na, who often wanted to consult with the sage. So he could seek advice at any time, the king built this wat for the monk in 1380. Along with the temple, tunnels were constructed and decorated with paintings, fragments of which may still be seen. Beyond the chedi is a pond filled with hungry carp. Throughout the grounds the trees are hung with snippets of wisdom such as "Time unused is the longest time." ⊠ *Off Suthep Rd., past Wat Suan Dok.*

GREATER CHIANG MAI

Beyond the highway that surrounds Chiang Mai you will find plenty to hold your attention. The most famous sight is Wat Phra That Doi Suthep, the mountaintop temple that overlooks the city. The mountain road that skirts Doi Suthep, winding through the thickly forested Mae Sa Valley, is lined with tourist attractions for much of its way, from bungee-jumping towers to orchid farms. Several operators have created a network of zip lines through the forest, enabling more adventurous visitors to swing Tarzan-style for more than a mile through the jungle at tree-top level.

TOP ATTRACTIONS

FAMILY **Chiang Mai Night Safari.** Modeled on Singapore's famous game park, the Chiang Mai Night Safari realized a long-held dream of Thaksin Shinnawatra, the country's former prime minister (he was deposed in a military coup in September 2006). The 800-acre reserve on the edge of Doi Suthep-Pui National Park, 10 km (6 miles) from downtown Chiang Mai, has more than 100 species of wild animals, including tigers, leopards, jaguars, and elephants. For a real thrill, board one of the special trams and tour the grounds after dark. ⊠ *Km 10, Chiang Mai–Hod Rd.* ⊕ *www.chiangmainightsafari.com* 🕾 *B100 until 4 pm, B500 after 6 pm* ⊙ *Daily 11 am–10:30 pm.*

Phuping Palace. The summer residence of the royal family is a serene mansion that shares an exquisitely landscaped park with the more modest mountain retreats of the crown prince and princess. The palace itself cannot be visited, but the gardens are open to the public. Flower enthusiasts swoon at the sight of the roses—among the lovely blooms is a variety created by the king himself. A rough, unpaved road left of the palace brings you after 4 km (2½ miles) to a village called Doi Pui Meo, where most of the Hmong women seem busy creating finely worked textiles (the songthaew return fare there is B300). On the mountainside above the village are two tiny museums documenting hill tribe life and the opium trade. ⊠ *Off Huay Kaew Rd., 6 km (4 miles) past Wat Phra That Doi Suthep* 🕾 *Gardens B50* ⊙ *Gardens daily 9–5, except when royal family in residence (usually Jan.).*

Fodor's Choice **Wat Phra That Doi Suthep.** As in so many chapters of Thai history, an
★ elephant is closely involved in the legend surrounding the foundation of Wat Phra That, northern Thailand's most revered temple and one of only a few enjoying royal patronage. The elephant was dispatched from Chiang Mai carrying religious relics from Wat Suan Dok. Instead of ambling off into the open countryside, it stubbornly climbed up Doi

Most boys are ordained as monks at least temporarily, often for the three-month Rains Retreat.

Suthep. When the elephant came to rest at the 3,542-foot summit, the decision was made to establish a temple to contain the relics at that site. Over the centuries the temple compound grew into the glittering assembly of chedis, bots, viharns, and frescoed cloisters you see today. The vast terrace, usually smothered with flowers, commands a breathtaking view of Chiang Mai. Constructing the temple was quite a feat—until 1935 there was no paved road to the temple. Workers and pilgrims alike had to slog through thick jungle. The road was the result of a vast community project: individual villages throughout the Chiang Mai region contributed the labor, each laying 1,300-foot sections.

You can find songthaews to take you on the 30-minute drive to this temple at Chuang Puak Gate, the Central Department Store on Huay Kaew Road, or outside the entrance to Wat Phra Singh. When you arrive, you are faced with an arduous but exhilarating climb up the broad, 304-step staircase flanked by 16th-century tiled balustrades that take the customary form of nagas (mythical snakes believed to control the irrigation waters in rice fields). ■TIP→ A funicular railway provides a much easier way to the top. But the true pilgrim's way is up the majestic steps. ⊠ *Huay Kaew Rd.* 🚌 *B70 (includes funicular)* ⊗ *Daily 6–6.*

WORTH NOTING

FAMILY **Chiang Mai Zoo.** On the lower slopes of Doi Suthep, this zoo's cages and enclosures are spaced out along paths that wind leisurely through shady woodlands. If the walk seems too strenuous, you can hop on an electric trolley or a monorail car that stop at all the sights. The monorail system runs through a "twilight" area of the zoo, where you're assured of seeing the animals emerge for their evening prowls to their watering holes. The most popular animals are two giant pandas, Lin Hui and Chuang Chuang and their female offspring, Lin Bing—the only ones in captivity in Southeast Asia. Koala bears from Australia are also a big attraction—kids are invited to cuddle them. ⊠ *100 Huay Kaew Rd.* ☏ *053/221179* ⊕ *www. chiangmaizoo.com* ☞ *B100, additional B100 to view pandas and B150 to ride monorail* ☉ *Daily 8–9.*

Elephant Nature Park. There are several elephant reserves north of Chiang Mai, but for a truly authentic up-close experience this one is hard to beat. More than 30 elephants, including four youngsters, roam freely in the natural enclosure formed by a narrow mountain valley an hour's drive away. Visitors can stroll among the elephants, feeding and bathing them in the river that runs through the park. There are no elephant rides or circus-like shows; Ford Foundation laureate Sangduen ("Lek") Chailert, who runs the reserve, insists that the animals in her care live as close to nature as possible. ⊠ *1 Ratchamanka Rd., Pra Singh, City office* ☏ *053/272855, 053/208246 and 053/208247* ⊕ *www.elephantnaturepark.org.*

FAMILY **Elephant Training Center.** The pachyderms here are treated well and seem to enjoy showing off their skills. They certainly like the dip they take in the river before demonstrating log-rolling routines and giving rides. ⊠ *Mai Sa Valley Rd. between Mae Rim and Samoeng* ☏ *053/206247* ⊕ *www.maesaelephantcamp.com* ☞ *B150, B800 for ½-hr elephant ride* ☉ *Shows daily at 8, 9:40, noon, and 1:30.*

FAMILY **Mae Sa Snake Farm.** If you're fascinated by slithering creatures, you'll find them not only at Chiang Mai Zoo but at this snake farm on the Mae Sa Valley road. There are cobra shows between 9 and 5, during which the snakes are "milked" for their venom. ⊠ *Mae Rim–Samoeng Rd.* ☏ *053/860719* ☞ *B200* ☉ *Daily 9–5.*

THE MAE SA VALLEY

This beautiful upland valley winds behind Chiang Mai's Doi Suthep and Doi Pui mountain ranges. A well-paved 100-km (60-mile) loop begins and ends in Chiang Mai, and is lined by resorts, country restaurants, tribal villages, an elephant center, a tiger reserve, a snake farm, a monkey colony, orchid hothouses, and the Queen Sirikit Botanical Gardens. The route follows Highway 1001 north from Chiang Mai, turning left at Mae Rim onto Highway 1096 and then 1269, returning to Chiang Mai from the south on Highway 108.

NEED A BREAK?

Mae Sa Valley Resort. If you're visiting the Elephant Training Center or the Mae Sa Snake Farm, stop for lunch at Mae Sa Valley Resort. It's a pretty place, with thatched cottages in beautifully tended gardens. The owner's honey-cooked chicken with chili is particularly good. If you're traveling back to Chiang Mai via Mae Rim, call in and have tea or coffee with the big cats at the Tiger Kingdom, a large reserve just before the Mae Sa Valley road rejoins the main 107 highway south. From the center's raised and open-sided terrace-restaurant, you can admire the tigers in their large enclosures and for a large fee (B1,500) prowl around among them and even

The History of Chiang Mai

Chiang Mai's rich history stretches back 700 years to the time when several small tribes, under King Mengrai, banded together to form a new nation called Anachak Lanna Thai. Their first capital was Chiang Rai, but after three decades they moved it to the fertile plains near the Mae Ping River to a site they called Napphaburi Sri Nakornping Chiang Mai.

The Lanna Thai eventually lost their independence to Ayutthaya and, later, to expansionist Burma. Not until 1774—when the Burmese were finally driven out—did the region revert to the Thai kingdom. After that, the region developed independently of southern Thailand. Even the language is different, marked by a more relaxed tempo. In the last 50 years the city has grown well beyond its original moated city walls, expanding far into the neighboring countryside.

---

get up close and personal—a great photo opportunity. ⊠ *Mae Rim–Samoeng Rd.* ☎ *053/290051, 053/290052* ⊕ *www.maesavalleyresort.com.*

Sankamphaeng Hot Springs. Among the most spectacular in northern Thailand, these hot springs include two geysers that shoot water about 32 yards into the air. The spa complex, set among beautiful flowers, includes an open-air pool and several bathhouses of various sizes. There's a rustic restaurant with a view over the gardens, and small chalets with hot tubs are rented either by the hour (B200) or for the night (B800). Tents and sleeping bags can also be rented for B80. The spa is 56 km (35 miles) north of Chiang Mai, beyond the village of San Kamphaeng. Songthaews bound for the spa leave from the riverside flower market in Chiang Mai. ⊠ *Moo 7, Tambon Ban Sahakorn, Mae On* ☎ *053/929077, 053/929099* 🎫 *B20* ☉ *Daily 8–6.*

WHERE TO EAT

All the city's top hotels serve reasonably good food, but for the best Thai cuisine go to the restaurants in town. The greatest variety—from traditional Thai to French nouvelle cuisine—are to be found within the Old City, although Nimmanhemin Road, about 2 km (1 mile) northwest of downtown, is rapidly becoming a star-studded restaurant row. The best fish restaurants, many of them Chinese-run, are found at the Anusan Market, near the Night Bazaar. Chiang Mai also has northern Thailand's best European-cuisine restaurants, and some of its French, Italian, and Mediterranean fusion restaurants rival those of Bangkok. *Prices in the reviews are the average cost of a main course at dinner or, if dinner is not served, at lunch.*

Use the coordinate (✛ B2) at the end of each listing to locate a site on the Where to Eat and Stay in Chiang Mai map.

THE OLD CITY

$$$ ✕ **Ginger Kafe.** The former House restaurant—ranked one of Chiang Mai's best—has transferred its kitchen and dining room to the adjacent Ginger Kafe, which is part of the same property, overlooking the city moat. The formal fine dining experience has become much more relaxed, with guests invited to make themselves comfortable on plump, plush armchairs and sofas and even on large cushions scattered over the polished teak floor. The cuisine remains distinctly eclectic "House," however, with old favorites such as its tapas selections and innovative salads still on the menu. [$] *Average main: B300* ✉ *199 Moon Muang Rd.* ☎ *053/419011* 🌐 *www.thehousethailand.com* 👔 *Jacket and tie* ✥ *E3.*

$ THAI ✕ **Huen Phen.** The small rooms in this restaurant, once a private home, are full of handicrafts that are typical of the region. Select a table in any of the dining rooms or out among the plants of the garden. The house and garden are open only in the evening; lunch is served in a street-front extension packed daily with hungry Thais. The *kaeng hang led* (pork curry) with *kao nio* (sticky rice) is a specialty. The *larb nua* (spicy ground beef fried with herbs) and deep-fried pork ribs are two more dishes you won't want to miss. [$] *Average main: B150* ✉ *112 Rachamankha Rd.* ☎ *053/814548* ✥ *C4.*

$ THAI ✕ **Tha Nam.** The crumbling old building that once housed this picturesque restaurant has been demolished and a brand new Tha Nam has opened for business a few hundred yards along the river. Faithful regulars complain that the restaurant has lost much of its former charm, with formal tables and chairs replacing the antique furniture that matched the historic setting of the old establishment. Yet the menu is basically the same (try the *hang led* pork and ginger curry or chicken in pandana leaves) and the riverside location is perhaps more attractive than before. A classical trio plays most nights. [$] *Average main: B150* ✉ *71 Pradaet Rd.* ☎ *053/275–1251* 🌐 *www.tharnthonglodges.com* ✥ *F6.*

$ ECLECTIC ✕ **Writers Club & Wine Bar.** You don't have to be a journalist to dine at Chiang Mai's unofficial press club—the regulars include not only media types but also anyone from hard-up artists and eccentric local characters to successful entrepreneurs. Local venison, wild boar, and rainbow trout frequently appear on the ever-changing menu, which also has an extensive Thai section. The house wines are good and sensibly priced. Reservations are essential on Friday and Sunday. [$] *Average main: B150* ✉ *141/3 Ratchadamnoen Rd.* ☎ *053/814187* ✍ *Reservations essential* 💳 *No credit cards* 🕒 *Closed Sat.* ✥ *D4.*

BEYOND THE OLD CITY

$ THAI ✕ **Arun Rai.** This simple, open-sided restaurant has prepared such traditional northern dishes as frogs' legs fried with ginger for more than 30 years. Try the *tabong* (boiled bamboo shoots fried in batter) and *sai ua* (pork sausage with herbs). There's also a take-out service for customers in a hurry. [$] *Average main: B100* ✉ *45 Kotchasarn Rd.* ☎ *053/276947* ✍ *Reservations not accepted* 💳 *No credit cards* ✥ *E4.*

$$ INTERNATIONAL 🍴 **Chez Marco.** Chiang Mai's expanding list of French-influenced restaurant is topped by this sophisticated establishment, which has become one of the city's most successful, packed most nights with customers drawn by the exceptional "price quality" factor of its extensive menu, where Chiang Mai's best coq au vin can be enjoyed for B300 and creamy pâtés add a further B100 or so to the bill. The restaurant, open only evenings and run with Gallic flair by Franco-Japanese chef Marco, began as a modest shophouse, but has doubled in size with the acquisition of neighboring premises, while keeping its tiny, stylishly intimate street terrace. [$] *Average main: B300* ✉ *15/7 Loi Kroh Rd.* ☎ *053/207032* 🕓 *Closed Sun.* ✥ *E4.*

$$ ECLECTIC 🍴 **Chiengmai Gymkhana Club.** The son of the author of *Anna and the King of Siam* was among the founders of this delightfully eccentric place in 1898. Polo is no longer played, but a country-club crowd gathers regularly at the restaurant for lunch and dinner. The food is remarkably good, with a variety of local and foreign dishes—the traditional fish-and-chips are among Chiang Mai's tastiest. Sporty types can enjoy a round of golf on the 9-hole course or a set or two of tennis. [$] *Average main: B220* ✉ *349 Chiang Mai–Lamphun Rd.* ☎ *053/241035, 053/247352* ✥ *H5.*

$ ECLECTIC 🍴 **The Gallery.** Awards have been heaped on this attractive riverside restaurant, both for its architecture (a combination of Chinese and Lanna styles) and its cuisine, which embraces dishes from Asia, Europe, and the United States. Guests enter through a gallery (a small exhibition of local antiques and handicrafts), cross a secluded courtyard with an open-air barbecue, and proceed into a teak-floored dining area with eggplant-color linens. A northern Thai string ensemble plays most evenings, and a subtly integrated bar-café offers some of Chiang Mai's best jazz and blues. [$] *Average main: B200* ✉ *25–29 Charoen Rat Rd.* ☎ *053/248601* 🌐 *www.thegallery-restaurant.com/home.html* ✥ *G3.*

$ ECLECTIC 🍴 **The Good View.** The name of this waterfront restaurant is an homage to its sweeping view of the Ping River, which, along with the food and live music, attracts a big nightly crowd. It's no place for a quiet evening—partying Thais tend to occupy the maze of tables. Stick to the excellent Thai menu rather than settling for the rather indifferent Western cuisine—the pad thai and grilled perch are particularly recommended. [$] *Average main: B200* ✉ *13 Charoen Rat Rd., Ping River* ☎ *053/241866* 🌐 *goodview.co.th* ✥ *G4.*

$ ASIAN 🍴 **Hinlay Curry House.** Tucked away in a corner of a former Chiang Mai businessman's mansion, this small, open-sided Asian restaurant specializes in inexpensive curry dishes from India, Burma, Malaysia, Indonesia, and Thailand. Daily specials, accompanied by two varieties of rice or a selection of Indian breads, are written on a blackboard. The tiny terrace overlooks the grounds of the mansion, whose present owners also run the restaurant. [$] *Average main: B120* ✉ *8/1 Na Watket Rd., Soi 1, Wat Ket* ☎ *053/242621* 💳 *No credit cards* ✥ *G3.*

$ THAI 🍴 **Just Khao Soy.** Northern Thailand's favorite dish, *khao soy,* has been turned into a work of art at Shane Beary's stylish, brick-floored restaurant one block from the river. The bowl of meat soup topped with crispy fried noodles is served on an artist's palette, with the various condiments

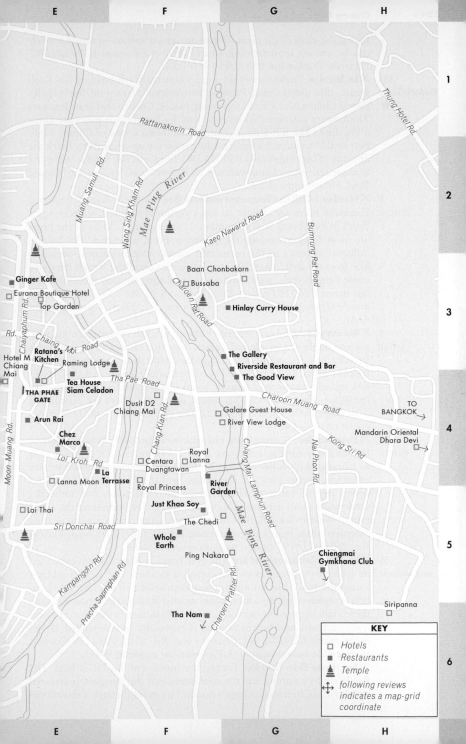

taking the place of the paint. Diners are issued aprons—eating khao soy can be messier than tackling lobster. [$] *Average main: B200* ⊠ *108/2 Charoen Prathet Rd.* ☎ *053/818641* ✦ *F5.*

$$$ ✕ **La Terrasse.** Tucked away on a quiet courtyard off bustling Loi Kroh
Fodor's Choice   Road, this unassuming Parisian bistro-style restaurant has rapidly
★   joined Chiang Mai's list of top eating places. Owner-chef Jean Jeacques Thine keeps it simple but inspired and his homemade pâtés are alone a big draw. The B295 three-course fixed menu is one of Chiang Mai's best deals. An adjacent French-run bar serves up aperitifs to spark the appetite. [$] *Average main: B300* ⊠ *59/5 Loi Kroh Rd.* ☎ *083/762–6065* ⊕ *www.laterrassechiangmai.com* ⌕ *Reservations essential* ⊙ *Closed Wed. Dinner only.* ✦ *E4.*

$ ✕ **Number 1 Chill Out Restaurant and Beer Garden.** More than 50 imported
ECLECTIC   European beers are on offer at this riverside restaurant, supporting its claim to be Chiang Mai's "number 1" beer garden. Most of the beers are from Belgium because the co-owner, Fred, is Belgian. The Belgian influence extends to the restaurant menu, which features specialties like Brussels-style meatballs and croquettes. And the french fries also come Belgian style, with mayonnaise replacing tomato sauce. [$] *Average main: B200* ⊠ *Pradaet Rd. 21, Moo 3* ☎ *081/034–3417* ⊕ *www.number1beergarden.com* ▭ *No credit cards* ⊙ *Daily 3 pm–midnight* ✦ *A6.*

$ ✕ **Ratana's Kitchen.** Looking rather like an English village tearoom, with
BRITISH   a white clapboard facade and a rustic door that chimes as you enter, this friendly little restaurant on Chiang Mai's main shopping street draws in tourists with a menu packed with more than 50 low-priced U.K. favorites, including bangers and mash, beans on toast, and a big, British-style breakfast. There's also a Thai menu, where the prices are even lower. [$] *Average main: B150* ⊠ *320–322 Tha Pae Rd.* ☎ *053/874173* ▭ *No credit cards* ✦ *E4.*

$$$ ✕ **River Garden.** A crumbling old teak-built property was torn down
ECLECTIC   to make way for this handsome Lanna-style restaurant complex next to Chiang Mai's historic "Iron Bridge." The spacious outside terrace commands great views of the bridge and the Ping River. The menu covers the full range of Thai dishes, which are pricey but authentic, while steaks and a plate of succulent spare ribs command the selection of Western food. Lovers of Japanese cuisine are catered to with an extensive sushi bar. [$] *Average main: B300* ⊠ *33/12 Charoen Prathet Rd.* ☎ *053/234493* ⌕ *Reservations essential* ✦ *F4.*

$$ ✕ **Riverside Restaurant and Bar.** The ever-popular Riverside has expanded
INTERNATIONAL its waterfront premises to encompass a modern and elegant address across the road. The informal, noisy atmosphere of the riverside location is replaced here by a more sophisticated dining experience, although there's still nightly live music. A candlelight dinner in the romantic central courtyard on a warm evening is especially recommended. [$] *Average main: B250* ⊠ *9/11 Charoen Rat Rd.* ☎ *053/243239* ⊕ *www.theriversidechiangmai.com* ⌕ *Reservations essential* ✦ *G3.*

✕ **Tea House Siam Celadon.** Escape the hustle and bustle of busy Tha Pae Road by stepping into the cool interior of this exquisitely restored century-old Chinese merchant's house. You enter through a showroom of fine celadon pottery and an adjoining courtyard flanked by tiny boutiques selling Lanna fabrics. The fan-cooled tearoom is a teak-floored salon furnished with wrought iron and glass. The menu is limited, mostly sandwiches and salads (try the avocado and prawns), but the pastries and fruitcake are among Chiang Mai's best. It opens at 9 am. [$] *Average main: B150* ✉ *158 Tha Pae Rd.* ☎ *053/234518, 053/234519* ▭ *No credit cards* ⏲ *No dinner* ⊕ *E4.*

$ 🍴 **Whole Earth.** On the second floor of an attractive old house, this long-
VEGETARIAN time favorite serves delicious and healthy foods. It's mostly vegetarian fare, but there are a few meat dishes for the carnivorous, such as *gai tahkhrai* (fried chicken with lemon and garlic). Many of the favorites here, including the tasty eggplant masala, are Indian dishes. The dining room is air-conditioned, and the garden terrace that surrounds it takes full advantage of any breezes. The service is sometimes slow. Reservations are recommended for groups of four or more. [$] *Average main: B200* ✉ *88 Sri Donchai Rd.* ☎ *053/282463* ⊕ *F5.*

GREATER CHIANG MAI

$ 🍴 **9 Moo 9.** A 30-minute taxi ride from downtown Chiang Mai brings
ECLECTIC you to this exquisite garden restaurant, hidden away in a subtropical setting below the foothills of the Doi Suthep mountain. Owner Siripann Kidd is an authority on fabrics and when she's not busy in her kitchen she is organizing exhibitions in the restaurant's adjoining gallery. Her daily changing menu is small but totally reliant on fresh produce—her outstanding lemon tart, for instance, is made with fruit from the restaurant's own citrus grove. [$] *Average main: B200* ✉ *Doitamm, Namphrae, Hang Dong* ☎ *086/184–2356* ▭ *No credit cards* ⏲ *No dinner Mon.–Wed.* ⊕ *A6.*

WHERE TO STAY

Soaring tourist numbers—particularly young Chinese visitors with newly acquired wealth and the urge and freedom to travel—have fueled an unprecedented hotel building boom in recent years. The majority are in the traditional so-called Lanna style and the most luxurious of these rival hotels in Bangkok. One, the Mandarin Oriental Dhara Devi, justly claims to be among Asia's finest. Prices are nonetheless far lower than in the capital (outside the December-to-February high season). Charming, modestly priced guesthouses and small hotels abound, and some are right on the water. ■ **TIP→ Watch out for guesthouses that advertise cheap room rates and then tell you the accommodation is only available if you book an expensive tour.** Always ask if there's any tour requirement with your room rate. All hotels and most guesthouses accept dollars, but if you are paying in greenbacks check the offered exchange rate carefully; it can be as much as 10 percent less than obtainable in banks and exchange booths.

Prices in the reviews are the lowest cost of a standard double room in high season. For expanded hotel reviews, visit Fodors.com.

Use the coordinate (✣ B2) at the end of each listing to locate a site on the Where to Eat and Stay in Chiang Mai map.

THE OLD CITY

$ B&B/INN **The 3 Sis Vacation Lodge.** A sacred Bhodi tree stands sentinel outside this attractive hotel, which looks out directly onto one of Chiang Mai's most historic temples, Wat Chedi Luang. **Pros:** famous Sunday market is right outside; three leading temples within walking distance; 24-hour convenience store next door. **Cons:** temple dogs can be noisy; busy main road location; limited parking. [$] *Rooms from: B56* ✉ *150 Phrapokklao Rd., Old City* ☎ *053/273243* 🌐 *www.3sisbedandbreakfast.com* 🛏 *39 rooms* 🍴 *No meals* ✣ *D4.*

$ B&B/INN **Banjai Garden.** A French restaurateur and his Thai wife refurbished this sturdy old Chiang Mai house into a comfortable guesthouse in 2012. **Pros:** easy access to bars and restaurants; shady garden; bicycle rental. **Cons:** difficult to park in tiny lane; barking dogs; insects. [$] *Rooms from: $30* ✉ *45 Prapokklao Rd., Soi 3, City Center* ☎ *085/716–1635, 085/653–1971* 🛏 *8 rooms.* ✣ *C4.*

$$ HOTEL **De Naga.** This latest addition to Chiang Mai's collection of Lanna-style "boutique" hotels within the old city is ideally located, surrounded by bars and restaurants. **Pros:** excellent service by English-speaking staff; good restaurant; shady terrace with comfortable garden furniture. **Cons:** nighttime noise from neighboring bars; small pool; unreliable Internet. [$] *Rooms from: $100* ✉ *21/2 Moon Muang Rd., Old City* ☎ *053/209030* 🌐 *www.denaga.com* 🛏 *55 rooms* 🍴 *Breakfast* ✣ *D4.*

$ HOTEL **Eurana Boutique Hotel.** The former S.P. Hotel has blossomed into one of Chiang Mai's most attractive boutique hotels, a haven of peace and understated luxury on a quiet lane near busy Sompet Market. **Pros:** secluded Old City location; cool and leafy garden; nearby market. **Cons:** noisy dogs; rowdy neighborhood bars; insects. [$] *Rooms from: $35* ✉ *Moon Muang Rd., Soi 7* ☎ *053/219402* 🌐 *www.euranaboutiquehotel.com* 🛏 *72 rooms* 🍴 *Breakfast* ✣ *E3.*

$ B&B/INN Fodor's Choice ★ **Gap's House.** This inn is both well placed for exploring the Old City and removed from the hustle and bustle, sunk dreamily in a backstreet tropical oasis. **Pros:** tours are reliable; luxuriant garden; total seclusion. **Cons:** moody owner; noisy plumbing; no parking. [$] *Rooms from: $13* ✉ *3 Ratchadamnoen Rd., Soi 4* ☎ *053/278140* 🌐 *www.gaps-house.com* 🛏 *19 rooms* 💳 *No credit cards* 🍴 *Breakfast* ✣ *D4.*

$ B&B/INN **Gap's House 2.** The popular Gap's House has spawned this second guesthouse on the western edge of the city moat. **Pros:** airy, comfortable lobby-lounge; Internet café; great tours. **Cons:** fronts a busy street with traffic noise; small rooms; no pool. [$] *Rooms from: $13* ✉ *43/2 Arak Rd., A. Muang* ☎ *053/274277* 🌐 *www.gaps-house2.com* 🛏 *21 rooms* 🍴 *Breakfast* ✣ *B4.*

$ HOTEL **Hotel M Chiang Mai.** Ideally located directly adjacent to the Tha Pae Gate and bordering the moat, this refurbished old favorite has a terrace that hums with activity on the weekend. **Pros:** central location; cozy rooms; bright ground-floor café. **Cons:** no pool; some traffic noise in rooms facing moat; limited parking. [$] *Rooms from: $57* ✉ *2–6 Ratcha-*

damnoen Rd. ☎ *053/211069, 053/418480* 🌐 *www.hotelthailand.com/chiangmai/montri* 🛏 *75 rooms* 🍴 *Breakfast* ✥ *E4.*

$ B&B/INN 🏨 **Lanna Moon Guest House.** Ask at this stylish guesthouse for one of the west-facing rooms which command good views of Chiang Mai's Doi Suthep mountain and its temple. **Pros:** cable TV in all rooms; swimming pool; short walk to Night Market. **Cons:** noisy neighborhood; proximity to seedy bars and massage parlors not ideal for families; heavy road traffic. [$] *Rooms from: $20* ✉ *17/2 Loi Kroh Rd.* ☎ *053/271169* 🌐 *www.lannamoon.com* 🛏 *18 rooms* 🍴 *Breakfast.* ✥ *E4*

$ B&B/INN 🏨 **Minicost Guesthouse.** A retired Australian police officer runs this attractive little guesthouse, so top security is guaranteed, down to the "swipe" cards issued to guests and the presence of closed-circuit TV cameras. **Pros:** coffee shop; massage center; friendly, helpful owners. **Cons:** no parking; noisy neighborhood dogs; small rooms. [$] *Rooms from: $30* ✉ *19/4 Ratchadamnoen Rd.* ☎ *053/418787* 🛏 *15 rooms* 🍴 *Breakfast.* ✥ *D3.*

$$$ HOTEL 🏨 **Rachamankha.** On a quiet lane near Wat Pra Singh, the Rachamankha is visually an extension of the temple compound, a series of hushed brick courtyards enclosed by triple-eaved Lanna-style buildings. **Pros:** cool, peaceful setting; helpful, knowledgeable receptionists; pool. **Cons:** shabby neighborhood; noisy temple dogs; rooms too spartan for some. [$] *Rooms from: $200* ✉ *Rachamanka Rd., Soi 9* ☎ *053/904111* 🌐 *www.rachamankha.com* 🛏 *24 rooms, 1 suite* 🍴 *Breakfast* ✥ *B4.*

$$ HOTEL 🏨 **Sri Pat Guest House.** This family-run, spotlessly clean and stylishly furnished little hotel sits on a cobbled lane a short walk from the moat, and is one of the best deals in the Old City. **Pros:** friendly, helpful Thai owner; lively village street scene; proximity to market. **Cons:** noisy neighborhood dogs; no double beds; no parking. [$] *Rooms from: $100* ✉ *16 Moon Muang Rd., Soi 7* ☎ *053/218716* ✉ *sri-pat@sri-patguesthouse.com* 🛏 *24 rooms* 🍴 *Breakfast* ✥ *D3.*

$$$ HOTEL 🏨 **Tamarind Village.** A canopy of towering, interlaced bamboo leads to the main entrance of this stylish, village-style hotel in the center of the Old City. **Pros:** quiet, secluded location; short walk to center of Old City; good restaurant. **Cons:** relatively small rooms; some may find rooms spartan; insects. [$] *Rooms from: $166* ✉ *50/1 Ratchadamnoen Rd.* ☎ *053/418896 up to 9* 🌐 *www.tamarindvillage.com* 🛏 *40 rooms* ✥ *C3.*

$$$ HOTEL 🏨 **U Chiang Mai.** Located in the exact center of the Old City, this Lanna-style boutique hotel, opened in June 2008, was constructed around a century-old teak house, home of a former governor which now serves as the lobby, spa, and reading room. **Pros:** 24-hour room rate, so if you arrive at 10 pm, you don't have to leave until the same time the next day; spa and massage; helpful tour desk. **Cons:** exposed pool that's open to view from most rooms; no parking; high bar and restaurant prices. [$] *Rooms from: $120* ✉ *70 Ratchadmanoen Rd.* ☎ *053/327000* 🌐 *www.uhotelsresorts.com/uchiangmai* 🛏 *41 rooms* 🍴 *Breakfast* ✥ *D3.*

6

BEYOND THE OLD CITY

$
B&B/INN

⊡ **Baan Chonpakorn.** Sandwiched between art galleries, boutiques, restaurants, and two temples in the heart of Chiang Mai's former Chinese quarter, this modest, teak-built inn is easily overlooked but is one of the most attractive budget options in this area of the city. **Pros:** main market and riverside restaurants a short walk away; free all-day tea and coffee; Internet corner with terminals. **Cons:** on busy main road; no breakfast; limited parking. Ⓢ *Rooms from: $27* ⊠ *122 Charoen Rat Rd., T. Wat Ket, City Center* ☎ *053/240161* ☞ *13 rooms.* ✛ *G3.*

$
B&B/INN
Fodor'sChoice
★

⊡ **Bussaba.** A former 19th-century Chinese trader's home has been beautifully converted into a snug bed-and-breakfast inn at the heart of a riverside road lined by similar reminders of a bygone era. **Pros:** Chiang Mai's main market and riverside bars and restaurants are a short walk away; home-away-from-home atmosphere of the inn; friendly and helpful owners. **Cons:** on busy street, front-facing upper rooms suffer from traffic noise; no restaurant; limited parking. Ⓢ *Rooms from: $35* ⊠ *124–128 Charoen Rat Rd., T. Wat Ket, City Center* ☎ *053/244067, 081/999–2504* ⊕ *www.bussababedbreakfast.com* ☞ *8 rooms* ⦿| *Breakfast.* ✛ *F3.*

$$
HOTEL

⊡ **Centara Duangtawan.** The 24-floor Centara dominates the city center and the busy Night Bazaar, with a modern exterior that leads through a vast entrance to a lofty, elegant lobby. **Pros:** the Night Bazaar is on the doorstep; underground parking; well-equipped fitness center. **Cons:** noisy tour groups; sometimes delays checking in and out; anonymous chain-hotel atmosphere Ⓢ *Rooms from: $70* ⊠ *132 Loi Kroh Rd., City Center* ☎ *053/905000* ⊕ *www.centarahotelsresorts.com* ☞ *507 rooms* ⦿| *Breakfast* ✛ *F4.*

$$$$
HOTEL
Fodor'sChoice
★

⊡ **The Chedi.** Chiang Mai's finest waterfront hotel sits in isolated splendor between the Mae Ping River and one of the city's busiest streets, with rooms and suites that are furnished in an eclectic mix of traditional styles and sleek modern lines. **Pros:** faultless service; riverside location; traditional "English" afternoon teas on the terrace. **Cons:** some find the metallic, rust-color facade ugly; nearby streets dingy; water features could be better lighted at night. Ⓢ *Rooms from: $230* ⊠ *123 Charoen Prathet Rd.* ☎ *053/253333* ⊕ *www.ghmhotels.com* ☞ *84 rooms* ⦿| *Breakfast* ✛ *F5.*

$$
HOTEL

⊡ **Chiang Mai Orchid.** With teak pillars lining the lobby, the Chiang Mai Orchid is a grand hotel in the old style, with tastefully furnished rooms trimmed with hardwoods. **Pros:** busy Huay Kaew Road is on the doorstep; lively in-house bar scene; ample parking. **Cons:** pool and exercise room used by nonguests; some rooms in need of renovation; preferred hotel of large Chinese tour groups. Ⓢ *Rooms from: $76* ⊠ *23 Huay Kaew Rd.* ☎ *053/22209 through 9, 02/714–2521 in Bangkok* ⊕ *www. chiangmaiorchid.com* ☞ *266 rooms* ✛ *A2.*

$$$
HOTEL

⊡ **Dusit D2 Chiang Mai.** Chiang Mai's most daringly modern hotel is a complete break from the traditional Lanna style that's so in vogue. **Pros:** in the thick of the nightlife scene; short stroll to Night Market; excellent buffet lunch deals. **Cons:** small pool; rooms aren't spacious; modern style won't appeal to those looking for traditional Thai charm.

$ *Rooms from: $166* ✉ *100 Chang Klan Rd., T. Chang Klan, A. Muang* ☎ *053/999999* 🌐 *www.dusit.com* 🛏 *131 rooms* 🍴 *Breakfast* ✥ *F4.*

$ HOTEL **Galare Guest House.** The location is the envy of many of the city's top hotels—its gardens lead right down to the Mae Ping River and is a short walk from the Night Bazaar. **Pros:** riverside location; airy terrace restaurant; secluded garden. **Cons:** no pool; many rooms overlook busy parking lot; insects. $ *Rooms from: $40* ✉ *7 Charoen Prathet Rd., Soi 2* ☎ *053/818887* 🌐 *www.galare.com* 🛏 *35 rooms* 🍴 *Breakfast* ✥ *F4.*

$$ HOTEL **Kantary Hills.** Chiang Mai's glitzy Nimmanhemin Road district is dominated by this vast but stylish hotel complex, a showpiece of the 15-hotel Kantary Group. **Pros:** free coffee, tea, and snacks in the reading room; live music in the restaurant; boutiques. **Cons:** noisy neighborhood; discos and bars; heavy road traffic; gridlock at night. $ *Rooms from: $100* ✉ *44 Nimmanheim Rd., Soi 12* ☎ *053/222111* 🌐 *www.kantarycollection.com* 🛏 *100 rooms, 70 suites* 🍴 *Breakfast* ✥ *A2.*

$ HOTEL **Lai Thai.** This rambling guesthouse on a busy thoroughfare just outside the moat is a budget traveler's favorite, so book far ahead. **Pros:** efficient travel service; courtyard pool; good value; open-air café and restaurant. **Cons:** rooms have thin walls; some night noise also from partying backpackers; drab neighborhood. $ *Rooms from: $27* ✉ *111/4-5 Kotchasarn Rd.* ☎ *053/271725* 🌐 *www.laithai.com* 🛏 *110 rooms* 🍴 *No meals* ✥ *E5.*

$$$$ HOTEL **Ping Nakara Hotel.** It's hard to believe that this stunning addition to the riverside area of Chiang Mai was built only in 2009; it's a masterpiece of old colonial architecture, furnished throughout with exquisite antiques. **Pros:** quiet corners; peaceful ambience; garden teatime service. **Cons:** drab, main road neighborhood; rooms on the main-road side of the building can be noisy; restaurant gets mixed reviews. $ *Rooms from: $240* ✉ *135/9 Charoenprathet Rd., A. Muang* ☎ *053/252999* 🌐 *www.pingnakara.com* 🛏 *19 rooms* 🍴 *Breakfast.* ✥ *G5.*

$$ HOTEL **Raming Lodge.** Sandwiched between cheap bars and massage shops, this stylish hotel offers a touch of class in the mostly seedy Loi Kroh Road area. **Pros:** lively restaurant and bar scene; short walk to Night Market; muay thai stadium is just across the road. **Cons:** families might be offended by the neighborhood sex bars; noisy late-night revelers; busy street traffic. $ *Rooms from: B100* ✉ *17 Loi Kroh Rd.* ☎ *053/271777* 🌐 *www.raminglodge.com* 🛏 *76 rooms* 🍴 *Breakfast.* ✥ *E4*

$$ HOTEL **River View Lodge.** Facing a grassy lawn that runs down to the Mae Ping River, this lodge lets you forget the noise of the city. **Pros:** riverside location; breezy poolside gazebo; river views. **Cons:** small pool; small parking lot with narrow access; service can be less than attentive. $ *Rooms from: $67* ✉ *25 Charoen Prathet Rd., Soi 4* ☎ *053/271109* 🌐 *www.riverviewlodgch.com* 🛏 *35 rooms* ✥ *G4.*

$ HOTEL **Royal Lanna.** Truly regal in its proportions, the Royal Lanna rises high over the downtown night market scene. **Pros:** immediate proximity to night market; close to bars and restaurants; large car park. **Cons:** soulless atmosphere in public rooms; favored by tour groups; service can be slow and unhelpful. $ *Rooms from: B67* ✉ *119 Loi Kroh Rd.* ☎ *053/818773* 🌐 *www.royallannahotelchiangmai.com* 🛏 *274 rooms* 🍴 *No meals.* ✥ *F4.*

$$ HOTEL **Royal Princess.** This centrally located hotel is ideal if you'd like to step out of the lobby and right into the tumult of downtown Chiang Mai. **Pros:** central location; close to Night Bazaar; helpful travel desk. **Cons:** noisy street scene; package-tour clientele; service can be patchy. [$] *Rooms from: $100* ✉ *112 Chang Klan Rd.* ☎ *053/281033* 🌐 *chiangmai.royalprincess.com* 🛏 *182 rooms, 16 suites* ✣ *F4.*

$ B&B/INN **The Saithong Guesthouse.** The friendly little Saithong has 10 air-conditioned and well-furnished rooms. **Pros:** central location; short walk to moat and Sunday market; helpful travel desk. **Cons:** no parking; noisy neighborhood music bars; patchy Internet. [$] *Rooms from: $30* ✉ *Ratchadamnoen Rd., Soi 3, Old City* ☎ *053/418672* 🌐 *www.saithongguesthouse.com* 🛏 *10 rooms* 🍴 *No meals* ✣ *D4.*

$$$$ HOTEL **Siripanna Villa Resort and Spa.** A new addition to Chiang Mai's growing collection of luxurious Lanna-style hotel-resorts, this attractive ensemble of detached villas nestles within tropical gardens on a large site on the southern edge of the city, near the celebrated Gymkhana Club. **Pros:** two stylish restaurants; attentive service; gymkhana sports facilities (including golf course) nearby and available to visitors. **Cons:** isolated location; unreliable transport to town; insects. [$] *Rooms from: $216* ✉ *36 Rat Uthit Rd.* ☎ *053/371999* 🌐 *www.siripanna.com* 🛏 *76 villas* 🍴 *Breakfast.* ✣ *H6.*

$ B&B/INN **Top Garden Boutique Guest House.** Small and intimate, this friendly guest house has the feel of a boutique hotel. **Pros:** secluded; close to the bar and restaurant scene, helpful owners. **Cons:** no pool; no parking; traffic noise. [$] *Rooms from: $17* ✉ *13 Chaiyapoom Rd, Old City* ☎ *082/183–8598* 🌐 *www.topgarden-chiangmai.com* 🛏 *10 rooms* 🍴 *Breakfast.* ✣ *E3.*

GREATER CHIANG MAI

$$$$ RESORT Fodor's Choice ★ **Four Seasons.** One of the finest hotels in Southeast Asia, the magnificent Four Seasons commands 20 acres of tropical countryside above the lush Mae Rim Valley. **Pros:** peaceful mountain setting; idyllic pool; impeccable, attentive service. **Cons:** limited access for those with mobility problems; 40-minute drive from town; little nightlife. [$] *Rooms from: $700* ✉ *Mae Rim–Samoeng Old Rd.* ☎ *053/298181, 800/545–4000 in U.S.* 🌐 *www.fourseasons.com/chiangmai* 🛏 *98 suites* 🍴 *Breakfast* ✣ *C1.*

$$$$ RESORT Fodor's Choice ★ **Mandarin Oriental Dhara Devi.** A Thai billionaire has turned 60 acres of farmland on the eastern outskirts of Chiang Mai into one of Asia's most extraordinary hotels, re-creating a walled Lanna city surrounded by a moat. **Pros:** total seclusion; beautiful grounds; spa treatments. **Cons:** shabby neighborhood; getting around the complex can be difficult, despite the buggy and horse-drawn carriages; little nightlife. [$] *Rooms from: $540* ✉ *51/4 Chiang Mai–San Kampaeng Rd., Moo 1, Tambon Tasala* ☎ *053/888888, 053/888929* 🌐 *www.mandarinoriental.com/chiangmai* 🛏 *54 suites, 69 residences* 🍴 *Breakfast* ✣ *H4.*

NIGHTLIFE

This being Thailand, Chiang Mai has its share of Bangkok-style hostess bars. If you don't want to be hassled, there are also dozens of places where you can grab a beer and listen to live music. Many restaurants, such as the Good View, double as bars later in the evening.

BARS

BEYOND THE OLD CITY

The western end of Loi Kroh Road, the southern end of Moon Muang Road, and the vast **Bar Beer Center** next to the Top North Hotel on Moon Muang Road have bars where the "working girls" usually outnumber the customers, but pool tables and dartboards are valid rival attractions.

Olde Bell. A jolly Welshman named Pedr runs one of Chiang Mai's most popular expat bars, the Olde Bell. The large, friendly bar and dining area—described as a "British pub"—serve excellent versions of traditional fare like beef stew, sausages and mash, and liver and bacon. Come for the Sunday lunch roast, with beef and Yorkshire pudding. ⊠ *25/1 Loi Kroh Rd.* ☎ *087/811–9468.*

O'Malley's Irish Pub. This pub serves draft Guinness. Regulars say it's Chiang Mai's most authentic Irish bar. ⊠ *Anusarn Market, Chang Klan Rd.* ☎ *053/271921.*

The Pub. Step through the gnarled door of The Pub and you could be anywhere in rural England. The bar area is hung with the usual pub paraphernalia. The adjacent restaurant area serves good "pub grub," favored by the large expat clientele. ⊠ *189 Huay Kaew Rd.* ☎ *053/211550.*

U.N. Irish Pub & Restaurant. This pub has a nightly entertainment program, varying from live music, quiz games, and live sports broadcasts. The upstairs bar, with French doors onto the street, and a small side garden are cool places to while away a warm evening. ⊠ *24 Ratvithee Rd.* ☎ *053/214554* ⊕ *www.unirishpub.com.*

Wine Connection. Most bars serve wine, but very few have made it their specialty. In reality a wine retail store, this well-stocked spot at the Nim City Daily Plaza has outside bistro tables where customers can sample the wines until late. It's a new idea that has attracted the attention of a widening circle of wine buffs, who crowd the tables most evenings. Food can be ordered from a neighboring bistro. ⊠ *Nim City Daily Plaza, Mahidol Rd.* ☎ *053/808688* ⊕ *www.wineconnection.co.th.*

Writers Club & Wine Bar. The Writers Club & Wine Bar is Chiang Mai's unofficial press club, but open to anyone who enjoys networking in good company. The decor is "eclectic colonial." ⊠ *141/3 Ratchadamnoen Rd.* ☎ *053/814187.*

DANCE CLUBS

Empress Hotel lobby bar. The stylish Empress Hotel lobby bar has live music most nights. ⊠ *199/42 Chang Klan Rd.* ☎ *053/270240.*

6

The Four Seasons' spa offers body treatments and massage in luxurious open-air suites.

Horizon Club. The centrally-located Horizon Club, in the basement of the Central Duang Tawan Hotel, is a popular local night spot. ⊠ *Loy Kroh Rd.* ☎ *053/905000.*

Hot Shots. If you prefer to remain anonymously unobtrusive on the disco floor, then Hot Shots is the place to be, where the spotlights pierce the gloom only at the 2 am closing time. It adjoins the Pornping Tower Hotel. ⊠ *Pornping Tower, Charoen Prathet Rd.* ☎ *053/270099.*

Monkey Club. This club has a large, shady garden, packed most nights with young Thais, and an indoor music stage and bar. ⊠ *Nimmanhemin Rd., Soi 9* ⊕ *www.monkeyclub2000.com.*

Opium Den. In the Chiang Mai Orchid Hotel, the Opium Den caters to a stylish, sophisticated crowd. ⊠ *23 Huay Kaew Rd.* ☎ *053/222099.*

Warm Up. Local "tuppies" (Thai yuppies) crowd the discotheques and music bars of the Nimmanhemin Road area, fast becoming Chiang Mai's major night scene. Visiting ravers under 40 won't feel out of place in haunts like Warm Up. ⊠ *40 Nimmanhemin Rd.* ☎ *053/400676.*

KHANTOKE

Khantoke (or *kantoke*) originally described a revolving wooden tray on which food is served, but it has now come to mean an evening's entertainment combining a seemingly endless menu of northern cuisine and presentations of traditional music and dancing. With sticky rice, which you mold into balls with your fingers, you sample delicacies like *kap moo* (spiced pork skin), *nam prik naw* (a spicy dip made with onions, cucumber, and chili), and *kang kai* (a chicken-and-vegetable curry).

Kantoke Palace. An ever-popular place for khantoke is Kantoke Palace. ✉ *288/19 Chang Klan Rd.* ☎ *053/272757.*

Khum Khantoke. Among the best of places offering khantoke is the sumptuously temple-like Khum Khantoke. ✉ *Chiang Mai Business Park, 139 Moo 4, Nong Pakrung* ☎ *053/304121 up to 3* ⊕ *www.khantoke.com.*

Old Chiang Mai Cultural Center. This fine ensemble of traditional teak-built houses offers a multicourse dinner accompanied by traditional music and dancing, at an all-in charge of B520. ✉ *185/3 Wualai Rd.* ☎ *053/275097.*

MUSIC

Despite controversial official restrictions on performances by non-Thai musicians, Chiang Mai has a lively music scene, catering for every taste, from hard rock to mainstream and modern jazz. The problems involved in engaging professional foreign performers have led to the rapid entrance on the scene of highly talented Thai musicians, such as the internationally known and respected Lek, who takes center-stage at the Brasserie around midnight. Bluegrass and Western country fans crowd a new city haunt, Tiger Kingdom in Town, which features a house band fronted by a young woman violin virtuoso. Most music bars are found in the Old City and along the Ping River, mainly concentrated in a small lane off Ratchaphakhinai Road.

Babylon. A rough, unnamed alleyway off Ratchaphakinai Road is a magnet for local night owls, who nightly pack the dozen or so open-air or open-sided music bars. The best of them are Babylon, **Heaven Beach**, and **Rock and Reggae**. The soi (lane) is difficult to find—follow Ratchaphakinai Road northward, cross the traffic light junction, and take the first lane on the right.

Brasserie. This venue has moved from its riverside site to a new location on the edge of the Old City. Otherwise, nothing has changed and star guitarist Lek still draws the crowds. ✉ *Chaiyapoom Rd.* ☎ *053/241665.*

Gallery. A café-bar adjacent to the Gallery restaurant has some of the city's best jazz Thursday to Sunday nights. ✉ *31–35 Charoen Rat Rd.* ☎ *053/248601.*

The Good View. The east bank of the Ping River between Nawarat Bridge and Nakorn Ping Bridge resounds after dark with live rock, jazz, and Motown oldies. Most of the decibels come from the Good View, which has a variety of bands that play nightly. ✉ *13 Charoen Rat Rd.* ☎ *053/241866.*

North Gate. Jazz aficionados call Chiang Mai Thailand's New Orleans, and some say it offers better quality music at lower prices than Bangkok. The leading jazz haunts are in the city center, some grouped around the Old City moat. The North Gate is the city's most popular music bar. Tuesday is jam session night, but the place is packed every night of the week. ✉ *Sriphum Rd. opposite Chiang Phuak Gate.*

Rasta Art Bar. Rasta Art Bar plays reggae and soft rock. ✉ *Sriphum Rd. between Sois 1 and 2.*

Tiger Kingdom in Town. More Mediterranean than Thai in its decor and ambience, this hugely popular restaurant has nightly music played on an open terrace overlooking the moat. Highlight of the evening's program is a Thai group headed by a virtuoso woman violinist who experiments expertly with bluegrass and other American country numbers. ⊠ *Moonmuang Rd.* ☎ *053/276861 up to 3* ⊕ *www.tigerkingdom.com.*

SPORTS AND THE OUTDOORS

BOATING

Book ahead for boat tours via phone if possible.

Mae Ping River Cruise. Two-hour Mae Ping River cruises depart daily between 8:30 and 5 from the landing at Wat Chai Mongkol, Charoen Prathet Road (just downriver from the Iron Bridge). An evening cruise includes dinner. ⊠ *133 Charoen Prathet Rd.* ☎ *01/8844621, 01/8850663* ⊕ *www.maepingrivercruise.com.*

Scorpion-tailed Boat River Cruises. For a taste of how the locals used to travel along the Ping River, take a ride in a scorpion-tail boat, so called because of the large rudder at the stern of this sturdy Siamese craft. Services run from the east bank of the river, between Nawarat Bridge and Rattanakosin Bridge. Scorpion-tailed Boat River Cruises has several trips daily between 9 and 5. Passengers get a running commentary from English-speaking guides and free refreshments. For dinner cruises, contact the Hanwood Restaurant, Chang Klan Road (053/274822). ⊠ *Charoen Rat Rd.* ☎ *081/960–9398* ⊕ *www.scorpiontailed.com.*

DANCE

Thai Dance Institute. Surprise your friends by learning the ancient art of Thai dancing at the Thai Dance Institute. A two-hour course teaching you a few of the graceful movements costs B900. ⊠ *53 Kohklong Rd., Nonghoy* ☎ *053/801375 and 6* ⊕ *www.thaidanceinstitute.com.*

GOLF

Chiang Mai is ringed by championship golf courses that challenge players of all levels.

Alpine Golf Resort. The Chiang Mai-Lamphun Golf Club has become a luxurious golf resort, offering family weekends where nonplayers can enjoy spa treatments or stroll in the subtropical grounds. A round of golf costs B2,500, not including caddy. ⊠ *San Khamphaeng* ☎ *053/880888* ⊕ *www.alpinegolfresort.com.*

Chiang Mai Driving Range. All Chiang Mai's golf courses have a driving range, with clubs for hire and B50 buckets of balls, but Chiang Mai Driving Range is the most conveniently located, virtually a 300-yard tee shot from the airport and nearby shopping mall. There's a good restaurant and coffee shop on-site. ⊠ *Mahidol and Hang Dong rds.* ⊕ *None.*

Chiangmai Highlands Golf and Spa Resort. A foot massage for tired golfers is included in the three-day, two-night offer at this scenic golf course and resort in the uplands east of Chiang Mai. Two rounds of golf and airport transfers are also included in the B26,500 deal. A single round of golf costs B3,000. ✉ *Mae On, San Khamphaeng* ☎ *053/261354 up to 9* ⊕ *www.chiangmaihighlands.com.*

Chiengmai Gymkhana Club. The Chiengmai Gymkhana Club, the city's oldest sports club (founded in 1898) and located on the Chiang Mai–Lamphun road, has a 9-hole course just 2 km (1 mile) from the city center; greens fees are B400 per day. ☎ *053/241035.*

Golfasian. Several specialist agencies offer tours of the best golf courses around Chiang Mai. The most comprehensive is Golfasian, established in Bangkok in 1997. A one-week tour, including accommodations in top hotels, costs B39,000. ✉ *29 Bangkok Business Center, Soi Ekamai-Sukhumvit 63, Unit 1105* ☎ *02/714–8470* ⊕ *www.golfasian.com.*

HORSEBACK RIDING

J & T Happy Riding. North of Chiang Mai, J & T Happy Riding sponsors trail rides through the beautiful Mae Sa Valley. Beginners are welcome. The stables are opposite the Mae Sa Orchid Farm. ✉ *Mae Rim–Samoeng Rd.* ☎ *081/5957–1137.*

Travel Shoppe. Horseback tours along trails around Chiang Mai are offered by Travel Shoppe. ✉ *2/2 Chaiyapoom Rd., near Thapei Gate* ☎ *053/874091* ⊕ *www.travel-shoppe.com.*

ROCK CLIMBING

The Peak Adventure Tour Company. The Peak Adventure Tour Company takes groups, including beginners, on tours to a variety of rock faces in the mountains around Chiang Mai. One-day tours cost B1,800, and six-day intensive training, including accommodation, can be booked for B6,500. The company also offers a one-day jungle survival course for B1,200. ✉ *302/4 Chkang Mai–Lamphun Rd.* ☎ *053/800567* ⊕ *www.thepeakadventure.com.*

THAI BOXING

Tha Pae Boxing Stadium. Professional muay thai contestants square off every Thursday night at the Tha Pae Boxing Stadium and every Saturday at the Loi Kroh stadium on Loi Kroh Road. The program at both venues starts at 9 pm. Tickets cost B400 to B600. ✉ *Beer Bar Center, Moon Muang Rd., beside the Top North Hotel.*

YOGA

Weena Yoga Studio. Located in the glitzy Nimmanhemin Road district, this modest yoga center offers a day's course for B800 and a program of 10 classes for B1,800. ✉ *The Ring, Nimmanheim Rd., Soi 17* ☎ *085/353–8108* ⊕ *www.weenayoga.com*

The Yoga Tree. The former Yoga Center has expanded into a yoga and meditation center offering a wide range of courses. A 90-minute yoga class costs B250, while a 10-class session can be booked for B2,000. ✉ *65/1 Arak Rd.* ☎ *081/724–7308* ⊕ *www.theyogatree.com.*

Yogasala. The Yogasala has a five-day yoga course that costs B1,500. ✉ *48/1 Rachamankha Rd.* ☎ *05/208452* ⊕ *www.cmyogasala.com.*

ZIP LINING

Flight of the Gibbon. Flying Tarzan-style through the jungle of Northern Thailand is the ultimate adventure trip for many visitors. Several operators maintain ziplines in stretches of thick forest north of Chiang Mai. "Flight of the Gibbon" has been established the longest and is reputedly the most reliable. Its treetop route is more than 3 miles long. You probably won't see a gibbon but you'll certainly feel like one. ✉ *Mae Sa Valley Rd.* ☎ *053/010660 up to 64, 089/970–5511* ⊕ *www. treetopasia.com.*

SHOPPING

Day-to-day life in Chiang Mai seems to revolve around shopping. The delightful surprise is that you don't have to part with much of your hard-earned money—even the most elaborately crafted silver costs a fraction of what you'd expect to pay at home. Fine jewelry weighed and priced at just above the current market value, as well as pewter, leather, and silk, are all on display all around the city.

COOKING CLASSES

Baan Thai Cookery School. Among the best Thai cooking cooking classes on offer is the Baan Thai Home Cookery School. A one-day course costs B900. ✉ *11 Ratchadamnoen Rd., Soi 5* ☎ *053/357339* ⊕ *www. cookinthai.com.*

Chiang Mai Thai Cookery School. Run by renowned TV chef Sompon Nabinan, Chiang Mai Thai Cookery School has a good reputation. A one-day beginner's course costs B1450. ✉ *42/7 Moon Muang Rd.* ☎ *053/206388* ⊕ *www.thaicookeryschool.com.*

Gap's House. One of the city's most popular budget lodgings, Gap's House also runs an excellent cooking school. A one-day beginner's course costs B900. ✉ *4 Ratchadamnoen Rd., Soi 3* ☎ *053/278140, 053/270143* ⊕ *www.gaps-house.com.*

STREET MARKETS

Kalare Night Bazaar. A permanent bazaar, the Kalare Night Bazaar is in a big entertainment complex on the eastern side of the Night Market on Chang Klan Road; it's clearly marked. It's packed with boutiques, stalls, cheap restaurants, and a beer garden featuring nightly performances of traditional Thai dances. ✉ *Chang Klan Rd.*

Fodor's Choice **Night Bazaar.** The justifiably
★ famous Night Bazaar, on Chang
Klan Road, is a kind of open-air
department store filled with stalls
selling everything from inexpensive souvenirs to pricey antiques.
In the afternoon and evening traders set up tented stalls, confusingly
known as the Night Market, along
Chang Klan Road and the adjoining streets. You're expected to bargain, so don't be shy. Do, however,
remain polite. ■TIP→ Many vendors believe the first and last customers of the day bring good luck,
so if you're after a real bargain (up
to 50% off) start your shopping
early in the day. ✉ *Chang Klan Rd.*

"Walking streets." Chiang Mai has

two so-called "walking streets," closed off to traffic to make way for
weekly markets. One is held on **Wualai Road** (the "silver street") on
Saturday evening. The other, much larger one, takes up the whole of
Ratchadamnoen Road and surrounding streets on Sunday. Both are
cheaper and far more authentic than the market on Chang Klan Road.

SPECIALTY STORES

ANTIQUES

If you follow certain common-sense rules—examine each item very
carefully for signs of counterfeiting (new paint or varnish, tooled damage marks) and ask for certificates of provenance and written guaran-
tees that the goods can be returned if proved counterfeit—shopping
for antiques should present few problems. ■TIP→ Reputable stores
will always provide certificates of provenance, aware that penalties
for dishonest trading are severe (if you're ever in doubt about a deal,
contact the Tourist Police).

Lanna Antiques. The Night Bazaar in Chiang Mai has two floors packed
with antiques, many of which were manufactured yesterday (and hence
come with no guarantee of authenticity). Some stalls have the genuine
article, among them Lanna Antiques. It's the second booth on the second floor. ✉ *Chang Klan Rd.*

The road south to Hang Dong (take the signposted turn before the
airport) is lined with antiques shops. Just outside Hang Dong you'll
reach the craft village of Ban Tawai. You could spend an entire morning
or afternoon rummaging through its antiques shops and storerooms.

ART

Chiang Mai has a vibrant artists' scene, and several small galleries dot
the city.

The Gallery. A number of restaurants feature displays of Thai art. One of the best of them is the Gallery. ✉ *25–29 Charoen Rat Rd.* ☎ *053/248601* ⊕ *www.thegalleryrestaurant.com/home.html.*

Suvannabhumi Art Gallery. Burmese art is on permanent display at the Suvannabhumi Art Gallery, run by a charming and knowledgeable Burmese art lover, Mar Mar, who mounts regular exhibitions of work by her country's leading artists. ✉ *116–11 Charoen Rat Rd.* ☎ *053/260173* ⊕ *www.suvannabhumiartgallery.com.*

Wattana Art Gallery. In 2012, the celebrated Thai artist Wattana opened his own art gallery, exhibiting a wide and eclectic collection of works that display the full range of Thailand's artistic expression. ✉ *100/1 Soi Wat Umong* ☎ *053/278747, 089/429–1883* ⊕ *www.wwattanapun-art.com.*

Writers Club and Wine Bar. The Writers Club and Wine Bar organizes regular exhibitions by local and Burmese artists. ✉ *141/3 Ratchadamnoen Rd.* ☎ *053/814187.*

> **ALL FOR ONE**
>
> To encourage each *tambon* (community) to make the best use of its special skills, the government set up a program called OTOP. The program, which stands for "One Tambon, One Product," has been a great success. Its center has a two-story showroom with a collection that rivals many of the city's galleries and museums. The ground floor has an exquisite display of furniture and decorative items. Upstairs are smaller items—baskets, carvings, ceramics, and textiles. ✉ *22/19 Singharat Rd.* ☎ *053/221174, 053/223164* ⊕ *www.otop5star.com.*

HANDICRAFTS

For two of Chiang Mai's specialties, lacquerware and exquisite paper products, take a taxi or songthaew to any of the outlets along San Kamphaeng Road (also known as the Golden Mile). Large emporiums that line the 10-km (6-mile) stretch sell a wide variety of items. Whole communities here devote themselves to their traditional trades. One community rears silkworms, for instance, providing the raw product for the looms humming in workshops.

Outside the city center, the highways running south and east of Chiang Mai—those leading to Hang Dong and San Kamphaeng—are lined for several miles with workshops stocked with handicrafts of every description. They're a favorite destination for tuk-tuk drivers, who receive a commission on goods bought by their passengers. ⚠ **Be very specific with tuk-tuk drivers about what you're looking for before setting out— otherwise you might find yourself ferried to an expensive silverware outlet when all you want to buy is an inexpensive souvenir.**

For local handicrafts, head to Tha Pae Road and Loi Kroh Road. Across the Nawarat Bridge, Charoen Rat Road is home to a row of refurbished old teak houses with a handful of boutiques selling interesting crafts such as incense candles and carved curios. Farther afield, along Nimmanhemin Road, a whole neighborhood of crafts shops has developed. The first lane on the left, Soi 1, has some of the most rewarding ones.

Baan Mai Kham. Beyond the Hang Dong–Ban Tawai junction is a large Lanna-style crafts center called Baan Mai Kham. ⊠ *122 Chiang Mai–Hod Rd.* ☎ *04/040–5007.*

Ban Tawai. Near Hang Dong, 12 km (7 miles) from the city center, is the crafts village of Ban Tawai, whose streets are lined with antiques shops. ⊠ *Near Hang Dong, Chiang Mai.*

Ban Tawai Tourist Village. Four kilometers (2½ miles) beyond Ban Tawai is the Ban Tawai Tourist Village, an entire community of shops dealing in antiques and handicrafts. At workshops you can see teak, mango, rattan, and water hyacinth being worked into an astonishing variety of attractive and unusual items. If you end up buying a heavy piece of teak furniture, the dealers here will arrange for its transport. ⊠ *Near Hang Dong, Chiang Mai.*

Hilltribe Products Promotion Center. The money you pay for a woven mat or carved mask goes directly to the local communities at the Hilltribe Products Promotion Center, a government-supported crafts store. Here you can discover a wide range of handicrafts made by Akha, Hmong, Karen, Lahu, Lisu, and Yao people in their native villages. ⊠ *21/17 Suthep Rd.* ☎ *053/277743.*

Hill Tribes Handicraft Center. Chiang Mai's second government-supported store, Hill Tribes Handicraft Center stocks a wide range of products, from elaborate silver jewelry to key rings. Fine examples of hill tribe textiles hang in frames on the center's walls, and can be bought for around B2,000. ⊠ *1 Moon Muang Rd.* ☎ *053/274877.*

Living Space. Living Space, on Tha Pae Road, is worth seeking out for its original and aesthetically pleasing collection of home decor items. ⊠ *276-278 Tha Pae Rd.* ☎ *053/874276 up to 8* ⊕ *www.living spacedesigns.com.*

Northern Village. This massive store, Chiang Mai's largest handicrafts retail outlet, takes up two floors of the Central Airport Plaza Shopping Center, which is northern Thailand's largest shopping mall. The selection here is astounding: silks and other textiles, ceramics, jewelry, and carvings. ⊠ *Hang Dong and Mahidol rds.* ☎ *081/764–6645.*

Thai Tribal Crafts. Thai Tribal Crafts has more than 25 years' experience in retailing the products of northern Thailand's hill tribe people. The organization prides itself on its "fair trade" policy and the authenticity of its products. It has three outlets in Chiang Mai. ⊠ *208 Bumrungrat Rd., Moonmuang Rd. and Central Airport Plaza* ☎ *053/241043* ⊕ *www.ttcrafts.co.th.*

Umbrella Making Center. Among the crafts you can find at this large sales outlet in the village of Bor Sang, 10 miles east of Chiang Mai, are hand-painted umbrellas made from lacquered paper and tree bark. Hundreds of these are displayed at the Umbrella Making Center. The artists at the center will paint traditional designs on anything from a T-shirt to a suitcase—travelers have discovered that this is a handy way of helping identify their luggage on an airport carousel. ⊠ *11/2 Moo 3, Bor Sang, East of Chiang Mai* ☎ *053/338324.*

JEWELRY

Chiang Mai is renowned for its gems and semiprecious stones. △ Avoid the unscrupulous dealers at the Night Market and head to any of the more reputable stores. If gold is your passion, make for the Chinese district. All the shops that jostle for space at the eastern end of Chang Moi Road are reliable, invariably issuing certificates of authenticity. The city's silver district, Wualai Road, is lined for several hundred yards with shops where you can sometimes see silversmiths at work.

At Eaze. Located on the second floor of the Central Airport Plaza, At Eaze has a good selection of tiny orchid blooms set in gold, as well as other locally-made fine jewelry. ⊠ *Central Airport Plaza, 2nd fl.*

Hirunyakorn Silverware. This dealer has one of the street's best selections of handcrafted silver. ⊠ *27–29 Wualai Rd.* ☏ *053/272750.*

Nova. This reliable jewelry shop has an attached jewelry school. ⊠ *201 Tha Pae Rd.* ☏ *053/273058* ⊕ *www.nova-collection.com.*

Nova Artlab. One- to five-day courses in jewelry making are offered at Nova Artlab. You can also study sculpture, leatherwork, painting, and photography—all for B1,400 a day. ⊠ *179 Tha Pae Rd.* ☏ *053/273058* ⊕ *www.nova-collection.com.*

Orchid Jade Factory. The Orchid Jade Factory claims to be the world's largest retailer of jadeite. The hard-sell tactics here can be slightly annoying, but the showrooms display a wealth of fabulous jade jewelry and ornaments, and visitors are invited to watch the craftspeople at work. ⊠ *7/7 Srivichai Rd., opposite the entrance to Doi Suthep* ☏ *053/295021 up to 3.*

Shiraz. This small, specialized shop has been in business for 20 years and has built up an unchallenged reputation for reliability, expertise, and good value. If the owner, Mr. Nasser, is behind the counter or at work in his office workroom, you're in luck—you won't find a more knowledgeable gems expert in Chiang Mai. ⊠ *170 Tha Pae Rd.* ☏ *053/252382* ☉ *Mon.–Sat., 8–7.*

Siam Royal Orchid Collection. An attractive Chiang Mai specialty features orchid blooms or rose petals set in 24-karat gold. There's a spectacular selection at the Siam Royal Orchid Collection booth in the Central Airport Plaza shopping mall. ⊠ *Central Airport Plaza, 2nd fl.* ☏ *053/245598* ⊕ *www.royalorchidcollection.com.*

Sherry. This small trove of a boutique is crammed in between the bars and restaurants of one of the city's busiest streets. ⊠ *59/2 Loi Kroh Rd.* ☏ *053/273529.*

PAPER

The groves of mulberry trees grown in northern Thailand aren't only used to feed the silkworms—their bark, called *saa*, produces a distinctive, fibrous paper that is fashioned into every conceivable form: writing paper and envelopes, boxes, book covers, and picture frames.

HQ PaperMaker. The biggest and best paper outlet in Chiang Mai, its first floor is a secluded gallery whose works include paintings done by elephants at the Elephant Conservation Center near Lampang. ⊠ *3/31 Samlan Rd.* ☎ *053/814717.*

Siam Promprathan. This dealer has a wide selection of saa paper products. ⊠ *95/3 Moo 4, Ratchawithi Rd., San Kamphaeng* ☎ *053/331768, 053/392214.*

TEXTILES

Chiang Mai and silk are nearly synonymous, and here you can buy the product *and* see it being manufactured. Several companies along San Kamphaeng Road open their workrooms to visitors and explain the process of making fine silk, from the silkworm to the loom. △ These shops are favorite destinations of package tours, so prices tend to be higher than in other parts of town or at the Night Market.

At Eaze. Located in a leading Chiang Mai shopping mall, the Central Airport Plaza, At Eaze has an eclectic display of textiles and decorative items. ⊠ *2nd fl., Central Airport Plaza* ☎ *053/262786.*

Shinawatra Thai Silk. Silk and other local textiles can be reliably bought at Shinawatra Thai Silk. ⊠ *18 Huay Kaew Rd.* ☎ *053/221076, 053/888535* ⊠ *Mandarin Oriental Dhara Devi, 51/4 Chiang Mai–San Kampaeng Rd., Moo 1, Tambon Tasala* ☎ *053/888535.*

Studio Naenna. Tucked on a heavily forested slope of Doi Suthep mountain, Studio Naenna is run by a renowned authority on local textiles, Patricia Naenna. ⊠ *138 Huay Kaew Rd., Soi 8,* ☎ *053/226042* ⊕ *www. studio-naenna.com.*

Vaniche. Its wide selection of silk and other textiles is complemented by its own individually designed jewelry. ⊠ *133 Boonraksa Rd.* ☎ *053/262786* ⊕ *www.vaniche.com.*

SPAS

Chiang Mai has no shortage of massage parlors (the respectable kind), where the aches of a day's strenuous sightseeing can be kneaded away with a traditional massage. Your hotel can usually organize either an in-house massage or recommend one of the city's numerous centers. Chiang Mai also has dozens of spas specializing in Thai massage and various treatments involving traditional herbs and oils.

There are also several options if you wish to learn the art of Thai massage yourself.

Ban Sabai Spa Village. At the Ban Sabai Spa Village you can get your massage in a wooden Thai-style house or in a riverside sala. Treatments of note include a steamed herb massage, wherein a bundle of soothing herbs is placed on the body, and various fruit-based body masques like honey-tamarind or pineapple. Two hours of this pampering costs around B2,000, depending on the kinds of treatments you choose. ⊠ *216 Moo 9, San Pee Sua* ☎ *053/854778 and 053/854779, 082/7628310.*

Continued on page 346

SILKWORMS & COCOONS:

SILK-MAKING IN THAILAND

by Dave Stamboulis

According to legend, the Chinese empress His-Ling discovered silk nearly 5,000 years ago when a cocoon fell into her teacup, and she watched it unwind into a fine filament. As China realized the value of these threads, the silk trade was born, spreading through Asia, along what became known as the Silk Road.

For centuries, the Chinese protected the secret of silk production, beheading anyone who tried to take silkworm eggs out of the country. But, eventually, smuggled worms, along with silk-making knowledge, made it to other parts of Asia. As the demand for silk grew, Chinese traders searched for the best climates in which to cultivate worms; historians believe that these traders brought sericulture, or silk-making, to Thailand about 2,000 years ago. Archaeologists have found silk remnants in the ruins of Baan Chiang near Udon Thani.

Though silkworms thrived, the silk business did not take on a large scale in Thailand, because Buddhist Thais were reluctant to kill the silkworms—an unavoidable part of the process. But a few families in Isan did continue to produce silk, using native plants like Palmyra Palm and jackfruit to make natural bleaches and dyes. After World War II, American businessman Jim Thompson discovered Thailand's cottage industry and helped expand it, founding the Thai Silk Company in 1951 (⇨ *Jim Thompson Thai Silk Company, Chapter 2*). Queen Sirikit, King Bhumibol's wife, has also been a long-term supporter of sericulture through her SUPPORT organization, which teaches traditional crafts to rural Thais.

Silk cocoons in the final stage of incubation, Surin.

HOW SILK IS MADE

Adult female bombyx mari.

Female moth laying eggs.

Larvae eating mulberry leaves.

Silk cocoons.

Boiling cocoons to remove silk.

Woman sifting through cocoons.

Silkworms are really the caterpillars of bombyx mari, the silk moth. The process begins when a mature female moth lays eggs—about 300 at once. When the eggs hatch 10 days later, the larvae are placed on trays of mulberry leaves, which they devour. After this mulberry binge, when the worms are approximately 7 cm (2.75 in) long, they begin to spin their cocoons. After 36 hours the cocoons are complete.

Before the worms emerge as moths—destroying the cocoons in the process—silk makers boil the cocoons so they can unravel the intact silk filament. The raw silk, which ranges in color from gold to light green, is dried, washed, bleached, and then dyed before being stretched and twisted into strands strong enough for weaving. The course, knotty texture of Thai silk is ideal for hand-weaving on traditional looms—the final step to creating a finished piece of fabric.

DID YOU KNOW?

Thai silk moths reproduce 10 or more times per year—they're much more productive than their Japanese and Korean counterparts, which lay eggs only once annually.

A worm can eat 25,000 times its original weight over a 30-day period, before encasing itself in a single strand of raw silk up to 900 m (3,000 ft) long.

CHECK IT OUT

In Bangkok, the Naj Collection has an excellent reputation and top quality products, and the Jim Thompson outlets are quite good, as is Shinawatras.

Naj Collection
✉ 42 Convent Rd. (Opposite BNH Hospital), Silom, Bangkok ☎ 662/632–1004-6 ⊕ www.najcollection.com.

Jim Thompson Outlet
✉ 9 Surawong Rd., Suriyawong, Bangrak, Bangkok ☎ 02/632–8100, 02/234–4900 ⊕ www.jimthompson.com.

Shinawatra Thai Silk
✉ 94 Sukhumvit Soi 23, North Klong Toei, Wattana, Bangkok ☎ 02/258-0295-9 ⊕ www.tshinawatra.com

Man works a traditional loom.

VARIETIES OF THAI SILK
Most Thai silk is a blend of two different colors, one for the warp (threads that run lengthwise in a loom) and the other for the weft (strands that are woven across the warp.) Smoother silk, made with finer threads, is used for clothing, while rougher fabric is more appropriate for curtains. To make "striped" silk, weavers alternate course and smooth threads. Isan's famous mudmee silk, which is used mainly for clothing, consists of threads that are tie-dyed before they are woven into cloth.

Mudmee silk.

6

IN FOCUS SILKWORMS & COCOONS

SHOPPING TIPS

Appraising silk quality is an art in itself. But there are a few simple ways to be sure you're buying pure, handmade fabric.

■ Examine the weave. Hand-woven, authentic silk has small bumps and blemishes—no part of the fabric will look exactly like any other part. Imitation silk has a smooth, flawless surface.

■ Hold it up to the light. Imitation silk shines white at any angle, while the color of real silk appears to change.

■ Burn a thread. When held to a flame, natural fibers disintegrate into fine ash, while synthetic fabrics melt, smoke, and smell terrible.

■ Though this isn't a foolproof method, consider the price. Genuine silk costs five to 10 times more than an imitation or blended fabric. You should expect to pay between B250 and B350 a meter for high-quality, clothing-weight silk. Men's shirts start at B800 but could be more than B2,000; women's scarves run from B350 to B1,500. At Bangkok shops that cater to westerners, you'll pay considerably more, though shops frequented by Thais have comparable prices throughout the country.

Fine Thai silk on bobbins.

Chetawan Thai Traditional Massage School. Courses cost B800 a day at this affiliate of Bangkok's famous Wat Po massage school. The school can accommodatefemale students. ⊠ *7/1–2 Soi Samut Lana* ☎ *053/410360* ⊕ *www.watpomassage.com.*

Oasis Spa. Oasis Spa has two first-class establishments in Chiang Mai. Both offer a full range of different types of massage from Swedish to traditional Thai and a slew of mouthwatering body scrubs like Thai coffee, honey and yogurt, or orange, almond, and honey. ⊠ *102 Sirimungklajan Rd.* ☎ *053/980111* ⊕ *www.chiangmaioasis.com* ⊠ *Samlan Rd.*

Rada. Good massages with or without accompanying herbal treatments are given at Rada. A one-hour full-body massage costs B300. ⊠ *2/2 Soi 3, Nimmanhemin Rd.* ☎ *089/9556–1103.*

Thai Massage School. The Thai Massage School, one of Thailand's oldest such establishments, is authorized by the Thai Ministry of Education. A 30-hour course costs B5,000. ⊠ *Old Medicine Hospital., 238/1 Wualai Rd.* ☎ *053/201663* ⊕ *www.thaimassageschool.ac.th.*

SIDE TRIPS FROM CHIANG MAI

DOI INTHANON NATIONAL PARK

90 km (54 miles) southwest of Chiang Mai.

GETTING HERE AND AROUND

Although there are minibus services from the nearest village, Chom Tong, to the summit of Doi Inthanon, there is no direct bus route from Chiang Mai. So the most convenient way to access the park is to either book a tour with a Chiang Mai operator or hire a car and driver in Chiang Mai for around B2,000. If you're driving a rental car (about B1,000 per day), take Highway 108 south (the road to Hot), and after 36 km (22 miles) turn right at Chom Thong onto the minor road 1099, a sinuous 48-km (30-mile) stretch winding to the mountain's summit. ■ TIP➜ The ashes of Chiang Mai's last ruler, King Inthawichayanon, are contained on Road 1099 in a secluded stupa that draws hundreds of thousands of pilgrims annually.

SAFETY AND PRECAUTIONS

The regular flow of visitors to the mountain ensures that it's a perfectly safe destination, although you should stick to marked paths and forest trails. A guide (obtainable at the national park headquarters) is recommended if you plan a long hike on the thickly forested mountain slopes.

TIMING

Doi Inthanon is a full day's outing from Chiang Mai. Chalets near the national park headquarters are available if you plan to stay overnight (dawn on the mountain is an unforgettable experience, with the tropical sun slowly penetrating the upland mist against a background of chattering monkeys, barking deer, and birdsong).

EXPLORING

FAMILY

Fodor's Choice

★

Doi Inthanon National Park. Doi Inthanon, Thailand's highest mountain (8,464 feet), rises majestically over a national park of staggering beauty. Many have compared the landscape—thick forests of pines, oaks, and laurels—with that of Canada. Only the tropical vegetation on its lower slopes, and the 30 villages that are home to 3,000 Karen and Hmong people, remind you that this is indeed Asia. The reserve is of great interest to nature lovers, especially birders who come to see the 362 species that nest here. Red-and-white rhododendrons run riot, as do other plants found nowhere else in Thailand.

Hiking trails penetrate deep into the park, which has some of Thailand's highest and most beautiful waterfalls. The Mae Klang Falls, just past the turnoff to the park, are easily accessible on foot or by vehicle, but the most spectacular are more remote and involve a trek of 4 to 5 km (2½ to 3 miles). The Mae Ya Falls are the country's highest, but even more spectacular are the Siribhum Falls, which plunge in two parallel cataracts from a 1,650-foot-high cliff above the Inthanon Royal Research Station. The station's vast nurseries are a gardener's dream, filled with countless varieties of tropical and temperate plants. Rainbow trout—unknown in the warm waters of Southeast Asia—are raised here in tanks fed by cold streams plunging from the mountain's heights, then served at the station's restaurant. The national park office provides maps and guides for trekkers and bird-watchers. ■TIP→ Accommodations are available: B1,000 for a two-person chalet, B6,500 for a villa for up to eight people. The park admission fee is collected at a tollbooth at the start of the road to the summit. ⊠ *Amphur Chomthong* ☎ *053/286728, 053/286730* ⊕ *www.dnp.go.th/parkreserve* ⊠ *B200 per person, plus B30 per car* ☉ *Daily 9–6.*

6

LAMPHUN

26 km (16 miles) south of Chiang Mai.

Lamphun claims to be the oldest existing city in Thailand (but so does Nakhon Pathom). Originally called Nakhon Hariphunchai, it was founded in AD 660. Its first ruler was a queen, Chamthewi, who has a special place in Thailand's pantheon of powerful female leaders. There are two striking statues of her in the sleepy little town, and one of its wats bears her name. Queen Chamthewi founded the eponymous dynasty, which ruled the region until 1932. Today the compact little city is the capital of Thailand's smallest province, and also a textile and silk production center.

The TAT office in Lamphun, opposite the main entrance to Wat Hariphunchai, has irregular hours, but is generally open weekdays 9 to 5. Several Chaing Mai travel agencies offer day trips to Lamphun, including Cattleya Tour and Travel Service and Chiang Mai Tic Travel.

GETTING HERE AND AROUND
BUS TRAVEL

The provincial buses from Chiang Mai to Lampang stop at Lamphun, a 40-minute drive south on Highway 106, a busy but beautiful and shady road lined by 100-foot-tall rubber trees. The buses leave half-hourly from Chiang Mai's city bus station and from a stop next to the TAT office on the road to Lamphun. Minibus songthaews also operate a service to Lamphun. They leave from in front of the TAT office. Fares for all services to Lamphun are about B20. Lamphun has no bus station; buses stop at various points around town, including at the TAT office and outside Wat Haripunchai.

TRAIN TRAVEL

One slow daily Bangkok–Chiang Mai train stops at Lamphun, where a samlor (pedicab) can take you the 3 km (2 miles) into town for about B30, but the bus is more practical.

TUK-TUK AND SONGTHAEW TRAVEL

Lamphun is a compact city, easy to tour on foot, although Wat Chamthewi is on the outskirts and best visited by tuk-tuk or songthaew.

SAFETY AND PRECAUTIONS

Lamphun knows little street crime, although the usual precautions are recommended if walking the city streets at night—leave valuables in your hotel safe or with the management. Women visitors are advised to carry handbags on the side away from the street.

TIMING

One day is sufficient for Lamphun, which is less than an hour from Chiang Mai. The tiny provincial capital has very little nightlife (although that's part of its charm), few restaurants, and only one hotel of international standard.

EXPLORING LAMPHUN

Lamphun has two of northern Thailand's most important monasteries, dating back more than 1,000 years. The smallest of them guards the remains of the city's fabled 8th-century ruler, Queen Chamthewi. The other, Wat Phra That Hariphunchai, is a walled treasure house of ancient chapels, chedis, and gilded Buddhas.

Ku Chang. Lamphun has one of the region's most unusual cemeteries—literally an elephant's graveyard—called Ku Chang. The rounded chedi is said to contain the remains of Queen Chamthewi's favorite war elephant. ⊠ *Ku Chang Rd.*

National Museum. Just outside Wat Phra That Hariphunchai, the National Museum has a fine selection of Dvaravati-style stuccowork. There's also an impressive collection of Lanna antiques. ⊠ *Inthayongyot Rd.* ☎ *053/511186* ☞ *B30* ☉ *Wed.–Sun. 9–4.*

Fodor'sChoice ★ **Wat Chamthewi.** Lamphun's architectural treasures include two monasteries. About 2 km (1 mile) west of the town's center is Wat Chamthewi, often called the "topless chedi" because the gold that once covered the spire was pillaged sometime during its history. Work began on the monastery in AD 755, and despite a modern viharn added to the side of the complex, it retains an ancient, weathered look. Suwan Chang Kot, to the right of the entrance, is the most famous of the two chedis, built by King Mahantayot to hold the remains of his mother, the legendary Queen Chamthewi. The five-tier sandstone chedi is square; on each tier are Buddha images that get progressively smaller. All are in the 9th-century Dvaravati style, though many have obviously been restored. The other chedi was probably built in the 10th century, though most of what you see today is the work of 12th-century King Phaya Sapphasit. **■TIP➜ You'll probably want to take a samlor down the narrow residential street to the complex. Since this is not an area where samlors generally cruise, ask the driver to wait for you.** ✉ *Lamphun–San Pa Tong Rd.*

Fodor'sChoice ★ **Wat Phra That Hariphunchai.** The temple complex of Wat Phra That Hariphunchai is dazzling. Through the gates guarded by ornamental lions is a three-tier, sloping-roof viharn, a replica of the original that burned down in 1915. Inside, note the large Chiang Saen–style bronze image of the Buddha and the carved *thammas* (Buddhism's universal principals) to the left of the altar. As you leave the viharn, you pass what is reputedly the largest bronze gong in the world, cast in 1860. The 165-foot Suwana chedi, covered in copper and topped by a golden spire, dates from 847. A century later King Athitayarat, the 32nd ruler of Hariphunchai, added a nine-tier umbrella, gilded with 14 pounds of gold. At the back of the compound—where you can find a shortcut to the center of town—there's another viharn with a standing Buddha, a sala housing four Buddha footprints, and the old museum. ✉ *Inthayongyot Rd.* 🎫 *B40* ⏲ *Daily 6–8 pm.*

WHERE TO EAT

$ THAI 🍴 **Add Up Coffee Bar.** This attractive riverside haunt, next door to the visitor information center, is more than just a coffee shop. The menu has the usual Thai dishes, but its list of Western specialties is full of surprises. The ice cream is made under American license and is delicious. A vegetarian-only annex under the same management, Spa Food, is next door. [$] *Average main: B120* ✉ *22 Lobmuangnai Rd.* ☎ *053/530272* ⏲ *Open daily 9–9.*

$ ASIAN 🍴 **Lamphun Ice.** The odd name of this restaurant seems to come from its origins as an ice-cream parlor. The interior has cozy booths that give it the feel of a vintage soda fountain. The Chinese, Thai, and Indian food served here is the real thing—try the sensational Indian-style crab curry. [$] *Average main: B115* ✉ *Chaimongkon Rd. opposite southern gate of Wat Phra That Hariphunchai* ☎ *053/511452.*

$ THAI 🍴 **Ton Fai.** This restaurant, named for the colorful flame tree, occupies an ancient house and its shady backyard. Inside, you can climb the stairs to a teak-floored dining room with tables set beneath the original rafters. The river breeze wafting in through the shuttered windows cools the room. The menu is simple, but has plenty of tasty northern Thai

6

specialties. [$] *Average main: B90* ✉ *183 Chaimongkol Rd., Tambon Nai Muang* ☎ *053/530060* ▭ *No credit cards.*

WHERE TO STAY

$ HOTEL 🏨 **Lamphun Will.** Most people visit Lamphun only as a day trip, but if you're going to stay, this is the town's top hotel, and wouldn't look out of place in central Chiang Mai. **Pros:** the café-terrace has great views of Wat Chamthewi. **Cons:** remote location, on the edge of town. [$] *Rooms from: $30* ✉ *204/10 Charmmathewi Rd., Tumbol Naimuang, Amphur Muang* ☎ *053/534865* 🌐 *www.lamphunwillhotel.com* 🛏 *79 rooms* 🍴 *Breakfast.*

SHOPPING

Lamphun's silk and other fine textiles make a visit to this charming city worthwhile. It has its own version of Venice's Rialto Bridge, a 100-yard-long covered wooden bridge lined on both sides with stands selling mostly silk, textiles, and local handicrafts. The bridge is opposite the main entrance to Wat Phra That Hariphunchai, Inthayongyot Road. The market is open daily 9 to 6.

Lampoon Thai Silk. Eight kilometers (5 miles) from Lamphun on the main Lampang highway is one of the area's largest silk businesses, Lampoon Thai Silk, where you can watch women weave at wooden looms. ✉ *8/2 Panangjitawong Rd., Changkong* ☎ *053/510329* 🌐 *www.thaisilk.th.com.*

LAMPANG

65 km (40 miles) southeast of Lamphun, 91 km (57 miles) southeast of Chiang Mai.

At the end of the 19th century, when Lampang was a thriving center of the teak trade, the well-to-do city elders gave the city a genteel look by buying a fleet of English-built carriages and a stable of nimble ponies to pull them through the streets. Until then, elephants had been a favored means of transport—a century ago the number of elephants, employed in the nearby teak forests, nearly matched the city's population. The carriages arrived on the first trains to steam into Lampang's fine railroad station, which still looks much the same as it did back then. More than a century later, the odd sight of horse-drawn carriages still greets visitors to Lampang. The brightly painted, flower-bedecked carriages, driven by hardened types in Stetson hats and cowboy boots, look touristy, but the locals also use them to get around the city, albeit for considerably less than the B150 visitors are usually charged for a short city tour.

Lampang's tourist office is on Thakhraonoi Road near the clock tower. It keeps irregular hours; officially it's open daily 9 to 5, but as in Lamphun, you might find the office closed on weekends and even on some afternoons.

GETTING HERE AND AROUND
AIR TRAVEL
Lampang Airport, which handles domestic flights, is just west of downtown. Songthaews run to the city center for around B50. Thai Airways fly twice daily from Bangkok's Souvarnabhumi Airport. Fares for the one-hour flight are about B2,000.

BUS TRAVEL
Buses from Chiang Mai to Lampang (stopping at the Elephant Conservation Center) leave every half hour from near the Tourism Authority of Thailand office on the road to Lamphun. Lampang's bus station is 2 km (1 mile) south of the city, just off the main highway to Bangkok. Faster VIP buses from Bangkok to Chiang Mai—operated by various companies—stop at Lampang; they leave Chiang Mai's Arcade Bus Station about every hour throughout the day. Fares from Chiang Mai range from about B40 to B150.

SONGTHAEW AND CARRIAGE TRAVEL
Within Lampang, songthaews are the cheapest way of getting around, though traveling via the city's horse-drawn carriages is much more thrilling. Carriages are at various city stands, most of them outside the Wiengthong Hotel.

TRAIN TRAVEL
All Bangkok–Chiang Mai trains stop at Lampang, where a samlor can take you the 3 km (2 miles) into town for about B30. By train, Lampang is about 2½ hours from Chiang Mai and 11 hours from Bangkok. First-class fares from Bangkok range from B1,300 (for a sleeper) to B600 or B800 (for a day train).

ESSENTIALS
TOURS
Two travel agencies offer tours of the temples and the city's old quarter: Lampang Holiday and List Travel.

Lampang Holiday Tours ✉ *260/22 Chatchai Rd.* ☎ *054/310403.*

SAFETY AND PRECAUTIONS
Lampang is a famously friendly city, with a sizable expat population, mostly teachers and retirees. There are few cases of street crime or theft involving foreigners. The usual precautions are nevertheless advised, particularly if walking on less busy streets at night—leave valuables in your hotel room safe or with the management.

TIMING
Lampang is worth at least one overnight stay. It has a quite large selection of comfortable hotels and a few restaurants (notably the Riverside) where a pleasant evening can be spent.

EXPLORING LAMPANG
Apart from some noteworthy temples and a smattering of fine teak shophouses and private homes, not much else remains of Lampang's prosperous heyday. An ever-dwindling number of sturdy 19th-century teak houses can be found among the maze of concrete. Running parallel to the south bank of the Wang River is a narrow street of ancient shops and homes that once belonged to the Chinese merchants who catered

Elephants embrace at the Lampang Elephant Conservation Center.

to Lampang's prosperous populace. ■ TIP→ The riverfront promenade is a pleasant place for a stroll; a handful of cafés and restaurants have terraces overlooking the water.

FAMILY
Fodor'sChoice
★

Elephant Conservation Center. On the main highway between Lampang and Chiang Mai is Thailand's internationally known Elephant Conservation Center. So-called training camps are scattered throughout the region, but many of them are little more than overpriced sideshows. This is the real thing: a government-supported research station. Here you can find the special stables that house the 10 white elephants owned by the king, although only those who are taking the center's mahout training course are allowed to see them. The 36 "commoner" elephants (the most venerable are more than 80 years old) get individual care from more than 40 mahouts. The younger ones evidently enjoy the routines they perform for the tourists—not only the usual log-rolling, but painting pictures (a New York auction of their work raised thousands of dollars for the center). There's even an elephant band—its trumpeter is truly a star. The elephants are bathed every day at 9:30 and 1:15, and perform at 10, 11, and 1:30. You can even take an elephant ride through the center's extensive grounds, and if you fancy becoming a mahout you can take a residential course in elephant management. The center's hospital, largely financed by a Swiss benefactor, is a heart-rending place, treating elephants injured by mines sown along the Burmese border. Its latest mine victim won international renown in 2008 by becoming the first elephant in the world to be fitted successfully with an artificial leg. ⊠ *Baan Tung Kwian, Km 28–29, Lampang–Chiang Mai Hwy., Hang Chat* ☎ *054/829333* ⊠ *B200* ☼ *Daily 8–4.*

Wat Phra Kaew Don Tao. Near the banks of the Wang River is Wat Phra Kaew Don Tao, dominated by its tall chedi, built on a rectangular base and topped with a rounded spire. More interesting, however, are the Burmese-style shrine and adjacent Thai-style sala. The 18th-century shrine has a multitier roof. The interior walls are carved and inlaid with colored stones; the ornately engraved ceiling is painted with enamel. The sala, with the traditional three-tier roof and carved-wood pediments, houses a Sukhothai-style reclining Buddha. Legend has it that the sala was once home to the Emerald Buddha, which now resides in Bangkok. In 1436, when King Sam Fang Kaem was transporting the statue from Chiang Rai to Chiang Mai, his elephant reached Lampang and refused to go farther. The Emerald Buddha is said to have remained here for the next 32 years, until the succeeding king managed to get it to Chiang Mai. ✉ *Phra Kaew Rd.*

Fodor's Choice ★ **Wat Phra That Lampang Luang.** Near the village of Ko Khang is Wat Phra That Lampang Luang, one of the most venerated temples in the north. It's also one of the most striking. Surrounded by stout laterite defense walls, the temple has the appearance of a fortress—and that's exactly what it was when the legendary Queen Chamthewi founded her capital here in the 8th century. The Burmese captured it two centuries ago, but were ejected by the forces of a Lampang prince (a bullet hole marks the spot where he killed the Burmese commander). The sandy temple compound has much to hold your interest, including a tiny chapel with a hole in the door that creates an amazing, inverted photographic image of the Wat's central, gold-covered chedi. The temple's ancient viharn has a beautifully carved wooden facade; note the painstaking workmanship of the intricate decorations around the porticoes. A museum has excellent wood carvings, but its treasure is a small emerald Buddha, which some claim was carved from the same stone as its counterpart in Bangkok. ✉ *15 km (9 miles) south of Lampangm in Koh Kha district* ⏲ *Tues.–Sun. 9–4.*

Wat Sri Chum. Workers from Myanmar were employed in the region's rapidly expanding logging business, and these immigrants left their mark on the city's architecture. Especially well preserved is Wat Sri Chum, a lovely Burmese temple. Pay particular attention to the viharn, as the eaves are covered with beautiful carvings. Inside you can find gold-and-black lacquered pillars supporting a carved-wood ceiling. To the right is a bronze Buddha cast in the Burmese style. Red-and-gold panels on the walls depict temple scenes. ✉ *Sri Chum Rd.*

WHERE TO EAT

$ THAI 🍴 **Rim Wang.** This simple Thai restaurant sits on the banks of the Wang River, is 2 km (1 mile) down the main 1034 highway, in the village of Ko Kha. Fresh fish is a daily specialty, but try the plump fish cakes or a crispy version of *larb,* a popular minced pork-based dish. [$] *Average main: B3* ✉ *Hwy. 1034, Ko Kha* ☎ *054/281104* 💳 *No credit cards.*

$ ECLECTIC 🍴 **The Riverside.** A random assortment of wooden rooms and terraces gives this place an easygoing charm—perched above the sluggish Wang River, it's a great place for a casual meal. The moderately priced Thai and European fare is generally excellent (although the steak, from local beef, is to be avoided), and on weekends the chef serves up a very passable

Thailand's Elephants

The United States has its eagle. Britain acquired the lion. Thailand's symbolic animal is the elephant, which has played an enormous role in the country's history through the ages. It even appeared on the national flag when Thailand was Siam. It's a truly regal beast—white elephants enjoy royal patronage, and several are stabled at the National Elephant Institute's conservation center near Lampang.

But the elephant is also an animal of the people, domesticated some 2,000 years ago to help with the heavy work and logging in the teak forests of northern Thailand. Elephants were in big demand by the European trading companies, which scrambled for rich harvests of teak in the late 19th century and early 20th century. At one time there were nearly as many elephants in Lampang as people.

Early on, warrior rulers recognized their usefulness in battle, and "Elephants served as the armored tanks of pre-modern Southeast Asian armies," according to the late American historian David K. Wyatt. The director of the mahout training program at the Lampang conservation center believes he is a reincarnation of one of the foot soldiers who ran beside elephants in campaigns against Burmese invaders.

While many of Thailand's elephants enjoy royal status, the gentle giant is under threat from the march of progress. Ivory poaching, a cross-border trade in live elephants, and urban encroachment have reduced Thailand's elephant population from about 100,000 a century ago to just 2,500 today. Despite conservation efforts, even these 2,500 face an uncertain future as mechanization and

a 1988 government ban on private logging threw virtually all elephants and their mahouts out of work. Hundreds of mahouts took their elephants to Bangkok and other big cities to beg for money and food. The sight of an elephant begging for bananas curbside in Bangkok makes for an exotic snapshot, but the photo hides a grim reality. The elephants are kept in miserable urban conditions, usually penned in the tiny backyards of city tenements. It's been estimated that the poor living conditions, unsuitable diet, and city pollution combine to reduce their life expectancy by at least five years.

A nationwide action to rescue the urban elephants and resettle them in the country—mostly in northern Thailand—is gathering pace. The National Elephant Institute near Lampang is a leader in this field, thanks largely to the efforts of an American expert, Richard Lair, and two young British volunteers. The 40 or so elephants that have found refuge at the center actually pay for their keep by working at various tasks, from entertaining visitors with shows of their logging skills to providing the raw material (dung) for a papermaking plant. The center has a school of elephant artists, trained by two New York artists, and an elephant orchestra. The art they make sells for $1,000 and more on the Internet, and the orchestra has produced two CDs. Several similar enterprises are dotted around northern Thailand. All are humanely run. The alternative—a life on the streets of Bangkok or entertaining Pattaya nightclub patrons in degrading cabaret shows—is just too depressing to consider.

pizza. Most nights a live band performs, but there are so many quiet corners that you can easily escape the music. Quietest corner of all is the Riverside's own guest house, a cozy ensemble of teak rooms just a short walk from the restaurant. [$] *Average main: B7* ✉ *328 Tipchang Rd.* ☎ *054/221861.*

WORD OF MOUTH

"The Thai elephant training camp in Lampang was special. The two-day mahout camp gave us a real taste for the animals—they are obviously well treated. The best part was the morning of the second day—you wake up very early, and take a long walk in the forest to get your elephant. You feed him snacks and then ride him back to camp as the mist lifts up from the forest. Fabulous." —4bams

WHERE TO STAY

For expanded hotel reviews, visit Fodors.com.

$ HOTEL 🏨 **Asia Lampang.** Although this hotel sits on a bustling street, most of the rooms are quiet enough to ensure a good night's sleep. **Pros:** central location; open-sided restaurant with view of busy street scene. **Cons:** dismal lobby; some rooms need refurbishing. [$] *Rooms from: $35* ✉ *229 Boonyawat Rd.* ☎ *054/227844 up to 47, 02/642–5497* in *Bangkok for reservations* 🌐 *www.asialampanghotel.com* 🛏 *71 rooms.*

$$ RESORT 🏨 **Lampang River Lodge.** Nature-lovers are well catered to at this remote lodge, a simple riverside resort isolated in woodland and a 15-minute drive south of Lampang's bright lights. **Pros:** beautifully landscaped grounds; magical riverside bar; ample parking. **Cons:** far from Lampang city center, and shuttle bus is infrequent; noisy frogs; patchy restaurant service. [$] *Rooms from: $90* ✉ *330 Moo 11, off Chiang Mai–Lampang Hwy. 11, Tambon Champoo* ☎ *054/336640* 🌐 *www.lampangriverlodge.com* 🛏 *60 rooms.*

$$ HOTEL 🏨 **Lampang Wiengthong.** One of the city's best hotels, this modern high-rise has a number of luxuriously appointed rooms and suites. **Pros:** central location; bathrooms with tubs; horse-carriage stand in front of hotel. **Cons:** chain hotel atmosphere; package tour groups. [$] *Rooms from: B50* ✉ *138/109 Phaholyothin Rd.* ☎ *054/225801* 🌐 *www.lampangwiengthong.co.th* 🛏 *235 rooms.*

$ B&B/INN Fodor's Choice ★ 🏨 **Riverside Guest House.** Under the same management as the nearby Riverside restaurant, this utterly enchanting little place has the same rustic coziness. **Pros:** homey atmosphere; garden hammocks; river views. **Cons:** noisy neighborhood dogs; insects; no restaurant. [$] *Rooms from: $40* ✉ *286 Talad Kao Rd.* ☎ *054/227005* 🌐 *www.theriverside-lampang.com* 🛏 *19 rooms.*

SHOPPING

Lampang is known for its blue, white, and orange pottery, much of it incorporating the image of a cockerel, the city's emblem. The city has a Saturday evening street market, on Talad Kao Road, where vendors sell the local pottery, fabrics, and handicrafts. ■ **TIP→ You can find the best bargains at markets a few miles south of the city on the highway to Bangkok, or north of the city on the road to Chiang Mai.**

Indra Ceramic. The biggest pottery outlet is 2 km (1 mile) west of the city center, on the road to Phrae, at Indra Ceramic. You can see the ceramics being made and also paint your own designs. The extensive show-rooms feature a ceramic model city. ✉ *382 Vajiravudh Damnoen Rd., Lampang–Phrae Hwy., 2 km (1 mile) from Lampang* ☎ *054/315591* ⊕ *www.indraceramic.com.*

Srisawat Ceramics. In Lampang proper, Phaholyothin Road has several small showrooms. The best place in central Lampang for pottery is Srisawat Ceramics. ✉ *316 Phaholyothin Rd.* ☎ *054/218139* ⊕ *www. tcie.com.*

NORTHERN
THAILAND

WELCOME TO NORTHERN THAILAND

TOP REASONS TO GO

★ **Natural Wonders:**
Northern Thailand means mountains. Beyond Chiang Mai, they rise to the borders of Myanmar and Laos, crisscrossed by deep valleys and fast-flowing rivers. National parks welcome hikers and campers to wild areas of outstanding natural beauty and hill tribe villages lost in time. At the southern edge of the region lie the ruins of Sukhothai, a cradle of Siamese civilization.

★ **Shopping:** The region is world famous for its silks, and the night markets of Mae Hong Son and Chiang Rai have an astonishing range of handicrafts, many of them from hill tribe villages.

★ **Eating:** The region's cuisine is said to be the country's tastiest. Chiang Rai and Pai have excellent restaurants, but even the simplest food stall can dish up delicious surprises.

★ **Temples:** The golden spires of thousands of temples dot the region. Each can tell you volumes about Buddhist faith and culture—particularly the haunted ruins of Sukhothai.

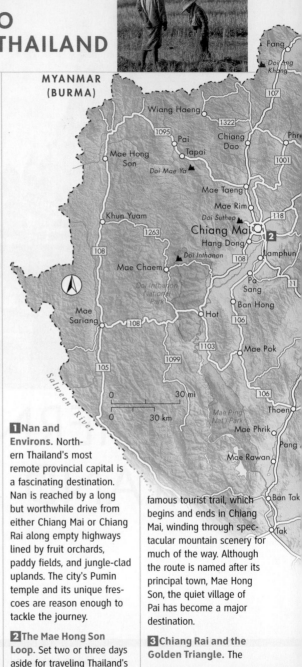

1 Nan and Environs. Northern Thailand's most remote provincial capital is a fascinating destination. Nan is reached by a long but worthwhile drive from either Chiang Mai or Chiang Rai along empty highways lined by fruit orchards, paddy fields, and jungle-clad uplands. The city's Pumin temple and its unique frescoes are reason enough to tackle the journey.

2 The Mae Hong Son Loop. Set two or three days aside for traveling Thailand's famous tourist trail, which begins and ends in Chiang Mai, winding through spectacular mountain scenery for much of the way. Although the route is named after its principal town, Mae Hong Son, the quiet village of Pai has become a major destination.

3 Chiang Rai and the Golden Triangle. The

Tachilek
Mae Sai
Golden Triangle
Chiang Saen
Dot
Mae Salong
Mae Chan
Chiang Khong
Houay Say (Houayxay)

LAOS

1089
3
1
1020

Chiang Rai
Wiang Chai
Thoeng

Mekong River

18
Mae Suai
Phan
1

Wang Nua
Phayao
Song Khwae

1120
Tha Wang Pha

1035
Ngao
1
Nan

101
Wiang Sa
103

Lampang
101
Phrae

11
Wiang Kosa National Park
11

101
Uttaradit

Satchanalai torical Park
Si Satchanalai
Phae

hung Saliam
Ban Dara
11
Sawankhalok
Nong Makhang

4
New Sukhothai
Wang Thong
Sukhothai istorical Park
Phitsanulok
Buddha Statue Temple

Chae Son National Park

GETTING ORIENTED

A journey through northern Thailand feels like venturing into a different country from the one ruled by far-off Bangkok: the landscape, the language, the architecture, the food, and even the people of this region are quite distinct. Chiang Mai is the natural capital of the north, but Chiang Rai is developing rapidly. Both cities are not smaller versions of Bangkok, but bustling regional centers in their own right. Just beyond each of them rises the mountain range that forms the eastern buttress of the Himalayas, and the region overall has some of the country's most dramatic scenery. The northernmost part of the region borders both Myanmar (Burma) and Laos, and improved land crossings into Laos from here have made forays into that country popular side trips.

northernmost region of Thailand is mostly known for its former role as the center of the opium trade; it has a museum devoted to the subject that's a worthy side trip. Beyond its fascinating past, the area has much to recommend it: mountain scenery, boat trips on the Mekong River, and a few luxurious resorts.

4 Sukhothai and Environs. To history buffs, the soul of the country is to be found in the cities of Sukhothai and Sri Satchanalai. These strongholds of architecture and culture evoke Thailand's ancient civilizations, while Sukhothai's well-developed tourist industry makes it the natural hub for exploring the region.

7

EATING AND DRINKING WELL IN NORTHERN THAILAND

To most foodies, the north of Thailand is the country's most interesting culinary hotbed (and take that literally!). The distinctive Laotian and Burmese influences, spicy salads, and grilled river fish are unlike any Thai food you've tasted in the West. Through rice paddies, across plains, and along the majestic Mekong, a healthy peasant's diet of fresh river fish, sticky rice, sausage, and spicy salads replaces the richer shellfish and coconut curries of Thailand's center and south.

Thailand's expansive north encompasses various ethnicities and immigrant groups, making it hard to pigeonhole the food. Universal, however, are searingly sour curries centering on sharp herbs and spices rather than coconut milk; salt-rubbed river fish grilled over open coals; and salads integrating lime, fermented shrimp, and dried chili.

Westerners may not like the frogs, lizards, and even rice-paddy rats that are often added to spicy curry. Snakehead fish with mango salad (above).

CLEVER COOKING IN NORTHERN THAILAND

The food of the far north is distinctly different from that of the rest of Thailand. In this poorer region of the country, cooks are sometimes inspired by whatever's on hand. Take salted eggs for example. They're soaked in salt and then pickled, preserving a fragile food in the hot environment and adding another tasty salty and briny element to dishes.

PLA DUK YANG

You'll find grilled river fish throughout the north, and snakehead fish is one of the region's most special treats. As opposed to the south, where fish is sometimes deep-fried or curried, here it is usually stuffed with big, long lemongrass skewers and grilled over an open fire, searing the skin. Add the spicy, sour curry that's served atop the fish—and throw in *som tam* salad and sticky rice for good measure—and you've got a quintessential northern meal.

SOM TAM

Som tam, a classic, ragingly hot green-papaya salad prepared with a mortar and pestle, is found all over Thailand, but its homeland is really the north. Tease out the differences between three versions: *som tam poo,* also found in Myanmar, integrating black crab shells (a challenging texture, to say the least); *som tam pla,* an Isan version with salt fish and long bean; and the traditional Thai *som tam,* ground with peanuts and tiny dried and fermented shrimp.

KHAO LAM

On highways, meandering rural roads, and at most markets you find women selling tubes of bamboo filled with sticky rice. The rice is steamed in bamboo, which adds a woodiness to the rice's rich, sweet, salty flavor. (Slowly peel off the bamboo to eat it.) The rice can be black or white, and sometimes is

cooked with minuscule purplish beans. In mango season, *khao neaw ma muang* (mango with sticky rice) is the ultimate salty-sweet dessert.

KHAO SOI

This comforting concoction of vaguely Burmese, vaguely Laotian, vaguely Muslim origins is ubiquitous in the north. Noodles swim in a hearty, meaty broth fortified with coconut milk and perked up with chili and lime. It's a lovely textural experience, especially when the noodles are panfried: they become soggy in the broth—great for slurping. Get it from a street-food vendor, where portions are incredibly cheap.

GAENG HANG LED

Another northern favorite, this mild pork curry gets its flavor not from chilies but a subtle mix of tamarind, ginger, and groundnuts. The result is a fairly sweet curry, but with sour back notes and chunks of pork. There's no coconut milk in the mix, but then again, it's not needed to temper any flames in this curry. It's almost always served with a side dish of sticky rice.

Updated by
Robert Tilley

Northern Thailand begins where the flat rice-growing countryside above Bangkok rises slowly to the mountains that border Myanmar and Laos. It's a vast region of Thailand, about the size of the state of Kentucky, that bears striking geographic and cultural differences from the south. The mountains that are the distinguishing feature of the north contribute to the region's distinctly different character, protecting its mostly rural people, and particularly its hill tribes, from too rapid an advance of outside influences.

The north has its own language ("Muang"), cuisine, and traditional beliefs and rituals (many of them animist) and a sturdy architectural style that has come to be known as Lanna ("a million rice fields"). All these features contrast strikingly with the distinguishing features of the rest of Thailand, where the strict practices of Buddhism have a greater hold on the people and where western influences have made greater inroads.

Although Chiang Mai is the natural capital of northern Thailand it's not the only city of this region deserving inclusion in any Thailand itinerary; Chiang Rai, Chiang Saen, Mae Hong Son, Phrae, and Nan have enough attractions, particularly historic temples, to make at least overnight visits worthwhile. The ancient city of Sukhothai, with its stunning ensemble of temple ruins, is a stand-alone destination in its own right but can be easily integrated into a tour of the north. The mountains and forested uplands that separate these fascinating cities are studded with simple national park lodges and luxury resorts, hot-water spas, elephant camps—the list is endless.

Chiang Rai is a particularly suitable base for exploring the region further—either on treks to the hill tribe villages that dot the mountainsides or on shorter jaunts by elephant. The fast-flowing mountain rivers offer ideal white-water rafting and canoeing. The truly adventurous

GREAT ITINERARIES

To really get a feel for northern Thailand, plan on spending at least a week here.

If You Have 2 Days. Spend your first day exploring the streets of Chiang Mai. On the second day rise early and drive up to Wat Phra That Doi Suthep. In the afternoon, visit Chian Rai and its mountainous surroundings.

If You Have 5 Days. Begin your stay in the north in Chiang Mai, flying from there to Mae Hong Son and take a tour of a nearby Karen village. Set out the next day (by hired car or bus) for Chiang Rai, stopping over for one night at Pai. On the third day, en route for Chiang Rai, you might consider overnighting in Tha Ton or Chiang Dao. On the fourth and fifth days make a circular tour to Chiang Saen to see its excavated ruins and meet the Mekong River, then to Ban Sop Ruak to visit the magnificent Hall of Opium museum. Finally, head to Mae Sai for a look at Burmese crafts in the busy local markets.

If You Have 7 Days. If you're lucky enough to have a week or more in northern Thailand, you'll have plenty of time to stay a night with a hill tribe family. Treks to these mountain villages, often done on elephants, can be arranged from Chiang Mai, Chiang Rai, Mae Hong Son, and other communities. Sukhothai, a must-see destination, is a day's journey to the south, so the best way to include it in your itinerary is to return to Chiang Mai and catch a long-distance VIP bus to Sukhothai, where a tour of the well-preserved ruins of ancient Siam's most advanced and most civilized kingdom will take up one day. From Sukhothai, another six-hour bus ride returns you to Bangkok.

7

may want to head for one of the region's national parks, which offer overnight accommodations and the services of guides.

From Chiang Rai, circular routes run through the city's upland surroundings and deep into more remote mountains, where descendants of Chinese soldiers who fled after the Communist takeover of their country grow coffee and tea. Nan, tucked away in the mountainous corner bordering Laos; and Mae Hong Son and Mae Sariang, where Myanmar lies just over the nearest range. The so-called Mae Hong Son Loop, a spectacular road starting and ending in Chiang Mai, runs through a small market town, Pai, that has developed over the years into a major tourist destination. First discovered by backpackers doing the "Loop," the town's simple guesthouses are now making way for smart resorts designed for Bangkok businesspeople seeking a quiet weekend in the north.

PLANNING

WHEN TO GO

Northern Thailand has three seasons. The region is hottest and driest from March to May. The rainy season is June to October, with the wettest weather in September. Unpaved roads are often impassable at this time of year. November to March is the best time to visit, when days are warm, sunny, and generally cloudless, and nights pleasantly cool. (At higher altitudes, it can be quite cold in the evening.) Book hotel accommodation a month or two ahead of the Christmas and New Year holiday periods and the Songkran festival in mid-April (Thailand's New Year celebration; also known as the Water Festival, because revelers douse each other with water).

GETTING HERE AND AROUND

Northern Thailand appears to be a very remote area of Asia, around 700 km (420 miles) from the country's capital, Bangkok, and far from other major centers. In fact, this region—bounded on the north, east, and west by Myanmar and Laos—is easily accessible. Chiang Mai and Chiang Rai are northern Thailand's major centers.

AIR TRAVEL

Main cities and towns are linked to Bangkok by frequent and reliable air services. There are more than 25 flights a day from Bangkok to Chiang Mai and Chiang Rai, and regular flights from the capital to Mae Hong Son, and Nan. Flight schedules to these two towns change with frustrating regularity, so check with your airline or travel agent for the very latest information.

BUS TRAVEL

An excellent regional bus service links towns and remote villages via a network of highways. The country's main north–south artery, Highway 1, connects Bangkok with Chiang Rai and the Golden Triangle. Highway 11 branches off for Chiang Mai at Lampang, itself a major transport hub with a long-distance bus terminal, railroad station, and airport. From Chiang Mai you can reach the entire region on well-paved roads, with travel times not exceeding eight hours or so. The journey on serpentine mountain roads to Mae Hong Son, however, can be very tiring, requiring a stopover in either the popular resort town of Pai or quieter Mae Sariang. Chiang Rai is a convenient stopover on the road north to the Golden Triangle.

CAR TRAVEL

Driving in Thailand is not for the faint of heart; hiring a car and driver is usually a better option (⇨ *Car Travel in Travel Smart Thailand*). ⚠ Between Christmas and New Year's the highway between Chiang Mai, Chiang Rai, Pai, and Mae Hong Son may be packed with bumper-to-bumper traffic.

MOTORCYCLE TRAVEL

Motorcycles are a cheap and popular option for getting around cities and towns. Rental agencies are numerous, and most small hotels have their own.

ESSENTIALS

SAFETY AND PRECAUTIONS

Malaria and other mosquito-borne diseases are rare in northern cities, but if you're traveling in the jungle during the rainy season (June to October), consider taking antimalarials. If you're trekking in the mountains or staying at hill tribe villages, pack mosquito repellent. Spray your room about a half hour before turning in, even if windows have screens and beds have mosquito nets.

Chiang Rai and other communities in northern Thailand are generally safe. However, it's a good idea to leave your passport, expensive jewelry, and large amounts of cash in your hotel safe. Keep a copy of your passport with you at all times, as police can demand proof of identification and levy a fine if you don't produce it. Always walk holding bags on the side of you facing away from the street. In a medical emergency, head to Chiang Rai or Chiang Mai. The police hotline is 191.

MONEY MATTERS

ATMs are everywhere in Chiang Rai and Pai, and most towns and larger villages have at least one machine. Every bank has at least one ATM, but if there are no convenient banks, head for a branch of the ubiquitous convenience store chain 7-Eleven, where an ATM is invariably to be found next to the entrance. Banks are open weekdays 9:30 to 3:30, closing on weekends and public holidays. All banks have an exchange counter; money can also be exchanged at some outlets in central Chiang Rai. Most businesses and restaurants accept credit cards (usually preferring MasterCard or Visa). Simpler Thai restaurants accept only cash.

RESTAURANTS

Northern cuisine differs significantly from cuisine in the rest of Thailand, although most restaurants serve both. You'll have no problem finding plain *khao suay* (steamed rice) or fragrant jasmine rice, for example, though locals prefer the glutinous *khao niao* (sticky rice). A truly northern and very popular Muslim specialty is *khao soy,* a delicious pork or chicken curry with crispy and soft noodles, served with pickled cabbage and onions; lively debates take place at Chiang Mai dinner tables on the best restaurants to find it.

Another scrumptious northern specialty is *hang led,* a pork curry spiced with ginger. Chiang Mai's sausages are nationally famous—try *sai ua* (crispy pork sausage) and *mu yo* (spicy sausage). Noodles of nearly every variety can be bought for a few baht from food stalls everywhere, and some fried-noodle dishes, particularly *pad thai,* have found their way onto many menus. Other northern dishes to try include *nam pik ong* (pork, chilies, and tomatoes), *gaeng ke gai* (chicken curry with chili leaves and baby eggplant), and *kap moo* (crispy pork served with *nam pik num,* a mashed chili dip). Western food is served at all larger hotels and at all international restaurants, although the local version of a western breakfast can be a bit of a shock.

Prices in the reviews are the lowest cost of a main course at dinner, or, if dinner is not served, at lunch.

HOTELS

Northern Thailand has the full range of accommodation, from simple guesthouses to five-star resorts. Optimistic prognoses by Thailand's tourist authorities led to a boom in hotel construction in recent years, mostly in Chiang Mai and Chiang Rai but also studding the region's mountains with resorts and spas, many of them lacking none of the luxury and facilities of Chiang Mai's top hotels. Chiang Rai, Sukhothai, and Pai, particularly, are witnessing the construction of so-called "boutique" hotels—small, comfortable, and well-appointed establishments of no more than 40 or so rooms. Most of these are built in "Lanna" style, reminiscent of this region's earlier architecture, with the accent on dark teak and white stucco. Some of the top hotels are internationally known for embracing a "contemporary Asian" look, combining sleek lines with decorative Oriental features.

Prices in the reviews are the lowest cost of a standard double room in high season.

VISITOR INFORMATION

Tours of northern Thailand are offered by Bangkok travel agencies, but it's best to book with one of the many reliable companies in Chiang Mai or Chiang Rai, which are likely to have a deeper local knowledge of the region. Mountain tours of one or two days, which pack in elephant riding, whitewater rafting, jungle trekking, and visits or overnights in hill tribe villages are popular. They are invariably led by guides with close knowledge of their region and with acceptable English. If you're touring alone or as a couple, you can draw up your own itinerary (omitting, for instance, visits to "Long Neck" villages, a controversial issue in Thailand), but it's far more fun to join a group—and, of course, it's cheaper (B800–B1,000 a day). Tours are also arranged by the Tourism Authority of Thailand (or TAT; ⊕ *www.tourismthailand.org*), which has offices in Chiang Mai, Chiang Rai, Mae Hong Son, and Nan.

NAN AND ENVIRONS

Visitors looking for off-the-beaten-track territory usually head north from Chiang Mai and Chiang Rai to the Golden Triangle or west to Mae Hong Son. Relatively few venture east, toward Laos, but if time permits, it's a region that's well worth exploring. The center of the region is a provincial capital and ancient royal residence, Nan, some 70 km (42 miles) from the Laotian border. The city is very remote; roads to the border end in mountain trails, and there are no frontier crossings, although there are ambitious, long-term plans to run a highway through the mountains to Luang Prabang.

Two roads link Nan with the west and the cities of Chiang Mai, Chiang Rai, and Lampang—they are both modern highways that sweep through some of Thailand's most spectacular scenery, following river valleys, penetrating forests of bamboo and teak, and skirting upland terraces of rice and maize. Hill tribe villages sit on the heights of the surrounding Doi Phu Chi (Phu Chi Mountains), where dozens of waterfalls, mountain river rapids, and revered caves beckon travelers with time on their hands. Here you can find Hmong and Lahu villages untouched by commercialism, and jungle trails where you, your elephant, and mahout beat virgin paths through the thick undergrowth.

The southern route from Chiang Mai to Nan passes through the ancient town of Phrae, the center of Thailand's richest teak-growing region and a pleasant overnight stop. An alternative route to Chiang Mai passes through the town of Phayao, beautifully located on a shallow, shimmering lake with a waterside promenade where restaurants feature freshly caught fish on their daily menu specialties. The region has three wild, mountainous national parks: Doi Phak Long, 20 km (12 miles) west

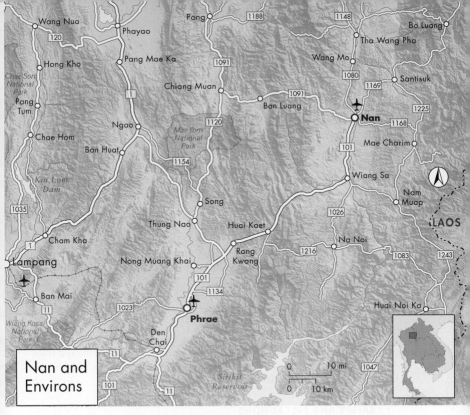

Nan and Environs

of Phrae on Route 1023; Doi Luang, south of Chiang Rai; and Doi Phukku, on the slopes of the mountain range that separates Thailand and Laos, some 80 km (48 miles) northeast of Nan.

NAN

318 km (198 miles) southeast of Chiang Mai, 270 km (168 miles) southeast of Chiang Rai, 668 km (415 miles) northeast of Bangkok.

Near the border of Laos lies the city of Nan, a provincial capital founded in 1272. According to local legend, Lord Buddha, passing through the Nan Valley, spotted an auspicious site for a temple to be built. By the late 13th century Nan was brought into Sukhothai's fold, but, largely because of its remoteness, it maintained a fairly independent status until the last few decades.

Tourist information about Nan Province, Nan itself, and Phrae is handled by the Tourism Authority of Thailand's regional office in Chiang Rai.

GETTING HERE AND AROUND

AIR TRAVEL

A new domestic airline, Kan Air, operates a weekly service from Chiang Mai to and from Nan. The 45 minute flight in Beachcraft propeller aircraft is every Thursday. Songthaews meet incoming flights and charge about B50 for the 3-km (2-mile) drive south into central Nan.

Kan Air ☎ *02/551–1445, 053/283311 in Chiang Mai.*

BUS TRAVEL

Several air-conditioned buses leave Bangkok and Chiang Mai daily for Nan, stopping en route at Phrae. The 11-hour journey from Bangkok to Nan costs B400 to B600; it's 8 hours from Chiang Mai to Nan and the cost is B300 to B400. Air-conditioned buses also make the five-hour journey from Lampang to Nan. There's local bus service between Nan and Phrae.

CAR TRAVEL

Hiring a car and driver is the easiest way to get to Nan from Lampang or Chiang Mai, but it will cost about B1,200 per day.

TAXI AND TUK-TUK TRAVEL

City transport in Nan is provided by tuk-tuks, songthaews, and samlors. All are cheap, and trips within the city should seldom exceed B30.

TRAIN TRAVEL

Nan is not on the railroad route, but a relatively comfortable way of reaching the city from Bangkok is to take the Chiang Mai–bound train and change at Den Chai to a local bus for the remaining 146 km (87 miles) to Nan. The bus stops en route at Phrae.

ESSENTIALS

SAFETY AND PRECAUTIONS

The mountainous border between Thailand and Laos is just an hour's drive from Nan, and until recently was a haven for smugglers, keeping local police busy. Foreign visitors rarely encounter reminders of this picaresque past, and street crime is rare. But elementary precautions are advised—such as leaving valuables in the hotel safe or with the hotel management.

TIMING

Nan is worth visiting for the Wat Pumin frescoes alone, but otherwise has little to keep a visitor for more than a day or two. The surrounding countryside and the nearby mountains have a wild beauty and a day tour is recommended.

TOURS

Trips range from city tours of Nan and short cycling tours of the region to jungle trekking, elephant riding, and white-water rafting. Nan is the ideal center from which to embark on treks through the nearby mountains, as well as raft and kayak trips along the rivers that cut through them. Khun Chompupach Sirsappuris has run Nan's leading tourist agency, Fhu Travel and Information, for more than 20 years, and knows the region like her own backyard. She speaks fluent English, and has an impressive Web site describing tours and prices.

Contacts Fhu Travel ✉ *453/4 Sumondhevaraj Rd.* ☎ *054/710636* ⊕ *www. fhutravel.com.* **River Raft** ✉ *50/6 Norkam Rd.* ☎ *054/710940* ⊕ *www. nanriverraft.com.*

EXPLORING NAN

Nan is rich in teak plantations and fertile valleys that produce rice and superb oranges. The town of Nan itself is small; everything is within walking distance. Daily life centers on the morning and evening markets. ■TIP➜ The Nan River, which flows past the eastern edge of town, draws visitors at the end of Buddhist Lent, in late October or early November, when traditional boat races are held. Each longtail boat is carved out of a single tree trunk, and at least one capsizes every year, to the delight of the locals. In mid-December Nan honors its famous fruit crop with a special Golden Orange and Red Cross Fair—there's even a Miss Golden Orange contest. It's advisable to book hotels ahead of time for these events.

National Museum. To get a sense of the region's art, visit the National Museum, a mansion built in 1923 for the prince who ruled Nan, Chao Suriyapong Pharittadit. The house itself is a work of art, a synthesis of overlapping red roofs, forest green doors and shutters, and brilliant white walls. There's a fine array of wood and bronze Buddha statues, musical instruments, ceramics, and other works of Lanna art. The revered "black elephant tusk" is also an attraction. The 3-foot-long, 40-pound tusk is actually dark brown in color, but that doesn't detract at all from its special role as a local good-luck charm. ✉ *Phalong Rd.* ☎ *054/710561* 💲 *B100* ⊙ *Wed.–Sun. 9–5.*

Wat Chang Kham. Wat Chang Kham has one of only seven surviving solid-gold Buddha images from the Sukhothai period. Its large chedi is supported by elephant-shape buttresses. ✉ *Suriyaphong Rd.*

Wat Hua Wiang Tai. Nan is dotted with other wats. Wat Hua Wiang Tai is the gaudiest, with a naga running along the top of the wall and lively murals painted on the viharn's exterior. ✉ *Sumonthewarat Rd.*

Wat Ming Muang. Wat Ming Muang contains a stone pillar erected at the founding of Nan, some 800 years ago. ✉ *Suriyaphong Rd.*

Fodor'sChoice
★ **Wat Pumin.** Nan has one of the region's most unusual and beautiful temples, Wat Pumin, whose murals alone make a visit to this part of northern Thailand worthwhile. It's an economically constructed temple, combining the main shrine hall and viharn, and qualifies as one of northern Thailand's best examples of folk architecture. To enter, you climb a short flight of steps flanked by two superb nagas, their heads guarding the north entrance and their tails the south. The 16th-century temple was extensively renovated in 1865 and 1873, and at the end of the 19th century murals picturing everyday life were added to the inner walls. Some have a unique historical context—like the French colonial soldiers disembarking at a Mekong River port with their wives in crinolines. A fully rigged merchant ship and a primitive steamboat are portrayed as backdrops to scenes showing colonial soldiers leering at the pretty local girls corralled in a palace courtyard. Even the conventional Buddhist images have a lively originality, ranging from the traumas of hell to the joys of courtly life. The bot's central images are

7

also quite unusual—four Sukhothai Buddhas locked in conflict with the evil Mara. ✉ *Phalong Rd.* ☉ *Daily 8–6.*

Wat Suan Tan. Wat Suan Tan has a 15th-century bronze Buddha image. It's the scene of all-night fireworks during the annual Songkran festival in April. ✉ *Tambon Nai Wiang.*

WHERE TO EAT

$ ✗**Ruen Kaew.** Its name means Crystal House, and this riverside restau-
THAI rant, open seven days a week, really is a gem. Guests step in through a profusion of bougainvillea onto a wooden deck directly overlooking the Nan River. A Thai band and singers perform from 6:30 every night. The Thai menu has some original touches—the chicken in a honey sauce, for instance, is a rare delight. $ *Average main: B240* ✉ *1/1 Sumondhevaraj Rd.* ☎ *054/710631, 089/558–2508.*

$ ✗**Suriya Garden.** This substantial restaurant on the banks of the Nan
THAI River is a larger version of the nearby Ruen Kaew, with a wooden deck overlooking the water. Like its neighbor, it has added some interesting specialties to its conventional Thai menu—Chinese-style white bass or pig's trotters, for instance. A band and solo vocalists perform nightly. $ *Average main: B200* ✉ *9 Sumondhevaraj Rd.* ☎ *054/710687.*

WHERE TO STAY

For expanded hotel reviews, visit Fodors.com.

$ 🏨 **City Park Hotel.** Nan's top hotel is a low-rise, ranch-style complex of
HOTEL buildings on the outskirts of the city, set in 12 acres of gardens. **Pros:** clean, well-maintained pool; shady gardens; friendly service. **Cons:** far from town center; insects; some rooms lack privacy. $ *Rooms from: $25* ✉ *99 Yantarakitkosol Rd.* ☎ *054/741343 up to 52* ⊕ *www. thecityparkhotel.com* ⇆ *129 rooms.*

$ 🏨 **Dhevaraj.** Built around an attractive interior courtyard, which is
HOTEL romantically lighted for evening dining, the Dhevaraj has all the comforts and facilities of a top-class hotel. **Pros:** cool interior courtyard; central location; large rooms. **Cons:** lousy breakfast; patchy service; street noise. $ *Rooms from: $35* ✉ *466 Sumondhevaraj Rd.* ☎ *054/751577* ⊕ *www.dhevarajhotel.com* ⇆ *160 rooms.*

$ 🏨 **Nan Boutique Hotel.** So-called "boutique" hotels are rare in rural
HOTEL Thailand, but this recent addition to Nan's limited choice of accommodation fully lives up to its name. **Pros:** free bicycles; busy restaurant with international menu; friendly service. **Cons:** no pool; long walk to town center; rooms with double beds can be suddenly unavailable. $ *Rooms from: $60* ✉ *1/11 Kha Luang Rd., city* ☎ *054/775532* ⊕ *www.nanboutiquehotel.com* ⇆ *32 rooms* ❑ *Breakfast.*

PHRAE

110 km (68 miles) southeast of Lampang, 118 km (73 miles) south-west of Nan.

A market town in a narrow valley, Phrae is well off the beaten path. It's a useful stopover on the 230-km (143-mile) journey from Lampang to Nan, but has little to offer the visitor apart from ruined city walls, some attractive and historic temples, and sturdy teak buildings that attest to its former importance as a center of the logging industry.

GETTING HERE AND AROUND

The domestic airline Nok Air flies four times weekly (Monday, Tuesday, Thursday and Saturday; one hour) between Bangkok and Phrae. Daily air-conditioned buses from Bangkok and Chiang Mai headed for Nan stop at Phrae. It's a 10-hour journey from Bangkok and five hours from Chiang Mai (B400 to B600). Air-conditioned buses travel between Lampang and Phrae (three hours) daily. There's local bus service between Phrae and Nan, an uncomfortable but cheap journey of two to three hours between each center. Hiring a car and driver in Lampang or Chiang Mai is the easiest way to get here (about B1,200 per day).

ESSENTIALS

SAFETY AND PRECAUTIONS

Phrae is a friendly place, where everybody knows everybody and where the police rarely have more to do than ticket wrongly parked motorists. You're perfectly safe to walk the streets at night, although you might like to leave valuables in the hotel safe or with the management. You're not likely to need to carry much cash—there's not much to spend it on in Phrae.

TIMING

Phrae has little to keep the visitor apart from a comfortable room as a stopover on the road to Nan.

VISITOR INFORMATION

Fhu Travel and Information ☎ 054/710636 ⊕ www.fhutravel.com.

EXPLORING PHRAE

The town's recorded history starts in the 12th century, when it was called Wiang Kosai, the Silk City. It remained an independent kingdom until the Ayutthaya period. Remains of these former times are seen in the crumbling city walls and moat, which separate the Old City from the new commercial sprawl.

Ban Prathap Chai. Phrae is renowned in northern Thailand for its fine teak houses. There are many to admire all over the city, but none to match what is claimed to be the world's largest teak structure, the Ban Prathap Chai, in the hamlet of Tambon Pa Maet near the southern edge of Phrae. Like many such houses, it's actually a reconstruction of several older houses—in this case, nine of them supported on 130 huge centuries-old teak posts. The result is remarkably harmonious. A tour of the rooms open to public view gives a fascinating picture of bourgeois life in the region. The space between the teak poles on the ground floor of the building is taken up by stalls selling a variety of handicrafts, including much carved teak. ⊠ *Hwy. 1022, 10 km (6 miles) east of Phrae* ⊠ *B40* ☉ *Daily 8–5.*

Wat Chom Sawan. On the northeastern edge of town stands Wat Chom Sawan, a beautiful monastery designed by a Burmese architect and built during the reign of King Rama V (1868–1910). The bot and viharn are combined to make one giant sweeping structure. ⊠ *Yantrakitkoson Rd.*

Wat Luang. Phrae's oldest building is Wat Luang, within the Old City walls. Although it was founded in the 12th century, renovations and expansions completely obscure so much of the original design that the only section from that time is a Lanna chedi with primitive elephant statues. A small museum on the grounds contains sacred Buddha images, swords, and texts. ✉ *Kham Lue Rd.*

WHERE TO EAT

For a quick bite, there's a night market at Pratuchai Gate with numerous stalls offering cheap, tasty food.

$ THAI 🍴 **Ban Jai.** For authentic Lanna cuisine, you can't do better than this simple but superb restaurant. You're automatically served *kanom jin* (Chinese noodles) in basketwork dishes, with a spicy meat sauce, raw and pickled cabbage, and various condiments. If that's not to your taste, then order the *satay moo,* thin slices of lean pork on wooden skewers, served with a peanut sauce dip. In the evening every table has its own brazier for preparing the popular northern specialty *moo kata,* a kind of pork stew. The open-sided, teak-floored dining area is shaded by ancient acacia trees, making it a cool retreat on warm evenings. [$] *Average main: B100* ✉ *3 Chatawan Rd.* 💳 *No credit cards.*

WHERE TO STAY

For expanded hotel reviews, visit Fodors.com.

$$ HOTEL 🏨 **Nakorn Phrae Tower.** A curious but effective combination of a conventional high-rise and a Lanna-style aesthetic distinguishes this comfortable central Phrae hotel. **Pros:** center of Phrae's muted nightlife; friendly service; large rooms. **Cons:** favored by tour groups; traffic noise; no pool. [$] *Rooms from: $35* ✉ *3 Muanghit Rd.* ☎ *054/521321* 🛏 *139 rooms* 🍽 *Breakfast.*

THE MAE HONG SON LOOP

Remote Mae Hong Son is reached along a mountainous stretch of road known to travelers as "the Loop." The route runs from Chiang Mai to Mae Hong Son via Pai if you take the northern route, and via Mae Sariang if you take the southern one. Which route offers the best views is the subject of much heated debate. The entire Loop is about 600 km (360 miles) long. ■ **TIP→ Allow at least four days to cover it—longer if you want to leave the road occasionally and visit the hot springs, waterfalls, and grottos found along the way.**

PAI

160 km (99 miles) northwest of Chiang Mai, 110 km (68 miles) east of Mae Hong Son.

Disastrous floods and mud slides in the surrounding mountains devastated this popular tourist haunt in 2005, but the town rapidly recovered, and now the only reminders of the catastrophe are a few high-water marks on the walls of some buildings and empty swathes of riverside land. A building boom is again in full swing as the former market town

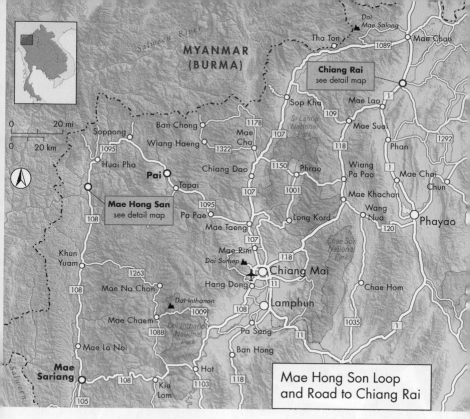

Mae Hong San
see detail map

Chiang Rai
see detail map

Mae Hong Son Loop
and Road to Chiang Rai

struggles to cope with another annual flood—the thousands of visitors who outnumber the locals in high season.

It was exhausted backpackers looking for a stopover along the serpentine road between Chiang Mai and Mae Hong Son who discovered Pai in the late 1980s. In 1991 it had seven modest guesthouses and three restaurants; now its frontier-style streets are lined with restaurants and bars of every description, cheap guesthouses and smart hotels, art galleries, and chic coffeehouses, while every class of resort, from back-to-nature to luxury, nestles in the surrounding hills. Thus far, Pai has managed to retain its slightly off-the-beaten-path appeal, but that may change as Bangkok property investors pour money into its infrastructure and flights arrive daily from Chiang Mai.

GETTING HERE AND AROUND
AIR TRAVEL

The new domestic airline Kan Air flies three times a week between Chiang Mai and Pai and daily during the Christmas–New Year holiday period. The flight takes less than a half hour in a 12-seater Cessna aircraft, an excellent alternative to the long, torturous drive.

BUS TRAVEL

Buses traveling between Mae Hong Son and Chiang Mai stop in Pai. They take four hours for the 120-km (75-mile) journey from Chiang Mai and an additional five hours to cover the 130 km (81 miles) from Pai to Mae Hong Son. Fares for each stretch vary from about B100 to B200. Buses stop in the center of Pai.

CAR TRAVEL

A hired car does the trip from Chiang Mai to Pai one hour faster than the buses, and cuts the journey time from Pai to Mae Hong Son by about the same margin. Cars and four-wheel-drive vehicles can be hired from many companies in Chiang Mai for around B1,000 to B1,200 a day. A driver costs about B1,000 extra per day.

ESSENTIALS

SAFETY AND PRECAUTIONS

Pai had a crime problem—but it was caused by drug-taking young foreign visitors, not by the locals. A police crackdown appears to have cleaned up the town, although keep your wits about you when visiting the local bars.

TIMING

Some foreign visitors come to Pai intending to stay a few days and never leave. It's that kind of place. There's not much to do in Pai besides exploring the surrounding countryside by day and partying by night, so if trekking, bike tours, river rafting, and late nights are not your thing, you'll want to get going again after one or two days.

TOURS

Thai Adventure Rafting organizes tours of the area as well as wild-water rafting on mountain rivers around Pai. Another reliable company is Pai Laguna. Ask for Charlie, who knows the area like the back of his hand.

Contacts Pai Laguna ☏ *081/733–9055* ⊕ *www.pailaguna.com.* **Thai Adventure Rafting** ☏ *053/699111* ⊕ *www.thaiadventurerafting.com.*

EXPLORING PAI

Although Pai lies in a flat valley, a 10-minute drive in any direction brings you to a rugged upland terrain with stands of wild teak, groves of towering bamboo, and clusters of palm and banana trees hiding out-of-the-way resorts catering to visitors who seek peace and quiet. At night the surrounding fields and forest seem to enfold the town in a black embrace. As you enter Pai from the direction of Chiang Mai, you'll pass by the so-called World War II Memorial Bridge, which was stolen from Chiang Mai during the Japanese advance through northern Thailand and rebuilt here to carry heavy armor over the Pai River. When the Japanese left, they neglected to return the bridge to Chiang Mai. Residents of that city are perfectly happy, as they eventually built a much more handsome river crossing.

WHERE TO EAT

$ ✕**All About Coffee.** One of Pai's historic merchant houses has been con-
CAFÉ verted into a coffee shop that could grace any fashionable city street in the world. More than 20 different kinds of java are on the menu, which is also packed with delicacies from the café's own bakery. The mezzanine

floor has a gallery of works by local artists. $ *Average main: B100* ✉ *100 Moo 1, Chaisongkram Rd.* ☎ *053/699429* ⊟ *No credit cards* ⊗ *Closes at 6 pm.*

$
THAI
✕**Baan Pai Terrace Restaurant.** The town's central meeting point is this airy, teak restaurant, which prides itself in using mostly organic products from the estates of the royal horticultural project. Western dishes tend to crowd out the Thai specialties, but the customers seem to come to this friendly hangout more for the atmosphere than for the food. $ *Average main: B150* ✉ *7 Moo 3, Rungsiyanon Rd., Baan Pakham, Tambon Viengtai* ☎ *053/699912.*

$
ECLECTIC
✕**Café del Doi.** There's nowhere better in Pai to watch the sun sink

PAI: DEMURE HAMLET OR PARTY TOWN?

Pai has a sizable Muslim population, which is why some of the guesthouses post notices asking foreign visitors to refrain from public displays of affection. Immodest clothing is frowned on, so bikini tops and other revealing garb is definitely out. The music bars close early, meaning that by 1 am the town slumbers beneath the tropical sky. Nevertheless, quiet partying continues behind the shutters of the teak cabins that make up much of the tourist lodgings. This is, after all, backpacker territory.

over the surrounding mountains than this bustling bar-restaurant on a hillside just outside the town limits. The owners ran a similarly successful establishment in Chiang Mai before settling in Pai, and many of their old regulars join the nightly crowds drawn by the live bands that perform regularly. The menu is eclectic—ranging from hill tribe food to Tex-Mex and Italian. In winter months under-floor heating is provided by water from the nearby hot springs. $ *Average main: B200* ✉ *Pai–Chiang Mai Rd., Km 5* ☎ *09/851–9621, 053/699948* ⊕ *www.cafedeldoi.com* ⚠ *Reservations not accepted.*

$
ECLECTIC
✕**Edible Jazz.** The international menu at this friendly little café, which includes chili con carne and good burritos, matches the flavor of the music. It's one of few places in Pai where you can hear live jazz. $ *Average main: B150* ✉ *Tambon Viengtai, 24/1, Chaisongkram Rd.* ☎ *053/714–6968* ⊕ *www.ediblejazz.com* ⊟ *No credit cards.*

$$
ECLECTIC
✕**Pai Corner.** This formerly German-run restaurant, a local favorite, passed into Thai hands in 2012, but the menu is still strongly Teutonic, featuring many of the specialties that made it so popular. Nevertheless, classic northern Thai dishes such as *khao soy* (spicy soup with crispy noodles and chicken) can also be found. Breakfast is served beginning at 7:30. $ *Average main: B250* ✉ *53 Moo 4, Raddamrong Rd.* ☎ *081/764–2334.*

$
BURGER
✕**Ping's Burger Queen.** Pai entrepreneur Ping returned from 10 years in Britain to open a highly successful burger restaurant in her home town. Her burgers are packed with the best local beef and are served with hand-cut choice potatoes. The modest establishment is also the place to catch up with travel tips from the crowds that gather there nightly. $ *Average main: B150* ✉ *Tedsaban Rd.* ☎ *081/381–9141.*

WHERE TO STAY
For expanded hotel reviews, visit Fodors.com.

$$ RESORT Fodor's Choice ★ [H] **Belle Villa.** This appealing resort's 45 teak chalets (traditional outside, pure luxury inside) are perched on stilts in a tropical garden that blends seamlessly with the neighboring rice paddies and the foothills of the nearby mountains. **Pros:** infinity pool, giving impression of swimming in a rice paddy; horse-and-buggy transport to town; airy restaurant. **Cons:** 15-minute drive from town; insects; noisy frogs. [$] *Rooms from: $120* ✉ *113 Moo 6, Huay Poo–Wiang Nua Rd., Tambon Wiang Tai* ☎ *053/698266, 053/698267, 02/693–2895 in Bangkok* 🌐 *www.bellevillaresort.com* ⇐ *45 chalets.*

WORD OF MOUTH

"We stayed in Pai about two years ago when driving the [Mae Hong Son] loop from Chiang Mai and loved it. There were a few hippy types about but it was nothing like the Khao San Road. There are quite a few backpackers' hostels in the center but we stayed just outside of town at the Belle Villa and it was very peaceful. A great place to stay for a few days. In fact I preferred it to MHS." —crellston

$ B&B/INN [H] **Brook View.** The brook babbles right outside your cabin window if you ask for a room with a view at this well-run little resort. **Pros:** near town, but still "away from it all"; ample parking; pretty breakfast gazebo. **Cons:** some cabins are small, with no river view; staff keep a low profile; uninteresting neighborhood. [$] *Rooms from: $50* ✉ *132 Moo 1, Tambon Wiang Tai* ☎ *053/699366* ✉ *brookviewpai@yahoo.com* ⇐ *18 rooms and villas* 💳 *No credit cards* 🍴 *No meals.*

$ RESORT [H] **Cave Lodge.** The chatter of gibbons wakes you up at this remote mountain lodge between Pai and Mae Hong Son. **Pros:** bread and pastries from the wood-fired oven; nature. **Cons:** snakes on the grounds; Pai an hour drive away. [$] *Rooms from: $17* ✉ *15 Moo 1, Pang Mapa, Mae Hong Son* ☎ *053/617203* 🌐 *www.cavelodge.com* ⇐ *17 rooms* 💳 *No credit cards.*

$$ HOTEL [H] **Paivimaan Resort.** Vimann means "heaven," and this fine resort, opened in 2006, certainly commands a heavenly spot on the banks of the Pai River. **Pros:** friendly family welcome; four-poster beds in "deluxe" rooms; close to town center. **Cons:** villa rooms are small; noise from riverside developments; insects. [$] *Rooms from: $120* ✉ *Moo 3, Tetsaban Rd.* ☎ *053/699403* 🌐 *www.paivimaan.com* ⇐ *12 rooms, 5 villas.*

$$ RESORT [H] **Tree House.** The rooms with the best views at this riverside "hotel" outside Pai are only for the most adventurous travelers—they're nestled in the upper branches of an enormous rain tree. **Pros:** terrace bar-restaurant; fine river views; peaceful location. **Cons:** 20-minute drive from town; popular for seminars; can get crowded. [$] *Rooms from: $70* ✉ *90 Moo 2, Tambon Machee* ☎ *081/911–3640* 🌐 *www.paitreehouse.com* ⇐ *19 rooms.*

NIGHTLIFE

Bepop. In high season Pai is packed with backpackers looking for a place to party. Pai's top music bar is Bepop, which throbs nightly to the sounds of visiting bands. ✉ *188 Rangsiyannon Rd., Moo 8, Tambon Viengtai* ☎ *053/699128.*

7

Phu Pai Art Cafe. At popular backpacker hangout Phu Pai Art Cafe, bands perform every night beginning at 9:30. ⊠ *21 Rangsiyannon Rd., Tambon Viangtai* ☎ *084/209–8169.*

Ting Tong ("crazy") Bar. A good place to chill out in the early evening is the aptly named Ting Tong ("crazy") Bar. On warm, rainless evenings you can lie on cushions and count the stars. ⊠ *55 Moo 4, Tambon Viengtai* ☎ *048/073781.*

SPORTS AND THE OUTDOORS

Pai in the Sky Rafting. While in Pai you can join a whitewater rafting trip sponsored by Pai in the Sky Rafting. The two-day outing on the Khong River sends you through steep-sided gorges, past spectacular waterfalls, and over 15 sets of rapids. An overnight stop is made at the Pai in the Sky camp, near the confluence of the Pai and Kohong rivers, before reaching the end point outside Mae Hong Son. The trips, costing B2,000, are made daily June to February, when the rivers are at their peak. ⊠ *114 Moo 4, Tambon Viengtai* ☎ *053/698145, 084/174–6157.*

MAE HONG SON

245 km (152 miles) northwest of Chiang Mai via Pai, 368 km (229 miles) via Mae Sariang.

Stressed-out residents of Bangkok and other cities have transformed this remote, mountain-ringed market town into one of northern Thailand's major resort areas. Some handsome hotels have arisen in recent years to cater to them. Overseas travelers also love the town because of its easy access to some of Thailand's most beautiful countryside.

GETTING HERE AND AROUND

AIR TRAVEL

Two domestic carriers, Nok Air and Kan Air, fly several times daily between Chiang Mai and Mae Hong Son (40 minutes; about B1,700). The Mae Hong Son Airport is at the town's northern edge. Songthaews run to the city center for around B50. In March and April smoke from slash-and-burn fires often causes flight cancellations.

BUS TRAVEL

Chiang Mai's Arcade Bus Terminal serves Mae Hong Son. Several buses depart daily on an eight-hour journey that follows the northern section of the Loop, via Pai. Buses stop in the center of town.

CAR TRAVEL

If you choose to rent a car, you'll probably do it in Chiang Mai, but Avis also has an office at Mae Hong Son Airport, if needed.

TOUR TRAVEL

A tourist info kiosk (with erratic hours) stands on the corner of Khunlum Prapas and Chamnan Salit roads. An efficient travel agency, Amazing Mae Hong Son, has an office at the airport. In the center of town, Discover Mae Hong Son offers day tours of local hill tribe villages.

■TIP→ **The road to Mae Hong Son from Chiang Mai has more than 1,200 curves, so make sure your rental car has power steering.** The most comfortable way to travel the route and enjoy the breathtaking mountain scenery is to let somebody else do the driving. The Loop road brings you here from either direction: the northern route through Pai (six hours) is a more attractive trip; the southern route through Mae Sariang (eight hours) is easier driving.

Contacts Amazing Mae Hong Son ☎ *620650.* **Discover Mae Hong Son** ☎ *053/611537.*

ESSENTIALS
SAFETY AND PRECAUTIONS
Mae Hong Son, lying close to the often-disputed Myanmar border, has a lawless history, and around 50 years ago was a place of internal exile for political dissidents. But those days lie long in the past, and today Mae Hong Son is a quiet backwater with little street crime. You can safely walk even its unlit lanes at night.

TIMING
It's possible to spend a restful week or so in Mae Hong Son, but most visitors overnight here while traveling the Loop, a popular route that also takes in Pai and Mae Sariang. The Burmese temples can occupy a morning or afternoon of sightseeing, but the town has little else to offer. It is, however, a good base from which to visit the hill tribe villages of the region.

EXPLORING MAE HONG SON
For a small town, Mae Hong Son has some notable temples, thanks to immigrants from nearby Myanmar, where Burmese architecture and decorative arts were historically more advanced. Two of the temples, Wat Chong Kham and Wat Kham Klang, sit on the shore of a placid lake in the center of town, forming a breathtakingly beautiful ensemble of golden spires. Within a short drive are dozens of villages inhabited by the Karen, the so-called "long-neck" people. Fine handicrafts are produced in these hamlets, whose inhabitants trek daily to Mae Hong Son to sell their wares at the lively morning market and along the lakeside promenade.

Although Mae Hong Son offers a welcome cool retreat during the sometimes unbearably hot months of March and April, the mountains can be obscured during that part of the year by the fires set by farmers to clear their fields. One of the local names for Mae Hong Son translates as "City of the Three Mists." The other two are the clouds that creep through the valleys in the depths of winter and the gray monsoons of the rainy season.

TOP ATTRACTIONS
Wat Chong Klang. This temple is worth visiting to see a collection of figurines brought from Burma more than a century ago. The teak-wood carvings depict an astonishing range of Burmese individuals, from peasants to nobles. ⊠ *Chamnansathit Rd.*

Wat Hua Wiang. Mae Hong Son's most celebrated Buddha image—one of the most revered in northern Thailand—is inside this temple. Its origins are clear—note the Burmese-style long earlobes, a symbol of the Buddha's omniscience. ⊠ *Panishwatana Rd.*

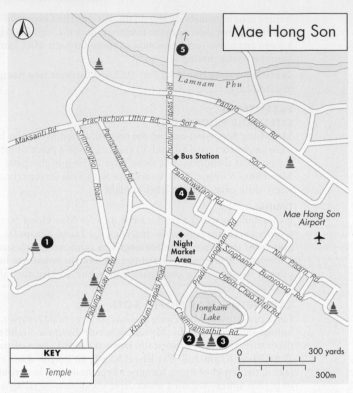

Mae Hong Son

Lamnam Phu

Prachachon Uthit Rd.

Maksanti Rd.

Khunlum Prapas Road

Panglo Nikon Rd.

Soi 2

Panishwatana Rd.

Srimongkol Road

◆ Bus Station

Soi 2

Panishwatana Rd.

❹

Mae Hong Son
Airport

❶

◆ Night
Market
Area

Pradit Jongkam   Singhanat   Niva Pisarn Rd.

Bumroong Rd.

Padung Muay To Rd.

Khunlum Prapas Road

Udom Chao Niter Rd.

Jongkam
Lake

Chamnansathit Rd.

❷   ❸

KEY

▲   *Temple*

| 0 | | 300 yards |
| 0 | | 300m |

Wat Phra That Doi Kong Mu. On the top of Doi Kong Mu, this temple has a remarkable view of the surrounding mountains. The temple's two chedis contain the ashes of 19th-century monks. ☒ *West of Mae Hong Son.*

WORTH NOTING

FAMILY **Thampla-Phasua Waterfall National Park.** About 16 km (10 miles) from Mae Hong Son, on the Pai road, this park has one of the region's strangest sights—a grotto with a dark, cisternlike pool overflowing with fat mountain carp. The pool is fed by a mountain stream that is also full of thrashing fish fighting to get into the cave. Why? Nobody knows. It's a secret that draws thousands of Thai visitors a year. Some see a mystical meaning in the strange sight. The cave is a pleasant 10-minute stroll from the park's headquarters. ☒ *70 Moo 1, Huay Pa* ☎ *053/619036* ☒ *Free.*

Wat Chong Kham. A wonderfully self-satisfied Burmese-style Buddha, the cares of the world far from his arched brow, watches over the temple, which has a fine pulpit carved with incredible precision. ☒ *Chamnansathit Rd.*

WHERE TO EAT

$ ✕ **Bai Fern.** Mae Hong Son's main thoroughfare, Khunlum Prapas Road,
THAI is lined with inexpensive restaurants serving local cuisine. Bai Fern is among the best. In the spacious dining room you eat in typical Thai

style, amid solid teak columns and beneath whirling fans. Among the array of Thai dishes, pork ribs with pineapple or roast chicken in pandanus leaves stand out as highly individual and tasty creations. An adjoining coffee corner offers free Wi-Fi. $ *Average main: B150* ✉ *87 Khunlum Prapas Rd.* ☎ *053/611374.*

$$
ITALIAN ✗ **La Tasca.** Mae Hong Son's only Italian restaurant serves excellent pastas, pizzas and a much-acclaimed calzone. Unusual for an Italian restaurant, it also has an extensive Thai menu. The wine list is also impressive. On cool

> ### SUNSET VIEWS
>
> For a giddy view of Mae Hong Son and the surrounding mountains, take a deep breath and trudge up Doi Kong Mu, a hill on the western edge of town. It's well worth the effort—from here you can see the mountains on the border of Myanmar (it's particularly lovely at sunset). There's another shade of gold to admire—a flame-surrounded white-marble Buddha in a hilltop temple called Wat Phra That Doi Kong Mu.

evenings, take a table on the small terrace overlooking Mae Hong Son's main street. $ *Average main: B250* ✉ *88/4 Khunlumpapas Rd.* ☎ *053/611344.*

WHERE TO STAY

For expanded hotel reviews, visit Fodors.com.

$ 🏨 **Ban Farang Guesthouse.** If you're visiting the Japanese War Museum
B&B/INN at Khun Yuam or just needing an overnight stop on the Mae Hong Son Loop, this modest guesthouse offers clean rooms and a simple restaurant. **Pros:** adjacent to Japanese War Museum; breakfast included; pleasant countryside walks. **Cons:** plumbing can be unreliable; shabby neighborhood; no nightlife. $ *Rooms from: $24* ✉ *499 Moo 1, Khun Yuam, Mae Sariang* ☎ *051/622086* ⊕ *www.banfarang-guesthouse.com* ⇩*20.*

$$
RESORT 🏨 **Fern Resort.** The room rate is relatively expensive, but it buys unexpected luxury in the midst of beautiful countryside outside Mae Hong Son. **Pros:** regular barbecue nights; fine mountain views; friendly owners. **Cons:** 15-minute drive from town, though there's a shuttle bus; mosquitos; small bathrooms. $ *Rooms from: $100* ✉ *10 Ban Hua Nam Mae Sakut, Tambon Pha Bong* ☎ *053/686110, 053/686111* ⊕ *www. fernresort.info* ⇩ *30 rooms.*

$$
HOTEL 🏨 **Imperial Tara Mae Hong Son.** Set amid mature teak trees, this fine hotel was designed to blend in with the surroundings—bungalows in landscaped gardens have both front and back porches, giving the teak-floored and bamboo-furnished rooms a light and airy feel. **Pros:** pleasant walks in the grounds; large rooms; satellite TV. **Cons:** some rooms need refurbishing; long walk from town, although hotel offers regular shuttle-bus service; insects. $ *Rooms from: $75* ✉ *149 Moo 8, Tambon Pang Moo* ☎ *053/611473, 02/261–9000 in Bangkok* ⊕ *www. imperialhotels.com/taramaehongson* ⇩ *104 rooms* ⏐❍⏐*Breakfast.*

$ 🏨 **Panorama Hotel.** This centrally located hotel lives up to its name with
HOTEL upper-floor rooms that have sweeping views of the mountains surrounding the city. **Pros:** central location; helpful tour desk; good restaurant. **Cons:** some rooms showing their age; cleaning service could be more

efficient; traffic noise. $ *Rooms from: B33* ⊠ *51 Khunlum Prapas Rd.* ☎ *053/611757 up to 62* ⌁ *463 rooms* ⎁ *Breakfast.*

$
RESORT **Rim Nam Klang Doi.** This retreat, about 7 km (4 miles) outside Mae Hong Son, is especially good value. **Pros:** helpful tour service; fine local walks; good restaurant. **Cons:** shuttle-bus service to town is erratic; small bathrooms; unreliable plumbing. $ *Rooms from: $30* ⊠ *108 Ban Huay Dua* ☎ *053/612142* ⌁ *39 rooms.*

$$
HOTEL **Rooks Holiday Hotel & Resort.** Mae Hong Son's largest hotel also claims to be the "biggest entertainment center in town," with 11 karaoke rooms, a "music hall," and a grand piano in the lounge. **Pros:** unexpected luxury; lively nighttime scene; well-equipped spa. **Cons:** karaoke rooms can be noisy; lots of tour groups; chain-hotel atmosphere. $ *Rooms from: $34* ⊠ *114/5–7 Khunlumprapas Rd.* ☎ *053/612324 up to 9* ⌁ *184 rooms* ⎁ *Breakfast.*

MAE SARIANG

175 km (109 miles) southwest of Chiang Mai, 140 km (87 miles) south of Mae Hong Son.

The southern route of the Loop runs through Mae Sariang, a neat little market town that sits beside the Yuam River. With two comfortable hotels and a handful of good restaurants, the town makes a good base for trekking in the nearby Salawin National Park or for boat trips on the Salawin River, which borders Myanmar.

GETTING HERE AND AROUND

Buses from Chiang Mai's Chiang Phuak bus station take about four hours to reach Mae Sariang. Fares range from B200 to B300. A few songthaews ply the few streets of Mae Sariang, but the town is small and compact, and can be covered easily on foot.

Tours of the border region around Mae Sariang are offered by travel agencies in Mae Hong Son. Two of the leading ones are Amazing Mae Hong Son and Discover Mae Hong Son.

ESSENTIALS

SAFETY AND PRECAUTIONS

Despite its proximity to the sometimes disputed Myanmar border, Mae Sariang is perfectly safe for visitors. There is also little crime, although elementary precautions are advised—leave valuables and large amounts of cash in your hotel safe or with the management.

TIMING

Mae Sariang is a beautiful, laid-back little town, so if you're looking for relaxation a stay of two or three days provides a welcome break on the long Mae Hong Son Loop route.

TOURS

Contacts Amazing Mae Hong Son ☎ *053/620650.* **Discover Mae Hong Son** ☎ *053/611537.*

EXPLORING MAE SARIANG

Near Mae Sariang the road winds through some of Thailand's most spectacular mountain scenery, with seemingly endless panoramas opening up through gaps in the thick teak forests that line the route. You'll pass hill tribe villages where time seems to have stood still, and Karen women go to market proudly in their traditional dress.

World War II Memorial Museum. In the village of Khun Yuam, 100 km (62 miles) north of Mae Sariang, you can find one of the region's most unusual and, for many, most poignant museums, the World War II Memorial Museum, part of a newly created Cultural Center. The museum commemorates the hundreds of Japanese soldiers who died here on their chaotic retreat from the Allied armies in Burma. Locals took in the dejected and defeated men. A local historian later gathered the belongings they left behind: rifles, uniforms, cooking utensils, personal photographs, and documents; they provide a fascinating glimpse into a little-known chapter of World War II. Outside is a graveyard of old military vehicles, including an Allied truck presumably commandeered by the Japanese on their retreat east. ✉ *Mae Hong Son Rd.* 🎫 *B40* 🕐 *Daily 8–4.*

WHERE TO EAT

$$$
THAI
Fodor'sChoice
★

✕ Coriander in Redwood. An early 20th-century English log-trader's home has been carefully restored into one of the region's most attractive restaurants. The house, restaurant, and bar are completely constructed of redwood, which lends a warm, lamplit glow to the dinner table. Tables are also ranged under the trees of a leafy garden. The restaurant attracts a regular clientele, who come from far afield for its steaks of locally reared beef. $ *Average main: B300* ✉ *12 Moo 2, Langpanich Rd.* 🕿 *053/683309* ⊕ *www.riversidehotels.com/coriander* 🍴 *Reservations essential.*

$
THAI

✕ Riverside Restaurant and Guesthouse. This restaurant, on the open-air terrace of an inexpensive guesthouse, is on a bend of the Yuam River, commanding an impressive view of rice paddies and the mountains beyond. The menu is simple, but the panoramic view is reason enough to eat here. The guesthouse, a rambling wooden building cluttered with antique bits and bobs ranging from worm-eaten farm implements to antlers, has 18 reasonably comfortable rooms ($12). $ *Average main: B150* ✉ *85 Langpanich Rd.* 🕿 *053/681188, 053/682592.*

WHERE TO STAY

For expanded hotel reviews, visit Fodors.com.

$$
HOTEL

🖼 Riverhouse Guesthouse. Cooling breezes from the Yuam River waft through the open-plan reception area, lounge, and dining room of this attractive hotel, built so completely of teak that even the snug bathrooms are timber-walled. **Pros:** cozy; timber-walled bathrooms; homey public lounge area; river views. **Cons:** limited restaurant menu; no nightlife; traffic noise. $ *Rooms from: $68* ✉ *77 Langpanich Rd.* 🕿 *053/621201* ⊕ *www.riverhousehotels.com* 🛏 *12 rooms.*

$
HOTEL

🖼 River House Resort. The pink facade of this modern hotel might appear to be an incongruous intrusion in this neat little border town, but it hides a smart and comfortable interior. **Pros:** riverside garden; fine

7

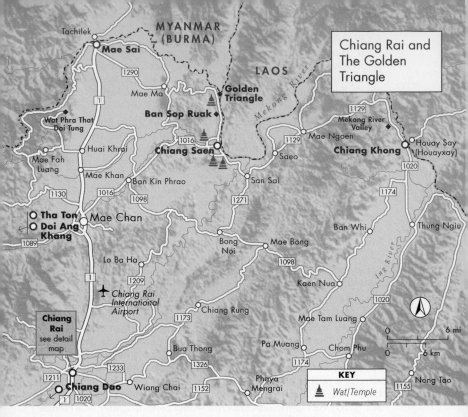

views; ample parking. **Cons:** disappointing breakfast; long walk to town center; insects. $ *Rooms from: $58* ✉ *6/1 Moo 2, Langpanich Rd.* ☎ *053/683066* ⊕ *www.riverhousehotels.com* ➟ *44 rooms* ❑ *Breakfast.*

CHIANG RAI AND THE GOLDEN TRIANGLE

This fabled area is a beautiful stretch of rolling uplands that conceal remote hill tribe villages and drop down to the broad Mekong, which is backed on its far side by the mountains of Laos. Although some 60 km (37 miles) to the south, Chiang Rai is its natural capital and a city equipped with the infrastructure for touring the entire region.

The region's involvement in the lucrative opium trade began in the late 19th century, when migrating hill tribes introduced poppy cultivation. For more than 100 years the opium produced from poppy fields was the region's main source of income. Even today, despite vigorous official suppression and a royal project to wean farmers away from the opium trade, the mountains of the Golden Triangle conceal isolated poppy plantations.

Despite its associations with the opium trade, the Golden Triangle is still the term used to refer to the geographical region, varying in size and interpretation from the few square yards where the borders of Thailand, Myanmar, and Laos actually meet to a 40,000-square-km (15,440-square-mile) region where the opium-yielding poppies are still cultivated. That region includes much of Thailand's Chiang Rai Province, where strenuous and sometimes controversial police raids have severely curbed opium production and trade. The royal program to encourage farmers to plant alternative crops is also paying dividends.

Whatever the size of the actual triangle is thought to be, its apex is the riverside village of Ban Sop Ruak, once a bustling center of the region's opium trade. An archway on the Mekong riverbank at Ban Sop Ruak invites visitors to step symbolically into the Golden Triangle, and a large golden Buddha watches impassively over the river scene. In a nearby valley where poppies once grew stands a huge museum, the Hall of Opium, which describes the history of the worldwide trade in narcotics.

Winding your way from Chiang Mai to Chiang Rai, the hub of the fabled Golden Triangle, will take you past Chiang Dao, best known for its astonishing cave complex; Tha Ton, a pretty riverside town on the Myanmar border, which has many outdoor activities; and Doi Ang Khang, a small, remote settlement—with one fancy resort.

> ## THE STORY OF THE NAME
>
> U.S. Assistant Secretary of State Marshall Green coined the term "Golden Triangle" in 1971 during a preview of the historic visit by President Richard Nixon to China. The Nixon Administration was concerned about the rise of heroin addiction in the United States and wanted to stem the flow of opium from China, Thailand, Myanmar, and Laos. The greatest source of opium was the wild territory where the Mekong and Ruak rivers formed porous borders between Thailand, Myanmar, and Laos—the "golden triangle" drawn by Green on the world map.

CHIANG DAO

72 km (40 miles) north of Chiang Mai.

The dusty, rather dilapidated village of Chiang Dao has two claims to fame: Thailand's third-highest mountain, 7,500-foot Doi Chiang Dao, which leaps up almost vertically from the valley floor; and the country's most spectacular caves, which penetrate more than 10 km (6 miles) into the massif. If you want to explore more of the mountain, hire a guide.

GETTING HERE AND AROUND

Hourly bus services run from Chiang Mai's Chiang Phuak Bus Terminal. The fare is B100 to B200, depending on the type of service (express, air-conditioned, etc.). Buses stop right on the main road in town.

If you need information about Chiang Dao, the best source is Khun Wicha of the Chiang Dao Nest. She knows the town and its attractions so well that she has produced a charming map for visitors.

ESSENTIALS

SAFETY AND PRECAUTIONS

Chiang Dao is a small village where everybody knows his or her neighbor, so safety is absolutely no problem.

TIMING

Chiang Dao's famous caves can be explored in a couple of hours, but many visitors are so captivated by the mountain scenery that they stay for a few days—the hike to the top of Chiang Dao mountain takes at least six hours, and most trekkers bivouac overnight at the top.

TOURS

ContactKhun Wihataya, Chiang Dao Nest ☎ *053/456242* 🌐 *www.chiangdao.com/nest.*

EXPLORING CHIANG DAO

Caves have a mystic hold over Buddhist Thais, and foreign visitors to Chiang Dao's famous caverns find themselves vastly outnumbered by the locals. If you're at all claustrophobic, join a group of Thais to explore the caves, which are thought to penetrate more than 10 km (6 miles) into the small town's guardian mountain, Doi Chiang Dao. Only a few hundred yards are lighted; if you want to explore further, hire a local guide with a lantern (about B100). The mountain can be scaled without difficulty in a day, but even just an hour or two of tough walking can bring you to viewpoints with amazing panoramas.

Chiang Dao Caves. Thailand's most famous caves run deep into the mountain that broods over the small town of Chiang Dao. The caverns, only some of which are lighted, contain spectacular stalagmites and stalactites and hundreds of Buddha statues and other votive items, placed there by devout Buddhists, for whom caves have a deep religious significance. ■ **TIP→ About half the caves have electric lights, but make sure you have a flashlight in your pocket in case there's a power failure.** Guides can be hired for B100. ✉ *About 3 km (2 miles) west of town* ☎ *053/248604* 🎫 *B20* 🕐 *Daily 7–5.*

WHERE TO STAY

For expanded hotel reviews, visit Fodors.com.

$ RESORT Fodor's Choice ★ 🏨 **Chiang Dao Nest.** Describing itself as a mini-resort, the Nest has grown over the years from one modest collection of chalets to two separate ones, a mile apart and nestling at the foot of the Chiang Dao mountain. **Pros:** total seclusion; great food; bicycles available. **Cons:** dim lighting makes bedtime reading difficult; insects; unheated pool water can be cold in winter. [$] *Rooms from: $30* ✉ *144/4 Moo 5* ☎ *053/456242* 🌐 *www.chiangdao.com/nest* 🛏 *23 chalets.*

$ RESORT 🏨 **Rim Doi Resort.** Rim Doi means "on the edge of the mountain," so it's fitting that two extraordinary peaks loom over this peaceful little resort near Chiang Dao. **Pros:** pleasant walks on the grounds; well-stocked lake for perch fishing, open-air restaurant. **Cons:** staff have limited English-language skills, chalet accommodation is very basic, insects. [$] *Rooms from: $30* ✉ *46 Moo 4, Muang Ghay* ☎ *053/375028, 053/375029* 🌐 *www.rimdoiresort.com* 🛏 *18 rooms, 22 chalets.*

DOI ANG KHANG

60 km (36 miles) north of Chiang Dao.

Ang means "bowl," and that sums up the mountaintop location of this remote corner of Thailand. A tiny, two-street settlement shares the small valley with the orchards and gardens of a royal agricultural project, which grows temperate fruits and vegetables found nowhere else in Thailand.

GETTING HERE AND AROUND

From Chiang Dao take Highways 1178 and 1340 north to Doi Ang Khang. Local bus services connect the two towns, stopping in the center of Doi Ang Khang. Tony Smile Travel organizes day trips to Doi Ang Khang.

ESSENTIALS

SAFETY AND PRECAUTIONS

This is a tiny, remote community and crime is virtually unknown.

TIMING

Doi Ang Khang is for nature lovers, who tend to relax for a few days amid its orchards and gardens. It's a long drive from either Chiang Mai or Chiang Rai, so at least an overnight stay is recommended. There's no nightlife, however, and after 9 the small community is wrapped in slumber.

TOURS

Tony Smile Travel ☎ *053/744762, 081/998–5719* 🌐 *tonysmile.asia/Website/tonysmile.asia.html.*

EXPLORING DOI ANG KHANG

The orchards, gardens, and hothouses of the royal project are open to the public, and at various times of the year you can buy pears, apples, plums, and peaches harvested directly from the trees. Not many tourists find their way into this border territory, so you'll get a warm welcome from the people who inhabit the dusty little village.

WHERE TO STAY

For expanded hotel reviews, visit Fodors.com.

$$ RESORT 🏨 **Ang Khang Nature Resort.** This stylish country resort in the mountains near Doi Ang Khan is now part of the OAM group of hotels. **Pros:** good restaurant, the Camellia, with first-class cuisine using products from the neighboring royal project gardens; open log fire in the lobby in cool season; pretty gardens. **Cons:** 2 km (1 mile) from the village center; no nightlife; insects. [$] *Rooms from: $80* ✉ *1/1 Moo 5, Baan Koom, Tambon Mae Ngon, Amphoe Fang* ☎ *053/450110* 🌐 *www.oamhotels.com/angkhang* 🛏 *72 rooms, 2 suites.*

THA TON

90 km (56 miles) north of Chiang Dao.

North of Chiang Dao lies the pretty resort town of Tha Ton, which sits on the River Kok right across the border from Myanmar. The local temple, Wat Tha Ton, is built on a cliff overlooking the town. From

Northern Thailand Then and Now

As late as 1939, northern Thailand was a semiautonomous region of Siam, with a history rich in tales of kings, queens, and princes locked in dynastic struggles and wars. The diversity of cultures you find here today is hardly surprising, because the ancestors of today's northern Thai people came from China, and the point where they first crossed the mighty Mekong River, Chiang Saen, became a citadel-kingdom of its own as early as 773. Nearly half a millennium passed before the arrival of a king who was able to unite the citizens of the new realm of Lanna ("a thousand rice fields").

The fabled ruler King Mengrai (1259–1317) also established a dynasty that lasted two centuries. Mengrai's first capital was Chiang Rai, but at the end of the 13th century he moved his court south and in 1296 founded a new dynastic city, Chiang Mai. Two friendly rulers, King Ngarm Muang of Phayao and King Rama Kampeng of Sukhothai, helped him in the huge enterprise, and the trio sealed their alliance in blood, drinking from a chalice filled from their slit wrists. A monument outside the city museum in the center of Chiang Mai's Old City commemorates the event. Nearby, another monument marks the spot where King Mengrai died, in 1317, after being struck by lightning in one of the fierce storms that regularly roll down from the nearby mountains.

Lanna power was weakened by waves of attacks by Burmese and Lao invaders, and for two centuries—from 1556 to the late 1700s—Lanna was virtually a vassal Burmese state. The capital was moved south to Lampang, where Burmese power was finally broken

and a new Lanna dynasty, the Chakri, was established under King Rama I.

Chiang Mai, nearby Lamphun (also at the center of Lanna-Burmese struggles), and Lampang are full of reminders of this rich history. Lampang's fortified Wat Lampang Luang commemorates with an ancient bullet hole the spot where the commander of besieging Burmese forces was killed.

To the north is Chiang Rai, a regal capital 30 years before Chiang Mai was built. This quieter, less-developed town is slowly becoming a base for exploring the country's northernmost reaches. In the far north Chiang Saen, site of the region's first true kingdom, is being excavated, its 1,000-year-old walls slowly taking shape again. Chiang Saen is on the edge of the fabled Golden Triangle. This mountainous region, bordered by Myanmar to the west and Laos to the east, was once ruled by the opium warlord Khun Sa, whose hometown, Ban Sop Ruak, has a magnificent museum, the Hall of Opium, that traces the story of the spread of narcotics.

Chiang Mai and Chiang Rai are ideal bases for exploring the hill tribe villages, where people live as they have for centuries. The communities closest to the two cities have been overrun by tourists, but if you strike out on your own with a good map you may still find some that haven't become theme parks. Most of the villages are bustling crafts centers, where the colorful fabrics you see displayed in Bangkok shop windows take shape before your eyes. The elaborately costumed villagers descend into Chiang Mai and Chiang Rai every evening to sell their wares in the night markets.

the bridge below boats set off for trips on the River Kok, some of them headed for Chiang Rai, 130 km (81 miles) away.

Tha Ton is a pleasant base for touring this mountainous region. The 1089 and 1130 highways that run north, close to the Myanmarborder, pass through villages that are more Chinese than Thai, inhabited by descendants of Kuomintang nationalist forces who fled here from Mao Tse-tung's army in the civil war that gave birth to the People's Republic of China. The largest community is Mae Salong.

GETTING HERE AND AROUND

Six buses a day leave Chiang Mai's Chiang Phuak bus station for the four-hour journey to Tha Ton. Fares range from B150 to B250. Boats leave Chiang Rai for the four-hour upstream journey to Tha Ton at 12 am. The single fare is B350.

For information about Tha Ton and its beautiful surroundings, inquire at the Maekok River Village Resort, where proprietors Bryan and Rosie Massingham are knowledgeable and helpful hosts.

ESSENTIALS

SAFETY AND PRECAUTIONS

Tha Ton is a small town, which knows virtually no crime. You're perfectly safe walking its one main street at night.

TIMING

Travelers on the northern route from Chiang Dao to Chiang Rai find it convenient to overnight in Tha Ton, but the town has little to justify a longer stay.

TOURS

Maekok River Village Resort ✉ *Tha Ton–Chiang Rai Rd.* ☎ *053/053628, 053/801257* 🌐 *www.maekok-river-village-resort.com.*

WHERE TO STAY

For expanded hotel reviews, visit Fodors.com.

$$ RESORT 🏨 **Mae Salong Flower Hills Resort.** The border hills of Myanmar lie just beyond the grounds of this resort hotel on the outskirts the mountaintop village of Mae Salong, first settled by remnants of the Chinese Nationalist forces fleeing their homeland after the Communist victory in the 1949 civil war. **Pros:** Chinese restaurant; ceremonial tea-time on the resort terrace; tropical gardens. **Cons:** erratic bathroom plumbing; long walk from village center; no nightlife. [$] *Rooms from: B67* ✉ *779 Moo 1, Doi Mae Salong, Mae Salong* ☎ *053/765495* 🌐 *www.maesalongflowerhills.com* 🛏 *45 chalets* 🍴 *Breakfast.*

$$$ RESORT FAMILY 🏨 **Maekok River Village Resort.** This remarkable resort, a combination of hotel and outdoor education center, is in a beautiful location on the Kok River, with sweeping views of the winding waterway, rice paddies, maize fields and orchards, and the mountains beyond. **Pros:** snug bar with open fireplace for winter evenings; friendly and knowledge able British management; fine open-sided restaurant. **Cons:** kids at the education center can be noisy; some rooms are cramped; tour buses call regularly. [$] *Rooms from: $110* ✉ *1 km (½ mile) from Tha Ton on road to Chiang Rai* ☎ *053/053628* 🌐 *www.maekok-river-village-resort.com* 🛏 *36 rooms.*

CHIANG RAI

180 km (112 miles) northeast of Chiang Mai, 780 km (485 miles) north of Bangkok.

Once again, an elephant played a central role in the foundation of an important Thai city. Legend has it that a royal elephant ran away from its patron, the 13th-century king Mengrai, founder of the Lanna kingdom. The beast stopped to rest on the banks of the Mae Kok River. The king regarded this as an auspicious sign, and in 1256 built his capital, Chiang Rai, on the site. But little is left from those heady days: the Emerald Buddha that used to reside in Wat Phra Keo is now in Bangkok's Grand Palace, and a precious Buddha image in the 15th-century Wat Phra Singh has long since disappeared.

Chiang Rai suffers for being the "poor cousin" of Chiang Mai, despite the recent addition of a handful of luxury hotels to its range of accommodation. It's certainly a quieter, less lively city, but therein many find its charm. It's also a green city, a big contrast to Chiang Mai, which can boast just one urban park.

GETTING HERE AND AROUND

AIR TRAVEL

Thai Airways has six daily flights from Bangkok to Chiang Rai. The single fare for the 90-minute flight is around B2,000. Chiang Rai International Airport is 6 km (4 miles) northeast of the city. Incoming flights are met by songthaews and tuk-tuks, which charge about B50 for the journey to central Chiang Rai.

BOAT AND FERRY TRAVEL

Longtail boats and rafts set off daily from Tha Ton for the 130-km (81-mile) trip downstream to Chiang Rai.

BUS TRAVEL

Chiang Rai is served by buses that leave regularly from Chiang Mai's two terminals (three to four hours; B80 to B200). Buses to Chiang Rai also leave regularly between 8 am and 7:15 pm from Bangkok's Northern Bus Terminal (12 hours; B600 to B700). Express buses also leave hourly from Chiang Mai's Arcade Terminal (B180).

CAR TRAVEL

Roads are well paved throughout the Golden Triangle, presenting no problem for drivers. The area is bisected by the main north–south road, Highway 110, and crisscrossed by good country roads. In Chiang Rai the most prominent companies are Avis, National, and Budget.

TAXI AND TUK-TUK TRAVEL

Tuk-tuks are the common way of getting around Chiang Rai, and a trip across town costs B40 to B50. Songthaews can also be hailed on the street and hired for trips to outlying areas. The fare inside the city is B15—farther afield is a matter of negotiation.

Travel desks are found in all Chiang Rai hotels and they are generally efficient and reasonably priced.

ESSENTIALS
SAFETY AND PRECAUTIONS
Take the usual urban precautions when visiting Chiang Rai: leave valuables either in your room safe or with the hotel management. Carry only a copy of your passport. The small, ill-lighted lanes around the central market can seem a bit threatening at night, but there's actually little crime.

TIMING
Chiang Rai is an ideal base for exploring the surrounding upland countryside and mountains, and a stay of at least two or three days is recommended. The city lacks the buzz of Chiang Mai, but it has enough restaurants and bars to keep night owls happy.

TOURS
The major hotels in Chiang Rai and the Golden Triangle Resort in Chiang Saen also organize minibus tours of the region, and their travel desks will arrange treks to the hill tribe villages. Track of the Tiger is a pioneer of soft-adventure tourism from rock climbing and biking to cooking and golf. The TAT's Chiang Rai branch (⇨ *below*) is a good resource.

Contacts Golden Triangle Tours ✉ *590 Phaholyothin Rd.* ☎ *053/713918, 053/740478* ⊕ *www.goldenchiangrai.com.* **Track of the Tiger** ✉ *Maekok River Village Resort, Box 3, Mae Ai* ☎ *053/053628, 053/801257* ⊕ *www.maekok-river-village-resort.com.*

Tour Information Tourist Authority of Thailand (Chiang Rai) ✉ *448/16 Singhaklai Rd.* ☎ *053/700051, 053/700052, 053/717433, 053/717434* ⊕ *www.tourismthailand.org/chiang-rai.*

EXPLORING CHIANG RAI
Chiang Rai attracts more and more visitors each year, and it's easy to see why. Six hill tribes—the Akha, Yao, Meo, Lisu, Lahu, and Karen—all live within Chiang Rai Province. Each has different dialects, customs, handicrafts, and costumes, and all still venerate animist spirits despite their increasing acquaintance with the outside world. As in Chiang Mai, they make daily journeys to the markets of Chiang Rai. The best of these is a night bazaar, just off Phaholyothin Road, which has a cluster of small restaurants and food vendors.

■ TIP→ Climbing to the top of Doi Tong, a modest hill on the northeastern edge of Chiang Rai, is a great way to learn the lay of the land. From the grounds of a 13th-century temple called Wat Doi Tong, you have a fine view of the Mae-Kok River and the mountains beyond. Chiang Rai has few sights of note, so a leisurely walk around town will take at most a few hours.

TOP ATTRACTIONS
Hilltribe Museum & Education Center. The culture, way of life and crafts of the many hill tribe people that populate the Chiang Rai region are graphically explained and displayed at this exemplary museum in the city center. The museum also supports its own travel service, PDA Tour, which organizes visits to hill tribe villages under the motto "We don't

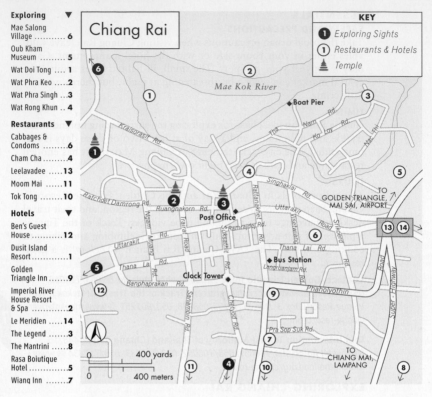

support human zoos!" ✉ *620/25 Thanalai Rd., 3rd fl., PDA Bldg.* ☎ *053/740088* ⊕ *www.pdacr.org.*

Oub Kham Museum. Lanna history and culture are vividly described in this jewel of a museum on the outskirts of Chiang Rai. The eclectic private collection of fascinating exhibits from several centuries of local history are displayed in an attractive ensemble of historic old buildings. They include the throne and coronation robes of a 16th-century Lanna ruler. ✉ *81/1 Rai Mai Luang Rd.* ☎ *B300* ☉ *Daily 8–6.*

Mae Salong Village. Visit this remote mountain village, 48 km (30 miles) northwest of Chiang Rai along a serpentine road, Highway 1234, and you could be excused for believing you'd strayed over a couple of borders and into China. The one-street hamlet (the mountainside has no room for further expansion) is the home of descendants of Chinese Nationalist troops who fled through Burma from the advancing communist army of Mao Tse-tung in 1949. They brought many Chinese traditions and skills with them, and now live mostly from cultivating tea, coffee, and fruit. Orchards and tea and coffee plantations drape the mountainsides, while visitors crowd the slopes in December and January to admire the cherry blossoms and swaths of sunflowers. Call at any of the numerous tea shops for a pot of refreshing Oolong. A local bus service runs from Chiang Rai to Mae Salong, and most Chiang Rai travel agents offer day-tours for around B3,000. ✉ *48 km (30 miles) northwest of Chiang Mai via Hwy. 1234.*

Wat Rong Khun. One of Thailand's most astonishing temples, Wat Rong Khun stands like a glistening, sugar-coated wedding cake beside the A-1 Chiang Rai–Bangkok motorway, 11 km (7 miles) south of Chiang Rai. Popularly called the White Temple because of its lustrous snow-white exterior, the extraordinary structure is being built by internationally renowned Thai artist Chalermchai Kositpipat, assisted by a team of more than 40 young artists, craftsmen, and construction workers, as a Buddhist act of winning merit. They have been working on the massive project for 10 years, and Chalermchai doesn't expect it to be finished in his lifetime. The glistening effect comes from thousands of reflective glass mosaics set into the white stucco. Even the fish in the temple's ornamental pool are white Chinese carp. A songthaew ride to the temple from Chiang Mai costs about B50. ✉ *11 km (7 miles) south of Chiang Mai on A-1 Chiang Rai–Bangkok motorway* 🎫 *Free* 🕑 *Daily 8–6.*

WORTH NOTING

Wat Doi Tong. Near the summit of Doi Tong, this temple overlooks the Mae Kok River. The ancient pillar that stands here once symbolized the center of the universe for devout Buddhists. The sunset view is worth the trip. ✉ *Winitchaikul Rd.*

Wat Phra Keo. The Emerald Buddha, which now sits in Thailand's holiest temple, Wat Phra Keo in Bangkok, is said to have been discovered when lightning split the chedi housing it at this similarly named temple at the foot of the Doi Tong in Chiang Rai. A Chinese millionaire financed a jade replica in 1991—although it's not the real thing, the statuette is still strikingly beautiful. ✉ *Trairat Rd.*

7

Wat Phra Singh. This 14th-century temple is worth visiting for its viharn, distinguished by some remarkably delicate woodcarving and for colorful frescoes depicting the life of Lord Buddha. A sacred Indian Bhoti tree stands in the peaceful temple grounds. ✉ *Singhaklai Rd.*

WHERE TO EAT

$ THAI 🍴 **Cabbages & Condoms.** Most of the modest price of your meal at this provocatively named restaurant (one of three in Thailand) goes toward the country's leading nongovernmental organization that specializes in HIV/AIDS education. A live band plays there at lunchtime and in the evenings. [$] *Average main: B220* ✉ *Thanalai Rd. 620/1, City Center* ☎ *053/740657.*

$ THAI 🍴 **Cham Cha.** Climb the stairs at this busy restaurant to avoid the lunchtime crowds and take an upstairs table overlooking a garden dominated by the handsome cham cha tree that gives the place its name. Jettison the Western dishes on the menu and go for traditional northern Thai specialties such as *tom djuet,* a delicious soup laced with tofu and tiny pork dumplings. Find the restaurant next to the Chiang Rai tourist office. [$] *Average main: B150* ✉ *447/17 Singhaklai Rd.* ☎ *053/744191* 💳 *No credit cards* 🕑 *Closed Sun. No dinner.*

$ THAI 🍴 **Leelavadee.** The name of this attractive open-sided restaurant signifies the strongly perfumed frangi-pangi trees that frame its riverside

Continued on page 401

HILL TRIBES
OWNERS OF THE
MOUNTAINS

by Robert Tilley

Thailand's hill tribes populate the remote, mountainous regions in the north. They welcome visitors, and their villages have become major attractions—some are even dependent on tourist dollars. But other villages, especially those that are harder to reach, have retained an authentic feel; a knowledgeable guide can take you to them.

Hill tribes are descendants of migratory peoples from Myanmar (Burma), Tibet, and China. There are at least 10 tribes living in northern Thailand, and they number a little over half a million, a mere 1% of Thailand's population. The tribes follow forms of ancestral worship and are animists: that is, they believe in a world of spirits that inhabit everything—rivers, forests, homes, and gardens. Historically, some tribes made a living by cultivating poppies for opium, but this practice has mostly died out.

Many tribespeople claim to be victims of official discrimination, and it is indeed often difficult for them to gain full citizenship. Although the Thai government has a program to progressively grant them citizenship, the lack of reliable documentation and the slow workings of the Bangkok bureaucracy are formidable obstacles. However, Thais normally treat hill tribe people with respect; in the Thai language they aren't called "tribes" but Chao Khao, which means "Owners of the Mountains."

Visiting the Chao Khao is a matter of debate. Some of the more accessible villages have become Disneyland-like, with tribespeople, clad in colorful costumes, who are eager to pose in a picture with you—and then collect your baht. In general, the farther afield you go, the more authentic the experience.

Even if you don't visit a village, you'll likely encounter tribespeople selling their crafts at markets in Chiang Mai, Chiang Rai, and Mae Hong Son.

The four tribes you're likely to encounter in northern Thailand are the Karen, Hmong, Akha, and Lisu.

(left) Long neck woman, Chiang Mai; (top) Akha girls wearing ornate headdresses.

KAREN

ORIGINS: Myanmar

POPULATION: 400,000

DID YOU KNOW? The famous "long necks" are actually the Paduang tribe, a subdivision of the Karen.

CRAFTS THEY'RE KNOWN FOR: weaving, beaded jewelry, handmade drums.

The majority of Thailand's hill tribe population is Karen, and there are an estimated 7 million of them living in Myanmar as well. The Karen are the most settled of the tribes, living in permanent villages of well-constructed houses and farming plots of land that leave as much of the forest as possible undisturbed. Though Karen traditionally hold Buddhist and animist beliefs, many communities follow Christianity, which missionaries introduced in colonial Burma.

(top) Karen woman weaving; (bottom) Padaung girls.

LONG NECKS

Traditionally, Paduang women have created the illusion of elongated necks—considered beautiful in their culture—by wrapping brass coils around them. The process begins when a girl is about 5 years old; she will add rings each year. The bands, which can weigh up to 12 lbs, push down on the collarbone, making the neck appear long.

Some human rights groups call the Paduang villages "human zoos" and say that you should not visit because tourism perpetuates the practice of wearing neck coils, which can be harmful. But, most of Thailand's Paduang are refugees who have fled worse conditions in Myanmar, and Thailand's three Paduang villages depend on tourism. Some Paduang women object not to tourism but to the fact that they earn as little as $50 a month from tour operators who profit handsomely. If you go, try to find an operator who treats the Paduang equitably.

HMONG

ORIGINS: China

POPULATION: 80,000

DID YOU KNOW? The Hmong wear elaborate silver lockets to keep their souls firmly locked into their bodies.

CRAFTS THEY'RE KNOWN FOR: needlework, batik, decorative clothing and headdresses.

At the night markets of Chiang Mai and Chiang Rai, you'll recognize Hmong women by their colorful costumes and heavy silver jewelry. There are two divisions of Hmong, White and Blue; White Hmong women wear baggy black pants and blue sashes, while Blue Hmong women wear knee-length pleated skirts. But the divisions "white" and "blue" don't refer to traditional Hmong costumes. "Blue" is a translation of the Hmong word "ntsuab," which also means "dark," a description given to a branch of Hmong whose members once practiced cannibalism. Hmong communities that rejected cannibalism were described as "dlawb," which means "innocent" or "white."

(right) Hmong children.

AKHA

ORIGINS: Tibet

POPULATION: 33,000

DID YOU KNOW? Akha villages are defined by a set of wooden gates, often decorated with charms meant to ward off evil spirits.

CRAFTS THEY'RE KNOWN FOR: silver belt buckles and bracelets, decorative hats and clothing, *saw oo* (fiddles).

The Akha once thrived on opium production, shielded from outside interference by the relative inaccessibility of the remote mountaintop sites they chose for their settlements. Today, all but the most remote communities grow alternative crops, such as rice, beans, and corn. They're a gentle, hospitable people whose women wear elaborate headdresses decorated with silver, beads, and feathers. Akha men wear hollow bracelets containing a silver bead, which they believe keeps them in touch with ancestral spirits.

Akha women wearing traditional headdresses.

7

IN FOCUS HILL TRIBES: OWNERS OF THE MOUNTAINS

LISU

ORIGINS: Tibet

POPULATION: 25,000

DID YOU KNOW? The Lisu pass their history from generation to generation in the form of a song.

CRAFTS THEY'RE KNOWN FOR: silver belt buckles, saw oo, large beaded hats.

Though they're not the most numerous, the business-like Lisu are the tribe you're most likely to meet on day trips out of Chiang Mai and Chiang Rai. More than any other hill tribe, the Lisu have recognized the earning power of tourism. As tourist buses draw up, women scramble to change from their everyday clothes into the famous multicolored costumes they normally wear only on high days and holidays.

Lisu women.

THE SHAN

Though sometimes referred to as a hill tribe, the Shan, who live predominantly in Myanmar, are actually a large minority (there are an estimated 6 million) who have been fighting for their own state for decades. They have lived in the area for 1,000 years and are believed to be descendents of the Tai people, the original inhabitants of the region. The Shan who reside in Thailand have fled persecution in Myanmar. Unlike the hill tribes, the Shan are predominantly Buddhist. Shan craftspeople make some of the silver jewelry and ornaments you'll find at markets.

Shan women wearing traditional bamboo hats.

VISITING HILL TRIBE COMMUNITIES

(top) Akha woman with children;
(bottom) Karen woman.

ETIQUETTE

Hill-tribe people tend to be conservative, so do follow a few simple guidelines on your visit.

- Dress modestly.
- Keep a respectful distance from religious ceremonies or symbols, and don't touch any talismans without asking first.
- Avoid loud or aggressive behavior and public displays of affection.
- Always ask permission before taking a person's picture.

TREKKING

Meeting and staying with tribespeople is one of the main attractions of trekking in northern Thailand. Some day trips include brief stops at villages, which are often little more than theme parks. But if you book a trek of three days or more you're sure to encounter authentic hill tribes living as they have for centuries.

Chao Khao are hospitable to westerners, often organizing spontaneous parties at which home-brewed rice whiskey flows copiously. If you stay overnight, you'll be invited to share the community's simple food and sleep on the floor in one of their basic huts.

Virtually all travel operators offer tours and treks to hill tribe villages. The **Mirror Foundation** (✉ *106 Moo 1, Ban Huay Khom, T. Mae Yao, Chiang Rai,* ☎ *053/737412* ⊕ *www.themirrorfoundation.org*), an NGO that works to improve the lives of hill tribes near Chiang Rai, can arrange culturally respectful tours. The foundation's current projects include bringing volunteer teachers to tribal villages and preventing the exploitation of hill tribe women and children.

■ **TIP→** To avoid being taken to a tourist trap instead of an authentic village, ask the operator to identify the tribes you'll visit and to describe their culture and traditions. It's a good sign if the operator can answer your questions knowledgeably; the information will also add greatly to the pleasure of your trip.

DAY TRIPS

You can also take daytrips to see hill tribes from Chiang Mai, Chiang Rai, or Mae Hong Son. The villages appear on few maps, so it's not advisable to set out on your own; a guide or driver who knows the region well is a better bet. You can easily hire one for about B1,000 per day; ask the TAT in Chiang Mai or Chiang Rai for recommendations.

Several Chiang Mai operators offer "three country" one-day tours of the Golden Triangle: a boat trip to a Laotian island in the Mekong River; a brief shopping trip to the tax-free Burmese border town of Tachilek; and a stop at a Thai hill tribe village on the way home. The fare of B800 to B1,000 includes lunch. These tours are likely to feel fairly touristy.

SHOPPING FOR HILL TRIBE CRAFTS

Embroidered textiles at a market near Chiang Mai.

Over the past few decades, the Thai royal family has worked with the government to wean hill tribe farmers off cultivating opium poppies. One initiative has been financing workshops for manufacturing traditional handicrafts, such as basketry, weaving, and woodworking. Some of these royal projects, located near hill tribe villages, offer both employment and on-site training. The workshops also prevent the crafts from dying out and create a market for products that were originally only distributed within the tribal communities.

WORKSHOPS

The Doi Tung mountain, 40 km (25 mile) north of Chiang Rai, is home to 26 hill tribe villages as well as the **Doi Tung Development Project** (☎ *053/767001* ⊕ *www.doitung.org*), a royal project based at the late Queen Mother's former summer palace. The tribes living in the mountain villages produce handicrafts; the project workshops also employ hill tribe craftsmen and women. Both the villages and the project welcome visitors. Daily tours of the project grounds are available for B100; tribespeople sell crafts at a shop and at stalls on the grounds.

Though it's not for the faint of heart, a very curvy 16-km (10-mile) road leads to the top of Doi Tung from the village of Huai Krai, 20 km (12 mile) south of Mae Sai via Highway 101. Local buses and songthaews from Huai Krai will take you here; you can also hire a driver or a guide.

MARKETS & STORES

Although hill tribe crafts are abundant at the night markets in Chiang Mai, Chiang Rai, and Mae Hong Son, serious collectors prefer government-run stores whose products come with certificates of authenticity. There are two stores in Chiang Mai—the **Thai Hill Tribe Products Promotion Center**, and the **Hill Tribes Handicraft Center** (⇨ *Shopping in Chiang Mai, above*). Prices are fixed at these stores but are comparable to what you'll pay at markets (upscale hotel boutiques, however, inflate prices substantially). Expect to pay at least B500 for a silver ring or belt buckle and as much as B2,500 for a bracelet or necklace; around B300 for a meter of woven cloth; and B300 to 400 for a simple wooden instrument like a bamboo flute.

setting. The menu is authentically Northern Thai and features fresh fish from the Kok and Maekong Rivers. If you're really daring, try the curried frogs' legs. $ *Average main: B200* ⊠ *58 Moo 19, Kaew Wai Rd.* ☎ *089/999–8444* ⋒ *Reservations essential.*

$

THAI

✕ **Moom Mai.** A garden panorama of ceramic dolls and other tiny figures greets you at this enchanting restaurant, where the tables are distributed among the shrubs and ornamental trees. Many of the dining areas are half-hidden thatched bowers. The locals love the place for its informality, its nightly live folk music, and the excellence of its Thai menu, which features northern Thai specialties and Chinese-influenced dishes such as deep-fried chopped prawns in dumplings. $ *Average main: B150* ⊠ *64 Sankhongluang Rd., Moo 16, Tambon Robwiang* ☎ *053/716416* ▭ *No credit cards.*

$

THAI

✕ **Tok Tong.** Chinese specialties and Northern Thai cuisine dominate the extensive menu at this timber-built traditional restaurant in a garden setting on Chiang Rai's main street. The curries can be spicy so make sure the serving staff are aware of your tastes. A traditional Thai ensemble plays nightly. $ *Average main: B150* ⊠ *45/12 Phahalyotin Rd.* ☎ *053/756369, 053/756367.*

WHERE TO STAY

For expanded hotel reviews, visit Fodors.com.

$

B&B/INN

⊡ **Ben's Guest House.** This family-run inn has repeatedly won accolades for its comfortable and extremely reasonable accommodations. **Pros:** friendly staff with deep knowledge of the region; lively evening scene; pool. **Cons:** cheaper rooms are very basic; thin walls; young clientele can be noisy. $ *Rooms from: $18* ⊠ *351/10 San Khong Noi Rd., Soi 4* ☎ *053/716775* ⤳ *30 rooms.*

$$

RESORT

⊡ **Dusit Island Resort.** This gleaming white high-rise, which sits on an island in the Mae Kok River, has tons of amenities, including the largest outdoor pool in northern Thailand. **Pros:** great breakfast; bathrooms with tubs; river views. **Cons:** some guests say it's showing its age; far from town; insects. $ *Rooms from: $115* ⊠ *1129 Kraisorasit Rd.* ☎ *053/607999, 02/238–4790 in Bangkok* ⊕ *www.dusit.com* ⤳ *270 rooms* ⭢⊙⊢ *Breakfast.*

$

B&B/INN

⊡ **Golden Triangle Inn.** If you're willing to tolerate erratic bathroom plumbing, this friendly inn is an ideal, centrally located base for exploring Chiang Rai. **Pros:** central location; parking; airy terrace. **Cons:** bathrooms need upgrading; mosquitos; haphazard signposting can make it difficult to find your room at night. $ *Rooms from: $20* ⊠ *590-2 Phaholyothin Rd.* ☎ *053/711339* ⤳ *39 rooms.*

$$$$

RESORT

⊡ **Imperial River House Resort and Spa.** Now part of the Imperial hotel group, this stylish, formerly privately owned riverside hotel has retained its individual character while avoiding any "chain hotel" characteristics. **Pros:** views; massage; tropical gardens. **Cons:** far from town; insects; golfers have made the hotel a Chiang Rai base and tend noisely to take over the bar. $ *Rooms from: $200* ⊠ *482 Moo 4, Mae Kok Rd., Amphoe Muang* ☎ *053/750829* ⊕ *www.imperialriverhouse-chiangrai. com* ⤳ *36 rooms.*

$$$$

RESORT

⊡ **Le Meridien.** Chiang Rai's largest and most luxurious hotel commands a stretch of the Kok River and views of the northern mountain range.

7

Pros: shuttle bus service until 10 pm; library; helpful tour desk. **Cons:** shabby neighborhood; slow room service; insects. [$] *Rooms from: $170* ✉ *221/2 Moo 20, Kwaewai Rd.* 🌐 *lemeridienchiangrai.com* 🛏 *159 rooms.*

$$$ RESORT Fodor's Choice ★ 🏨 **The Legend.** With its large, tastefully furnished rooms, vast bathrooms, separate toilets, secluded terraces, open-air gourmet restaurant, and unrestricted views of the distant mountains, the river side Legend lives up to its name. **Pros:** elegant and peaceful; impeccably designed; reliable airport pickup. **Cons:** standard rooms have no bathtubs; city center is a 10-minute drive away; confusing signposting can make it difficult to find your room at night. [$] *Rooms from: $130* ✉ *124/15 Kohloy Rd., A. Muang* ☎ *053/910400, 053/719649, 02/642–5497 in Bangkok* 🌐 *www.thelegend-chiangrai.com* 🛏 *79 rooms.*

$$ HOTEL 🏨 **The Mantrini.** Only the tropical vegetation hints that this highly stylish hotel is in Thailand and not a boutique establishment in central Milan or Munich. **Pros:** beautifully designed; shady pool area; friendly staff. **Cons:** shabby neighborhood; noisy bars nearby; 15-minute drive to city center. [$] *Rooms from: $100* ✉ *292/13 Moo 13, Robwiang, A. Muang* ☎ *053/601555 up to 9* 🌐 *www.mantrini.com* 🛏 *63 rooms* 🍴 *Breakfast.*

$$ HOTEL 🏨 **Rasa Boutique Hotel.** The former White House Hotel has undergone a dramatic transformation, discarding its tired old look and exchanging it for a completely new, exotic appearance. **Pros:** secluded swimming pool; good restaurant. **Cons:** shabby neighborhood; far from city center. [$] *Rooms from: $65* ✉ *789/7 Phaholyothin Rd.* ☎ *053/717454* 🌐 *www.rasaboutiquehotelchiangrai.com* 🛏 *30 rooms.*

$$$$ 🏨 **River House Resort & Spa.** A lofty, spacious lobby that also serves as an art gallery sets the tone for this elegant new hotel (opened in 2008) on the banks of the Kok River. **Pros:** views across the Kok River to Chiang Rai; infinity swimming pool; excellent restaurant. **Cons:** loud golfers tend to take over the bar. [$] *Rooms from: $65* ✉ *482 Moo 4, Mae Kok Rd., Rimkok, A. Muang* ☎ *053/750829 up to 34* 🌐 *www.riverhouse-chiangrai.com* 🛏 *36 rooms.*

$ HOTEL 🏨 **Wiang Inn.** In the heart of downtown, this sleek, modern hotel is among the best in central Chiang Rai. **Pros:** best facilities of in-city hotels; good restaurant; central location. **Cons:** standard rooms have only single beds; impersonal "chain hotel" atmosphere; karaoke room noise can be disturbing. [$] *Rooms from: $50* ✉ *893 Phaholyothin Rd.* ☎ *053/711533* 🌐 *www.wianginn.com* 🛏 *260 rooms.*

SHOPPING

Chiang Rai has a **night market,** on Robviang Nongbua Road, and although it's much smaller than Chiang Mai's, there is a large variety of handicrafts and textiles on offer. A central section of Thanalai Road is closed to traffic on Saturday nights for a "walking street" market, and San Khon Noi Road is also made a pedestrian-only area for a Sunday market.

T.S. Jewelry & Antiques. This shop has a very large selection of jewelry and antiques from northern Thailand and neighboring Myanmar and Laos. ✉ *877–879 Phaholyothin Rd.* ☎ *053/711050.*

SPORTS AND THE OUTDOORS

Chiang Rai is an excellent base from which to set out on tours trekking through the nearby mountains or canoeing and rafting on the region's rivers. Tour operators charge about B800 a day (including overnight stops in hill tribe villages).

Phu Sang. Some 90 km (56 miles) due east of Chiang Rai is perhaps the region's most beautiful national park, Phu Sang, which has one of Thailand's rarest natural wonders, cascades of hot water. The temperature of the water that tumbles over the 85-foot-high falls never drops below 33°C (91°F), and a nearby pool is even warmer. The park has some spectacular caves, and is crisscrossed by nature trails teeming with birdlife. One hour's drive north lies the mountainous border with Laos, straddled by 5,730-foot-high Phu Chee Fah, a favorite destination for trekkers and climbers. You reach Phu Sang National Park via Thoeng, 70 km (43 miles) east of Chiang Rai on Route 1020. The park rents cabins for B500 a night. Entrance to the park costs B200, and B30 for a vehicle. Call or make contact through the website for reservations. ☎ *054/401099* ⊕ *www.dnp.go.th*.

BOATING

For something adventurous, catch a bus to the border town of Tha Ton and board a high-powered longtail boat there and ride the rapids 130 km (81 miles) to Chiang Rai. Boats leave from a pier near the town bridge at noon and take about three to four hours to negotiate the bends and rapids of the river, which passes through thick jungle and past remote hill tribe villages. The single fare is B350. For a more leisurely ride to Chiang Rai, board a raft, which takes two days and nights to reach the city, overnighting in hill tribe villages. Fares start at B1,000. ■TIP→ Take bottled water, an inflatable cushion, and (most important) a hat or umbrella to shade you from the sun. The best time to make the trip is during October and November, when the water is still high but the rainy season has passed.

Four Lens Tour ⊠ *131/6 Moo 13, Mae Korn Intersection* ☎ *053/700617 to 20* ⊕ *www.4lens.com*.

GOLF

Santiburi Country Club. Chiang Rai has one of northern Thailand's finest golf courses, the Santiburi Country Club, laid out by the celebrated Robert Trent Jones Jr. The par-72, 18-hole course is set among rolling hills 10 km (6 miles) outside Chiang Rai. The ranch-style clubhouse has an excellent restaurant and coffee shop, and the facilities also include a sauna. Visitors are welcome, and clubs, carts, and shoes can be rented. Weekday greens fee is B1,580, while weekend golfers pay B2,150. Reservations are requested. ⊠ *12 Moo 3, Huadoi-Sobpao Rd.* ☎ *053/662821 up to 6* 🖷 *053/717377*.

EN ROUTE

Doi Tung. If you're traveling north from Chiang Rai on Highway 110, watch for the left-hand turn at Km 32 to Doi Tung. The road winds 42 km (26 miles) to the summit, where an astonishing view opens out over the surrounding countryside. The temple here, Wat Phra That Doi Tung, founded more than a millennium ago, is said to be the repository of some important relics of Lord Buddha, including a collarbone.

7

The shrine attracts pilgrims from as far away as India and China, for whom its huge Chinese Buddha figure is a vastly important symbol of good fortune. On the mountain slopes below the temple is the summer home built for the king's late mother. The fine mansion is closed to the public, but the gardens, an explosion of color in all seasons, are open unless particularly important guests are staying.

CHIANG SAEN

59 km (37 miles) north of Chiang Rai, 239 km (149 miles) northeast of Chiang Mai, 935 km (581 miles) north of Bangkok.

On the banks of the Mekong River sits Chiang Saen, a one-road town that in the 12th century was home to the future King Mengrai. Only fragments of the ancient ramparts survived the incursion by the Burmese in 1588, and the rest of the citadel was ravaged by fire when the last of the Burmese were ousted in 1786. Chiang Saen is now being developed as a major Mekong River port, and it's the embarkation point for river trips to Myanmar, Laos, and China.

GETTING HERE AND AROUND

The ubiquitous songthaews provide the local transport service. They charge B20. Two buses daily run between Chiang Mai's Chiang Phuak bus station and Chiang Saen, taking 4½ hours. The fare is about B150; buses stop in the center of town and at the boat piers.

ESSENTIALS

SAFETY AND PRECAUTIONS

Chiang Saen is a river port and something of a smugglers' haven, and the local police are kept busy. But foreign visitors are left alone, although the usual precautions are advised when walking the riverside promenade at night. Leave valuables in your hotel safe or with the hotel or guesthouse management.

TIMING

Chiang Saen is an ideal base from which to explore the Golden Triangle region, so plan on staying two or three days—longer if the town's ancient ruins and museum attract your interest.

ESSENTIALS

Tour Information Golden Shan Travel ☎ *053/784198* ⊕ *www. goldenshantravel.com.*

EXPLORING CHIANG SAEN

Only two ancient chedis remain standing to remind the visitor of Chiang Saen's ancient glory, although government-financed excavation is gradually uncovering evidence of the citadel built here in the 12th century by King Mengrai, who later founded Chiang Mai. Ancient flooring and walls have been exposed, and give a fascinating idea of the extent of what was one of the region's first royal palaces.

National Museum. Next door to Wat Phra That Luang is the National Museum, which houses artifacts from the Lanna period, as well as some Neolithic discoveries. The museum also has a good collection of carvings and traditional handicrafts from the hill tribes. ⊠ *Road to*

Chiang Rai, 1 km (½ mile) from town center ☎ *053/777102* ⌂ *B40* ⊙ *Wed.–Sun. 9–4.*

Wat Pa Sak. Just outside the city walls is the oldest chedi, Wat Pa Sak, whose name refers to the 300 teak trees (Ton Sak) that were planted in the surrounding area. The stepped temple, which narrows to a spire, is said to enshrine holy relics brought here when the city was founded.

Wat Phra That Luang. Inside the city walls stands the imposing octagonal Wat Phra That Luang. Scholars say it dates from the 14th century.

WHERE TO STAY

For expanded hotel reviews, visit Fodors.com.

$ | HOTEL | ▣ **Chiang Saen River Hill Hotel.** Part of the Old City wall guides the way to this stylish, quiet hotel with a tropical garden a short walk from the local boat jetty. **Pros:** a small market abuts the hotel; shady garden; ample parking. **Cons:** noisy tour groups tend to take over; long walk to town center; insects. $ *Rooms from: $60* ⌂ *714 Moo 3, Tambon Wiang* ☎ *053/777396* ⌖ *60 rooms* ⦿ *Breakfast.*

$$$$ | RESORT | ALL-INCLUSIVE | **Fodor's** Choice | ★ | ▣ **Four Seasons Tented Camp Golden Triangle.** Elephant lovers, beware— you may never want to leave this pachyderm haven. **Pros:** unique, up-close elephant experiences; beautiful setting; interesting regional activities; luxury with a touch of adventure. **Cons:** location might be too remote for some (requires car and boat rides); some tents are far from the main buildings and up steep paths, so may not be suitable for all guests; insects. $ *Rooms from: $2200* ⌂ *499 Moo 1, Tumbol Wieng Amphur* ☎ *053/910200* ⊕ *www.fourseasons.com/goldentriangle* ⌖ *15 tents* ⦿ *All-inclusive.*

$ | B&B/INN | ▣ **Gin's Guest House.** Local lawyer Khun Gin and his wife run this charming guesthouse, which is a true home away from home. **Pros:** friendly owners steeped in knowledge of the area; riverside walks; "country cottage" atmosphere. **Cons:** 10-minute drive from Chiang Saen; upperstory rooms are only accessible on a steep staircase; insects. $ *Rooms from: $30* ⌂ *71 Moo 8, Ban Hua, Ban Sop Ruak Rd.* ☎ *053/650847* ⌖ *9 rooms* ⊟ *No credit cards* ⦿ *Breakfast.*

CHIANG KHONG

53 km (33 miles) northeast of Chiang Rai.

This small Mekong River town is gearing up to become a main waystation on the planned Asian Highway, and a bridge is being built across the Mekong River to the Laotian harbor town of Houayxay. Until its completion (held up because of budgetary problems), small skiffs carry people across the Mekong between Chiang Khong and Houayxay, from whose pier daily boats set off for the two-day trip to the World Heritage town of Luang Prabang in Laos. Chiang Khong is a convenient overnight stop before boarding.

GETTING HERE AND AROUND

The paved road east out of Chiang Saen parallels the Mekong River for much of the way en route to Chiang Khong and a half-way point commands a magnificent view of the wide river valley far below. A refreshment stall and tables cater to thirsty travelers. Songthaews ply the route for about B100, but you can also hire a speedboat (B500) to go down the river, a thrilling three hours of slipping between the rocks and rapids. Not too many tourists make the journey, especially to villages inhabited by the local Hmong and Yao tribes. The rugged scenery along the Mekong River is actually more dramatic than that of the Golden Triangle. A few Chiang Khong travel agencies offer tour programs that include short cruises on the Mekong River. The two leading ones are Chiang Khong Thai-Lao Travel and Chiang Khong Travel.

ESSENTIALS

SAFETY AND PRECAUTIONS

Despite its location on the Laotian border and the occasional arrest of a smuggler or two, Chiang Khong is safe for foreign visitors. Nevertheless, caution is advised when walking the riverside promenade at night—leave valuables and excess cash in your hotel safe or with the management.

TIMING

Chiang Khong is the official border crossing to Laos, and few visitors linger longer than one night, waiting for the Mekong River ferry.

TOURS

Chiang Khong is the embarkation point for the Laotian pier where boats for Luang Prabang are moored. Most Chiang Khong guesthouses have travel desks where tickets for the river cruise to the Laotian World Heritage site can be bought.

Ann Tours. A 15-day Laos visa can be acquired in Chiang Khong from Ann Tours, which specializes in tours not only of Northern Thailand but Laos, Vietnam, and Cambodia. ✉ *166 Moo 8, Saiklang Rd.* ☎ *053/655198* 🌐 *www.anntours.com.*

EXPLORING CHIANG KHONG

Chiang Khong, where a bridge will eventually connect with Laos and a Chinese-built section of the Asian Highway, is developing rapidly into a major river port, incorporating some hideous industrial sites. The town has little to attract the visitor apart from magnificent vistas from its riverside towpath to the hills of Laos across the Mekong. Its one 300-year-old temple has an interesting Chiang Saen–style chedi but is in need of repair. Textiles from China and Laos can be bought cheaply in the town's market.

WHERE TO STAY

For expanded hotel reviews, visit Fodors.com.

$ HOTEL 🏨 **Nam Khong River Side.** Chiang Khong's best hotel sits on the south bank of the Mekong River, with most of its rooms, including the rooftop Fai Ngeng restaurant, commanding unobstructed views to the hills of Laos on the other side. **Pros:** free Wi-Fi throughout; helpful travel desk can organize boat trips to Luang Prabang in Laos; fine views from the terrace. **Cons:** small bathrooms; drab neighborhood; traffic noise. [$] *Rooms from: $50* ✉ *174–176 Moo 8, Tambon Wiang* ☎ *053/791796, 053/791801* 🌐 *www.namkhongriverside.com* 🛏 *40 rooms* 🍴 *Breakfast.*

Elephants flank the ruined chedi at Wat Chedi Luang.

BAN SOP RUAK

8 km (5 miles) north of Chiang Saen.

Ban Sop Ruak, a village in the heart of the Golden Triangle, was once the domain of the opium warlord Khun Sa. Thai and Burmese troops hounded him out in 1996 and he spent the remaining years until his death in 2007 under house arrest in Yangon, where he lived comfortably in the company of a personal seraglio of four young Shan women. His picaresque reputation still draws those eager to see evidence of the man who once held the region under his thumb.

GETTING HERE AND AROUND

Songthaews (about B50) are the only transport service from Chiang Saen to Ban Sop Ruak. A taxi service is operated by Golden Shan Travel (⊠ *587 Ban Sop Ruak High St.* ☎ *053/784198*), which also offers tours of the Golden Triangle, Mae Salong, Doi Tung, and hill tribe villages for B3,000 and B3,500.

ESSENTIALS

SAFETY AND PRECAUTIONS

Although Ban Sop Ruak was once the center of the Golden Triangle illegal narcotics trade, it's a law-abiding little town now, and the one main street is perfectly safe, even late at night. Nevertheless, it's advisable to leave valuables in your hotel safe or with the hotel or guesthouse management.

TIMING

Ban Sop Ruak is the Golden Triangle, with enough points of interest to warrant a stay of at least two or three days. The Hall of Opium alone is extensive enough to take up a whole day, while boat trips to Burma and Laos beckon.

TOURS

Golden Shan Travel occupies the ground floor of a modest guesthouse, the Mekong Riverside, which has eight simple but comfortable rooms directly overlooking the river.

Golden Shan Travel ☎ *053/784198, 086/915–4604.* **Rimnam Guesthouse Travel Desk** ✉ *Ban Sop Ruak main street, Sai Klang* ☎ *053/655680.*

EXPLORING BAN SOP RUAK

This simple riverside town has one main street, 1 km (½ mile) in length, that winds along the southern bank of the Mekong River and is lined with stalls selling souvenirs and textiles from neighboring Laos. Waterfront restaurants serve up fresh catfish, and provide vantage points for watching the evening sun dip over the mountains to the west.

Hall of Opium. Opened in 2004, the magnificent Hall of Opium is a dazzling white stucco, glass, marble, and aluminum building nestling in a valley above the Mekong. The site of the museum is so close to former poppy fields that a plan is still being considered to extend the complex to encompass an "open-air" exhibit of a functioning opium plantation. The museum traces the history of the entire drug trade (including a look at how mild stimulants like coffee and tea took hold in the West). It even attempts to give visitors a taste of the "opium experience" by leading them through a 500-foot-long tunnel where atmospheric music wafts between walls bearing phantasmagoric bas-relief scenes. The synthetic smell of opium was originally pumped into the tunnel but the innovation was dropped after official complaints.

The entrance tunnel emerges into a gallery of blinding light, where the nature of the opium-producing poppy is vividly described on an information panel erected in front of an imitation field of the insidiously beautiful flower. It's an arresting introduction to an imaginatively designed and assembled exhibition, which reaches back into the murky history of the opium trade and takes a long, monitory look into a potentially even darker future. ■**TIP➔ The Hall of Opium is so large in scope and scale that two days are hardly enough to take it all in. A visit is ideally combined with an overnight stay at one of two hotels within walking distance: the Hall's own Greater Mekong Lodge (double rooms from B1,800, including breakfast) or, for a sheer splurge, at the luxurious Anantara, just across the road.** ✉ *Main street* ☎ *053/784444* ⊕ *www.maefahluang.org* ▦ *B300* ☉ *Tues.–Sun. 10–3:30.*

Imperial Golden Triangle Resort. Even if you don't stay overnight, pay a visit to the sumptuous Imperial Golden Triangle Resort, which has the best views over the confluence of the Mae Sai, Ruak, and Mekong rivers. ⊕ *www.imperialhotels.com.*

Longtail excursion boats. Longtail excursion boats captained by experienced river men tie up at the Ban Sop Ruak jetty, and the B500 fee covers a 90-minute cruise into the waters of Myanmar and Laos and a stop at a Laotian market. You can take a short trip into Myanmar by visiting the Golden Triangle Paradise Resort, which sits in isolated splendor on the Burmese bank of the Mekong, about 1 km (½ mile) upstream from the Golden Triangle. The Thai immigration office at the Ban Sop Ruak jetty makes a photocopy of your passport for the Burmese authorities for B200.

Opium Museum. Opium is so linked to the history of Ban Sop Ruak that the small town now has two museums devoted to the subject. The smaller one, Opium Museum, is in the center of town. A commentary in English details the growing, harvesting, and smoking of opium. Many of the exhibits, such as carved teak opium boxes and jade and silver pipes, are fascinating. ✉ *Main street* 🎟 *B30* ⏲ *Daily 7–6.*

WHERE TO STAY

For expanded hotel reviews, visit Fodors.com.

$$$$ RESORT Fodor's Choice ★ 🏨 **Anantara Golden Triangle Resort & Spa.** The Anantara is one of the Golden Triangle's top addresses, a true symphony of styles created by Thailand's leading interior designer Bill Bensley. **Pros:** truly stunning place to stay; great restaurant; particularly fine views from the rooms; huge bathrooms. **Cons:** access to some rooms involves much stair climbing, isolated position far from village center, steep bar prices. [$] *Rooms from: $1250* ✉ *229 Moo 1, Chiang Saen* ☎ *053/784084, 02/476–0022 in Bangkok* 🌐 *www.anantara.com* 🛏 *106 rooms, 4 suites* 🍴 *Breakfast.*

$ HOTEL 🏨 **De River Boutique Resort.** Most rooms at this small, Lanna-style hotel halfway between Chiang Saen and Ban Sop Ruak directly overlook the Mekong, with sweeping views across its swirling waters to the hills of Laos on the opposite bank. **Pros:** sunrise from one's private balcony; riverside walks; wonderful views. **Cons:** staff have poor English skills; Chiang Saen or Ban Sop Ruak both a 15-minute drive away; no transport. [$] *Rooms from: $45* ✉ *455 Moo 1, Chiang Saen* ☎ *053/784488* 🌐 *www.deriverresort.com* 🛏 *18 rooms.*

$ B&B/INN 🏨 **Golden Home.** The Mekong River is just across the road from this small resortlike guesthouse. **Pros:** central location; pleasant garden; good restaurants and shopping nearby. **Cons:** small, basic rooms; staff lack English skills; traffic noise. [$] *Rooms from: $20* ✉ *41 Moo 1, Wiang, Chiang Saen* ☎ *053/784205* 🛏 *7 cabins* 💳 *No credit cards* 🍴 *Breakfast.*

$$ HOTEL 🏨 **Imperial Golden Triangle Resort.** From the superior rooms in this high-eaved, Lanna-style hotel you are treated to magnificent views of three rivers rushing together. **Pros:** spectacular sunsets over the Mekong; excellent travel service; pleasant restaurant terrace. **Cons:** many rooms involve flights of stairs; service staff can be off-hand; poor language skills. [$] *Rooms from: $85* ✉ *222 Ban Sop Ruak* ☎ *053/784001 up to 5, 02/261–9000 in Bangkok for reservations* 🌐 *www.imperialhotels.com* 🛏 *73 rooms* 🍴 *Breakfast.*

7

MAE SAI

25 km (16 miles) west of Ban Sop Ruak, 60 km (37 miles) north of Chiang Rai.

From Ban Sop Ruak you can travel west on a dusty road to Mae Sai, a Thai-Burmese border town that straddles the Mae Sai River. A lively trade takes place at markets on both sides of the border.

GETTING HERE AND AROUND

Buses leave six times daily from Chiang Mai's Chiang Phuak bus station for the five-hour journey to Mae Sai. The fare is about B150. Regular bus service also runs between Chiang Rai and Mae Sai (one hour; B50). Around town songthaews are the only means of getting around other than via organized tour (for which two travel agencies are recommended: Mae Khong Travel and Mandalay Travel Service).

ESSENTIALS

SAFETY AND PRECAUTIONS

There are occasional bomb attacks by Burmese anti-regime activists in Tachilek, the Burmese town separated from Mae Sai by only a bridge. Hostilities between Burmese and Thai troops sometimes break out, closing the border. But Mae Sai itself is safe for foreign visitors, although it's advisable to leave valuables, excess cash, and passports in your hotel safe or with the management.

TIMING

Mae Sai is essentially a day-trip destination, and many travel there from Chiang Mai or Chiang Rai just to shop at the markets in Tachilek. You'll also meet many expats who cross the border on visa runs—some of them shadier characters than any Thai you'll encounter.

TOURS

Mae Khong Travel ☎ 053/642517 ⊕ www.maekhongtravel.com. **Mandalay Travel Service** ✉ 382, Moo 7, Phaholyotin Rd. ☎ 053/640086, 053/640087.

EXPLORING MAE SAI

Mae Sai attracts a steady flow of foreign residents of Thailand who cross the Myanmar border on the edge of the town in order to renew their visas. But the cross-border trip is also the town's main tourist attraction. The market that nestles next to the border bridge is packed with jewelry stalls, where the careful buyer can find some bargains, including rubies and jade from Myanmar.

Kengtung. For $30 you can get a three-night visa that lets you travel 63 km (39 miles) north to Kengtung, a quaint Burmese town with colonial-era structures built by the British alongside old Buddhist temples.

Thachilek. Foreigners may cross the river to visit Thachilek on a one-day visa, obtainable at the Burmese immigration office at the bridge for US$10. It's a smaller version of Mae Sai, but with a vast tax-free emporium, a busy market, and no fewer than three casinos packed with Thai gamblers.

Wat Phra That Doi Wao. For the best view across the river into Myanmar, climb up to Wat Phra That Doi Wao—the 207-step staircase starts from behind the Top North Hotel.

WHERE TO EAT

$ THAI 🍴 **Rabiang Kaew.** Set back from the main road by a wooden bridge, this restaurant built in the northern style has an unmistakable charm. Antiques adorning the dining room add to its rustic style.The Thai fare is tasty and expertly prepared. [$] *Average main: B120* ✉ *356/1 Phaholyothin Rd.* ☎ *053/731172.*

WHERE TO STAY

For expanded hotel reviews, visit Fodors.com.

$ B&B/INN 🏨 **Mae Sai Guest House.** Travelers on a tight budget rank this riverside guesthouse, about 2 km (1 mile) west of the bridge, as the best in Mae Sai. **Pros:** views into Myanmar; riverside walks; friendly staff. **Cons:** rooms are fairly spartan; long walk into town; no parking. [$] *Rooms from: $20* ✉ *688 Wiengpangkam* ☎ *053/732021* 🛏 *20 bungalows* 💳 *No credit cards* 🍽 *No meals.*

$ HOTEL 🏨 **Piyaporn Pavilion.** Mae Sai's most modern hotel lacks any Thai character, offering instead standard Western-styled rooms and furnishings. **Pros:** pleasant riverside walks; helpful travel desk; large bathrooms with tubs. **Cons:** no restaurant; "chain hotel" atmosphere; street noise. [$] *Rooms from: $28* ✉ *925/36 Moo 1, Wiang Pang Kham* ☎ *053/734511 up to 13, 053/642113 up to 15* 🌐 *www.pavilion-place.com* 🛏 *80 rooms* 🍽 *Breakfast.*

$ HOTEL 🏨 **Top North Hotel.** Renovated in 2010 (although some guests might object to the green-dominated decor), this centrally located hotel is now one of Mae Sai's most comfortable and well appointed. **Pros:** authentic northern Thai food; central location; Wi-Fi throughout. **Cons:** not much authentic Thai character; service staff could be friendlier; street-side rooms can be noisy. [$] *Rooms from: $25* ✉ *306 Phaholyothin Rd.* ☎ *053/731955* 🛏 *24 rooms* 🍽 *No meals.*

$ HOTEL 🏨 **Wang Thong.** This riverside high-rise hotel was originally intended to cater to business executives trading across the nearby Thai-Burmese border, but now the guests are mostly travelers. **Pros:** pleasant riverside walks; panoramic views from the restaurant; large pool. **Cons:** noisy tour groups tend to take over the public rooms and outside terrace; anonymous "chain hotel" atmosphere; staff lack English language skills. [$] *Rooms from: $45* ✉ *299 Phaholyothin Rd.* ☎ *053/733388* 🌐 *www.wangthong.com* 🛏 *150 rooms.*

SHOPPING

Thais take household goods and consumer products across the river, where the Myanmar trade them for sandalwood, jade, and rubies. Though you may want to see Myanmar, the prices and quality of the goods will not be better than in Mae Sai.

■ TIP→ Rubies aren't the only red gems here. Mae Sai is also justifiably proud of its sweet strawberries, which ripen in December or January, found at local markets and as far away as Chiang Rai and Chiang Mai.

Mengrai Antique. Near the bridge, Mengrai Antique has a matchless reputation. ✉ *Phaholyothin Rd.* ☎ *053/731423, 081/949–1493.*

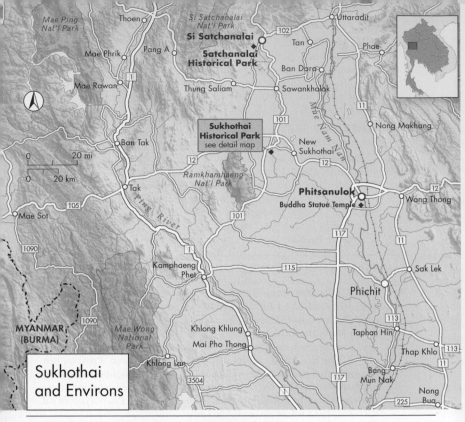

Sukhothai and Environs

SUKHOTHAI AND ENVIRONS

In the valley of the Yom River, protected by a rugged mountain range in the north and richly forested mountains in the south, lies Sukhothai. Here laterite (red porous soil that hardens when exposed to air) ruins mark the birthplace of the Thai nation and its emergence as a center for Theravada Buddhism.

North of Sukhothai is its sister city of Si Satchanalai, which is quieter and more laid-back, but no less interesting—its Historical Park has the remains of more than 200 temples and monuments.

To complete your tour of the north with a visit to Sukhothai and its ruins, head for Chiang Mai and board a long-distance bus for the six-hour journey—the route most visitors follow. If you're driving, take the Bangkok-bound motorway M1 and head 150 miles south from Chiang Mai until the town of Tak where the number 12 highway branches off to Sukhothai. Sukhothai has a small airport but it's owned and used exclusively by Bangkok Airways. Flights from Bangkok to nearby Phitsanulok are more frequent, taking just 50 minutes. Phitsanulok is an historic town thatin many ways makes the best base for exploring the area. Despite its historical relevance as the regional capital for 25 years, the birthplace of King Narai the Great, and residence of the

Ayutthayan crown princes, Phitsanulok has grown away from its roots. This onetime military stronghold has stamped over its past, leaving only a few reminders like Wat Phra Si Rattana Mahathat and the revered Phra Buddha Chinnarat image. Phitsanulok now serves as a center for commerce, transportation, and communication. In addition, its blend of entertainment and access to outward-bound excursions make it an enjoyable diversion.

PHITSANULOK

377 km (234 miles) north of Bangkok, 60 km (37 miles) southeast of Sukhothai.

For a brief span in the 14th century, after the decline of Sukhothai and before the rise of Ayutthaya, Phitsanulok was the kingdom's capital. Further back in history, Phitsanulok was a Khmer outpost called Song Kwae—today only an ancient monastery remains of that incarnation. The new city, which had to relocate 5 km (3 miles) from the old site, is a modern provincial administrative seat with few architectural blessings. There are outstanding attractions, however, such as the Phra Buddha Chinnarat inside Wat Phra Si Rattana Mahathat. And make sure to walk along the Nan River, lined with tempting food stalls in the evening. On the far side are many houseboats, which are popular among Thais.

GETTING HERE AND AROUND

AIR TRAVEL

Nok Air and Kan Air have daily flights from Bangkok to Phitsanulok, (50 minutes). The airport is just 1 km (½ mile) from town.

BUS TRAVEL

Buses to Phitsanulok regularly leave Bangkok's Northern Terminal. Fares on an air-conditioned "VIP" bus start at around B260 for the six-hour trip. The terminal also has buses for travel to and from Chiang Mai via Lampang or via Phrae and Phayao, and to Mae Sot via Tak. The terminal is downtown, just 1 km (½ mile) from Wat Phra Si Mahatat (known locally as Wat Yai).

Between Phitsanulok and Sukhothai there are regular buses for pennies, which depart roughly every hour; the trip takes about 1½ hours.

Bus Contacts Bus station ⊠ *Mittaparp Rd.* ☎ *055/242430, 055/242030.*

CAR TRAVEL

A car is a good way to get around the region. Highway 12 from Sukhothai is a long, straight, and reasonably comfortable 59-km (37-mile), one-hour drive. To get to the Phitsanulok from Bangkok, take the four-lane Highway 117; the drive from Bangkok takes about 4½ hours. Both Avis and Budget have desks at the Phitsanulok airport. Costs for renting economy cars up to SUVs range from B1,500 to B3,500 per day without drivers; count on an additional B1,000 a day for a car and driver. Make sure to request an English-speaking driver. Bigger hotels in Phitsanulok offer chauffeur services at similar prices, but are more tour-oriented and generally offer no more than a one-day trip.

7

SAMLOR TRAVEL

There's a cheap, cramped, tin-can bus service within Phitsanulok, but unless ovens are your thing, you're best off using the open-sided song-thaews, the motorized samlors, or the more eco-friendly pedal-powered samlors.

ESSENTIALS

MONEY MATTERS

There are plenty of ATMs and exchange kiosks in town; Naresuan Road has most of Phitsanulok's banks.

SAFETY AND PRECAUTIONS

Take elementary precautions when visiting Phitsanulok. Leave valuables, unneeded cash, and your passport either in the room safe or with the management.

TIMING

Apart from its historic temples and some interesting museums, Phitsanulok has a pleasant riverside promenade that invites the visitor to linger, particularly in one of the several waterfront restaurants. The city is worth at least an overnight stay.

TOURS

The local office of the Tourism Authority of Thailand, TAT, recommends several local travel agents, including Nanthaphon Tour and Rang Thong Tour.

Contacts Rang Thong Tour ✉ *55/37 Surasi Commercial Center* ☎ *055/259973.* **Tourist Authority of Thailand (TAT)** ✉ *209/7–8 Boromtrailokanat Rd., Surasi Trade Center* ☎ *055/252743* ⊕ *www.tourismthailand.org/Phitsanulok* ⊙ *Daily 8:30–4:30.*

EXPLORING PHITSANULOK

With its wide choice of comfortable, modern hotels and some good riverside restaurants, Phitsanulok is an ideal base for exploring the region. Most of the sights in Phitsanulok are within walking distance, but samlors are easily available. Bargain hard—most trips should be about B30. Taxis are available for longer trips; you can find a few loitering around the train station.

Sgt. Maj. Thawee Folk Museum. Phitsanulok also has a little-known museum, the Sgt. Maj. Thawee Folk Museum, that alone would justify a visit to the city. In the early 1980s Sergeant-Major Khun Thawee traveled to small villages, collecting traditional tools, cooking utensils, animal traps, and handicrafts that were rapidly disappearing, and crammed them into a traditional house and barn. For a decade nothing was properly documented; visitors stumbled around tiger traps and cooking pots, with little to help them decipher what they were looking at. But Khun Thawee's daughter came to the rescue and now the marvelous artifacts are systematically laid out, all 10,000 of them. You can now understand the use of everything on display, from the simple wood pipes hunters played to lure their prey, to elaborately complex rat guillotines. Thawee was honored with two university doctorates for his work in preserving such rare artifacts. He also took over a historic foundry, which casts brass Buddhas and temple bells. The museum is a 15-minute walk south of the railway station, on the east side of the tracks, and the foundry is directly opposite. ✉ *Wisut Kasat Rd.* ☎ *055/212749 055/258715 foundry (phone ahead)* 🎟 *B100* 🕒 *Tues.–Sun. 8:30–4:30.*

Wat Phra Si Rattana Mahathat. Naresuan Road, named after the city's most illustrious son, the 16th-century Prince Naresuan the Great, runs from the railway station to the Nan River. North of this street you can find Wat Phra Si Rattana Mahathat, a temple commonly known as Wat Yai (the Great Temple). Built in the mid-14th century, Wat Yai has developed into a large monastery with typical ornamentation. Particularly noteworthy are the viharn's wooden doors, inlaid with mother-of-pearl in 1756 at the behest of King Boromkot. Behind the viharn is a 100-foot corn-cob-style prang with a vault containing Buddha relics. The many religious souvenir stands make it hard to gain a good view of the complex, but the *bot,* or chapel, is a fine example of the traditional three-tier roof with low sweeping eaves, designed to diminish the size of the walls, accentuate the nave, and emphasize the image of the Buddha. Within the viharn is what many consider the world's most beautiful image of the Buddha, Phra Buddha Chinnarat. It was probably cast in the 14th century, during the late Sukhothai period. Its mesmerizing beauty and the mystical powers ascribed to it draw streams of pilgrims—among the most notable of them was the Sukhothai's King Eka Thossarot, who journeyed here in 1631. According to folklore, the king applied with his own hands the gold leaf that covers the Buddha. Many copies of the image have been made, the best-known one residing in Bangkok's Marble Temple. ✉ *Off Ekethosarot Rd.* 🕒 *Daily 8–6.*

WHERE TO EAT

Phitsanulok has a good range of dining options, from its popular pontoon and riverside restaurants to some great little daytime canteen-style restaurants near the central clock tower on Phayalithai Road. The Muslim restaurants on Pra Ong Dam Road, opposite the town's mosque, are great for curry and roti breakfasts. The night bazaar promenade banking the Nan River contains some basic early-evening places to enjoy the sunset, including the infamous "flying vegetable restaurants," where you can have the province's famed *pak bung fire dang* (stir-fried morning glory). And the veggies do fly here—when the cooks fling the morning glory to waiters, who deftly catch the food on their plates. Akathodsarod Road near Topland Hotel is a good bet for late-night noodles.

$ SEAFOOD 🍴 **Boo Bpen Seafood.** Although not on the river, this upbeat seafood restaurant has the edge on the competition because of its spacious bench seating and garden atmosphere. Live bands play on a small central stage. House specialties include *gai khua kem* (roasted chicken with salt) and *boo nim tort gratium* (crab fried in garlic), and are worth a nibble, but for something more substantial, the barbecue prawns are a must, sampled with the chili, lime, and fish-sauce dip. [$] *Average main: B150* ✉ *Sanambin Rd.* ☎ *055/211110.*

$ SEAFOOD 🍴 **Phraefahthai.** This floating teak Thai-style house on the Nan River is the more popular of the pontoon eateries in Phitsanulok; it draws the majority of tourists, as well as local businesspeople and their families.

7

It's strikingly lighted up at night, impossible to miss from anywhere on the river. An extensive menu in English makes it the most comfortable riverside experience. The emphasis is on fresh seafood—the *pla tap-tim* (St. Peter's fish, a delicious freshwater variety found everywhere in Thailand) is particularly recommended, served steamed with a spicy lemon-and-lime sauce. Ⓢ *Average main: B200* ⊠ *100/49 Phutabucha Rd.* ☎ *055/242743.*

WHERE TO STAY
For expanded hotel reviews, visit Fodors.com.

$$
HOTEL **Grand Riverside Hotel.** The name is no misnomer—this impressive hotel is very grand indeed. **Pros:** plentiful free parking; shopping mall; nearby market. **Cons:** unreliable Wi-Fi; some rooms beginning to show their age; staff lack English language skills. Ⓢ *Rooms from: $85* ⊠ *59 Praroung Rd.* ☎ *055/248333* ⊕ *www.tgrhotel.com* ⇆ *79 rooms* ⦿❘ *Breakfast.*

$
HOTEL **La Paloma.** This vast complex is Phitsanulok's best-value high-end option. **Pros:** clean and comfortable rooms; fitness room and massage; snooker table. **Cons:** far from city center; shabby neighborhood; tour groups delay reception desk service. Ⓢ *Rooms from: B38* ⊠ *103 Srithumtripdork Rd.* ☎ *055/217930* ⇆ *239 rooms, 10 suites.*

$
HOTEL **Pailyn Hotel.** The rooms at this white high-rise are quite large, with picture windows adding plenty of light—rooms on the higher floors have the best view of the river. **Pros:** convenient location; friendly service; tour desk. **Cons:** no Wi-Fi in rooms; noisy discotheque; tour groups delay attention at reception desk. Ⓢ *Rooms from: $50* ⊠ *38 Boroma-trailokart Rd.* ☎ *055/252411, 02/215–7110 in Bangkok* ⇆ *247 rooms.*

$$$
RESORT **Pattara Resort & Spa.** Phitsanulok's newest luxury hotel, which opened in October 2009, is an attractive ensemble of Sukhothai-style chalets built around a palm-fringed tropical lagoon. **Pros:** central yet peaceful location; shady pool area; massage. **Cons:** slow room service; small bathrooms; mosquitoes. Ⓢ *Rooms from: B200* ⊠ *349/40 Chaiyanupap Rd.* ☎ *055/282966* ⊕ *www.pattararesort.com* ⇆ *64 rooms* ⦿❘ *Multiple meal plans.*

SUKHOTHAI

Fodor's Choice *56 km (35 miles) northwest of Phitsanulok, 427 km (265 miles) north*
★ *of Bangkok, 1 hour by bus from Phitsanulok.*

Sukhothai, which means "the dawn of happiness," holds a unique place in Thailand's history. Until the 13th century most of Thailand consisted of many small vassal states under the thumb of the Khmer Empire based in Angkor Wat. But the Khmers had overextended their reach, allowing the princes of two Thai states to combine forces. In 1238 one of the two princes, Phor Khun Bang Klang Thao, marched on Sukhothai, defeating the Khmer garrison commander in an elephant duel. Installed as the new king of the region, he took the name Sri Indraditya and founded a dynasty that ruled Sukhothai for nearly 150 years. His youngest son became the third king of Sukhothai, Ramkhamhaeng, who ruled from 1279 to 1299. Through military and diplomatic victories he expanded

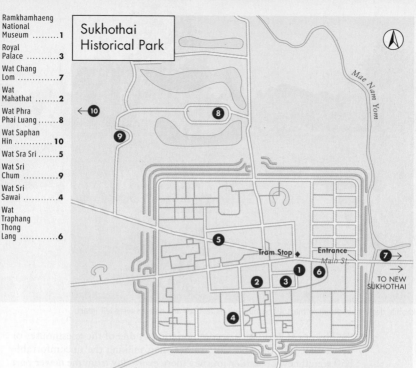

the kingdom to include most of present-day Thailand and the Malay Peninsula.

By the mid-14th century Sukhothai's power and influence had waned, and Ayutthaya, once its vassal state, became the capital of the Thai kingdom. Sukhothai was gradually abandoned to the jungle, and a new town grew up about 14 km (9 miles) away. In 1978 a 10-year restoration project costing more than $10 million created the Sukhothai Historical Park. The vast park (70 square km [27 square miles]) has 193 historic monuments. Sukhothai is busiest during the Loi Krathong festival, which is celebrated in the Historical Park each year on the full moon in November. Its well-orchestrated, three-day light-and-sound show is the highlight. At this time the town's hotels and guesthouses are booked weeks in advance.

New Sukhothai, where all intercity buses arrive, is a quiet town where most inhabitants are in bed by 11 pm. Its many guesthouses are a magnet for tourists coming to see the ruins, and you'll see quite a few *farang* (foreigners), especially young British, German, and American couples, wandering around amid the locals, drinking at the bars or browsing the sidewalk food stalls. New Sukhothai's night market is sleepy by the standards of the region, and in short, you can't expect much of an urban cultural experience here. If you've come specifically to visit

Sukhothai declined in power in the 15th century, but its temples and palaces were left intact.

the Historical Park, seek accommodation at one of the guesthouses or hotels that ring the Old City, rather than making the uncomfortable B50 songthaew or samlor journey there every day from the newer part of town.

GETTING HERE AND AROUND

AIR TRAVEL

Bangkok Airways flies daily from Bangkok to Sukhothai, which is roughly equidistant from its own exclusively operated airport (a beautiful open-air terminal) and the one in Phitsanulok, which is served by Nok Air and Kan Air and less than an hour away by taxi or bus. Single fares from Bangkok to Sukhothai or Phitsanulok are around B2,000.

Contacts Sukhothai Airport ☎ *02/134–3960.*

BUS TRAVEL

Buses to Sukhothai depart from Bangkok's Northern Bus Terminal (Mo Chit) daily from 7 am to 11 pm, leaving roughly every 20 minutes. There are five main companies to choose from, but all charge about the same, most with prices under B300. One company, Win Tours, operates "super VIP" buses that offer comfort and service comparable to business-class air travel. The journey takes about seven hours. Buses from Sukhothai's new bus terminal on the bypass road depart at the same times and for the same prices.

Contacts Sukhothai ✉ *Bypass Rd.* ☎ *055/614529.*

CAR TRAVEL

Highway 12 from Phitsanulok leads to Sukhothai and is a long, straight, and reasonably comfortable 59-km (37-mile), one-hour drive. Car rentals are available at Sukhothai airport. The drive from Bangkok, along the four-lane Highway 117, is about 440 km (273 miles), or roughly seven hours.

SAMLOR AND SONGTHAEW TRAVEL

Sukhothai does not have local buses, and most of the population gets around in souped-up samlors or songthaews.

ESSENTIALS

SAFETY AND PRECAUTIONS

Although Sukhothai is as safe as any other provincial Thai city, most hotels recommend that you leave valuables, passport, and excess cash in your room safe or with the management.

TIMING

At least two days are needed to tour the magnificent ruins of the Sukhothai Historical Park and a further morning or afternoon is claimed by even the most cursory visit to the Ramkhamhaeng National Museum. If you use Sukhothai as a base for exploring the ruins of Si Satchanalai and the potteries and museum of Sawankhalok, at least an additional two days are mandatory.

TOURS

In the Old City the main travel agency is run by the Vitoon guesthouse, whose owner, Kuhn Michael, is a knowledgeable guide who speaks good English. The guesthouse has fleets of bicycles and motorbikes and runs a taxi service.

TAT (Sukhothai) ✉ *130 Charodwithitong Rd.* ☎ *055/616228* ⊕ *tourismthailand. org/sukhothai* ⊗ *Daily 8:30–4:30.* **Vitoon Guesthouse** ☎ *055/697045* ⊕ *www. vitoonguesthouse.com.*

EXPLORING SUKHOTHAI

Because the sights are so spread out, the best way to explore the park is by bicycle; you can rent one for about B40 a day from outlets opposite the entrance to the Historical Park. You can also book a tour with a guide. Either way, bring a bottle of water with you—the day will get hotter than you think.

Depending on your means of transportation, a tour of the city could take a few hours or the better part of a day. It's best to come in the late afternoon to avoid the midday sun and enjoy the late evening's pink-and-orange hues. Crowds generally aren't a problem.

TOP ATTRACTIONS

Ramkhamhaeng National Museum. Most of the significant artifacts from Sukhothai are in Bangkok's National Museum, but this open, airy museum has more than enough fine pieces to demonstrate the gentle beauty of this period. You can learn how refinements in the use of bronze let artisans create the graceful walking Buddhas. ✉ *Charodwithitong Rd., just before entrance to Historical Park* 🖼 *B40* ⊗ *Daily 9:30–4.*

Continued on page 428

THE BUDDHA IN THAILAND

Buddhism plays a profound role in day-to-day Thai life. Statues of the Buddha are everywhere: in the country's 30,000 *wats* (temples), in sacred forest caves, in home shrines, and in cafés and bars. Each statue is regarded as a direct link to the Buddha himself and imparts its own message—if you know what to look for.

by Howard Richardson

The origins of Buddhism lie in the life of the Indian prince Siddhartha Gautama (563 BC– 483 BC), who became the Buddha (which simply means "awakened"). Statues of the Buddha follow ancient aesthetic rules. The Buddha must be wearing a monastic robe, either covering both shoulders or leaving the right shoulder bare. His body must display sacred marks, or *laksanas*, such as slender toes and fingers, a full, lion-like chest, and long eyelashes. Many statues also have elongated earlobes, a reminder of the Buddha's original life as a prince, when he wore heavy earrings. Buddha statues are in one of four positions: sitting, standing, walking, or reclining.

Detail of Reclining Buddha's head.

Statues of the Buddha have their hands arranged in a *mudra* or hand position. The mudras, which represent the Buddha's teachings or incidents in his life, were created by his disciples, who used them to enhance their meditation. There are about 100 mudras, but most are variations on six basic forms.

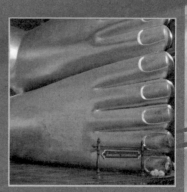

Reclining Buddha,
Wat Po, Bangkok.

Detail of top of Reclining Buddha's feet.

Detail of bottom of Reclining Buddha's foot.

WHAT THE BUDDHA TAUGHT

Gautama taught that there are three aspects to existence: *dukkha* (suffering), *anicca* (impermanence), and *anatta* (the absence of self). He believed that unfulfilled desire for status, self-worth, and material possessions creates dukkha, but that such desire is pointless because anicca dictates that everything is impermanent and cannot be possessed. Therefore, if we can learn to curb desire and cultivate detachment, we will cease to be unhappy.

The ultimate goal of Buddhism is to reach enlightenment or nirvana, which is basically the cessation of struggle—this happens when you have successfully let go of all desire (and by definition, all suffering). This signals the end to *samsara*, the cycle of reincarnation that Buddhists believe in. Buddhists also believe in karma, a law of cause and effect that suggests that your fate in this life and future lives is determined by your actions. Among the ways to improve your karma—and move toward nirvana—are devoting yourself to spirituality by becoming a monk or a nun, meditating, and *tham boon*, or merit making. Making offerings to the Buddha is one form of tham boon.

Thai painting of monks listening to the Buddha speak at a temple.

THE MIDDLE WAY

Gautama's prescription for ending dukkha is an attitude of moderation towards the material world based on wisdom, morality, and concentration. He broke this threefold approach down further into eight principles, called the Noble Eightfold Path or the Middle Way.

Wisdom:

Right Understanding: to understand dukkha and its causes.

Right Thought: to resist angry or unkind thoughts and acts.

Morality:

Right Speech: to avoid lying, speaking unkindly, or engaging in idle chatter.

Right Action: to refrain from harming or killing others, stealing, and engaging in sexual misconduct.

Right Livelihood: to earn a living peacefully and honestly.

Concentration:

Right Effort: to work towards discipline and kindness, abandoning old, counterproductive habits.

Right Mindfulness: to be aware of your thoughts, words, and actions; to see things as they really are.

Right Concentration: to focus on wholesome thoughts and actions (often while meditating.)

DID YOU KNOW?

Burmese invaders damaged many Buddha statues when they sacked Ayutthaya in 1767. The head of one statue became lodged in the roots of a tree at Wat Phra Mahathat, where it remains today.

THE BUDDHA'S POSITIONS

Standing Buddha in saffron robes, Bangkok.

STANDING

The Buddha stands either with his feet together or with one slightly in front of the other. The standing posture is often accompanied by certain hand positions to signify driving away fear or appealing to reason.

⇨ Wat Phra Mahathat, Sukhothai, Ch. 7; Wat Benjamabophit, Bangkok, Ch. 2.

RECLINING

Many scholars believe that reclining sculptures depict the Buddha dying and simultaneously reaching nirvana. According to another story, the Buddha is showing a proud giant who has refused to bow to him that he can lie down and still make himself appear larger than the giant. The Buddha then took the giant to the heavens and showed him angels that made the Buddha himself appear small, teaching the giant that there are truths beyond the realm of our own experience.

⇨ Wat Po, Bangkok, Ch. 2.

Reclining Buddha ornament.

SITTING

Seated Buddhas are the most common. The Buddha can sit in three different postures: adamantine or lotus, with legs crossed and feet resting on opposite thighs; heroic, a half-lotus position with one leg folded over the other; or western, with legs hanging straight down, as if sitting in a chair.

⇨ Wat Suthat, Bangkok (heroic style), Ch. 2.

THE LAUGHING BUDDHA

The Laughing Buddha, whose large belly and jolly demeanor make him easy to recognize, is a folkloric character based on a 9th century Chinese monk known for his kindness. The Laughing Buddha does not figure into Thai Buddhism but you may see him at temples in Bangkok's Chinatown. And because he represents good fortune and abundance, some Thai shops sell Laughing Buddhas as lucky charms. Laughing Buddha statues often carry sacks full of sweets to give to children.

Seated Buddha, Wat Suthat, Bangkok.

WALKING

Walking statues represent the Buddha going into the community to spread his teachings. Traditionally, walking Buddhas were constructed in relief. The first walking-Buddha statues were created in Sukhothai, and you can still see a few in the city's ruins.

⇨ Wat Sra Sri, Sukhothai and Wat Phra Phai Luang, Sukhothai, Ch. 7.

Walking Buddhas, Wat Phra Mahathat, Sukhothai.

WHAT DO THE BUDDHA'S HANDS MEAN?

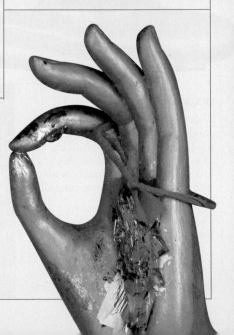

SETTING THE WHEEL IN MOTION

In this mudra, the Buddha's thumbs and forefingers join to make a circle, representing the Wheel of Dharma, a symbol for Buddhist law.

⇨ Cloisters of Wat Benjamabophit, Bangkok, Ch. 2; Phra Pathom Chedi, Nakhon Pathom, Ch. 3.

MEDITATION

The Buddha's hands are in his lap, palms pointing upwards. This position represents a disciplined mind.

⇨ National Museum, Bangkok, Ch. 2; Phra Pathom Chedi, Nakhon Pathom, Ch. 3.

REASONING

This posture, which signifies the Buddha's preference for reason and peace rather than hasty or thoughtless action, is similar to the absence of fear mudra, but the Buddha's thumb and forefinger are touching to form a circle.

⇨ Cloisters of Wat Benjamabophit, Bangkok, Ch. 2; Sukhothai Historical Park, Ch. 7.

SUBDUING MARA

Mara is a demon who tempted the Buddha with visions of beautiful women. In this posture, the Buddha is renouncing these worldly desires. He sits with his right hand is on his right thigh, fingers pointing down, and his left hand palm-up in his lap.

⇨ Wat Suthat, Bangkok, Ch. 2; Wat Mahathat, Sukhothai, Ch. 7; Phra Pathom Chedi, Nakhon Pathom, Ch. 3.

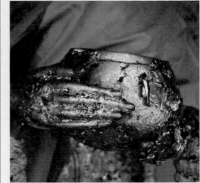

Hand and alms bowl detail; Nakhon Pathom Chedi, Nakon Pathom.

CHARITY

Buddhas using this mudra are usually standing, with their right arm pointing down, palm facing out, to give or receive offerings. In some modern variations, the Buddha is actually holding an alms bowl.

⇨ National Museum, Bangkok, Ch. 2.

ABSENCE OF FEAR

One or both of the Buddha's arms are bent at the elbow, palms facing out and fingers pointing up (like the international gesture for "Stop!") In this attitude the Buddha is either displaying his own fearlessness or encouraging his followers to be courageous.

⇨ Cloisters of Wat Benjamabophit, Bangkok Ch. 2.

Wat Mahathat. Sitting amid a tranquil lotus pond, Wat Mahathat is the largest and most beautiful monastery in Sukhothai. Enclosed in the compound are some 200 tightly packed chedis, each containing the funeral ashes of a member of the Sukhothai nobility. Towering above them is a large central chedi, notable for its bulbous, lotus-bud prang. Wrapping around the chedi is a frieze of 111 monks, their hands raised in adoration. Probably built by Sukhothai's first king, Wat Mahathat owes its present form to King Lö Thai, who in 1345 erected the lotus-bud chedi to house two important relics brought back from Sri Lanka by the monk Sisatta. This Sri Lankan–style chedi became the symbol of Sukhothai and classical Sukhothai style. Copies of it were made in the principal cities of its vassal states, signifying a magic circle emanating from Sukhothai, the spiritual and temporal center of the empire. ⊠ *In Old City* ☜ *B150 to all sights inside Old City walls* ☉ *Daily 8:30–4:30.*

THE TRACES OF A NATION

The optimism that accompanied the birth of the nation at Sukhothai is reflected in the art and architecture of the period. Strongly influenced by Sri Lankan Buddhism, the monuments left behind by the architects, artisans, and craftsmen of those innovative times had a light, often playful touch. Statues of the Buddha show him as smiling, serene, and confidently walking toward a better future. The iconic image of the walking Buddha originated in Sukhothai. Note also the impossibly graceful elephants portrayed in supporting pillars.

Wat Sri Chum. Like many other sanctuaries, Wat Si Chum was originally surrounded by a moat. The main structure is dominated by a breathtaking statue of the Buddha in a seated position. The huge but elegant stucco image is one of the largest in Thailand, measuring 37 feet from knee to knee. Enter the *mondop* (pillared pavilion) through the passage inside the left inner wall. Keep your eyes on the ceiling: more than 50 engraved slabs illustrate scenes from the *Jataka*, which are stories about the previous lives of Lord Buddha. ⊠ *East of Old City walls* ☜ *B150 for admission to all Historical Park sites.*

WORTH NOTING

Royal Palace. Thais imagine Sukhothai's government as a monarchy that served the people, stressing social needs and justice. Slavery was abolished, and people were free to believe in their local religions, Hinduism and Buddhism (often simultaneously), and to pursue their trades without hindrance. In the 19th century a famous stone inscription of King Ramkhamhaeng was found among the ruins of the palace across from Wat Mahathat, and is now in the National Museum in Bangkok. Sometimes referred to as Thailand's Declaration of Independence, the inscription's best-known quote reads: "This city Sukhothai is good. In the water there are fish, in the field there is rice. The ruler does not levy tax on the people who travel along the road together, leading their oxen on the way to trade and riding their horses on the way to sell. Whoever wants to trade in elephants, so trades. Whoever wants to trade in horses, so trades." ⊠ *In Old City* 🔲 *B150 for all sights in Historical Park* ⊙ *Daily 8–4:30.*

Wat Chang Lom. South of the park off Chotwithithong Road is one of Sukhothai's oldest monasteries. Its bell-shape pagoda, thought to have been built in the latter part of the 14th century, is of Sri Lankan influence and is perched on a three-tiered square base atop damaged elephant buttresses. In front of the chedi are a viharn and solitary pillars; the remains of nine other chedis have been found within this complex. ⊠ *Chotwithithong Rd., about 4 km (2½ miles) before entrance to Historical Park, reached by turning north down small lane over smaller bridge.*

Wat Phra Phai Luang. This former Khmer structure, once a Hindu shrine, was converted to a Buddhist temple. Surrounded by a moat, the sanctuary is encircled by three laterite prangs, similar to those at Wat Sri Sawai—the only one that remains intact is decorated with stucco figures. In front of the prangs are the remains of the viharn and a crumbling chedi with a seated Buddha on its pedestal. Facing these structures is the *mondop*, a square structure with a stepped pyramid roof, built to house religious relics. ⊠ *North of Old City walls on Donko Rd., opposite Tourist Information Center* 🔲 *B150 for all sights in Historical Park* ⊙ *Daily 8:30–4:30.*

Wat Saphan Hin. This pretty wat is reached by following a slate pathway and climbing a 656-foot hill. An amazing standing Buddha, nearly 40 feet tall, gazes down on the mere mortals who complete the climb. ⊠ *North of Old City walls* 🔲 *Free.*

Wat Sra Sri. This peaceful temple sits on two connected islands within a lotus-filled lake. The lake, called Traphong Trakuan Pond, supplied the monks with water and served as a boundary for the sacred area. A Sri Lankan–style chedi dominates six smaller chedis, and a large stucco seated Buddha looks down a row of columns, past the chedis, and over the lake to the horizon.

Especially wondrous is the walking Buddha beside the Sri Lankan–style chedi. The walking Buddha is a Sukhothai innovation, and the most ethereal of Thailand's artistic styles. The depiction of the Buddha is often a reflection of political authority, and is modeled after the ruler. Under the Khmers, authority was hierarchical, but the kings of Sukhothai represented the ideals of serenity, happiness, and justice. The walking Buddha is the epitome of Sukhothai's art; he appears to be floating on air, neither rooted on Earth nor placed on a pedestal above the reach of the common people. ⊠ *In Old City* 🔲 *B150 for all sights inside Old City walls* ⊙ *Daily 8:30–4:30.*

Wat Sri Sawai. Sukhothai's oldest structure may be this Khmer-style one with three prangs—similar to those found in Lopburi—surrounded by a laterite wall. The many stucco Hindu images and scenes suggest that Sri Sawai was probably first a Hindu temple, later converted to a Buddhist monastery. ⊠ *In Old City* 🔲 *B150 for all sights inside Old City walls* ⊙ *Daily 8:30–4:30.*

Wat Traphang Thong Lang. The square mondop of Wat Traphang Thong Lang is the main sanctuary, the outer walls of which boast beautiful stucco figures in niches—some of Sukhothai's finest art. The north side depicts the Buddha returning to preach to his wife. On the west side he preaches to his father and relatives. Note the figures on the south wall, where the story of the Buddha is accompanied by an angel descending from heaven. ✉ *Just north of Old City walls* ☾ *Daily 8:30–4:30.*

WHERE TO EAT

Some of the best food in town can be found at the local food stalls that line the main street before and after the bridge. If you're in the mood for something sweet, look for the stand selling delicious Thai crepes filled with condensed milk, right at the bridge on the city-center side. But it's hard to go wrong almost anywhere in or near the night market or along that street.

$$ ✕**Celadon.** In the Ananda Museum Gallery Hotel, the open-air Celadon
THAI restaurant, overlooking gardens and rice paddies, is one of Sukhothai's most stylish. Copies of works from Sukhothai's ancient celadon factories are on display, and the menu is full of equally historic traditional dishes—*yam tua pool,* for instance, a spicy salad of shrimps and tiny beans. ⑨ *Average main: B300* ✉ *Charodwitrhitong Rd.* ☎ *055/622428 up to 31* ⊕ *www.ananda-hotel.com/restaurant.*

$ ✕**Dream Café.** While waiting for your meal, feast your eyes on the
THAI extraordinary collection of antiques that fills this charming restaurant, which first opened its gnarled doors more than 20 years ago. The rustic tile floor, the glowing teak tables and chairs, and the nooks and crannies packed with fascinating odds and ends—everything from old lamps to fine ceramics—combine in a perfect harmony to endow the Dream Café with a superlative atmosphere. The modified Thai food is not quite up to snuff, however; be sure to tell your waiter you want things spicy, not farang-style, and even then, don't expect much. Behind the restaurant are four rustic but romantic rooms ($), aptly named Cocoon House, set in a fairy-tale garden. ⑨ *Average main: B150* ✉ *86/1 Singhawat Rd.* ☎ *055/612081.*

WHERE TO STAY

For expanded hotel reviews, visit Fodors.com.

$$$ ⊡ **Ananda Museum Gallery Hotel.** The Ananda has redefined the con-
HOTEL cept of luxury lodging in Sukhothai; as you might expect from a hotel that is also an art gallery, room design is informed by a deep sense of minimalism along with a healthy dose of feng shui. **Pros:** aesthetic surroundings; fine furnishings, elegant restaurant. **Cons:** located on busy highway; taxi fare to town is expensive; museum-like stillness at night might trouble some guests. ⑨ *Rooms from: $165* ✉ *10 Moo Banlum, Charodwithitong Rd.* ☎ *055/622428 up to 31* ⊕ *www.ananda-hotel. com* ⇆ *32 rooms, 2 suites* ⧦ *Breakfast.*

$$ ⊡ **The Legendha Sukhothai Resort.** This attractive Sukhothai-style resort
HOTEL hotel blends so perfectly with the outskirts of the Historical Park that
Fodor's Choice it could easily pass for a creation of the aesthetic King Ramkhamhaeng
★ himself. **Pros:** welcome fruit basket; friendly, helpful staff; chlorine-free pool. **Cons:** inconvenient location, between Historical Park entrance and the new city center; expensive hotel transport; insects. ⑨ *Rooms from: $85* ✉ *214 Moo 3, Tambon Muangkao, Old City* ☎ *055/697249*

CLOSE UP

Loi Krathong

On the full moon of the 12th lunar month, when the tides are at their highest and the moon at its brightest, the Thais head to the country's waterways to celebrate Loi Krathong, one of Thailand's most anticipated and enchanting festivals.

Loi Krathong was influenced by Diwali, the Indian lantern festival that paid tribute to three Brahman gods. Thai farmers adapted the ceremony to offer tribute to Mae Khlong Kha, the goddess of the water, to thank her for blessing the land with water.

Ancient Sukhothai is where the festival's popular history began, with a story written by King Rama IV in 1863. The story concerns Naang Noppamart, the daughter of a Brahman priest who served in the court of King Li-Thai, grandson of King Ramkhamhaeng the Great. She was a woman of exceptional charm and beauty who soon became his queen. She secretly fashioned a *krathong* (a small float used as an offering), setting it alight by candle in accordance with her Brahmanist rites. The king, upon seeing this curious, glimmering offering embraced its beauty, adapting it for Theravada Buddhism and thus creating the festival of Loi Krathong.

Krathong were traditionally formed by simply cupping banana leaves and offerings such as dried rice and betel nut were placed at the center along with three incense sticks representing the Brahman gods. Today krathong are more commonly constructed by pinning folded banana leaves to a buoyant base made of a banana tree stem; they're decorated with scented flowers, orange candles (said to be representative of the Buddhist monkhood), and three incense sticks, whose meaning was changed under Li-Thai to represent the three forms of Buddhist existence.

Today young Thai couples "loi" their "krathong" to bind their love in an act almost like that of a marriage proposal, while others use the ceremony more as a way to purge any bad luck or resentments they may be harboring. Loi Krathong also commonly represents the pursuit of material gain, with silent wishes placed for a winning lottery number or two. The festival remains Thailand's most romantic vision of tradition, with millions of Thais sending their hopes floating down the nearest waterway.

Although it's celebrated nationwide, with events centered around cities such as Bangkok, Ayutthaya, Chiang Mai, and Tak, the festival's birthplace of Sukhothai remains the focal point. The Historical Park serves as a kind of Hollywood back lot, with hundreds of costumed students and light, sound, and pyrotechnic engineers preparing for the fanfare of the annual show, which generally happens twice during the evening. With the Historical Park lighted and Wat Mahathat as its stage, the show reenacts the story of Sukhothai and the legend of Loi Krathong; then governors, dignitaries, and other celebrity visitors (which recently included a former Miss USA who is idolized in Thailand) take part in a spectacular finale that includes sending off the krathong representing the king and queen, and fireworks.

—Warwick Dixon

7

🌐 *www.TheLegendhaSukhothai.com* 🛏 *62 rooms* 🍴 *Breakfast.*

$ RESORT 🏨 **Lotus Village.** French owner Michel Hermann has expanded his modest guesthouse into one of Sukhothai's finest resort hotels, adding a spa with massage rooms and a sauna. **Pros:** helpful owners; lovely grounds; nearby market and ethnic restaurants; massage. **Cons:** shabby neighborhood; long walk through dark streets to town; river views blocked by ugly (though eminently prudent) flood-protection walls. [$] *Rooms from: $40* ✉ *170 Ratchathanee Rd.* ☎ *055/621484* 🌐 *www.lotus-village.com* 🛏 *10 rooms.*

SHOPPING

Because a relatively small number of travelers venture this way, fewer crafts are for sale here than elsewhere in the country. One notable exception is around Sukhothai and Si Satchanalai, where you can find reproductions of the pottery made here when this was the capital of the country.

$ HOTEL 🏨 **Pailyn Sukhothai Hotel.** The staff is proud to point out that King Bhumibol Adulyadej has spent the night here; a vast building with a subtle contemporary Thai look, including a typical stepped roof. **Pros:** attractive modern decor; atrium lounge; pool. **Cons:** unattractive neighborhood; expensive taxi ride to town or Historical Park; tour groups can be noisy. [$] *Rooms from: $35* ✉ *10/2 Moo 1, Jarodvithithong Rd.* ☎ *055/633335 up to 9, 02/215–5640 in Bangkok* 🌐 *www.pailynhotelssukhothai.com* 🛏 *230 rooms* 🍴 *Breakfast.*

$ HOTEL 🏨 **Rajthanee Hotel.** The traditional Thai entrance of this well-run hotel fronts a modern building; there's a terrace where you can also enjoy a Thai whisky and a stylish restaurant that serves good Asian cuisine. **Pros:** reasonable price; airy terrace; ample parking. **Cons:** drab, dark lobby and public rooms; uninteresting neighborhood; traffic noise in street-facing rooms. [$] *Rooms from: $24* ✉ *229 Jarodvithithong Rd.* ☎ *055/611031, 055/611308* 🛏 *83 rooms* 🍴 *Breakfast.*

$$ HOTEL 🏨 **Thai Village House.** This cluster of thatch bungalows is usually jammed with tour groups. **Pros:** tropical garden setting; great location; dining alfresco. **Cons:** noisy tour groups; atrocious fluorescent lighting; few frills. [$] *Rooms from: $80* ✉ *214 Jarodvithithong Rd., Muang Kao* ☎ *055/647249* 🛏 *80 rooms* 🍴 *Breakfast.*

SI SATCHANALAI

80 km (50 miles) north of Sukhothai.

Si Satchanalai, a sister city to Sukhothai, was governed by a son of Sukhothai's reigning monarch. Despite its secondary position, the city grew to impressive proportions, and the remains of no fewer than 200 of its temples and monuments survive, most of them in a ruined state but many well worth seeing.

GETTING HERE AND AROUND

Most visitors to Si Satchanalai reach it as part of a tour from Sukhothai (most hotels can set you up with a guide). If you want to go on your own, hop on a bus bound for the town of Sawankhalok. The ride from Sukhothai takes 1½ hours and costs around B40. Take a taxi from Sawankhalok to the Historical Park, asking the driver to wait while you visit the various temples. You can also tour the site by bicycle or on top of an elephant, if that's your choice of transportation. The Vitoon Guesthouse in Sukhothai also offers day trips to Si Satchanalai and Sawankhalok; it's opposite the entrance to the Sukhothai Historical Park.

SAFETY AND PRECAUTIONS
Although you might find yourself alone in the Si Satchanalai ruins, the area is perfectly safe.

TIMING
The Si Satchanalai Historical Park is a day's outing from Sukhothai.

ESSENTIALS
Tour Information Vitoon Guesthouse ☎ *055/697045* ⊕ *www.vitoonguesthouse.com.*

EXPLORING SI SATCHANALAI
With its expanse of neatly mowed lawns, Sukhothai is sometimes criticized for being too well groomed. But Si Satchanalai, spread out on 228 acres on the banks of the Mae Yom River, remains a quiet place with a more ancient, undisturbed atmosphere. It isn't difficult to find the ruins of a temple where you won't be disturbed for hours. Accommodations near the park are limited, so most visitors stay in Sukhothai, but the historical park has plenty of casual dining spots where you can get lunch.

Sawankhaworaranayok Museum. Sukhothai grew wealthy on the fine ceramics it produced from the rich earth around the neighboring town of Sawankhalok. The ceramics were so prized that they were offered as gifts from Sukhothai rulers to the imperial courts of China, and they found their way as far as Japan. Fine examples of 1,000-year-old Sawankhalok wares are on display at the Sawankhaworaranayok Museum, about 1 km (½ mile) from the town. The exhibits include pieces retrieved from the wrecks of vessels that sank in typhoons and storms on their way to China and Japan centuries ago. ⊠ *Wang Phinphat, Sawankhalok, Rte. 1201* 🖃 *B40* ⊙ *Daily 8:30–2.*

Wat Chang Lom. Near the entrance, Wat Chang Lom shows strong Sri Lankan influences. The 39 elephant buttresses are in much better condition than at the similarly named temple in Sukhothai. The main chedi was completed by 1291. As you climb the stairs that run up the side, you can find seated images of the Buddha.

Wat Chedi Jet Thaew. The second important monument, Wat Chedi Jet Thaew, is to the south of Wat Chang Lom. The complex has seven rows of ruined chedis, some with lotus-bud tops that are reminiscent of the larger ones at Sukhothai. The chedis contain the ashes of members of Si Satchanalai's ruling family.

Wat Nang Phya. Located to the southeast of Wat Chedi Jet Thaew, Wat Nang Phya has well-preserved floral reliefs on its balustrade and stucco reliefs on the viharn wall.

Wat Suam Utayan. As you leave the park, stop at Wat Suam Utayan to see a Si Satchanalai image of Lord Buddha, one of the few still remaining.

CAMBODIA

WELCOME TO CAMBODIA

TOP REASONS TO GO

★ **Angkor Temple Complex:** Hands-down Southeast Asia's most magnificent archaeological treasure, Angkor has hundreds of ruins, many still hidden deep in the jungle.

★ **Education and Enlightenment:** You'll learn a heap about history, warfare and human tragedy, science, and archaeology.

★ **Off-the-Beaten-Path Beaches:** Along the Gulf of Thailand lie a few of Southeast Asia's most unspoiled beaches and (generally) unpolluted waters. You'll eat some delicious seafood here.

★ **Philanthropy:** Work with street kids, give blood, buy a cookie to support the arts—if you're looking to do good while you travel, you'll find plenty of exciting and meaningful opportunities here.

★ **Southeast Asia's Rising Star:** Gradually earning worldwide attention, Siem Reap is developing into one of the hippest cities in Southeast Asia.

1 Phnom Penh and Environs. In the capital, you'll find a great deal to see and do: a palace and war monuments, great food and fine wine, and ample opportunities for people-watching along the breezy riverfront. It's an eye-opening place—a city that's come a long way in postwar recovery. And the stories its residents have to tell are both tragic and optimistic.

2 North of Phnom Penh. As you travel north, you'll see some of Asia's last remaining jungles where wildlife populations are actually increasing. Get a glimpse of the rare Irrawaddy dolphin at Kratie. There are still hill tribes in the far north in Ratanakkiri Province.

3 Siem Reap and Angkor Temple Complex. Angkor Wat is the largest religious structure ever built, and it's but one temple in a complex of hundreds. Siem Reap, a rapidly growing city, is the gateway to Angkor and other adventurous excursions.

4 Southern Cambodia. The once-sleepy coast has perked up. Whether you stay at a high-end resort, in a hillside bungalow, or in an island hut, it remains a treat to enjoy the laid-back beach ambience. Sihanoukville is now a bustling party-land while Kep is beginning to reemerge as a stylish destination.

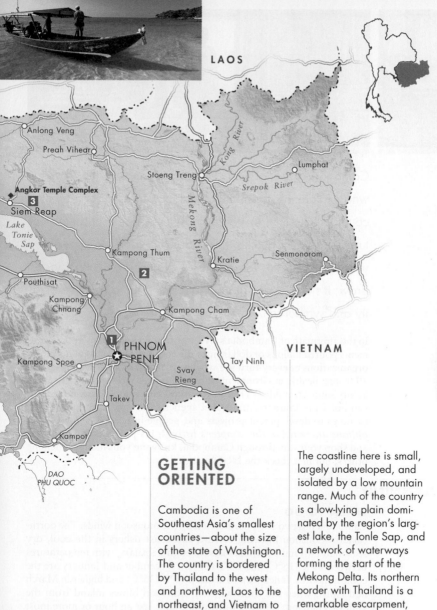

LAOS

Anlong Veng

Preah Vihear

Kong River

Stoeng Treng

Lumphat

Srepok River

Angkor Temple Complex

3

Siem Reap

Lake Tonle Sap

Mekong River

Kampong Thum

Kratie

Senmonorom

2

Pouthisat

Kampong Chnang

Kampong Cham

VIETNAM

1

Kampong Spoe

PHNOM PENH

Svay Rieng

Tay Ninh

Takev

Kampot

DAO PHU QUOC

8

GETTING ORIENTED

Cambodia is one of Southeast Asia's smallest countries—about the size of the state of Washington. The country is bordered by Thailand to the west and northwest, Laos to the northeast, and Vietnam to the east and southeast. In the south, Cambodia faces the Gulf of Thailand, which provides access to the Indian and Pacific oceans.

The coastline here is small, largely undeveloped, and isolated by a low mountain range. Much of the country is a low-lying plain dominated by the region's largest lake, the Tonle Sap, and a network of waterways forming the start of the Mekong Delta. Its northern border with Thailand is a remarkable escarpment, rising from the plains to heights of up to 1,800 feet—a natural defensive border and the site of many ancient fortresses.

Cambodia spins of web of intrigue around the travelers who explore this fascinating and increasingly sophisticated country. Take time to get to know the people and their culture, and you'll quickly fall under the spell. Be sure not to miss Angkor Wat, the country's crown jewel and biggest draw; it's a spectacular example of the merging of spirituality and symbolism.

In the aftermath of Cambodia's civil war foreign aid groups and governments poured billions of dollars into the country. Hundreds of nonprofit organizations at every turn are working toward a better Cambodia on all fronts: health, environment, safety, women's rights, civil rights, disability support, children's rights, economy, education. Many nonprofits run hotels, restaurants, and travel agencies that give a chunk of their earnings to development projects and people in need. *Do-good travel options are noted in this chapter's listings.* It's possible to wine, dine, and shop your way through Cambodia, knowing your money is helping others, but first check the NGO is legit.

PLANNING

WHEN TO GO

Cambodia has two seasons, affected by the monsoon winds. The northeastern monsoon blowing toward the coast ushers in the cool, dry season in November, which lasts through February, with temperatures between 65°F (18°C) and 80°F (27°C). December and January are the coolest months. It heats up to around 95°F (35°C) and higher in March and April, when the southwestern monsoon blows inland from the Gulf of Thailand, bringing downpours that last an hour or more most days. This rainy, humid season runs through October, with temperatures ranging from 80°F (27°C) to 95°F (35°C). The climate in Phnom Penh is always very humid. Thanks to climate change, Cambodia now experiences rainstorms in the dry season, cool temps in the hot season, and a lot of unpredictability. Bring your umbrella, although higher-end resorts usually offer one along with your bathrobe and slippers.

It's important to book in advance if you plan on visiting during mid-April's New Year celebrations or for the Water Festival in Phnom Penh in November. Strangely, the New Year is one of the best times to see the capital—at least in terms of lower rates and crowds—because the majority of Phnom Penh residents come from somewhere else and they all go home for the holidays.

GETTING HERE AND AROUND

AIR TRAVEL

After many years of "semi aviation isolation" Phnom Penh is opening up to the rest of the world, with Qatar Airways being one of the first international carriers to fly here. Regular air service links Phnom Penh and Siem Reap to Bangkok and Vientiane. Domestic flights run between Phnom Penh and Siem Reap. Air Asia, Bangkok Airways, Lao Airlines, Royal Khmer Airlines, Siem Reap Airways, and Thai Airways have flights to Cambodia (⇨ *Air Travel in Travel Smart Thailand*).

BOAT TRAVEL

From Phnom Penh, ferries called "bullet boats" travel along the Tonle Sap to reach Siem Reap and Angkor; they also ply waters between Sihanoukville and Koh Kong. You can buy tickets from a tour operator, your hotel's concierge, or at the port in Phnom Penh. ⚠ **Bullet boats, though fast, can be dangerous.** Smaller ferries travel daily between Siem Reap's port and Battambang, on the Sangker River. Ask about water levels before booking a ticket; in dry season the water can get so low the boat may get stuck for hours at a time.

BUS TRAVEL

Cambodia has a comprehensive bus network, and bus travel is cheap and generally of good standard. It's also generally the safest cross-country transportation, aside from flying. Travel from neighboring countries is easy, reliable, and cheap. Buses from Thailand and Vietnam operate daily.

Bus Contacts Giant Ibis ✉ *3E0, Road 106, Sangkat Doun Penh, Khan Doun Penh, Phnom Penh* ☎ *023/987808* ⊕ *www.giantibis.com*. **GST Bus** ✉ *13 St. 142, Phnom Penh* ☎ *023/218114, 012/895550*. **Hua Lian** ✉ *Hua Lian Bus Station, near Olympic Stadium, Phnom Penh* ☎ *023/223025*. **Mekong Express** ✉ *87E0 Sisowath Quay, S.K Wat, Phnom Penh* ☎ *023/427518, 012/257599*. **Neak Krorhorm Travel** ✉ *127 St. 108, Phnom Penh* ☎ *023/219496*.

CAR TRAVEL

If you want to get to a destination quickly, hiring a driver with a car is probably the most effective way, but it can be a hair-raising ride. A hired car with a driver costs about $50 a day, but agree on the price beforehand. ⚠ **We strongly advise against driving yourself.** Foreign drivers licenses are not valid here, rules of the road aren't observed, and most drivers drive dangerously.

8

MOTO AND TUK-TUK TRAVEL

Within cities and for shorter journeys, *motos* (motorcycle taxis), and *tuk-tuks* (three-wheeled cabs), are the best and cheapest ways of getting around. Tuk-tuk drivers will greet (or hassle) you at every street corner, providing you with the opportunity of learning to haggle.

BORDER CROSSINGS

The following border points are open with Thailand (Thai border towns in parentheses): Koh Kong (Hat Lek), Pailin (Ban Pakard), Duan Lem (Ban Laem), Poipet (Aranyaprathet), O'Smach (Chong Jom), and Anlong Veng (Chong Sa Ngam). From Laos you can cross at Dom Kralor (Voeung Kam). Overland crossings through Poipet and Koh Kong are the most popular, but bear in mind that Cambodian roads remain arduous, particularly in the rainy season. Coming from Laos overland, the only way to continue into Cambodia is by boat or bus to Stung Treng, then on from there the following morning.

PASSPORTS AND VISAS

One-month tourist visas, which cost $20, are available at all border crossings *listed below* and at the airports. You'll need two passport photos—if you don't have any with you, it's an added $5 to have them made there (no added wait). ■TIP➔ If you want to cross into Laos from Cambodia, you'll need to secure your visa to Laos in advance, as they are not available at the border. Border crossings are open daily 7:30 to 11:30 and 2 to 5.

Unfortunately, travelers report corruption at many border crossings. Cambodian authorities often will ask for a $1 fee at the Laos border, or for Thai B1,200 or more (well above the legal $20 fee for a tourist visa) at the Thailand crossings. Ignore them and head straight to the border (a short walk from where the buses leave you) where you will find the appropriate offices and authorities—and in high season, several long queues. You need one completely blank page in your passport in order to get a tourist Visa.

MONEY MATTERS

The Cambodian currency is the riel, but the U.S. dollar is more widely accepted, with many high-end businesses actually requiring payment in dollars. *All prices are given in dollars in this chapter.* Thai baht are usually accepted in bordering provinces.

The official exchange rate is approximately 4,000 riel to one U.S. dollar and 100 riel to the Thai baht. It's possible to change dollars to riel just about anywhere. Banks and businesses usually charge 2% to cash traveler's checks.

ATMs are available in Phnom Penh, Siem Reap, and Sihanoukville, mostly at ANZ and Canadia banks, although there are numerous other banks starting to install them. Using an ATM will cost you $5 per withdrawal. Credit cards are accepted at major hotels, restaurants, and at some boutiques. Cambodian banking hours are shorter than in many Western countries, generally from 8 am until 3 or 4 pm. ATMs are available 24 hours.

HEALTH AND SAFETY

If a real health emergency arises, evacuation to Bangkok is the best option.

Cambodia is far safer than many people realize, but you still need to exercise common sense. Most violence occurs against Cambodians. A decade ago, tourists were often mugged and sometimes even killed in Phnom Penh and on the beaches of Sihanoukville. Keep most of your cash, valuables, and your passport in a hotel safe, and avoid walking on side streets after dark—also it's best to avoid abrupt or confrontational behavior overall. Siem Reap has less crime than the capital, but that's starting to change. ⚠ **Avoid motos late at night. Moto theft is one of Cambodia's most widespread crimes.**

Land mines laid during the civil war have been removed from most major tourist destinations. Unexploded ordnance is a concern, however, around off-the-beaten-track temples, where you should only travel with a knowledgeable guide. As a general rule, never walk in uncharted territory in Cambodia, unless you know it's safe.

Cambodia has one of Asia's most atrocious road records. Accidents are common in the chaotic traffic of Phnom Penh and on the highways, where people drive like maniacs, and will not hesitate to make speedy U-turns on a busy two-way street. The better the road, the scarier the driving. Unfortunately, chauffeurs are some of the worst offenders. Wear a seat belt if they're available, and if you rent a moto, wear a helmet. If you are in a tuk-tuk, just hold on tight.

> ### BEGGARS
>
> Beggars will sometimes approach you in Cambodia. Many NGO workers who work with the homeless advise against giving handouts on the street. Instead, you should acknowledge the people who greet you, politely decline, and make a donation to an organization that operates larger-scale programs to aid beggars and street kids.

TOURS AND PACKAGES

5oceans Travel ✉ *147 St. 51 (Pasteur), Phnom Penh* ☎ *023/986920, 023/221537* ⊕ *www.5oceanscambodiatours.com.*

Beyond Unique Escapes. Well-planned, ethical, locally run tours all round Cambodia. ✉ *At Sivutha Blvd. and Alley West, Old Market, Siem Reap* ☎ *077/562565* ⊕ *www.beyonduniqueescapes.com.*

Hanuman Travel. Tailors your trip to suit your needs. ✉ *12 Street 310, Sangkat Tonle Bassac, Phnom Penh* ☎ *023/218396* ⊕ *www.hanuman. travel.*

oSmoSe Conservation Ecotourism Education. Birders enjoy oSmoSe Conservation Ecotourism Education, which offers tours to the Prek Toal Biosphere Reserve, mainland Southeast Asia's most important waterbird nesting territory. ✉ *27th St., Wat Bo, Siem Reap* ☎ *012/832812, 063/963710* ⊕ *www.osmosetonlesap.net.*

Pepy Tours. An award-winning tour operator, Pepy Tours offers somewhat quirky but socially responsible travel options. ✉ *Group 5, Village Sala Kangseng, Commune Svay Kangseng, Siem Reap* ✎ *info@pepytours.com* ⊕ *www.pepytours.com.*

8

Scuba Nation. This dive operator is the oldest and still probably the best. ✉ *Mohachai Guesthouse, Serendipity Beach, Sihanoukville* ☎ *034/933700, 012/604680* ⊕ *www.divecambodia.com.*

VISITOR INFORMATION

Andy Brouwer (⊕ *www.andybrouwer.blogspot.com* or *www. andybrouwer.co.uk*), a longtime traveler to Cambodia, has dedicated a good part of his life to informing people about the country where he lives. **Tales of Asia** (⊕ *www.talesofasia.com*) is an excellent source of information, with travelers' stories, road reports, and up-to-date travel information.

Once you arrive, pick up a visitor's guide (separate editions for Phnom Penh, Siem Reap, and Sihanoukville), as well as any of the various Cambodia Pocket Guides, widely available free at airports, hotels, and restaurants.

The **Ministry of Tourism** (⊕ *www.tourismcambodia.org*) has some information on its website. **Tourism Cambodia** (⊕ *www.tourismcambodia. com*) has more detailed descriptions of top attractions.

PHNOM PENH AND ENVIRONS

Cambodia's capital is also the country's commercial and political hub, a busy city amid rapid change. Over the past few years the number of international hotels, large restaurants, sidewalk cafés, art galleries, boutiques, Internet cafés, and sophisticated nightclubs has increased dramatically. So has the city traffic: motorbikes and tuk-tuks fight for space with cars and SUVs.

Phnom Penh is the natural gateway to anywhere in Cambodia: a slew of the north's accessible towns, far-off Ratanakkiri Province in the northeast, the beaches of Sihanoukville and Kep, and Kampot nearby in the south. Cambodia's roads have come a long way in recent years, but many in rural areas remain potholed and difficult in the rainy season (particularly heading toward the Thai border). Roads heading out of the capital lead to day-trip destinations like the beaches of Tonle Bati, a small lake with a couple of temples nearby, the lovely temple at Phnom Chisor to the south, and the pagoda-topped hill of Udong and the Mekong island of Koh Dach in the north.

PHNOM PENH

The capital of Cambodia, Phnom Penh is strategically positioned at the confluence of the Mekong, Tonle Sap, and Bassac rivers. The city dates back to 1372, when a wealthy woman named Penh, who lived at the eastern side of a small hill near the Tonle Sap, is said to have found four Buddha statues hidden in a large tree drifting down the river. With the help of her neighbors, she built a hill (a *phnom*) with a temple on top, and invited Buddhist monks to settle on its western slope. In 1434 King Ponhea Yat established his capital on the same spot and constructed a brick pagoda on top of the hill. The capital was later moved twice,

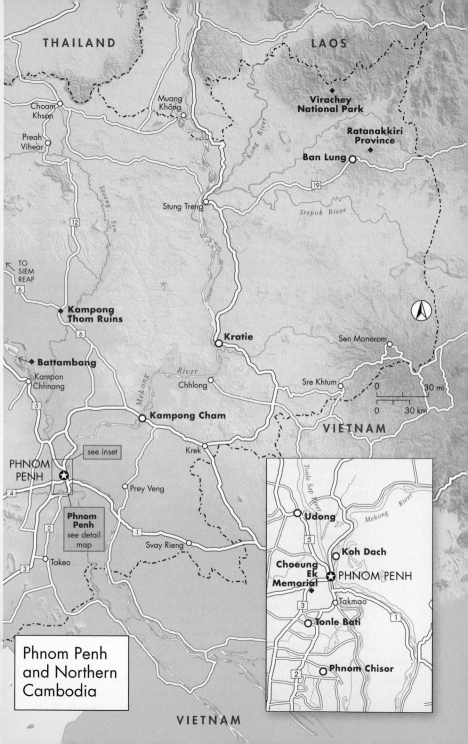

THAILAND

LAOS

Choam
Khsan

Muang
Không

Virachey
National Park

Preah
Vihear

Ratanakkiri
Province

Ban Lung

12

19

Stung Treng

Srepok River

Strong Sen

TO
SIEM
REAP
6

Kampong
Thom Ruins

6

Kratie

Sen Monorom

Battambang

River

Chhlong

Sre Khtum

Kampon
Chhnang

Mekong

0   30 mi

5

0   30 km

Kampong Cham

VIETNAM

see inset

Krek

PHNOM
PENH

4

Prey Veng

Tonle Sap River

Mekong
River

Phnom
Penh
see detail map

Udong

2

Svay Rieng

5

Koh Dach

Takeo

Choeung
Ek
Memorial

PHNOM PENH

3

Takmao

3

1

Tonle Bati

Phnom
Penh
and Northern
Cambodia

2

Phnom Chisor

1

VIETNAM

first to Lovek and later to Udong. In 1866, during the reign of King Norodom, the capital was moved back to Phnom Penh.

It was approximately during this time that France colonized Cambodia, and the French influence in the city is palpable—the legacy of a 90-year period that saw the construction of many colonial buildings, including the grandiose post office and railway station (both still standing, though the latter is threatened by potential development plans). Some of the era's art-deco architecture remains, in varying degrees of disrepair. Much of Phnom Penh's era of modern development took place after independence in 1953, with the addition of tree-lined boulevards, large stretches of gardens, and the Independence Monument, built in 1958.

Today Phnom Penh has a population of about 2 million people. But during the Pol Pot regime's forced emigration of people from the cities, Phnom Penh had fewer than 1,000 residents. Buildings and roads deteriorated, and most side streets are still a mess. The main routes are now well paved, however, and the city's wats (temples) have fresh coats of paint, as do many homes. This is a city on the rebound, and its vibrancy is in part due to the abundance of young people, many of whom were born after the war years. Its wide streets are filled with motorcycles, which weave about in a complex ballet, making it a thrilling achievement merely to cross the street (the best way is to screw up your courage and step straight into the flow, which should part for you as if by magic). If you're not quite that brave (and people have been hit doing this), a good tip is to wait for locals to cross and cross with them.

There are several wats and museums worth visiting, and the Old City has some attractive colonial buildings scattered about, though many disappear as time goes on. The wide park that lines the waterfront between the Royal Palace and Wat Phnom is a great place for a sunset stroll, particularly on weekend evenings when it fills with Khmer families, as do the other parks around town: Hun Sen Park, the Vietnamese monument area, and the promenade near the monstrous new Naga Casino. On a breezy evening you'll find hundreds of Khmers out flying kites.

GETTING HERE AND AROUND

AIR TRAVEL Thai International Airways flies twice daily from Bangkok to Phnom Penh, and Bangkok Airways has three flights a day. The trip takes about an hour and costs around $200 round-trip. Siem Reap Airways and AirAsia also have service between Bangkok and Phnom Penh. Lao Airlines flies from Vientiane and Pakse in Laos to Phnom Penh. Siem Reap Airways and Royal Khmer Airlines provide service between Cambodian cities. (⇨ See Air Travel in Travel Smart Thailand for airline contacts.)

Phnom Penh's modern Pochentong Airport is 10 km (6 miles) west of downtown. The international departure tax is $25, and the charge for domestic departures is $5 to $15. A taxi from the airport to downtown Phnom Penh costs $10. ■TIP➜ Motorcycles and tuk-tuks are cheaper than taxis (around $3), but it's a long, dusty ride.

BOAT TRAVEL (⇨ See Cambodia Planner for boat information)

BUS TRAVEL Phnom Penh has a half dozen or more private bus companies with regular service from all major Cambodian cities. Major bus stations include the Central Market, Sisowath Quay near the ferry port, and the

Hua Lian Station near the Olympic Stadium. Mekong Express charges a little more than other bus companies, but routes are direct and buses are clean and comfortable, with onboard tour guides and a bathroom (bring your own paper, which is a golden rule anywhere public in Cambodia). Most long-distance bus tickets cost $3 to $18, depending on the destination and distance. Newcomer bus company Giant Ibis also provides free Wi-Fi.

Tickets can be purchased at the bus companies' offices or through most hotels and guesthouses.

Note that some bus companies advertise a direct Phnom Penh–Bangkok ticket, but that trip takes 20 hours on rough roads, including several bothersome stops, so it's not recommended. Minivans are often a better (yet still very cramped) way to travel, but ensure that the driver doesn't oversell the space. Minivans go to all major, and some minor, destinations within Cambodia. Minivans travel between the Lao border (at the Cambodian immigration point) and Stung Treng (about two hours), where you can catch a bus to Phnom Penh.

CAR TRAVEL A hired car with a driver costs about $50 a day, but settle on the price before setting off. You can arrange to hire a car with driver through any hotel.

TAXI, MOTO, AND CYCLO TRAVEL The most common forms of transportation are the moto (motorcycle taxi) and tuk-tuk. They cruise the streets in abundance, and gather outside hotels and restaurants—wherever you walk, you'll attract them. The standard fare for a short trip on a moto is $1 to $2; tuk-tuks run a little higher, up to $4, but with a little haggling you can quickly reach an agreed amount. Taxis don't cruise the streets, but there are usually a couple parked outside large hotels, and the receptionist can call one. Almost all drivers speak varying degrees of English, some fluently.

ESSENTIALS

ANZ Royal Bank has several ATM machines throughout the city. Canadia Bank also has an ATM at the airport.

Bank Contacts ANZ Royal Bank ⊠ *100 Sihanouk* ☎ *023/726900.* **Canadia Bank** ⊠ *265–269 Street 214* ☎ *023/214868, 012/776592.*

Visitor and Tour Information Diethelm Travel ⊠ *65 Street 240* ☎ *023/219151* ⊕ *www.diethelmtravel.com/cambodia.* **Exotissimo** ⊠ *6th fl., SSN Center, No. 66, Norodom Blvd.* ☎ *023/218948* ⊕ *www.exotissimo.com.*

Guides can also be hired right at the Royal Palace and National Museum.

EXPLORING PHNOM PENH

Phnom Penh is an easy place to navigate and explore. There are markets, museums, and historical sites to visit. You will be able to explore the highlights of the city's tourist attractions in three to four days. All hotels will be able to arrange a range of transport options for your tours around the city.

TOP ATTRACTIONS

Choeung Ek Memorial (*Killing Fields*). In the mid- to late 1970s thousands of Khmer Rouge prisoners who had been tortured at the infamous Tuol Sleng prison were taken to the Choeung Ek extermination camp

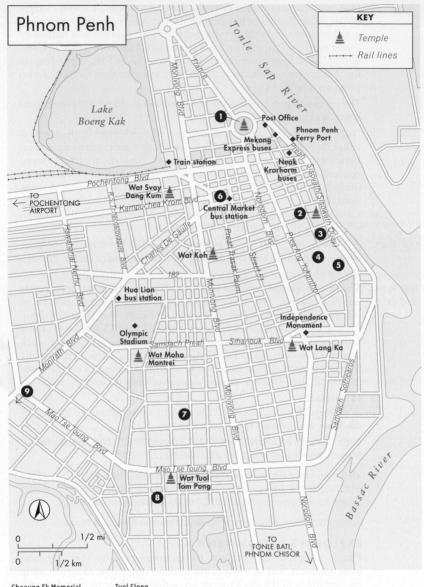

Phnom Penh

KEY

🔺 Temple

↟↟↟ Rail lines

Tonle Sap River

Lake Boeng Kak

① Wat Phnom

Post Office

Phnom Penh Ferry Port

Mekong Express buses

◆ Train station

Neak Krorhorm buses

Pochentong Blvd

← TO POCHENTONG AIRPORT

Wat Svay Dang Kum 🔺

Kampuchea Krom Blvd

⑥ Central Market bus station

② 🔺

③

④

⑤ 🔺

🔺 Wat Koh

182

◆ Hua Lian bus station

◆ Olympic Stadium

Samdach Preah

Independence Monument

🔺 Wat Moha Montrei

Sihanouk Blvd

🔺 Wat Lang Ka

⑦

⑨ ←

Mao Tse Toung Blvd

Mao Tse Toung Blvd

🔺 Wat Tuol Tom Pong

⑧

Bassac River

TO TONLE BATI, PHNOM CHISOR

🔆 (compass)

0 ——— 1/2 mi

0 ——— 1/2 km

TOURING PHNOM PENH

Start your tour early, just as the sun rises over the Tonle Sap. Take a tuk-tuk to **Wat Phnom**. Then climb the staircase and head for the temple, where King Ponhea Yat is venerated. After descending the hill, head east to the Tonle Sap and walk south along the riverfront promenade. Across the street you are greeted by a plethora of breakfast options; pick the restaurant of your choice. After eating, return to the riverfront, where you have a fine view of the Chroy Changvar Peninsula. The cobbled riverside path leads you to **Wat Ounalom**, one of Phnom Penh's largest and oldest pagodas.

After visiting the wat, continue south on Sisowath Quay, past a busy strip of bars and restaurants, and on to a huge lawn in front of the cheerful yellow **Royal Palace**. On the grounds of the palace is the must-see **Wat Preah Keo Morokat**, aka the Silver Pagoda. The palace closes for lunch from 11 am to 2 pm, so plan accordingly. On the northern side of the palace a side street leads to the traditional-style **National Museum**, which is a peaceful and quiet place to spend an hour or two.

By now you might be hungry again. As you exit the museum, head north on Street 13 to **Friends the Restaurant** for a light lunch and tasty drink. From there, if you think you can hack it, catch a tuk-tuk to the **Tuol Sleng Genocide Museum,** which will require an hour or more with a clear head. It's a somber, sobering experience, and most locals wouldn't dream of visiting. Afterward, head to the trendy Street 240 for some good food and interesting shopping.

for execution. Today the camp is a memorial, and the site consists of a monumental glass stupa built in 1989 and filled with 8,000 skulls, which were exhumed from mass graves nearby. It's an extremely disturbing sight: many of the skulls, which are grouped according to age and sex, bear the holes and slices from the blows that killed them. The site is at the end of a rough and dusty road, and can be reached in 30 minutes by motorbike, tuk-tuk ($10 is a reasonable price), or car. ■ TIP→ Admission including an excellent audio tour is only $5. ⊠ *15 km (9 miles) southwest of downtown Phnom Penh* ☎ *No phone* ⊕ *www. phnompenh.gov.kh* ⊠ *$2–$5* ☉ *Daily 7:30–5:30.*

National Museum. Within this splendid, Khmer-style rust-red landmark lie many archaeological treasures. Exhibits chronicle the various stages of Khmer cultural development, from the pre-Angkor periods of Fu Nan and Zhen La (5th to 8th century) to the Indravarman period (9th century), the classical Angkor period (10th to 13th century), and post-Angkor period. Among the more than 5,000 artifacts and works of art are 19th-century dance costumes, royal barges, and palanquins. A palm-shaded central courtyard with lotus ponds houses the museum's showpiece: a sandstone statue of the Hindu god Yama, the Leper King, housed in a pavilion. Guides, who are usually waiting just inside the entrance, can add a lot to a visit here. ■ TIP→ This is one of Cambodia's two main museums, and houses impressive archaeological relics that have survived war, genocide, and widespread plundering. ⊠ *Junction* *of sts. 178 and 13, next to Royal Palace* ☎ *023/217647, 023/217648* ⊕ *cambodiamuseum.info* 🖃 *$3* ⊘ *Daily 8–5.*

Phsar Tuol Tom Pong (*Russian Market*). This popular covered market earned its nickname in the 1980s, when the wives and daughters of Russian diplomats would often cruise the stalls on the lookout for curios and antiques. Today the market has a good selection of Cambodian handicrafts. Wood carvings and furniture abound, as do "spirit houses" used for offerings of food, flowers, and incense. Colorful straw mats and hats, as well as baskets, are in high demand. The market is the city's best source for art objects, including statues of the Buddha and Hindu gods; you can also buy valuable old Indochinese coins and paper money printed during different times of Cambodia's turbulent modern history. A jumble of stalls concentrated at the market's south side sells CDs, videos, and electronics. It's also a great place to buy overstock clothes from Cambodia's numerous garment factories at a fraction of their official retail price. ⊠ *South of Mao Tse Tung Blvd., between sts. 155 and 163* ⊘ *Daily 7–5.*

Royal Palace. A walled complex that covers several blocks near the river, the official residence of current King Preah Norodom Sihamoni and former residence of King Sihanouk and Queen Monineath Sihanouk is a 1913 reconstruction of the timber palace built in 1866 by King Norodom. The residential areas of the palace are closed to the public, but within the pagoda-style compound are a number of structures worth visiting. These include Wat Preah Keo Morokat (⇨ *below*); the Throne Hall, with a tiered roof topped by a 200-foot-tall tower; and a pavilion donated by the Emperor Napoleon III and shipped here from France. Guides can be hired at the entrance for $8. ⊠ *Sothearos between sts. 184 and 240* 🖃 *$3–$6.50 with video* ⊘ *Daily 7:30–11 and 2–5.*

Tuol Sleng Genocide Museum. This museum is a horrific reminder of the cruelty of which humans are capable. Once a neighborhood school, the building was seized by Pol Pot's Khmer Rouge and turned into a prison and interrogation center, the dreaded S-21. During the prison's four years of operation, some 14,000 Cambodians were tortured here; most were then taken to the infamous Killing Fields for execution. The four school buildings that made up S-21 have been left largely as they were when the Khmer Rouge left in January 1979. The prison kept extensive records and photos of the victims, and many of the documents are on display. Particularly chilling are the representations of torture scenes painted by S-21 survivor Vann Nath. Locals generally reveal they have never set foot here. ⊠ *St. 113 (Boeng Keng Kang) and St. 350* 🖃 *$3–$5 with video* ⊘ *Daily 8–5.*

Fodor's Choice **Wat Preah Keo Morokat** (*Temple of the Emerald Buddha*). Within the
★ Royal Palace grounds is Phnom Penh's greatest attraction: the Temple of the Emerald Buddha, built 1892 to 1902 and renovated in 1962. The temple is often referred to as the **Silver Pagoda** because of the 5,329 silver tiles—more than 5 tons of pure silver—that make up the floor in the main *vihear* (temple hall). At the back of the vihear is the venerated **Preah Keo Morokat** (Emerald Buddha)—some say it's carved from jade, whereas others maintain that it's Baccarat crystal. In front of the

The Royal Palace's Throne Hall is used today for ceremonies like coronations and royal weddings.

altar is a 200-pound solid-gold Buddha studded with 2,086 diamonds. Displayed in a glass case are the golden offerings donated by Queen Kossomak Nearyreath (King Sihanouk's mother) in 1969; gifts received by the royal family over the years are stored in other glass cases. The gallery walls surrounding the temple compound, which serves as the royal graveyard, are covered with murals depicting scenes from the Indian epic, the *Ramayana*. Pride of place is given to a bronze statue of King Norodom on horseback, completed in Paris in 1875 and brought here in 1892. There's a nearby shrine dedicated to the sacred bull Nandi. ✉ *Sothearos between sts. 240 and 184* 🖃 *Included in $3 admission to Royal Palace* ☉ *Daily 7:30–11 and 2–5.*

WORTH NOTING

Phsar Thmei (*Central Market*). An inescapable sightseeing destination in Phnom Penh is the colonial-era Central Market, built in the late 1930s on land that was once a watery swamp. This wonderfully ornate building with a large dome retains some of the city's art deco style. The market's Khmer name, Phsar Thmei, translates as "new" market to distinguish it from Phnom Penh's original market, Phsar Chas, near the Tonle Sap River; it's popularly known as Central Market, however. Entry into the market is through one of four grand doors that face the directions of the compass. The main entrance, facing east, is lined with souvenir and textile merchants hawking everything from cheap T-shirts and postcards to expensive silks, handicrafts, and silverware. Other stalls sell electronic goods, mobile phones, watches, jewelry, household items, shoes, secondhand clothing, flowers, and just about anything else you can imagine. Money changers mingle with beggars and war veterans with disabilities asking for a few hundred riel. ✉ *Blvd. 128, at St. 76* ⏲ *Daily 5–5.*

Wat Ounalom. The 15th-century Wat Ounalom is now the center of Cambodian Buddhism. Until 1999 it housed the Institute Buddhique, which originally contained a large religious library destroyed by the Khmer Rouge in the 1970s. Wat Ounalom's main vihear, built in 1952 and still intact, has three floors; the top floor holds paintings illustrating the lives of the Buddha. The central feature of the complex is the large stupa, **Chetdai,** which dates to Angkorian times and is said to contain hair from one of the Buddha's eyebrows. Four niche rooms here hold priceless bronze sculptures of the Buddha. The sanctuary is dedicated to the Angkorian king Jayavarman VII (circa 1120–1215). In much more recent times the wat served as a temporary sanctuary for monks fleeing cops and soldiers in post-election political riots. ✉ *Riverfront, about 250 yards north of National Museum* ☎ *012/773361* 🎟 *Free* ⏲ *Daily 6–6.*

Wat Phnom. According to legend, a wealthy woman named Penh found four statues of the Buddha hidden in a tree floating down the river, and in 1372 she built this hill and commissioned this sanctuary to house them. It is this 90-foot knoll for which the city was named: Phnom Penh means "Hill of Penh." Sixty years later, King Ponhea Yat had a huge stupa built here to house his ashes after his death. You approach the temple by a flight of steps flanked by bronze friezes of chariots in battle and heavenly *apsara* (traditional Khmer dancing figures). Inside the vihear are some fine wall paintings depicting scenes from the Buddha's lives, and on the north side is a charming Chinese shrine. The bottom of the hill swarms with vendors selling everything from devotional candles, to flowers to swallows (which you buy to set free). ✉ *St. 96 and Norodom Blvd.* 🎟 *$2* ⏲ *Daily 7–6:30.*

WHERE TO EAT

Phnom Penh is quickly becoming one of the top culinary cities in Asia. With delectable Khmer food at all levels, from street stalls to five-star establishments, plus an influx of international restaurants, you'll eat well every night in Phnom Penh. The country's colonial history means you'll find many French-inspired restaurants, too.

🍴 **Deco.** The two-tone color scheme, and art deco (as the name suggests) dining area, is the ideal place to enjoy a top-notch lunch or dinner. Deco reflects the changing face of Phnom Penh. Seasonal produce sourced locally, coupled with top-grade quality produce from around the world, are transformed by chef Casper von Hofmannsthal into modern European dishes infused with tastes of Asia. As for the cocktails, it's worth coming here just to sample the classic Negroni or the popular Deco Bramble (a mix of Bombay Sapphire, and homemade blackberry syrup finished with a dash of lemon). [$] *Average main: $11* ✉ *At sts. 57 and 352* ☎ *017/577327* 🌐 *www.decophnompenh.com* ✍ *Reservations essential* ⏲ *Lunch Tues.–Sat. noon–2; dinner Mon.–Sat. 5:30–10.*

$$ CONTEMPORARY

🍴 **FCC.** You don't have to be a journalist to join the lively international crowd that gathers here every day. In fact, it's not really a Foreign Correspondents Club, but it does attract a fair foreign following. People drop

CAMBODIAN CUISINE

Cambodian cuisine is distinct from that of neighbors Thailand, Laos, and Vietnam, although some dishes are common throughout the region. Fish and rice are the mainstays, and some of the world's tastiest fish dishes are to be had in Cambodia. The country has the benefit of a complex river system that feeds Southeast Asia's largest freshwater lake, plus a coastline famous for its shrimp and crab. Beyond all that, Cambodia's rice paddies grow some of the most succulent fish around. (Besides fish, Cambodians also eat a lot of pork, more so than beef, which tends to be tough.)

Be sure to try *prahok*, the Cambodian lifeblood: a stinky cheeselike fermented fish paste that nourishes the nation. *Amok*, too, is a sure delight. Done the old-fashioned way, it takes two days to make this fish-and-coconut concoction, which is steamed in a banana leaf.

Down south, Kampot Province grows world-renowned aromatic pepper. If you're coming from a northern climate, try a seafood dish with whole green peppercorns on the stalk. You won't find it (not fresh, anyway) in your home country.

Generally, the food in Cambodia is far tamer and less flavorsome that of Thailand or Laos, but seasoned heavily with fresh herbs. Curried dishes, known as *kari*, show the ties between Indian and Cambodian cuisine. As in Thailand, it is usual in Cambodian food to use fish sauce in soups, stir-fried cuisine, and as a dipping sauce. There are many variations of rice noodles, which give the cuisine a Chinese flavor. Beef noodle soup, known simply as *kuyteav*, is a popular dish brought to Cambodia by Chinese settlers. Also, *banh chiao*, a crepelike pancake stuffed with pork, shrimp, and bean sprouts and then fried, is the Khmer version of the Vietnamese *bánh xèo*. Cambodian cuisine uses many vegetables. Mushrooms, cabbage, baby corn, bamboo shoots, fresh ginger, Chinese broccoli, snow peas, and bok choy are all found in Cambodian dishes from stir-fry to soup.

Usually, meals in Cambodia consist of three or four different dishes, reflecting the tastes of sweet, sour, salty, and bitter. The dishes are set out and you take from which dish you want and mix with your rice. Eating is usually a communal experience, and it is appropriate to share your food with others.

8

in as much for the atmosphere of the French-colonial building and its open river views as for the tasty food, which is as eclectic as the diners. The beer is always cold, and you can grab a reliable burger or pizza if you're in need of a change from Khmer fare. If you find it difficult to leave this pleasant corner of Phnom Penh, you're in luck: there are even rooms for overnight guests. $ *Average main: $10 ⊠ 363 Sisowath Quay* ☏ *023/724014* ⊕ *www.fcccambodia.com* ☉ *7 am–midnight.*

$ ✕ **Friends the Restaurant.** Before Romdeng *(⇨ see Phnom Penh Dining)*,
TAPAS there was Friends the Restaurant. This extremely popular nonprofit
Fodor's Choice café near the National Museum serves a huge range of small tapas, fruit
★ juices, salads, and international dishes. Admire the colorful artwork, then visit the Friends store next door, filled with souvenirs and trinkets,

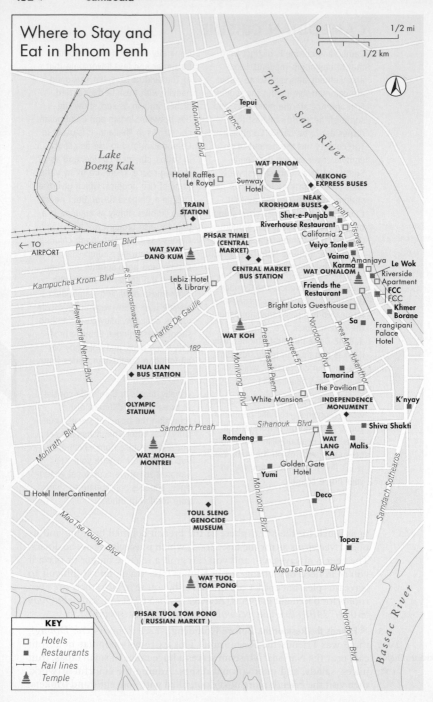

Where to Stay and Eat in Phnom Penh

0   1/2 mi

0   1/2 km

Lake Boeng Kak

Tonle Sap River

Tepui

Moniyong Blvd

France

WAT PHNOM

Hotel Raffles Le Royal

Sunway Hotel

MEKONG EXPRESS BUSES

Preah Sisovath

NEAK KRORHORM BUSES

Sher-e-Punjab

Riverhouse Restaurant

California 2

TRAIN STATION

← TO AIRPORT

Pochentong Blvd

PHSAR THMEI (CENTRAL MARKET)

WAT SVAY DANG KUM

Veiyo Tonle

Vaima

Karma

Amanjaya

Le Wok

CENTRAL MARKET BUS STATION

WAT OUNALOM

Riverside Apartment

Kampuchea Krom Blvd

R.S. Tcheroslovaquie Blvd

Lebiz Hotel & Library

Charles De Gaulle

Friends the Restaurant

FCC

FCC

Khmer Borane

Bright Lotus Guesthouse

Sa

Frangipani Palace Hotel

Hawaharial Nerhru Blvd

182

WAT KOH

Preah Trasak Paem

Street 51

Norodom Blvd

Prea Ang Yukanthor

HUA LIAN BUS STATION

Moniyong Blvd

Tamarind

OLYMPIC STATIUM

White Mansion

The Pavilion

INDEPENDENCE MONUMENT

K'nyay

Monirath Blvd

Samdach Preah

Sihanouk Blvd

Romdeng

WAT LANG KA

Shiva Shakti

Malis

Samdach Sothearos

WAT MOHA MONTREI

Yumi

Golden Gate Hotel

Hotel InterContinental

Mao Tse Toung Blvd

Deco

TOUL SLENG GENOCIDE MUSEUM

Moniyong Blvd

Topaz

Mao Tse Toung Blvd

Norodom Blvd

WAT TUOL TOM PONG

Bassac River

PHSAR TUOL TOM PONG (RUSSIAN MARKET)

KEY

□ Hotels

■ Restaurants

┼ Rail lines

▲ Temple

whose proceeds help the NGO provide much-needed assistance to street children. Best to book ahead as it is usually packed—prepare to queue. $ *Average main: $3* ✉ *215 Street 13* ☎ *012/802072* ⊕ *www. mithsamlanh.org* ⚲ *Reservations essential* ▭ *No credit cards* ⊗ *Daily 11–9* ⊗ *Closed Mon.*

$
CAMBODIAN

✗ **Karma.** Located on the riverfront, Karma offers tasty Khmer and western fare, well-sized portions that are great value for money. Karma is one of the better restaurants to become acquainted with local cuisine (the fish amok and pork loc lak are recommended), if you happen to start your Cambodian adventure in Phnom Penh. $ *Average main: $4* ✉ *273c Sisowath Quay* ☎ *089/788841* ⊗ *Daily 7 pm–midnight.*

$
CAMBODIAN

✗ **Khmer Borane.** This casual, breezy riverfront café on the bottom floor of an old colonial-era building attracts a steady crowd. Try something from the extensive list of classic Khmer dishes; the pomelo salad and fish soup with lemon and herbs are both good choices. If those don't please your palate, Khmer Borane also offers a wide variety of western dishes at reasonable prices. $ *Average main: $5* ✉ *389 Sisowath Quay* ☎ *012/290092* ▭ *No credit cards* ⊗ *Daily 11–11.*

$
CAMBODIAN
Fodor's Choice
★

✗ **K'nyay.** Khmer cuisine doesn't get much better than at K'nyay. This elegantly designed restaurant serves modern, simple but tasty dishes, offering a great range of veggie and vegan choices. Not surprisingly, it has become a favorite of the local expat community who also come to enjoy the peaceful setting. Next door is the newly opened K2, a cool little bar run by the same owners. $ *Average main: $6* ✉ *25K Suramarit Blvd., St. 268, near Independence Monument* ☎ *023/225225* ⊗ *Tues.– Sat. 7 am–9 pm.*

$$
CAMBODIAN

✗ **Le Wok.** The restaurant serves well thought-out and beautifully presented Asian and European fusion food, in a quietly sophisticated ambience. Try the creamy pumpkin ravioli or grouper and scallop terrine as an appetizer and the chocolate mousse for dessert, or opt for one of the Escale or Decouverte set menus if your appetite is alive and kicking. Welcoming, professional service in a modern, Asian-inspired space. $ *Average main: $8* ✉ *Street 178, across National Museum* ☎ *092/821857.*

$$
CAMBODIAN

✗ **Malis.** The Phnom Penh elite frequent this upscale traditional Khmer restaurant in a peaceful garden, as its chef Luu Meng is a Cambodian celebrity who has worked on TV with the likes of Gordon Ramsay. The long menu features a great variety of fresh fish and seafood, soups, complex curries, and grilled meats. The prices are a little high by Cambodian standards, but it makes for an enjoyable change if you're looking for something out of the ordinary. $ *Average main: $12* ✉ *136 Street*

8

41, Norodom Blvd. ☎ *023/221022* ✍ *Reservations essential* ⏲ *Daily 6 am–midnight.*

$$ MEDITERRANEAN 🍴 **Riverhouse Restaurant.** The Riverhouse evokes a French bistro, with sidewalk seating and a daily set menu. It's on a corner across the street from the northern end of the waterfront park, with half the tables outside, behind a potted hedge, and half beneath the ceiling fans of the open-air dining room. The menu is eclectic, ranging from couscous to tagines to stewed rabbit. It's a good idea to reserve ahead. ■ **TIP→ With a balcony overlooking the street and river, the upstairs bar is a great place for a drink or a game of pool.** [$] *Average main: $10* ✉ *6E St. 110, at Sisowath Quay* ☎ *023/212302, 012/751291* 🌐 *saenterprises.asia/riverhousecambodia/RiverhouseAsianBistro* ⏲ *Daily 10–2.*

$ CAMBODIAN 🍴 **Romdeng.** Some of the country's tastiest provincial Khmer dishes are served at this gorgeously redesigned house in a residential area. The adventurous can try the three flavors of *prahok,* Cambodia's signature fermented fish paste, or even fried spiders. If those don't suit your tastes, Romdeng (which means "galangal" in Khmer) offers plenty of piquant soups, curries, salads, and meat dishes. Have a glass of palm wine to sip with the meal, and enjoy the paintings on the walls—artwork by former street kids. The restaurant is part of the Mith Samlanh (Friends) group, so your dollars will help the former street kids who have been trained to work here. [$] *Average main: B5* ✉ *21 St. 278* ☎ *092/219565* 💳 *No credit cards* ⏲ *Mon.–Sat. 11–9* ⏲ *Closed 1–5 Wed. and Fri.*

$ INDIAN Fodor's Choice ★ 🍴 **Sher-e-Punjab.** Follow the aroma of pungent spices into this restaurant and prepare for a hearty curry and all the essential sides at the capital's best Indian restaurant. The accommodating staff and exotically spiced fare more than compensate for the modest appearance of this much raved-about restaurant. Complementary popadoms, dips, and chutney satiate the hunger pangs as you mull over the varied menu. Try the melt-in-your-mouth Tandoori chicken and don't miss out on the freshly baked naan. [$] *Average main: $5* ✉ *16 St. 130* ☎ *023/210695, 023/992901* 💳 *No credit cards* ⏲ *Daily 9 am–11 pm.*

$$ INDIAN 🍴 **Shiva Shakti.** Succulent samosas, vegetable *pakoras* (fritters), spicy lamb masala, butter chicken, and prawn *biryani* (with rice and vegetables) are among the favorites served at this small Indian restaurant. In the pleasant dining room a statue of the elephant-headed Hindu god Ganesha stands by the door, and reproductions of Mogul art line the walls. There are also a few tables on the sidewalk next to their little bar. It's just east of the Independence Monument. [$] *Average main: $9* ✉ *70E Sihanouk Blvd.* ☎ *012/813817* ⏲ *Tues.–Sun. 11–2 and 6–10:30.*

$$$$ SOUTH AMERICAN Fodor's Choice ★ 🍴 **Tepui.** Built in 1903, Chinese House (home to Tepui) is among the few colonial houses in Phnom Penh that remains in its original state; a mix of Chinese and French colonial architecture. But don't let the location's name mislead you, the food is combination of South American and Asian tastes with specialties such as corn empanadas filled with beef picadillo and goat cheese cream, or red tuna tartare with wasabi emulsion. An impressive painting of a Chinese girl with ruby red lips is the centerpiece in this sophisticated restaurant. There is a lively bar on the ground floor. ■ **TIP→ Have your tuk-tuk wait for you outside to avoid any delays after dinner.** [$] *Average main: $16* ✉ *Chinese House, 45*

Sisowath Quay, at St. 84, in front of Phnom Penh Port ☎ 023/991514 ⊕ www.chinesehouse.asia ⌕ Reservations essential ⊘ Mon.–Sat. 6 pm–10:30 pm.

$$$
FRENCH

✗ **Topaz.** The first-class French specialties and extensive wine list at this fine restaurant make it a long-time Phnom Penh favorite. Though it's no longer one of the most feted places to dine in the city's growing restaurant scene, it is still a reliable choice for an intimate, candlelight meal. ⓢ Average main: B14 ⊠ No. 182, Norodom Blvd. ☎ 023/221622 ⊕ www.topaz-restaurant.com ⊘ Daily 11:30–2 and 6–11.

> ### STOCKING THE FRIDGE
>
> **Veggy's.** If your room or suite has a kitchenette or an ample mini-fridge, check out Veggy's, which features fine wines, cheeses, and meats from around the world. It also supplies imported dry goods and fresh veggies, as the name indicates. ⊠ 23 St. 240 ☎ 023/211534 ⊘ Daily 8 am–10 pm.

$
CAMBODIAN

✗ **Veiyo Tonle.** This Khmer-owned and -operated nonprofit restaurant on the riverfront serves excellent traditional Khmer dishes, pizzas (39 varieties!), pastas, and more. Proceeds go toward an orphanage established by the owner. Visit on a Saturday or Monday night and enjoy a performance by kids dancing traditional dances. ⓢ Average main: $4 ⊠ 237 Sisowath Quay ☎ 012/847419, 011/737670 ▤ No credit cards ⊘ Daily 6 pm–midnight.

$$
JAPANESE

✗ **Yumi.** Although somewhat challenging to locate, Yumi is well worth the effort. Housed in a trendily converted old garage with a little courtyard, Yumi serves fresh, delectable Japanese tapas. The compact menu provides numerous set options ideal for couples or small groups to get to sample a variety of shared dishes, accompanied by some creative cocktails. ⓢ Average main: $8 ⊠ 29a St. 288, between Monivong and St. 63, Boeung Keng Kang 1 ☎ 092/163903 ⌕ Reservations essential ⊘ Daily 11–2 and 5–10.

WHERE TO STAY

These days the capital offers a plethora of accommodations for all budgets. Phnom Penh has several international-standard hotels, including the Raffles refurbishment of a 1929 beauty. Clean and comfortable boutique or trendy guesthouses have sprung up across the city, particularly in the Boeung Kak area. Most charge less than $20 a night. If you haven't found what you're looking for, wander the riverfront and its side streets. You're bound to discover something to your liking among the dozens upon dozens of options. ■TIP➜ When booking a hotel, always ask for the best price. Often just asking for a discount will yield a rate that's half the listed price. If you're doing business in Cambodia, be sure to say so, as additional discounts may apply.

For expanded hotel reviews, visit Fodors.com.

$$$$
HOTEL

⬚ **Amanjaya.** With chic rosewood furnishings and Khmer silk textiles in-room, Amanjaya is the classiest hotel on the banks of the Tonle Sap River. **Pros:** glorious riverside location; great restaurant and bar; breakfast included. **Cons:** noisy traffic all day; no pool; patchy Wi-Fi.

8

$ *Rooms from: $178* ⊠ *1 Street 154, Sisowath Quay* ☎ *023/214747* ⊕ *www.amanjaya-pancam-hotel.com* ⇌ *21 suites* ⦿ *Breakfast.*

$
B&B/INN
⌗ **California 2.** Clean, cheerful, and good value, with a bar that doubles as the reception and somewhat sets the tone of this easygoing, friendly guesthouse. **Pros:** close to bus stops; bar draws in a good crowd; friendly staff **Cons:** rooms a little on small side; no lift; not central. $ *Rooms from: $27* ⊠ *79 Sisowath Quay* ☎ *077/503144* ⊕ *www.cafecaliforniaphnompenh.com* ⇌ *10 rooms.*

$$
HOTEL
⌗ **FCC.** Ideally located on the riverfront and across the National Museum, the FCC is well known as a hub for expats and visitors who hang out at its lively restaurant-bar on the second and third floors, cooled by the river breezes. **Pros:** charm of old-style correspondent's digs; lively restaurant-bar; excellent location. **Cons:** a little ragged around the edges; street noise; patchy hot water. $ *Rooms from: $90* ⊠ *363 Sisowath Quay* ☎ *023/991641, 023/210142* ⊕ *www.fcccambodia.com* ⇌ *9 rooms* ⦿ *Breakfast.*

$$
HOTEL
⌗ **Frangipani Palace Hotel.** Completed in 2012, the Frangipani Palace Hotel is the fifth in a local chain, and is currently the only hotel in Phnom Penh with a rooftop pool, from where one can enjoy lovely panoramic views of the capital, especially during sunset. **Pros:** scenic rooftop pool and bar; good spa; high-end restaurant. **Cons:** not all rooms have a view; piped music throughout; only one elevator for eight floors. $ *Rooms from: $85* ⊠ *27 St. 178, Sangkat Cheychumneas, Khan Daun Penh* ☎ *023/223320, 023/223340* ⊕ *www.frangipanipalacehotel.com* ⇌ *60 rooms* ⦿ *Breakfast.*

$
HOTEL
⌗ **Golden Gate Hotel.** Long popular with faithful clients and frequent visitors, the Golden Gate offers rooms by the night or month. **Pros:** central location; free airport pickup; laundry and parking. **Cons:** facilities in two separate buildings; better suited to long-term business guests; impersonal. $ *Rooms from: $28* ⊠ *9 St. 278, Sangkat Bengkengkang 1* ☎ *023/427618, 023/721161* ⊕ *www.goldengatehotels.com* ⇌ *40 rooms* ⦿ *Breakfast.*

$$$$
HOTEL
⌗ **Hotel InterContinental.** One of Phnom Penh's finest hotels is on the far edge of town, where it's long been a favorite of business travelers and tycoons requiring VIP treatment. **Pros:** many amenities and services (including a concierge and executive floor); good selection of bars and restaurants; dramatic views. **Cons:** location in business district; far from city's main attractions; Internet charge. $ *Rooms from: $136* ⊠ *296 Blvd. Mao Tse Tung* ☎ *023/424888* ⊕ *www.intercontinental.com* ⇌ *372 rooms* ⦿ *Breakfast.*

$$$$
HOTEL
⌗ **Hotel Raffles Le Royal.** Phnom Penh's ritziest hotel first opened in 1929, was practically destroyed during the Khmer Rouge years, and was meticulously restored by the Raffles group in 1996. **Pros:** great location; exemplary service; sumptuous luxury. **Cons:** expensive; style may not be to everyone's tastes. $ *Rooms from: $240* ⊠ *92 Rukhak Vithei Daun Penh* ☎ *023/981888, 800/637–9477 in U.S., 800/6379–4771 in U.K.* ⊕ *www.raffles.com* ⇌ *170 rooms* ⦿ *Multiple meal plans.*

$$
HOTEL
⌗ **Lebiz Hotel and Library.** This boutique hotel's futuristic urban-chic decor is geared mainly to hip professionals; large blaringly white rooms are activated by splashes of bright colors and decked out with techy

facilities such as DVD player, LCD screen, and iPod dock. **Pros:** affordable designer comfort; cool minimalist style; friendly staff. **Cons:** breakfast somewhat lacking; location central but requires a good walk; decor too clinical for some. *Rooms from: $78 ✉ 79F St. 128 ☎ 023/998608 🌐 www.lebizhotel.com 27 rooms.*

$$ HOTEL Fodor's Choice ★ **The Pavilion.** A discreet green oasis in the heart of bustling Phnom Penh, the Pavillion is in a lovingly restored building of the raging 1920s, with a swimming pool and spa. **Pros:** limo pickup service from airport with treats (for a little extra); pool; great location. **Cons:** rooms and bathrooms are a little small; no children under 16 allowed; fills quickly. *Rooms from: $50 ✉ 227 St. 19, Khan Daun Penh ☎ 023/222280 🌐 www.thepavilion.asia 21 rooms.*

$$ HOTEL **Sunway Hotel.** This hotel near Wat Phnom and the U.S. Embassy is a primary choice among business travelers. **Pros:** in the heart of the business district; excellent lounge bar, no-smoking room option. **Cons:** slightly dated architecture; high-speed Internet charged. *Rooms from: $99 ✉ 1 St. 92, Sangkat Wat Phnom ☎ 023/430333 🌐 phnompenh.sunwayhotels.com 138 rooms Breakfast.*

$$$ HOTEL **White Mansion Hotel.** This glossy hotel on the hip, upmarket 240 Street has suites on the top floors with balconies overlooking great vistas of the city, while rooms on the ground floor have a terrace that leads directly to the pool. **Pros:** spacious rooms; child-friendly; nice monochrome design. **Cons:** open showers can be messy; elevator only goes up to third floor; not central. *Rooms from: $100 ✉ 26 St. 240 ☎ 023/5550955 🌐 www.hotelphnompenh-whitemansion.com 30 rooms Breakfast.*

NIGHTLIFE AND THE ARTS

NIGHTLIFE

What makes the nightlife here enjoyable is how easy it is to get from place to place in this compact city. Most of the dusk-to-dawn nightspots are near the Tonle Sap riverside, along Street 240 and Street 51. ⚠ **Keep your wits about you after dark in Phnom Penh—robberies are common, and although foreigners aren't specifically targeted, they are certainly not exempt from the rise in crime.**

Blue Chilli. Phnom Penh is a gay-friendly city, and Blue Chilli is one of the most popular and oldest bars for locals, expats, and tourists. The lively, friendly bar hosts entertaining live drag shows and other performances throughout the week, as well as DJ sets that will keep you dancing until the early hours. *✉ 36EO St. 178, behind National Museum ☎ 012/566353 🌐 www.bluechillicambodia.com.*

Bouchon Wine Bar. A novel addition to the Phnom Penh nightlife scene, Bouchon serves a dapper selection of more than 40 French wines and accompanying light meals or finger food, in a buzzily sophisticated, industrial nouveau-pub atmosphere that attracts an eclectic international crowd. Wine labels are also stamped on the wooden tables, and you can sample different varieties by the bottle or by the glass. *✉ 3 St. 246 ☎ 077/881103.*

Pontoon Club and Lounge. The only club in the Cambodian capital that brings over top DJs from around the world for happening live sets that

8

Cambodia's Festivals

Like many Southeast Asian nations, Cambodia celebrates a lot of important festivals. Quite a few of them are closely tied to Buddhism, the country's predominant religion.

Meak Bochea: On the day of the full moon in February, this festival commemorates the Buddha's first sermon to 1,250 of his disciples. In the evening, Buddhists parade three times around their respective pagodas.

Khmer New Year: Celebrated at the same time as the Thai and Lao lunar new year (mid April), it's a new-moon festival spread over the three days following the winter rice harvest. People celebrate by cleaning and decorating their houses, making offerings at their home altars, going to Buddhist temples, and splashing lots and lots of water on each other. Be forewarned: Foreigners are fair game.

Visakha Bochea: This Buddhist festival on the day of the full moon in May celebrates the Buddha's birth, enlightenment, and death.

Chrat Preah Nongkol: The Royal Ploughing Ceremony, a celebration of the start of the summer planting season, is held in front of the Royal Palace in Phnom Penh in May. The impressive ceremony includes soothsaying rites meant to predict the outcomes for the year's rice harvest.

Pchum Ben (All Souls' Day): In mid-October the spirits of deceased ancestors are honored according to Khmer tradition. People make special offerings at Buddhist temples to appease these spirits.

Bonn Om Touk: The Water Festival ushers in the fishing season, and marks the "miraculous" reversal of the Tonle Sap waters. It's celebrated in November throughout the country: longboat river races are held, and an illuminated flotilla of *naga*, or dragon boats, adds to the festive atmosphere. The biggest races are held in Phnom Penh in front of the Royal Palace, where the King traditionally presides.

---

draw accidental as well as dedicated music-loving punters. ✉ *80 St. 172* ☎ *016/779966.*

Score Sports Bar & Grill. Open till 2 every morning, this sports haunt is a favorite of expats, locals, and tourists what want to watch their game live on one of many LCD screens, while enjoying a tipple among a laidback, enthusiastic crowd. The food leaves a lot to be desired so don't come here with a satisfying meal in mind. ✉ *5 St. 282* ☎ *023/221357.*

THE ARTS

Various Phnom Penh theaters and restaurants offer programs of traditional music and dancing. Many of these shows are organized by nonprofit groups that help Cambodian orphans and disadvantaged kids, or disabled individuals. Siem Reap perhaps has more venues, but many there are run by for-profit companies in the tourism industry.

Chaktomuk Theater. Chaktomuk Theater is an architectural landmark that hosts performances, organized by the Ministry of Culture, of traditional music and dance, while also hosting business events such as conferences. The dates and times of shows are listed in the English-language newspaper the *Cambodia Daily* and the *Phnom Penh Post.* ⊠ *Sisowath Quay north of St. 240* ☎ *023/725119.*

Plae Pakaa. A rotating show organized by the Marion Insitute with Cambodian Living Arts, Plae Pakaa was established to create work opportunities for talented local artists. It's hosted in the National Museum gardens and runs from Monday to Saturday at 7 pm, featuring beautifully staged performances that showcase the rich diversity of Cambodian culture, from Apsara dances to traditional ceremonies, theater, music, and contemporary dance performances. ⊠ *The National Museum, St. 3, corner of St. 178* ☎ *023/986032* ⊕ *www.marioninstitute. org/cambodian-living-arts/about-cambodian-living-arts.*

Sovanna Phum Khmer Art Association. The privately run Sovanna Phum Khmer Art Association organizes educational workshops for young Cambodians in dance, music, theater, and hosts performances featuring shadow puppets, folk dances, and traditional music every Friday and Saturday at its theater. ⊠ *111 St. 360* ☎ *023/987564, 012/837056* ⊕ *shadow-puppets.org.*

Veiyo Tonle restaurant. The nonprofit Veiyo Tonle restaurant sponsors an orphanage, and twice a week the kids put on beautiful dance performances. ⊠ *237 Sisowath Quay* ☎ *012/847419.*

These days Phnom Penh has a number of remarkably good art and photo galleries to browse.

Reyum. Reyum, an NGO run by the Institute of Arts and Culture, helps educate and launch careers for young Cambodians in the arts via its Art School, and commissions new artists' work. It also presents exhibitions of traditional Khmer art and architecture. ⊠ *47 St. 178, across from National Museum* ☎ *023/217149* ⊕ *www.reyum.org.*

8

SHOPPING

The city has many shops and a few markets selling everything from fake antiques to fine jewelry, while several polished boutiques sell items made with local materials and offer sustenance to socially disadvantaged individuals. Prices are generally set at shops, so save your bargain-hunting for the markets. The best shops are to be found on streets 178 and 240.

Psar Reatrey Night Market. This lively riverfront market attracts locals and tourists alike for basic clothing, traditional handmade souvenirs, accessories, and gift shopping until midnight. Several stalls sell freshly made local dishes as well as drinks such as sugarcane and bean juices, and there is a large sitting area covered in rattan mats. ⊠ *Sisowath Quay between sts. 106 and 108.*

Psar Thmei. The largest market in Phnom Penh is Psar Thmei, popularly known as the Central Market, an art deco–style structure in the center of the city that sells foodstuffs, household goods, fake antiques, and some silver and gold jewelry. You're expected to bargain—start off by offering half the named price and you'll probably end up paying about 70%. It's busiest in the morning. ⊠ *Blvd. 128 (Kampuchea Krom), at St. 76.*

Psar Tuol Tom Pong. A popular location for discovering some of the best bargains in town, the Psar Tuol Tom Pong, or Russian Market, sells a great variety of Cambodian handicrafts, traditional Krama scarves, Khmer wood carvings, baskets, knock-off electronics, and much more. ⊠ *Russian Market, adjacent to Wat Tuol Tom Pong at sts. 155 and 163.*

ANTIQUES
AND FINE ART

Bazar Art de Vivre. Bazar Art de Vivre includes some rare Chinese pieces among its eclectic collection of contemporary Asian art, small furniture, and antiques. ⊠ *28 Sihanouk Blvd.* ☎ *012/843043.*

Couleurs d'Asie. As well as presenting regular exhibitions of contemporary and classic-style Khmer art, Couleurs d'Asie sells beautifully crafted accessories and home decor items made by local artists in sumptuous silks and other locally sourced materials. ⊠ *19 St. 360* ☎ *023/221075* ⊕ *www.couleursdasie.net.*

Le Lezard Bleu. Like its newer twin in Siem Reap, Le Lezard Bleu is a boutique/gallery/shop featuring home decor creations inspired by Cambodian culture and made by local artisans, as well as a collection of antique *objets d'art.* ⊠ *61 St. 240* ☎ *023/986978.*

Lotus Pond. Lotus Pond provides a fine selection of quality Cambodian silks, artistic carvings and statues, spirit houses, and small furniture items, while also working on training local artisans and raising money for rural development projects. ⊠ *57 St. 178* ☎ *023/426782.*

Water Lily. Enter a world of humorous fantasy, quirky chic, and illustrative color at the jewelry workshop/store of French designer Christine Gauthier. Buttons, beads, wires and feathers shine in her eccentric designs, some of which are hidden like treasures in a chest with hundreds of little drawers for you to peek through. ⊠ *37 St. 240* ☎ *012/812469* ⊕ *www.waterlilycreation.com.*

LOCAL CRAFTS

Daughters of Cambodia Boutique. Located in Phnom Penh's red-light district and offering employment opportunities to sex trafficking victims, this boutique sells men's and women's clothing and accessories, children's toys, and home decor items. ⊠ *65 St. 178* ☎ *077/657678* ⊕ *daughtersofcambodia.org.*

Friends n Stuff. Trendy, playful, and eco-friendly accessories can be found at Friends n Stuff, next to the ultrapopular Friends restaurant. Here you can buy locally crafted laptop cases made from recycled bicycle tires, handbags made from food packets, glossy hardback books on Cambodia and other fun stuff, and all for the worthy cause of helping street children achieve a quality of life. ⊠ *215 St. 13, north of National Museum, Khan Daun Penh* ☎ *023/220596* ⊕ *www.mithsamlanh.org.*

Rajana. Rajana sells interesting, locally hand-crafted jewelry, silks, home decor items, stationery, and clothing. Proceeds go toward the Rajana Association, which trains local artisans. ■ **TIP➔ Check out the old warscrap necklaces and recycled spark-plug figurines.** The store has other locations in Sihanoukville and Siem Reap. ⊠ *Next to Russian Market, 170St. 450, at sts. 450 and 155* ☎ *023/993642* ⊕ *www.rajanacrafts.org.*

Watthan Artisans Cambodia. Watthan Artisans Cambodia, an organization worth supporting, produces attractive women's accessories, decorative objects and knickacks in silk, cotton, wood and clay that are made on site by people with physical disabilities. Watthan Artisans products can also be found at the great Colours of Life store behind the FCC.

Women parade near the Royal Palace in celebration of Bonn Om Touk, Cambodia's water festival.

✉ *Wat Than Pagoda, 180 Norodom Blvd.* ☎ *023/216321* ⊕ *www.wac.khmerproducts.com.*

SILK **Khmer Silk Village Communities Showroom.** Working with an association of 1,500 silk breeders and weavers around the country, the KSVCS sells stunning scarves and materials from their Mekong, Takeo, and Golden Silk collections, exclusively produced with fine Khmer silk. ✉ *St. 55 at St. 228, Sangkat Chak Tomuk, Khan Daun Penh* ☎ *023/997125.*

Sayon Silk Shop. Sayon Silk Shop has an collection of silks accessories, quilts, and home elements such as cushions and bolsters, in exquisite colors and patterns. The store offers employment to impoverished women from remote regions. ✉ *40 St. 178* ☎ *012/859380.*

TONLE BATI

33 km (20 miles) south of Phnom Penh.

On weekends Phnom Penh residents head for this small lake a half-hour drive south on Highway 2. It has a beach with refreshment stalls and souvenir stands. Note that you'll encounter many beggars and children clamoring for attention here. The nearby, but more remote, **Ta Phrom,** a 12th-century temple built around the time of Siem Reap's Angkor Thom and Bayon, is less chaotic. The five-chambered laterite temple has several well-preserved Hindu and Buddhist bas-reliefs. Nearby is an attractive, smaller temple, **Yeah Peau.** Both temples are free and open to the public at all times. Phnom Tamao, Cambodia's leading zoo, is about 11 km (7 miles) farther south, but it's not worth a detour.

Cambodia Then and Now

The Kingdom of Cambodia, encircled by Thailand, Laos, Vietnam, and the sea, is a land of striking extremes. Internationally, it's best known for two contrasting chapters of its long history. The first is the Khmer empire, which in its heyday covered most of modern-day Southeast Asia. Today the ruins of Angkor attest to the nation's immutable cultural heritage. The second chapter is the country's recent history and legacy of Khmer Rouge brutality, which left at least 1.7 million Cambodians dead. In 1993 the United Nations sponsored democratic elections that failed to honor the people's vote. Civil war continued until 1998, when another round of elections was held, and violent riots ensued in the aftermath. Cambodia's long-standing political turmoil—both on the battlefield and in much more subtle displays—continues to shape the nation's day-to-day workings. Through decades of war, a genocide, continued widespread government corruption, high rates of violence and mental illness, the provision of billions of dollars in international aid, and the disappearance of much of that money, Cambodia has suffered its demons. Yet Cambodians are a forward-thinking, sharp-minded and friendly people, whose warm smiles are not yet jaded by tourism and do not belie the inordinate suffering their nation has so recently endured. Though practically destroyed by the regional conflict and homegrown repression of the 1970s, individual Cambodians have risen from those disasters, and a new, hard-working and young middle class has blossomed. The streets of Phnom Penh are abuzz with a youthful vibrancy, and Siem Reap, near the Angkor ruins, has already become one of the world's hottest boutique resort holiday destinations.

More than half of Cambodia was once blanketed in forests, but the landscape has changed in recent decades thanks to ruthless and mercenary deforestation. The country is blessed with powerful waters: the Mekong and Tonle Sap rivers, and Tonle Sap lake, which feeds 70% of the nation. The surrounding mountain ranges, protecting Cambodia's long river valleys, are home to hill tribes and some of the region's rarest wildlife species.

The three ranges of low mountains—the northern Dangkrek, the exotically named Elephant Mountains in the south, and the country's highest range, the Cardamoms, in the southwest—formed natural barriers against invasion and were used as fortresses during the war years. Among these ranges is a depression in the northwest of Cambodia connecting the country with the lowlands in Thailand; by allowing communication between the two countries, this geographic feature played an important part in the history of the Khmer nation. In eastern Cambodia the land rises to a forested plateau that continues into the Annamite Cordillera, the backbone of neighboring Vietnam.

As the seat of the Khmer empire from the 9th to the 13th century, Cambodia developed a complex society based first on Hinduism and then on Buddhism. After the decline of the Khmers and the ascendancy of the Siamese, Cambodia was colonized by the French, who ruled from the mid 1860s until 1953.

Shortly after the end of World War II, during which the Japanese had occupied Cambodia, independence became the rallying cry for all of Indochina. Cambodia became a sovereign power with a monarchy ruled by King Norodom Sihanouk, who abdicated in favor of his father in 1955 and entered the public stage as a mercurial politician.

In the early 1970s the destabilizing consequences of the Vietnam War sparked a horrible chain of events. The U.S. government secretly bombed Cambodia, arranged a coup to oust the king, and invaded parts of the country in an attempt to rout the Vietcong. Civil war ensued, and in 1975 the Khmer Rouge, led by French-educated Pol Pot, emerged as the victors. A regime of terror followed. Under a program of Mao-Tse-tung-inspired reeducation centered on forced agricultural collectives, the cities were emptied and hundreds of thousands of civilians were tortured and executed. Hundreds of thousands more succumbed to starvation and disease. During the four years of Khmer Rouge rule, somewhere between 1 and 2 million Cambodians—almost one-third of the population—were killed.

By 1979 the country lay in ruins. Vietnam, unified under the Hanoi government, invaded the country in response to a series of cross-border attacks and massacres in the Mekong Delta by the Khmer Rouge. The invasion forced the Khmer Rouge into the hills bordering Thailand, where they remained entrenched and fighting for years. United Nations–brokered peace accords were signed in 1991. International mediation allowed the return of Norodom Sihanouk as king and the formation of a coalition government that included Khmer Rouge elements after parliamentary elections in 1993. But civil war continued.

In 1997 Second Prime Minister Hun Sen toppled First Prime Minister Norodom Ranariddh in a coup. During the following year's national elections, Hun Sen won a plurality and formed a new government, despite charges of election rigging. Pol Pot died in his mountain stronghold in April 1998, and the remaining Khmer Rouge elements lost any influence they still had.

It has taken years for the United Nations and the Cambodian government to establish a tribunal that will bring to justice the few surviving key leaders of the Khmer Rouge regime. Proceedings began in 2007, but only one former Khmer Rouge leader (Duch, the infamous head of Tuol Sleng) is in jail; Ta Mok, the so-called "Butcher," was the only other Khmer Rouge leader to be imprisoned, but he died in 2006. The others remain free; many have blended with ease into current society, and some remain in the folds of the Cambodian government.

Foreign investment and the development of tourism have been very strong in recent years, but it remains to be seen whether domestic problems can truly be solved by Prime Minister Hun Sen and his hard-line rule. In October 2004, Sihanouk's son, Sihamonie, a classically trained ballet dancer, was made King. Sihanouk, a cult figure in Cambodia, died in October 2012.

8

GETTING HERE AND AROUND

Hiring a car and driver in Phnom Penh is perhaps the easiest way to visit Tonle Bati, and if you do this, you can easily combine the trip with Phnom Chisor. The drive takes about 30 minutes. Nearly hourly GST and Neak Krorhorm buses head to Tonle Bati. Buses drop you within walking distance of the lake, but there are also moto-taxis available.

Diethelm Travel *(⇨ Essentials in Phnom Penh)* arranges tours to Tonle Bati.

PHNOM CHISOR

55 km (34 miles) south of Phnom Penh.

A trip to Phnom Chisor is worth the drive just for the view from the top of the hill of the same name. There's a road to the summit, but most visitors prefer the 20-minute walk to the top, where stunning vistas of the Cambodian countryside unfold. At the summit the 11th-century temple, which is free and open to the public, is a Khmer masterpiece of laterite, brick, and sandstone.

GETTING HERE AND AROUND

Though the (decent) bus ride is cheap, you can combine Tonle Bati and Phnom Chisor in one trip if you hire a car and driver (about $50 per day), perhaps the easiest way to visit Phnom Chisor. The drive takes about 20 minutes from Tonle Bati or 40 minutes from Phnom Penh. Takeo-bound GST and Neak Krorhorm buses (departing from Phnom Penh every hour) stop at Prasat Neang Khmau; from there you can hire a moto to take you up the hill. The whole trip should take no more than an hour.

Diethelm Travel *(⇨ Essentials in Phnom Penh)* and Hanuman Travel *(⇨ Cambodia Planner)* arrange tours to Phnom Chisor.

KOH DACH

30 km (19 miles) north of Phnom Penh.

This Mekong River island's main attractions are its beach and its handicrafts community of silk weavers, wood-carvers, potters, painters, and jewelry makers. The beach isn't spectacular by Southeast Asian standards, but it is convenient for Phnom Penh getaways. In all, the trip over to the island is quick; most people spend about half a day on this excursion, but you can dwell longer if you want a relaxing beach day.

GETTING HERE AND AROUND

Any tuk-tuk or moto driver can take you to Koh Dach from Phnom Penh. Alternatively, you can hire a car and driver for the day (about $40 per day). The trip takes approximately two hours each way, and involves a ferry trip to the island.

Diethelm Travel *(⇨ Essentials in Phnom Penh)* and Hanuman Travel *(⇨ Cambodia Planner)* arrange tours to Koh Dach.

UDONG

45 km (28 miles) north of Phnom Penh.

This small town served as the Khmer capital from the early 1600s until 1866, when King Norodom moved the capital south to Phnom Penh. Today it's an important pilgrimage destination for Cambodians paying homage to their former kings. You can join them on the climb to the pagoda-studded hilltop, site of the revered Vihear Prah Ath Roes assembly hall, which still bears the scars of local conflicts from the Khmer Rouge era.

GETTING HERE AND AROUND

Udong is best reached by catching a GST or Neak Krorhorm bus to Kampong Chhnang from the Central Bus Station and getting off at the junction at the Km 37 mark. Motos and tuk-tuks will then take you to the temples. The bus costs around $1.

You can also take a boat from Phnom Penh; this can be arranged through your hotel or any travel agent.

Diethelm Travel, Exotissimo *(⇨ Essentials in Phnom Penh)*, and Hanuman Travel *(⇨ Cambodia Planner)* arrange tours to Udong.

NORTH OF PHNOM PENH

If you're looking to go even farther afield, you can visit the ancient ruins of Kampong Thom or Kampong Cham; see highly endangered freshwater Irrawaddy dolphins at Kratie; or head to the remote and largely undeveloped provinces of Ratanakkiri or Mondulkiri, both of which offer trekking opportunities among hill tribes. The city of Battambang (Cambodia's second largest) may be closer to Siem Reap on the map, but Phnom Penh is the logical jumping-off point for a visit there. Note that many of these destinations are quite removed from one another or accessed via different routes, and thus can't be combined in one tour. ■ TIP➔ During rainy season the road to Ratanakkiri is often hazardous.

KAMPONG CHAM

125 km (78 miles) northeast of Phnom Penh.

Cambodia's third-largest city was also an ancient Khmer center of culture and power on the Mekong River, and it has a pre-Angkorian temple, **Wat Nokor.** (Sadly, the temple itself is in a state of disrepair and the $2 entry fee unmerited.) Just outside town are the twin temple-topped hills, Phnom Pros and Phnom Srei (included in the price). Ask a local guide to explain the interesting legend surrounding their creation. In the ecotourism village of Cheungkok, about 5 km (3 miles) south of town, you can see silk-making, carving, and other traditional crafts in progress and also buy the wares directly from villagers. All profits are reinvested in the village.

Kampong Cham can be visited in a few hours, but with Cheungkok it is an all-day trip.

GETTING HERE AND AROUND

You can get to Kampong Cham from Phnom Penh by taxi or bus; the trip takes about three hours. Any guesthouse or hotel can arrange for a taxi. Expect to pay $6 for a single bus ticket and $50 for a taxi from Phnom Penh. The buses (GST, Hua Lian Mekong Express, and Neak Krorhorm) leave hourly from the bus station at the Central Market.

WHERE TO STAY

Kampong Cham has the usual local food stalls and shophouses, but no restaurants of note.

For expanded hotel reviews, visit Fodors.com.

$ HOTEL 🏨 **Monorom VIP Hotel.** The heavy, sculpted wooden furniture and ruffled curtains of the large rooms may be too much for some, but it's apparent that the owners of this hotel have made a real effort to create a pleasant and polished environment. **Pros:** central, riverside location; comfortable beds; nice views. **Cons:** bored, inattentive staff; no breakfast; not all rooms have views. [$] *Rooms from: $20* ✉ *Mort Tunle St.* ☎ *097/733–2526, 092/777102.*

$ B&B/INN FAMILY 🏨 **Rana.** Rana offers a one-of-a-kind, well-organized experiential homestay for adults or families in the Cambodian countryside. **Pros:** unique window into local life; culturally educational; friendly owners. **Cons:** no electricity; no running water; two-night maximum stay. [$] *Rooms from: $25* ✉ *Srey Siam* ☎ *No phone* 🌐 *rana-ruralhomestay-cambodia.webs.com* 🛏 *2* 💳 *No credit cards.*

KOMPONG THOM RUINS

160 km (99 miles) north of Phnom Penh.

These ruins, exactly halfway between Phnom Penh and Siem Reap, are even older than those at Angkor. They are all that remain of the 7th-century Sambor Prei Kuk, the capital of Zhen La, a loose federation of city-states. The ruins, which are free and open to the public at all times, are near the Stung Sen River, 35 km (22 miles) northeast of the provincial town of Kampong.

GETTING HERE AND AROUND

The ruins are a day trip by taxi from Siem Reap (two hours; $50) or Phnom Penh (three hours; $24, or $6 per person, shared). The journey can be dusty and hot in the dry season and muddy and wet in the rainy season. You can catch a bus to the town of Kompong Thom from Siem Reap ($5) or Phnom Penh ($5), and arrange local transport via tuk-tuk or moto (about $25 for the full tour of the ruins).

KRATIE

340 km (217 miles) northeast of Phnom Penh.

Kratie is famous for the colony of freshwater Irrawaddy dolphins that inhabits the Mekong River some 15 km (9 miles) north of town. ■ **TIP→ The dolphins are most active in the early morning and late afternoon.** Taxis and hired cars from Kratie charge about $10 for the journey to the stretch of river where the dolphins can be observed.

You will likely have to hire a local boatman to take you to where the dolphins are, as they move up and down the river.

GETTING HERE AND AROUND

Several bus companies from Phnom Penh's Central Bus Station offer regular service to Kratie (six to seven hours; $10). Expect delays in the wet season. You can also get a share taxi or hire your own driver, but as always buses are a far safer option.

Diethelm Travel (⇨ *Essentials in Phnom Penh*) arranges tours to Kratie.

WHERE TO STAY

Kratie has an abundance of local food shops. Most guesthouses have simple menus, and there is a lively food-stall scene in town.

For expanded hotel reviews, visit Fodors.com.

$$
RESORT
🏨 **Rajabori Villas Resort.** After the long bus-taxi trip to Kratie, it is another 20 minutes of boat and tuk-tuk to get to Rajabori Villas Resort, so getting here is not for the fainthearted. **Pros:** cheap bike rentals for exploring the island; peaceful location; nature all around. **Cons:** breakfast not included; food and drinks overpriced; getting to and from the resort can be challenging. 💲 *Rooms from: $55* ⊠ *Koh Trong* 📞 *012/770150, 012/959115* ⊕ *www.rajabori-kratie.com* ➘ *10 rooms.*

$
B&B/INN
🏨 **Santepheap Hotel.** Ask for a room with a river view at this hotel across the road from the boat pier. **Pros:** clean rooms; river views from the front rooms; near bus stop. **Cons:** accommodations a little basic; in need of a makeover. 💲 *Rooms from: $6* ⊠ *River Rd., Rue Preah Suramarit St.* 📞 *072/971537* ➘ *24 rooms* ⊟ *No credit cards* ⏏ *Breakfast.*

RATANAKKIRI PROVINCE

8

Ban Lung is 635 km (395 miles) northeast of Phnom Penh.

Both Ratanakkiri and neighboring Mondulkiri provinces are mountainous and covered with dense jungle, and together they are home to 12 different Khmer Loeu ethnic-minority groups. The government has developed four community-based projects in the region. The eventual aim is to reinvent large sections of the area as ecotourism destinations, making them self-sufficient and helping the communities reduce the impact on the natural resources by creating an ecotourism destination.

GETTING HERE AND AROUND

From Phnom Penh there's daily bus service to Ban Lung (12-plus hours; $10) on GST bus lines. The journey is much improved from a few years ago with the opening of the resurfaced road, but construction is still ongoing. Minibuses are faster and only a little more expensive ($13). There are no scheduled flights available, but charter companies do the trip regularly; visit any travel agent for details. Share-taxis are always an option (unattractive as that option may be—it's an arduous drive).

Diethelm Travel (⇨ *Essentials in Phnom Penh*) arranges tours to Ratanakkiri.

In Ban Lung you can hire a jeep (preferably with a driver-guide) or, if you're very adventurous, a motorcycle, to visit the fascinating destinations an hour or two away.

Religion in Cambodia

As in neighboring Thailand, Laos, and Vietnam, Buddhism is the predominant religion in Cambodia. But animism and superstition continue to play strong roles in Khmer culture and society. Many people believe in powerful *neak ta,* or territorial guardian spirits. Spirit shrines are common in Khmer houses as well as on temple grounds and along roadsides. The Khmer Loeu hill tribes, who live in the remote mountain areas of Ratanakkiri and Mondulkiri provinces, and some tribes of the Cardamom Mountains are pure animists, believing in spirits living in trees, rocks, and water.

The main layer of Cambodian religion is a mix of Hinduism and Buddhism. These two religions reached the country from India about 2,000 years ago and played a pivotal role in the social and ideological life of the earliest kingdoms. Buddhism flourished in Cambodia in the 12th to 13th century, when King Jayavarman VII embraced Mahayana Buddhism. By the 15th century, influenced by Buddhist monks from Siam and Sri Lanka, most Cambodians practiced Theravada Buddhism.

Cambodian religious literature and royal classical dance draw on Hindu models, such as the *Reamker,* an ancient epic about an Indian prince searching for his abducted wife and fighting an evil king. Brahman priests still play an important role at court rituals.

Cambodia's Muslim Chams, who number a few hundred thousand, are the descendants of the Champa Kingdom that was based in what is today Vietnam. Many have lived in this area since the 15th century, when they were forced from the original kingdom. The country's 60,000 Roman Catholics are mainly ethnic Vietnamese. A small Chinese minority follows Taoism.

EXPLORING RATANAKKIRI PROVINCE

Ratanakkiri Province is remote, but it is slowly building a reputation as an ecotourism destination, and the government is trying hard to promote tourism to this part of Cambodia. Intrepid travelers will find natural and cultural attractions, including waterfalls, jungle treks, lakes, and villages.

Ban Lung. The provincial capital of Ban Lung is a small, sleepy town. It holds a certain romance as a far-flung capital away from the influence of Phnom Penh, but otherwise offers little more than slow-paced local life and clouds of red dust in the dry season—or mud in the wet season. Arrive with everything you need, as Western goods are sometimes difficult to obtain.

Bokeo. A visit to the gem mines of the Bokeo area, 30 km (20 miles) east of Ban Lung, can be arranged through your hotel, or any moto driver in Ban Lung can take you there. The mines are shallow, mainly for semiprecious stones such as zircon.

Virachey National Park. The lush and scenic jungle of Virachey National Park, 35 km (22 miles) northeast of Ban Lung, is home to the two-tiered Bu Sra Waterfall and lots of wildlife. Tuk-tuks and motos will take you there from Ban Lung ($15). Admission is $5 and all treks and eco-activities should be prearranged in Ban Lung at the park's visitor information center.

Yeak Laom Lake. Mystical Yeak Laom Lake, 5 km (3 miles) from Ban Lung, is sacred to many of the Khmer Loeu hill tribes. Lodged in a volcanic crater, the lake is a half mile in diameter and 154 feet deep. Take a tuk-tuk ($3 round-trip) or moto from Ban Lung.

WHERE TO EAT AND STAY
For expanded hotel reviews, visit Fodors.com.

$$
INTERNATIONAL

✗ **Gecko House Restaurant.** Asian dishes such as curries, sweet-and sour chicken and salads, and western fare such as burgers and sandwiches are decent, if not outstanding. The quirkily contemporary restaurant (check out the gravel floor) turns into a fun bar serving refreshing ice-cold beers most nights of the week, and there is free, speedy Wi-Fi. $ *Average main: $8* ⊠ *Ban Lung,* ☎ *012/422228* ▭ *No credit cards* ☉ *Daily noon–11.*

$$
HOTEL
Fodor's Choice
★

▥ **Terres Rouge Lodge and Restaurant.** The former residence of the governor of Ratanakkiri Province has been transformed into a tranquil, scenic resort with a beautifully landscaped tropical garden. **Pros:** spacious rooms; beautiful, colonial building; good restaurant and bar. **Cons:** limited facilities in rooms; staff somewhat apathetic; some rooms a little rough around the edges. $ *Rooms from: $86* ⊠ *Boeung Kan Siang Lake, Ban Lung* ☎ *012/770650* ⊕ *www.ratanakiri-lodge.com* ⤙ *14 rooms.*

$
B&B/INN
▥ **Yaklom Hill Lodge.** This popular lodge, which prides itself on an eco-friendly philosophy, offers 15 clean, well-cared for wooden cottages and a traditional hill-tribe house in a jungle setting outside the city. **Pros:** lush natural location; friendly staff; ecological. **Cons:** no hot water most of the day; basic facilities only; definitely off the beaten track. $ *Rooms from: $15* ⊠ *Outside Ban Lung* ☎ *011/790510* ⊕ *yaklom.blogspot.com* ⤙ *15 cottages, 1 house* ▭ *No credit cards.*

BATTAMBANG

290 km (180 miles) northwest of Phnom Penh.

Cambodia's second-largest city straddles the Sanker River in the center of the country's rice bowl. Dusty Battambang is bypassed by most visitors to Cambodia, but it's an interesting city to explore. ■**TIP**➜ **The French left their mark here with some fine old buildings, more than you'll find in most Cambodian cities these days.**

GETTING HERE AND AROUND

BUS TRAVEL
All the major bus companies depart daily from Phnom Penh's Central Market to Battambang (five hours; $5–$9), and in some cases, on to Poipet.

BOAT TRAVEL
For the more adventurous, lovely but lengthy boat trips are a good option. The ride to Siem Reap can take anywhere between 5 and 10 hours ($20).

CAR TRAVEL
A hired car with a driver costs about $50 a day, but settle on the price before setting off.

ESSENTIALS

Banks ANZ/Royal Bank Battambang ✉ *2, 4, and 6 St. 1, Svay Poa Commune* 🌐 *www.anzroyal.com.*

Emergencies Makalin Clinic Branch 1 ✉ *Rd. No 1, along Maot Steung St., next to old Spean Dek, 20 Usaphea Village, Sangkat Svay Por* ☎ *012/381376.*

Visitor and Tour Information Capitol Tours ✉ *739 La Ae St., near Boeung Chhouk Market* ☎ *053/953040, 092/277561* 🌐 *www.capitoltourscambodia.com.*

EXPLORING BATTAMBANG

The few sights to see in and around town include some Angkor-era temple ruins and the Khmer Rouge "killing caves." The town is walkable, and strolling down to the river in the evening is a pleasant way to pass the time.

Phnom Banan. In the countryside outside the city is the 11th-century hilltop temple Phnom Banan, with five impressive towers.

Phnom Sampeou. Perhaps Battambang's most interesting site is the mountain, Phnom Sampeou, on which stands a temple and a group of "killing caves" used by the Khmer Rouge. In one, which contains the skeletal remains of some of the victims, you can stand on the dark floor and look to a hole in the cave ceiling with sunlight streaming through. The Khmer Rouge reportedly pushed their victims through that hole to their deaths on the rocks below.

Psar Nath Market. Psar Nath Market, like most local markets, is a decent enough place for souvenir hunting. The market is known for its gems and Battambang's famous fruit, but it also sells everything from fresh produce to electronics imported from China. Some stalls sell textiles, but most of these are imported. ✉ *On the Sangker River* 🕒 *Daily 7–5.*

Wat Ek Phnom. Long before the French arrived, Battambang was an important Khmer city, and among its many temples is an 11th-century Angkorian structure, Wat Ek Phnom. The temple has some fine stone carvings in excellent condition. Get here via tuk-tuk or moto (around $15); negotiate a price before you set out. 🎫 *$2.*

WHERE TO STAY

There is a good selection of restaurants in town, including some western cuisine. The places to eat here are all at the lower end of the price range. A Khmer food market opens down by the river in late afternoon or early evening.

For expanded hotel reviews, visit Fodors.com.

$$ RESORT 🏨 **Battambang Resort.** A small paradise, this tranquil resort has a lush garden where you can find a hammock to relax in among exotic fruit trees and organically grown herbs, flowers, and vegetables, all used by its restaurant to create healthy Asian and European dishes. **Pros:** friendly service; holistic concept; lovely pool. **Cons:** a little out of the way; marriage venue nearby can be noisy; bring mosquito repellent. [$] *Rooms from: $55* ✉ *Wat Ko Village* ☎ *012/510100, 053/666–7001* 🌐 *www.battambangresort.com* 🛏 *10 rooms.*

$ B&B/INN 🏨 **Chez Sam.** This inn is something like a homestay, offering guests the opportunity to get to know the goings-on of the local community

8

through activities and tours guided by the gracious and knowledgeable host Sarom (Sam), a Cambodian who spent a few years living in France. **Pros:** an authentic local experience; well-located; tasty Khmer food. **Cons:** only four rooms; no shower or toilet in-room; not all rooms have a/c. [$] *Rooms from: $10* ✉ *4 Groupe 1 Pong Preah Beit Tchan, Sangkat* ☎ *077/875911* 🛏 *4 rooms* 💳 *No credit cards.*

$$ HOTEL 🏨 **La Villa.** This boutique hotel is in a beautifully restored 1930s colonial house, with well-maintained, spacious rooms that have an old-world charm and quaint art deco feel—all are elegantly embellished with antique furnishings and objets d'art. **Pros:** beautiful architecture; lovely riverfront location; large, clean pool. **Cons:** not many facilities; service can lack attention to detail; could do with some maintenance. [$] *Rooms from: $70* ✉ *185 Pom Romchek 5 Kom* ☎ *017/411880* ✉ *lavilla@online.com.kh* 🌐 *www.lavilla-battambang.net* 🛏 *7 rooms.*

SIEM REAP AND ANGKOR TEMPLE COMPLEX

The temples of Angkor, hailed as "the eighth wonder of the world" by some, constitute one of the world's great ancient sites and Southeast Asia's most impressive archaeological treasure. The massive structures, surrounded by tropical forest, are comparable to Central America's Mayan ruins—and far exceed them in size. Angkor Wat is the world's largest religious structure—so large that it's hard to describe its breadth to someone who hasn't seen it. And that's just one temple in a complex of hundreds.

Siem Reap was once a small, provincial town known only for the nearby Angkor ruins. In recent years it has grown tremendously, becoming a high-profile tourism hub critical to the Cambodian economy.

It's well worth spinning through the countryside around Siem Reap to get a feel for the way Cambodian farmers and fishermen live. Take a day to tour floating villages, some of the outlying temples, or Kulen Mountain, a sacred place for modern Cambodians, with tremendous views. Naturalists won't be sorry with a trip to see the birdlife at Prek Toal, near Tonle Sap, especially when birds are nesting (November or December). Local guesthouses and tour companies can arrange most trips.

SIEM REAP

315 km (195 miles) north of Phnom Penh.

Siem Reap, which means "Siam defeated," based on a 15th-century battle with Cambodia's neighbors to the west, has emerged as a modern, friendly and elegantly low-key city with highly sophisticated shopping, dining, and nightlife options. After a long day at the temples you'll be happy to spend your evening strolling along the Siem Reap River, and dining at an outdoor table on a back alley in the hip old French quarter or Alley West off the more boisterous Pub Street, which is closed to traffic in the evening.

The Old Market area is a big draw and the perfect place to shop for souvenirs; dig through the silk, wood and silver ornaments and accessories

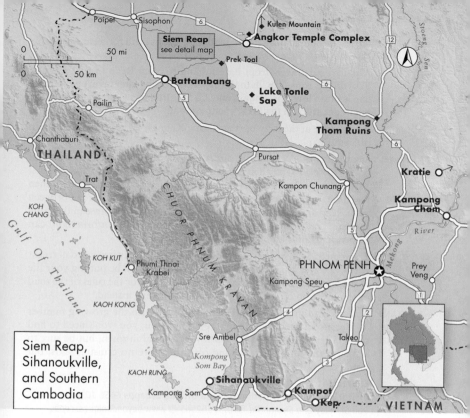

and you may find your treasure. Many of the colonial buildings in the area were destroyed during the Khmer Rouge years, but many others have been restored and turned into world-class resorts and restaurants.

You could spend an entire afternoon in the Old Market area, wandering from shop to shop, café to café, gallery to gallery. It changes every month, with ever more delights in store. Long gone are the days when high-end souvenirs (the legal kind) came from Thailand. Today numerous shops offer high-quality Cambodian silks, Kampot pepper and other Cambodian spices, and herbal soaps and toiletries made from natural Cambodian products.

GETTING HERE AND AROUND

AIR TRAVEL — Bangkok Airways flies six times daily between Siem Reap and Bangkok (one hour; $300 round-trip). Lao Air flies three times a week to Siem Reap from both Pakse (50 minutes; $150 one-way) and Vientiane (80 minutes; also $150 one-way), in Laos. Royal Khmer Airlines and Angkor Air fly between Phnom Penh and Siem Reap (one hour; from $65 and up one-way). Siem Reap International Airport is 6 km (4 miles) northwest of town. The taxi fare to any hotel in Siem Reap is $5.

BOAT TRAVEL — The road to Phnom Penh was upgraded several years ago, but some tourists still prefer the six-hour boat trip on the Tonle Sap. High-speed ferries, or "bullet boats," depart from Phnom Penh for Siem Reap daily (⇨ *Cambodia Planner*).

A daily boat travels from Battambang to Siem Reap (5 to 10 hours; $20) on the Tonle Sap. ⚠ In the dry season, the water level on the Tonle Sap is often low. Passengers may be required to switch boats, or boats might get stuck in the lake, a long ordeal.

Boats arrive at the ferry port at Chong Khneas, 12 km (7½ miles) south of Siem Reap.

BUS TRAVEL Siem Reap is accessible by direct bus from Phnom Penh (five to six hours; $5 to $13) on all major lines, and from Bangkok (10 to 12 hours; $15 and not in one vehicle—the first bus drops you at the border, then you have to navigate your way to Cambodia and on). The road between Siem Reap and the border is usually a slow-moving morass in the rainy season. Neak Krorhorm Travel (⇨ *Visitor and Tour Information*) can help you arrange all bus trips.

CAR TRAVEL The road to Siem Reap from Phnom Penh has greatly improved in recent years, and the trip by taxi is four hours. But you'll be putting your life in the hands of daredevil drivers with little care for the rules of the road or the function of the brake pedal. Take the bus instead.

MOTO AND TUK-TUK TRAVEL Tuk-tuk and moto drivers have kept apace with the growing number of tourists visiting Siem Reap: they'll find you; you won't need to find them. They cost about $1 to $3 for a trip within town, but be sure to settle on the fare before setting off. There are no cruising taxis, but hotels can order one.

ESSENTIALS

Visitor and Tour Information Beyond Unique Escapes ⊠ *St. 10, corner Pub St. Alley and Sivatha Rd.* ☎ *077/562565* ⊕ *www.beyonduniqueescapes. com.* **Hanuman Travel** ⊠ *12 St. 310, Sangkat Tonle Bassac, Phnom Penh* ☎ *023/218356, 012/807657* ✑ *marketing@hanumantourism.com* ⊕ *www. hanuman.travel.* **Neak Krorhorm Travel** ⊠ *127 St. 108, Phnom Penh* ☎ *023/219496.* **oSmoSe Conservation Ecotourism Education** ⊠ *0552, Group 12, Wat Bo Village* ☎ *012/832812* ⊕ *www.osmosetonlesap.net.*

EXPLORING SIEM REAP

Siem Reap is the base to use for exploring the temples at Angkor, however the town does have great places to see in itself. You can wander around the new and contemporary Angkor National Museum, take a cooking class, visit a rural village, explore a myriad of art galleries, try a gourmet restaurant or take a stroll down the central Pub Street. There's plenty to keep the temple-weary traveler occupied for two or three days—in fact today's visitors find themselves lingering on for up to, or over, a week, as there is something seductive about the city.

Fodor's Choice
★ **Angkor National Museum.** This modern, interactive museum (opened in 2008) gracefully guides you through the rise and fall of the Angkorian Empires, covering the religions, kings, and geopolitics that drove the Khmer to create the monumental cities whose ruins are highly visible in modern day Cambodia. With more than 1,300 artifacts on glossy display, complemented by multimedia installations, this museum experience helps demystify much of the material culture that visitors

encounter at the archaeological parks and sites. The atmosphere is set in the impressive gallery of a thousand Buddhas, which plunges you into the serene spirituality that still dominates the region. Seven consequent galleries, set up chronologically, highlight the Funan and Chenia pre-Angkorian epochs, followed by the golden age of the Angkorian period lead by the likes of King Soryavarman II, who built Angkor Wat. The final two galleries showcase stone inscriptions documenting some of the workings of the empires and statues of Apsara, shedding light on the cult and fashions of these celestial dancers. ■ **TIP→ The audio tour is excellent and well worth the extra $2.** ✉ *No. 968, Vithei Charles de Gaulle, Khrum 6, Phoum Salakanseng, Khom Svaydangum* ☎ *063/966601* 🌐 *www.angkornationalmuseum.com* 🎟 *$12* 🕒 *May–Sept., daily 8:30–6; Oct.–Apr., daily 8:30–6:30.*

Cambodia Land Mine Museum. Be sure to visit the Cambodia Land Mine Museum, established by Akira, a former child soldier who fought for the Khmer Rouge, the Vietnamese, and the Cambodian Army. Now he dedicates his life to removing the land mines he and thousands of others laid across Cambodia. His museum is a must-see, a socio-political eye-opener that portrays a different picture of Cambodia from the glorious temples and five-star hotels. Any tuk-tuk or taxi driver can find the museum. When in the Old Market area, visit the Akira Mine Action Gallery for more information on land mines and ways to help land-mine victims go to college. ✉ *Off road to Angkor, 6 km (4 miles) south of Banteay Srey Temple, 25 km (15 miles) from Siem Reap* ☎ *012/598951* 🌐 *www.cambodialandminemuseum.org* 🎟 *$2* 🕒 *Daily 7:30–5.*

WHERE TO EAT

$$ INTERNATIONAL 🍴 **Abacus.** Ideal for a romantic garden dinner or a fun, elegant night out with friends, Abacus offers an eclectic choice of French-international fusion cuisine. Through a menu presented on a giant blackboard (a testament to how it changes weekly), chefs and co-owners Renaud and Pascal combine their creative talents and refined expertise to provide a high-quality, welcome change from traditional restaurants or bland hotel fare. Regulars swear by the juicy Abacus burger, but there are always plenty of options to suit any taste or disposition. The restaurant also has a bar that welcomes guests for an aperitif or a postdinner digestif. [$] *Average main: B14* ✣ *Rd. No. 6 to airport, pass Angkor Hotel, turn right at ACLEDA Bank. After 100m turn left to find restaurant.* ☎ *855/63763660, 855/12644286* 🌐 *cafeabacus.com.*

$$ FRENCH 🍴 **Chez Mathieu.** The compelling draws here are the restaurant's unusual location, which is right across Angkor Wat along a dark dirt road (ideally, ask your tuk-tuk driver to wait as you dine), and its renowned eccentric French owner and executive chef Mathieu, who offers an enjoyable, sometimes unique take on traditional Khmer cuisine, such as the famous Amok curry. Alternatively you can opt to go completely French, sampling imported confit of duck. Though a little overpriced, this place is well worth visiting for a change of scene. For dinner, make sure to book in advance. [$] *Average main: $10* ✉ *Across Angkor Wat (no need for entry card), Trapeang Ses Village* ☎ *012/858003* ✍ *Reservations essential* 💳 *No credit cards.*

8

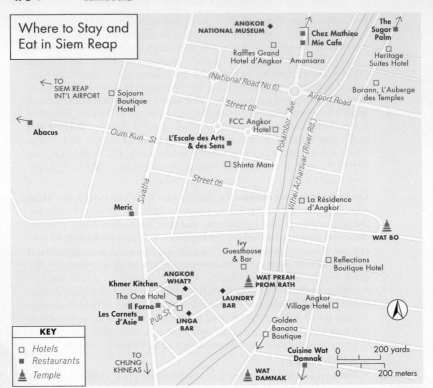

Where to Stay and Eat in Siem Reap

KEY

□ Hotels
■ Restaurants
▲ Temple

$$
ECLECTIC
Fodor's Choice
★   ✕ **Cuisine Wat Damnak.** Cuisine Wat Damnak is one of the most unique restaurants in Siem Reap, offering a real journey for the tastebuds. Beyond the apparent ambition for trendy sophistication in the indoor sala and romantic garden, the concept here is Cambodian food remodeled into creative modern dishes that lead you through a sensory experience. The restaurant serves only two set menus of five to seven dishes each, as created by French chef Joannes Riviere. Exclusively local, fresh, and seasonal ingredients are a grand priority for Riviere, whose knowledge of the area allows him to source ingredients that are otherwise not easy to come by, such as shellfish unique to the Mekong and Tonle Sap lake, fresh lotus seeds, wild lily stems and edible flowers. ■**TIP➜** Interested in learning more about Riviere's culinary philosophy and techniques? Ask for his cookbook, sold in-house. $ *Average main: $26* ⊠ *Between Psa Dey Hoy market and Angkor High School, Commune Svay Kangseng* ☎ *855/77347762* ⊕ *www.cuisinewatdamnak.com* ⌖ *Reservations essential* ⊗ *Closed Sun.–Mon.*

$
ITALIAN   ✕ **Il Forno.** Considered the best Italian eatery and winery in Siem Reap, Il Forno offers an enjoyable change from the Southeast Asian delights on offer at every turn. Just off Pub Street and near the Old Market, this "little corner of Italy" uses its Neopolitan woodfire oven to make delicious pizza and calzone specialties. An authentic variety of pasta dishes, platters for one or for sharing, and primi piatti are also on

offer, all made using quality imported ingredients, and washed down with good regional wines. The stone walls and aged-effect saffron walls are indeed reminiscent of a rustic Italian village, as is the hospitality that creates a warmly familial ambience. $ *Average main: $7 ✉ Pari's Alley, 16 The-Lane, Old Market ☎ 092/238914 ⊕ www. ilfornorestaurantsiemreap.com.*

$ ✕ **Khmer Kitchen.** By now a staple of Siem Reap dining, the newly
CAMBODIAN expanded and very centrally located Khmer Kitchen is basic (in its cuisine as well as its decor) yet pleasantly authentic, serving tasty local dishes and even offering cooking classes to those interested in learning how to prepare some of the traditional dishes they have on offer. Try their fresh spring rolls, Lo Lak beef curry or baked pumpkin among a colorful variety of options. $ *Average main: $5 ✉ Mondul I, Sangkat Svay Dangkum, alley off Pub St ☎ +855/63964154, +855/12763468* ▭ *No credit cards.*

$ ✕ **Mie Cafe.** Mie Cafe reflects the upbeat, forward-thinking new gen-
ASIAN eration of postdisaster Cambodia, represented by its visionary young owner Siv Pola, whose sheer determination to become a chef led him to running his own top-notch restaurant in Cambodia's hottest city. His somewhat out-of-the-way, open-air garden restaurant offers sweet respite from noisier parts of Siem Reap, while the proudly low-budget, basic Asian-chic decor creates a traditional atmosphere with a contemporary twist. Although he also uses imported products, Pola makes fresh, local, seasonal ingredients a priority. Try the popular spicy tuna tartare with mango, and the hot, creamy chocolate cake he learned while training at Doumande Chateaux Vieux, although the more traditional Khmer dishes are also prepared with love, creativity, and skill. $ *Average main: $7 ✉ 0085 Phum Treng, Khum Slorgram ☎ +855/12791371, +855/69999096 ⊕ miecafe-siemreap.com.*

$$ ✕ **The Sugar Palm.** One of the most favorable, no-frills restaurants in
CAMBODIAN Siem Reap, the Sugar Palm is infused with the owner's colorful enthusiasm for traditional Khmer cuisine taught to her by her mother and grandmother. After years in exile in New Zealand during the Khmer Rouge regime, Kethana returned to her homeland determined to create a familial place where diners could enjoy her favorite dishes, such as her uniquely soufflélike fish amok, which is made to order. As you wait, sample a flavorful variety of starters such as crispy shrimp cakes with black pepper sauce or banana blossom salad with chicken. The restaurant is on the second floor of a traditional-style timber house, and its food as well as its airy, modern-traditional atmosphere has drawn all varieties of guests, including superstar chef Gordon Ramsay, who filmed a cooking show here. $ *Average main: $7 ✉ Ta Phul Rd. ☎ +855/12818143, +855/63964838 ☉ Daily 11–11.*

WHERE TO STAY

For expanded hotel reviews, visit Fodors.com.

$$$$ ⊞ **Amansara.** The jewel in the crown of Siem Reap hotels, Amansara
RESORT offers exceptional service, atmosphere, and accommodations in an
Fodor'sChoice ambience of understated luxury. **Pros:** simple yet sophisticated restau-
★ rant menu renewed daily; rooftop open-air cinema; impressive attention to detail by friendly management and staff. **Cons:** a little out of the way;

8

expensive; TV-lovers can't watch in-room. $ *Rooms from: $1000* ⊠ *Road to Angkor, behind Tourism Dept.* ☎ *063/760333* ⊕ *www.amanresorts.com* ↝ *24 suites.*

$$$ **Angkor Village Hotel.** This oasis
HOTEL of Khmer-style wooden buildings, lush gardens, and pools filled with lotus blossoms lies along a stone path a couple of blocks from the river in a green neighborhood. **Pros:** central location and easy access to tuk-tuks; spa with traditional therapies; the hotel organizes activities and trips. **Cons:** road can congest during the rainy season; no TV in-room; some rooms a little rough around the edges. $ *Rooms from: $174* ⊠ *Wat Bo Rd.* ☎ *063/963361* ⊕ *www.angkorvillage.com* ↝ *38 rooms* ⦿ *Breakfast.*

$$ **Borann, l'Auberge des Temples.** The accommodations are attractive and
RESORT the rates reliable at this tranquil, small hotel, a couple of blocks east of the river. **Pros:** large rooms; traditional decor; terrace for every room. **Cons:** small pool; no generator; no TV. $ *Rooms from: $69* ⊠ *Wat Bo St., north of N6, aast of river, behind La Noria* ☎ *063/964242* ⊕ *www.borann.com* ↝ *20 rooms* ⊟ *No credit cards.*

$$$ **FCC Angkor Hotel.** Yet another in a line of resorts with black-and-white
HOTEL decor, the FCC Angkor takes a former French consulate and turns it into an inviting retreat along the river. **Pros:** sleek contemporary design; riverside location; fun crowd. **Cons:** not within walking distance of town; pool area is limited; poor lighting in some rooms. $ *Rooms from: $200* ⊠ *Pokambor Ave. next to Royal Palace* ☎ *063/760280* ⊕ *www.fcccambodia.com* ↝ *29 rooms, 2 suites* ⦿ *Breakfast.*

$ **Golden Banana Boutique Hotel and B&B.** This gem of a getaway is one
B&B/INN of the best budget accommodations around; each room is a duplex—bedroom and bathroom downstairs, and a sitting room upstairs. **Pros:** good prices; friendly staff; good value. **Cons:** not central; poor road access; small swimming pool. $ *Rooms from: $30* ⊠ *Wat Damnak area* ☎ *012/885366* ⊕ *www.goldenbanana.info* ↝ *43 rooms* ⦿ *Breakfast.*

$$$ **Heritage Suites Hotel.** In a quiet neighborhood but still close to the
HOTEL town center, this boutique hotel offers a calm and relaxing stay. **Pros:** quiet atmosphere; good restaurant and bar; good spa facilities. **Cons:** not suitable for families; hidden in Siem Reap's backstreets; service can be sluggish. $ *Rooms from: $185* ⊠ *Wat Polanka* ☎ *063/969100* ⊕ *www.heritagesuiteshotel.com* ↝ *29 rooms.*

$ **Ivy Guesthouse & Bar.** The Ivy offers cheap accommodations at a short
B&B/INN walking distance to most central spots. **Pros:** central location; cheap prices; near all local nightlife. **Cons:** rooms somewhat tatty around the edges; no breakfast included; very basic. $ *Rooms from: $8* ⊠ *Old Market* ☎ *012/800860* ↝ *6 rooms* ⊟ *No credit cards.*

$$$$ **La Résidence d'Angkor.** Swathed in ancient Angkor style, this luxury
RESORT ury retreat is packed into a central walled compound on the river.

There are about 200 faces of Lokesvara, the bodhisattva of compassion, on Bayon's towers.

Pros: attractive riverside location; excellent restaurant; attentive service. **Cons:** out of town; some rooms may have less than spectacular views; can get busy in peak season. [$] *Rooms from: $400* ✉ *River Rd. (east side)* ☎ *063/963390* 🌐 *www.residencedangkor.com* 🛏 *62 rooms* 🍴 *Breakfast.*

$$$$ HOTEL 🏨 **The One Hotel.** The One Hotel has but one suite, but it's on the one street in town where you'd want to be. **Pros:** prime location; ultimate in personal attention; unique experience. **Cons:** must be reserved months in advance; limited space. [$] *Rooms from: $250* ✉ *Pub St. area across from Linga Bar* ☎ *012/755311* 🌐 *www.theonehotelangkor.com* 🛏 *1 room.*

$$$$ HOTEL 🏨 **Raffles Grand Hotel d'Angkor.** Built in 1932 and still featuring the cage elevator from that year in the lobby, this grande dame was restored and reopened after near-destruction by occupying Khmer Rouge guerillas. **Pros:** picturesque gardens; excellent restaurant; nicely designed and decorated. **Cons:** somewhat dependent on their name and former glory; more impersonal than smaller hotels; outside the center of Siem Reap. [$] *Rooms from: $350* ✉ *1 Vithei Charles de Gaulle, Khum Svay Dang Kum* ☎ *063/963888* 🌐 *www.raffles.com/siem-reap* 🛏 *117 rooms* 🍴 *Multiple meal plans.*

NIGHT FLIGHTS

Around sunset, the sky fills with thousands of large bats, which make their homes in the trees behind the Preah Ang Chek Preah Ang Chorm Shrine, near the gardens in front of the Raffles hotel.

\$\$ ☎ **Reflections Boutique Hotel.** From
HOTEL the hotel gate, featuring the lyrics
of John Lennon's "Imagine," to the
sofa in the lobby made of hundreds
of teddy bears, and the masses of
deliberately kitsch overcluttered
artworks and decor details. **Pros:**
bursting with creativity; very central, yet quiet; strong Wi-Fi connection. **Cons:** staff have poor
English; rooms lack finesse; food
prices a little high. $ *Rooms from:
$60* ✉ *0545 Wat Bo St., Sang-
kat Salakamreuk* ☎ *063/6402224*
⊕ *www.reflections-cambodia.com*
🛏 *16 rooms* ⦿ *Breakfast.*

\$\$\$\$ ☎ **Shinta Mani.** Not only will you
HOTEL sleep and eat in luxurious style,
your money will also help support
projects bringing clean water, transportation, and jobs to underprivi-
leged communities, via the Shinta
Mani Foundation. **Pros:** proceeds go to a charitable cause; good location; great facilities. **Cons:** the hotel has been squeezed into a relatively small space; no room service after 11 pm; no disability access.
$ *Rooms from: $200* ✉ *Oun Khum and 14th sts.* ☎ *063/761998*
⊕ *www.shintamani.com* 🛏 *39 rooms.*

\$\$\$ ☎ **Sojourn Boutique Villas.** The layout of these 10 villas, each with a pool
RESORT or garden view, offers privacy and relaxation in lovingly maintained
Fodor's Choice verdant grounds. **Pros:** poolside restaurant serves succulent Khmer spe-
★ cialties; extremely knowledgeable management; quality spa. **Cons:** a
10-minute tuk-tuk ride from town center; you either love or hate the
1980s-style swim-up pool bar; garden not very big. $ *Rooms from:
$200* ✉ *Treak Village Rd., Treak Village* ☎ *+855/12 923 437* ⊕ *www.
sojournsiemreap.com* 🛏 *11 rooms.*

> **THE BEST OF THE BEST**
>
> Reliable international chains have
> begun to open along the road to
> Angkor, and both the dusty airport
> road and the town's noisy thor-
> oughfares are clogged with upper-
> end accommodations. However,
> why settle for a lousy location?
> Siem Reap offers several superb
> options in the quaint and quiet
> river area, where lush gardens
> are the norm and birds and but-
> terflies thrive. Booking a room in
> a high-price hotel in this quarter
> means that your view of the hotel
> pool won't include the neighbors'
> laundry line, and will delight you
> with natural splendor instead of
> traffic jams.

NIGHTLIFE

Most of Siem Reap's nightlife is concentrated around the Old Market,
particularly on vibrant Pub Street, which has become popular. Just get
a little lost, and you're sure to find a hangout that fits your style.

Angkor What? Graffiti-splattered Angkor What? was one of the first
pumping dance clubs in the old quarter, and it still lures in the cool
twentysomethings nightly. Techno, trance, dance, and ambient sounds
hypnotize the crowds and keep them going until the early hours. You
can also graffiti your personal philosophy on the walls. ✉ *Pub St.*
☎ *012/490755.*

Asana. A grown-up playground strewn with hammocks, wooden bar
stools, and tree trunk tables, Asana is uniquely located in the one of
the few remaining old traditional Khmer houses in Siem Reap. The
bar attracts a fun, artsy crowd and hosts live piano performances and

Linga Bar is Siem Reap's first gay-friendly nightlife spot, but it attracts a mixed crowd.

other artistic events. Among a list of regular snacks and drinks, try the signature cocktail—tamarind sauce, made with rum, tamarind juice, kaffir leaf, and lemony rice-paddy herbs. ⊠ *7 Sivatha St., north of Park Hyatt Hotel* ☎ *092/987801.*

Laundry Bar. The Laundry Bar is a favorite among visitors and expats yearning for a place to chill out, far from the madding crowds of Pub Street. It's especially popular for its creative cocktails and funky global sounds. ⊠ *Old Market area* ☎ *016/962026.*

Linga Bar. Known for its inventive cocktails, gay-friendly Linga Bar is named after the archaic phallus that was broadly worshipped in Angkorian times. The bar welcomes a mixed crowd of all ages and hosts regular drag shows and live DJ sets. ⊠ *Pub St. alley, across from John McDermott Gallery Annex, Old Market* ☎ *012/246912, 012/540548* ⊕ *lingabar.com.*

Fodor's Choice **Miss Wong.** A favorite haunt of creative types, eclectic expats and guests ★ from exclusive resorts, this bar stands out with its sexy 1920s Shanghai kitsch aesthetic: red walls, gold lanterns, and low lighting. Immersed in an era of glamorous decadence, guests are easily seduced into tasting cocktails made using local herbs, such as the apricot liqueur and kaffir lime-infused gin martini. Dim Sum and Asian-fusion fingerfood are also on the menu. ⊠ *The Lane* ☎ *092/428332.*

Nest Angkor. For a change of scene head to this restaurant-bar located in a landscaped garden, where guests are invited to sip their designer cocktails lying on canopied loungers. ⊠ *Sivatha Blvd., Siem Reap* ☎ *063/966381* ⊕ *nestangkor.com.*

Picasso Tapas Bar. A real hub for foreign residents, barrel-shape Picasso is a fun option for those who crave a few tasty Spanish tapas dishes to keep them going late into the night. ⊠ *The Alley West, Old Market.*

Fodor'sChoice ★ **The Yellow Submarine.** This off-the-wall, four-story gastropub is the owners' gushing tribute to the Beatles, whose memorabilia and even personal objects such as toys, paintings, and family photos deck practically every surface. Wacky cocktails such as the bubblegum martini are complemented by snacks such as crunchy popcorn-crusted prawns. ⊠ *9A The Lane, Old Market* ☎ *069/509911.*

SHOPPING

Angkor Night Market. A fun, lively flea market to get lost in and practice your bargaining skills in a maze that includes a food hall, massage stands, bars, an enormous variety of clothes, accessories, souvenirs, food and cosmetic products, jewelry and more. ⊠ *Sivatha Blvd. near Pub St.* ⊕ *www.angkornightmarket.com.*

Artisans Angkor. With 38 workshops in Siem Reap, and more than 800 craftspeople employed around the country, Artisans Angkor offers a dazzling selection of Cambodian fine arts and crafts objects, accessories, and silverware from all over Thailand. ⊠ *Stung Thmey St.* ⊕ *www.artisansdangkor.com.*

Eric Raisina. Madagascar-born, French-raised fashion designer Eric Raisina welcomes clients to his atelier, where he presents his impeccably stylish couture designs. The world-acclaimed designer uses stunning Khmer silks to create clothing and accessories that clearly stand a head above the rest. By appointment only. ⊠ *53 Veal Village* ☎ *063/965207* ⊕ *www.ericraisina.com.*

Mekong Quilts. Offering employment opportunities to disadvantaged women, Mekong Quilts sells beautiful handmade, durable quilts of all designs, colors, styles, and sizes. ⊠ *5 Sivutha Blvd., Old Market area.*

Psar Chaa Old Market. Perfect for last-minute shopping, this venue that has everything—from clothes to traditional wood, cloth, and ceramic home decor items, kitschy souvenirs, attractive silverware, clothing, and all varieties of freshly cooked or packaged foods.

Senteurs d'Angkor. This store transforms spices and herbs used traditionally in Cambodia into delightful cosmetic or deli food products. Here you can find Kampot pepper, Rattanakiri coffee, and soaps made with lemongrass, turmeric, jasmine or mango. ⊠ *Opposite Old Market* ⊕ *www.senteursdangkor.com.*

Theam's House. Theam's House specializes in unique lacquerware designs such as polychrome paintings and their trademark colored elephants, as well as elegant traditional wood-carved Buddhas and home decor items. ⊠ *25 Phum Veal* ⊕ *www.theamshouse.com.*

AROUND SIEM REAP

TONLE SAP

10 km (6 miles) south of Siem Reap.

Covering 2,600 square km (1,000 square miles) in the dry season, Cambodia's vast Tonle Sap is the biggest freshwater lake in Southeast Asia. Its unique annual cycle of flood expansion and retreat dictates Cambodia's rice production and supplies of fish. During the rainy season the Mekong River backs into the Tonle Sap River, pushing waters into the lake, which quadruples in size. In the dry season, as the Mekong lowers the Tonle Sap River reverses its direction, draining the lake. Boats make the river journey to the lake from Phnom Penh and Battambang, tying up at Chong Khneas, 12 km (7½ miles) south of Siem Reap. Two-hour tours of the lake, costing $10 to $15, set out from Chong Khneas.

Prek Toal Biosphere Reserve. Between Chong Khneas and Battambang is the Prek Toal Biosphere Reserve, which is mainland Southeast Asia's most important waterbird nesting site. It's a spectacular scene if you visit at the start of the dry season (November and December), when water remains high and thousands of rare birds begin to nest. Visits can be booked through **oSmoSe Conservation Ecotourism Education** (⇨ *Visitors and Tour Information in Siem Reap*). Day tours and overnight stays at the Prek Toal Research Station can be arranged. Prices vary.

GETTING HERE AND AROUND

Boats make the river journey to the lake from Phnom Penh ($30) and Battambang ($20; usually during the wet season, May to October only), tying up at Chong Khneas, 12 km (7½ miles) south of Siem Reap.

Two-hour tours of the lake ($10) set out from Chong Khneas; arrange them at any travel agent in Siem Reap.

Transport to and from the Tonle Sap can be arranged at any hotel or travel agent. Alternatively, ask any tuk-tuk or moto ($7 to $12).

KULEN MOUNTAIN

50 km (31 miles) north of Siem Reap.

King Jayavarman II established this mountain retreat 50 km (31 miles) northeast of Siem Reap in AD 802, the year regarded as the start of the Angkor dynasty. The area is strewn with the ruins of Khmer temples from that time. The mountain was revered as holy, with a hallowed river and a waterfall. Admission to the area costs $20, it is not included in the ticket price to the Angkor Temple Complex.

GETTING HERE AND AROUND

Tuk-tuks, motos, and local taxis can take you to Kulen Mountain; negotiate a price prior to departure, or ask your hotel to handle it (expect to pay around $20 for the trip). The journey should take no more than 50 minutes. Siem Reap tour companies also go here.

8

Continued on page 496

ANGKOR

by Christina Knight

The scale of the ruins, the power of the encroaching jungle, and the beauty
of the architecture have made Angkor one of the world's most celebrated
ancient cities. This was the capital of the mighty Khmer empire (present-day Thailand, Laos, Vietnam, and Cambodia). The vast complex

contains more than 300 temples and monuments that four centuries of
kings built to honor the gods they believed they would become after they
died. It's not just the size of the structures that takes your breath away; it's
the otherworldly setting and a pervading sense of mystery.

THE CITY OF ANGKOR

Silk-cotton tree roots growing over the ruins at Ta Prohm.

CONSTRUCTION

Angkor, which simply means "city," was founded in 839 AD when King Jayavarman II completed the first temple, Phnom Bakheng, using sandstone from the Kulen mountains, northeast of Angkor. Jayavarman II had established the empire in 802, uniting various principalities, securing independence from Java (in present-day Indonesia), and declaring himself the world emperor as well as a "god who is king," or *devaraja*.

Over the next 400 years, each successive Khmer emperor added to Angkor, erecting a *wat*, or temple, to worship either Shiva or Vishnu. The Khmer empire was Hindu except during the rule of Jayavarman VII (1181–1220), who was a Mahayana Buddhist. Theravada Buddhism became the dominant religion in Cambodia after the decline of the Khmer empire, in the 15th century.

Kings situated buildings according to principles of cosmology and numerology, so the center of the city shifted over the centuries. Only the wats, built with reddish-brown laterite, ochre brick, or gray sandstone, have survived; wooden structures perished long ago.

Historians estimate that the royal city had a population of 100,000 in the late 13th century; at that time, London's population was roughly 80,000. The royal city was ringed by a larger medieval city about 3,000 square km (1,150 square mile)—the world's largest pre-industrial settlement and more than twice the size of present-day Los Angeles, with an estimated population of 1 million. At its height, the Khmer empire covered about 1 million square km (400,000 square mile), stretching east from the Burmese border to southern Vietnam and north from Malaysia to Laos.

Archaeologists have only excavated the largest of the hundreds of temples that once dotted the royal city, and even fewer have been restored. The most impressive and best preserved temple, Angkor Wat, is also the world's largest religious monument; it covers approximately 2 square km (¾ square mile), including its moat.

Apsara bas-relief on a wall of Angkor Wat.

Angkor Wat.

DECLINE AND REDISCOVERY

In 1431, Thailand's Ayutthaya kingdom invaded and sacked Angkor. The following year, the declining Khmer empire moved its kingdom to Phnom Penh, 315 km (195 mile) south. Though a handful of foreign adventurers visited Angkor in the following centuries, it wasn't until 1861, when Frenchman and naturalist Henri Mouhot published a book about the site, that Angkor became famous. By this time, looting foreigners and the insistent forces of time and nature had taken a toll on the complex. Restoration efforts began in the early 20th century but were interrupted by the Cambodian Civil War in the 1960s and '70s; in 1992, UNESCO declared Angkor a World Heritage Site. Since that time the number of visitors has risen dramatically to 4 million in 2012. You won't have the place to yourself, but it's unlikely to feel crowded in comparison to famous European sites.

PLANNING YOUR VISIT

Elephant statue at East Mebon.

The sunset from atop Phnom Bakheng.

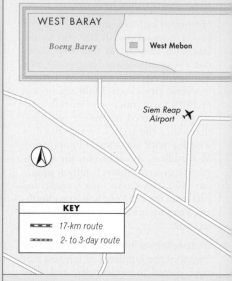
WEST BARAY

Boeng Baray   West Mebon

Siem Reap Airport ✈

KEY
17-km route
2- to 3-day route

You can see most of the significant temples and monuments in a one-day sprint, although a three-day visit is recommended. If you have just one day, stick to a 17-km (11-mile) route that takes in the south gate of Angkor Thom, Bayon, Baphuon, the Elephant Terrace and the Terrace of the Leper King, and Ta Prohm, ending with a visit to Angkor Wat itself in time to catch the sunset. Leave the most time for the Bayon and Angkor Wat.

If you have two or three days, cover ground at a more leisurely pace. You can also tack on additional sites such as Preah Khan, Neak Pean, Pre Rup (a good sunset spot), Phnom Bakheng, or farther-flung Banteay Srei. Another option is East Mebon, a 10th-century ruin in the East Baray, a former reservoir. Alternatively, visit the West Baray, once Angkor's largest reservoir—it still fills with water during the rainy season (June to October).

The best way to experience Angkor is with a guide, who can help you decode the bas-reliefs and architectural styles.

■ TIP→ If you buy your ticket at 5 PM, you'll be admitted for the remaining open hour, in time to see the sunset from Phnom Bakeng or to catch the last rays setting Angkor Wat aglow. Your ticket will also count for the following day.

ESSENTIALS

HOURS & FEES The Angkor complex is open from 5:30 AM to 6 PM. Admission is $20 for one day, $40 for three consecutive days, and $60 for a week. You'll receive a ticket with your photo on it. Don't lose the ticket—you'll need it at each site and to access the restrooms.

WHEN TO GO Most people visit the east-facing temples of Bayon and Baphuon in the morning—the earlier you arrive, the better the light and the smaller the crowd. West-facing Angkor Wat gets the best light in the late afternoon, though these temples can also be stunning at sunrise. You can visit the

Eastern entrance to Banteay Srei.

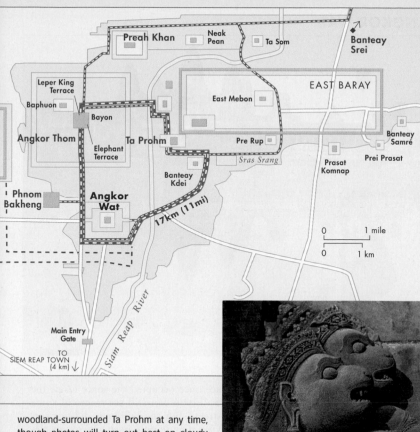

Preah Khan

Neak Pean

Ta Som

Banteay Srei

Leper King Terrace

Baphuon

Bayon

EAST BARAY

East Mebon

Angkor Thom

Ta Prohm

Elephant Terrace

Pre Rup

Banteay Samré

Prasat Komnap

Prei Prasat

Banteay Kdei

Sras Srang

Phnom Bakheng

Angkor Wat

17km (11mi)

0   1 mile

0   1 km

Main Entry Gate

Siem Reap River

TO SIEM REAP TOWN (4 km)

8

IN FOCUS ANGKOR

Bas-relief detail in red sandstone at Banteay Srei.

woodland-surrounded Ta Prohm at any time, though photos will turn out best on cloudy days; the distant Banteay Srei is prettiest in late-afternoon light. If quiet is your priority, beat the crowds by visiting sunset spots in the morning and east-facing temples in the afternoon.

GETTING AROUND The entrance to the complex is 4 km (2 ½ mile) north of Siem Reap; you'll need to arrange transportation to get here and around. Most independent travelers hire a car and driver ($35–50 per day), moto (motorcycle) driver ($12–18), or tuk-tuk ($20–35, seats up to four). Renting bicycles ($3–5) or electric bikes ($5–8) is also an option if you're up for the exertion in the heat. Tourists may not drive motorized vehicles in the park. If you hire a driver, he'll stick with you for the whole day, ferrying you between the sites. However, going with a guide is strongly recommended.

DRESS Skimpy clothes, such as short shorts and backless tops, violate the park's dress code. Shield yourself from the sun with light fabrics, and bring a wide-brimmed hat or even a shade umbrella. Drivers remain with the vehicle so you can leave items you don't want to carry.

ON THE GROUND You'll find food and souvenir stalls inside the park near the temples; children also roam the sites selling trinkets and guidebooks. But you'll get templed out if you don't take a break from sightseeing; consider breaking up the day by swinging back to Siem Reap for lunch or to your hotel for an afternoon rest. Make sure to drink plenty of water, which you can buy inside the park.

ANGKOR WAT

A monk looking at Angkor Wat across the moat.

The best-preserved temple has become shorthand for the entire complex: Angkor Wat, built by King Suryavarman II in the early 12th century. The king dedicated Angkor Wat to Vishnu (the preserver and protector), breaking with tradition—Khmer kings usually built their temples to honor Shiva, the god of destruction and rebirth, whose powers the kings considered more cosmically essential than Vishnu's.

It helps to think of the ancient city as a series of concentric protective layers: a 190-m- (623-ft-) wide moat surrounds an outer wall that's 1,024 by 802 m (3,359 by 2,630 ft) long—walking around the outside of the wall is a more than 2-mi stroll. A royal city and pal-

ace once occupied the space inside the wall; you can still see traces of some streets, but the buildings did not survive. The temple itself sits on an elevated terrace that takes up about a tenth of the city.

APPROACHING THE TEMPLE

You'll reach the temple after crossing the moat, entering the western gateway (where you'll see a 10-foot, eight-armed Vishnu statue), and walking nearly a quarter of a mile along an unshaded causeway. Angkor Wat originally had nine towers (an auspicious number in Hindu mythology), though only five remain. These towers, which took 30 years to complete, are shaped like

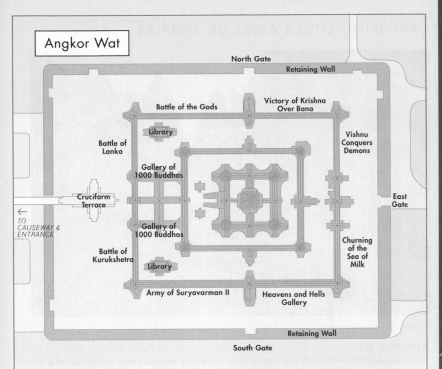

Angkor Wat

North Gate

Retaining Wall

Battle of the Gods

Victory of Krishna
Over Bana

Library

Vishnu
Conquers
Demons

Battle of
Lanka

Gallery of
1000 Buddhas

Cruciform
Terrace

East
Gate

← *TO CAUSEWAY & ENTRANCE*

Gallery of
1000 Buddhas

Churning
of the
Sea of
Milk

Battle of
Kurukshetra

Library

Army of Suryavarman II

Heavens and Hells
Gallery

Retaining Wall

South Gate

closed lotuses and form the center of the temple complex. Their ribbed appearance comes from rings of finials that also take the form of closed lotuses. These finials, along with statues of lions and multi-headed serpents called *nagas*, were believed to protect the temple from evil spirits.

Like the other major monuments at Angkor, the complex represents the Hindu universe. The central shrines symbolize Mt. Meru, mythical home of the Hindu gods, and the moats represent the seven oceans that surround Mt. Meru.

THE GALLERIES

Nearly 2,000 *Apsara*—celestial female dancers—are scattered in bas-relief on the outer entrances and columns of galleries. Inside the shaded galleries, 600 m (2,000 ft) of bas-reliefs tell

Bas-relief depicting a historical Khmer battle.

epic tales from the *Ramayana*, the *Churning of the Sea of Milk* (gods and demons join forces to find the immortality elixir), the punishments of the 32 hells, and the less-imaginative rewards of the 37 heavens.

EXPLORING OTHER ANGKOR TEMPLES

Banteay Srei temple complex.

ANGKOR THOM

King Jayavarman VII built the massive city known as Angkor Thom in 1181 and changed the state religion to Buddhism (although subsequent kings reverted to Hinduism). At the center of the city stands the 12th-century **Bayon**, a large, ornate state temple that rises into many towers (37 remain today), most of which are topped with giant, serene, smiling boddhisattva faces on four sides. These faces, the most photogenic and beatific in all of Angkor, resemble both the king and the boddhisattva of compassion—a Buddhist twist on the king-as-a-god tradition.

On the walls of Bayon's central sanctuary are 1½ km (1 mile) of marvelous bas-relief murals depicting historic sea battles scenes from daily life, and Hindu gods and mythical crea-tures. You can pick out the Khmers in the reliefs because they are depicted with long earlobes; they frequently warred with the Cham, whose warriors wear headpieces that curl towards the jawline. Jayavarman VIII, a later king, added the Hindu iconography and destroyed some of his predecessor's Buddhist statuary.

Just to the north of the Bayon is the slightly older **Baphuon**, which King Udayadityavarman II built in the mid-11th century as part of a small settlement that predated Angkor Thom. The king built the temple on a hill without proper supports, so it collapsed during a 16th-century earthquake. In that same century, a magnificent reclining Buddha was added to the three-tiered temple pyramid, which was originally a Shiva sanctuary. The temple is undergoing reconstruction and is not open to the public; however, the exterior gate and elevated walkway are open.

King Jayavarman VII.

Once the foundation of the royal audience hall, the **Elephant Terrace** is adorned with carvings of *garudas* (birdlike creatures), lion-headed figures, and elephants tugging at strands of lotuses with their trunks.

Located at the north end of the Elephant Terrance, the **Terrace of the Leper King** area is named after a stone statue found here that now resides in the National Museum (⇨ *Phnom Penh, above*); a copy remains here. Precisely who the Leper King was and why he was so named remains uncertain, though several legends offer speculation. (One theory is that damage to the sculpture made the figure look leprous, leading people in later generations to believe the person depicted had been ill.) Today the terrace's two walls create a maze lined some seven layers high with gods, goddesses, and nagas.

TA PROHM

Jayavarman VII dedicated this large monastic complex to his mother. It once housed 2,700 monks and 615 royal dancers. Today the moss-covered ruins lie between tangles of silk-cotton and strangler fig trees whose gnarled offshoots drape window frames and grasp walls. This gorgeous, eerie spot gives you an idea of what the Angkor complex looked like when westerners first discovered it in the 19th century. Another famous mother—Angelina Jolie—shot scenes of *Lara Croft: Tomb Raider* here.

Sculptures of *devas* leading to Angkor Thom.

Two-storeyed pavilion at Preah Khan.

PHNOM BAKHENG

One of the oldest Angkor structures, dating from the 9th century, Bakheng temple was carved out of a rocky hilltop and occupied the center of the first royal city site. Phnom Bakheng is perhaps the most popular sunset destination, with views of the Tonle Sap Lake and the towers of Angkor Wat rising above the jungle. Climb a shaded trail or ride an elephant up the hill. You'll still have to climb steep stairs to reach the top of the temple.

PREAH KHAN

Dedicated to the Jayavarman VII's father, mossy Preah Khan was also a monastery. Its long, dim corridors are dramatically lit by openings where stones have fallen out. Preah Khan is the only Angkor site with an annex supported by rounded, not square, columns.

BANTEAY SREI

This restored 10th-century temple, whose name means "citadel of women," lies 38 km (24 mile) northeast of Siem Reap. Its scale is small (no stairs to climb), but its dark pink sandstone is celebrated for its intricate carvings of scenes from Hindu tales including the Ramayana. The site is at least a 40-minute, somewhat-scenic drive from other Angkor sites; your driver will charge extra to take you here.

GOING WITH A GUIDE

A guide can greatly enrich your visit to Angkor's temples, helping you decode action-packed reliefs and explaining the juxtaposition of Hindu and Budhhist elements at sites that were transformed over the centuries. You can always ask your guide for a little free time; another option is to spend two days with a guide and return on the third day with a tuk-tuk driver to wander solo.

HIRING A GUIDE

The tourism office on Pokambor Avenue, across from the Raffles Grand Hotel d'Angkor, can provide a list of English-speaking guides. The best way to find a guide, however, is through word of mouth. Most guides who work for tour companies are freelancers, and you'll usually pay less if you hire them independently. Find a younger staffer at your hotel or guesthouse and tell him or her what you want to learn and any particular interests. You don't need to worry about ending up with an amateur; only certified, highly trained guides are permitted to give tours. Prices usually run around $30–40 per person (not including transportation) for eight hours with a very well-informed guide fluent in English. Fancy hotels often have guides who work for them fulltime; a day with one of these guides is around $45–55 per person.

If you feel more comfortable booking through a travel company, Beyond

Stupa in the center of Preah Khan.

Unique Escapes, corner of Sivutha Blvd and Alley West ☎ 077562565 ⊕ www.beyonduniqueescapes.com is an excellent choice. The company has established a foundation to help eradicate poverty in rural Cambodia. Their guides are $55 per person per day, but some of your dollars will go towards wells, water filters, and mosquito nets.

WHAT TO EXPECT

Your guide will meet you at your hotel, along with a tuk-tuk or car driver, whom you'll need to pay separately ($12–$15 per day for a tuk-tuk; $25 for a car). Guides, who are almost always men, will typically cater to your interests and know how to avoid crowds. You aren't expected to join your guide for lunch. Usually your driver will drop you and your guide at a temple and pick you up at another entrance, meaning you won't have to double back on yourself.

Bayon temple in Angkor Thom.

8

IN FOCUS ANGKOR

Cambodia's Endangered Species

In an ironic contrast to the Khmer Rouge atrocities, at least some of Cambodia's wildlands and wildlife populations emerged from that period intact, and therefore the country has a far different scenario than that faced by its neighbors, where the rarest of species were expunged years ago.

The Prek Toal Biosphere Reserve is Southeast Asia's most important waterbird nesting site, home to several endangered species. Near Sre Ambel, in what was a Khmer Rouge hotbed, conservationists are working to save the Cambodian royal turtle, which was thought extinct until early

2000s. In Kratie, some of the world's last Irrawaddy dolphins swim the Mekong in another area long held by the Khmer Rouge; and in Mondulkiri, conservationists report an increase in wildlife species in recent years.

The more tourists who express interest in Cambodia's natural environment, the better the outlook for these species and others. The jungles remain threatened by illegal logging (just visit Stung Treng and Ratanakkiri), and poaching is common. But if those in charge begin to see serious tourist dollars connected to conservation, there may be hope yet.

SIHANOUKVILLE AND SOUTHERN CAMBODIA

The beaches of Sihanoukville are quickly becoming a top Cambodian tourist destination (after Angkor, of course). Much of the country's stunning coastal area is currently under intense development, but some parts remain relatively undiscovered, a natural draw for those who tire of the crowds on neighboring Thai islands. Sihanoukville lies some 230 km (143 miles) southwest of Phnom Penh, a four-hour bus ride from the capital.

THE ROAD TO THE COAST

The four-hour bus journey from Phnom Penh to Sihanoukville along Highway 4 is an interesting one, winding through uplands, rice paddies, and orchards. Once you drive past Phnom Penh's Pochentong Airport and the prestigious Cambodia Golf & Country Club, and on through the area of Kompong Speu, the landscape turns rural, dotted with small villages where a major source of income seems to be the sale of firewood and charcoal. Somewhere around the entrance to Kirirom National Park all buses stop for refreshments at a roadside restaurant.

The halfway point of the journey lies at the top of the **Pich Nil mountain pass,** guarded by dozens of colorful spirit houses. These spirit houses were built for the legendary deity Yeah Mao, guardian of Sihanoukville and the coastal region. Legend has it that Yeah Mao was the wife of a village headman who worked in far-off Koh Kong, an island near today's border with Thailand. On a journey to visit him, Yeah Mao died when the boat transporting her sank in a storm—an all-too-believable story to anyone who has taken the boat from Sihanoukville to Koh Kong. Her spirit became the guardian of local villagers and fisherfolk.

At the small town of Chamcar Luang, a side road leads to the renowned smuggling port of Sre Ambel. The main highway threads along **Ream National Park,** with the Elephant Mountains as a backdrop. The national park is a highlight of Sihanoukville, with its mangroves, forests, waterfalls, and wildlife. The park is, unusually for Cambodia, well protected from the vagaries of modern development. The sprawling Angkor Beer brewery heralds the outskirts of Sihanoukville and the journey's end.

GETTING HERE AND AROUND

You can hire a private car and driver through your hotel or guesthouse for the trip to the coast from Phnom Penh. The price varies, but starts at approximately $50, and can be split with other passengers if you prefer. The drive (three to four hours) is often an alarmingly fast and dangerous ride along the well-maintained highway. However, it is common to see tourists who have rented motorcycles in Phnom Penh zipping past.

All major bus companies go to the coast, and Hunaman Traveland oSmoSe Conservation (⇨ *Visitor and Tour Information in Siem Reap)* do tours.

SIHANOUKVILLE

230 km (143 miles) southwest of Phnom Penh.

A half a century ago, Cambodia's main port city, Sihanoukville, was a sleepy backwater called Kampong Som. Then a series of world-shattering events overtook it and gave rise to the busy industrial center and coastal resort now prominent on every tourist map.

The French laid the foundations of Kampong Som back in the mid-1950s, before they lost control of the Mekong Delta and its ports following their retreat after the French-Indochina War. The town was renamed Sihanoukville in honor of the then king. A decade later, Sihanoukville received a further boost when it became an important transit post for weapons destined for American forces fighting in the Vietnam War. In the mid-1970s Sihanoukville itself came under American attack and suffered heavy casualties after Khmer Rouge forces captured the SS *Mayaguez,* a U.S. container ship.

Today Sihanoukville presents a relatively peaceful face to the world as Cambodia's seaside playground. It has seven primary tourist beaches, all easily accessible from downtown by motorbike taxi or even a rented bicycle.

GETTING HERE AND AROUND

Air-conditioned buses from Phnom Penh run several times daily (four hours; $5), departing from the Central Market or the Hua Lian Station near Olympic Stadium. Buses from Bangkok (10 hours; from $25) and other towns on Thailand's eastern seaboard connect to Sihanoukville via Koh Kong.

You can hire a private car and driver through your hotel or guesthouse for the trip to the coast from Phnom Penh (three to four hours; starting at $50 excluding gas). △ The highway to Sihanoukville is one of the most dangerous in the country. Buses are almost as quick and often safer.

KHMER: A FEW KEY PHRASES

A knowledge of French may get you somewhere in francophone Cambodia, but these days it's far easier to find English speakers. The Cambodian language, Khmer, belongs to the Mon-Khmer family of languages, enriched by Indian Pali and Sanskrit vocabulary. It has many similarities to Thai and Lao, a reminder of their years as vassal lands in the Khmer empire.

The following are some useful words and phrases:

Hello: joom reap soo-uh

Thank you: aw-koun

Yes: bah (male speaker), jah (female speaker)

No: aw-te

Excuse me: som-toh

Where?: ai nah?

How much?: t'lay pohn mahn?

Never mind: mun ay dtay

Zero: sohn

One: muay

Two: bpee

Three: bay

Four: buon

Five: bpram

Six: bpram muay

Seven: bpram pull

Eight: bpram bay

Nine: bpram buon

Ten: dop

Eleven: dop muay

Hundred: muay roi

Thousand: muay poan

Food: m'hohp

Water: dteuk

Expensive: t'lay nah

Morning: bprek

Night: youp

Today: tngay nee

Tomorrow: tngay sa-ik

Yesterday: mus'el mun

Bus: laan ch'nual

Ferry: salang

Village: pum

Island: koh

River: tonle

Doctor: bpet

Hospital: moonty bpet

Bank: tia-nia-kia

Post Office: praisinee

Toilet: baan tawp tdeuk

EXPLORING SIHANOUKVILLE

Sihanoukville is a beach town without a center. There is a market area with a surrounding business area that has all the banks and other basic facilities; however, the town's accommodations are spread out along the coast. There is a national park to visit that has mangroves and rivers, and is teeming with birdlife.

Fodor's Choice ★ **Koh Rong Samlem.** The Sihanoukville coast is flanked by several islands (many untouristed and lightly populated by Khmer fishermen) accessible by boat. Koh Rong Samlem, **Koh Tas,** and **Koh Russei** are popular day-trip destinations for snorkeling and picnicking. ■TIP→ Local guides can arrange overnight stays in places like Lazy Beach and other rustic bungalows on some of these islands.

Ream National Park. Ream National Park encompasses 210 square km (81 square miles) of coastal land 16 km (10 miles) north of Sihanoukville, including mangrove forests, the Prek Tuk Sap estuary, two islands, isolated beaches, and off-shore coral reefs. Macaques, pangolin (scaly anteaters), sun bears, and muntjac (barking deer) live in the forest. ⊠ *Airport Rd. (near naga statue), across from entrance to airport* ☎ *012/875096, 016/767686* ✉ *Walking tour $6 for 2 hrs, $10 for 5 hrs, full day boat trip $50* ◷ *Daily 7–5.*

BEACHES

Hawaii Beach. This lovely beach, where the foundations of Sihanoukville were dug in the early 1950s, almost meets the promise of its name. Popular with the Phnom Penh crowd, it quickly gets packed on weekends, but is pleasantly quiet during the week. A huge bridge has just been built connecting the bordering headland with Snake Island, which is a bit of an eyesore. **Amenities:** food and drink; water sports. **Best for:** swimming. ⊠ *Southern end of Victory Beach.*

Independence Beach. Once a local favorite, there is little of the beach actually open to the public anymore. Independence Beach, also known as 7-Chann Beach, is now only accessible at the northern end, but even this 500-meter strip (close to Independence Hotel, after which the beach was named) makes for a nice little oasis away from the crowded Ochheuteal beach. **Amenities:** food and drink. **Best for:** escaping the throngs. ⊠ *In front of Thnou St.*

Ochheuteal Beach. This is the busiest beach in the area, littered with loungers and umbrellas and its fair share of beggars and hawkers. The beach itself is a little narrow and not so clean but there are plenty of activities for the young at heart, as the bars close late every night, and often throw beach parties. After dusk, roadside eateries open up on 23 Tola Street (one of the roads flanking the beach) selling barbecued seafood and meats. **Amenities:** food and drink; water sports. **Best for:** partiers; sunset; swimming. ⊠ *Ochheuteal St.*

Otres Beach. Otres has managed to maintain the natural, peaceful vibe of a truly chilled-out beach holiday. The beach is split into two parts with a beautiful 1½ km of empty beach in between—usually lighted at night and with a paved side-path. Otres I is the busier of the two, with some good bars and restaurants, as well as a smattering of accommodations. Otres II is developing quickly but for now is still the more laid back and peaceful of the two. **Amenities:** food and drink; water sports. **Best for:** swimming; sunsets.

Serendipity Beach. Bordering Ochheuteal, this is a favorite with backpackers. Over the past few years a slew of bungalows, cheap guesthouses, and earthy restaurants have been added to the landscape. The beach is moving upmarket, and there are always rumors, but so far big resort developments have stayed away. **Amenities:** food and drink. **Best for:** partiers. ⊠ *North of Ochheuteal Beach.*

8

Sokha Beach. Some of the best swimming can be enjoyed at Sokha Beach, site of Cambodia's first international-class beach resort, the Sokha Beach Resort. Everyone can access the beach and the beautiful singing sand (it squeaks under foot). Good food can be had at the resort's beachside restaurant. **Amenities:** food and drink. **Best for:** swimming; walking. ⊠ *2 Thnou St.*

Victory Beach. Victory Beach is named after the Vietnamese victory over the Khmer Rouge regime in 1979. It is separated from Hawaii beach by an outcrop on top of which sits the actual victory monument. The beach itself has lots of hotels; it was a popular backpacker spot but now hosts a midrange crowd. Victory Hill, also known as Weather Station Hill, has grown from a small Khmer neighborhood 15 years ago to a bustling sprawl of guesthouses, cafés, pubs, and music dens, much like those on neighboring Thai islands. **Amenities:** food and drink; massage. **Best for:** sunsets; family swimming; water sports. ⊠ *North end of town, in front of Krong St.*

WHERE TO EAT
The most inexpensive guesthouses, restaurants, and other tourist services are on Victory (Weather Station) Hill, Serendipity Beach, and Ochheuteal Beach. Some of the lodgings in these areas are quite attractive, although over the years these locations have become somewhat corrupted by mass tourism.

$$ ╳ **Cafe Sushi.** Fish your own dinner right out of the Gulf of Siam in a
JAPANESE trip arranged by this restaurant. Take a class to learn how to prepare it
FUSION or choose whether to have it grilled or made into a tartare, sushi, nigiri, or tempura. By far the most authentic Japanese food in Sihanoukville, with a menu heavily reliant on the Japanese owner's mood and the fish caught that day, also offering bento boxes, okonomiyaki, and other delights. $ *Average main: $6* ⊠ *25 Ekareach St., Sangkat 4, Khan Mittapheap* ☎ *012/940368* ⊟ *No credit cards.*

$ ╳ **Chhne Meas Restaurant.** Dine on the edge of Victory Beach, next to
SEAFOOD the crashing waves, at this lovely indoor-outdoor Chinese restaurant. All manner of fresh fish and seafood, from stir-frys to clay pots to barbecues and curries, is available. Locals dine here—always a good sign. $ *Average main: $6* ⊠ *Near New Beach Hotel and port* ☎ *012/340060* ⊟ *No credit cards.*

$$ ╳ **The Deck.** In the Sokha Beach Resort, this outdoor beachfront res-
INTERNATIONAL taurant is an idyllic dinner-and-drinks spot, from the dreamy sunset hour to late at night. The tapas menu is innovative and trendy, while Japanese dishes are authentic and refined. A wonderful selection of international wines and inventive cocktails make for a great accompaniment. $ *Average main: $5* ⊠ *Sokha Beach Resort, Street 2 Thnou, Sokha Beach* ☎ *034/935999.*

$ ╳ **Holy Cow.** With an easygoing bar on the ground floor and the restau-
INTERNATIONAL rant above, Holy Cow offers pleasant views of the surrounding garden with a a budget-friendly menu of authentic Khmer and western dishes. $ *Average main: $3* ⊠ *Ekareach St., between Ochheuteal beach and town center* ☎ *012/478510* ⊟ *No credit cards.*

$ ╳ **Manoha.** Simple, unpretentious, Manoha serves French-Khmer cui-
CAMBODIAN sine with a sophisticated air, prepared by a Cambodian chef who likes

to make the best of fresh local ingredients and the catch of the day. Excellent value for the money, with delicate dishes like fish carpaccio and tartare at $3. [$] *Average main: $3* ✉ *Serendipity Beach Rd.* 💳 *No credit cards.*

$ MODERN EUROPEAN 🍴 **Mushroom Point.** A bar-restaurant with a delightfully relaxed atmoshere and the most offbeat architectural style on Otres beach—it looks like a miniscule village of mushroom-shape huts. Great for a sunset aperitif with your toes in the sand followed by a creamy Khmer curry or a large salad. [$] *Average main: $5* ✉ *Otres I Beach* ☎ *097/7124635.*

$ CAFÉ 🍴 **Starfish Bakery and Cafe.** Try a shake, homemade yogurt or brownie, indulge in a massage, and learn about volunteering opportunities in Sihanoukville. The café has Wi-Fi and a handicrafts shop upstairs. It's not the easiest of places to find—it's hidden down a dirt road behind the Samudera Market in town—but it's well worth the trek. It's open from 7 am to 5 pm. Proceeds from this delightful little garden cafe go toward the Starfish Project, which supports individuals in need. [$] *Average main: $4* ✉ *On unmarked road off 7 Makara St.* ☎ *012/952011* 💳 *No credit cards.*

WHERE TO STAY

For expanded hotel reviews, visit Fodors.com.

$ HOTEL 🏨 **Coolabah Hotel.** Apart from its pleasantly simple decor and sense of spaciousness, maybe the best feature of Coolabah is the lovely bistro, where the seafood platter is a highlight of a mainly French-inspired menu that also includes a good wine list. **Pros:** friendly staff; good eats; good value. **Cons:** can get noisy at night; not the best beach; not all rates include breakfast. [$] *Rooms from: $45* ✉ *14 Mithona St., Ochheuteal Beach Road* ☎ *017/678218* 🌐 *coolabah-hotel.com* 🛏 *30 rooms.*

$$ HOTEL FAMILY 🏨 **Don Bosco Hotel School.** As the name suggests, this lodging doubles up as a school for trainees of the service industry, selected from a pool of local underprivileged young adults, but far from feeling like a guinea pig at a training facility, guests enjoy a high level of service and care. **Pros:** big swimming pool; shuttle service to town and beaches; excellent food. **Cons:** inconvenient location; part of a larger complex; somewhat impersonal. [$] *Rooms from: $30* ✉ *Group 13, Sangkat 4, Ou 5* ☎ *034/934478, 016/919834* 🌐 *www.donboscohotelschool.com* 🛏 *23 rooms.*

$$$ HOTEL 🏨 **Independence Hotel.** First opened in 1963 with the interior designed by King Sihanouk, the Independence established itself as the premier destination of the era. **Pros:** wonderful mix of historic and modern design; great views; lush gardens. **Cons:** not necessarily family-friendly; slow service; a little isolated. [$] *Rooms from: $90* ✉ *St. 2 Thnou, Sangkat 3, Khan Mittapheap* ☎ *034/934300 up to 3* 🌐 *www.independencehotel.net* 🛏 *88 rooms.*

$ B&B/INN Fodor's Choice ★ 🏨 **Lazy Beach, Koh Rong.** Jump on the hotel's boat from Ochheuteal Beach at midday and two hours later marvel at this beautiful tropical hideout, made up of wooden bungalows stretched out along the powdery beige sand. **Pros:** peaceful getaway; pretty, natural setting; friendly management and staff. **Cons:** a two-hour boat ride; no electricity; not much to do (except relax). $ *Rooms from: $40* ☎ *016/214211, 017/456536* ⊕ *lazybeachcambodia.com* ⟲ *10 rooms* ⊟ *No credit cards.*

$ · **Orchidee Guesthouse.** This brick-and-stucco lodging is one of Siha-
HOTEL · noukville's oldest and consistently popular choices. **Pros:** great facilities for the price; nice pool; no-smoking rooms. **Cons:** away from the
beach; hot water in the bathrooms not always a given; a little rough
around the edges. $ *Rooms from: $18* ⊠ *Ochheuteal Beach, 23 Tola
St.* ☎ *012/380300, 034/933639* ⊕ *www.orchidee-guesthouse.com* ⟲ *69
rooms* ⊟ *No credit cards.*

$ · **Small Hotel.** If you're looking for a budget hotel in Sihanoukville
HOTEL · town that doesn't cater to bar girls and their clientele, this is it. **Pros:**
small boutique style; clean; family feel. **Cons:** far from the beach;
not the largest rooms; breakfast not in room price. $ *Rooms from:
$20* ⊠ *Behind Caltex station off Sopheakmongkol St.* ☎ *034/6306161*
✎ *thesmallhotel@yahoo.com* ⊕ *thesmallhotel.info* ⟲ *11 rooms* ⊟ *No
credit cards.*

$$$$ · **Sokha Beach Resort.** This is the top address in Sihanoukville, a first-
RESORT · class resort hotel with all the facilities required for a fun-filled beach
FAMILY · holiday. **Pros:** great for families; private beach; nice location. **Cons:**
not geared to romantic getaways; a bit short of the luxury status
it claims; showing some age. $ *Rooms from: $200* ⊠ *Sokha Beach,
2 Thnou St.* ☎ *034/935999* ⊕ *www.sokhahotels.com* ⟲ *188 rooms*
Ol Breakfast.

$$$$ · **Song Saa Private Island.** Barefoot luxury are the buzz words most
RESORT · used to describe Song Saa, the first private island luxury resort in Cam-
Fodor'sChoice · bodia. **Pros:** created with sustainability in mind; surrounding waters
★ · are part of a marine park; discrete staff. **Cons:** isloated; limited acco-
modation so book early; pricey. $ *Rooms from: $1500* ⊠ *Koh Ouen*
☎ *0236/860360, 0239/890009* ✎ *reservations@songsaa.com* ⊕ *song-
saa.com* ⟲ *27 rooms.*

SPORTS AND THE OUTDOORS

Most hotels and guesthouses arrange boat trips, which include packed
lunches, to the many offshore islands. Several companies offer diving
and snorkeling; two of the most popular dive centers are EcoSea Dive
and Scuba Nation.

Contact Information Scuba Nation. Scuba Nation Diving Center was Cambodia's first certified PADI dive center. ⊠ *Mohachai Guesthouse, Serendipity Beach
Rd.* ☎ *012/604680, 034/933700* ⊕ *www.divecambodia.com.*

KAMPOT

*110 km (68 miles) east of Sihanoukville, 150 km (93 miles) south of
Phnom Penh.*

This attractive, if somewhat bland, riverside town at the foot of the
Elephant Mountain range, not far from the sea, is known for its French-
colonial architecture remnants—and for salt and pepper. In the dry
season, laborers can be seen along the highway to Kep, working long
hours in the salt fields; pepper plantations are scattered around the
province. Kampot is the departure point for trips to the seaside resort

Jayavarman VII built Preah Khan in 1191 to commemorate the Khmers' victory over Cham invaders.

of Kep and Bokor Hill Station. The coastal road from Sihanoukville to Kampot is somewhat rough, but has spectacular views. Several limestone caves speckle the landscape from Kampot to Kep to the Vietnam border. Plan at least a morning or afternoon excursion to see the cave at Phnom Chhnork.

GETTING HERE AND AROUND
To get here, take a taxi or bus, or hire a car and driver through your hotel. The journey from Phnom Penh takes approximately four hours. A single bus ticket starts from $4 from Phnom Penh's Central Market. Prices for a taxi or a car with driver start at $30. Hotels are the best source for tour information in and around Kampot.

EXPLORING KAMPOT
Kampot has enough to keep the intrepid traveler busy for a couple of days. The town is sleepy and relaxed, with a wide river marking the center of the town's dining and lodging area. Kampot is the stepping-off point for nearby Kep, and it has rapids and a few caves to explore. Don't forget the world-renowned salt and pepper production. Bokor Hill Station remains the largest draw for visitors and is earmarked for a new spate of development.

Phnom Chhnork Caves. The limestone Phnom Chhnork caves shelter a pre-Angkorian ruin, over which the stalagmites and stalactites are gradually growing. The less appealing cave of Phnom Sia (flashlight required) is more for the fun of exploring in the depths of a cave. The white elephant cave or Cave of Sasear has a shrine where worshippers pray to an elephant-shape limestone formation. ⊠ *On Kampot–Kep rd.*

Phnom Voul Natural Pepper Plantation. Kampot's world-renowned aromatic pepper is sold all around the town and surrounding areas, but there's nothing quite like visiting where it's grown, sampling it right off the plant and paying its producers in person for a certified 100% organic product. One of the most respectable producers is Phnom Voul Natural Pepper Plantation, where you can buy white, red, or black pepper in half- or one-kilogram bags. It's not cheap, but quality is guaranteed. ■TIP➔ As most pepper plantations are in the countryside along dusty, rocky roads, it's best to arrange a taxi ride—tuk-tuks across this kind of terrain can be exhausting. ⊠ *Chom Ka 3 Village, Pong Tek Commune, Domnak Er district.*

WHERE TO EAT

$$ ✕ **Cafe Espresso Kampot.** Caffeine-lovers rejoice, for at Cafe Espresso
CAFÉ you are guaranteed to find the perfect, most elegantly presented cup of coffee. The news gets even better as the coffee beans are locally grown, home roasted, and ground fresh for each order. The café, where you can enjoy free Wi-Fi in a trendy, upbeat atmosphere, also serves fantastic breakfasts and brunches that include delights such as eggs Benedict and bagels. Vegetarians will also be pleased to find exciting options such as tofu or veggie burgers, falafel, crispy dumplings, and Mexican wraps. Ⓢ *Average main: B5* ⊠ *#17 down side street from Epic Arts Cafe* ☎ *092/388736* ⊕ *espressokampot.blogspot.gr.*

$ ✕ **Epic Arts Cafe.** Created as a positive, dynamic means of raising aware-
CAFÉ ness and generating work opportunities for deaf or disabled people in the region, many of whom now work here, Epic Arts Cafe serves a good selection of tasty homemade breakfast, including options like porridge, as well as lunch (try the BLT), dessert, and children's dishes, fresh fruit smoothies and iced coffees brewed from local beans. Ⓢ *Average main: $3* ⊠ *Across new Kampot market, Sovann Sakor, Kompong Kandal* ☎ *033/555–5201* ⊕ *www.epicarts.org.uk* ▭ *No credit cards* ⊙ *No dinner.*

$$ ✕ **La Java Bleu.** Fresh fish sourced daily from the local market and skill-
CAMBODIAN fully barbecued or cooked in other inventive styles is what makes this restaurant, which is in a nicely renovated Chinese building near the river, so popular. The seafood-inspired menu, which does include some meat and chicken dishes, as well as a few vegetarian options, has French and Khmer influences. Try the grilled barracuda or the seafood platter with a good bottle of white from the restaurant's fine international wine selection. Ⓢ *Average main: $7* ⊠ *27 Phoum Ouksophear Sangkat, French Quarter* ☎ *033/6676679.*

$ ✕ **Mea Culpa.** Set in the attractive garden of the Mea Culpa guesthouse,
PIZZA 50 meters from the riverside, this friendly restaurant offers a break from traditional cuisine (although there are well-prepared Khmer dishes on the menu as well) and serves what many consider to be the best pizza in the area, made with a thin, crispy crust in a wood-fired oven. There's also homemade bread, and a choice of tasty salads and starters. Ⓢ *Average main: $8* ⊠ *44 Sovansokar, behind Governor's Mansion* ☎ *012/504769* ⊕ *www.meaculpakampot.com* ▭ *No credit cards.*

$ ✕ **Rikitikitavi.** This cheery second-floor terrace restaurant has a youth-
INTERNATIONAL ful vibe, and serves European and American favorites such as burgers,

bruschetta, and salads, but the cuisine also has a strong Khmer undercurrent; try the creamy Saraman beef curry with peanuts, local herbs, and spices. Many ingredients are seasonal and locally sourced. Vegetarians take note: the only option is very non-Khmer (but tasty) vegetable burritos. Rikitikitavi also rents clean and affordable rooms. $ *Average main: $8* ⊠ *Riverside Rd., next to post office* ☏ *012/235102* ⊕ *www. rikitikitavi-kampot.com* ⊙ *Daily noon–10.*

WHERE TO STAY
For expanded hotel reviews, visit Fodors.com.

$ ⊡ **Blissful Guesthouse.** This two-story renovated colonial house has fan-
B&B/INN cooled rooms (some with attached bathrooms, but with no hot water) with balconies, which are extremely basic but generally clean and at low prices. **Pros:** friendly atmosphere; good for budget travellers; central. **Cons:** away from the riverside; no air-conditioning; no hot water. $ *Rooms from: $4* ⊠ *Across from Orchid Guesthouse, near Acleda Bank* ☏ *092/494331* ✎ *blissfulguesthouse@yahoo.com* ⇥ *9 rooms* ⊟ *No credit cards.*

$ ⊡ **Bokor Mountain Lodge.** Ideally located on the banks of Kampong Bay
HOTEL River in a beautifully restored colonial building, this centrally located boutique hotel offers a handful of clean, spacious, and affordable rooms. **Pros:** nice views; great restaurant; management knowledgeable about the area. **Cons:** more expensive than other nearby budget options; light sleepers may be irked by the noisy next-door pub. $ *Rooms from: $35* ⊠ *Riverfront Rd. near Rusty Keyhole* ☏ *033/932314* ⊕ *www. bokorlodge.com* ⇥ *6 rooms.*

$$ ⊡ **Ganesha Riverside Eco Resort.** Named after the Hindu elephant-headed
RESORT deity who removes and creates obstacles, this little heaven for nature-lovers offers a choice of budget rooms in the main house, tribal huts on stilts, riverside yurts, and a tower (for up to four persons) with glorious 360-degree views of the river, the elephant mountain range, and rice fields. **Pros:** in the heart of nature; good service; yoga and meditation on offer. **Cons:** a little out of the way ($4 tuk-tuk ride); not much to do here. $ *Rooms from: $25* ⊠ *Kampong Krang* ☏ *092/724612* ⊕ *www. ganesharesort.com* ⇥ *8 rooms.*

$ ⊡ **Orchid Guesthouse.** This quiet but quaint little guesthouse on a neigh-
B&B/INN borhood street offers bungalows and a patio in a pleasant garden setting. **Pros:** cheap; friendly staff; free Wi-Fi. **Cons:** away from the river; a little tacky; converted garage room is uncomfortable. $ *Rooms from: $10* ⊠ *Across from Acleda Bank and Blissful Guesthouse* ☏ *092/226996* ✎ *orchidguesthousekampot@yahoo.com* ⊟ *No credit cards.*

KEP

25 km (16 miles) east of Kampot, 172 km (107 miles) south of Phnom Penh.

You'll never find another seaside getaway quite like Kep, with its narrow pebble and sand coastline bordered by the ghostly villa ruins of the Khmer Rouge era. What once was the coastal playground of Cambodia's elite and the international glitterati was destroyed in decades

Cambodia's Early History

The earliest prehistoric site excavated in Cambodia is the cave of Laang Spean in the northwest. Archaeologists estimate that hunters and gatherers lived in the cave 7,000 years ago. Some 4,000 years ago this prehistoric people began to settle in permanent villages. The Bronze Age settlement of Samrong Sen, near Kampong Chhnang, indicates that 3,000 years ago people knew how to cast bronze axes, drums, and gongs for use in religious ceremonies; at the same time, they domesticated cattle, pigs, and water buffaloes. Rice and fish were then, as now, the staple diet. By 500 BC ironworking had become widespread, rice production increased, and circular village settlements were surrounded by moats and embankments. It was at this stage that Indian traders and missionaries arrived—in a land then called Suvarnabhumi, or Golden Land.

Legend has it that in the 1st century AD the Indian Brahman Kaundinya arrived by ship in the Mekong Delta, where he met and married a local princess named Soma. The marriage led to the founding of the first kingdom on Cambodian soil. Archaeologists believe that the kingdom's capital was at Angkor Borei in Takeo Province.

In the 6th century the inland kingdom of Zhen La emerged. It comprised several small city-states in the Mekong River basin. A period of centralization followed, during which temples were built, cities enlarged, and land irrigated. Power later shifted to Siem Reap Province, where the history of the Khmer empire started when a king of uncertain descent established the Devaraja line by becoming a "god-king." This royal line continues today.

of war. Ever so slowly investors are refurbishing what's salvageable; most of the villas were bought in the early 1990s for next to nothing by people now turning them into resorts. When you arrive, tuk-tuk drivers and tour guides are sure to find you. Not much traffic comes through Kep, so the locals know the bus schedule. They're sure to offer you a tour of a nearby pepper plantation, which can be a rewarding experience but also a long, bumpy ride along dusty rural roads (a 4x4 or regular car is a better choice). Kep grows some of the world's best pepper, which you can enjoy in its green, red, black and white phases in a multitude of traditional dishes—the crab with Kampot pepper is especially good.

The beach in town is small and a popular picnic spot for locals who come to relax at the water's edge. Offshore, **Rabbit Island** is a beautiful spot that has attracted a lot of tourists over the last few years, and unfortunately as a result become somewhat polluted. You can hire a boat to take you there for $7 to $10. If you are a true nature adventurer and choose to stay at one of the 30 or so bungalows here, be warned there is no electricity and the wildlife is not for the fainthearted, but the tropical paradise can inspire you to conquer your fears.

GETTING HERE AND AROUND

To get here, take a taxi or bus, or hire a car and driver through your hotel. The journey from Phnom Penh takes approximately 3½ hours. A single bus ticket is $5 from Phnom Penh's Central Market. Hiring a taxi or a car with driver will cost at least $40.

WHERE TO EAT

$ CAMBODIAN 🍴 **The Crab Market.** A strip of simple eateries mainly run by local fishermen and their families can be found in the seafront Crab Market area. Here you can take your pick of these local haunts, each serving tons of fresh seafood dishes—mainly finger lickin' crab—from fresh salads and crunchy patties to succulent, spicy curries starring the famously flavorsome green, red, or black pepper from neighboring Kampot. Ideally, arrive around sunset to watch the fishermen returning with their catch, and to enjoy the mesmerizing colors play on the ocean before tucking into your dinner. Don't expect anything fancy from these basic restaurants; overall, hygeine standards are adhered to, and service is polite. [$] *Average main: $5* ✉ *Phsar Kdam Khan, Kep* 💳 *No credit cards.*

$ INTERNATIONAL FAMILY 🍴 **Sailing Club.** A great way to combine seaside eating and fun, especially for families, the Knai Bang Chatt hotel's Sailing Club is open throughout the day and welcomes all visitors for seafood BBQs, a popular Sunday brunch and light meals as well as beach volley, sailing, Hobie Cat rentals and kayaking. Linger on until the evening to sip a cocktail and take in the stunning sunset views. [$] *Average main: $6* ✉ *Phum Thmey, Sangkat Prey Thom, Kep* ☎ *078/333685* 🌐 *www.knaibangchatt.com* 🕒 *Closed Mon.*

WHERE TO STAY

For expanded hotel reviews, visit Fodors.com.

$ B&B/INN 🏨 **Beach House.** Perched on a hillside overlooking the tree-lined coast, the Beach House offers picturesque perspectives of Kep, the sea, and a nice pool set in pretty gardens. **Pros:** enjoyable saltwater pool and jacuzzi; centrally located; lovely ocean views. **Cons:** lower floor room views obstructed by electrical wires; beach narrow and rocky in places; service can be sluggish. [$] *Rooms from: $40* ✉ *On beach road in central Kep* ☎ *012/712750* 🌐 *www.thebeachhousekep.com* 🛏 *16 rooms* 💳 *No credit cards.*

$$ HOTEL FAMILY 🏨 **Jasmine Valley.** Below the National Park on a jungly mountain near the Vietnam border, Jasmine Valley is an ecologically responsible hotel, which runs completely on solar power that guests can regulate for their own rooms. **Pros:** uniquely eco-friendly; stunning natural location and views; friendly management and staff. **Cons:** no hot water; a little remote; restaurant could be improved. ■ **TIP→ If (you or) your teenager is craving action, Jasmine Valley has built its own skateboarding bowl.** [$] *Rooms from: $30* ☎ *077/599248, 0977/917636* 🌐 *www.jasminevalley.com* 🛏 *10 rooms* 💳 *No credit cards.*

$$$$ RESORT Fodor's Choice ★ 🏨 **Knai Bang Chatt.** Knai Bang Chatt reflects the laissez-faire glamor of Kep in the 1960s and 1970s, when it was a fashionable seaside escape for Cambodian royalty and the international elite. **Pros:** exclusive and luxurious; scenic beach location; old-fashioned elegance. **Cons:** a bit

8

isolated; beach is less than ideal; staff can be slow in clearing things away. ■ **TIP→ Ask to find out about the owner's worthy Hand In Hand education initiatives such as the school created for disadvantaged local children.** [$] *Rooms from: $225* ✉ *Phum Thmey, Sangkat Prey, Thom Khan* ☎ *078/888556* 🌐 *www.knaibangchatt.com* ⇨ *18 rooms.*

$$ RESORT 🏨 **Le Bout du Monde.** The comfortable, attractively furnished, and spacious thatch-roofed bungalows with wraparound balconies are built in traditional Khmer style from local wood and stone and stand on stilts, overlooking magnificent panoramic views of lush landscapes, Bokor mountain and the Gulf of Siam. **Pros:** eco-friendly approach; wonderfully scenic; truly tranquil ambience. **Cons:** in-room humidity can be challenging in wet season; mattresses are a little hard. [$] *Rooms from: $60* ☎ *012/801968* ⇨ *6 rooms.*

LAOS

WELCOME TO LAOS

TOP REASONS TO GO

★ **Natural beauty:** It may not have the sheer variety of Thailand, but Laos is a beautiful country. Take a multiday trek or bike ride, or enjoy the scenic bus ride from Luang Prabang to Vang Vieng.

★ **Archaeological wonders:** The country's most unusual attraction is the Plain of Jars, which has 5-ton stone-and-clay jars of mysterious origin. Wat Phu, pre-Angkor Khmer ruins, is Laos's most recent UNESCO World Heritage Site.

★ **Buddhist customs:** Observing or participating in morning alms in Luang Prabang is a magical experience; so, too, is sitting in a temple to chat with a novice monk, surrounded by the sounds of chanting and chiming bells.

★ **The Mekong:** The Mekong is the lifeline of Laos. You can travel down the mighty river and stop at one of 4,000 islands for a chance to spot freshwater dolphins.

1 Vientiane and Environs. Vientiane is a curiosity—more like a small market town than a national capital—but it has some fine temples, many French-colonial buildings, and a riverside boulevard unmatched elsewhere in Laos. Vang Vieng, a short bus ride north, has beautiful mountains, caves, waterfalls, and a laid-back, rural vibe.

2 Luang Prabang and Northern Laos. Luang Prabang is the country's major tourist destination, thanks to its royal palace (now a museum), temples, French-colonial architecture, and the villagelike ambience it has managed to retain and refine. Hill tribes, Buddhist rituals, and Lao textiles are also major draws of the northern part of the country, as are trekking and river-rafting adventures.

CHINA

VIETNAM

MYANMAR (BURMA)

Muang Sing

Phong Saly

Dien Bie Phu

Luang Nam Tha

Meung

Pak Mong

Oudomxay

Huay Xai

Pak Ou

Pakbeng

2 Luang Prabang

Phonesavanh

PLAIN OF JARS

Vang Vieng

Phu Bic 2820 n

1 VIENTIANE

THAILAND

3 **Southern Laos.** Few tourists venture to the far south of the country, but Pakse is an interesting town and a convenient base from which to explore ancient Khmer ruins, such as the fabulous Wat Phu. Fishing villages line the lower reaches of the Mekong River, a water wonderland with islands, countless waterfalls, and the rare Irrawaddy dolphin.

GETTING ORIENTED

Boxed in by China, Myanmar (Burma), Thailand, Cambodia, and Vietnam, Laos is geographically divided into three regions, each with its chief city: northern Laos and Luang Prabang, central Laos and Vientiane, southern Laos and Pakse. About 90% of Laos is mountainous, so once you leave Vientiane, Luang Prabang, and the southern lowlands you're in true off-the-beaten-track territory. Luang Prabang is the best base for single or multi-day trekking, biking, and river-rafting expeditions.

9

Map of Laos with surrounding regions:

ieng haw

Hua Muang

7

Pakxan

13   8   Khamkeut

Mekong

12

Tha Khaek

VIETNAM

9   9

Savannakhet

River

13

3   BOLAVEN PLATEAU

Pakse

100 mi

100 km

◆ Wat Phu   Attapeu

13

CAMBODIA

Updated by Dave Stamboulis

Despite a limited infrastructure, Laos is a wonderful country to visit. The Laotians are some of the friendliest, gentlest people in Southeast Asia—devoutly Buddhist and traditional in many ways. Not yet inured to countless visiting foreigners, locals volunteer assistance and a genuine welcome.

And because this landlocked nation is so sparsely populated—fewer than 7 million people in an area larger than Great Britain—its countryside is dominated by often impenetrable forested mountains. Laos has a rich culture and history, and though it's been a battleground many times in the past, it's a peaceful, stable country today.

Although Laos has opened itself up to international trade and tourism, it's still a secondary destination on most itineraries. Tourism professionals in Thailand and Laos have been energetically pushing a joint cooperation program, making it considerably easier for visitors to Thailand to plan a side trip to Laos. Much of the Thai part of this program is based in Chiang Mai, from which Luang Prabang and Vientiane are easily reached by air in 60 to 80 minutes. Most travel agents in Chiang Mai can set you up with a tour to Laos for as little as $500 (including airfare). You can also fly to Vientiane and Luang Prabang from Bangkok, or cross the Mekong over bridges at Nong Khai and Ubon Ratchathani, in eastern Isan. Ferries link Chang Kong, in northern Thailand, with the Lao river port of Huay Xai.

PLANNING

WHEN TO GO

Laos has a tropical climate with two distinct seasons: the dry season from November through May, and the rainy season from June to October. The cooler winter months of the dry season (November–February) is the more comfortable time to tour Laos. In the rainy season, road and air travel can be slower and days can get very hot and sticky; August and September see the most rain. But the country is greener and less crowded during the rains and prices are lower.

The yearly average temperature is about 82°F (28°C), rising to a maximum of 100°F (38°C) during the rainy season. In the mountainous areas around Luang Nam Tha, Phonsavan, and Phongsaly, however, temperatures can drop to 59°F (15°C) in winter and sometimes hit the freezing point at night.

Laos has a busy festival calendar and Vientiane and Luang Prabang, in particular, can get very crowded during the most important of these festivals (such as the That Luang Festival in Vientiane in November), so book your hotel room early.

GETTING HERE AND AROUND
AIR TRAVEL
Most of the country's mountainous terrain is impenetrable jungle; the only practical way to tour the country in less than a week is by plane. Bangkok Air has daily flights from Bangkok to Luang Prabang; Thai Air flies to Vientiane; and Lao Airlines runs frequent (and slightly more expensive) flights from Bangkok to Luang Prabang and Vientiane, as well as provincial cities including Pakse and Savannakhet. (⇨ Air Travel in Travel Smart Thailand).

■ TIP➜ A cheap and convenient route to is to fly Air Asia from Bangkok to either Ubon Ratchatani or Udon Thani and then cross the border by land, putting you in Vientiane or Pakse in less than an hour.

BOAT TRAVEL
Running virtually the entire length of the country, the Mekong River is a natural highway. Because all main cities lie along the Mekong, boats offer an exotic but practical way to travel. The most popular water route is between Huay Xai (on the Thai border) and Luang Prabang (⇨ River Journey to Huay Xai). More adventurous travelers can board boats in Huay Xai or Pak Tha to travel up the Nam Tha River to Luang Nam Tha. Two luxury vessels ply the Mekong: the Vat Phu (⇨ Pakse) and the Luang Say (⇨ River Journey to Huay Xai).

BUS TRAVEL
A network of bus services covers almost the entire country. Though cheap, bus travel is slow and not as comfortable as in Thailand. VIP buses, which connect Vientiane, Luang Prabang, and Pakse, are somewhat more comfortable—they have assigned seats and more legroom, and make fewer stops. Minivans have also become common between cities, and are priced about the same as buses and a bit quicker, not to mention they pick up directly from hotels. ■ TIP➜ There are now sleeper buses between Vientiane and Pakse, though beds are less than 6 feet long and tall folks may want to buy both spots (in what is essentially one shared small bed).

CAR TRAVEL
Although it's possible to enter Laos by car or motorbike and drive around on your own, it's not recommended, as driving conditions are difficult: nearly 90% of the country's 14,000 km (8,700 miles) of roads are unpaved; road signs are often indecipherable; and accidents will invariably be considered your fault. A better alternative is to hire a car and driver for about $50 per day.

9

SONGTHAEW AND TUK-TUK TRAVEL

Tuk-tuks and songthaews cruise the streets and are easy to flag down in most towns. Lao tuk-tuk drivers can be unscrupulous about fares, especially in Luang Prabang and Vientiane. ■TIP→ Do not believe the "official" prices placard displayed by drivers in Vientiane. Don't get into a tuk-tuk before you've agreed on a fare and don't negotiate in dollars (get a quote in kip or baht). Finally, never pay more than you would for a comparable ride in Thailand.

BORDER CROSSINGS

In addition to the international airports in Vientiane, Luang Prabang, and Pakse, there are numerous land and river crossings into Laos. The busiest is the Friendship Bridge, which spans the Mekong River 29 km (12 miles) east of Vientiane. Other border crossings from Thailand to Laos are: Chiang Khong to Huay Xai (by ferry across the Mekong River); Nakhon Phanom to Tha Khek; Mukdahan to Savannakhet; and Chongmek to Vang Tao. You can also enter Laos from Cambodia at Voeung Kam; and from Mohan, in China's Yunnan Province, at Boten.

Border crossings are open daily 8:30 to 5, except for the Friendship Bridge, which is open daily 6 to 10.

MONEY MATTERS

The currency is the Lao kip (LAK), which comes in relatively small notes (the largest denomination equals about $12). Though the kip has stabilized in recent years, and most prices are now listed in kip, we've chosen to list all hotel rates in U.S. dollars. The Thai baht is accepted in Vientiane, Luang Prabang, and border towns. It's best to carry most of your cash in dollars or baht and exchange relatively small amounts of kip as you travel. At this writing, the official exchange rate is approximately 260 kip to the Thai baht and 8,000 kip to one U.S. dollar.

There are now ATM machines throughout the country so changing money isn't a big issue anymore.

Credit cards are accepted in most hotels and some restaurants, but few shops. Banks in major tourist destinations will provide a cash advance on a MasterCard or Visa, typically for a 5% service charge. Western Union has branches in Vientiane and other major towns.

HEALTH AND SAFETY

⚠ Laos's health care is nowhere near to Thailand's. If you will be traveling extensively, consider buying international health insurance that covers evacuation to Thailand.

Take the same health precautions in Laos that you would in Thailand (⇨ *Health in Travel Smart Thailand*). Pharmacies are stocked with Thai antibiotics and often staffed with assistants who speak some English. Vientiane is malaria-free, but if you're visiting remote regions, consider taking prophylactics. HIV is widespread in border areas. Reliable Thai condoms are available in Laos.

Laos is fairly free of crime in tourist areas. Pickpocketing is rare, but you should still be careful in crowded areas. Never leave luggage unattended.

Penalties for drug possession are severe. Prostitution is illegal, and $500 fines can be levied against foreigners for having sexual relations with Lao citizens (how this is enforced is unclear, but even public displays of affection may be seen as shady behavior).

⚠ In the countryside, trekkers should watch out for unexploded ord-nance left over from the Vietnam War, especially in Xieng Khuang and Hua Phan provinces, and in southern Laos. Don't wander off well-trav-eled trails. Better yet, trek with a qualified guide. Do not photograph anything that may have military significance, like airports or military installations.

PASSPORTS AND VISAS

You'll need a passport and a visa to enter Laos. Visas are now available on arrival at most entry points, but if you're taking the cross-border bus to Vientiane from Udon Than or Nong Khai in Thailand, you'll need to get a visa in advance. You can do this at the Lao embassy in Bang-kok (⇨ *Getting Here and Around in Vientiane*) or consulate in Khon Kaen in an hour or through an embassy or travel agency before you leave home. Tourist visas are good for 30 days, cost $35 for Americans, and can be paid for in U.S. dollars (if you are buying a visa at the Lao border or in a Lao embassy or consulate in Thailand, you can pay in baht, but you will be charged B1,500 which is much more than $35). You'll need to have two passport-size photos (one photo if buying at the border) with you—bring these from home or get them in Bangkok. In the past Lao border officials have been able to accommodate trav-elers who don't have extra photos for an additional fee. Occasionally immigration officials ask to see evidence of sufficient funds and a plane ticket out of the country. Showing them credit and ATM cards should be proof enough of funds. ⚠ Regulations change without warning, so check with the Lao embassy in your own country before setting out.

Lao Embassy (Bangkok) ✉ *502/502/1–3 Soi Sahakarnpramoon, Pracha Uthit Rd., Wangthonglang, Bangkok, Thailand* ☏ *02/539-6667* ⊕ *www.laoembassybkk. com.*

TOUR OPERATORS

Travel agents in Chiang Mai can set you up with any number of tour packages.

Diethelm Travel. Diethelm Travel is one of the oldest and most-respected travel agencies offering package trips to Laos, and a good source for travel information and tours in Laos. ✉ *Kian Gwan II Bldg., 140/1 Wireless Rd., Bangkok, Thailand* ☏ *02/660–7000* ⊕ *www. diethelmtravel.com* ✉ *Setthathirat Rd. at Nam Phu Fountain Sq., Vien-tiane* ☏ *021/215129, 021/215920.*

Green Discovery Laos. Green Discovery Laos is the top eco- and adven-ture-tour operator in Laos, offering a staggering array of adventure, eco, and cultural tours throughout the country with well-trained guides and is the best source for local information. ✉ *54 Setthathirat Rd., Nam Phou, Vientiane* ☏ *021/223022* ⊕ *www.greendiscoverylaos.com.*

9

Lao Youth Travel. Lao Youth Travel does tours around Laos and can answer questions. ✉ *024 Fa Ngum Quay, Ban Mixay, Vientiane* ☎ *021/240939* ⊕ *www.laoyouthtravel.com.*

National Tourism Authority of the Lao People's Democratic Republic. The National Tourism Authority of the Lao People's Democratic Republic has offices in Vientiane and all other provinces in Laos; they provide some printed materials, and try their best to be helpful, but you are probably better off going to private travel agencies for more detailed information. ✉ *BP 3556, Ave. Lane Xang, Vientiane* ☎ *021/212248, 021/212251* ⊕ *www.tourismlaos.org.*

RESTAURANTS

For such a sleepy, somewhat-off-the-beaten-path country, Laos has some excellent dining options. Choices in Luang Prabang and Vientiane are endless (high-end French restaurants, Japanese, Thai, Indian, and pizza, not to mention fantastic bakeries and coffee shops). In smaller spots you may have to make do with sticky rice and grilled meats or fish, but most towns do have at least one or two fancier places with decent menus. Lao food is similar to Thai, but not quite as spicy or varied. Vietnamese pho noodles can be found in most spots, and the same goes for baguette sandwich vendors, which are a convenient option for bus trips.

Prices in the reviews are the average cost of a main course at dinner or, if dinner is not served, at lunch.

HOTELS

Luang Prabang has some of the most elegant resorts in the world. Vientiane also has a classic colonial luxury hotel, a few boutique options, and several business-style hotels of international standards. Otherwise, fancy resorts in Laos are few and far between, though there are perfectly adequate facilities in Pakse and the Plain of Jars. New resorts are starting to spring up, but in the more off-the-beaten-path spots like Phongsaly, Muang Ngoi, 4,000 Islands, things like Wi-Fi or cable TV are not guaranteed, and in some spots hot water or even 24-hour electricity may be missing.

Prices in the reviews are the lowest cost of a standard double room in high season.

VIENTIANE AND ENVIRONS

Vientiane is not only the capital of Laos but also the logical gateway to the country, as it's far more accessible to the outside world than Luang Prabang. The city sits along the Mekong River, with Thailand just across the water. A 20-minute ride by taxi or tuk-tuk brings you to the Friendship Bridge, which links Laos and Thailand. Crossing the bridge is a mere formality. On the Thai side of the bridge is the riverside frontier town of Nong Khai, which has direct rail services to Bangkok and a bus terminus serving the Thai capital and most cities in eastern Isan. Many tourists choose this route from Thailand into Laos, although Vientiane is easily and cheaply reached by air from Bangkok, Chiang Mai, and most Southeast Asian cities.

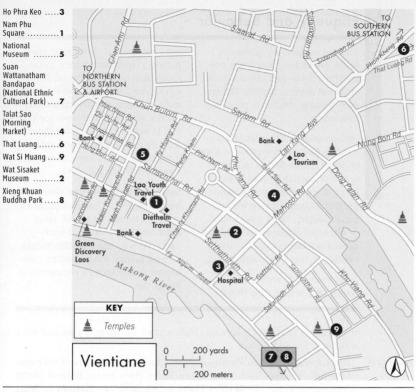

VIENTIANE

Vientiane is the quietest Southeast Asian capital, with a pace as slow as the Mekong River, which flows along the edge of town. It doesn't have the kind of imposing sights you find in Bangkok, but neither does it have the air pollution and traffic jams. That's not to say that Vientiane isn't changing at all—though there are still many more bicycles and scooters than cars on its streets, several of the main thoroughfares are beginning to bustle.

The abundance of ugly cement-block buildings in urgent need of paint gives the town a superficially run-down appearance, but scattered among these eyesores are some remnants of elegant French colonial architecture. There are also dozens of temples—ornate, historic Buddhist structures that stand amid towering palms and flowering trees. First-time visitors often find Vientiane a drab, joyless city, but you only have to arrive in the midst of the weeklong That Luang Festival in November to be reminded that first impressions can be misleading.

GETTING HERE AND AROUND

AIR TRAVEL Vientiane's Wattay International Airport is about 4 km (2½ miles) from the city center. You can take a metered taxi from the airport into the city for 60,000 kip; get a taxi voucher from the kiosk in the arrivals hall. The ride to the city center takes about 15 minutes. Alternatively,

Etiquette and Behavior

Laotians are generally gentle and polite, and visitors should take their lead from them—avoiding any public display of anger or impolite behavior. Even showing affection in public is frowned-on.

Laotians traditionally greet others by pressing their palms together in a sort of prayer gesture known as a *nop*; it is also acceptable for men to shake hands. If you attempt a nop, remember that it's basically reserved for social greetings; don't greet a hotel or restaurant employee this way. The general greeting is *sabai di* ("good health"), invariably said with a smile.

Avoid touching or embracing a Laotian, and keep in mind that the head has spiritual significance; even patting a child affectionately on the head could be misinterpreted. Feet are considered "unclean," so when you sit, make sure your feet are not pointing directly at anyone, and never use your foot to point in any situation. Shoes must be removed before you enter a temple or private home, as well as some restaurants and offices.

Shorts and sleeveless tops should not be worn in temple compounds. When visiting a temple, be careful not to touch anything of spiritual significance, such as altars, Buddha images, or spirit houses. Ask permission from anyone before taking a photograph of him or her.

---

if you don't have much luggage, walk out of the airport gate and take a tuk-tuk for 40,000 kip.

BUS TRAVEL The best way to get to Vientiane from Thailand via bus is to take one of the hourly buses from either Udon Thani (two hours; B80) or Nong Khai (one hour; B55). ■TIP→ These buses take you straight to Talat Sao, Vientiane's Morning Market, but you cannot board them unless you already have a Lao visa.

If you don't have an advance visa, you can take a bus from Udon Thani to Nong Khai, then a tuk-tuk to the border (B30 to B50), cross the Friendship Bridge on a B20 shuttle bus, and take a taxi (B350), tuk-tuk (B150), or public bus (B20) from the Lao side of the border into Vientiane.

The Northern Bus Terminal for trips to and from northern Laos is 3 km (2 miles) northwest of the center, while southern buses leave from the Southern Bus Station, which is out on Highway 13. The Talat Sao (Morning Market) Bus Station handles local departures.

Although there's city bus service in Vientiane, schedules and routes are confusing for visitors, so it's best to stick to tuk-tuks and taxis. The city bus station is next to the Morning Market.

TAXI AND TUK- You can cover Vientiane on foot, but tuk-tuks and jumbos, their larger
TUK TRAVEL brethren, are easy to flag down. Be sure to negotiate the price before setting off; you can expect to pay about 20,000 to 40,000 kip for a ride within the city if you are a firm negotiator. Taxis are available, but must be reserved, which you can do through your hotel or at the Morning

Market. For day trips outside the city, ask your hotel or guesthouse to book a car with a driver.

SAFETY AND PRECAUTIONS

Vientiane is very safe, but beware of being taken to the cleaners by tuk-tuk drivers. Ask a local for correct fares.

TIMING

Vientiane does not have an abundance of sights aside from That Luang and a few other monuments. However, it has a wonderfully sleepy ambience, quaint restaurants, and is a good place to enjoy creature comforts and a Beerlao on the Mekong before heading out into the wilds. Most people stay just a few days; if you throw in some day trips to Nam Ngun or nearby national parks, you could make it a few more. Vientiane is also the place to take care of any business (onward visas, fax and computer connections, etc.).

EMERGENCIES

Mahosot Hospital International Clinic in Vientiane is the best medical center in the country. ■TIP➔ For anything major, consider crossing the border to Thailand and going to Wattana Hospital in Nong Khai or Udon Thani.

ESSENTIALS

Air Contacts Lao Airlines ☎ *021/212050 up to 4 for international flights, 021/212057, 021/212058 for domestic flights* ⊕ *www.laoairlines.com.* **Thai Airways International** ☎ *021/222527 up to 29 in Vientiane* ⊕ *www.thaiair.com.*

Banks Bank of Lao PDR. Bank of Lao PDR has Western Union transfer services. ✉ *Nam Phou Square* ☎ *021/213300, 021/213301* ⊕ *www.bol.gov.la.* **Banque Pour le Commerce Exterieur Lao (BCEL)** ✉ *Pang Kham Rd., 1 block south of Nam Phu Square* ☎ *021/213200* ⊕ *www.bcellaos.com.*

Car-Rental Agency Eurocar ✉ *Setthatirat Rd. at Wat Mixay, Ban Mixay* ☎ *021/217493, 021/223867* ✎ *info@europcar.com* ⊕ *www.europcarlaos.com.*

Emergencies Mahosot Hospital International Clinic ✉ *Fa Ngum Quay* ☎ *021/214018.* **Wattana Hospital in Nong Khai** ✉ *1159/4 Moo 2, Prajak Rd., Nongkhai* ☎ *042/465201 up to 8* ⊕ *admin@wattanahospital.net.* **Wattana Hospital in Udon Thani** ✉ *70/7–8 Suppakitjunya Rd.* ☎ *042/325999* ⊕ *www.wattanahospital.net.* **U.S. Embassy** ✉ *Rue Bartholoni* ☎ *021/267000, 021/212581.*

Visitor and Tour Information Diethelm Travel ✉ *Setthathirat Rd. at Nam Phu Fountain Sq.* ☎ *021/215920, 021/215129* ⊕ *www.diethelmtravel.com.* **Green Discovery Laos** ✉ *54 Setthathirat Rd., Nam Phou* ☎ *021/223022, 021/218373* ⊕ *www.greendiscoverylaos.com.* **Lao Youth Travel** ✉ *039 Fa Ngum Quay, Ban Mixay* ☎ *021/240939* ⊕ *www.laoyouthtravel.com.*

EXPLORING VIENTIANE

Laos's capital is a low-key, pleasant city thanks to its small size, relative lack of traffic, and navigable layout. Outside of That Luang, there aren't too many must-sees, but the promenade along the Mekong and the wats scattered throughout town are great to explore by bicycle. Good restaurants and old French colonial architecture make it an enjoyable place to stop for a day or two.

TOP ATTRACTIONS

Ho Phra Keo. There's a good reason why Ho Phra Keo, one of the city's oldest and most impressive temples, has a name so similar to the wat in Bangkok's Grand Palace. The original Ho Phra Keo here was built by King Setthathirat in 1565 to house the Emerald Buddha, which he had taken from Chang Mai in Thailand. The king installed the sacred statue first in Luang Prabang and then in Vientiane at Ho Phra Keo, but the Buddha was recaptured by the Siamese army in 1778 and taken to Bangkok. The present temple was restored in 1936, and has become a national museum. On display are Buddha sculptures of different styles, some wonderful chiseled images of Khmer deities, and a fine collection of stone inscriptions. The masterpiece of the museum is a 16th-century lacquered door carved with Hindu images. ⊠ *Setthathirat Rd. at Mahosot St.* ☎ *021/212621* ≊ *5,000 kip* ⊙ *Daily 8–noon and 1–4.*

> ### THE RISE OF THE MOON CITY
>
> Originally named Chanthaburi (City of the Moon), Vientiane was founded in the 16th century by King Setthathirat near a wide bend of the Mekong River, on the grounds of a Khmer fortress dating to the 9th to 13th centuries. In 1828 the Siamese army from Bangkok razed the city. But the old part of Vientiane is still an attractive settlement, where ancient temples that survived the Siamese attack, museums, and parks are all just a short distance from one another.

Talat Sao (Morning Market) (*Morning Market*). To truly immerse yourself in Vientiane, visit this vast indoor bazaar that is, despite its name, actually open all day. The bright, orderly emporium holds everything from handwoven fabrics and wooden Buddha figures to electric rice cookers and sneakers. Most of the shops cater to locals, but there's still plenty to interest travelers: handicrafts, intricate gold-and-silver work, jewelry, T-shirts, and bags and suitcases to accommodate all your extra purchases. Many products are imported from abroad. Fruits, confections, and noodle soups are sold at open-door stalls outside, where Vietnamese shoemakers also ply their trade. The market, which is near the main post office, is now housed in a brand new department store, Laos' first, and spills out into the surrounding area. ⊠ *Lane Xang Ave. at Khu Vieng St.* ⊙ *Daily 7–6.*

That Luang. The city's most sacred monument, this massive, 147-foot-high, gold-painted stupa is also the nation's most important cultural symbol, representing the unity of the Lao people. It was built by King Setthathirat in 1566 (and restored in 1953) to guard a relic of the Buddha's hair and to represent Mt. Meru, the holy mountain of Hindu mythology, the center and axis of the world. Surrounding the lotus-shape stupa are 30 pinnacles on the third level and a cloistered square on the ground with stone statues of the Buddha. The complex is flanked by two brilliantly decorated temple halls, the survivors of four temples that originally surrounded the stupa. On the avenue outside the west gate stands a bronze statue of King Setthathirat erected in the 1960s by a pious general. ■ TIP→ That Luang is the center of a major weeklong

Lao Festivals

Laos has many fascinating festivals, quite a few of which are steeped in Buddhism. Be sure to book hotels in advance if you're planning on visiting during festival time, particularly in the big cities.

Bun Bang Fai: The Rocket Festival is held in the middle of May. Rockets are fired and prayers are said in the paddy fields to bring rain in time for the planting of the rice seedlings.

Bun Khao Padab Din: This is a special rice ceremony held in August (the exact date depends on the harvest schedule). People make offerings at local temples to keep alive the memory of spirits who have no relatives.

Bun Khao Salak: This is a similar rice ceremony in September (the exact date depends on the harvest schedule), wherein people visit local temples to make offerings to their ancestors. Boat races are held on the Mekong, especially in Luang Prabang and Khammuan Province.

Bun Ok Pansa: The day of the full moon in October marks the end of Buddhist Lent, and is celebrated with donations to local temples. Candlelight processions are held, and colorful floats are set adrift on the Mekong River. The following day, boat races are held in Vientiane, Savannakhet, and Pakse.

Bun Pimai: Lao New Year takes place April 13 to 15. This is a water festival

similar to Thailand's celebrated Songkran, when all the important Buddha images get a cleaning with scented water (and the general public gets wet in the bargain). The festivities are particularly lively in Luang Prabang.

Bun Visakhabucha (Buddha Day): On the day of the full moon in May, candlelight processions are held in temples to mark the birth, enlightenment, and death of the Buddha.

That Ing Hang Festival: This takes place in Savannakhet in December, and lasts several days on the grounds of the ancient Wat That Inhang, just outside the city. There are performances of traditional Lao music and dance, sports contests, and a spectacular drumming competition.

That Luang Festival: This is a week-long event in Vientiane in November, which ends with a grand fireworks display. Hundreds of monks gather to accept alms. The festival runs concurrently with an international trade fair showcasing the products of Laos and other countries of the Greater Mekong Subregion (GMS).

Wat Phu Festival: Also known as Makhabucha Day, this festival is held during the day of the first full moon in February at Wat Phu, near Champasak. A full schedule of events includes elephant races, buffalo fights, cockfights, and traditional Lao music-and-dance performances.

9

festival during November's full moon. It's on the north end of town (a 10-minute songthaew ride from the center). The monument is also short songthaew ride away from the riverside. Be sure to head to the riverbank in the late afternoon to experience one of Vientiane's most spectacular sights—sunset over the Mekong. ⊠ *North end of That Luang Rd.* 🚍 *5,000 kip* ⊙ *Daily 8–12 and 1:30–4.*

Thai invaders destroyed That Luang in 1828; it was restored in the 20th century.

Xieng Khuan Buddha Park. The bizarre creation of an ecumenical monk, Luang Pa Bunleua Sulilat, who dreamed of a world religion embracing all faiths, this park is "peopled" by enormous Buddhist and Hindu sculptures spread across an attractive landscape of trees, shrubs, and flower gardens. Keep an eye out for the remarkable 165-foot-long sleeping Buddha. The park was laid out by the monk's followers in 1958 on the banks of the Mekong, opposite the Thai town of Nong Khai. Get there by taking public bus no. 14 from the Talat Sao bus station. ⊠ *Km 27–28 on Tha Deua Rd.* 📧 *5,000 kip, 3,000 kip camera fee* 🕙 *Daily 7–6.*

WORTH NOTING

Nam Phu Square (*Fountain Square*). An attractive square with a nice but nonfunctioning circular fountain in the middle, this used to be one of several reminders in the city of French colonial influence—reinforced further by the presence on the square's perimeter of some very Gallic restaurants. Unfortunately the central square has been renovated and the fountain is now part of a fancy new restaurant. However, the surrounding plaza still contains many eateries with some charm.

National Museum. A modern, well-laid-out, two-story building houses interesting geological and historical displays. Exhibits touch on Laos's royal history, its colonial years, and its struggle for liberation. The museum also highlights the country's 50 main ethnic groups, and indigenous instruments. ⊠ *Sam Sen Tai Rd.* ☎ *021/212460, 021/212461, 021/212462* 📧 *10,000 kip* 🕙 *Mon.–Sat. 8–noon and 1–4.*

Suan Wattanatham Bandapao (*National Ethnic Cultural Park*). The attraction at this park near the river (and 20 km [12 miles] from Vientiane near the Thai border) is a model village of miniature Lao houses. Sculptures of Lao heroes dot the grounds. There's also a small zoo in one corner. Take a short stroll downstream and admire the sleek lines of the Friendship Bridge and pop into one of the many restaurants lining the riverbank. Get here with public bus no. 14 from the Talat Sao bus station. ✉ *Km. 20 on Tha Deua Rd.* 🎫 *5,000 kip* 🕓 *Daily 8–4.*

Wat Si Muang. This wat, built in 1956, guards the original city pillar, a revered foundation stone dating to the 16th century. In a small park in front of the monastery stands a rare memorial to Laos's royal past: a large bronze statue of King Sisavang Vong. ✉ *Setthathirat Rd. and Samsenthai Rd.* 🎫 *Free* 🕓 *Daily 7–5.*

Wat Sisaket Museum. This interesting museum complex is made up of a crumbling temple and monastery compound across the road from Ho Phra Keo. Built in 1818 by King Anu, the temple survived the destruction of the city by the Siamese army in 1828. The monastery stands intact in its original form, and is one of the most frequented in the city. Inside the main compound the courtyard walls have hundreds of little niches and large shelves displaying 6,840 Buddha statues. Although it's in need of more work, the impressive temple hall underwent some restoration in 1938. The paintings that once covered its interior walls have largely been destroyed by the ravages of time, but the intricately carved wooden ceiling and doors are still intact. There's also an intriguing wooden library that stores palm-leaf manuscripts. ✉ *Setthathirat Rd. at Mahosot St.* ☎ *021/212622* 🎫 *5,000 kip* 🕓 *Daily 8–noon and 1–4.*

WHERE TO EAT

$ ECLECTIC 🍴 **Khop Chai Deu.** A French-colonial structure houses this very popular downtown restaurant and bar, which serves as an excellent meeting point for happy-hour cocktails or dinner. The long menu is crammed with Lao, Asian, and international dishes, and a daily buffet is also served. For a tasty introduction to traditional Lao cuisine, try the Lao Discovery, a set menu including *larb,* a semi-spicy salad; *tom yum,* a sour chili-and-lemongrass fish soup; *khao niaw,* Lao sticky rice; and a glass of *lao-lao* (rice whisky). Draft beer is on tap, live music plays in the bar nightly, and the kitchen is open until 11. [$] *Average main: $10* ✉ *54 Setthathirat Rd.* ☎ *021/263829* 🌐 *www.inthira.com.*

$ LAO 🍴 **Kualao.** In a fading mansion one block southeast of Nam Phu Square, this is one of Vientiane's best Lao restaurants. The food is quite good, and the vast menu ranges from *mok pa fork* (banana-leaf-wrapped steamed fish cooked with eggs, onions, and coconut milk) to *gaeng panaeng* (a thick red curry with chicken, pork, or beef). Servings are small, so most people order several entrées or set menus with seven to nine dishes, plus dessert and coffee. Photos and English descriptions facilitate the ordering process. There's Lao folk dancing nightly from 7 to 9. [$] *Average main: $10* ✉ *134 Samsenthai Rd.* ☎ *021/214813* 🌐 *www.kualaorestaurant.com* 🕓 *Daily 3–5.*

$$$ FRENCH Fodor's Choice ★ 🍴 **La Signature.** For truly fine dining in Vientiane, visit the charming new La Signature, located in a hidden lane in the boutique Ansara Hotel. Serving authentic French cuisine in a romantic garden setting, sample the degustation menu, which features grilled salmon and foie gras, or indulge in a Canard Deux Façons, fried duck and foie gras. There are

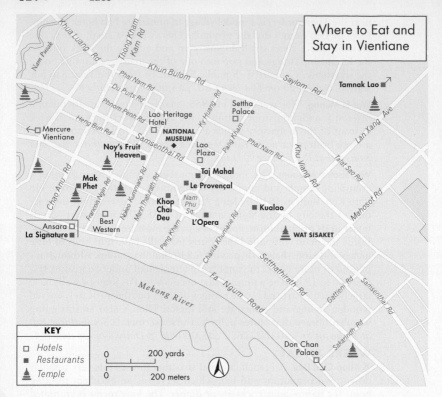

Where to Eat and Stay in Vientiane

KEY

☐   *Hotels*
■   *Restaurants*
▲   *Temple*

daily chef's plates along with an excellent selection of fine wines to complement your meal. $ *Average main: $17* ✉ *Box 622, Quai Fa Ngum, Ban Vat Cham Tha, Hom 5, Vientiane* ☎ *021/213514* ⏱ *Daily 11:30–2 and 6:30–9:30.*

$$ ✕ **Le Provençal.** A local family that lived in France for many years runs
FRENCH   this little bistro behind Nam Phu Square. Chef Daniel's menu is almost exclusively French, although there's a hybrid pizza à la française. Try the beef-based terrine du maison to start, then sink your teeth into chicken niçoise, frogs' legs à la lyonnaise, or fillet of fish à la Provençale. Save room for such desserts as crème caramel and chocolate mousse. On sunny days you can sit on the terrace overlooking the square. $ *Average main: $12* ✉ *73/1 Pang Kham Rd.* ☎ *021/219685* ⏱ *Daily 11:30–2 and 5–10. No lunch Sun.*

$$ ✕ **L'Opera.** Vientiane's best Italian restaurant serves authentic pastas,
ITALIAN   baked entrées, and fresh salads. Try the Pizza de Laos (made with chilies and Lao sausage) if you're in the mood for fusion. There are also espresso and cappuccinos, plus an extensive wine list to choose from. Tables at the small front terrace look out on all the action on Nam Phu Square. $ *Average main: $12* ✉ *PO Box 5575, 12 Nam Phu Fountain Sq.* ☎ *021/215099.*

$ ✕ **Mak Phet.** This nonprofit restaurant serves modern Lao food. Its prof-
LAO   its go to providing street kids with an education or some sort of training.

Lao Cuisine

CLOSE UP

It may not be as famous as Thai food, but Lao cuisine is similar and often just as good, though usually less spicy. Chilies are used as a condiment, but Lao cuisine also makes good use of ginger, lemongrass, coconut, tamarind, crushed peanuts, and fish paste. Because so much of the country is wilderness, there's usually game, such as venison or wild boar, on the menu. Fresh river prawns and fish—including the famous, massive Mekong catfish, the world's largest freshwater fish—are also standard fare, along with chicken, vegetables, and sticky rice.

As in Isan, *larb* (meat salad with shallots, lime juice, chilies, garlic, and other spices) is a staple, as are sticky rice and *tam mak hu,* the Lao version of green-papaya salad. Grilled chicken, pork, and duck stalls can be found in every bus station and market in the country. Northern Laos, especially

Luang Prabang, is noted for its distinctive cuisine: specialties include grilled Mekong seaweed, sprinkled with sesame seeds and served with a spicy chili dip; and *orlam,* an eggplant-and-meat stew with bitter herbs. Sticky rice, served in bamboo baskets, is the bread and butter of Laos. Locals eat it with their hands, squeezing it into a solid ball or log and dipping it in other dishes.

Throughout the country you'll find *pho,* a Vietnamese–style noodle soup, served for breakfast. Fresh baguettes, a throwback to the French-colonial days, are also available everywhere, often made into sandwiches with meat pâté, vegetables, and chili sauce. Laotians wash it all down with extra-strong Lao coffee sweetened with condensed milk, or the ubiquitous Beerlao, a slightly sweet lager.

The restaurant is staffed and run by the very people that past profits have helped. The food is excellent; the staff well-trained, happy, and motivated. Eating here is one big feel-good story! $ *Average main: $10* ⊠ *Behind Wat Ong Teu, parallel to Sethathirat Rd.* ☎ *021/260587* ⊙ *Mon.–Sat. 11–9, Tues. and Thurs. closed 2–6.*

$ **✕ Noy's Fruit Heaven.** This cute little café serves up gourmet sandwiches,
CAFÉ such as imported feta, Camembert, or goat cheese melted onto fresh baguettes, and various breakfast options, as well as any sort of tropical fruit smoothie you can dream up. The lively owner Noy also rents bicycles, sells traditional crafts, and gives impromptu Lao lessons upon request. A great hangout spot to meet other travelers. $ *Average main: $4* ⊠ *Heng Boun Rd., Ban Haysok* ☎ *030/996–0913* ▭ *No credit cards.*

$ **✕ Taj Mahal.** People in the know love this slightly hidden away and
INDIAN nondescript Indian eatery that serves knockout food at ridiculously cheap prices. Excellent tandoori naan breads, a good selection of dal and meat and fish curries, and other northern Indian favorites top the wide array of menu choices. $ *Average main: $2* ⊠ *Setthathirath Rd. behind Cultural Hall, Chantabury* ☎ *020/5561–1003.*

$ **✕ Tamnak Lao.** Classical Lao dances are performed every evening at this
LAO fine outdoor restaurant specializing in the cuisine of Luang Prabang. Many dishes, such as the *pla larb* (minced fish with herbs), are prepared with fish fresh from the Mekong River. Note that dinner service doesn't

begin until 6. $ *Average main: $10* ✉ *100 That Luang Rd., Ban Phon Xay* ☎ *021/413562.*

WHERE TO STAY

For expanded hotel reviews, visit Fodors.com.

$$$
B&B/INN
Fodor's Choice
★
🏨 **Ansara Hotel.** Vientiane's newest upscale property, the Ansara is a charming small boutique hotel in a small quiet lane near the Mekong River and all attractions. **Pros:** extremely quiet; free laptop notebooks in room; free minibar replenished daily. **Cons:** expensive; a bit hard to find the first time around; lack of extra amenities (swimming pool, spa, etc). $ *Rooms from: $133* ✉ *Box 622, Quai Fa Ngum, Ban Vat Cham Tha, Hom 5, Vientiane* ☎ *021/213514* ⊕ *www.ansarahotel.com* ⇔ *14 rooms* ❄ *Breakfast.*

$$
HOTEL
🏨 **Best Western Vientiane.** With a convenient location in the heart of town near the Mekong River, and comfort at competitive rates, this hotel is popular with business travelers. **Pros:** fitness center and Jacuzzi; quiet pool area; great location near river and restaurants. **Cons:** small pool; no views; rooms feel slightly worn. $ *Rooms from: $77* ✉ *2–12 Francois Nginn Rd., Ban Mixay* ☎ *021/216906 up to 09* ⊕ *www.bestwesternvientiane.com* ⇔ *44 rooms* ❄ *Multiple meal plans.*

$$$$
HOTEL
🏨 **Don Chan Palace.** The tallest building in Laos, Don Chan Palace has spectacular views of Vientiane and of Thailand across the Mekong River. **Pros:** fantastic river views; large fitness center and pool; abundant and attentive staff. **Cons:** pool area is covered and doesn't get sun; isolated; way overpriced for value. $ *Rooms from: $180* ✉ *Unit 6, Piawat Village* ☎ *021/244288* ⊕ *www.donchanpalacelaopdr.com* ⇔ *230 rooms* ❄ *Breakfast.*

$
B&B/INN
🏨 **Lao Heritage Hotel.** Set in a quaint restored colonial home on a quiet side street, the Heritage Hotel offers teak-floored traditional rooms above a lovely peaceful garden. **Pros:** quiet neighborhood; lovely garden; a real colonial feel. **Cons:** rooms on the small side; some rooms lack windows and are dim; hotel hard to find (on small side street that many tuk-tuk drivers don't know). $ *Rooms from: $23* ✉ *125 Phnom Penh Rd., Anou Village* ☎ *021/265093, 020/550–5840* ⊕ *www.laoheritagehotel.com* ⇔ *9 rooms* ▬ *No credit cards* ❄ *Breakfast.*

$$$$
HOTEL
🏨 **Lao Plaza.** Something of a local landmark, Lao Plaza stands six stories tall in the center of town. **Pros:** large swimming pool and terrace; enormous beds; great central location. **Cons:** way overpriced for what you get; on very busy street; constant hassle from tuk-tuk drivers outside. $ *Rooms from: $188* ✉ *63 Samsenthai Rd, PO Box 6708* ☎ *021/218800, 021/218801* ⊕ *www.laoplazahotel.com* ⇔ *142 rooms* ❄ *Breakfast.*

$$$
HOTEL
🏨 **Mercure Vientiane.** Although Vientiane's Mercure is a five-minute drive from the airport, it has a pleasant location in front of Fa Ngum Park. **Pros:** tennis courts; one of the few hotels in Laos that have all amenities, good Web discounts. **Cons:** out of town center; on very busy road; expensive. $ *Rooms from: $103* ✉ *Unit 10, Samsenthai Rd., Vientiane* ☎ *021/213570* ⊕ *www.accorhotels-asia.com* ⇔ *172 rooms.*

$$$$
HOTEL
Fodor's Choice
★
🏨 **Settha Palace.** This colonial landmark has been through many changes: it was built by the French at the turn of the 19th century, converted into a hotel in the 1930s, and expropriated by the communist government in the 1970s. **Pros:** elegant and private; gorgeous furnishings; beautiful

pool garden. **Cons:** often fully booked; no elevator; only four stan-dard rooms. $\boxed{\$}$ *Rooms from: $152 $\boxtimes$ 6 Pang Kham Rd. $\textcircled{a}$ 021/217581, 021/217582 $\oplus$ www.setthapalace.com $\rightleftharpoons$ 29 rooms $\lozenge$ Breakfast.*

NIGHTLIFE

The after-dark scene in Vientiane is very subdued, mostly confined to some of the more expensive hotels and a handful of bars and pubs along the Mekong River boulevard.

Bor Pen Yang. Vientiane's most popular bar (and also a restaurant), Bor Pen Yang occupies a prime spot on the Mekong, with great views from the rooftop setting, music, international cuisine, and plenty of beer and cocktails. Most nights it's packed with locals and travelers. $\boxtimes$ *Fah Ngum Quay, Ban Wat Cham* $\textcircled{a}$ *021/261373.*

The Bowling Alley. Believe it or not, the bowling alley on Khun Bulom Road, around the corner from Settha Palace, is a happening after-hours spot, serving food and drinks to a rowdy mix of locals, expats, and travelers. It is open from 9 until midnight. $\boxtimes$ *Khun Bulon Rd.* $\textcircled{a}$ *021/218661.*

Jazzy Brick. In a town not known for highbrow nightlife, Jazzy Brick is a welcome addition. Full of rattan chairs, a sophisticated vibe, and a staggering drink menu (150 cocktails!), the brick-and-wood-paneled club is popular among foreign NGO workers and does occasionally host live jazz, as well as staying open until the wee hours. Shorts and sleeveless tops are not allowed here. $\boxtimes$ *038 Setthathirat, Vientiane* $\textcircled{a}$ *021/771–1138.*

SHOPPING

Caruso Lao. For exquisite handwoven Lao silk and fine wood carvings, head to one of Lao's best craft shops, Caruso, on the riverside near the Don Chan Palace Hotel. $\boxtimes$ *008 Fah Ngum Quai, Ban Phiavath, Vientiane* $\textcircled{a}$ *021/223644 $\oplus$ www.carusolao.com.*

Carol Cassidy Lao Textiles. Lao handwoven silk is world renowned; Carol Cassidy Lao Textiles, a beautiful weaving studio housed in an old French home, sells some particularly high-quality fabrics, as well as scarves, shawls, and wall hangings. Open Monday to Saturday 8 to noon and 1 to 5. $\boxtimes$ *84–86 Th. Nokeo Khumman* $\textcircled{a}$ *021/212123* $\oplus$ *www.laotextiles.com.*

Phaeng Mai Silk Gallery. Phaeng Mai Silk Gallery, located in the old weaving district, is another shop with handwoven silk. Open Monday to Saturday from 8 to 5. $\boxtimes$ *110 Ban Nongbuathong Tai* $\textcircled{a}$ *021/243121.*

Small and Medium Enterprises Promotion Center (*SMEPC*). If you're still looking for that something special and you can't find it at Talat Sao, try the Small and Medium Enterprises Promotion Center handicrafts center. $\boxtimes$ *Phokheng Rd.* $\textcircled{a}$ *021/416736.*

Talat Sao (*Morning Market*). With crafts, jewelry, T-shirts, and more, the Talat Sao should satisfy all your shopping needs. The new indoor shopping mall area also has tons of mobile phone sellers and plenty of electronics. $\boxtimes$ *Lane Xang Ave. at Khao Vieng St.*

NAM NGUM LAKE

90 km (56 miles) north of Vientiane via Phonhong on Hwy. 13.

Nam Ngum Lake. Forested mountains surround this island-dotted reservoir lake, which is accessible by car from Vientiane. Floating restaurants here serve freshly caught lake fish, and there's a large hotel complex, the Dansavanh Nam Ngum Resort. Visitors who have built substantial amounts of time into their itineraries to explore Laos may want to skip this trip as there are others that are far better. But those who only have a few days in the country will enjoy this side trip as a way to see a bit of Laos's countryside without having to travel too far from Vientiane. You can get here by time-consuming public transport, but its better to take a tour. Green Discovery Laos (⇨ *Laos Planner)* offers excellent day trips that include a boat ride on the lake.

GETTING HERE AND AROUND

There is public transport from Talat Sao Bus Station to the "Talat" bus stop where songthaews continue on to Nam Ngun (15,000 kip) that take about three hours, but to really take in the area, it is best to do an adventure tour with Green Discovery Laos. Hiring a car and driver will run upward of $60 per day. If you're driving, take Highway 10 north from Vientiane to the Lao Zoo; from there, follow the road for the Dansavanh Resort.

SAFETY AND PRECAUTIONS

This is a safe place, but visitors should take the usual precautions with valuables.

TIMING

This trip is best done as a day tour, but if you have extra time, spend the night and take advantage of the many lodges in this area.

ESSENTIALS

Tours and Packages Green Discovery Laos ✉ *54 Setthathirat Rd., Vientiane* ☎ *021/223022, 021/218373* ⊕ *www.greendiscoverylaos.com.*

PHU KHAO KHOUAY

40 km (25 miles) northeast of Vientiane on Hwy. 10

Phu Khao Khouay. "Buffalo Horn Mountain" lies in a national park—a dramatic area of sheer sandstone cliffs, river gorges, abundant wildlife, and the Ang Nam reservoir. The park's three rivers empty into the Mekong. The banks of the reservoir have several simple restaurants and refreshment stands.

GETTING HERE AND AROUND

The park is about three hours from Viantiane, via Highway 13 south to Tha Bok and then via a side road north from there. Green Discovery Laos (⇨ *Laos Planner)* runs reasonably priced one- to two-day treks and homestays; this is a good way to see the park, since hiring a car and driver is pricey. If coming on your own, buses run from Talat Sao to Tha Bok (15,000 kip); from there, songthaews go to Ban Hat Khai, where you can arrange treks.

Vientiane and Environs

SAFETY AND PRECAUTIONS
Phu Khao Khouay is a safe place, but take the usual precautions with your money and belongings.

TIMING
One day or an overnight trip is enough time to see the area.

PLAIN OF JARS

390 km (242 miles) northeast of Vientiane, 270 km (162 miles) southeast of Luang Prabang.

Plain of Jars. One of the world's major archaeological wonders, the Plain of Jars is also one of the world's most tantalizing mysteries. The broad, mountain-ringed plain northeast of Vientiane is littered with hundreds of ancient stone and clay jars, some estimated to weigh 5 or 6 tons. The jars are said to be at least 2,000 years old, but to this day nobody knows who made them or why. They survived heavy bombing during the Vietnam War, and their sheer size has kept them out of the hands of antiquities hunters.

The jars are scattered over three main areas, but only the Ban Ang site is accessible and worth visiting. Here you can find some 300 jars dotting a windswept plateau about 12 km (7½ miles) from Phonsavanh,

According to legend, the Plain of Jars was once inhabited by giants who built the jars to brew rice wine.

capital of Xieng Khuang Province. This is true Hmong territory: you pass Hmong villages on the way from Phonsavanh to Ban Ang and on Highway 7, which leads east to the Vietnamese border at Nong Het. There's much of interest in this remote area along Highway 7, including hot mineral springs at Muang Kham. From Muang Kham, a road leads to Vieng Xay, which has more than 100 limestone caves, some of them used as hideouts by the revolutionary Pathet Lao during the war years.

UXO Visitor Center. Along with the adjoining Mines Advisory Group office, the Center has a small exhibition that provides very sobering insight into the horrifying realities of unexploded ordnance, much of which still litters the Plain of Jars area. Several documentary films are shown each afternoon, and a visit here is a must for anyone exploring the region. ✉ *Xaysana Rd., Phonsavan* 🎫 *Free* 🕐 *Weekdays 8–8, Weekends 4–8.*

GETTING HERE AND AROUND

A hard day's drive along Highway 7 from either Vientiane or Luang Prabang, the vast plain is difficult to reach. Travel operators in both cities, such as Diethelm Travel and Lao Youth Travel *(⇨ Laos Planner)*, offer tours. You'll fly into Xieng Khuang Airport in Phonsavanh, which is 3 km (2 miles) outside town. Lao Airlines flies daily from Vientiane in the high season and every other day the rest of the year for about $80. Most hotels and guesthouses in Phonsavanh can arrange trips to the jar sites for $20 to $25 per person in a minivan or jeep; you can also take a taxi to the sites for about $30.

The bus to Phonsavanh from Luang Prabang costs 100,000 kip, and takes seven hours. From Vientiane it is 120,000 kip and is 10 hours or more.

SAFETY AND PRECAUTIONS

Stay on marked paths, and don't stray off into the countryside without a guide; the Plain of Jars area is still littered with unexploded ordnance.

TIMING

One day is enough to see the jar sites and visit some local villages. However, Phonsavanh is a friendly place that doesn't see many tourists other than visitors to the jars, and it may be worthwhile to spend an extra day exploring the pretty surrounding countryside, hot springs, and local villages.

TOURS

Sousath Travel is the best tour operator in town. Run by the Maly Hotel family, they offer a large selection of trips around the area, from basic Plain of Jars tours to more exciting propositions, such as going by boat to Luang Prabang. Their local bicycle trips to the jars and local villages are an excellent way to experience rural Laos.

ESSENTIALS

Emergencies Lao Mongol Hospital ✉ *Phonsavanh* ☎ *061/312018.*

Tour Information Sousath Travel ✉ *Xaysana Rd., Box 1105A, Phonsavan* ☎ *020/296–7213, 020/511–3791.*

WHERE TO EAT AND STAY

For expanded hotel reviews, visit Fodors.com.

$ LAO 🍴 **Maly Restaurant.** Housed in the hotel of the same name, the Maly serves a large selection of both Lao and western dishes, which are surprisingly good given Phonsavan's remoteness. Staples include different kinds of larb and decent curries, along with some western dishes. You can also try matsutake mushrooms here, pine mushrooms that are widely grown in the area and are considered a delicacy. It's about a kilometer or two south of the main road, so take a tuk-tuk. [$] *Average main: $6* ✉ *Muang Phouan Rd., Phonsavan* ☎ *061/312031* 🌐 *www.maly-hotel.com/resturant.html.*

$ INDIAN **Fodor's Choice** ★ 🍴 **Nisha.** Who would ever have thought that some of the best food in Laos would be found in remote Phonsavanh, and Indian food at that! Yet hole-in-the-wall Nisha serves up some fantastic Indian cuisine, thanks to its amiable owners from Tamil Nadu (whose family runs branches in Luang Prabang and Vang Vieng). An entire chicken tikka or tandoori costs only 25,000 kip, but we recommend the chicken *lessani,* marinated overnight in yogurt and spices. A full vegetarian menu is also on tap. Located at the east end of Phonsavan's main street. [$] *Average main: $4* ✉ *Xaysana Rd., Phonsavan* ☎ *020/5569–8140* 💳 *No credit cards.*

$$ B&B/INN 🏨 **Auberge Plaine des Jarres.** These charming rustic cabins, set on a hill in a pine forest overlooking the surrounding area, will make you feel like you are in a "wild west" film rather than Southeast Asia. **Pros:** most scenic spot in town; romantic; fireplaces in rooms. **Cons:** far from town; no fans or air-conditioning; transportation in the evening

is scarce. $ *Rooms from: $60* ✉ *Domaine de Phouphadeng, Phonsavan* ☎ *020/2353333* ⊕ *auberge_plainjars@yahoo.fr* ⤴ *15 rooms* ▭ *No credit cards* ❘◎❘ *Breakfast.*

$ ▦ **Maly Hotel.** The folks at Maly are jacks and jills of all trades in far-
HOTEL flung Phonsavan. **Pros:** in-house tour agency is excellent; good restaurant on premises; discounts often available if the hotel isn't full. **Cons:** deluxe rooms overpriced; a bit of a hike to the center of town; in-room Wi-Fi is spotty. $ *Rooms from: $45* ✉ *Muang Phouan Rd., Box 649A, Phonsavan* ☎ *061/312031* ⊕ *www.maly-hotel.com* ⤴ *26 rooms* ❘◎❘ *Breakfast.*

VANG VIENG

Fodor's Choice *160 km (99 miles) north of Vientiane.*
★
The town of Vang Vieng was discovered in the mid-1990s by backpackers traveling between Vientiane and Luang Prabang on Highway 13. It's not only a convenient stopover, but also a town bordered by some of the most attractive scenery and countryside in Laos, including the Nam Song River and a dramatic range of jagged limestone mountains. During the Vietnam War the United States maintained an airstrip in the town center; there are rumors that the abandoned tarmac will someday field direct flights from Luang Prabang or elsewhere. These days the town center is jam-packed with bars and backpacker hangouts, but you can escape the noise and the crowds by making for the river, which is lined with guesthouses and restaurants catering to both backpackers and those on a more flexible budget. The river is clean and good for swimming and kayaking, and the mountains beyond are riddled with caves and small pleasant swimming holes. River trips and caving expeditions are organized by every guesthouse and hotel. ⚠ **Note that the treks to the caves can be fairly arduous, and some are only accessible by motorbike.** The less-adventurous adventurer can rent an inner tube for $7 and float down the river for a few hours. ⚠ **Vang Vieng has been famous for its rope-swing party bars along the river, attracting a huge backpacker crowd. In 2012, due to a huge number of deaths caused by drinking, drugs, and drowning, the Lao government closed the bars along the river. Today, Vang Vieng is starting to move slightly more upscale and trying to disassociate itself with the backpacker party scene.**

GETTING HERE AND AROUND
BUS TRAVEL From Vientiane you can take a minibus, which takes three to four hours to reach Vang Vieng, and costs 50,000 kip.

If you're coming from Luang Prabang, VIP buses headed back to Vientiane stop here three times a day—the journey takes seven hours and costs 100,000 kip. Minivans to Vang Vieng can be arranged at travel agencies in both cities for about the same price as a VIP bus ticket.

A daily bus also goes to Phonsavan (Plain of Jars) for 100,000 kip (six hours).

SONGTHAEW Songthaews run from the bus station, 2 km (1 mile) north of town, to
TRAVEL all hotels for 10,000 kip per person. They can also be hired for excursions farther afield; prepare to bargain.

The pretty village of Vang Vieng is surrounded by spectacular limestone cliffs.

SAFETY AND PRECAUTIONS
Always double-check prices in Vang Vieng, as merchants are notorious for overcharging. Make sure to shop around and compare, as quotes for identical services may vary wildly.

The river can be fast-flowing during rainy season. All but the strongest swimmers are advised to wear a life vest and take the necessary precautions when innertubing or kayaking.

Do not under any circumstances accept offers for smoking marijuana or other drugs in Vang Vieng. Dealers are usually informants with the police, and those caught face a very large bribe or jail time.

TIMING
This backpacker town is not pleasant, but the surrounding countryside is wonderful. One day to explore the caves and go farther afield, and one day to relax on the river should be plenty.

TOURS
Green Discovery Laos. Green Discovery offers a unique way to travel from Vang Vieng to Vientiane. Starting downstream from Vang Vieng, you get in a kayak for the four-hour paddle to Vientiane, stopping for lunch and a 33-foot rock jump into the river. You're picked up riverside outside Vientiane in the afternoon, reunited with your luggage, and dropped off in Vientiane around 5 pm. In addition to the kayak trip you can also do (or combine it with) a new canopy-zip-line/trekking option along the way. The one-way trip costs $81 per person if there are two people, but drops to $56 if there are four. ⊠ *Ban Savan, Vang Vieng* ☎ *023/511230* ⊕ *www.greendiscoverylaos.com.*

ESSENTIALS

Emergencies Provincial Hospital ✉ *Ban Vieng Keo* ☎ *023/511604.*

WHERE TO EAT AND STAY

For expanded hotel reviews, visit Fodors.com.

$ ECLECTIC 🍴 **La Verandah Riverside.** In a town noted for extremely bland food, this beautifully situated restaurant right on the river inside the Villa Nam Song Resort serves up a nice blend of Thai, Lao, French, and Western dishes. The penang curry is aromatic and full of flavor, as is the spaghetti *pad kee mao* (drunken noodles, with basil and chili sauce). On the French menu are coq au vin, ratatouille, and fresh organic salad. A fine French wine list complements the menu, and if you still have room, there is even homemade ice cream. [$] *Average main: $9* ✉ *Riverside Rd., Ban Viengkeo* ☎ *023/511637.*

$ B&B/INN 🏨 **Ban Sabai Bungalows.** Some of the sleekest rooms in town are in traditional Lao-style thatch-roof bungalows that are raised on stilts. **Pros:** rustic rooms; private decks with river views; charming restaurant on river. **Cons:** small rooms; often fully booked; rooms fairly basic for price. [$] *Rooms from: $38* ✉ *Nam Song River Rd.* ☎ *023/511088* 🌐 *www.inthira.com/hotel_about.php?hid=2* 🛏 *13 bungalows* 🍽 *Breakfast.*

$ RESORT 🏨 **Elephant Crossing Hotel.** Almost every room at this modern four-story hotel has a river view, a balcony, hardwood floors, and wooden trim constructed of recycled bits of old Lao houses. **Pros:** excellent river views; free Wi-Fi; private balcony in each room. **Cons:** small rooms; fair walk to town center; often crowded with tour groups. [$] *Rooms from: $45* ✉ *Ban Viengkeo (Namsong Riverside)* ☎ *023/511232, 020/560–2830* 🌐 *www.theelephantcrossinghotel.com* 🛏 *35 rooms* 🍽 *Breakfast.*

$$$ RESORT Fodor's Choice ★ 🏨 **Riverside Boutique Resort.** Upscale boutique lodging has finally arrived in Vang Vieng—with the best riverside viewpoint in town, overlooking fabulous mountain scenery and the atmospheric wooden bridge. **Pros:** best viewpoint in Vang Vieng; best swimming pool; quiet and away from the backpacking crowd. **Cons:** not all rooms have good river views; breakfast buffet a bit bland; quite expensive for the area. [$] *Rooms from: $135* ✉ *Ban Viengkeo, Box 360, Vang Vieng* ☎ *023/511726, 023/511727* 🌐 *www.riversidevangvieng.com* 🛏 *34 rooms* 🍽 *Breakfast.*

$ B&B/INN 🏨 **Saysong Guest House.** This is one of the cheapest deals in town, and its lovely riverside location can't be beat. **Pros:** excellent location in heart of town; river views from some rooms; super value. **Cons:** cheaper rooms rather dark and very basic; west-facing rooms get very hot in afternoon. [$] *Rooms from: $30* ✉ *Ban Savang* ☎ *023/511130* ✉ *riverviewbungalows@hotmail.com* 🌐 *www.river-view-bungalows.com* 🛏 *38 rooms* 🍽 *Breakfast.*

$$ RESORT 🏨 **Villa Nam Song.** The Mediterranean-style rooms at this hotel have wooden floors and ceilings, yellow concrete walls, and wooden beds, desks, and chairs. **Pros:** excellent location next to river; quiet; unusually good hot water supply. **Cons:** rooms smell like cleaning products; a bit of a walk from town center, not the best value in town. [$] *Rooms from: $100* ✉ *Unit 9, Ban Viengkeo* ☎ *023/511637* 🌐 *www.villanamsong.com* 🛏 *16 rooms* 🍽 *Breakfast.*

LUANG PRABANG AND NORTHERN LAOS

For all its popularity as a tourist destination, Luang Prabang remains one of the most remote cities in Southeast Asia. Although a highway now runs north to the Chinese border, the hinterland of Luang Prabang is mostly off-the-beaten-track territory, a mountainous region of impenetrable forests and deep river valleys. Despite Luang Prabang's air links to the rest of the country and the outside world, the Mekong River is still a preferred travel route. Passenger craft and freight barges ply the river's length as far as China in the north and near the Cambodian border in the south.

LUANG PRABANG

390 km (242 miles) north of Vientiane.

This is Laos's religious and artistic capital, and its combination of impressive natural surroundings, historic architecture, and friendly inhabitants make it one of the region's most pleasant towns. The city's abundance of ancient temples led UNESCO to declare it a World Heritage Site in 1995, and since then it's been bustling with construction and renovation activity.

But the charm of Luang Prabang is not exclusively architectural—just as pleasant are the people, who seem to spend as much time on the streets as they do in their homes. Children play on the sidewalks while matrons gossip in the shade, young women in traditional dress zip past on motor scooters, and Buddhist monks in saffron robes stroll by with black umbrellas, which protect their shaven heads from the tropical sun.

⚠ Despite scores of guesthouses, finding accommodations here can be a challenge in the peak season. And when you visit the top attractions, be prepared for crowds of tourists.

GETTING HERE AND AROUND

AIR TRAVEL There are direct flights to Luang Prabang from both Bangkok and Chiang Mai. Lao Airlines operates a thrice-weekly service from Bangkok to Luang Prabang and five flights weekly from Chiang Mai to Luang Prabang. Bangkok Airways flies direct twice daily from Bangkok to Luang Prabang, and onward to Siem Reap.

Lao Airlines also has at least three flights a day between Vientiane and Luang Prabang, plus three weekly flights from Vientiane to Huay Xai.

Luang Prabang International Airport is 4 km (2½ miles) northeast of the city. The taxi ride to the city center costs 50,000 kip.

BIKE TRAVEL Biking is one of the best ways to visit all the interesting sights within Luang Prabang, and many hotels provide bicycles for guests, or if not, one can rent them from shops in town for 20,000 to 30,000 kip per day.

BOAT AND FERRY TRAVEL In Luang Prabang you can find a boat for hire just about anywhere along the entire length of the road bordering the Mekong River; the main jetty is on the river side of Wat Xieng Thong.

BUS TRAVEL Buses from Vientiane arrive four to five times daily and take between 8 and 11 hours. You have your choice of VIP (usually with air-conditioning and toilets aboard), express, and regular buses; prices range

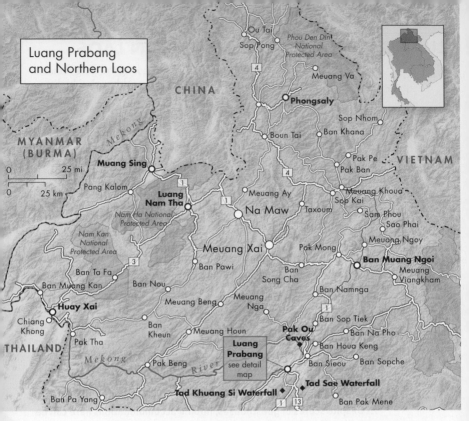

Luang Prabang and Northern Laos

from 100,000 to 130,000 kip. ■TIP→ You'll pay more if you buy your ticket from an agency in town. There is now a new minivan station opposite the Southern Bus Terminal, where you access all bus destinations for just about the same price, though minivans are far quicker, more comfortable, and include pickup from your hotel. There are also buses to Phonsavanh (eight hours; 100,000 kip), Vang Vieng (five hours; 135,000 kip), Oudomxay (four hours; 60,000 kip), and Luang Nam Tha (nine hours; 100,000 kip), among other places. There are two bus terminals in Luang Prabang, the Northern Bus Terminal, out near the airport, and the Ban Naluang Southern Bus Terminal, in the south of town, with services to respective destinations.

CAR TRAVEL   Although you can drive from Vientiane to Luang Prabang, it takes eight to nine hours to make the 365-km (240-mile) trip along the meandering, but paved, road up into the mountains.

TAXI, TUK-TUK, AND SONGTH- AEW TRAVEL   Tuk-tuks and songthaews make up Luang Prabang's public transport system. They cruise all the streets and are easy to flag down. Plan on paying around 10,000 to 20,000 kip for a trip within the city. The few taxis in town must be booked through your hotel or guesthouse.

SAFETY AND PRECAUTIONS
Luang Prabang is safe, but beware of unscrupulous tuk-tuk drivers.

Emergencies International Clinic. For medical and police emergencies, use the services of your hotel or guesthouse. ⊠ *Ban Thongchaloen* ☎ *071/254023.*

TIMING

Unless you are a temple addict, three to four days in Luang Prabang is more than enough. If you have the extra time, try to get farther north, where there are fewer tourists and fantastic nature.

TOUR INFORMATION

Shangri Lao. Shangri Lao is a new luxury tour that takes you, by elephant and horseback via an old explorers trail, to fancy safari-style camp resorts on the Nam Khan River. It's a great way to have an old-fashioned jungle adventure in style. All-inclusive trips run $600 for 2 persons for two days. ⊠ *Ban Xieng Lam* ☎ *071/252417* ⊕ *www. shangri-lao.com.*

Green Discovery Laos, Lao Youth Travel, and **Diethelm Travel** *(⇨ Laos Planner)* have Luang Prabang branches.

Visitor and Tour Contacts Shangri Lao ⊠ *Sisavangvong Rd., Ban Xieng Lom* ☎ *071/252417* ⊕ *www.shangri-lao.com.* **White Elephant Adventures** ⊠ *Sisavangvong Rd.* ☎ *030/514–0243* ⊕ *www.white-elephant-adventures-laos.com.*

EXPLORING

Some 36 temples are scattered around town, making Luang Prabang a pleasant place to explore on a rented bicycle or on foot. When you need a break from temple-hopping, there are plenty of appealing eateries and fashionable boutiques. Waking early one morning to watch the throngs of monks make their alms runs at dawn is highly recommended. Your hotel should be able to tell you what time to get up and suggest a good viewing spot.

TOP ATTRACTIONS

Phu Si Hill. Several shrines and temples and a golden stupa crown this forested hill, but the best reason to ascend its 328 steps is to enjoy the view from the summit: a panorama of Luang Prabang, the Nam Khan and Mekong rivers, and the surrounding mountains. It's a popular spot for watching the sunset (just be sure to bring insect repellent), but the view from atop old Phu Si is splendid at any hour. ■ TIP→ If you're not up for the steep climb up the staircase, try the more enjoyable hike up the trail on the "back" side of the hill. ⊠ *Rathsavong Rd.* ⊡ *10,000 kip* ⊙ *Daily 6–6.*

Royal Palace. In a walled compound at the foot of Phu Si Hill stands this palace, the former home of the royal Savang family. Built at the beginning of the 20th century, the palace served as the royal residence until the Pathet Lao took over Laos in 1975 and exiled Crown Prince Savang Vatthana and his children to a remote region of the country (their fate has never been established). It still has the feel of a large family home—a maze of teak-floor rooms surprisingly modest in scale. The largest of them is the **Throne Room,** with its gilded furniture, colorful mosaic-covered walls, and display cases filled with rare Buddha images, royal regalia, and other priceless artifacts.

The walls of the **King's Reception Room** are decorated with scenes of traditional Lao life painted in 1930 by the French artist Alex de

A GOOD WALK (OR RIDE)

Touring the city's major sights takes a full day—maybe longer if you climb Phu Si Hill, which has particularly lovely views at sunset. The evening bazaar on Sisavangvong Road starts around 6. Though the distances between these attractions are walkable, you may not want to do this all on foot if it's really hot out. Rent a bike, or break this into a few shorter walks, and stay out of the sun during the heat of the day.

Start your tour of Luang Prabang at the pulsing heart of the city: the **Tribal Market** at the intersection of Sisavangvong Road and Setthathirat Road. From here, head northeast along Sisavangvong, stopping on the left at one of the city's most beautiful temples, **Wat Mai.** Magnificent wood carvings and golden murals decorate the main pillars and portico entrance to the temple. Continue down Sisavangvong to the compound of the **Royal Palace,** with its large bronze statue of King

Sisavangvong. On leaving the palace grounds by the main entrance, climb the staircase to **Phu Si Hill.** The climb is steep and takes about 15 minutes, but you'll be rewarded with an unforgettable view of Luang Prabang and the surrounding countryside.

Back in front of the Royal Palace, follow Sisavangvong toward the confluence of the Mekong and Nam Khan rivers, where you can find another fascinating Luang Prabang temple, **Wat Xieng Thong.** Leaving the compound on the Mekong River side, walk back to the city center along the romantic waterside road, which is fronted by several French-colonial houses and Lao traditional homes. Passing the port area behind the Royal Palace, continue on to the intersection with Wat Phu Xay; turn right here to return to the Tribal Market. Every evening there's a local night bazaar, stretching from the Tribal Market to the Royal Palace.

Fautereau. The **Queen's Reception Room** contains a collection of royal portraits by the Russian artist Ilya Glazunov. The room also has cabinets full of presents given to the royal couple by visiting heads of state; a model moon lander and a piece of moon rock from U.S. president Richard Nixon share shelf space with an exquisite Sevres tea set presented by French president Charles de Gaulle and fine porcelain teacups from Chinese leader Mao Tse-tung. Other exhibits in this eclectic collection include friezes removed from local temples, Khmer drums, and elephant tusks with carved images of the Buddha.

The museum's most prized exhibit is the **Pha Bang,** a gold image of the Buddha slightly less than 3 feet tall and weighing more than 100 pounds. Its history goes back to the 1st century, when it was cast in Sri Lanka; it was brought to Luang Prabang from Cambodia in 1359 as a gift to King Fa Ngum. This event is celebrated as the introduction of Buddhism as an official religion to Laos, and Pha Bang is venerated as the protector of the faith. An ornate temple called Ho Pha Bang, near the entrance to the palace compound, is being restored to house the image.

Tucked away behind the palace is a crumbling wooden garage that houses the royal fleet of aging automobiles. ■TIP➔ You'll need about two hours to work through the Royal Palace's maze of rooms. ⊠ *Sisavangvong Rd. across from Phu Si Hill* ☏ *071/212470* 💰 *30,000 kip* ⊘ *Wed.–Mon. 8:30–11 and 1:30–4.*

Wat Xieng Thong. Luang Prabang's most important and impressive temple complex is Wat Xieng Thong, a collection of ancient buildings near the tip of the peninsula where the Mekong and Nam Khan rivers meet. Constructed 1559 to 1560, the main temple is one of the few structures to have survived centu-

ries of marauding Vietnamese, Chinese, and Siamese armies, and it's regarded as one of the region's best-preserved examples of Buddhist art and architecture. The intricate golden facades, colorful murals, sparkling glass mosaics, and low, sweeping roofs of the entire ensemble of buildings (which overlap to make complex patterns) all combine to create a feeling of harmony and peace.

The interior of the main temple has decorated wooden columns and a ceiling covered with wheels of dharma, representing the Buddha's teaching. The exterior is just as impressive thanks to mosaics of colored glass that were added at the beginning of 20th century. Several small **chapels** at the sides of the main hall are also covered with mosaics and contain various images of the Buddha. The bronze 16th-century reclining Buddha in one chapel was displayed in the 1931 Paris Exhibition. The mosaic on the back wall of that chapel commemorates the 2,500th anniversary of the Buddha's birth with a depiction of Lao village life. The chapel near the compound's east gate, with a gilded facade, contains the royal family's funeral statuary and urns, including a 40-foot-long wooden boat that was used as a hearse. ⊠ *Sisavangvong Rd.* ☏ *071/212470* 💰 *20,000 kip* ⊘ *Daily 6–6.*

WORTH NOTING

Night Market. The night market is a real hub of activity, full of colorful local souvenirs, delicious and cheap food, and a meeting place for locals and tourists. Sisavangvong Road is closed to vehicles from the tourist office down to the Royal Palace starting in the late afternoon, and a tented area is set up, thronged with vendors selling lanterns, patterned cushion covers, Lao coffee and tea, hand-stitched bags, and many other local crafts. Small side streets are lined with food stalls selling everything from fried chicken to Mekong seaweed and other treats at a fraction of the price you'll pay in a restaurant. It's worth strolling here just for the atmosphere. ⊠ *Sisavangvong Rd., Luang Prabang* ⊘ *Daily 4:30–9.*

Wat Mai. This small but lovely temple next to the Royal Palace compound dates from 1796. Its four-tier roof is characteristic of Luang Prabang's religious architecture, but more impressive are the magnificent wood carvings and gold-leaf murals on the main pillars and portico entrance to the temple. These intricate panels depict the last life of the

9

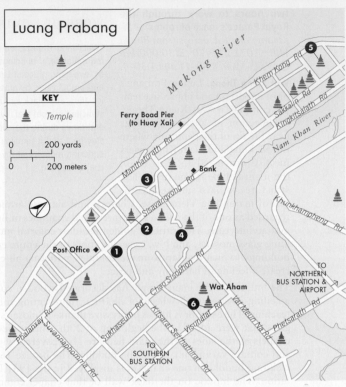

Luang Prabang

KEY

🔺 *Temple*

0 — 200 yards
0 — 200 meters

Mekong River

Nam Khan River

Ferry Boad Pier
(to Huay Xai) ◆

● Bank

Post Office ◆

Wat Aham

TO
NORTHERN
BUS STATION &
AIRPORT

TO
SOUTHERN
BUS STATION

Buddha, as well as various Asian animals. During the Bun Pimai festival
(Lao New Year), the Prabang sacred Buddha image is carried from the
Royal Palace compound to Wat Mai for ritual cleansing ceremonies.
⊠ *Sisavangvong Rd.* 🖃 *10,000 kip* ⊙ *Daily 6–6.*

Wat Visun. The 16th-century Wat Visun and neighboring **Wat Aham**
play a central role in Lao New Year celebrations, when ancestral masks,
called *phu gneu gna gneu,* are taken from Wat Aham and displayed in
public. Wat Visun was built in 1503, during the reign of King Visunalat, who had the temple named after himself. Within the compound
is a large and unusual watermelon-shape stupa called **That Makmo**
(literally Watermelon Stupa). The 100-foot-high mound is actually a
royal tomb, where many small precious Buddha statues were found
when Chin Haw marauders destroyed the city in the late 19th century (these statues have since been moved to the Royal Palace). The
temple hall was rebuilt in 1898 along the lines of the original wooden
structure, and now houses an impressive collection of Buddha statues,
stone inscriptions, and other Buddhist art. ⊠ *Visunalat Rd.* 🖃 *10,000
kip* ⊙ *Daily 6–6.*

WHERE TO EAT

$$ INTERNATIONAL

✕**Apsara Restaurant.** Occupying a lovely spot overlooking the Nam Khan River, Apsara serves fine Western and Eastern cuisine, ranging from baguette sandwiches for lunch to elegant set dinners featuring fresh fish and meat dishes such as tajine of young goat with braised prunes and couscous or grilled fillet of buffalo. There's an extensive top wine list, and the quiet location is an excellent place for a leisurely meal. In high season you may need a reservation. $ *Average main: $11* ✉ *Kingkitsarath St., Baan Wat Sene* ☎ *071/254670* ⊕ *www.theapsara. com.*

$ ECLECTIC

✕**Auberge and Cafe 3 Nagas.** The *tom hom pak e-leup,* betel leaf soup with dried buffalo, or the *mok het,* steamed mushrooms in coconut mousse, are just two of local specialties served in one of Luang Prabang's most appealing eateries. The atmospheric restaurant is opposite the 3 Nagas Hotel. They also do Western dishes on the hotel side of the site, under the same management. $ *Average main: $9* ✉ *Sakkalin Rd., Box 722* ☎ *071/253888* ⊕ *www.3-nagas.com.*

$ LAO

✕**Indochina Spirit.** For a hearty meal, head to this eclectic Thai-run restaurant housed in a 1920s residence that once belonged to a royal physician, where a selection of Lao specialties costs just $6. Start with an appetizer of Mekong seaweed or banana-flower salad, followed by steak. Italian-style pastas and pizza are also on the menu, and delicious pancakes are served for breakfast. $ *Average main: $6* ✉ *50–51 Ban Wat That* ☎ *071/252372, 020/567–0198.*

$ CAFÉ

✕**Joma Bakery Cafe.** Canadians run this cheap, friendly self-service restaurant, where an in-house bakery turns out delicious pastries, pizzas, salads, and French bread. The homemade soups are excellent, as are the breakfast burritos and wraps. $ *Average main: $3* ✉ *Chao Fa Ngum Rd.* ☎ *071/252292* ⊕ *www.joma.biz* ☐ *No credit cards.*

$$$ INTERNATIONAL Fodor'sChoice ★

✕**Kitchen by the Mekong at Xiengthong Palace.** This quaint Mekong riverside restaurant in the former royal residence (now a luxury boutique hotel) serves up some excellent food in a charming and serene location. Try the divine Mekong Boat, which is a salad with croutons, bacon, and feta cheese tossed in a vinaigrette and wrapped in a toasted Mekong seaweed (a specialty of Luang Prabang) boat. Entrees include duck Shiraz, New Zealand lamb, and Tasmanian salmon served with mushroom risotto and sundried tomato salsa. Lao dishes such as whisky-flavored buffalo steak are also on the menu, and make sure to leave room for dessert. The ebony chip chocolate mousse heated with Bailey's cream is

---

A JACK OF ALL TRADES

L'etranger Books and Tea. L'etranger Books and Tea has a bit of everything for those in search of a break. The first floor contains a collection of new and used books in a variety of languages for sale or for loan (2,000 kip per hour or 5,000 kip per day). Upstairs, 20 years of *National Geographic* magazines line the walls and patrons sip on tea, coffee, and smoothies or nibble on snacks while reclining on comfortable floor pillows. In the evening, the place fills for DVD screenings. An adjoining gallery on the second floor features local artists. ✉ *Ban Aphay next to Hive Bar* ☎ *020/2299-3332.*

9

The Prabang Buddha

But for a few simple facts, the Pha Bang Buddha image, the namesake of Luang Prabang, is shrouded in mystery. This much *is* known: the Prabang image is approximately 33 inches tall and weighs 110 pounds. Both hands of the Buddha are raised in double *abhaya mudra* position (the meaning of which has predictably ambiguous symbolic interpretations, including dispelling fear, teaching reason, and offering protection, benevolence, and peace). Historically, the Prabang Buddha has been a symbol of religious and political authority, including the legitimate right to rule the kingdom of Laos. Beyond that, there is much speculation.

It is believed that the image was cast in bronze in Ceylon (Sri Lanka) between the 1st and 9th century, although it has also been suggested that it is made primarily of gold, with silver and bronze alloys. Regardless of its composition, the double-raised palms indicate a later construction (14th century), and a possibly Khmer origin.

Nonetheless, in 1359 the Prabang was given to Fa Ngum, the son-in-law of the Khmer king at Angkor, and brought to Muang Swa, which was subsequently renamed Luang Prabang, the capital of the newly formed kingdom of Lang Xang. The Prabang Buddha became a symbol of the king's legitimacy and a means of promoting Theravada Buddhism throughout Laos.

In 1563 the Prabang image was relocated, along with the seat of power, to the new capital city of Vientiane. In 1778 Siamese invaders ransacked Vientiane and made off with both the Prabang and Emerald Buddhas. The Prabang was returned to Laos in 1782 after political and social unrest in Siam was attributed to the image. Similar circumstances surrounded the subsequent capture and release of the Prabang by the Siamese in 1827 and 1867.

Following its return to Laos, the Prabang was housed in Wat Wisunalat, Luang Prabang's oldest temple, and then at Wat Mai. In 1963, during the reign of Sisavang Vatthana, Laos's final monarch, construction began on Haw Pha Bang, a temple to house the Prabang on the grounds of the palace.

However, in 1975 the communist Pathet Lao rose to power, absolved the monarchy, and installed a communist regime. The communist government, having little respect for any symbol of royalty *or* Buddhism, may have handed over the Prabang to Moscow in exchange for assistance from the Soviet Union. Other accounts of the image have it spirited away to Vientiane for safekeeping in a vault, where it may still reside today.

Regardless, there is a 33-inch-tall Buddha statue, real or replica, housed behind bars in an unassuming room beside the entrance to the Royal Palace Museum (until Haw Pha Bang is completed). On the third day of every Lao New Year (April 13–15), the image is ferried via chariot to Wat Mai, where it is cleansed with water by reverent Laotians.

As for its authenticity, a respectable and reliable source told me simply this: "People believe that it is real because the Prabang Buddha belongs in Luang Prabang."

—Trevor Ranges

COOKING CLASSES

Tamnak Lao. Restaurant Tamnak Lao (⇨ *Where to Eat)* doesn't just serve tasty Laotian food, it also teaches you how to cook it yourself. The restaurant's school comprehensively explains Lao cuisine, cultural influences, and provides ingredients for 12 recipes. Full-day (from 10 to 6) classes of no more than eight students each are held daily at 250,000 kip per person. ✉ *Sakkarin Rd, Ban Vat Sene* ☎ *071/252525* 🌐 *www.tamnaklao.net.*

Tum Tum Cheng. Tum Tum Cheng now offers cooking classes. You can spend a half day learning one of their 150 recipes. Classes run from 8:30 in the morning until 2 and cost 250,000 kip. ✉ *Sakkarine Rd., Ban Xieng Thong 4/42* ☎ *071/253187, 020/2242–5499* 🌐 *tumtumcheng@yahoo.com.*

particularly lovely. [$] *Average main: $16* ✉ *Kounxoau Rd., Ban Phonehueng, Luang Prabang* ☎ *071/213200* 🌐 *www.xiengthongpalace.com.*

$ FRENCH 🍴 **Le Café et Restaurant Ban Vat Sene.** Sidewalk seating and a retractable brown-striped awning contribute to the traditional French café atmosphere here. Freshly made quiche, baguettes, and *grandes tartines* (large slices of homemade bread with various toppings) are the highlights of the menu. Across from Villa Santi on the northern end of town, the café is a relaxing place for a meal or simply a cup of coffee and some pastries. [$] *Average main: $6* ✉ *Sakkarin Rd.* ☎ *071/252482.*

$$$ FRENCH 🍴 **L'Elephant Restaurant Français.** When you can't face another serving of rice or spicy sauces, it's time to walk down the hill from the Villa Santi to this pleasant corner restaurant. The menu is traditional French, with a bit of Lao influence, especially when it comes to the ingredients. Consider, for example, the *chevreuil au poivre vert* (local venison in a pepper sauce). There are always the three-course set meal and several daily specials, which usually include fish fresh from the Mekong. Seating is available in the bright, airy dining room or on the sidewalk, behind a barrier of plants. [$] *Average main: $18* ✉ *Ban Wat Nong, Box 812* ☎ *071/252482* 🌐 *www.elephant-restau.com.*

$ CAFÉ 🍴 **Luang Prabang Bakery.** It would be difficult not to eventually wander into Luang Prabang Bakery—it has a great central location and the most enticing atmosphere of the several outdoor-seating restaurants in this part of town. It certainly is a great spot for a cool drink and some prime people-watching. The restaurant also serves more than 20 different Laotian dishes, such as *jo mart len pak lae kout noi* (steamed fresh vegetables with a spicy grilled-tomato sauce), and you can also satisfy a craving for western food with a tasty hamburger, a pizza, some pasta, or even a steak. The menu includes a variety of French and Australian wines. [$] *Average main: $6* ✉ *Sisavangvong Rd.* ☎ *071/254844* 🌐 *luangprabang-bakery-guesthouse.com.*

$ ASIAN 🍴 **Pak Huay Mixay.** *Mok pa,* steamed fish with spices wrapped in a banana leaf, is the dish of choice at this long-established Asian restaurant, a favorite with locals. Enjoy other Lao dishes, such as *tom yum* soup (with lemongrass, coriander, chilies, and chicken or fish), or *sai oua* (Luang Prabang sausage) and end your meal with a glass of *lao-lao.*

9

$ *Average main: $6* ✉ *75/6 Sothikhoummane Rd., Ban Xieng Muan* ☎ *071/212260, 020/551–1496* ▭ *No credit cards.*

$ ✗ **Roots and Leaves.** Near the Amantaka in a charming garden setting
LAO with outdoor tables set next to a lotus pond and surrounded by jackfruit and tamarind trees, Roots and Leaves offers inexpensive traditional Lao fare and selected Thai specialties. Try the buffalo stew or frogs' leg salad if you're adventuresome, or just stick with the usual favorites like green curry or grilled pork. The restaurant also has a free dinner performance with traditional Lao dance and music with a multicourse set menu, and also offers cooking classes during the day. $ *Average main: $6* ✉ *Setthathirath Rd., Box 586* ☎ *071/254870* ⊕ *www.rootsinlaos.com.*

$ ✗ **Tamnak Lao.** If you're looking for excellent Lao food, this noted res-
LAO taurant and cooking school (and book exchange!) is the place to start. Try a set menu to sample a variety of the country's cooking styles, or order from the lengthy menu that includes *kaipan,* a crispy dried Mekong River plant covered with sesame seeds and served with a local chutney (the local equivalent of chips and salsa), and *orlam,* an eggplant "casserole" that can be compared to an exotic *gaeng kiew waan* (Thai green curry) and is a local favorite. $ *Average main: $6* ✉ *Sakkarin Rd.* ☎ *071/252525* ⊕ *www.tamnaklao.net* ☽ *Closed 4–6.*

$ ✗ **Tum Tum Cheng.** This popular restaurant also runs a well-known cook-
LAO ing school. Even if you don't take a class (250,000 kip per day, sign up one day in advance), come for the delicious citronella Mekong catfish, sautéed chicken in banana leaf, or eggplant with chili sauce. $ *Average main: $7* ✉ *Sakkarine Rd., Ban Xieng Thong 4/42* ☎ *071/253187, 020/2242–5499* ▭ *No credit cards.*

WHERE TO STAY

New hotels are shooting up in Luang Prabang to accommodate the growing numbers of tourists. Many of the most attractive of them are in converted buildings dating from French-colonial days, and two old favorites are former royal properties.

For expanded hotel reviews, visit Fodors.com.

$$$$ 🏨 **Hotel 3 Nagas.** This turn-of-the-19th-century mansion stands under
HOTEL official UNESCO World Heritage Site protection, thanks in no small
Fodor's Choice measure to the efforts of the French owner to retain its weathered but
★ handsome colonial look. **Pros:** private patios and gorgeous garden; spacious bathrooms with claw-foot tubs; $50 discounts in low season. **Cons:** often fully booked; poor lighting around bed; 20% service charge. $ *Rooms from: $174* ✉ *Sakkarin Rd., Ban Wat Nong, Box 722* ☎ *071/253888* ⊕ *www.3-nagas.com* ⇜ *15 rooms* ⦿ *Breakfast.*

$$$$ 🏨 **Amantaka.** The Amantaka raises the bar for defining luxury. **Pros:**
RESORT perfectly situated and close to everything; spacious and private suites;
Fodor's Choice excellent food served in the atmospheric restaurant; enormous pool.
★ **Cons:** extra 20% tax and service charge added to rates; mandatory per-day half-board/activities charge levied in addition to room rate; on the flight path into the LP airport, so jet noise when planes fly in. $ *Rooms from: $800* ✉ *55/3 Kingkitsarath Rd., Ban Thongchaleun, Box 1090* ☎ *071/860333* ⊕ *www.amanresorts.com* ⇜ *24 rooms* ⦿ *Some meals.*

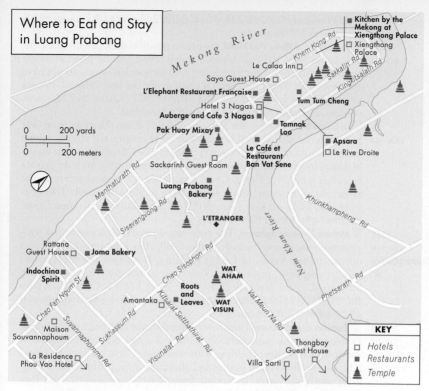

Where to Eat and Stay in Luang Prabang

Kitchen by the Mekong at Xiengthong Palace
Xiengthong Palace
Mekong River
Khem Kong Rd
Sakkalin Rd
Kingkitsalath Rd
Le Calao Inn
Sayo Guest House
L'Elephant Restaurant Française
Tum Tum Cheng
Hotel 3 Nagas
Auberge and Cafe 3 Nagas
Tamnak Lao
Pak Huay Mixay
Apsara
Le Rive Droite
Le Café et Restaurant Ban Vat Sene
Manthaturath Rd
Sackarinh Guest Room
Luang Prabang Bakery
Khunkhamphengh Rd
Sisavangvong Rd
L'ETRANGER
Nam Khan River
Rattana Guest House
Joma Bakery
Chao Sisophon Rd
Indochina Spirit
Phetsarath Rd
WAT AHAM
Chao Fan Ngum St
Roots and Leaves
Amantaka
WAT VISUN
Vat Meun Na Rd
Kisarai Setthathirat Rd
Sukhaseum Rd
Suvannaphomma Rd
Maison Souvannaphoum
Visunalat Rd
Thongbay Guest House
La Residence Phou Vao Hotel
Villa Sarti

0   200 yards
0   200 meters

KEY

- □ Hotels
- ■ Restaurants
- ▲ Temple

$$$
B&B/INN
Apsara. With its white facade and balustrades and its riverside location, this French-style *maison* would be at home in southern France; instead, it's the trendiest boutique hotel in Luang Prabang. **Pros:** quiet riverside location; beautifully furnished rooms; rain-style showerheads in some bathrooms. **Cons:** downstairs rooms have no views; standard rooms a bit dark; often fully booked. ⓢ *Rooms from: $130* ✉ *Ban Wat Sene, Kingkitsarat Rd.* ☎ *071/254670* ⊕ *www.theapsara.com* ➮ *13 rooms* ⧉ *Breakfast.*

$$$$
B&B/INN
Apsara Rive Droite. For those looking for something even more glamorous and exclusive than the Aspara, the lovely Apsara Rive Droite across the Nam Khan River continues the owner's attention to detail and charm, featuring a swimming pool, private verandas, and a free 24-hour shuttle-boat service to take guests across the river. **Pros:** luxurious isolation; quiet; nice swimming pool **Cons:** across the river; two-night stay required; only nine rooms, so may be full. ⓢ *Rooms from: $190* ✉ *Ban Phanluang* ☎ *071/254670, 071/213053* ⊕ *www.theapsara. com* ➮ *9 rooms* ⧉ *Breakfast.*

$
B&B/INN
Ban Homsawan. This new and cozy guesthouse (the former Pinekham Douangnaly guesthouse) a few steps down from the Tourist Office is the cleanest, most welcoming, and easily best-value option for nesting a night or two in Phongsaly (70,000 kip a room). ⓢ *Rooms from:*

$9 ✉ *Phongsaly* ☎ *020/2239–5018, 020/2299–9924* 🛏 *8 rooms* 💳 *No credit cards* 🍴 *No meals.*

$$$$ RESORT 🏨 **La Residence Phou Vao Hotel.** Its prime position on Kite Hill gives this sumptuous hotel the best views in town. **Pros:** infinity pool; excellent restaurant; discounts for longer stays. **Cons:** garden rooms do not have great views; 20% tax and service charge; not the best value. [$] *Rooms from: $480* ✉ *Phu Vao Hill 3, Box 50* ☎ *071/212530 up to 33* 🌐 *www.residencephouvao.com* 🛏 *34 rooms* 🍴 *Breakfast.*

$$ B&B/INN 🏨 **Le Calao Inn.** Fronting the Mekong and just down the street from Wat Xieng Thong is this small hotel, which was resurrected from a ruined mansion built by a Portuguese merchant in 1904. **Pros:** quiet spot on the Mekong; lovely Mediterranean restaurant; upstairs rooms have private balconies with river views. **Cons:** almost always booked; interiors not as elegant as exterior; some rooms have unpleasant smell. [$] *Rooms from: $80* ✉ *Khem Kong Rd.* ☎ *071/212100* 🌐 *www.calaohotel.com/lpb.html* 🛏 *6 rooms* 🍴 *Breakfast.*

$$$$ B&B/INN Fodor's Choice ★ 🏨 **Maison Souvannaphoum.** The once-run-down residence of Prince Souvannaphoum, prime minister in the 1960s, has been transformed into one of the top hotels in Luang Prabang. **Pros:** spa; beautiful photo gallery; exclusive, private feel. **Cons:** views not inspiring; on a fairly busy road; often booked. [$] *Rooms from: $180* ✉ *Chao Fa Ngum Rd.* ☎ *071/254609* 🌐 *www.angsana.com/en/maison_souvannaphoum/* 🛏 *24 rooms* 🍴 *Breakfast.*

$ HOTEL 🏨 **Rattana Guest House.** Family-run guesthouses are common in Luang Prabang, but this one certainly makes you feel right at home. **Pros:** spotlessly clean; new building with teak floors; firm mattresses. **Cons:** a bit of a walk to main dining and shopping area; rooms in new wing a bit small; no views. [$] *Rooms from: $30* ✉ *Koksack St., 3/2 Ban What That* ☎ *071/252255* 🌐 *www.rattanaguesthouse.com* 🛏 *14 rooms* 🍴 *Breakfast.*

$ HOTEL 🏨 **Sackarinh Guest Room.** This friendly place in the center of town is the ideal Luang Prabang guesthouse—it's spotless and it's super cheap. **Pros:** ideal location; very clean; friendly staff. **Cons:** some rooms dark; low ceilings; often booked in high season. [$] *Rooms from: $19* ✉ *Sisavangvong Rd., Ban Xieng Mouane* ☎ *071/254512, 020/544–2001* 🛏 *11 rooms* 💳 *No credit cards* 🍴 *No meals.*

$$ B&B/INN 🏨 **Sayo Guest House.** An elegant white colonial-style hotel with green shutters, Sayo Guest House is almost prototypical Luang Prabang style. **Pros:** serene riverside location; spacious, well-furnished rooms, some with balconies. **Cons:** some rooms lack big windows; often full in high season; a walk from central area. [$] *Rooms from: $60* ✉ *Khem Kong Rd., Ban Phone Meuang* ☎ *071/212484* 🌐 *www.sayoguesthouse.com* 🛏 *13 rooms* 💳 *No credit cards* 🍴 *Breakfast.*

$ B&B/INN 🏨 **Thongbay Guest House.** Thongbay is just outside town, but it's right on the Nam Khan River and every bungalow has a deck with floor pillows and chairs from which to look out over the river or the beautiful gardens.The resort is a small village of well-built, comfortable thatch huts with fans. **Pros:** relaxing private deck areas; quiet, pretty location; friendly neighborhood. **Cons:** out of town; no air-conditioning; some rooms don't have river views. [$] *Rooms from: $48* ✉ *On small dirt*

Samlors (three-wheeled bicycle carriages) are a leisurely way to get around Luang Prabang.

road off 13 North Rd., near New Bridge, Ban Vieng Mai, Vat Sakem ☎ *071/253234* 🌐 *www.thongbay-guesthouses.com* 🛏 *16 rooms* 🍴 *No meals.*

$$$ B&B/INN 🏨 **Villa Santi.** This 19th-century royal residence in the heart of Luang Prabang was converted to a boutique hotel in 2001 by a local princess's son-in-law, who also built a resort outside town. **Pros:** main property has central location; quiet sidestreet; restaurant in pleasant garden. **Cons:** tiny bathrooms; no balconies or views; overpriced. [$] *Rooms from: $128* ✉ *Sakkarin Rd.* ☎ *071/252157* 🌐 *www.villasantihotel.com* 🛏 *20 rooms* 🍴 *Breakfast.*

$$$$ Fodor's Choice ★ 🏨 **Xiengthong Palace.** Luang Prabang's latest boutique residence used to be the Royal Palace, and has been renovated into one of the town's most luxurious and perfectly located places to stay. **Pros:** fantastic location; extremely quiet; elegant furnishings in the rooms. **Cons:** some tight corners and spaces in some rooms; not all rooms have Mekong views or plunge pools; no swimming pool or extras. [$] *Rooms from: $175* ✉ *Kounxoau Rd., Ban Phonehueng, Luang Prabang* ☎ *071/213200* 🌐 *www.xiengthongpalace.com* 🛏 *26* 🍴 *Breakfast.*

NIGHTLIFE AND THE ARTS

Luang Prabang's nightlife is limited. A number of bar-restaurants consisting of simple tables and chairs are set up on the hill above the Mekong River on Souvannakhamphong Road. On the other side of Phousi Hill are **Lao Lao Garden,** a casual, open-air restaurant and bar, **L'etranger Books and Tea,** and the **Hive Bar,** where young backpackers congregate within a dimly lighted interior or around small outdoor "campfires" to mix, mingle, and share tales of the road. The three are near the corner of Phou Si and Phommathay streets.

Dao Fa. When Muong Sua shuts down at 11:30 pm the party moves to Dao Fa, where Luang Prabang's young "nouveau riche" strut their stuff. ✉ *Across from National Stadium just near southern bus terminal* 🕿 *071/260789.*

Muong Sua. Locals head to the nightclub Muong Sua for Lao-style folk and rock music. If you need a dancing partner, the waiters will find you one. Otherwise, wait until the locals start line-dancing and simply get in line! It's located next to the Sanakeo Hotel. ✉ *Phu Vao Rd.* 🕿 *071/212263, 071/254478.*

Royal Ballet Theater Phralak-Phralam. Monday, Wednesday, and Saturday evenings at 6:00 the Royal Ballet Theater Phralak-Phralam performs at the Royal Palace museum. The program includes local folk songs, a local *bai-si* ceremony, classical dances enacting episodes from the Indian *Ramayana* epic, and outdoor presentations of the music and dances of Lao minorities. Admission is 100,000 to 150,000 kip. 🕿 *071/253705* ✉ *Sisavangvong Rd. across from Phu Si Hill.*

SPORTS AND THE OUTDOORS

Many of the tour operators in town offer interesting rafting and kayaking trips, plus cycling expeditions. Several shops rent bikes for about 25,000 kip a day.

White Elephant Adventures. The Canadian owners of White Elephant Adventures are as enthusiastic about sharing their adopted home country as they are about making sure each visitor's experiences are authentic and uncrowded. White Elephant ensures that the impact of these journeys on the local people and their environment is low. The tours are educational, led by local guides, and are constantly exploring new areas to provide a less touristy experience. Single- or multiday hiking, biking, and kayaking adventures are available for groups of two to nine people costing about $45 per head. ✉ *Sisavangvong Rd., just down the street from Luang Prabang Bakery on opposite side* 🕿 *030/514–0243* ⊕ *www.white-elephant-adventures-laos.com.*

SHOPPING

Luang Prabang has two principal markets where you can find a large selection of handicrafts: the Dara Central Market, on Setthathirat Road, and the Tribal Market, on Sisavangvong Road. In the evening, most of Sisavangvong Road turns into an open bazaar, similar to Thailand's night markets. It's a pleasant place to stroll, bargain with hawkers, and stop for a simple meal and a beer at one of many roadside stalls.

Pathana Boupha. Pathana Boupha is an antiques and textile shop and museum. It claims to produce the costumes and ornaments for the Miss New Year pageant in Luang Prabang (a seemingly prestigious endeavor). It has a dizzying array of goods on display, many of which are not for sale. Shoppers *can,* however, purchase textiles produced by a variety of different Laotian ethnic groups. ✉ *26/2 Ban Visoun* 🕿 *071/212262.*

Thitpheng Maniphone. Locally worked silver is cheap and very attractive. You can find a good selection at Thitpheng, which is located just around the corner from the Indochina Spirit restaurant. ⊠ *48/2 Ban Wat That* ☎ *071/212327.*

TAD SAE WATERFALL

15 km (9 miles) east of Luang Prabang.

Tad Sae Waterfall. Accessible only by boat, this spectacular waterfall is best visited in the rainy season, when the rivers are high and their waters thunder over the cascade. The waterfall features multilevel limestone formations divided into three steps with big pools beneath them—don't forget your bathing suit. There are some old waterwheels here and a small, simple resort nearby. ⌦ *10,000 kip.*

GETTING HERE AND AROUND

From Luang Prabang you can take a tuk-tuk east on Highway 13 for 13 km (8 miles) to the turnoff for the pristine Lao Lum riverside village of Ban Aen (20,000–30,000 kip). From Ban Aen, hire a boat (10,000 kip per person) for a two-minute trip upstream to the waterfall. However, it's easier to let one of Luang Prabang's many travel agencies arrange your trip for about 55,000 kip per person, including admission to the falls. Tours leave around 1 pm and return by 5. Adventure-tour agencies like White Elephant (⇨ *Sports and the Outdoors in Luang Prabang)* and Green Discovery (⇨ *Laos Planner)* also organize kayaking day trips to the falls.

SAFETY AND PRECAUTIONS

Be careful on the slippery paths around the falls.

TIMING

A few hours should give you enough time to see enjoy the area.

PAK OU CAVES

25 km (16 miles) up the Mekong from Luang Prabang.

Pak Ou Caves. Set in high limestone cliffs above the Mekong River, at the point where it meets the Nam Ou River from northern Laos, are two sacred caves filled with thousands of Buddha statues dating from the 16th century. The lower cave, **Tham Thing,** is accessible from the river by a stairway, and has enough daylight to allow you to find your way around. The stairway continues to the upper cave, **Tham Phum,** for which you need a flashlight. The admission charge of 20,000 kip includes a flashlight and a guide.

The town of Pak Ou, across the river from the caves and accessible by ferry, has several passable restaurants.

GETTING HERE AND AROUND

It takes 1½ hours to get to Pak Ou by boat from Luang Prabang. Many agencies in town organize tours for 80,000 kip per person, including admission to the caves. Tours leave Luang Prabang around 8 am and include visits to waterside villages for a look at the rich variety of local handicrafts, a nip of lao-lao, and perhaps a bowl of noodles. You can

CLOSE UP

Laos: Then and Now

Despite its limited infrastructure, Laos is a wonderful country to visit. The Laotians are some of the friendliest, gentlest people in Southeast Asia—devoutly Buddhist, and traditional in many ways. Not yet inured to countless visiting foreigners, locals volunteer assistance and a genuine welcome. And because this land-locked nation is so sparsely popu-lated—fewer than 6 million people in an area larger than Great Britain—its mountainous countryside has not yet been deforested or overdeveloped. Laos has a rich culture and history, and though it's been a battleground many times in the past, it's a peace-ful, stable country today.

Prehistoric remains show that the river valleys and lowland areas of Laos were settled as far back as 40,000 years ago, first by hunt-ers and gatherers and later by more developed communities. The mysterious Plain of Jars—a stretch of land littered with ancient stone and clay jars at least 2,000 years old—indicates the early presence of a sophisticated society skilled in the manufacture of bronze and iron implements and ceramics. Starting in the 3rd century BC, cultural and trad-ing links were forged with Chinese and Indian civilizations.

Between the 4th and 8th century, farming communities along the Mekong River began to organize themselves into communities called "Muang"—a term still used in both Laos and neighboring Thailand. This network of Muang gave rise in the mid-14th century to the first Lao monarchy, given the fanciful name of Lan Xang, or the "Kingdom of a Million Elephants," for the large herds of the pachyderms that roamed the land.

At the start of the 18th century, fol-lowing fighting over the throne, the kingdom was partitioned into three realms: Luang Prabang, Vientiane, and Champasak. Throughout the latter part of the 18th century Laos was under the control of neighbor-ing Siam. In the early 19th century Laos staged an uprising against the Siamese, but in 1828 an invading Siamese army under King Rama III sacked Vientiane and took firm control of most of Laos as a province of Siam. Siam maintained possession of Laos until the French established the Federation of French Indochina, which included Laos, Vietnam, and Cambodia, in 1893. In 1904 the Lao monarch Sisavang Vong set up court in Luang Prabang, but Laos remained part of French Indochina until 1949. For a brief period during World War II Laos was occupied by Japan, but reverted to French control at the end of the war. In 1953 the Lao PDR became an independent nation, which was confirmed by the passage of the Geneva Convention in 1954. The monarchy was finally dissolved in 1975, when the revolutionary group Pathet Lao, allied with North Vietnam's communist movement dur-ing the Vietnam War, seized power after a long guerrilla war.

During the Vietnam War the U.S. Air Force, in a vain attempt to disrupt the Ho Chi Minh Trail, dropped more tons of bombs on Laos than were dropped on Germany during World War II. Since the end of the Vietnam War the People's Democratic Party (formerly the Pathet Lao) has ruled the country, first on Marxist-Leninist lines and now on the basis of limited pro-market reforms. Overtures are being made to the outside, particularly to Thailand, Japan, and China, to assist in developing the country—not an easy task. The Friendship Bridge over the Mekong River connects Vientiane with Nong Khai in northeastern Thailand, making Laos more accessible to trade with neighboring countries.

Decentralization of the state-controlled economy began in 1986, resulting in a steady annual growth rate of around 6%. The country has continued to grow steadily: Vientiane, Luang Prabang, and Pakse have new airports; visitors from most countries can now get a visa on arrival, and those from some ASEAN (Association of Southeast Asian Nations) countries need no visa at all. New hotels are constantly opening. Nonetheless, infrastructure in the country remains primitive in comparison to the rest of the world. Laos has no railways; communications technology and electricity are common only in more densely populated areas (cell phones outnumber landlines five to one), and only 9 of the country's 44 airports and airstrips are paved. The road from the current capital, Vientiane, to Laos's ancient capital, Luang Prabang, has been paved and upgraded—though it still takes eight hours to make the serpentine, 320-km (198-mile) journey north, and nearly 90% of the nation's roads are unpaved. The upgraded road running south from Vientiane can now accommodate tour buses going all the way to the Cambodian border. Other border crossings have also opened up, especially along the Vietnamese border.

A low standard of living (the GDP per-capita of $1,900 is one of the world's lowest, and 34% of the population lives below the poverty line) and a rugged landscape that hampers transportation and communication have long made the countryside of Laos a sleepy backwater. But Luang Prabang, boosted by its status as a World Heritage Site, has become a busy and relatively prosperous tourist hub. Vientiane, despite its new hotels and restaurants, remains one of the world's sleepiest capital cities.

Despite their relative poverty, Lao people are frank, friendly, and outwardly cheerful people. Although Laos certainly has far to go economically, it is currently a member of the ASEAN trade group, has Normal Trade Relations status with the United States, and receives assistance from the European Union to help it acquire WTO membership. Growing investment in Laos and expanding numbers of tourists to both the main tourist centers and more remote areas should continue to benefit the people of Laos.

9

also take a tuk-tuk to the village of Pak Ou, and then a quick boat ride across the Mekong, but few people use this option, as it is less scenic and pricier than taking a tour.

SAFETY AND PRECAUTIONS
Watch your head and footing in the caves.

TIMING
A few hours is plenty of time.

TAD KHUANG SI WATERFALL

29 km (18 mi) south of Luang Prabang.

Tad Khuang Si Waterfall. A series of cascades surrounded by lush foliage, Tad Khuang Si is a popular spot with Lao and foreigners alike. Many visitors merely view the falls from the lower pool, where picnic tables and food vendors invite you to linger, but a steep path through the forest leads to pools above the falls that are perfect for a swim. The best time to visit the falls is between November and April, after the rainy season. ⊠ *20,000 kip.*

GETTING HERE AND AROUND
Tour operators in Luang Prabang offer day trips that combine Tad Kuang Si with a visit to a Khamu tribal village nearby for 55,000 kip. The drive, past rice farms and small Lao Lum tribal villages, is half the adventure. Taxi and tuk-tuk drivers in Luang Prabang all want to take you to the falls, quoting around 150,000 kip round-trip, but unless you have your own group, a tour is a better deal.

SAFETY AND PRECAUTIONS
Watch your footing around the falls.

TIMING
Half a day will give you enough time to enjoy the area

BAN MUANG NGOI

150 km (93 miles) northeast of Luang Prabang.

This picturesque river village sits on the eastern side of the Nam Ou River, which descends from Phongsaly Province in the north to meet the Mekong River opposite the famous Pak Ou Caves. The village, populated by Lao Lum and surrounded by unusual limestone peaks, has become a popular traveler hangout, with friendly locals, gorgeous scenery, and plenty of treks and river options to keep you busy for several days. Be aware that village only has electricity for three or four hours a night, so accommodations lack some amenities that you may be used to.

GETTING HERE AND AROUND
The journey here is an adventure in itself: a minivan takes you from Luang Prabang's Northern Bus Terminal to a pier at Nong Khiaw (four hours; 55,000 kip), where boats (25,000 kip) continue on a one-hour trip upstream to the village (boats leave Nong Khiaw at 11 am and 2 pm, and return from Muang Ngoi at 9:30 am daily, which means that you need to charter your own boat or go on a tour if you don't want to spend the night). Just about any travel agent in Luang Prabang can

arrange a guide or a tour. From Muang Ngoi, you can also continue upriver when the water is high enough to Muang Khoua and then onwards to Phongsaly.

SAFETY AND PRECAUTIONS

The village is safe, but take the usual precautions with your money and belongings.

TIMING

Two or three days will give you a chance to go for some hikes or boat trips and just relax in one of Laos's more tranquil spots.

WHERE TO STAY

For expanded hotel reviews, visit Fodors.com.

$ B&B/INN **Ning Ning Guesthouse.** Of the many simple guesthouses in Ban Muang Ngoi, this is probably the best. **Pros:** good mosquito nets; riverside restaurant; quiet. **Cons:** bungalows lack river views; hot water rarely works; no fans or air-conditioning. [$] *Rooms from: $10* ✉ *Ban Muang Ngoi* ☎ *020/2388–0122* *ningning_guesthouse@hotmail.com* *10 bungalows* *No credit cards* 🍴 *No meals.*

LUANG NAM THA

319 km (198 miles) north of Luang Prabang.

The capital of Laos's northernmost province, Luang Nam Tha is the headquarters of the groundbreaking Nam Ha Ecotourism. The program, a model for Southeast Asia, actively encourages the involvement of local communities in the development and management of tourism policies. You can join a two- or three-day trek (organized by Forest Retreat, Green Discovery, the Boat Landing Guesthouse, and a few other agencies) through the Nam Ha Protected Area, which provides some excellent opportunities for communing with nature, having outdoor adventures, and visiting ethnic minorities (Khamu, Akha, Lanten, and Yao tribes live in the dense forest).

9

GETTING HERE AND AROUND

Luang Nam Tha is tiny, and can be navigated on foot, although many places rent mountain bikes (10,000–25,000 kip per day) for exploring the surrounding countryside.

AIR TRAVEL Lao Airlines flies from Vientiane to Luang Nam Tha Monday, Wednesday, and Friday for $100. Tuk-tuks run from the airport and bus station into town for 10,000 kip per person.

BOAT TRAVEL Longtail boats can be arranged for the two-day trip on the Nam Tha River, running all the way down to Pak Tha, where the Nam Tha meets the Mekong, and on to Huay Xai. The same trip can also be done in reverse, although it makes more sense to go down river. A boat costs about 1,800,000 kip, and can take four to six passengers. Unless you speak Lao, it's best to make arrangements through the Boat Landing (⇨ *Where to Eat and Stay, below*) or Forest Retreat (⇨ *below*). Note that the boats can only travel the Nam Tha during times of high water, basically from July to October.

BUS TRAVEL The Luang Nam Tha bus station is 10 km (6 miles) out of town, past the airport. Buses go to Oudomxay three times a day (four hours; 40,000 kip); to Luang Prabang and Vientiane each morning (8 and 19 hours; 90,000 kip and 170,000 kip, respectively); and to Muang Singh every hour and a half (two hours; 25,000 kip). The mountainous terrain and bad roads, in addition to rental prices, make driving impractical.

SAFETY AND PRECAUTIONS
Be careful of snakes if trekking in the area, and know that leeches (harmless but very annoying) come out during the rainy season.

TIMING
Nam Tha town isn't very exciting, but give yourself a couple of days to do an ecotour, trek, kayak, bicycle, or explore the sights along the Nam Tha River and the Nam Ha Protected Area.

ESSENTIALS
Emergencies Provincial Hospital ✉ *Nam Tha Rd.* ☎ *086/211752.*

Visitor and Tour Information Green Discovery Laos ✉ *Nam Tha Rd.* ☎ *086/211484* ⊕ *www.greendiscoverylaos.com.*

Forest Retreat Laos. Run by a New Zealand couple and their Lao counterpart, this new agency (and excellent restaurant!) offer multiple tours in the area, with kayaking and trekking in the Nam Ha Protected Area, along with visits to ethnic minorities, and their professional services are highly recommended. ✉ *Ban Oudomsin, Luang Nam Tha* ☎ *020/5568–0031* ⊕ *www.forestretreatlaos.com.*

WHERE TO EAT AND STAY
For expanded hotel reviews, visit Fodors.com.

$ **✕ Aysha.** A welcome addition to a town with limited culinary options,
INDIAN Aysha is run by relatives of the popular Nisha chain, and serves up cheap, tasty Indian food. It makes for a nice change from larb and sticky rice. $ *Average main: $3* ✉ *Ban Oudomsin* ☎ *020/5684–1685, 020/9959–9674* ▭ *No credit cards.*

$ **✕ The Forest Retreat.** Luang Nam Tha has finally gone vogue—amazing
INTERNATIONAL to have outstanding wood fire pizza, real espresso and cappuccino,
Fodor's Choice fresh-baked bread, hummus, pesto, pasta, and much more in remote
★ northern Laos. A husband and wife team from New Zealand have opened this happening new eatery, which is also a highly recommended trekking agency working with local people to create sustainable tourism in the Nam Ha Protected Area. $ *Average main: $7* ✉ *Luang Nam Tha* ☎ *020/5568–0031* ⊕ *forestretreatlaos.com.*

$ **✕ Heuan Lao.** In a beautiful wooden guesthouse with an open-air dining
INTERNATIONAL room, Heuan Lao, at the northern end of Nam Tha Road, has great ambience and is the most popular place in town for officials and businesspeople. The extensive menu has plenty of Thai and Lao specialties, as well as a Western menu featuring steak and pizza. They serve Western breakfasts and even have bagels and cream cheese on the menu! $ *Average main: $4* ✉ *Nam Tha Rd.* ☎ *086/211111* ▭ *No credit cards.*

$ **⌂ Boat Landing Guesthouse.** Comfortable accommodations can be
B&B/INN found in the timber-and-bamboo bungalows furnished in rattan at this eco-friendly guesthouse. **Pros:** open-air restaurant with traditional

Most Lao men, like Thai men, join the *sangha* (monastic community) at least temporarily.

food; great source of local information; bicycles available. **Cons:** not at all convenient for town and restaurants, no Internet on premises; quite expensive for Luang Nam Tha. $ *Rooms from: $45* ⊠ *Box 28, Ban Kone* ☎ *086/312398* ⊕ *www.theboatlanding.com* ✈ *11 rooms* ⦿ *Breakfast.*

MUANG SING

60 km (37 miles) north of Luang Nam Tha.

In the late 19th century this mountain-ringed town on the Sing Mountain River was the seat of a Tai Lue prince, Chao Fa Silino; Muang Sing lost its regional prominence, however, when French-colonial forces occupied the town and established a garrison here. Muang Sing is known for its morning market, which draws throngs of traditional ethnic hill tribes. Shoppers from among the 20 different tribes living in the area, and even traders from China, visit the market to buy locally produced goods and handicrafts. The market is open daily throughout the day but it is best to go from 6 to 8 before the minority groups return to their villages.

GETTING HERE AND AROUND

The only way in and out of Muang Singh is by bus from Luang Nam Tha. There are five to six departures each day; the two-hour journey costs 25,000 kip.

SAFETY AND PRECAUTIONS

This is a safe place, but take the usual precautions with your money and belongings.

TIMING
Unless you're coming here to trek and visit the hill tribes, Muang Singh isn't worth more than a day. Its appeal lies in what is out of town.

RIVER JOURNEY TO HUAY XAI

297 km (184 mi) up the Mekong from Luang Prabang.

River Journey to Huay Xai. Growing rapidly in popularity is the 300-km (186-mile) Mekong River trip between Luang Prabang and Huay Xai, across the river from Chiang Khong in Thailand. It's a leisurely journey on one of the world's most famous stretches of river. Your boat drifts along the meandering Mekong past a constantly changing primeval scene of towering cliffs, huge mud flats and sandbanks, rocky islands, and riverbanks smothered in thick jungle, also swaths of cultivated land, mulberry trees, bananas, and tiny garlic fields. There are no roads, just forest paths linking dusty settlements where the boats tie up for refreshment stops.

The only village of note is a halfway station, Pakbeng, which has many guesthouses and restaurants along its one main street, and seems to exist solely to serve the boat passengers who arrive each night. ■**TIP→ Once you arrive in Huay Xai (which has little of interest in itself other than the Gibbon Experience), a good way to return to Thailand is to cross the river to Chiang Khong and then take a bus to Chiang Rai, 60 km (37 miles) inland.**

GETTING HERE AND AROUND
There are three ways to make the journey to Huay Xai from Luang Prabang on the river: by regular "slow" boat, which holds about 50 passengers; by speedboat, which seats about 4; and by luxury cruise.

The regular boat is at least a 12- to 14-hour journey over two days. You'll spend the night in Pakbeng, in basic guesthouses whose owners come to meet the boats and corral guests. The fare is about 240,000 kip per person; slow boats depart daily from the riverside near the morning market in Luang Prabang.

Speedboats make the journey between Luang Prabang and Huay Xai in six hours. ⚠ **Speedboats may be fun for the first hour, but they are not safe, and become extremely uncomfortable after the novelty wears off.** The seats are hard, the engine noise is deafening (earplugs are advised), and the wind and spray can be chilling. If you're determined to take one, bring a warm, waterproof windbreaker, and be sure to get a life jacket and crash helmet with a visor from the boat driver. Speedboats cost 350,000 kip per person, and leave daily from a pier on the outskirts of Huay Xai.

LuangSay. Much more comfortable than the regular boat and speedboat, but far more expensive, is the *LuangSay* luxury boat, which is specially designed for leisurely river travel. The river cruise includes accommodation in Pakbeng at the comfortable LuangSay Lodge. The *LuangSay* departs from Huay Xai on Monday, Thursday, Friday, and Sunday (Monday and Friday, October through April), and returns from Luang Prabang every Monday and Friday (Tuesday and Saturday, October through April; no boats in June). The cruise costs $500 all-inclusive ($390 from May to September). ✉ *50/4 Sakkarine Rd., Ban Vat Sene, Luang Prabang, Thailand* ☎ *071/252553* 🌐 *www.mekong-cruises.com.*

SAFETY AND PRECAUTIONS

See the above warning on speedboats.

TIMING

It's not worth lingering in Huay Xai, as it's just a border-crossing point and riverboat terminus.

ESSENTIALS

Visitor and Tour Information. Guesthouses in Huay Xai can answer most questions.

EXPLORING HUAY XAI

The Gibbon Experience. Certainly one of the most unique experiences one can have in Laos, let alone anywhere in Asia, the Gibbon Experience combines a visit to the Bokeo Nature Reserve with jungle trekking, sleeping in canopy-level treehouses, traveling among the trees by zip lines, and watching gibbons and other types of wildlife. Profits go toward gibbon rehabilitation and sustainable conservation projects. Be prepared to rough it a bit. Book ahead of time, as this is a popular activity and groups are small. ✉ *Huay Xai, Thailand* ☎ *084/212021* 🌐 *gibbonexperience.org* 🎟 *$250 for 3-day all-inclusive package.*

WHERE TO EAT AND STAY

For expanded hotel reviews, visit Fodors.com.

$ ASIAN 🍴 **Riverside Houayxay.** For a tasty meal in a prime spot along the Mekong, the Riverside Houayxai can't be bettered. The menu is enormous, featuring Thai and Lao dishes, along with Western breakfasts. In the evening, try the *dath* barbecue, or perhaps some steamed fish with lemon or curried crab. Popular with tour groups, the open-air eatery offers ample Mekong vistas and sits right above the boat landing to Thailand. [$] *Average main: $6* ✉ *168 Centre Road, Huay Xai, Thailand* ☎ *084/211064, 020/5420–2222.*

$ HOTEL 🏨 **Riverside Houayxay.** For a convenient night's rest just next to the Lao immigration and the boat to Chiang Khong, Thailand, the Riverside is a decent choice. **Pros:** centrally located; great Mekong views from some rooms; restaurant is a great spot with good food. **Cons:** very expensive for Huay Xai; river-facing rooms get very hot in the afternoon; often packed with noisy tour groups. [$] *Rooms from: $25* ✉ *168 Centre Rd., Huay Xai* ☎ *084/211064, 020/54202222* ✉ *riverside_huayxai_laos_@hotmail.com* 🛏 *40 rooms* 🍽 *No meals.*

PHONGSALY

425 km (264 miles) north of Luang Prabang.

If you're looking for off-the-beaten-track adventure, head for the provincial capital Phongsaly, in the far north of Laos. It's a hill station and market town nearly 5,000 feet above sea level in the country's most spectacular mountain range, Phu Fa. Trekking through this land of

Religion in Laos

The overwhelming majority of Laotians are Buddhists, yet as in neighboring Thailand, spirit-worship is widespread, blending easily with temple traditions and rituals. A common belief holds that supernatural spirits called *phi* have power over individual and community life.

Laotians believe that each person has 32 *khwan,* or individual spirits, which must be appeased and kept "bound" to the body. If one of the khwan leaves the body, sickness can result, and then a ceremony must be performed to reattach the errant spirit. In this ritual, which is known as *bai-si,* white threads are tied to the wrist of the ailing person in order to fasten the spirits. Apart from the khwan, there are countless other spirits inhabiting the home, gardens, orchards, fields, forests, mountains, rivers, and even individual rocks and trees.

Luang Prabang has a team of ancestral guardian spirits, the Pu Nyeu Na Nyeu, who are lodged in a special temple, Wat Aham. In the south, the fierce guardian spirits of Wat Phu are appeased every year with the sacrifice of a buffalo to guarantee an abundance of rain during the rice-growing season.

Despite the common belief in a spirit world, more than 90% of Laotians are officially Theravada Buddhists, a conservative nontheistic form of Buddhism said to be derived directly from the words of the Buddha. Buddhism arrived in Laos in the 3rd century BC by way of Ashoka, an Indian emperor who helped spread the religion. A later form of Buddhism, Mahayana, which arose in the 1st century AD, is also practiced in Laos, particularly in

the cities. It differs from Theravada in that followers venerate the bodhisattvas. This northern school of Buddhism spread from India to Nepal, China, Korea, and Japan, and is practiced by Vietnamese and Chinese alike in all the bigger towns of Laos. The Chinese in Laos also follow Taoism and Confucianism.

Buddhism in Laos is so interlaced with daily life that you have a good chance of witnessing its practices and rituals firsthand—from the early-morning sight of women giving alms to monks on their rounds through the neighborhood to the evening routine of monks gathering for their temple recitations. If you visit temples on Buddhist holy days, which coincide with the new moon, you'll likely hear monks chanting texts of the Buddha's teachings.

Christianity is followed by a small minority of mostly French-educated, elite Laotians, although the faith also has adherents among hill tribe converts in areas that have been visited by foreign missionaries. Missionary activity has been curbed in recent years, however, as the Lao government forbids the dissemination of foreign religious materials.

Islam is practiced by a handful of Arab and Indian businesspeople in Vientiane. There are also some Muslims from Yunnan, China, called Chin Haw, in the northern part of Laos. More recently, a very small number of Cham refugees from Pol Pot's Cambodia (1975–79) took refuge in Vientiane, where they have established a mosque.

forest-covered mountains and rushing rivers may be as close as you'll ever get to the thrill of exploring virgin territory.

GETTING HERE AND AROUND

Buses from Oudomxay make the nine-hour run to Phongsaly daily at 8 am (75,000 kip), with the journey getting slightly faster each year as the road gets upgraded. You can also get here by boat from Muang Khua when the water levels are high enough; the six-hour trip is 120,000 kip per person. In town, tuk-tuks can take you wherever you need to go for 5,000 kip.

SAFETY AND PRECAUTIONS

Always trek with a local guide. The terrain is mountainous jungle, and it's easy to get lost. It is also close to the Chinese border, which is not always clearly marked. English is not widely spoken here.

TIMING

The only reason to come to Phongsaly is to go trekking or take a boat ride down to Muang Khua and on to Muang Ngoi. Three days would be a minimum for any of these. If you're pressed for time, skip Phongsaly, as the journey is a difficult one.

TOURS

The Phongsaly Provincial Tourism office runs a good ecotourism program providing treks and homestays in hill tribe areas with English-speaking guides.

ESSENTIALS

Visitor and Tour Information Phongsaly Tourism Office ☎ 020/54284600 ⊕ www.phongsaly.net.

EXPLORING PHONGSALY

Tribal Museum. If you'd like to take a break from trekking, this local museum offers a fascinating glimpse into the lives and culture of the 25 different ethnic groups in the area. We like the kaleidoscopic display of tribal costumes. ☎ 020/5657–6050 ☎ 5,000 kip ☉ Weekdays 8:30–11:30 and 1:30–4:30.

WHERE TO EAT AND STAY

For expanded hotel reviews, visit Fodors.com.

OUDOMXAY

$ **✕ Souphailin's Restaurant.** Despite its humble appearances, this small
LAO thatched hut eatery just opposite the palatial neoclassical Bank of
Fodor'sChoice Laos and a few steps down the small side street serves up the best
★ food in Oudomxay. Mrs. Souphailin specializes in authentic northern Lao food and it's well worth it to come in early to preorder dishes #1 to #15 on the menu, which are all local specialties that need several hours of prep time. Try the delicious *mok het khao,* white mushrooms cooked in a banana leaf, or the *kaeng naw som sai sin gai,* bamboo soup with chicken. Truly authentic! $ *Average main: $5* ⊠ *Oudomxay* ☎ *081/211147, 020/606–2474* ⊟ *No credit cards.*

$ **⌂ Litthavixay Guesthouse.** Located right between the bus station and mar-
HOTEL ket on the main road, this is a good choice if you're spending the night in Oudomxay on the way to or from Phongsaly. **Pros:** centrally located; bicycle rental; Internet café. **Cons:** noisy street outside; minimal English

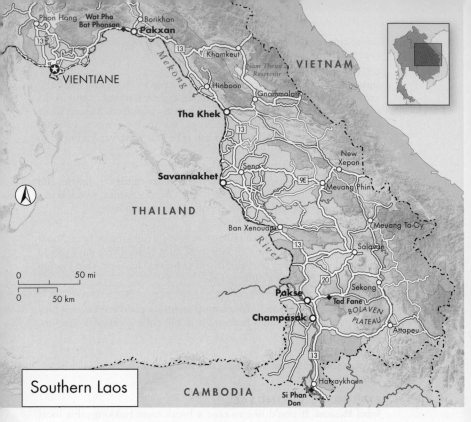

Southern Laos

spoken; west-facing rooms get quite hot in the afternoon. $ *Rooms from: $9* ✉ *Main rd., Oudomxay* ☎ *081/212175* ⊕ *litthavixay@yahoo.com* ⇗ *18 rooms* ▭ *No credit cards* ❍ *No meals.*

PHONGSALY

$

HOTEL

Phou Fa. Located in the old Chinese consulate, near the roundabout and governor's house, the Phou Fa is probably the best choice for a night of relative comfort in Phongsaly. **Pros:** great amenities for Phongsaly; decent selection of rooms; great views. **Cons:** up a hill; bit of a walk from town; power outages. $ *Rooms from: $19* ✉ *Old Chinese Consulate* ☎ *088/210031* ✐ *phoufahotel@yahoo.com* ⇗ *28 rooms* ▭ *No credit cards* ❍ *Breakfast.*

SOUTHERN LAOS

In some ways, Laos is really two countries: the south and north are as different as two sides of a coin. The mountainous north was for centuries virtually isolated from the more accessible south, where lowlands, the broad Mekong valley, and high plateaus were easier to traverse and settle. The south does have its mountains, however: notably the Annamite range, called Phu Luang, home of the aboriginal Mon-Khmer ethnic groups who lived here long before Lao farmers and traders arrived from northern Laos and China. The Lao were followed by

CLOSE UP

Lao: A Few Key Phrases

The official language is Lao, part of the extensive Thai family of languages of Southeast Asia spoken from Vietnam in the east to India in the west. Spoken Lao is very similar to the northern Thai language, as well as local dialects in the Shan states in Myanmar and Sipsongbanna in China. Lao is tonal, meaning a word can have several meanings according to the tone in which it's spoken.

In tourist hotels the staff generally speaks some English. You can find a smattering of English-speakers in shops and restaurants. A few old-timers know some French.

Here are a few common and useful words:

Hello: sabai di (pronounced *sa-bye dee*)

Thank you: khop chai deu (pronounced *cop jai dew*; use khop cheu neu in northern Laos)

Yes: heu (pronounced like deux) *or* thia

No: bo

Where?: iu sai (pronounced *you sai*)?

How much?: to dai (pronounced *taw dai*)?

Zero: sun (pronounced *soon*)

One: neung

Two: song

Three: sam

Four: si

Five: ha

Six: hok

Seven: tiet (pronounced *jee-yet*)

Eight: pet

Nine: kao

Ten: sip

Twenty: sao (rhymes with cow; different from Thai "yee sip")

Hundred: neung loi

Thousand: neung phan

To have fun: muan

To eat: kin khao (pronounced *kin cow*)

To drink: kin nam

Water: nam

Rice: khao

Expensive: peng

Bus: lot me (pronounced *lot may*)

House: ban

Road: thanon

Village: ban

Island: don

River: mae nam (pronounced *may nam*)

Doctor: maw

Hospital: hong mo (pronounced *hong maw*)

Post Office: paisani

Hotel: hong hem

Toilet: hong nam

9

French colonists, who built the cities of Pakxan, Tha Khek, Savan-nakhet, and Pakse. Although the French influence is still tangible, the southern Lao cling tenaciously to their old traditions, making the south a fascinating destination.

Pakse is the regional capital, and has an international airport with daily flights to Vientiane, as well as to Phnom Penh and Siem Reap in neighboring Cambodia. There's also overnight bus service to Pakse from Vientiane, plus good local service in the area.

SOUTH ALONG THE MEKONG

Highway 13 out of Vientiane penetrates as far as the deep south of Laos and the Cambodian border, a distance of 835 km (518 miles). It's paved all the way. The section between Vientiane and Pakse is not noted for sightseeing opportunities, but if you have time you can stop to savor the slow-paced, timeless river life here.

GETTING HERE AND AROUND

AIR TRAVEL   Lao Airlines flies from Vientiane to Savannakhet several times daily for 850,000 kip.

BUS TRAVEL   Local bus service connects all the towns on Highway 13, from Vientiane or Pakse. VIP buses traveling the Vientiane–Pakse route do not stop in the small towns; they will stop in Savannakhet and Tha Kaek, but they'll charge you the full fare to Vientiane or Pakse and you'll arrive in the middle of the night. Local buses depart hourly until midday for Savannakhet, Tha Kaek, Paksan, and all other destinations along the Mekong from Pakse's Northern Bus Station (about five hours; 45,000 kip) and from Vientiane's Southern Bus Station.

SAFETY AND PRECAUTIONS

Safety isn't an issue here, but take the usual precautions with your money and belongings.

TIMING

This area is only for those with extra time. There are some ecotourism and trekking projects that have sprung up in Tha Kaek and Savanna-khet, but one would need an extra three to five days to cover this area. Most visitors bypass it for the sights farther south.

ESSENTIALS

Emergencies Provincial Hospital ⊠ *Kanthabuli Rd., Savannakhet* ☎ *041/212051.*

Visitor and Tour Information Provincial Tourist Office ⊠ *Ratsaphanith Rd., Savannakhet* ☎ *041/212755.*

EXPLORING THE ROAD SOUTH TO PAKSE

Pakxan. Pakxan, 150 km (93 miles) south of Vientiane, in Bolikhamxay Province, is a former French-colonial outpost, a Mekong River port, and now the center of the Lao Christian community. Traveling south from Pakxan, Highway 13 crosses the Nam Kading River, for which the protected-forested NBCA (National Biodiversity Conservation Area Nam Kading) is named. About 90 km (56 miles) south of Pakxan High-way 13 meets Highway 8, which leads via Lak Sao to Nam Pho on the

The Bolaven Plateau's volcanic soil is ideal for farming.

Vietnamese border. From here the road leads to the Vietnamese coastal city of Vinh and other areas of north Vietnam.

Tha Khek. Tha Khek, 350 km (217 miles) south of Vientiane, in Khammuan Province, is a bustling Mekong River port, with some of its ancient city wall still intact. It's surrounded by stunning countryside and karst (limestone caverns and sinkholes). There are some spectacular limestone caves in the area—notably **Tham Khong Lor.** This cave is more than 6½ km (4 miles) long, and is so large that the Nam Hin Bun River runs through it. Opposite Tha Khek is Thailand's provincial capital of Nakhon Phanom. Ferries ply the waters between the two cities.

Wat Pha Bat Phonsan. The first stop of interest on Highway 13, about 80 km (50 miles) northeast of Vientiane, is the pilgrimage temple complex Wat Pha Bat Phonsan, which has a revered footprint in stone said to be that of the Buddha.

SAVANNAKHET

470 km (290 miles) south of Vientiane.

A former French-colonial provincial center, the pleasant riverside town of Savannakhet is today the urban hub of a vast rice-growing plain. It's distinguished by some fine examples of French-colonial architecture. There are some options for eco-trekking north of Savannakhet in Tha Kaek at the fantastic Khong Lor Cave, but given the distances and slow transport down here, this will take a lot of extra time. That said, the town itself is worth a daylong visit tops, and most visitors on a timetable bypass it for the more interesting options farther south.

Dinosaur museum. One of Savannakhet's curiosities is a dinosaur museum, which displays fossils discovered in the area. ⊠ *Khantaburi Rd.* 🕾 *041/212597* 🖅 *5,000 kip* ☉ *Weekdays 8–11:30 and 1–3:30.*

GETTING HERE AND AROUND

Lao Airlines flies from Vientiane to Savannakhet several times daily for 850,000 kip. From Pakse, buses depart hourly until midday for Savannakhet from the northern bus station (five hours; 45,000 kip). VIP buses (115,000 kip) from Vientiane's southern bus terminal to Savannakhet depart daily at 8:30 pm and arrive about seven hours later. A songthaew in town will cost around 20,000 kip to most any point

The Thai town of Mukdahan lies just across the Mekong River and is accessible by ferry or by crossing the second of three bridges connecting Thailand and Laos. The bridge, one of several established to create an East–West Economic Corridor connecting the Vietnamese port of Da Nang with Laos, Thailand, and Myanmar (Burma), also greatly facilitates tourist travel between Thailand and Laos. Eight to twelve buses shuttle passengers the 10 miles in either direction; buses depart daily 7 am to 5:30 pm, stopping briefly at the border, where passengers must pay a B10 fee.

ESSENTIALS

Banks Lao Development Bank ⊠ *Udomsin Rd.* 🕾 *041/212272.*

Emergencies Provincial Hospital ⊠ *Kanthabuli Rd.* 🕾 *041/212051.*

PAKSE

205 km (127 miles) south of Savannakhet, 675 km (420 miles) south of Vientiane.

Pakse is a former French-colonial stronghold, linked now with neighboring Thailand by a bridge 40 km (25 miles) away. It plays a central role in an ambitious regional plan to create an "Emerald Triangle"—a trade and tourism community grouping Laos, Thailand, and Cambodia. The city has few attractions, but is the starting point for tours to the Khmer ruins at Wat Phu, the 4,000 Islands, and the Bolaven Plateau, which straddles the southern provinces of Saravan, Sekon, Attapeu, and Champasak. The volcanic soil of the plateau makes the vast region ideal for agriculture: it's the source of much of the country's prized coffee, tea, and spices. Despite its beauty and central role in the Lao economy, the plateau has minimal tourist infrastructure, and is very much off-the-beaten-track territory.

GETTING HERE AND AROUND

AIR TRAVEL There are several Lao Airlines flights each day from Vientiane to Pakse, sometimes routed via Savannakhet; the flight takes an hour and costs around a million kip one way. Lao Airlines flights from Siem Reap, Cambodia, arrive every Wednesday, Friday, and Sunday. The price of a one-way ticket is similar. A tuk-tuk from Pakse International Airport (4 km [2 miles] west of town) to the city center costs 30,000 kip to 40,000 kip.

BOAT TRAVEL   You can charter a boat for 600,0000 kip up to six passengers to go to Champasak and visit Wat Phu from several agencies in town, a far more scenic alternative than traveling by road.

BUS TRAVEL   Pakse is the transportation hub for all destinations in the south. Comfortable VIP bed buses (using the VIP bus station near the evening market) make the overnight, 11-hour journey to and from Vientiane (200,000 kip from Vientiane, including transfer to bus station, 170,000 kip from Pakse to Vientiane). Buses leave Vientiane nightly at 8 or 8:30 pm and arrive in Pakse at 6:30 am; the times are the same from Pakse to Vientiane. Pakse's central bus station, a short walk east of the VIP terminal, has hourly departures to Savannakhet (five hours; 50,000 kip) and other points north.

Buses depart from the Southern Bus Station (known as Lo Lak Pert, due to its location at the Km 8 mark on the road east of Pakse) for the Si Phan Don area and Champasak. If you're headed to Si Phan Don, it's more convenient to take a minibus, which will pick you up at your hotel for 65,000 kip; all guesthouses sell tickets.

For international departures, you can get direct buses to Ubon in Thailand from Pakse as well as to Phnom Penh in Cambodia.

CAR TRAVEL   Any travel agent in town can arrange car rental with a driver.

TAXI, TUK-TUK, AND SONGTH-AEW TRAVEL   Tuk-tuks around town cost 10,000 kip (although you will be hard pressed to get this price as a tourist), and a charter out to the Southern Bus Station costs 40,000 kip. Songthaews to Champasak (two hours; 30,000 kip) leave from the Dao Heuang market.

TIMING

There's little in the way of sights here—it's more a place to book tickets, go to the bank, and deal with any kind of communications or business before moving on to Champasak, Tad Fane, or the 4,000 Islands. One night should be enough (unless using Pakse as a base for visiting Champasak or elsewhere as a day tour) although many visitors end up staying longer as Pakse has enough decent hotels, restaurants, and cafés to while away some time.

TOURS

Pakse's Provincial Tourism office can arrange boat and vehicle ecotours to Champasak and Si Phan Don as well as farther afield, with trained guides at competitive prices. However, the private Pakse Travel runs similar tours, and has excellent transportation options and is far busier and more willing to help. Day tours to the Boloven Plateau, homestays on Don Daeng and in ethnic villages, tea-and-coffee plantation tours ($180 for two) are just some of the options on offer.

ESSENTIALS

Banks BCEL ✉ 11 St. ☎ 31/212770.

Emergencies Provincial Hospital ✉ Ban Pakse ☎ 031/212844.

Visitor and Tour Information Champasak Provincial Tourism ✉ Th. 11, Ban Tasalakam ☎ 031/212021. **Pakse Travel** ✉ 108 Ban Thaluang ☎ 020/227–7277 ✎ pakse-travel@etllao.com.

EXPLORING PAKSE

Historical Heritage Museum. Pakse's Historical Heritage Museum displays stonework from the famous Wat Phu in Champasak, handicrafts from the Bolaven Plateau ethnic groups, and locally made musical instruments. ✉ *Hwy. 13* 🎟 *10,000 kip* ⏲ *Daily 8–11:30 and 1:30–4.*

CRUISING ON THE MEKONG

Mekong Cruises. A luxurious double-decker houseboat, the *Vat Phou,* operated by Mekong Cruises, plies the southern length of the Mekong between Pakse and Si Phan Don. The cruises, which last three days and two nights, depart from Pakse every Tuesday, Thursday, and Saturday in high season, and cost $635 to $670. ✉ *108 Haengboun Rd, Ban Anou, Chanthabouly, Vientiane* ☎ *021/215958, 031/251446* 🌐 *www.mekong-cruises.com, www.vatphou.com.*

WHERE TO EAT AND STAY

For expanded hotel reviews, visit Fodors.com.

$ INDIAN 🍴 **Jasmin.** This long-standing mainstay serves vegetarian and nonvegetarian Indian and Malay food. They do excellent dosas and curries, and have a good selection of western-style breakfasts starting at 6:30—perfect for the early-morning minivan crowd heading to the 4,000 Islands. The kind owner, Mr. Hajamaideen, also can arrange bus tickets and other travel services. [$] *Average main: $4* ✉ *385 Banthaluang, Rd. 13* ☎ *031/251002* 💳 *No credit cards.*

$ ASIAN FUSION 🍴 **Le Panorama.** Le Panorama not only has the best view in town, it has the best food as well. Start with a sunset cocktail on the romantic rooftop terrace, located on the 6th floor of the Hotel Pakse, and then move on to a romantic candlelight dinner. The *gai vat phou* (chicken breast stuffed with crabmeat) is divine, and the delicious pizzas are the most authentic in all southern Laos. [$] *Average main: $6* ✉ *6th fl., Pakse Hotel, Rd. 5, Ban Vat Luang, Pakse* ☎ *031/212131* 🌐 *www.hotelpakse.com/Pakse_hotel_bars_restaurants_en.php.*

$$ HOTEL 🏨 **Champasak Grand Hotel.** Pakse's newest and fanciest digs, the Champasak Grand sits right on the banks of the Mekong next to the Japanese-Lao Friendship Bridge. **Pros:** fantastic Mekong views; close to the airport; nice swimming pool. **Cons:** a bit far from downtown; next to the noisy and busy road going onto the bridge; not all rooms have Mekong views (even though they cost the same). [$] *Rooms from: $56* ✉ *Lao Nippon Bridge Riverside, Box 419* ☎ *031/255–111 up to 8* 🌐 *www.champasakgrand.com* 🛏 *215 rooms* 🍽 *Breakfast.*

$ HOTEL 🏨 **Champasak Palace.** On the banks of the Seddon River on the town's outskirts, this former residence of a local prince is impressive, though scarcely palatial. **Pros:** beautiful terrace over the river; huge beds; new bar overlooking the garden. **Cons:** not central; dirty walls in some rooms; better value to be had elsewhere. [$] *Rooms from: $44* ✉ *Ban Prabaht* ☎ *031/212263, 031/212779* 🌐 *www.champasakpalacehotel.com* 🛏 *114 rooms* 🍽 *Breakfast.*

$ HOTEL 🏨 **Pakse Hotel.** This well-cared-for central hotel now offers international standards of comfort and service with the most knowledgeable management and staff in southern Laos. **Pros:** great location in the heart of the city; clean, comfortable rooms with plenty of light; friendly and attentive staff. **Cons:** small elevator; far from provincial bus stations; busy with tour groups. [$] *Rooms from: $38* ✉ *Rd. 5, Ban Vat Luang* ☎ *031/212131* 🌐 *www.paksehotel.com* 🛏 *65 rooms* 🍴 *Breakfast.*

CHAMPASAK

40 km (25 miles) south of Pakse.

In the early 18th century the kingdom of Laos was partitioned into three realms: Luang Prabang, Vientiane, and Champasak. During the 18th and 19th centuries this small village on the west bank of the Mekong River was the royal center of a wide area of what is today Thailand and Cambodia.

GETTING HERE AND AROUND

Songthaews travel here from the Dao Heuang Market in Pakse three times each morning (two hours; 30,000 kip). Minibuses can be arranged via guesthouses and travel agencies in Pakse for 60,000 kip. While most tour agency minibuses take the road toward the 4,000 Islands and drop you off at the Ban Muang boat pier on the east bank of the Mekong, a new road down the west side cuts out the need for a boat ride across if coming via local songthaew. A car with a driver can be hired from all tour agencies in Pakse for about 500,000 kip. Tuk-tuks run to Wat Phu from Champasak for 10,000 kip per person.

SAFETY AND PRECAUTIONS

This is a safe town, but take the sensible precautions with your belongings.

TIMING

One day should be enough time to tour the ruins.

EXPLORING CHAMPASAK

Don Daeng Island. Don Daeng is a 9-km-long (5½-mile-long) long island in the middle of the Mekong opposite Wat Phu, and a fantastic place to escape the tourist crowds that are beginning to descend on the islands further south. It has gorgeous views of the river and the surrounding countryside. An ecotourism program and a long sandy beach have made it popular with visitors of Wat Phu as an alternative to staying in Pakse or Champasak. Bicycles can be rented on the island and homestays arranged at the Provincial Tourist Office in Pakse. There's also now a charming upscale hotel on the island to get away from it all.

Wat Phu. Wat Phu sits impressively on heights above the Mekong River, about 8 km (5 miles) south of Champasak, looking back on a centuries-old history that won it UNESCO recognition as a World Heritage Site. Wat Phu predates Cambodia's Angkor Wat—its hilltop site was chosen by Khmer Hindus in the 6th century AD, probably because of a nearby spring of freshwater. Construction of the wat continued into the 13th century, at which point it finally became a Buddhist temple. Much of the original Hindu sculpture remains unchanged, however, including representations on the temple's lintels of the Hindu gods Vishnu, Shiva, and Kala. The staircase is particularly beautiful, its protective *nagas* (mystical serpents) decorated with plumeria, the national flower of Laos.

Many of the temple's treasures, including pre-Angkor-era inscriptions, are preserved in an archaeology museum that is part of the complex. ■**TIP→** Every February, at the time of the full moon, the wat holds a nationally renowned festival that includes elephant racing, cockfighting, concerts, and lots of drinking and dancing.

✉ *8 km (5 miles) southwest of Champasak* ☎ *30,000 kip* ⊘ *Daily 8–4:30 (from 4:30 to 6 one can purchase special after-hours tickets for 40,000 kip).*

SI PHAN DON AND THE 4,000 ISLANDS

80 km (50 miles) south of Champasak, 120 km (74 miles) south of Pakse.

If you've made it as far south as Champasak, then a visit to the Si Phan Don area—celebrated for its 4,000 Mekong River islands and freshwater dolphins—is a must. *Don* means island, and several of them in particular are worth visiting: Don Daeng, Don Khon (and its connected counterpart, Don Det), and the similarly named Don Khong. Don Khong has some lovely open countryside and rice fields, and is very photogenic, but in terms of sights, Don Khon is the best option, combining river life with proximity to waterfalls and dolphins. Don Det, connected to Don Khon by a bridge, attracts the backpacker crowd. The area's most romantic lodging option, with a Robinson Crusoe feel, is La Folie on Don Daeng, an island that remains largely untouched by tourism and is an excellent base for visiting Wat Phu and Champasak. Most lodging options on Don Khon, Det, and Khong are not attractive or high in star rating, but this is changing as progress rapidly comes to the islands.

GETTING HERE AND AROUND

Any travel agency in Pakse can help you charter a boat to Don Khong or Don Khon for about 1,200,000 kip; the trip takes four to five hours. You can charter a boat from Champasak as well.

From Pakse you can take a minibus, arranged at any travel agency or guesthouse, to the boat crossing at either Hai Sai Khun (for Don Khong) or Nakasang (for Don Khon) with tickets for the small boat crossing to the islands included. The journey takes two to three hours and costs 60,000 to 70,000 kip depending which island you go to. Don Daeng is accessed from the Ban Muang pier, the same one as for Champasak.

Boat crossings from the mainland to Don Khon (from Nakasang) cost 20,000 kip and take 15 minutes; to Don Khong (from Hat Sai Khun) it's a five-minute trip and costs 5,000 kip.

SAFETY AND PRECAUTIONS

Take care when kayaking on the Mekong. The water may appear still, but the currents are actually quite strong, and there are some eddies that can suck you in. It's best to go with a guide. The name Liphi Falls means "spirit trap," and there's a lot of superstition surrounding them. It is considered offensive to swim here, so do refrain. Also, the rapids are strong, and there have been a number of tourist deaths in years past.

The Irrawaddy Dolphin

The freshwater Irrawaddy dolphin, known as *pla ka* in Lao, is one of the world's most endangered species; according to a 2008 study, fewer than 50 now remain in the Mekong. The Irrawaddy has mythical origins. According to Lao and Khmer legend, a beautiful maiden, in despair over being forced to marry a snake, attempted suicide by jumping into the Mekong. But the gods intervened, saving her life by transforming her into a dolphin.

Lao people do not traditionally hunt the dolphins, but the Irrawaddy have been casualties of overfishing, getting tangled in nets. New dams in the Mekong have altered their ecosystem, further threatening their survival.

Catching a glimpse of these majestic animals—which look more like orcas than dolphins—can be a thrilling experience. The least obtrusive way to visit the Irrawaddy is in a kayak or other nonmotorized boat. If you go by motorboat and do spot dolphins, ask your driver to cut the engine when you're still 100 yards or so away. You can then paddle closer to the animals without disturbing them. Do not try to swim with the dolphins, and—of course—don't throw any trash into the water.

TIMING

The major sights can be seen in one day, but it would be a shame to not budget in time to relax and enjoy the local pace of life. Ideally, a day or two in Don Daeng and two days in Don Khon would give a good feel for the area.

EXPLORING SI PHAN DON

Beautiful scenery and laid-back atmosphere are the reasons to come to Si Phan Don. The Khone Phapheng Falls near Don Khon are a highlight, and visiting them can be combined with seeing the Irrawaddy dolphins. (You'll find many boat operators happy to take you on this tour.) Don Khong has scenic rice fields and more upscale lodging choices, but is not as interesting or attractive as Don Khon. Don Det is another island adjoined to Don Khon by an old rail bridge. The two islands are similar, but Don Khon is closer to the sights, has fewer guesthouses and is slightly more upmarket. If you have the extra day, consider staying on Don Daeng up near Champasak, if you want an unspoiled Lao experience on a beautiful little island.

Don Khong. Don Khong is the largest island in the area, inhabited by a community of fisherfolk living in small villages amid ancient Buddhist temples.

Don Khon. You can hike or bicycle to the beautiful Liphi waterfall (entry fee 25,000 kip) on the island of Don Khon, though an even more stunning waterfall, Khone Phapheng, is just east of Don Khon on the mainland (day-trip tours that include visits to the dolphins set out from Don Khon). Also on Don Khon (and Don Det) are the remains of a former French-built railway.

Freshwater Irrawaddy dolphins. Downstream from Don Khon, at the border between Laos and Cambodia, freshwater Irrawaddy dolphins frolic in a protected area of the Mekong. Boat trips to view the dolphins set off from Veun Kham and Don Khon and cost 60,000 kip per person.

WHERE TO EAT AND STAY

For expanded hotel reviews, visit Fodors.com.

$ ✕ **Seng Ahloune Restaurant.** Located just west of the railway bridge on
LAO   Don Khon, this rickety restaurant on wooden planks sitting just above the Mekong may not look like much, but it delivers some of the more authentic and tastier Lao food on the island. The setting is intimate and romantic, although it can get busy with tour groups who stay in the family's decent guesthouse. $ *Average main: $6* ✉ *Don Khong Island* ☎ *031/260934* ⊕ *www.sengahloune.com* ▭ *No credit cards.*

$ ✕ **Villa Muong Khong.** Housed in a beautiful old wooden lodge on the
LAO   river, this restaurant has great ambience and tasty local food. Soft and succulent grilled fish is a specialty, along with spicy tom yum soup and papaya salad. Order baskets of sticky rice for a traditional Lao meal. There's also a well-stocked wine rack. $ *Average main: $7* ✉ *Don Khong Island* ☎ *031/213011* ▭ *No credit cards.*

$$$$ 🏨 **La Folie Lodge.** For a luxury Robinson Crusoe experience, you
B&B/INN   can't beat La Folie. **Pros:** fantastic views; unique escapist experience;
Fodor's Choice   extremely friendly and authentic local hospitality. **Cons:** no other
★   options for eating or going out; very expensive; lack of English spoken by most staff. $ *Rooms from: $172* ✉ *Don Daeng, Pathoumphone* ☎ *030/534–7603* ⊕ *www.lafolie-laos.com* ⇆ *24 rooms* ⧫○⧫ *Breakfast.*

$$ 🏨 **Sala Done Khone.** This charming resort on Don Khon offers French
B&B/INN   colonial–style rooms, newly renovated traditional Lao homes in a garden, or incredibly atmospheric "raftels," rooms that are actually floating on the Mekong. **Pros:** beautiful riverside location; most upmarket hotel on the island; some raftels have sunroofs. **Cons:** all rooms go quickly in high season; mosquitoes prevalent at sunset; power outages are still a source of annoyance on Don Khon. $ *Rooms from: $60* ✉ *Don Khon Island* ☎ *031/260940* ⊕ *www.salalao.com* ⇆ *25 rooms (11 traditional Lao, 6 French suites, 8 raftels)* ⧫○⧫ *Breakfast.*

$ 🏨 **Villa Muong Khong Hotel.** At this friendly family-run hotel on the island
HOTEL   of Don Khong you live alongside local Lao fisherfolk. **Pros:** fantastic location at quiet end of village; owners can arrange boat trips to nearby sights; peaceful area good for relaxing on the Mekong. **Cons:** not much to do in area; scenic countryside requires a long bike ride; dirty shower curtains. $ *Rooms from: $35* ✉ *Don Khong Island* ☎ *031/213011* ⇆ *52 rooms* ⧫○⧫ *Breakfast.*

9

TAD FANE

38 km (24 miles) east of Pakse.

Tad Fane is Laos's most impressive waterfall, pounding down through magnificent jungle foliage for almost 400 feet. It's set on the border of the Dong Hua Sao National Park and up in the cool air of the Bolaven Plateau, Laos's premiere coffee growing region. There's good hiking here, and the cool temperatures are a relief from the heat and humidity down on the Mekong. The area is accessible as a day trip from Pakse, though there is a somewhat run-down and overpriced resort at the base of the falls should you care to stay.

GETTING HERE AND AROUND

Buses and songthaews run from the Southern (Km 8) Bus Station in Pakse several times each morning. The trip up to Tad Fane and the Bolaven Plateau town of Paksong takes an hour and costs 30,000 kip.

SAFETY AND PRECAUTIONS

The trails around the falls are slippery and can be dangerous, especially during the rainy season (when the leeches come out). Proceed with caution and take a guide if you aren't sure.

TIMING

Take one day for the falls and possibly another day to do some hiking in the park or explore the area around Paksong.

EXPLORING TAD FANE

There are some excellent walks around Tad Fane. Aside from the easy stroll out to the viewing platform above the main falls, there are also guided walks down to the base of the falls, plus some more roundabout trails going up above the falls. These take in some minor falls and some fun swimming holes. Farther afield, the beautiful Tat Yuang falls can be reached via a one-hour trail from Tad Fane, or from a turnout at Km 40 on the main road. Inquire at the resort for guides and trail information.

MYANMAR

WELCOME TO MYANMAR

TOP REASONS TO GO

★ **Explore pagodas:** Slip off your shoes and stare slack-jawed at Bagan's staggering spread of 2,000-plus 11th- and 12th-century pagodas.

★ **Sweat it out:** Spicy curries, giant chili-soaked prawns, and piquant salads help you beat the heat.

★ **Travel back in time:** The turn-of-the-century colonial buildings that line Yangon's Strand Road stand just as they did during British rule.

★ **Get in early:** China opened up rapidly and became Disneyfied, and many fear the same will happen in Myanmar.

★ **Know kindness:** Burmese locals will welcome you warmly; some might even invite you into their homes.

1 Yangon (Rangoon). The one-time capital of British Burma, Japanese Burma, and the country formerly and often still known as Burma, this is the country's biggest, most bustling city.

2 Bagan. Along the sides of a dusty stretch of road, more than 2,000 11th- and 12th-century pagodas are waiting to be explored. Even with the surge in tourists, you can still find yourself alone among the stupas.

3 Inle Lake. It's shades of blue for miles at Inle Lake, where the main activity is floating lazily along in a long, narrow boat and taking in the natural scenery.

4 Mandalay and environs. The dusty roads here belie Mandalay's gems—the former royal palace, home to the last king of Burma, Mandalay Hill, and nearby hill station Pyin-U Lwin.

GETTING ORIENTED

Myanmar (Burma) is Southeast Asia's second-largest country (after Indonesia)—roughly the size of Texas. It's bordered to the southeast by Thailand and the northeast by China and also shares borders with India, Laos, and Bangladesh. Roughly a third of the country's perimeter is gorgeous coastline along the Bay of Bengal and Andaman Sea, a whopping 1,200 miles. Compared with neighboring Thailand, Myanmar's coastline is undeveloped. A number of mountain ranges cut through Myanmar, running from the Himalayas north to south. The country has three rivers that are divided by the mountain ranges, and of them, the 1,348-mile Irrawaddy is the longest.

10

Updated
by Sophie
Friedman

Myanmar (Burma) is amazing. This country of 60 million is rapidly emerging from more than 50 years of military dictatorship, blossoming into as worthy a stop as its popular neighbors. The people are more than friendly; they're thrilled to have tourists after being closed off to the West for so long. And it's safe; you won't constantly need to feel for your purse or hold your jewelry tightly.

Myanmar is a country straddling two worlds—there's Wi-Fi but just 5% of the population has a mobile phone. There are pristine 12th-century pagodas and beautiful beaux-arts buildings, though how long they'll be preserved remains to be seen, which makes now the time to go. A note about this guide: It is impossible to go to Myanmar and not indirectly give money to the government; the airlines and many of the better hotels are connected to the government. We encourage travelers to do their best to support independent businesses.

PLANNING

WHEN TO GO
PEAK SEASON: MID-OCTOBER TO FEBRUARY
The Burmese call this the cold season, but you'll still find yourself plenty toasty, with temperatures in the hotter areas hovering in the mid-90s°F (mid-30s°C) in October, down to the mid-80s°F (around 26°C) in February. Hotels fill up quickly and rates will be at their highest. Airline prices won't skyrocket but planes are quite small and book up quickly.

OFF-SEASON: LATE MAY TO LATE SEPTEMBER
Southwestern monsoons, particularly from July to September, leave the country drenched, particularly in the western Rakhine State. The problem is not so much the rain itself as the aftermath, when dirt roads become impassible fields of mud. This is certainly the least expensive time to go. Around Pyay and Mandalay, you should be able to sightsee without getting soaked.

SHOULDER SEASON: MARCH TO MAY

It's always hot and humid in Myanmar, but these are the months during which you'll roast if not careful. Temperatures in Yangon can easily top 100°F (38°F), with temperatures going even higher in Bagan and Mandalay. Still, because it's dry, hotel rates are not at their lowest, especially those with pools.

GETTING HERE AND AROUND

BORDER CROSSINGS

Foreigners can cross into Myanmar from Thailand but are only permitted to travel within the specific border region. As of this writing, the following border points are open with Thailand (Thai border towns in parenthesis). Myawaddy (Mae Sot): Foreigners can only access this crossing on foot and from the Thai side and cannot stay in Myanmar beyond 6 pm. No visa is required but an entry fee of either $10 or 500 baht must be paid. Tachileik (Mae Sai): Foreigners can cross this border from either side, but those entering into Myanmar will not be able to go beyond Kengtung. If you plan to cross here from Myanmar into Thailand, you will need to arrange for a permit at the state-owned Myanmar Travels and Tours office in Yangon.

AIR TRAVEL

There are direct flights to Yangon from a growing number of cities, including Bangkok, Singapore, Hong Kong, Doha, Guangzhou, and Seoul. Air Asia, Thai Airways, Myanmar Airways International, and Korean Airlines are just a few that run regular flights. From abroad, Mandalay can be reached from Bangkok (Air Asia and Thai Air) and Kunming (China Eastern Airlines). Myanmar has some half-dozen domestic airlines, including KBZ, Air Mandalay, Asian Wings Airways, and Yangon Airways, which run to all major tourist destinations and then some.

BOAT TRAVEL

There are two methods of boat travel in Myanmar—luxury riverboat cruises such as Orient Express, and regular ferries. The latter is further divided into two categories—slow, and what is called express but is still fairly slow. Ferries run Yangon to Mandalay and back, with stops in Bagan in Pyay. A ticket on the Mandalay–Bagan express ferry will cost you $35 (the Shwe Keinnery, daily) or $43 (the Malikha runs only certain dates; the schedule is announced a month in advance). ⇨ *For more information on cruise lines, see Irrawaddy River Cruise section.*

BUS TRAVEL

Myanmar has an extensive bus network and although many roads pretty rough, this is the cheapest way to get around. The quality of buses varies—there are the "luxury" buses that run the Mandalay–Yangon route, and then there's the rest of the lot. Because so many roads are in poor condition, trips take longer than advertised; the drive from Yangon to Mandalay should be around 12 hours and the fare no more than 11,000 kyat. When possible, opt for the air-conditioned buses (pack something in which to wrap yourself) and sit in the front next to a window, where it's least bumpy.

10

CAR TRAVEL

A car and driver can be hired for less money than you'd think. If you're staying at an upscale hotel, do not try to arrange one with the concierge or you will end up overpaying; see Tours and Packages for tour agency recommendations. You can also try your luck with taxi drivers, who may be eager for a much larger fare.

CYCLO, MOTO, AND TUK-TUK TRAVEL

Motos (motorcycle taxis), tuk-tuks or trishaws (three-wheeled cabs), and cyclos (pedal-powered trishaws) are popular forms of transportation in cities and towns across Myanmar except in Yangon, where motorcycles are illegal. Hiring a bicycle is easy but those wishing to hire their own moto or scooter will have a tougher time.

ESSENTIALS

ETIQUETTE

It's acceptable for women to wear short shorts on the street, but a *longyi* (traditional sarong) or long skirt is needed when entering pagodas and temples. Visitors are also required to remove shoes and socks. There's no need to hike up your skirt or sarong while you're walking around the temples; it's okay if it drags a bit on the ground.

Business-card customs here are the same as elsewhere in Asia. If you plan on doing business in Myanmar, have cards printed up with English on one side, Burmese on the other. Business cards are exchanged with two hands.

Be respectful of language difficulties. Although English is widely spoken, try and speak slowly and annunciate when talking to locals, especially over the phone.

PASSPORTS AND VISAS

Everyone needs a visa to enter Myanmar. As of this writing, visas on arrival arranged ahead of time through an agent are available. Tourist visas are good for 28 days, are not extendable, and must be used within three months from the date of issue. You'll need a passport that's valid for six months from the date of your arrival in Myanmar. If you are applying for your visa from within the United States, do so at least a month in advance. If you're applying from within Asia—Bangkok or Hong Kong, for example—you can get the visa in two working days, and the drop-off/pick-up process is quick and painless.

MONEY

Cash once ruled everything in Myanmar, but as of February 2013, there are now ATMs throughout the country that accept Visa and Master-Card, which visitors can use to withdraw the local currency, kyat. A fee of 5,000 kyat ($6) is charged for each transaction; 300,000 kyat ($353) can be withdrawn up to three times per day. Visitors will still need to change kyat into USD to pay for hotels. In Yangon and Mandalay, it's also possible to exchange euros, Chinese yuan, and Thai baht into local currency. Coins exist but are rarely given as change. Banknotes range from 50 pyas (cents) up to 10,000 kyat. An important note: Prices in Myanmar are rising rapidly; those in this chapter were correct at the time of writing.

HEALTH AND SAFETY

Myanmar is very hot for much of the year, and it's essential to stay hydrated and protect your skin. Tap water is fine for brushing your teeth, but when drinking, stick to bottled. Sunscreen is only occasionally available at supermarkets in Yangon, so we recommend bringing your own.

Malaria is a problem in rural Myanmar. Be vigilant about bug spray, which is available in supermarkets, and sleep with the windows closed or inside a mosquito net.

The state of health care in Myanmar is very poor. HIV/AIDS is prevalent; avoid getting shots at local hospitals.

Myanmar is extremely safe. Crime, especially against foreigners, is severely punished. Even petty crime, such as pickpocketing, is rare. Visitors do not need to be concerned about wearing backpacks or carrying open-top tote bags or purses. The Burmese, many who are devout Buddhists, are markedly friendly; the closest you will come to being truly scammed is paying too much for jade at the market.

RESTAURANTS

While Burmese homestyle cooking, drawing influence from its neighbors Thailand and India, is the most prevalent cuisine, Myanmar has quite a good variety, especially given that it was cut off from the west for so long. In Yangon, you'll find everything from sushi to slushies. The one-time capital has most of the country's upscale restaurants—we're talking just a handful—but it's the family-run establishments that are really worth a visit. When you inevitably tire of rice and curry, Bagan and Inle Lake's laid-back, open-air restaurants will lure you in with Dutch-style pancakes, shakes, and the holy grail for many western travelers: guacamole.

Prices in the reviews are the average cost of a main course at dinner or, if dinner is not served, at lunch.

HOTELS

Because demand far outweighs supply, hotels in Myanmar are significantly more expensive than in neighboring Thailand. Yangon has the biggest concentration of upscale accommodations—some tip the scale at $500 a night—including two classic colonial luxury hotels and a handful of international business hotels. Places in Yangon catering to foreigners almost always have 24-hour electricity and most have some degree of Wi-Fi. Mandalay has a few luxury big-box hotels, including one western chain, and several options considered midrange by Myanmar standards. Brownouts and brief blackouts are common but the more upscale hotels have generators. All of the hotels at Inle Lake and in Bagan are locally owned and, though power outages can be frequent albeit brief, there's no problem getting hot water.

Prices in the reviews are the lowest cost of a standard double room in high season.

10

TOURS

Myanmar is perfectly friendly to independent travelers, and there's enough infrastructure for tourists that you'll get where you want to go, one way or another. That said, at the time of publication, a trip to Myanmar—particularly during peak season—requires serious advance research and planning. Those wishing to either join a guided tour or have a tour arranged may contact the following agencies.

Bagan Horse Cart Driver, Ko That ⊠ *Horse cart no. 40* ☎ *09/402753856.*

Kengtung Trekking Guide, Sai Sam Tip ⊠ *Yangon (Rangoon)* ☎ *09/4100–6263* ✎ *saisamtip3@gmail.com.*

Fodor'sChoice
★
Myanmar Damsel Travels and Tours ⊠ *Bldg. B, 4A, 66–68 San Yeit Nyein 6 St.* ☎ *095/523583* ✎ *nwenwe.burma@gmail.com* ⊕ *www.itravel myanmar.com.*

Myanmar Shalom ⊠ *Moses Samuels, 70 31st St., Yangon (Rangoon)* ☎ *01/252814 Yangon office, 646/734–8472 New York office* ⊕ *www. myanmarshalom.com.*

Myanmar Travel and Tours (MTT). This is the government-run agency to which you come groveling if you want permits for traveling to restricted areas. If you plan to cross from Tachileik into Mae Sai, Thailand, you'll need a permit. MTT runs its own tours and manages state-owned hotels. ⊠ *118 Mahabandoola Garden St., Yangon (Rangoon)* ☎ *095/371286, 095/378376* ⊕ *www.myanmartravelsandtours.com.*

One Stop Travel and Tours ⊠ *160/3C Kyuntaw St., Yangon (Rangoon)* ☎ *01/523486* ✎ *info@onestop-myanmar.com* ⊕ *www.onestop-myanmar. com.*

Santa Maria Travels and Tours ⊠ *233–235 32nd St., 2nd fl., Yangon (Rangoon)* ☎ *01/256178, 01/384064* ✎ *sales.santamaria@mptmail.net.mm* ⊕ *www.myanmartravels.net.*

Shan Yoma Travel and Tours ⊠ *124–126 50th St., Yangon (Rangoon)* ☎ *01/295510, 01/299389, 01/204152* ✎ *info@exploremyanmar.com* ⊕ *www.exploremyanmar.com.*

Sun Far Travels and Tours ⊠ *27–31 38th St., Yangon (Rangoon)* ☎ *01/380211* ✎ *ho@sunfartravels.com* ⊕ *www.sunfartravels.com.*

VISITOR INFORMATION

Both the Myanmar Tourism Promotion Board and the Ministry of Hotels and Tourism are state-owned. We recommend using local, privately owned tour agencies—it's worth shopping around. ⇨ *See Tours and Packages.*

Ministry of Hotels and Tourism ⊠ *77–91 Sule Pagoda Rd., Yangon (Rangoon)* ☎ *01/285689* ✎ *mo.moht@mptmail.net.mm* ⊕ *www. myanmartourism.org.*

Myanmar Tourism Promotion Board ⊠ *Diamond Condo A, 497 Pyay Rd., Rm. 904, Yangon (Rangoon)* ☎ *01/242828* ✎ *mtpb@mptmail.net.mm.*

Admission to the Shwedagon Pagoda is free for locals and many come by night to pay their respects.

YANGON (RANGOON)

The capital city until 2006, Yangon (Rangoon) is Burma's largest and its commercial center. It is truly developing city and one full of juxtapositions: new hi-rises abut traditional Southeast Asian shop houses while down the street from a frozen yogurt bar, a sidewalk dentist goes to work. Yangon's rich collection of colonial architecture is one of its biggest draws; The Strand and its surrounding side streets look today much as they did at the turn-of-the-century, when Yangon—then Rangoon—was under British rule. Yangon's most iconic sight is unquestionably the enormous gilded Shwedagon Pagoda, but what makes it worth visiting beyond that is the rich, vibrant life that spills out of people's homes and onto the streets. Colorful and chaotic, Yangon is a feast for the senses. Grinning uniformed schoolchildren and pre-adolescent monks vie for sidewalk space as vendors hawk fried goods and longyi-wearing businessmen go off to work. On a street of Indian-run paint shops sits the country's only synagogue, a 19-century relic; blocks away rise the steeples of St. Mary's Cathedral, another reminder of the city's colonial past.

GETTING HERE AND AROUND

Most international flights to Myanmar land in Yangon, the country's largest city and former capital. Yangon is not difficult to navigate on foot, as most of downtown is laid out on a grid and the area where tourists go is quite compact. Addresses are easily recognizable, and it's simple to ask for directions. The area of Yangon that's the easiest to navigate is that which surrounds the Bogyoke Market, from Bogyoke Aung San Road south to The Strand, and from Aung Yadana Street east

Central Yangon

Theingottara Sacred Garden

Kyae Thoon Pagoda

Agriculture Museum

Aung San Statue

Bogyaka Aung San Park

Kandawgyi Nature Park

U Wisara's Roundabout

U Htaung Bo Road

U Htaung Bo Roundabout

Aquarium

Kan Daw Gyi Lake

Karaweik Palace

U Wisara's Statue

Maha Wizara Pagoda

Shwe Dagon Pagoda Road

Kan Yeik Thar Street

Kan Taw Mingalar Garden

Zoological Garden

Ah Pya Pagoda Street

Theinphyu Playground

Ba Nyar Dala

Myoma Kyaung Street

U Wisara Road

Natural History Museum

Tomb of the Last Moghul Emperor

Maw Kon Taik

Bo Min Khaung St.

Daw Thein Tin Street

Myanma Gone Yi St.

Myoma Ground

Pan Tra St.

Tatmadaw Hall

Na Wa Day St.

National Theatre

Yaw Min Gyi St.

Aung San Sports Ground & Stadium

Bo Min Yaung Road

Thein Phyu Rd.

Phayar Rd Station

Yangon Central Rail Station

Bogyoke Aung San Rd

Bogyoke Aung San Rd

0   ¼ mi

0   ¼ km

Anawrahta Rd

Anawrahta Rd

The Secretariat

Maha Bandoola Road

Shwe Dagon Pagoda Road

Shwe Bon Tha Road

Sule Pagoda Road

Pansodan Road

Bo Aung Kyaw Road

Thein Phyu Road

Bo Myat Tun Road

Sule Pagoda

Sule Pagoda Roundabout

Tourist Information

Independence Statue

High Court Building

Maha Bandoola Garden

Merchant Road

Shwe Taung Tan St. Jetty

Sint Oh Dan St. Jetty

Strand Road

Strand Road

Strand Hotel

Botahtaung Pagoda

Yangon River

to May Yu Road. Be careful walking around at night. Crime is not the issue—Myanmar is extremely safe—but many streets have large holes in the sidewalks and no streetlamps.

AIR TRAVEL

With the exception of China Eastern flights to Mandalay, all international flights go to Yangon, and quite a few airlines offer direct flights. China Southern Airlines and Myanmar Airways International fly from Guangzhou, Air Asia and Thai International Airways fly from Bangkok, Korean Airlines flies from Seoul, and Malaysia Airlines flies from Kuala Lumpur. From Cambodia, travelers can connect to Myanmar on Air Mandalay, Myanmar Airways International, and Malaysian Airlines. This is not an exhaustive list of flights to Yangon, and we predict that in the coming months, more airlines will add direct flights.

Yangon's airport, 30 minutes north of the city center, has domestic and international terminals less than 700 feet apart. The airport is small and simple, and customs is a breeze. A taxi downtown will run you 7,000 kyat, less if you bargain. Be aware that the porters are not airport volunteers and expect to be paid for their services; they will grab your bags unless you say otherwise. K500 per bag should suffice.

BOAT TRAVEL

Ferries leave from Yangon's jetty, just off Strand Road, running north and making stops in Mandalay, Bagan, and Pyay. There's also a ferry to Pathein (overnight) and ferries to Dallah, just across the Rangoon River (⇨ *Exploring Yangon*). All tickets can be purchased from the Inland Water Transport (☎ *095/380–753*) office on Strand Road, just across from the jetty.

BUS TRAVEL

Most tourists stick to cabs and cyclo rickshaws or get around on foot, but Yangon also has an extensive bus system. Don't try and navigate the bus system, but rather consider it an adventure and hop aboard. Tickets are 200 kyat. Regional buses leave from the Highway Bus Center.

CAR TRAVEL

A car and driver can be hired through any travel agency and will cost around $50 per day, but a hired vehicle is not necessary in Yangon.

TAXI, MOTO, AND CYCLO TRAVEL

Cabs and cyclos are abundant in Yangon. Neither are metered; a taxi ride within downtown should not run you more than 3,500 kyat and a cyclo ride will cost less. Taxis and cyclos can both be hired for touring, and in fact touring by cyclo is much more interesting than doing so in a car. Agree with the driver on a fair before you take off. You won't find any motorcycles.

ESSENTIALS

Arrive in Yangon with crisp, unmarked bills printed no earlier than 2006, including at least $10 in small bills, which you'll need for your cab ride from the airport. Yangon's airport has two ATMs that accept international cards, but there will be long lines to use them and whether they will be working properly when you arrive is impossible to predict. Creased U.S. bills will not be accepted; $100 bills will get you the best exchange rates, which fluctuate daily and from one location to the

10

next. The exchange rates at banks are not as good as they are at Bogy-oke Market—you should be able to get around 850 kyat to the dollar here—but neither are banks a total rip-off, and they'll do if you're far from the market.

Air Contacts Yangon International Airport ☎ 095/162712.

Bank Contacts CB Bank Head Office ✉ *Corner of Strand Rd. and 23rd St., Yangon (Rangoon)* ☎ *095/371848* ⊙ *Money changer services: weekdays 9:30–3* ✉ *797 Mahabandoola Rd., Yangon (Rangoon)* ☎ *095/212125* ⊙ *Money changer services: weekdays 9:30–3.* **KBZ Bank Kyauktada Branch** ✉ *Corner of Bank St. and Maharbandoola St., Yangon (Rangoon)* ☎ *095/373952* ⊙ *Weekdays 9:30–3* ✉ *Golden Gate Tower, 117–119 Upper Pazundaung Rd., Yangon (Rangoon)* ☎ *095/299774* ⊙ *Weekdays 9:30–3* ✉ *Block B, Unit 1, 6–7 Lanmadaw Rd., Yangon (Rangoon)* ☎ *095/212763* ⊙ *Weekdays 9:30–3.*

Bus Contacts The Highway Bus Centre (Aung Mingalar Bus Terminal) ✉ *Just southwest of the airport, off Pyay Rd.* ☎ *No phone.*

Visitor and Tour Information Tourist Information Office (Ministry of Hotel and Tourism) ✉ *77–91 Sule Pagoda Rd.* ☎ *095/252859.*

EXPLORING YANGON

Downtown Yangon is easily navigated on foot and the farther-flung areas can be reached without hassle by taxi or rickshaw. A fast-paced traveler could cover the best of Yangon in two days.

TOP ATTRACTIONS

FAMILY

Fodor'sChoice

★

Shwedagon Pagoda. This 325-foot-tall gilded pagoda is Yangon's top tourist attraction and, at 2,500 years old, the world's oldest pagoda. It is simply stunning. Admission is free for locals, and you'll see families, kids, groups of teenagers, and solo visitors milling around the pagoda all day, every day—praying, meditating, and just hanging out. The space is massive and never feels crowded. Women need a *longyi* (traditional sarong) or knee-length skirt to enter the pagoda, and all visitors are required to remove their shoes in the parking lot. During Yangon's hot days the pagoda glistens in the sun—it can be truly sweltering, and the floor can burn your bare feet. A better option is to come after the sun's gone down, when the Shwedagon is beautifully illuminated. ■TIP→ There is an elevator for those who do not wish to climb up. ✉ *Ar Za Nir Street, Yangon (Rangoon)* ⊕ *www.shwedagonpagoda.com* 💰 *$5* ⊙ *Daily 4 am–10 pm.*

Strand Road and Southern Yangon. This meandering walk through southern Yangon gives a good overview of the city's streets, leading you to the Strand Hotel on Yangon's southernmost boulevard, adjacent to the river. Your first stop is **Saint Mary's Cathedral** (Bogyoke Aung San Road and Bo Aung Kyaw Street), a Dutch-designed Gothic Revival structure dating back to 1899. The cathedral survived a 1930 earthquake and the World War II bombings, although its original stained-glass windows were shattered and have been replaced. There's a small swing set in the cathedral's yard. Backtracking a bit, walk south and west toward **Musmeah Yeshua Synagogue** (85 26th Street, near Maha

Monks stroll the grounds at the Myanmar's most sacred site, the Shwedagon Pagoda.

Bandoola Road), Burma's only remaining synagogue. Constructed in 1896, it's small but well maintained, with beautiful, simple stained-glass windows. Today its congregation contains just eight families; there remain in Yangon only 20 Jews. The street on which the synagogue sits is lined with Indian-run paint shops, and the shop houses are painted in gorgeous, eye-popping colors such as robin's egg blue, violet, and dark orange. From the synagogue, walk east and south to the **Strand Hotel** (92 Strand Rd. at 38th St.), which opened in 1901 and was frequented by Rudyard Kipling. Steep yourself in the hotel's rich history by enjoying traditional afternoon tea; both the classic English and a Burmese version are available. ✉ *Bogyoke Aung San Rd. and Bo Aung Kyaw St., Yangon (Rangoon).*

Yangon Circular Railway. There's no better bang for your buck in Yangon than a ride on the city's circle line. The three-hour tour covers 46 km (29 miles) and 39 stations on a railway loop that connects tiny towns and the suburbs with downtown Yangon. You'll see urban Yangon followed by shantytowns, grazing cows, ponds, barefoot giggling kids, and lots of greenery. The journey starts from the grand Yangon Central Station, whose style combines Colonial and traditional Burmese architectural elements and is itself a site. The train is the great unifier, with vegetable sellers, monks, kids, and commuters all hanging tight. Trains leave from Yangon Central platforms 4 and 7, one going clockwise and the other counterclockwise; the kindly ticket seller will personally guide you to the proper platform. Tickets are available at the station master's office at platform 7. You may be asked to show your passport to purchase tickets. ✉ *Yangon Central Station, Pansodan St. and Kun Can Rd., Yangon (Rangoon)* 🎫 *$1* 🕒 *Daily 4 am–10 pm.*

WORTH NOTING

Dallah and Twante. Just across the river from Yangon is the small village of Dallah, reached by ferry from the city's jetty. It's a 10-minute ride where you'll stand among vendors selling fruit, fried snacks, knickknacks, and fresh-rolled cheroots and cigarettes. Make a quick stop at the pagoda in Dallah before moving on to Twante (40-minute drive, go via cab, moto, or pick-up truck). Once there, hop a trishaw or a horse and buggy for a visit to the Shwesandaw Pagoda, a miniaturized version of the Shwedagon, and to the local pottery sheds. From Yangon, you can also go to Twante directly on the two-hour ferry. Tickets for both ferries are $1 each and can be purchased at the Pandosan Street Jetty, from which the boat leaves (across from Strand Hotel). ✉ *Yangon (Rangoon).*

FAMILY **Inya Lake.** The British created this artificial lake in 1883, and it's said to look much the same today as it did then. About 10 km (6 miles) north of downtown, the area surrounding the lake is home to the Yangon Sailing Club (established in 1924) and expensive homes belonging to Aung San Suu Kyi and the U.S. ambassador. You can circle the lake on foot in about two hours, and many of the paths are well shaded. Adjacent to the lake and next to Yangon University is the 37-acre Inya Park, enormously popular with young couples who come to canoodle, watch movies on their laptops, and gaze at the lake. There are small snack and drink shops near the parking lot and benches dotted all over. On the western side of the lake is Mya Kyuan Thar, a peninsula with a kids' playground and an amusement park. ✉ *Intersection of Inya Rd. and Pyay Rd., Yangon (Rangoon).*

WHERE TO EAT

There's not a single western chain eatery in Yangon, which has a varied and vibrant restaurant scene. The restaurants below are sit-down (to some degree).

$ ASIAN 🍴 **999 Shan Noodle Shop.** This pint-size, cheap-and-cheerful noodle stall is equally popular with locals and tourists. The friendly proprietors speak English well, and the picture menu has English descriptions. The noodles are those of the Shan ethnic group, and servings are available in soup or taken dry (e.g., fried-rice noodles with chicken). Rounding out the menu are sautéed vegetables, fried tofu, and pork skin. The owners can prepare plain and mild noodle dishes if you're not one for spice. Inexpensive local beer is available, too. [$] *Average main: B1000* ✉ *130B 34th St. near Anawrahta Rd., Yangon (Rangoon)* ✥ *South of Traders Hotel and just north of Sule Pagoda and City Hall* 💳 *No credit cards* 🕒 *Open until 7 but food will run out by 6:30.*

$$$ ASIAN 🍴 **Feel.** Just around the corner from the Governor's Residence and some of the embassies is this bustling Burmese restaurant with a sizeable buffet. There's not much English spoken, but the drill is a simple one: stand by the buffet, point to what you want, and they'll bring it out for you. Everything is served with heaps of white rice and a plate of mixed greens that changes depending on what's available but will include something

BURMESE CUISINE

Burmese cuisine is heavily influenced by its neighbors Thailand, China, and India. Steamed rice is always served along with some half-dozen small dishes, generally curry, vegetables, and fish. Chicken and fish are quite popular, as Buddhists avoid beef and Muslims pork, although you'll be able to order all four at any restaurant that's neither vegetarian nor halal. **Freshwater fish** and shrimp are served salted, fried, dried, fermented, and made into a paste. One of the loveliest things about Myanmar cuisine is the many salads (*a thoke*). One of the most popular is a Shan dish called *laphet,* made with pickled tea leaves, fried broad beans, peanuts and garlic, green chilies, tomato, and preserved ginger and tossed with peanut oil, fish sauce, and lime; it's tart, sharp, and refreshing.

There are overseas Chinese all over Myanmar, but the farther north you go toward the border, the more **Chinese cuisine** you'll see. In the areas that cater particularly to tourists, such as Bagan, restaurants serve a smattering of Chinese, Indian, Thai, and Burmese dishes. Mandalay has lots of Chinese and Indian restaurants, and it's here that you'll find some of the best Indian street food, including hot-off-the-grill chapatis and buttery naan.

In general, Burmese food is not as spicy as in Thailand or India, but those who like it hot can certainly ask for extra chilies. **Curry** is enormously popular in Myanmar, eaten with white rice, but it too is mild. Burmese curry tends to be oilier than its Indian and Thai cousins.

As in its neighboring countries, eating is a communal experience here; everyone will have rice, and then can serve themselves from the array of small plates on the table. At most Burmese restaurants, it's buffet, and the waitstaff will keep refilling your bowls until you're stuffed.

Although fruit shakes, including the excellent avocado, are quite popular, **desserts** aren't huge; tamarind sweets will often be served at the end of a meal, as will fruit.

The city is a feast for the eyes and the stomach. You'll see **street snack** vendors all over Yangon, with rows of them lining the sidewalk on both sides of Bogyoke Aung San Road near Bogyoke Market and Traders Hotel. The most common snacks include:

Shwe gye: This semi-sweet banana cake, sold in neatly sliced hunks, gets its distinct flavor from semolina and coconut milk. You'll be thinking about it long after you leave Yangon.

Dosa: The southern Indian snack is known in Burmese as *toshay* and also referred to as *khout mote* (literally, "folded snack") and *mont pyar thalet.* The crepes are made with rice flour and come in sweet (shredded coconut and palm sugar syrup, sometimes red bean) and savory (tomatoes, chickpeas, cabbage, and sometimes chili).

Buthi kyaw: Battered, deep-fried chunks of gourd are far from healthy but taste delicious dipped in the accompanying sauce (slightly sour and a little spicy).

Mohinga: Eaten nationwide, this popular breakfast dish is rice vermicelli in a fish broth made from fresh fish, onions, garlic, lemongrass, banana tree stem, and a dash of ginger.

10

like baby eggplants, bitter greens, and bean sprouts. Stand-out dishes include giant curried prawns and the ubiquitous and delicious tea-leaf salad (ask for garlic and chilies or this one will feel a bit tame). It's always crowded here, the tables packed with a mix of tourists, local Burmese, and embassy staff. $ *Average main: K4000* ⊠ *124 Pyi Htaung Su Yeikthar St., near Padonmar St., Yangon (Rangoon)* ☎ *01/210678* ⊕ *www.feelrestaurant.com.*

$$$$
CONTEMPORARY

✕ **Mandalay Restaurant.** The Governor's Residence is idyllic, but if you're staying there and enjoying the included breakfast buffet, it's well worth exploring what else Yangon has to offer for lunch and dinner. If you're *not* staying here, however, pack a swimsuit and head over. Come for lunch and enjoy an afternoon swim, or take a dip and then stay for dinner. Eschew Mandalay's tempting Continental options and instead try an upscale take on traditional Burmese food, accompanied by locally produced wine. Try the tongue-twisting *ah-mel thar pha yone thee*— beef and pumpkin curry with sesame cabbage and rice—and the spicy *lephet thoke,* a salad of pickled green tea leaves, butterbeans, peanuts, dry shrimp, and chili. $ *Average main: K19,000* ⊠ *The Governor's Residence, 35 Taw Win Rd., Yangon (Rangoon)* ☎ *01/229860* ⊕ *www. governorsresidence.com/web/pyan/mandalay_restaurant.jsp* ☉ *Daily noon–2:30 and 7–10:30.*

$$$
SEAFOOD
FAMILY

✕ **Minn Lan Seafood.** Pull up a chair near one of the fans here and order an avocado shake to suck down while you peruse the menu. Once you're finished, order another; you'll need something to cool your mouth down after a bite of the rice noodles in a fiery broth. Once your sinuses have been cleared, move on to the delectable grilled seafood; there's crab, oysters, prawns, squid, and shellfish to choose from and all come to the table expertly charred. ■**TIP**➔ The restaurant is at the northern tip of Inya Lake, just north of the American Club. $ *Average main: K3000* ⊠ *Pyay Rd. at Parami Rd., Yangon (Rangoon).*

$
INDIAN

✕ **Nilar Biryani.** Eating at this busy spot that's always packed with locals is a delicious, inexpensive affair. The menu is tiny, with just three types of biryani—chicken, mutton, and vegetable (which sells out the fastest). Be sure to order your meal with pickles. Service is fast and efficient; this is the place to grab a lassi and eat quickly before returning to sightseeing. ■**TIP**➔ Nilar Biryani is always crowded. If you can't get a table, head just down the street to the equally good New Delhi (Anawratha Road between Shwe Bontha and 28th Street), where the menu is longer and includes plenty of vegetarian dishes. Don't skip out on the potato chapati, daal, and very spicy curries. $ *Average main: K1300* ⊠ *216 Anawratha Rd., Yangon (Rangoon)* ⊟ *No credit cards* ☉ *No dinner.*

$$$
THAI
FAMILY

✕ **Sabai Sabai.** Ease into Burma at this clean, mid-market, Westerner-friendly restaurant popular with the expat and NGO worker set as well as upper-middle-class locals. The Thai food is plenty authentic and leans a bit into Burmese cuisine with excellent green curry. Be sure to order tom yum soup, any satay (the chicken in particular is very tender), and prawns. A full meal with soup, starter, main course, and drinks runs around 7,000 kyat per person. $ *Average main: K4000* ⊠ *232 Dhama Zedi Rd., Yangon (Rangoon)* ☎ *951/544724* ⊟ *No credit cards.*

$$ ITALIAN FAMILY 🍴 **Scoop.** If you decide to walk from Inya Lake back downtown, make a pit stop at gelato bar Scoop. There are half a dozen flavors to choose from, and the owner uses a combination of local fruits and imported ingredients. The mint and green tea are particularly delicious, but purists will be just as happy with good old standbys vanilla and chocolate. [$] *Average main: K1500* ✉ *Junction Shopping Center, between Pyay and Kyun Taw Rds., 1st fl., Yangon (Rangoon)* ☎ *09/7321–8321.*

$$$ INTERNATIONAL FAMILY 🍴 **Zawgyi House.** After a sweaty whirl through Bogyoke Market, take a load off at this neighboring restaurant. Zawgyi's back garden looks out onto the redbrick former railway headquarters, now abandoned; its front patio faces busy Bogyoke Aung San Road and is ideal for people watching. Is it cheating to plump for western food? We won't tell. The fare at Zawgyi is decent—sandwiches, crepes (sweet and savory), a few salads—but it's best for kicking back with a cold drink. The durian shake is smooth and creamy; the chocolate is closer to chocolate milk, but still refreshing. [$] *Average main: K4500* ✉ *372 Bogyoke Aung San Rd., Yangon (Rangoon)* ☎ *951/256355* 💳 *No credit cards.*

WHERE TO STAY

Hotel rooms are in high demand across Myanmar and prices reflect that. Yangon has some of the country's best and most expensive hotels, but there are still a few midrange options to be had.

$ HOTEL FAMILY 🏨 **East Hotel.** With hotels in Yangon more expensive than in neighboring Thailand, East offers an especially good value. **Pros:** smack-dab in the middle of downtown; free (but slow) Wi-Fi; complimentary bottled water. **Cons:** beaded curtains instead of bathroom doors; some rooms have plumbing problems and others are dim. [$] *Rooms from: $78* ✉ *234–240 Sule Pagoda Rd., Yangon (Rangoon)* ☎ *959/7313–5311* 🛏 *48 rooms* 💳 *No credit cards* 🍽 *Breakfast.*

$$$$ RESORT Fodor's Choice ★ 🏨 **The Governor's Residence.** It's a trip back in time at this 1920s colonial-style mansion on a quiet backstreet in the Embassy Quarter. **Pros:** quiet and serene; lovely pool; superb service; free, fast Wi-Fi. **Cons:** not within walking distance of downtown; condition of hailed taxis varies enormously. [$] *Rooms from: $370* ✉ *35 Taw Win Rd., Yangon (Rangoon)* ☎ *951/229860* 🌐 *www.governorsresidence.com* 🛏 *470 rooms* 🍽 *Breakfast.*

$ B&B/INN FAMILY 🏨 **Hotel Alamanda.** Quiet and quaint, this six-room former colonial home is just out of the city center, between Inya Lake and the Shwedagon Pagoda. **Pros:** delicious French-style breakfasts; tucked away in the quiet, residential Embassy District. **Cons:** you'll need a ride to go downtown; some guests find the owners to be aloof and curt. [$] *Rooms from: $80* ✉ *60B Shwe Taung Kyar Rd., Yangon (Rangoon)* ☎ *951/534513* 🌐 *hotel-alamanda.com* 🛏 *6 rooms* 💳 *No credit cards* 🍽 *Breakfast.*

$$ RESORT FAMILY 🏨 **MiCasa Hotel.** MiCasa offers a large pool, often empty, and plenty of space for kids to run around. **Pros:** kitchenettes make it easy to prepare your own meals; you can pay in advance with credit card; complimentary washing machines and dryers. **Cons:** removed from downtown; Wi-Fi isn't free; restaurant food is subpar. [$] *Rooms from: $206* ✉ *17 Kaba Aye Pagoda Rd., Yangon (Rangoon)* ☎ *951/650933*

⊕ *www.myanmar.micasahotel.com* ⊲⋾ *143 rooms* ⊟ *No credit cards* ⏐⊙⏐ *Breakfast.*

$ ⊡ **Seasons of Yangon Hotel.** A luxury hotel this is not, but it's a stone's
HOTEL   throw from the airport (a 25 to 30 minute drive from downtown). **Pros:**
FAMILY   across the street from airport; staff will pack you a to-go breakfast box
for early flights. **Cons:** it's a bit dingy around the edges; simple requests,
such as extra pillows, seem to cause staff some confusion. ⟮$⟯ *Rooms
from: $40* ⊠ *Airport Estate, Yangon (Rangoon)* ☏ *951/666699* ⊲⋾ *120
rooms* ⏐⊙⏐ *Breakfast.*

NIGHTLIFE AND THE ARTS

NIGHTLIFE

Yangon has Myanmar's best western-style nightlife; late-night boozing
just isn't the focus in this country (yet). There are still a handful of places
to get a tipple, though, often with a side of excellent conversation.

19th Street, Chinatown. For a whole barbecued fish, a cup of draft beer,
and a scene straight out of Mainland China, 19th street in Yangon's
Chinatown is unbeatable. There are restaurants along both sides of the
block, with little outdoor grills and plastic tables and chairs set up, the
stools often occupied by locals in their undershirts and pajama bot-
toms. Chicken, pork, and fish are the three main dishes, but you'll find
mushrooms, assorted sautéed greens, and of course, rice, too. BYOB is
perfectly acceptable so if draft beer's not your thing, you can pop open
that bottle of whisky you carried over from Thailand. ⊠ *19th St. near
Maha Bandula, Yangon (Rangoon).*

FAMILY   **50th Street.** That steak and Guinness pie at the next table over is not
Fodor'sChoice   an apparition. 50th Street is a proper pub, one that's been honing its
★   craft since it opened in 1997, a lone island of burgers adrift in a sea
of noodles. Today, the bilevel bar remains enormously popular with
expats, foreign tourists, and a few wealthy Burmese. In addition to
colonial favorites, the extensive menu includes a selection of pizzas.
Portions are hearty, the better to be washed down with smoothies,
cocktails, and draft beer. Beyond the food, 50th Street is somewhat
of a clubhouse for the city's expats, so you'll find them here nightly,
vying for pub quiz prizes or playing billiards. ⊠ *9–13 50th St., Yangon
(Rangoon)* ☏ *95/139–7060* ⊕ *50thstreetyangon.com* ⊟ *No credit cards*
*Mon.–Thurs. 11–2 and 5–midnight, Fri. 11–2 and 5–3, Sat. 10:30 am–3
am, Sun. 10:30 am–midnight.*

British Club. The first Friday of every month sees foreigners flocking
to the British Club for drinks and networking. The evening starts out
calm enough but quickly becomes raucous, accented voices fighting
to be heard over each other. Every expat in town will be here, along
with foreign visitors who want to do a little mingling. The event kicks
off at 7:30, but most people come around 9:30. Be sure to bring your
passport for admission. ⊠ *Alan Pya Pagoda Rd., north of Aung San
Stadium, Yangon (Rangoon).*

Sapphire Bar & Lounge. The Shwedagon Pagoda is at its most gorgeous
at night and, from Alfa Hotel's rooftop bar, you can see it clearly in

the distance, a gilded piece of history shining bright. It's a simple bar where people gather for a drink or two and quiet conversation. A local harpist places plays nightly from 7 to 9. Because the rooftop is not enclosed, the bar is closed during Myanmar's rainy season, roughly June to September. ✉ *Alfa Hotel, 41 Nawaday St., Yangon (Rangoon)* ☎ *095/137–7964* ⊘ *Daily 3–3.*

Strand Bar. When the Strand Hotel opened in 1901, its swanky bar was the place to see and be seen. Today, Rangoon is a very different place and the bar is still pretty, if pretty staid, except on Friday nights, when it comes alive with expats who giddily pack in for two-for-one happy hour, which runs 5 to 11. Waiters glide around with trays of snacks like pizza and kebabs, which are ravenously gobbled up by NGO workers. ✉ *Strand Hotel, 92 Strand Rd., Yangon (Rangoon)* ☎ *095/124–3377* ⊕ *www.lhw.com/hotel/The-Strand-Yangon-Yangon-Myanmar.*

THE ARTS

Myanmar's art scene may be small, but Yangon has a handful of plucky galleries. Several have been around for some three decades while others have opened in the last couple of years; all are worth a visit.

Inya Gallery of Art. Yangon native and self-taught artist Aung Myint opened this gallery in 1989. Aung was the first Burmese artist to win an ASEAN Art Award, and his work is in the permanent collections of the National Art Museum of Singapore and National Art Gallery of Malaysia, among others. Inya Gallery of Art showcases Aung's work as well as that of artists who work with similar themes. Most of the paintings are coloful, though Aung does have a series of black and whites. ✉ *50B Inya Rd., Yangon (Rangoon)* ☎ *095/524818* ✑ *inyaartgallery@yahoo.com* ⊕ *inyaartgallery.tripod.com.*

Lokanat Galleries. The motto of this gallery, which opened in 1971 and claims to be Myanmar's longest-running gallery, is "Truth, Beauty, Love." The NGO is dedicated to promoting local artists, and represents 21 of them. It hosts exhibitions every few months and also works with embassies and other NGOs to put on shows and fairs. ✉ *62 Pansodan St., Yangon (Rangoon)* ☎ *095/382269* ⊕ *www.lokanatgalleries.com* ⊘ *Closed Mon.*

New Treasure Art Gallery. Halfway between the Shwedagon Pagoda and Inya Lake is this gallery, which is owned in part by Min Wae Aung, Burma's best-selling artist, most well known for his highly detailed paintings of Buddhist monks. New Treasure's goal is to showcase the work of young Burmese artists, but Min Wae Aung also has a collection of 20th-century work from which today's artists draw much inspiration. ■ **TIP➔ Walk directly north and you'll reach the southern tip of Inya Lake; walk directly south and you can enter People's Park from the northern gate.** ✉ *84A Than Lwin Rd., Yangon (Rangoon)* ☎ *095/526776.*

FAMILY **New Zero Art Space.** This nonprofit works to promote young Myanmar artists and to bring together artists and the community at large. New Zero hosts regular exhibitions, seminars, and workshops on art and film. Friday to Sunday from 4 to 6 pm there are free art classes (donations accepted) for children and adults. The space also has a small

10

library with books and films about Myanmar's art scene. When it has the funds, New Zero also runs an artist-in-residency program to encourage Burmese artists to meet those from abroad. ⊠ *54 Bo Yar Nyunt St., 1-E, Yangon (Rangoon)* ☏ *095/7312–9520* ✑ *newzero.rog@gmail.com* ⊘ *Tues.–Sun. 9:30–5.*

Pansodan Gallery. Colorful paintings by local artists pack the walls at this gallery, which opened in 2008 and has frequently rotating exhibitions. The gallery is more than just a place where art hangs and is sold; it's a gathering place for Burmese artists both established and rising, as well as Yangon's expats and tourists. On Tuesday nights from 7:30 pm, Pansodan hosts a weekly gathering, with snacks, drinks, and usually one or two people playing guitar. The event is free, but donations are welcome. ⊠ *286 Pansodan St., 1st fl., Yangon (Rangoon)* ☏ *095/130846* ✑ *aungsoeminn@gmail.com* ⊕ *www.pansodan.com* ⊘ *Daily 10–6.*

SHOPPING

Yangon doesn't have tons in the way of traditional souvenir shopping, but you will definitely not leave empty handed. Because this is most visitors' last stop, it makes sense to shop here on your last day rather than carry everything all over the country.

Bogyoke Market. This market, which opened in 1926, is enormous but clean, well-organized, and—despite sweltering temperatures outside—not an oven. Come here on your first day in Yangon to peruse the offerings, pick up a longyi for temple visits, and exchange money. You'll get the best rate here, and it's not so much dedicated exchange windows that you'll find but vendors with bags of cash. Shops here sell stone and wood carvings; jade, silver, and gold jewelry; lacquerware; paintings by local artists; and a smattering of cosmetics and toiletries. ∎**TIP→** If you're buying jewelry, do your research beforehand. On the whole, sellers here are not pushy, but no matter what you purchase, be sure to haggle. ⊠ *27th St. and Bogyoke Aung San Rd., Yangon (Rangoon).*

FAMILY **City Mart.** This citywide chain of small hypermarkets offers the best selection of edible souvenirs. Among the many options in the grocery section of the store are the makings for pickled tea-leaf salad, which is served across the country (leaves and fried beans) and all manner of candy ranging from ginger chews to chocolates. There's also a shelf of tea with interesting packaging and, toward the back, several shelves full of local beer and liquor. ⊠ *Directly across from Bogyoke Market, Yangon (Rangoon).*

Fodor's Choice ★ **Pomelo.** Pomelo supports nonprofits in Myanmar that work with disadvantaged groups, including families in poverty, those with HIV, the mentally and physically disabled, and the homeless. The goods at this cute fair-trade boutique are made by those with whom the NGOs work, and the result are fantastic. Sein Na Garr Glass Factory, for example, makes its beautiful vases with recycled glass bought from Yangon's garbage collectors. Lovely beaded jewelry comes from the children at Hlaing Thar Yar Disability Centre. Action for Public works with women and children with HIV, and the sweet stuffed animals and chic wallets and ornaments that dot Pomelo were expertly sewn by them. This is one of Yangon's loveliest little shops and a great place to pick up meaningful souvenirs. ⊠ *85–87 Thein Byu Rd., Yangon (Rangoon)* ⊕ *www.pomeloyangon.com* ⊙ *Daily 10–9.*

BAGAN

Between the 9th and 13th centuries, Bagan (née Pagan), was the capital of the Kingdom of Pagan, once a tiny settlement that eventually gained power and, in doing so, united the neighboring territories to form Burma, present-day Myanmar. The 11th through mid-13th centuries were the height of the Kingdom of Pagan's prosperity, and it was during those 250 years that the then-10,000 stupas, temples, and pagodas were built. Today, just 2,000 remain, but their expanse is staggering. Bikes can be hired from every guesthouse for around K2,500, and visitors will find that on two wheels is the best way to get around. The stupas dot the sides of the long road that runs through Bagan, and the awe-inspiring larger temples are clustered across from Tharabar (née Tharbha) Gate, the only surviving section of Bagan's city wall. There are so many small stupas on either side of the road leading up to the larger temples that it's entirely possible to be completely alone and surrounded by hundreds of them. If your time in Myanmar is limited, skip Mandalay and head to Bagan, permeated by a laid-back, backpacker-style vibe.

GETTING HERE AND AROUND

Connecting the three main areas of Bagan—Old Bagan, New Bagan, and Nyuang-U—is the Bagan-Nyaung-U Road. On the side streets off the main road are a smattering of hotels and restaurants. It's possible to traverse Bagan on foot, and some tourists do, but it's a long walk from New Bagan up to Nyaung-U. A better and much more common option is hiring a bicycle and riding along Bagan-Nyaung-U Road, off the sides of which are plenty of stupas. Bicycles will cost between 2,000 and 5,000 kyat per day. Other available forms of transportation include hired cars (including taxis) or horse carts. Your hotel can arrange for both, or you can flag down both near Ananda Temple.

AIR TRAVEL

Bagan's airport is in Nyaung-U, a 15-minute drive the city. There are some half a dozen flights per day on domestic Burmese airlines. None can be booked online, although Air Mandalay is the easiest to deal with. Have your hotel or a travel agent book air tickets for you or, if you're starting in Yangon, go directly to the airlines' office. The flight from Yangon is 70 minutes and costs around $130; flights from Mandalay and Heho (Inle Lake) are shorter and cheaper.

BOAT TRAVEL

Taking a ferry from Yangon or Mandalay to Bagan is time-consuming but a unique experience you certainly won't get flying. From Mandalay, the Malikha Express costs $43, departs at 8 am, and should arrive at 6 pm, though it's been reported that journeys can take more than 12 hours.

BUS TRAVEL

Buses leave Yangon between 6 and 7:30 pm, arriving in Bagan between 3 and 5 am. Ask your hotel or an agent to book a ticket for you and then take to the station the receipt they give you to find your bus. Give

10

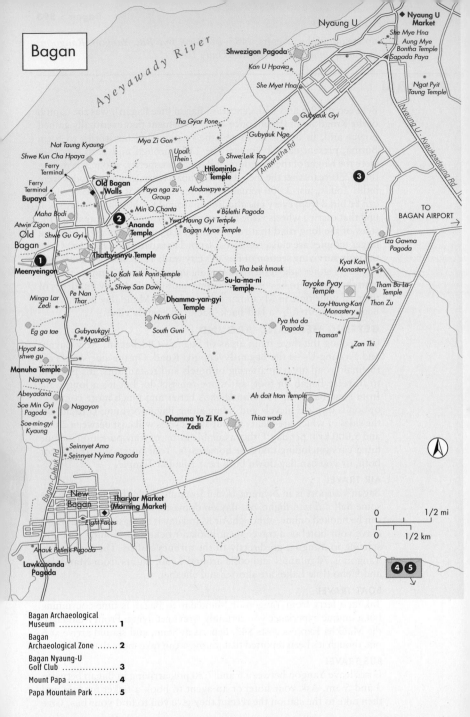

Bagan

Ayeyawady River

Nyaung U

◆ **Nyaung U Market**

Shwezigon Pagoda

She Mye Hna
Aung Mye
Bontha Temple
Sapada Paya

Kan U Hpawa

Ngat Pyit
Taung Temple

She Myet Hna

Tha Gyar Pone

Gubyauk Gyi

Mya Zi Gon

Gubyauk Nge

Nat Taung Kyaung

Upali
Thein

Shwe Kun Cha Hpaya

Shwe Leik Too

Ferry
Terminal

**Htilominla
Temple**

Anawratha Rd

❸

Ferry
Terminal

**Old Bagan
Walls**

Alodawpye

Paya nga zu
Group

Bupaya

Min O Chanta

Bulethi Pagoda

TO
BAGAN AIRPORT

Maha Bodi

❷

Ywa Haung Gyi Temple

Atwin Zigon

**Ananda
Temple**

Bagan Myoe Temple

Iza Gawna
Pagoda

Shwe Gu Gyi

**Old
Bagan**

Thatbyinnyu Temple

Tha beik hmauk

Kyat Kan
Monastery

❶

Lo Kah Teik Panr Temple

**Su-la-ma-ni
Temple**

Tham Bu La
Temple

Meenyeingon

Shwe San Daw

Tayoke Pyay
Temple

Minga Lar
Zedi

Pe Nan
Thar

**Dhamma-yan-gyi
Temple**

Thon Zu

Lay-Htaung-Kan
Monastery

North Guni

Pya tha da
Pagoda

Zan Thi

Eg ga tae

Gubyaukgyi
Myazedi

South Guni

Thaman

Hpyat sa
shwe gu

Manuha Temple

Nagayon

Nanpaya

Abeyadana

Ah dait htan Temple

Soe Min Gyi
Pagoda

Soe-min-gyi
Kyaung

**Dhamma Ya Zi Ka
Zedi**

Thisa wadi

Seinnyet Ama

Seinnyet Nyima Pagoda

Bagan-Chauk Rd

**New
Bagan**

**Tharyar Market
(Morning Market)**

Eight Faces

0   1/2 mi

0   1/2 km

Anauk Petleik Pagoda

**Lawkananda
Pagoda**

❹ ❺

yourself plenty of time to get your bearings, as the Yangon bus station is large and confusing. Tickets cost around 15,000 kyat. Bring earplugs and something with which to shield yourself from the air-conditioning. The overnight bus from Mandalay (13,000 kyat) departs at 8:30 pm, arriving at 4:30 am. Arrange to have your hotel come get you, as taxis will not be plentiful.

CAR TRAVEL

It's a long drive from Yangon to Bagan; you can hire a car and driver through a tour agency or, if you fancy trying your luck, ask a cab driver. The drive from Mandalay to Bagan takes about five hours without stops and costs around $100.

TRAIN TRAVEL

There's an overnight train from Yangon to Bagan, departing Yangon Central Railway Station at 4 pm and scheduled to arrive in Bagan at 9:30 am; tickets are $30, $40, and $50 for a standard seat, an upper-class seat, and a sleeper car, respectively. The trains are often delayed so don't have any plans hinging on your timely arrival. The train from Mandalay to Bagan is very slow; trains depart at 9 pm and are scheduled to arrive at 4:50 am, covering in that time just 111 miles. Tickets are $4, $7, and $10 for a standard seat, an upper-class seat, and a sleeper car, respectively.

ESSENTIALS

Running through most of Bagan is Bagan-Nyaung-U Road, and so it's easy to right yourself if you get lost. Simply find a local, tell them whether you're going to Old or New Bagan or Nyaung-U, and they'll send you off in the right direction.

Banks KBZ Nyaung-U Branch ⊠ *Corner of Anawrahta Rd. and Nyaung-U-Kyaukpatung Rd.* ☎ *061/61089* ⊕ *Weekdays 9:30–3.*

TOURS

Balloons over Bagan. Eastern Safaris' hot air balloon flights over the temples of Bagan and the Irrawaddy River offer unparalleled views and a truly unique experience. The British-made balloons are flown by U.K.-certified pilots, and passenger safety is the number one priority; balloons won't fly in winds exceeding 15 mph. Rides last 45 minutes to an hour and are followed by a light Champagne breakfast. The balloons go wherever the wind takes them, so which pagodas you'll see and where you'll end up landing are a surprise even to the pilots. ■TIP→ The rack rate is $330 per person, but travel agents can usually get a significant discount. Price includes a hotel transfer. ⊠ *Sedona Hotel, 1 Kaba Aye Pagoda Rd., Ste. 03–06, Yangon (Rangoon)* ☎ *01/652809* ⊕ *www.easternsafaris.com/balloonsoverbagan_home.html.*

Myanmar Travels and Tours. Those wishing to cross the Tachileik/Mae Sai border into Thailand will need to organize permits with State-owned MTT. As of this writing, you should allow yourself at least two weeks for permit processing. Those crossing from Mae Sai into Myanmar at the Tachileik check point do not need a permit from MTT. ⊠ *Bagan-Nyaung-U Rd. at Thiri Marlar St., Nyaung-U* ☎ *061/65040.*

10

Myanmar's growing tourism industry is centered on Bagan's collection of 11th- and 12th-century temples and stupas.

VISITOR INFORMATION
Ever Sky Information Service ✉ *Intersection of restaurant row and Thiripy-itsaya 5, Nyaung-U* ☎ *061/60895* ⊙ *Daily 7:30 am–9:30 pm.*

EXPLORING BAGAN

Visitors flock to Bagan for its staggering spread of 11th- and 12th-century pagodas, and the area where most are concentrated is best traversed by bicycle. The alternatives to biking are walking—not recommended during the hottest months—taxi or private car, and horse cart. The latter is a slow but unique and fun way to get around.

TOP ATTRACTIONS

Bagan Archaelogical Zone. Some 2,200 11th- and 12th-century ruins dot Bagan, an enormous amount but a mere fraction of the more than 10,000 that once stood. The temples, pagodas, and stupas are simply astonishing. Some are very large and have been renovated, while others are tiny and stand in disrepair among rambling grasses and brambles. The expanse of the ruins is staggering; from the side of a long, dusty dirt road they pop up, completely abandoned and yours for taking. Each and every stupa, temple, and pagoda is truly breathtaking, but visitors will find the liveliest is **Ananda Temple,** which has beautiful frescoes and houses four 31-foot-tall Buddha statues. Its location at the end of restaurant row means it gets busiest around lunch. 💵 *$10, paid at airport on arrival.*

WORTH NOTING

Bagan Archaeological Museum. Complement the stupa ogling with a visit to this museum, which is a short walk from Ananda Temple and Old Bagan's restaurant row. It's been woefully neglected and is a mess, but there are roughly 850 objects on display here, all pieces of Bagan's rich history. There are excellent wood carvings of Buddha, intricate bronze pieces, and even ancient coiffeurs used at the time by the chicest of women. It's interesting to see the frescoes here and then compare them to the real ones inside the temples. ✉ *Bagan-Nyaung-U Rd., near Ananda Temple, Old Bagan* ☎ *061/60048* 💲 *$5; kyat sometimes accepted* ⊘ *Daily 9–4.*

Bagan Nyaung-U Golf Club. This 18-hole (par-72) course may not be celebrity-designed or have hosted PGA tournaments, but it's got something with which no other course in the world can compete—a smattering of Bagan's pagodas dotted around the green. The course is government run and managed by Amazing Bagan Resort, but you do not have to be staying at the hotel to play. ✉ *Mandalay Division, Nyaung-U* ☎ *061/60035* ⊕ *www.bagangolfresort.net/golfclub.html* 💲 *$45, includes clubs and caddy* ⊘ *Daily 6–6.*

Mount Popa. If you've got an extra day in Bagan and have tired of the temples, this is an easy half-day trip. Fifty miles southeast of Bagan, Mount Popa stands nearly 5,000 feet above sea level. It's a 777-step-barefoot climb all the way to the top; along the stairwell are souvenir sellers and, at the top, a gilded pagoda. Beware of monkeys who can turn nasty if they sense you've got treats and whose droppings are everywhere; wet wipes are a must. A taxi (four passengers) from Bagan will run you around 37,000 kyat, and you can stop on your way at a palm sugar plantation and distillery. ■TIP→ Nearby Mt. Popa resort is lovely and offers great views, but is owned by government crony Tay Za.

Popa Mountain Park. If you're tiring of temple-hopping and fancy sticking around Mt. Popa for the afternoon, bring your hiking shoes in the car and take to the trails. There are a handful, some leading to the rim of the volcano crater and others to waterfalls. The word *popa* comes from the Sanskrit word for flower, and as you're hiking up, you'll see how lush it is, and how the vegetarian changes with the altitude. This is a good hike on which to follow a guide; your driver should be able to find you one or you can ask at Popa Mountain Resort. From there to the crater can take up to five hours.

10

WHERE TO EAT

Bagan has a good selection of restaurants clustered together across Old and New Bagan and Nyaung-U, so if your first choice is full, there's another option right next door. Among the cheerful Indian, Thai, and general backpacker-cuisine places are a handful of tasty, inexpensive Myanmar family-style restaurants.

$$$$

INDIAN

✕**Aroma 2.** Aroma 2 is one of a happening strip of restaurants, where you're likely to bump into friends you've made earlier in the day during temple hopping. These places are geared to tourists and so prices are inflated, but the "no good, no pay" offer at this Indian restaurant is hard to resist. Curries are quite good but mild, so definitely ask for more spice if you like a kick. All the breads are worth a try, especially the hot, fluffy naan. Aroma 2 gets packed so it's best to have your hotel make reservations. If it's full, there are plenty of other eateries from which to choose. $ *Average main: K5000* ⊠ *Yarkinnthar Hotel Rd., Nyaung-U* ☎ *09/204–2630* ⊟ *No credit cards.*

$$$
VEGETARIAN
FAMILY
✗ **Be Kind to Animals the Moon.** A charming little restaurant that wouldn't look out of place in a warm-weather college town in the west, Be Kind to Animals the Moon is constantly packed with ravenous temple-goers. The menu offers traditional Burmese dishes like a refreshing tea leaf salad alongside gussied up backpacker staples. Dip papadums into guacamole and cool down with refreshing shakes or the restaurant's top-notch lime, ginger, and honey juice. $ *Average main: K4000* ⊠ *Off Bagan-Nyaung U Rd., between Tharabar Gate and Ananda Temple, Old Bagan* ☎ *061/60481* ⊟ *No credit cards.*

$$$
INDIAN
✗ **Black Rose.** On New Bagan's restaurant row, Black Rose serves up Thai, Indian, and Chinese food to tourists staying in the nearby hotels. Most dishes are quite mild, so tell your waiter if you like your food on the spicy side. The chicken curry is excellent. The restaurant owners, a husband and wife duo, speak English well and are on hand, but service is extremely slow. Order a drink to start and sip slowly while you wait for your food. $ *Average main: K3500* ⊠ *Khayea Pin St. (main road), just south of Thiri Marlar, New Bagan* ⊟ *No credit cards.*

$$$
BURMESE
✗ **Golden Myanmar 2.** Part of the cluster of restaurants just north of Ananda Temple, Golden Myanmar 2 should not be confused with its sibling Golden Myanmar, which pales in comparison. Sit down, smile expectantly, and dishes will begin appearing on your table faster than you can wash the grime from your face. Mutton, pork, and chicken curries, fried fish, sautéed vegetables, Burmese salads (with pickled tea leaves), and rice will leave you stuffed, but then dessert comes out—short, squat bananas and sweet little tamarind candies. The friendly staff will keep refilling your plates unless you say otherwise. The buffet is 3,000 kyat per person, excluding drinks. $ *Average main: K3000* ⊠ *Off Bagan-Nyaung U Rd. near Ananda Temple, Old Bagan* ⊟ *No credit cards.*

$$$$
ITALIAN
FAMILY
✗ **San Carlo Italian and Chinese Restaurant.** Like a mirage, this enormously charming little space just pops up off the side of the unlit dirt road. Around the corner from a few budget guesthouses, including Kaday Aung Hotel, San Carlo is a most welcome reprieve. There are a scattering of tables outdoors and in, some shaded. The Chinese food is tasty but average, and you're coming here for the Western dishes, anyway. A mozzarella and tomato salad is filling enough for a meal; the smoky eggplant meaty. For dessert, the Dutch-style pancakes—thinner than their American cousin but thicker than crepes—are a happy ending to a lovely, unexpected meal. $ *Average main: K4500* ⊠ *D-14, Hnin Se St., near Kaday Aung Hotel, New Bagan* ☎ *61/65253* ⊟ *No credit cards.*

WHERE TO STAY

Visitors can choose from hotels in Old Bagan, closest to the big temples, New Bagan, which has more restaurants and budget accommodations, and Nyaung-U, which is more residential and has plenty of restaurants but is a 2-mile cycle from most of the temples.

$$$$ RESORT FAMILY **Bagan Thiripyitsaya Sanctuary.** Calling this hotel a sanctuary is a stretch, and the rooms are a bit dated, but the grounds and pool are expansive and well maintained, and the Irrawaddy River views during sunrise and sunset are truly stunning. **Pros:** gorgeous river views; a stone's throw from the stupas; spa is a bargain compared to the room rates. **Cons:** poor value during peak season; rooms could use updating; house restaurant food is middling. [$] *Rooms from: $380* ✉ *Bagan Archeological Zone, Old Bagan* ☎ *61/60048* 🌐 *www.thiripyitsaya-resort.com* 🛏 *68 rooms, 8 suites* 💳 *No credit cards* 🍴 *Breakfast.*

$$$ HOTEL FAMILY **Blue Bird.** Owned by a charming French-Burmese couple, this quaint 24-room boutique hotel packs in a motley crew of travelers. **Pros:** free Wi-Fi; pool is just the right temperature; owners on hand to help. **Cons:** extremely thin walls; outside noise; dependence on the hotel's cab service. [$] *Rooms from: $190* ✉ *10 Naratheinkha, New Bagan* ☎ *61/65051* 🌐 *www.bluebirdbagan.com* 🛏 *24 rooms* 💳 *No credit cards* 🍴 *Breakfast.*

$$$ RESORT **The Hotel at Tharabar Gate.** Touch-and-go service hasn't kept visitors from packing into this hotel, which has been described as an oasis; the well-manicured verdant lawns and trees provide guests with a much-needed break from the dust and dirt of the temples. **Pros:** prime location; superb breakfast; lush surroundings. **Cons:** mosquitoes; some problems with the pool water. [$] *Rooms from: $190* ✉ *Near Tharabar Gate, Old Bagan* ☎ *61/60037* 🌐 *www.tharabargate.com* 🛏 *80 rooms, 4 suites* 💳 *No credit cards* 🍴 *Breakfast.*

$ RESORT FAMILY **Kaday Aung Hotel.** Excellent value for money is what keeps travelers coming back to this midsize hotel. **Pros:** refreshing pool; short walk to the pagodas; good value. **Cons:** shoddy service; essential to double-confirm everything. [$] *Rooms from: $50* ✉ *Hninn Pann St., Hteeminyin Block, New Bagan* ☎ *61/65070, 626/320–4853 Los Angeles office* 🌐 *www.kadayaunghotel.com* 🛏 *48 rooms* 💳 *No credit cards* 🍴 *Breakfast.*

$$ HOTEL **Ruby True Hotel.** This simple, modest New Bagan hotel with excellent service and well-priced, comfortable rooms is a 15-minute stroll to the town's restaurant row. **Pros:** warm, friendly, extremely helpful staff; great value. **Cons:** a little isolated; could use a touch of updating; not many staff members speak English [$] *Rooms from: $85* ✉ *Myat Lay Rd., New Bagan* ☎ *061/65043* 🌐 *www.rubytrue.com* 🛏 *35 rooms* 💳 *No credit cards* 🍴 *Breakfast.*

NIGHTLIFE AND THE ARTS

There's no art scene to speak of in Bagan, and no real bar scene either, but all restaurants serve local beer and a few can put together mixed drinks.

Beach Bagan Restaurant and Bar. For sunset over the Irrawaddy with a drink in hand, Beach Bagan delivers. The bilevel restaurant, which can seat 400 people, including 100 in the garden, caters mainly to bus tours.

Those who've been tippling at other Bagan establishments will find the 3,500 kyat draft beer on the pricey side, but you're paying for the view. Book a seat either next to the river or on the rooftop and settle in for a cold beer and cool breezes. ✉ *12 Youne Tan Yat, Nyaung-U ✛ From Nyaung-U market, walk toward Lam Ma Daw 2 Rd., cross over Lam Ma Daw 3 Rd., and keep walking toward water* ☎ *061/60126* ⊕ *www. thebeachbaganrestaurant.com.*

Shwe Ya Su. This is a simple, unpretentious Burmese restaurant that also serves local draft beer and can concoct simple mixed drinks like rum and coke (no gin and tonics, though). Locals tuck into a bevy of dishes and watch soccer on a big screen indoors while tourists, exhausted from cycling all day, lounge in outdoor seating, surrounded by trees wrapped in strings of twinkling lights. The young servers are eager to please and the whole place has a lovely, laid-back vibe. ✉ *Yarkinnthar Hotel Rd., near Aroma 2, Nyaung-U* ◷ *Daily 7 am–10:30 pm.*

SHOPPING

Lacquerware is the big to-buy in Bagan; it's best purchased from work-shops in the Myinkaba area, half a mile south of Thiripyitsaya Sanctu-ary Resort, where the artists will show you how it's made and where the quality is higher. From the street vendors outside the temples, cute pottery pieces make good souvenirs. Be sure to compare prices and bargain for a discount of around 10%.

Bagan House. Come here if you've run out of cash and can't make it to the KBZ bank in Nyaung-U; this upmarket workshop accepts credit cards (plus 5% surcharge) if you spend more than $100. Bagan House sells a huge array of products fit for a (Burmese) king or queen. Options range from chic coasters to lamps that would look right at home in a pasha's opium den. ✉ *9 Jasmin Rd., 1 block south of Thiri Marlar St., Nyaung-U* ☎ *061/65133* ⊕ *www.baganhouse.com.*

Golden Cuckoo. The owners here have a workshop where visitors can see the lacquerware being made alongside a slew of vases, bowls, cups, and jewelry for sale. The family-run shop has been open since 1975, and the owner speaks English; one of the most impressive things in the shop (if it hasn't yet been snapped up) is a gorgeous five-panel fold-ing screen made by her father, each panel featuring Aung San Suu Kyi. ✉ *Just off main rd., behind Manuha Temple, Myinkaba* ☎ *061/65156* ✐ *goldencuckoo.bagan@gmail.com.*

Jasmine Family Lacquerware Workshop. This small, family-run business makes everything on-site and then sells its wares both directly to custom-ers and to larger lacquerware shops. Prices here are at least 20% cheaper than the more tourist-focused workshops, and the family themselves are quite lovely. Expect to pay around $25 for a 14-layer vase (the more lay-ers, the higher the quality). ✉ *Just off main rd., near Manuha Temple and Yaung Chi Oo Guest House, Myinkaba* ⊕ *jasminelacquer.notlong.com.*

Mani-Sithu Market. Locals do their produce shopping at this market, where the array of colorful fruits, vegetables, and flowers is simply gorgeous. Also for sale are souvenirs such as wood carvings, T-shirts, and assorted vintage odds and ends; treasures spotted include a 1970s Hot Wheels Camaro, a pair of pince-nez, and a knife shaped like a lizard. Textiles are also for sale here, and it's a good place to pick up inexpensive sheets of fabric that can be used as longyis to wear during temple visits. The market runs 6 am to 5 pm, but is at its most lively before noon. ⊠ *Anawrahta Rd. at Bagan-Nyaung-U Rd., Nyaung-U* ⊘ *Closed Sun.*

Shwe War Thein Handicrafts Shop. You'll find all manner of tchotchkes at this shop, which is slightly east of Tharabar Gate and the corresponding hotel. Peruse wood carvings, carved stone pieces, wind chimes, and leogryph figurines as well as puppets and assorted jewelry. There's also a small section of what the shop says are antique goods. There's lacquerware on sale but the offerings in Myinkaba are better. ⊠ *Off Bagan-Nyaung-U Rd., just east of Tharabar Gate, Myinkaba* ☎ *061/67032.*

INLE LAKE

Not for die-hard urbanites, tranquil Inle Lake is where visitors come to decompress after hot, dusty tours through the rest of the country's must-see spots. Myanmar's second-largest lake, Inle is located in Nyaung Shwe Township in Myanmar's Shan State, which borders China to the north, Laos to the east, and Thailand to the south. It's estimated that the country has some 100 ethnic groups, and most of the people living on and around the lake are Intha; they are self-sufficient farmers and practice a unique form of paddling called leg-rowing. It's the tiny village of Nyaung Shwe to which visitors arrive from, and depart for, the airport. Like Bagan's towns, it has evolved to cater to tourists. The activity of choice here is boating, floating around the lake on wooden canoes fitted with outboard motors. Diminutive wooden huts on stilts rise up from the water as women do their washing and kids run from one dwelling to the next. Following sunset, the lake quickly quiets, with just the faint whirring of motors as the last boatmen retire for the day.

GETTING HERE AND AROUND

AIR TRAVEL

The airport closest to Inle Lake is Heho, about an hour drive from the lake's jetty. There are half a dozen flights per day on domestic Myanmar airlines. The flight from Yangon is 75 minutes and costs around $110; flights from Mandalay and Bagan are cheaper and shorter. Even though you'll have arrived on a domestic flight, you will still have your passport checked on arrival in Heho. Once you exit the airport, you'll see a slew of vans waiting to fill up with passengers; if the van isn't full, you'll pay a minimum of 25,000 kyat ($30). If your driver can fill every seat, you're likely to pay around 18,000 kyat, and less if you're really good at bargaining. Just outside the town of Nyaung Shwe where the jetty is, you'll have your passport checked again and pay a $5 entrance fee.

BOAT TRAVEL

Unless you're staying on land, once you arrive at Inle Lake's jetty in Nyaung Shwe you'll need to board a boat to your hotel. These are long wooden canoes with seats like lawn chairs and run by outbound

10

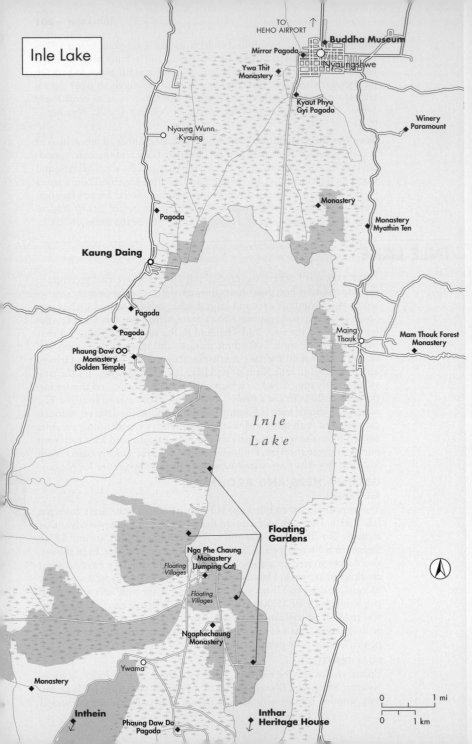

motors or, much more rarely, by leg rowers. These men (always men) stand on one leg and wrap the other around a paddle, using it to move the boat. Expect to pay around K13,500 for this trip alone; combine it with touring and you'll pay around K13,500 for a half day or K19,500 for a full day.

BUS TRAVEL

Buses leave Yangon daily between 4 and 5 pm arriving in Shwe Nyaung around 5 am. Tickets cost K13,000. From here you'll have to get a ride to Nyuang Shwe. These are two separate towns; Nyaung Shwe surrounds the lake's jetty, like Shwe Nyaung is about 12 kilometers north. There will be a few cars and a bus or two waiting to ferry passengers to Nyaung Shwe, but if you're traveling in a large group or you have heavy luggage, you should arrange with your guesthouse ahead of time to have someone come meet you at the bus station. As of this writing, a taxi will cost around K6,500; the bus will cost around K1,600. From Mandalay, the 11-hour overnight bus costs K11,000. From Bagan, there's the Bagan Minn Thar Express, a daily bus that departs at 7:30 am, arrives at 5:30 pm, and costs K13,000. Make sure you get off at Nyaung Shwe. Theoretically, tickets can be purchased on the bus, but it's easier to have your hotel help you book in advance, especially in peak season. Buses depart from a variety of locations; have your hotel or guesthouse confirm departure location.

CAR TRAVEL

Two types of hired cars and drivers can be had. The first is either through a travel agent or through your hotel. The second is a standard taxi; many cab drivers are happy to make a long journey in exchange for much more than they'd make in a day of staying in town. With a cabbie, you can negotiate—not so with the hotel or agency. The drive from Mandalay or Bagan to Inle Lake takes a bit over eight hours; going with a cab driver, you should pay around $180.

TRAIN TRAVEL

Trains run from Mandalay and Yangon to Shwen Yaung, 11 km (6.8 miles) from Inle Lake's jetty in Nyaung Shwe. The train from Yangon ($24/"upper class," $9/"ordinary") departs at 11 am, arriving at 2:45 pm the next day. There's another train from Yangon that has sleeper cars; it departs at 3 pm, gets you to Thazi just after 3 am, and leaves you with three hours to connect to the 6 am train bound for Shwen Yaung. Another option is the 6 am train from Yangon that gets to Thazi at 7 pm; you can stay overnight in Thazi and then take the aforementioned 6 am train. The train from Mandalay also connects in Thazi. As with the Shwe Nyaung bus stop, there will be cars and a pick-up truck or two waiting outside. Expect to pay around K9,500 for a cab and K2,000 per person for a seat in a pick-up truck. If you can walk 15 minutes, you can pick up a tuk tuk into town for around K7,000. To make things easier, reserve transport with your hotel or guesthouse ahead of time.

TAXI, MOTO, AND CYCLO TRAVEL

⇨ *For taxi information, see Car Travel.* From Heho Airport, it is possible to take a moto or cyclo to the jetty in Nyaung Shwe. Not for the faint of heart, it's a drive that takes an hour in a car and one that goes

Most of the villagers living on Inle Lake are self-sufficient farmers.

along a bumpy dirt road. One person can fit on a moto; two light people with little luggage can squeeze into a cyclo. Expect to pay around 15,000 kyats.

ESSENTIALS

Inle Lake has a few floating restaurants, but if you want to pick something up before you board the boat to your hotel, Nyaung Shwe is the only place to do it. Likewise, this is where you'll find the bank where you can exchange money; your hotel will accept USD but you'll need small kyat bills if you wish to buy souvenirs.

Air Contacts Heho Airport ⊠ *Off National Highway 4, Taunggyi District, Inle Lake* ☎ *No phone.*

Bank Contacts There's a KBZ bank in Nyaung Shwe, a 10-minute walk from the Inle Lake jetty.**KBZ Bank** ⊠ *30 Lanmadaw St., Nyaung Shwe* ☎ *081/209894.*

Visitor and Tour Information Inle Boy Travel Service ⊠ *Directly adjacent to jetty, Nyaung Shwe* ☎ *081/209806.*

EXPLORING INLE LAKE

The number-one activity at Inle Lake is cruising the water. Most visitors spend a day or two criss-crossing the lake in narrow wooden canoes powered by outboard motors, visiting different villages and taking in the scenery. It takes almost an hour to get to the southern end of the lake. If you're staying on land, you can explore the village of Nyaung Shwe, which has a backpacker vibe and which can be easily traversed on foot or by bike.

TOP ATTRACTIONS

Boating. Although the outboard motors make boat trips around Inle Lake loud (we recommend earplugs), they're still languid and, more importantly, the reason visitors come here in the first place. Inle is Myanmar's second largest lake, 44.9 square miles at an altitude of 2,900 feet. Boats leave from the jetty in the village of Nyaung Shwe, where you'll be dropped off after the trip in from the airport. Lining the narrow road where the airport vans leave you off are a handful of tiny travel agencies through which you can arrange boat trips, bicycle hire, and airport drop-off service. Expect to pay around $20 for a full-day boat tour and $14 for half a day. The only way to get to hotels on the lake is by boat; depending on how far south you are, expect to pay up to $14, though the price will drop significantly if you're using the same boatman (they are all men) for touring.

Inthar Heritage House. This beautiful wooden house, on stilts in the middle of Inle Lake, was completed in 2008 but appears older, thanks to reclaimed wood from which 80% of it is built. It's a wonderfully multiuse space. Downstairs is a cat sanctuary, where pampered Burmese felines lounge about lazily. The cats are the result of a two-year breeding program, an effort to reintroduce them to their native Myanmar. Upstairs from the cats is a re-creation of a traditional bedroom with impressive dark wooden period furniture. Then there's the art gallery, which hosts quarterly exhibitions of local artists' work, and then Inthar Restaurant, which is good—mostly Chinese dishes, with coffee, tea, shakes, and desserts—and a lovely, peaceful space. The restaurant's vegetables come from the house's own organic farm; cooking classes are also offered. ⊠ *Inpawkhon Village* ☎ *95/251232* ⊕ *www.intharheritagehouse.com.*

Inthein. Spending an hour or two meandering around this village, which is on land and reached by a narrow canal, is a nice way to break up monotonous, albeit pretty, Inle Lake cruising. The stupas start just behind the village proper with **Nyaung Ohak,** where a grouping of them stands in disrepair, surrounded by jungle. Keep going up the hill until you reach **Shwe Inn Thein Paya.** On the way up the stairs, you'll see vendors selling souvenirs, so bring some cash with you. The climb is worth it; you'll find a slew of 17th- and 18th-century stupas, some are crumbling but others have been lovingly renovated, so there's a nice contrast.

WORTH NOTING

Buddha Museum. The Shan ethnic group has its own unique culture but, because this is a government-run museum, you'll find no symbols of it here. Instead, eye Buddha images before turning your attention to the building itself, a teak-and-brick mansion that was once home to Sao Shwe Thaike; he was the 33rd and last Shan king and the first president of independent Burma, from 1948 to 1962, until the junta coup. ⊠ *Museum Rd. (Haw St.) near Myawady Rd.* ☜ *$2* ☉ *Wed.–Sun. 10–4.*

Floating Gardens. A far cry from the vegetable farms of the west, these floating gardens are a testament to the ingenuity of Inle Lake's villagers. The floating gardens are just north of Nampan (the southern end of the lake), and here Intha farmers grow a cornucopia of colorful produce using wooden trellises that rely on floating mats for support. Vegetables and flowers stand tall and strong on the trellises, which are lovingly tended by farmers floating by in their long wooden canoes. ✉ *Nampan Village.*

Kaung Daing. Five miles from Nyaungshwe is this sleepy village inhabited by the Intha ethnic group, who live around Inle Lake. Shan tofu is made here using not soybeans, but yellow split peas. Kaung Daing's big draw is its hot springs; there's a swimming pool and private bathhouses for men and women, and the water supply all comes from natural springs. It's a 45-minute bike ride here from Nyaungshwe, one that runs over a bridge, along a dirt road, and through marshes, eventually depositing you at the hot springs for a well-deserved soak. A boat here will take 30 minutes (K3,000–K3,500 each way), and a moto will do the round-trip for K5,000–K5,500. ✉ *Kaung Daing Village.*

WHERE TO EAT

If you're staying at a hotel on the lake, you'll be eating breakfast and dinner there. Lunch can be enjoyed at one of the restaurants on the lake, which, like the hotels, stand on stilts. If you're staying in or spending time in Nyaung Shwe, there are a dozen or so eateries, including the food stalls at Mingala Market.

$ BURMESE

🍴 **Food Stalls at Mingala Market.** Open for breakfast and lunch only, the food stalls at this colorful market are an experience for the senses. Everything is handmade and the sellers take pride in what they're offering. Featured dishes include Shan tofu salad, noodle soup, and enormous round rice crackers that will be devoured by those who've had a bit too much spice. Just across from the market are a few other food stalls where you'll find inexpensive plates of tea-leaf salad and spicy noodle soup. [$] *Average main: K1000* ✉ *Yoyng Gyi Rd. near Mong Li Chuang, Nyaung Shwe* ✣ *Walk from Viewpoint in direction of Paradise Hotel; market is about three-fourths of way there, on right side of main road* 💳 *No credit cards.*

$$$ EUROPEAN

🍴 **Inle Pancake Kingdom.** Inle Lake is unlikely to be your first stop in Myanmar, and so by this time a break from Burmese food is likely a top priority. Pancake Kingdom is a classic backpacker restaurant, with friendly service, inexpensive sweet and savory pancakes (really somewhere between crepes and American-style pancakes), Wi-Fi, and computers. Proximity to the docks, indoor and outdoor seating, and a general laid-back and quiet atmosphere make this popular with tourists looking for a little western flavor. [$] *Average main: K3000* ✉ *Just south of Yone Gyi Rd., near Phaung Daw Seiq Rd., Nyaung Shwe* ☎ *081/29288* 🌐 *inlepancakekingdom.com* 💳 *No credit cards.*

$$$ BURMESE

🍴 **Lotus Restaurant.** This diminutive, family-run space has just five tables and with so many tourists milling around town, it fills up quickly, and with good reason. Salads, which utilize pickled tea leaves, coriander, bits of chili and other assorted delicious odds and ends, have great texture and go down nicely alongside the restaurant's curries. Round out the meal with a refreshing fruit plate and a chat with the owner.

Rice-noodle fish soup Mohinga is considered Myanmar's national dish and is commonly eaten for breakfast.

$ *Average main: K4000* ✉ *Museum Rd. (Haw St.) and Myawady St., Nyaung Shwe* ⟷ *Close to Paradise Hotel* ▭ *No credit cards.*

$$$$ ✕ **Nice Restaurant.** This is indeed a nice place to hop off your boat when
ECLECTIC tooling around Inle Lake and tuck into Burmese and Western dishes,
some odd (pork cordon bleu has never seemed so out of place) and some
refreshing (avocado and prawn cocktail). The restaurant is open on all
sides though fully covered, so you're shaded but get a nice breeze. Beat
the hottest part of the day by making it a long lunch with the restaurant's K2,000 four-wine tasting, all locally produced. The restaurant's
quite big, but on the off chance it's full, float over to **Cherry Pann,**
directly across the water. $ *Average main: K5000* ✉ *Nampan Village*
☎ *081/22743* ▭ *No credit cards.*

$$$$ ✕ **Red Mountain Estate Vineyards.** There are nine varieties here, and the
ECLECTIC winemaking process is overseen by a Frenchman who joined the win-
ery in 2002. Tours are basic but give a good overview of Red Mountain's production process. Both wine and food are quite average, but
the K2,000 tasting menu paired with lovely views of the fields and
cool breezes makes for a very pleasant afternoon. Note that service
is molasses-slow, so budget at least an hour. ■TIP➔ The vineyard can
be reached by bike in about 20 minutes, and it's an easy ride save for
the very last uphill stretch. $ *Average main: K5000* ✉ *Taung Chay
Village Group* ☎ *081/209366* ⊕ *www.redmountain-estate.com* ▭ *No
credit cards.*

10

WHERE TO STAY

There are hotels on the lake and then there are those in Nyaung Shwe, the village surrounding the lake's jetty. The lake hotels are arguably better positioned for touring, but the hotels in Nyaung Shwe offer easy access to restaurants and services.

$$
B&B/INN
Fodor's Choice
★

Golden Island Cottages. This hotel is Inle Lake's most unique; it's run by the Pa-O minority group as a cooperative project: There are two outposts—the Thale-U branch, at the southern tip of the lake, about an hour ride from the jetty, and the the Nampan outpost, which is 10 miles from the jetty. **Pros:** reasonably priced; tasty food at in-house restaurants; warm service. **Cons:** noisy boat motors; Thale-U hotel is far from town. $ *Rooms from: $100 ⊠ Thale-U Village ☎ 081/209390 Nampan, 081/209389 Thale-U ⌁ 52 rooms ⊟ No credit cards ☉ www. gicmyanmar.com* ¶⊙¶ *Breakfast.*

$$
HOTEL

Hotel Amazing Nyaung Shwe. In the village of Nyaung Shwe, a 15-minute walk to the Inle Lake jetty, this hotel is ideally positioned for those who want to stretch their sea and land legs. **Pros:** plenty to see in the immediate area; very helpful staff. **Cons:** so popular it's hard to get a room; free Wi-Fi barely works. $ *Rooms from: $140 ⊠ Mong Li Chuang near Myawady Rd., Nyaung Shwe ☎ 081/209477 ⊕ www. hotelamazingnyaungshwe.com ⌁ 13 rooms, 3 suites* ¶⊙¶ *Breakfast.*

$$
RESORT

Inle Princess Resort. The quaint bungalows that make up this hotel are removed from the main lake to give you a quieter, more peaceful experience; rather than using noisy outboard motors to dock, boat drivers row. **Pros:** free Wi-Fi; a bang-up breakfast spread. **Cons:** a/c weak; so popular you need to book far in advance or find a well-connected travel agent. $ *Rooms from: $180 ⊠ Magyizin Village ☎ 081/209055 ✑ inleprincess@gmail.com, inleprincess@myanmar.com.mm ⊕ www. inleprincessresort.net ⌁ 45 suites ⊟ No credit cards* ¶⊙¶ *Breakfast.*

$$
B&B/INN

Paramount Inle Resort. Though by no means budget, this is one of the less expensive hotels on the lake proper. **Pros:** warm service; prime lake location. **Cons:** poor Wi-Fi signal; lake-facing rooms are loud; bathrooms need updating. $ *Rooms from: $100 ⊠ Nga Phe Chaung Village ☎ 094/936-0855 ⊕ www.paramountinleresort.com ⌁ 16 rooms, 12 suites ⊟ No credit cards* ¶⊙¶ *Breakfast.*

$$
RESORT
Fodor's Choice
★

ViewPoint Lodge. Of the hotels immediately off the jetty, this is the most upscale, and you'll see its weathered brown eaves as soon as you stumble from your airport van. **Pros:** beautiful rooms; warm service; delicious food. **Cons:** not all rooms have balconies; noise from the boats carries into the rooms; touch-and-go Wi-Fi. $ *Rooms from: $145 ⊠ Near Talk Nan Bridge and jetty, Nyaung Shwe ☎ 081/209062 ⊕ www.inleviewpoint.com ⌁ 20 suites* ¶⊙¶ *No meals.*

NIGHTLIFE AND THE ARTS

If you're staying on the lake, there are no bars to speak of, though your hotel restaurant will definitely serve wine, beer, and liquor. In Nyaung Shwe, not every restaurant serves alcohol, but many do and here you'll find visitors and some locals enjoying a drink.

FAMILY **Aung's Puppet Show.** Within a pocket-size theater, local puppeteer Aung (who is also a cab driver) puts on a nightly half-hour show in which he showcases his skills. It's cute and very entertaining, a nice evening activity in a place where there aren't any. Aung knows exactly what he's doing and his marionettes have the audience in constant giggles. On the premises is a puppet shop with marionettes and other souvenirs. Reservations are essential for the show. ⊠ *Opposite Nanda Wunn Hotel, 80 Yone Gyi Rd.* 🖃 *K3,000* ⊘ *Daily 7 and 8:30 pm.*

Min Min's. This sweet little eatery doubles as the town's only western-style watering hole. It's a family affair, with Min Min and his wife running things and their grade-school-age daughter Soe Soe acting as a runner. Visitors tuck into heaping plates of pasta with homemade pesto washed down with proper piña coladas, made with plenty of rum and fresh lime. Nearly 10,000 miles from Havana, Min Min's mojitos are spot on, a most welcome refreshment after a hot day of touring. ■TIP→ Min Min's also offers tour services, though we caution you not to sign up for any treks after your second mojito. ⊠ *Yone Gyi Rd. near Kyaung Taw Anouk Rd., Nyaung Shwe* ⊕ *www.min-mins.com.*

SHOPPING

Shopping at Inle Lake is limited to the workshops, which nicely showcase traditional handicrafts but are truly shops for tourists, and the markets, which are interesting and a good spot to purchase fresh produce.

Lakeside Workshops. Unless you tell him otherwise, your boat driver will without question take you to a series of workshops. Although these are certainly souvenir shops set up only for tourists, the employees aren't pushy and it's quite interesting to see how local goods are made. Swing by the cigar (cheeroot) workshop, followed by the goldsmith's and the blacksmith's, the handmade paper workshop, and the lotus silk workshop. Jewelry from the goldsmith's, delicate parasols from the paper workshop, and scarves and robes from the lotus silk workshop are among the most popular souvenirs.

Mingala Market. Mornings see this market packed with locals doing their shopping. What's on offer can be divided into three categories—groceries (fresh fish, produce), home goods (fishing supplies, bowls, the occasional knife), and handicrafts, which are sold at a few stalls. The market isn't too chaotic except every five days, when Inle's regular rotating market sets up shop here. Your hotel will be able to tell you when this is. ⊠ *Yone Gyi Rd. near Mong Li Chuang, Nyaung Shwe.*

Ywama. This is where to come if you're keen to purchase souvenirs. Ywama was the first of Inle Lake's many small villages to get a big tourism push and, as such, its waterways are more packed than the others. Ywama is still charming and has retained its authenticity—certainly families still live here and you'll see giggling kids running around—but there are also lots of tchotchke peddlers. Every five days, a floating market is held, when even more hawkers convene on Ywama. Thrown into the mix are a handful of farmers who continue selling vegetables to locals.

10

MANDALAY AND ENVIRONS

Myanmar's second largest city and its last royal capital, Mandalay is home to the rebuilt Mandalay Palace; the original, destroyed during WWII, was home to then-Burma's last monarchy. Downtown Mandalay is heavy on the concrete and urban sprawl; unlike Yangon, it looks nothing like it did when it was part British Burma. Mandalay is laid out on a grid, and from 35th St. north to the citadel walls can be easily traversed on foot or by bicycle. Bikes can be hired from your hotel for around $3 per hour. Mandalay offers a sharp contrast to Yangon and is interesting taken from both a historical and an urban planning point of view. A further juxtaposition to the big, dusty city is its nearby hill station Pyin U Lwin (née Maymo). Here is where Upper Burma's strongest colonial legacy lies, in the form of manicured gardens, horse-drawn carriages, and homes straight out of the English countryside.

GETTING HERE AND AROUND

Tourists' Mandalay has two distinct sections—Mandalay Hill and the palace entrance and downtown Mandalay. Although it is possible to walk between the two, a far easier way to go from the palace downtown to the restaurants is by bike, pick-up truck, or cab; coming back from downtown, you'll also have the option of a moto.

AIR TRAVEL

Half a dozen domestic flights land in Mandalay every day. The trip from Yangon takes 1 hour 25 minutes and costs around $116; the trips from Bagan and Heho (Inle Lake) are about half the time and less expensive. Air Asia and Thai Airways both fly in from Bangkok and China Eastern flies in from Kunming. Mandalay's airport is almost an hour from the city. Expect to pay at least K8,000; K6,000 if you're sharing.

BOAT TRAVEL

Boats arrive to and depart from the area around Gawein Jetty at 35th Street. The Malikha express ferry is the most popular, running between Mandalay to Bagan. Boats depart at 7 am, arriving in Bagan at 3:30 pm; tickets are $45 and a western breakfast, with lots of toast, is served on board. The ferry schedule is issued a month in advance. For a good schedule and information see ⊕ *www.myanmarrivercruises.com*.

BUS TRAVEL

There are half a dozen buses a day leaving Yangon for Mandalay and a couple from Bagan. Bus schedules can change, so have your hotel or guesthouse book tickets for you. Almost all buses from Yangon run overnight, leaving around 6 pm (K10,400). The trip from Bagan (K8,500) takes seven hours. Just outside the bus station you'll find a sea of taxis; bargain and you should be able to get a cab to your hotel for around K5,000.

CAR TRAVEL

From Bagan or Inle Lake to Mandalay, expect to spend around $180 and eight hours in the car. Within Mandalay, pick-ups trucks will drive between downtown and Mandalay Hill and the palace for around K5,000. A car out to Pyin-U Lwin will cost around K30,000 to K35,000, or K7,000 for a shared taxi.

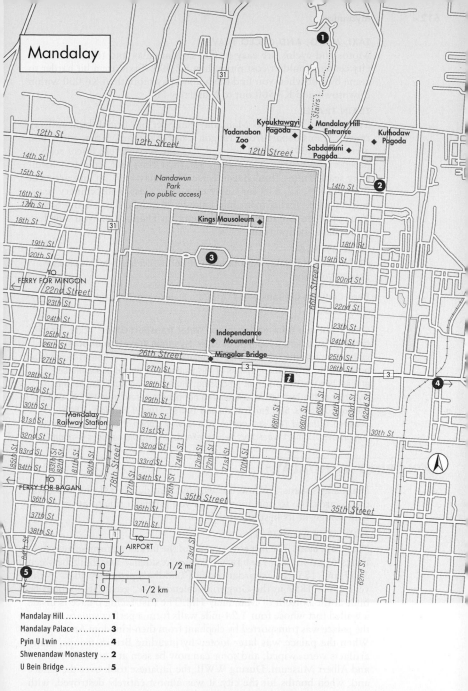

Mandalay

12th St
14th St
15th St
16th St
17th St
18th St
19th St
20th St
22nd Street
23rd St
24th St
25th St
26th St
27th St
28th St
29th St
30th St
31st St
32nd St
33rd St
34th St
36th St
37th St
38th St

31

12th Street
12th Street

Yadanabon
Zoo

Kyauktawgyi
Pagoda

Mandalay Hill
Entrance

Kuthodaw
Pagoda

Sabdamuni
Pagoda

14th St

2

Nandawun
Park
(no public access)

Kings Mausoleum

31

3

18th St
19th St
20th St
22nd St
23rd St
24th St
25th St
26th St

66th Street

TO
FERRY FOR MINGON

Independance
Moument

Mingalar Bridge

26th Street

3

i

3

4

Mandalay
Railway Station

27th St
28th St
29th St
30th St
31st St
32nd St
33rd St
34th St
35th Street

78th Street

80th St
81st St
82nd St
83rd St
85th St
37th St
72nd St
74th St
75th St
77th St

68th St
66th St
65th St
64th St
63rd St
62nd St

30th St

35th Street

62nd St

TO
FERRY FOR BAGAN

73rd St

TO
AIRPORT

0   1/2 mi

0   1/2 km

5

TAXI, MOTO, AND CYCLO TRAVEL

Motos and cyclos are easy to find in Mandalay and trips within the city center shouldn't cost more than K2,000. Taxis are a bit harder to come by, but when you find them don't pay more than K6,000 within downtown and K7,500 out to Mandalay Hill.

TRAIN TRAVEL

Trains from Yangon to Mandalay run over old British-built railway tracks. Trains depart from Yangon Central at 6 am, 3 pm, and 5 pm, arriving at 8:30 pm, 6:30 am, and 9:15 am, respectively. Prices are $33 (sleeper), $30 (upper class seat), $22 (first class seat), and $11 (ordinary seat). Trains from Bagan leave Mandalay at 7 am and arrive at 2:30 pm ($4, $7, $10 for upper class, first class, and ordinary seats, respectively). Trains from Inle Lake to Mandalay leave from Shwen Yaung (11 km [6.8 miles] from the jetty) to Thazi, where you switch to a Mandalay-bound train.

ESSENTIALS

Air Contacts Mandalay International Airport ⊠ *Off Naypyitaw–Mandalay Expy.* 🕾 *No phone.*

Bank Contacts CB Bank ⊠ *E-1, 2, 3 78th St. between 27th and 28th sts.* 🕾🕾 *02/69901.*

Visitor and Tour Information Inland Water Transport Office. Tickets for the ferries are sold here. ⊠ *35th St. at water.* **Myanmar Travels and Tours.** Those wishing to cross the Tachileik/Mae Sai border into Thailand will need to organize permits with state-owned MTT. As of this writing, you should allow yourself at least two weeks for permit processing. Those crossing from Mae Sai into Myanmar at the Tachileik checkpoint do not need a permit from MTT. ⊠ *Corner 68th and 27th sts.* **Sun Far Travels and Tours** ⊠ *Unit H, SY Bldg., 30th St. between 77th and 78th sts., across from railway station* 🕾 *02/69712* ⊕ *www. sunfartravels.com* ⊗ *Weekdays 9–5; weekends and public holidays 9–noon.*

EXPLORING MANDALAY

Mandalay's gems are few but worthy. Mandalay Hill and the royal palace are close to one another, but you'll need a ride to get out to U Bein Bridge, at its best at sunrise.

TOP ATTRACTIONS

Mandalay Palace. The last royal palace of the ultimate Burmese monarch, Kings Mindon and Thebaw's one-time residence was built between 1857 and 1859 in accordance with Buddha's prophecy that, in the year 2400 (1857 in the Gregorian calendar), a "great city" would be built at the bottom of Mandalay Hill. The east-facing palace is inside a walled fort whose four 1.24-mile walls form a perfect square. Part of the palace was transported by elephant from then-kingdom Amarapura. When the palace was later looted by invading British troops, many artifacts were swiped, and some can now be seen at London's Victoria and Albert Museum. During WWII, the Japanese took over the palace and, when bombs hit the city, it was almost entirely destroyed, with only the mint and one watchtower (which can be climbed today) surviving the attack. The structure that now stands was built in 1989 and is

Mandalay Palace, in Myanmar's last royal capital, one of the gems that reward exploration of Mandalay's dusty streets.

a faithful re-creation of the original. The palace itself is an important sight, but what's even more interesting is the village inside the citadel walls, where locals go about their daily business within spitting distance of what were once Burma's most hallowed halls. ⊠ *East Moat at 19th St.* 🎫 *$10 combination ticket includes Shwenandaw Monastery.*

FAMILY **Pyin U Lwin.** Pyin U Lwin is 42 miles from Mandalay and, at an elevation of 3,500 feet, feels much cooler than the stifling town. After capturing Mandalay during the Third Anglo-Burmese War, the British set upon Pyin U Lwin (then known as Maymo or May Town) and made it their hill station, and it remained as such until the end of British rue in 1948. The town is still quite charming and is best enjoyed by bicycle or perched in a colonial-style horse-drawn carriage. Start off in the town center where you'll see the **Purcell Clock Tower** (1936) and redbrick **All Saints' Church** (1912). Mandalay is a desert compared with Pyin U Lwin, so soak up the green at the 435-acre **National Kandawgyi Gardens,** which were built in 1915 and in which can be found nearly 500 plant species. There's a lovely lake, a butterfly museum, an orchid garden, an aviary, and a swimming pool. (Note that the gardens are owned by government crony Tay Za). The best place to see Pyin U Lwin's old colonial buildings is along roads **Circular and Forest,** which you can cycle or bump along in your horse-cart. Buildings run the style gamut from Tudor to plantation, and both the Candacraig Hotel (once the British Club) and the former Croxton Hotel are worth an ogle. ■TIP➔ A private car to Pyin U Lwin should cost K30,000–K35,000; a shared taxi, which leaves from downtown Mandalay (27th and 83rd streets) should cost K7,000 per person; the trip takes two hours. A more scenic, albeit bumpy, trip can be made by train, which leaves around 4 am and arrives just before 8 am; tickets are \$3. ⊠ *\$5.*

Fodor's Choice
★
U Bein Bridge. The world's longest teak bridge runs three-quarters of a mile over Taungthaman Lake in Amarapura, Burma's former capital and now part of Mandalay. More than 1,000 teak poles make up the bridge, each scavenged from the former Royal Palace by then mayor U Bein. During dry season (November to April) the lake is quite shallow but, during summer, it nearly doubles in height, with water reaching up to just below the bridge's planks. Around sunrise is the best time to come, when a stream of monks and villagers, some on bike, cross back and forth. Most visitors are dropped off at the western end and then walk across; at the eastern end is a small village where you can munch on hot, fresh chapatis and sip very sweet tea. ■TIP→ If you're staying near Mandalay Hill and heading to the bridge for sunrise, book a cab the night before; it will run you around K18,000.

WORTH NOTING

Mandalay Hill. The city's name is derived from this hill, which, at nearly 800 feet, can seem a lot more like a mountain when you're schlepping up it on a 100°F day. For those unable to make the climb, there's an elevator as well as a road to an escalator that leads up to the gilded Sutaungpyei Pagoda at the top of the hill. Burmese Buddhists have been coming here for nearly two centuries, paying their respects, and you'll still see monks here, mostly sweet teenage boys who are eager to chat with visitors and practice their (already quite good) English. On the way up, you'll see a giant standing Buddha, his right hand pointing to the city. Legend has it that when Buddha visited Mandalay Hill, he prophesied that in the year 2400 (Buddhist calendar), a "great city" would be founded at the bottom of the hill. In the Gregorian calendar, that year is 1857, exactly when King Mindon decreed that Mandalay would be Burma's new capital. Sunset over Mandalay is best viewed from the top of the hill, and the climb can take 40 minutes, so give yourself plenty of time. ■TIP→ Bring wet wipes to clean off your feet. ⊠ *Mandalay Hill* ⊠ *K1,000.*

Shwenandaw Monastery. King Mindon built this intricately carved structure in the mid 19th century as his apartment and then died there in 1878. His son Thebaw believed his father's ghost was still in the building, refused to live there, and had it taken down and moved outside the citadel walls and turned into a monastery. In doing so, he unknowingly saved it from pillaging by the British (1885) and certain ruin during the WWII Japanese invasion. At its inception, the building was more regal than it is today since gold plating and the exterior glass mosaics are now gone, but the interior remains in quite good shape. ⊠ *62nd St. near 14th St., next to university* ⊠ *\$10 combination ticket includes Mandalay Palace.*

WHERE TO EAT

There's some excellent Indian food in Mandalay, along with the Myanmar buffets available countrywide. Restaurants on the whole are inexpensive and offer good value for money.

$$ BURMESE 🍴 **84th and 23rd Streets Restaurants.** A handful of Shan restaurants have set up shop around this intersection. Both **Golden Shan** and **Lashio Lay** offer sizeable buffet spreads of standard Myanmar dishes like chicken curry and assorted sautéed greens, served with big helpings of white rice. Teashop **Karaweik** does excellent Shan noodles (K600, popular for breakfast) and sweet naan (K150) straight from the tandoor, best enjoyed alongside a cup of tea. [$] *Average main: K2500* ✉ *84th St. near 23rd St.* 💳 *No credit cards.*

$$$ VEGETARIAN FAMILY 🍴 **Marie Min.** Burmese, Indian, and western dishes pack the vegetarian menu here, so there's something for everyone. The all-day breakfast, with dishes like muesli and pancakes, are big with backpackers staying nearby, but most come here for lunch and dinner, snagging coveted seats on the upper level balcony. The menu includes dal and curries (the pumpkin is the best), guacamole and eggplant dip, and tart, fresh tomato salad. Wash it all down with lassis or chocolate–peanut butter milk shakes. ■ **TIP→ There have been several reports of intentional bill discrepancies; check yours carefully.** [$] *Average main: B3000* ✉ *27th St. between 74th and 75th sts.* ☎ *95/236234* 💳 *No credit cards* 🕒 *Daily 8:30 am–9 pm.*

$ INDIAN 🍴 **Nay Cafe.** Long after you've returned from Mandalay, visions of these chapatis will continue to dance in your head. This is the perfect place to sit back and watch the city go by, surrounded by hungry, happy locals and foreigners. Grab a sidewalk table and order the mutton, lamb, or mixed vegetable curries, best enjoyed with a couple mouthwatering chapatis, a side of dal and, to wrap it up, a cup of chai. [$] *Average main: K1700* ✉ *82nd St. at 27th St.* 💳 *No credit cards.*

$ CAFÉ FAMILY 🍴 **Nylon Ice Cream Bar.** The ice cream here is not the best you'll ever have, but you won't be able to find cold scoops anywhere else in Mandalay. The atmosphere is really the big draw, with locals and foreigners coming by all day to hang out at the sidewalk tables and people watch while sipping beer and shakes. The short flavor list includes chocolate, strawberry, vanilla, and durian, of which the durian is the best. Eco-warriors, beware: unless you specifically ask for a bowl or glass, scoops come served in little styrofoam containers. [$] *Average main: K1000* ✉ *83rd St. between 25th and 26th sts.* ☎ *95/232318* 💳 *No credit cards.*

$$$ BAKERY FAMILY Fodor's Choice ★ 🍴 **Simplicity Organic Food and Bakery.** Enormously charming and truly unique in Mandalay, this pint-size, family-run café is near Mandalay's jetty, an area otherwise devoid of much in the way of dining. The sweet owner and his son speak English well and are passionate and knowledgeable about organic food, the environment, and the use of MSG. There are delicious Chinese-style pastries, some ice cream and, like manna from heaven, proper coffee from a Swiss-made machine, available in several variations including iced (a dream come true) and even cappucinos. On the savory side are traditional Shan noodles, which the locals eat for breakfast, house-made dumplings, and simple stir-fry dishes like chicken with rice and vegetables. ■ **TIP→ 35th St. runs the length of downtown Mandalay, so be sure to indicate to whomever is driving you that you want to be near the jetty.** [$] *Average main: B3000* ✉ *35th St. between 91st and 92nd sts., near jetty* 💳 *No credit cards.*

WHERE TO STAY

Mandalay's more expensive hotels are near Mandalay Palace, but within the city are a few budget options that offer easier access to restaurants.

$ 🏨 **Ayarwaddy River View Hotel.** Set right along the river, this hotel
HOTEL   offers a nice alternative to the luxury behemoths and the comparably priced city hotels. **Pros:** river views; friendly and efficient service. **Cons:** some rooms can be loud; no dining options in the immediate area $ *Rooms from: $60* ✉ *Strand Rd. between 22nd and 23rd sts., Strand Rd. becomes Myo Pat Rd. and 22nd becomes Pinya* ☎ *02/72373* ⊕ *www.ayarwaddyriverviewhotel.com* ⟿ *56 rooms* ⊟ *No credit cards* ⫟⊙⫞ *Breakfast.*

$ 🏨 **Emerald Land Inn.** Though it looks a bit tired, this budget hotel (by
HOTEL   Myanmar standards) with its neatly tended gardens and swimming pool offers respite from downtown Mandalay. **Pros:** good value for money; attentive staff; plentiful hot water. **Cons:** far from most everything; road-facing rooms are noisy; power outages. $ *Rooms from: $70* ✉ *9 14th St., near 87th St.* ☎ *02/39471* ⟿ *38 rooms* ⫟⊙⫞ *Breakfast.*

$ 🏨 **Mandalay City Hotel.** Swimming pools at budget hotels are far and
HOTEL   few between, and Mandalay City delivers on that front. **Pros:** pool; downtown location; efficient service. **Cons:** loud rooms; no elevators; some rooms are small. $ *Rooms from: $56* ✉ *26th St. between 82nd and 83rd sts.* ☎ *02/61700* ⊕ *www.mandalaycityhotel.com* ⟿ *67 rooms* ⊟ *No credit cards* ⫟⊙⫞ *Breakfast.*

$$$ 🏨 **Mandalay Hill Resort.** A stone's throw from Mandalay Hill and a
RESORT   short jaunt to the royal palace, this Thai-owned big-box hotel offers
FAMILY   easy access to Mandalay's main sites. **Pros:** very close to Mandalay
Fodor's Choice   Hill and Royal Palace; great pool; lovely grounds. **Cons:** a cab ride
★   from downtown; two tiny elevators are extremely slow. $ *Rooms from: $200* ✉ *No. 9, 416.B Kwin, 10th St., near foot of Mandalay Hill* ☎ *02/35638* ✉ *mandalayhillresort1996@gmail.com* ⊕ *www. mandalayhillresorthotel.com* ⟿ *192 rooms, 14 suites* ⊟ *No credit cards* ⫟⊙⫞ *Breakfast.*

$$$$ 🏨 **Rupar Mandalar Resort.** Idyllic and full of local flavor, this resort is a
RESORT   ways from downtown but is a real oasis. **Pros:** lovely rooms, staff, and pool. **Cons:** far from the city but not from the dust, as new hotels are going up just next door. $ *Rooms from: $300* ✉ *Corner of 53rd and 30th Sts.* ☎ *02/61555* ⊕ *www.ruparmandalar.com* ⟿ *10 rooms, 5 suites* ⊟ *No credit cards* ⫟⊙⫞ *Breakfast.*

NIGHTLIFE AND THE ARTS

To say that nightlife in Mandalay is nonexistent would be a stretch; it's more than that there's little divide between restaurants and bars. Almost all eateries serve beer and you'll see locals sitting around enjoying drinks as the next table over has a full meal. (⇨ *Where to Eat*). Of all the big cities in Myanmar, however, Mandalay has the most active theater scene, made up of the famous Moustache Brothers, a marionette theater, and a dance troupe.

FAMILY   **Mandalay Marionettes.** Ma Ma Naing and Naing Yee Mar founded this theater in 1986 and, in 2000, performed in France, the Netherlands, and the U.S. The team also works with NGOs to put on puppet shows that aim at improving AIDS awareness. The expert manipulators here use colorful marionettes to tell classic Burmese tales, including love stories and one about a flying alchemist. Read the program so you understand more about what you're watching. The hour-long show starts nightly from 8:30 pm. ⊠ *66th St. between 26th and 27th sts.* ☏ *02/34446* ✐ *naing.yee.mar@mandalaymarionettes.com* ⊕ *www. mandalaymarionettes.com* ✏ *$8.*

FAMILY **Mintha Theater.** Accompanied by eight musicians, seven talented dancers kitted out in bright costumes perform classical Burmese routines. Twelve dances are on the rotating program, which changes nightly and highlights Myanmar's variety of traditional dances. The lively, colorful show runs an hour and kids who can sit for that long will certainly be entertained. The performance starts at 8:30 pm. ⊠ *27th St. between 66th and 65th sts.* ☏ *09/680–3607* ⊕ *www.minthatheater. com* ✏ *K8,000.*

Moustache Brothers. Two brothers and a cousin make up this comedic trio, which has suffered for critisizing the regime; 64-year-old Par Par Lay and his cousin 60-year-old Lu Zaw were imprisoned from 1996 to 2003. Today, all three continue to perform with several other family members, and their quirky variation of comedy—screwball meets political satire, with history lessons, traditional dance, and singing thrown in—can't be seen anywhere else in Myanmar. The hour-long show starts at 8:30 pm. ⊠ *39th St. between 80th and 81st sts.* ⊕ *www.facebook. com/TheMoustacheBrothers* ✏ *$10.*

SHOPPING

Shopping areas in Mandalay are a bit spread out, so hiring a taxi would be most convenient way to visit the stores we recommend. Mandalay is known for its handicrafts, especially puppets. These can be purchased at Moustache Brothers and Mandalay Marionettes *(⇨ Nightlife and the Arts)*. If you've got a ride and fancy some more shopping, there are rows of stone carvers' workshops west of Mahamuni Temple where slabs of stone are chipped, carved, and polished into Buddhas of varying sizes and into more manageable souvenirs like marble elephants. If you've got limited time in Mandalay, the easiest place to buy souvenirs is at Mandalay Hill, where there are vendors on the lower-level steps.

Gold Pounders' District. Local worshippers will often put gold leaves onto images of Buddha, and this is where the .00008-inch bits are made, each pounded between heavy blocks by muscular craftsmen. At **Golden Rose** (36th Street between 78th and 79th streets) and **King Galon** (36th Street between 77th and 78th streets), you can observe the craftsmen as the English-speaking staff explain the production process. The information is not a sales pitch, but the most popular thing to buy here is sheets of gold leaf (10 sheets for K2,500). ⊠ *36th St. from 77th to 79th sts.*

Jade Market. A warren of worktables, this jam-packed market is filled with jade traders inspecting uncut pieces and then having them cut, shaped, and polished to their specifications. The trading floor could give Wall Street a run for its money, with buyers and sellers bent over

10

tables, intently discussing business. Outside, on the eastern side of the market, the cutting and polishing continues. If you do want to buy jade, it's best to come here with a reputable guide. ⊠ *South of 38th St., near 87th St.* ☜ *$1, not always enforced.*

Soe Moe. For impressive embroidered tapestries, bronze sculptures, and carved wood and stone pieces, visit Soe Moe, where the staff can arrange for your purchases to be shipped to Yangon. ⊠ *36th St. between 77th and 78th sts.*

Sunflower. In the same building as vegetarian restaurant Marie Min, Sunflower sells attractive bronze and wood carvings. ⊠ *27th St. between 75th and 74th sts.*

Zegyo Market. Mandalay's oldest market dates back to King Mindon (father of Thebaw, the last king of Burma). The original structure has seen been replaced by a Chinese-style mall, but the hive of activity outside is more interesting than the household goods sold with in. A wide array of produce is available here, neatly grouped in colorful piles, and locals come out in full force to do their marketing. Dried shrimp and fish paste make good, nonperishable souvenirs. ⊠ *84th St. at 26th St.*

IRRAWADDY RIVER CRUISES

Not to be confused with the Irrawaddy River ferries *(⇨ Getting Here and Around for both Bagan and Mandalay)*, these cruises range in length from two-day/one-night to more than three weeks. The cruises can be classed as either upmarket or very upmarket; a less expensive alternative is the aforementioned ferries. There's no single departure point for Irrawaddy River cruises; most leave from Mandalay or Yangon, but others start in Bagan and even Bangkok (on land). All cruises include stops in Bagan and Mandalay (the shorter cruises run back and forth between the two). Beyond visiting land sights, the cruises themselves provide for an up-close look at the riverside villages that depend on the water for their livelihood.

ESSENTIALS

Meals and drinks are included in the cruise price but snacks are not. You'll be able to pick these up in Yangon or at the more populated port towns. Anything ordered on the ship not included in the meal plan must be paid for in cash. You will definitely need to bring your own sunblock.

You should arrive in your cruise's departure city one day before your ship is set to sail, even if your cruise doesn't depart until the following evening. Included in many cruises' pricing is one night in the departure city, but be sure to confirm with your individual operator.

CRUISE LINES

Most of the boats that ply the Irrawaddy are bilevel; some are cruise ships while others are colonial steam-ship style. Each ship has between five and 30 cabins, accommodating 10 to 60 people. The cruise lines stop in different places, but all cover Bagan and Mandalay. Unless otherwise indicated, all prices listed are per person for a double cabin during high season.

Abercrombie and Kent. Abercrombie and Kent is best known for its luxury excursions, and its 10-night, 11-day Myanmar's Burmese Heritage cruise (from $6,995) ensures guests' every whim is catered to. The tour meets in Bangkok, starts in Yangon, and ends with the reverse. In between, travelers cruise the Irrawaddy on luxury liner the Road to Mandalay, visiting Inle Lake, Mandalay, and Bagan. Day 5, between Mandalay and Bagan, is spent almost entirely on the water save for a brief stop in Sagaing, an important center of Buddhism. ⊠ *1411 Opus Pl., Downer's Grove, Illinois, USA* ☎ *888/611–4711* ⊙ *Weekdays 8–7, Sat. 9–1 CST* ⊕ *www.abercrombiekent.com.*

Amara River Cruise. Amara's two boutique boats, the Amara I and II, are built of strong, gleaming teak and have just seven and five rooms, respectively. Because the boats are so small, the service is extremely personalized and the entire boat can be chartered if a party so wishes. Amara offers three-night, four-day Mandalay–Bagan and Bagan–Mandalay cruises (€580/I, €690/II) and six-day, seven-night Mandalay–Bhamo and Bhamo–Mandalay (€1,200/I, €1,540/II). Bhamo is a town in Myanmar's northernmost state, Kachin, and is 40 miles from the border of Yunnan province, China. Visited by few tourists, it offers a real look at how Burmese villagers live along the river. ⊠ *6 Tayza Rd., Yangon (Rangoon)* ☎ *01/652191* ⊕ *www.amaragroup.net.*

Orient Express. Orient Express is the British group that manages Yangon hotel The Governor's Residence, and their cruises are just as luxe. In a nod to Rudyard Kipling, the massive ship is called the Road to Mandalay; there are 51 cabins, a spa, and two places to order a Pegu Club cocktail that would make *The Jungle Book* author proud. Tours are three, four, and seven nights long. All go to Bagan and Mandalay; the shorter trips also stop in Sagaing, an important center of Buddhism and the longer trip also brings you to Mt. Popa and Pyin-U Lwin (referred to as Maymo). Note that the boat does not run every month, particularly when water levels are too low. ⊠ *Fountain Valley, California, USA* ☎ *800/524–2420* ✉ *greatjourneys@oeh.com* ⊕ *www.orient-express.com.*

Pandaw River Expeditions in Asia. Singaporean-owned Pandaw has eight Irrawaddy River cruises. The shortest is seven nights—Prome to Mandalay with a stop in Bagan (from $2,452) or Mandalay to Katha (the setting for Orwell's *Burmese Days*) and back (same price). Visit Prome, which has a collection of 7th-century stupas, Thayetmyo, a former British Burma border town with a handful of old colonial buildings, and Minlah Fort, which were built by the Italians to keep the British out of what was then Royal Burma. Pandaw's longest cruise is a whopping 20 nights on the water, starting in Yangon and ending in Mandalay (from $7,056). It makes many stops in rural Myanmar, to tiny villages along the river, and to Katha, made famous by Orwell. Pandaw has a 10% discount for those who book early. Ten custom-built colonial steamship-style boats make up the fleet. The Pandaw Charity is the cruise operator's nonprofit arm, based in the U.K. and working mostly in Myanmar to build schools, an orphanage, and a hospice. A portion of the cruises' annual profits is donated to the charities; in

10

2012, this was more than $250,000. ☎ *044/203–287–6113 U.K. office, 061/280–067–013 Australia office* ⊕ *www.pandaw.com.*

Paukan Cruises by Ayravata Cruise Company. Paukan's fleet of three comprises a lovingly restored 1947 Scottish-built steamship and two newer vessels:, the 2007, which looks much like the 1947 outfit, and the sleek, teak 2012 model. Paukan is one of a few operators who have short cruises; there's a one-night trip from Mandalay to Bagan and a two-night trip that runs both the Bagan–Mandalay and Mandalay–Bagan routes (both from $780). One of the most popular tours is the four night Royal Myanmar (from $1,920), which starts in Bagan and ends in Mandalay following stops at Yandabo (a pot-making village, where the peace treaty for the First Anglo-Burmese war signed; we know how that ended), Monywa (caves with hundreds of Buddha statues), Ava (teak monastery and 88½-foot watchtower), and Amarapura (penultimate capital city). Paukan also offers 5-, 6-, and 10-night cruises. ⊠ *25 38th St., Yangon (Rangoon)* ☎ *01/380877* ⊕ *www.ayravatacruises.com.*

Value World Tours. This 14-day Golden Myanmar cruise (from $4,000) starts with a tour of Yangon before moving on to Mandalay, where passengers will board the 16-cabin, steamship-style boat and set off. This cruise makes the standard stops in Mandalay and Bagan, but also brings passengers to Yandabo Village, where the people specialize in making pottery; Minhla Fort, built by the Italians to keep the British out of upper Burma; and Prome and Pyu, home to ancient Buddhist artifacts dating from the 5th century. The village is also the site of a school and medical dispensary built by donations from cruise passengers. The cruise fees include not only all meals but also free-flowing tea, coffee, bottled water, soft drinks, and even alcohol. On board are lectures, cooking lessons, and other optional activities. ⊠ *17220 Newhope St., Ste. 203, Fountain Valley, California, USA* ☎ *800/795–1633 in California* ⊕ *www.rivercruises.net.*

Viking River Cruises. American cruise behemoth Viking has its own slice of the Myanmar-river-cruise pie with the 16-day Memories of Mandalay excursion. This Irrawaddy cruise kicked off in 2002 and the ship underwent refurbishment in 2013. The $5,000 tour starts and ends in Bangkok. Travelers spend two days in Yangon before heading to river town Pyay and boarding the luxury liner. From there, it's off to Thayetmyo, once the border between upper and British Burma and still home to a handful of colonial structures. Next is Minhla Fort, which the Italians built to keep the British out of upper Burma (things did not go according to plan). Before Bagan, the group stops at the Salé Monasteries, one of which teak structures was built in 1882. The tour winds down in Mandalay before passengers fly back to Bangkok. ⊠ *Yangon (Rangoon)* ☎ *800/706–1483 in California* ⊕ *www.vikingrivercruises.com.*

UNDERSTANDING
THAILAND

INTRODUCTION TO
THAI ARCHITECTURE

VOCABULARY

MENU GUIDE

INTRODUCTION TO THAI ARCHITECTURE

Though real architecture buffs are few and far between, you'd be hard-pressed to find a visitor to Thailand who doesn't spend at least a little time staring in slack-jawed amazement at the country's glittering wats and ornate palaces—and the elegant sculptures of the mythical beasts that protect them. As befits this spiritual nation, most of the fanfare is saved for religious structures, but you can find plenty to admire in the much simpler lines of the traditional houses of the Central Plains and northern Thailand.

Wats

Wat is the Thai name for what can range from a simple ordination hall for monks and nuns to a huge sprawling complex comprising libraries, bell towers, and meditation rooms. Usually the focal point for a community, it's not unusual for a wat to also be the grounds for village fêtes and festivals. Although most wats you come across symbolize some aspect of Thai-style Theravada Buddhism, examples of other architectural styles are relatively easy to find: Khmer ruins dot the Isan countryside to the east, while northern Thailand showcases many Burmese-style temples.

Wats are erected as acts of merit—allowing the donor to improve his karma and perhaps be reborn as a higher being—or in memory of great events. You can tell much about a wat's origin by its name. A wat *luang* (royal wat), for example, was constructed or restored by royals and may have the words *rat, raja,* or *racha* in its name (e.g., Ratburana or Rajapradit). The word *phra* may indicate that a wat contains an image of the Buddha. Wats that contain an important relic of the Buddha have the words *maha* (great) and *that* (relic) in their names. Thailand's nine major wat mahathats are in Chiang Rai, Chai Nat, Sukhothai, Phisanulk, Ayutthaya, Bangkok, Yasothon, Phetchaburi, and Nakhon Si Thammarat.

Thai wats, especially in the later periods, were seldom planned as entire units, so they often appear disjointed and crowded. To appreciate a wat's beauty you often have to look at its individual buildings.

Perhaps the most recognizable feature of a wat, and certainly a useful landmark when hunting them down, is the towering conelike *chedi*. Originally used to hold relics of the Buddha (hair, bones, or even nails), chedis can now be built by anyone with enough cash to house their ashes. At the base of the chedi you can find three platforms representing hell, earth, and heaven, while the 33 Buddhist heavens are symbolized at the top of the tallest spire by a number of rings.

The main buildings of a wat are the *bot*, which contains a Buddha image and functions as congregation and ordination hall for the monks, and the *viharn*, which serves a similar function, but will hold the most important Buddha image. Standard bot and viharn roofs will feature three steeply curved levels featuring red, gold, and green tiles; the outer walls range from highly decorated to simply whitewashed.

Other noticeable features include the *mondop, prang,* and *ho trai*. Usually square with a pyramid-shape roof, the mondop is reminiscent of Indian temple architecture and serves as a kind of storeroom for holy artifacts, books, and ceremonial objects. The prang is a tall tower similar to the chedi, which came to Thailand by way of the Khmer empire and is used to store images of the Buddha. Easily identifiable by its stilts or raised platform, the ho trai is a library for holy scriptures.

Roofs, which are covered in glazed clay tiles or wooden shakes, generally consist of three overlapping sections, with the lower roof set at gentle slopes, increasing to a topmost roof with a pitch of 60 degrees. Eave brackets in the form of a *naga* (snakes believed to control the irrigation waters of rice fields) with its head at the bottom often support the lower edges of the roofs. Along the eaves of many roofs are a row of small brass bells with clappers attached to thin brass pieces shaped like Bodhi tree leaves.

During the early Ayutthaya period (1350–1767), wat interiors were illuminated by the light passing through vertical slits in the walls (wider, more elaborate windows would have compromised the strength of the walls and, thus, the integrity of the structure). In the Bangkok period (1767–1932), the slits were replaced by proper windows set below wide lintels that supported the upper portions of the brick walls. There are usually five, seven, or nine windows on a side in accordance with the Thai preference for odd numbers. The entrance doors are in the end wall facing the Buddha image; narrower doors may flank the entrance door.

Principal building materials have varied with the ages. Khmer and Lopburi architects built in stone and laterite; Sukhothai and Lanna builders worked with laterite and brick. Ayutthaya and Bangkok architects opted for brick cemented by mortar and covered with one or more coats of stucco (made of lime, sand, and, often, rice husks). In early construction, walls were often several feet thick; as binding materials and construction techniques improved they became thinner.

The mid-13th century saw an enormous wave of men entering the monkhood as the Kingdom of Sukhothai adopted Hinayana Buddhism as its official religion. Consequently there was a need for bigger monasteries. Due to the lack of quality stone and brick available, wood became the building material of choice, marking a shift away from the exclusively stone structures of the Khmer period.

Sculpture

The Thai image of the Buddha usually features markedly long ears weighed down by heavy earrings in reference to his royal background, and is cast in bronze and covered in gold leaf by followers. He is typically depicted seated or standing; less common images are reclining Buddhas, acknowledging impending death, and walking Buddhas, which were favored during the Sukhothai period (13th to 15th century). Statues from the Lanna period of the 13th to 15th century and the present Ratanakosin era feature eyes fashioned from colored gems or enamel, while the Lopburi period of the 10th to 13th century favored metal.

A collection of 32 Pali *lakshanas,* descriptions used to identify future incarnations of the Buddha, popularly serve as a kind of blueprint for reproductions. The lakshanas include reference to wedge-shape heels, long fingers, and toes of equal length, legs like an antelope, arms long enough that he could touch either knee without bending, skin so smooth that dust wouldn't adhere to it, a body as thick as a banyan tree, long eyelashes like those of a cow, 40 teeth, a hairy white mole between his eyebrows, deep blue eyes, and an *ushnisha* (protuberance) atop his head—either a turban, a topknot, or a bump on his skull.

Palaces

Although King Bhumibol currently uses Chitlada Palace when in Bangkok, the Chakri Dynasty monarchs who preceded him used the showpiece Grand Palace as their official residence. Shots of the palace with its gleaming spires floodlighted up at night fill every postcard stand, and it's arguably Bangkok's single most important tourist attraction.

Built in 1782 when King Rama I chose Bangkok as Siam's new capital, the Grand Palace is the only remaining example of early Ratanakosin architecture—Rama II and III chose not to initiate any large-scale construction projects in the face of economic hardship. A primarily functional collection of buildings, the compound contains the Royal Thai Decorations and Coin Pavilion, the Museum of Fine Art, and the Weapons Museum.

Also worth checking out while in the capital is what is believed to be the world's largest golden teak-wood building. The three-story Vimanmek Palace was moved from Chonburi in the east to Bangkok's Dusit Palace, and contains jewelry and gifts given as presents from around the world.

Rama IV led the revival of palace construction in the second half of the 19th century, overseeing the building of several royal getaways. Perhaps the most impressive of these is Phra Nakhon Khiri in the southern town of Phetchaburi. Known locally as Khao Wang, the palace sits atop a mountain with wonderful panoramic views. Sharing its mountain home are various wat, halls, and thousands of macaque monkeys. Klai Kangwon in nearby Hua Hin is still used as a seaside getaway for the royal family and as a base when they visit southern provinces. Built in 1926 by Rama VI, the two-story concrete palace's name translates as Far From Worries and was built in the style of European châteaus.

Houses

Look around many Thai towns and you can see that this is a swiftly modernizing country: whitewashed apartment blocks, everything-under-one-roof shopping malls, and glass-fronted fast-food outlets are testaments to a growing economy and general rush to get ahead (as well as to the disappearance of Thailand's forests, which once provided cheap and sturdy building materials). However, peer a little closer and you will find Thailand's heritage staring right back at you.

Traditional Thai houses are usually very simple and essentially boil down to three basic components: stilts, a deck, and a sloping roof. Heavy, annual monsoon rains all over the country necessitate that living quarters be raised on stilts to escape flooding; in the dry season the space under the house is typically used as storage for farming equipment or other machinery. The deck of the house is essentially the living room—it's where you can find families eating, cooking, and just plain relaxing.

As with wats, it's often the roofs of houses that are the most interesting. Lanna-style (northern Thailand) roofs, usually thatched or tiled, are thought to have evolved from the Thai people's roots in southern China, where steeply pitched roofs would have been needed to combat heavy snows. Although there's no real chance of a snowball fight in Thailand, the gradient and overhang allows for quick runoff of the rains and welcome shade from the sun.

These basics are fairly uniform throughout the country, with a few small adjustments to accommodate different climates. For example, roofs are steepest in areas with more intense weather patterns, like the Central Plains, and northern Thai houses have smaller windows to conserve heat better.

VOCABULARY

Thai has several distinct forms for different social levels. The most common one is the street language, which is used in everyday situations. If you want to be polite, add "khrup" (men) or "kah" (women) to the end of your sentence. For the word "I," men should use "phom" and women should use "deeshan."

Note that the "h" is silent when combined with most other consonants (th, ph, kh, etc.). Double vowels indicate long vowel sounds (uu=oo, as in food), except for "aa," which is pronounced "ah."

BASICS

Hello/goodbye	Sa-wa-dee-khrup/kah.
How are you?	Sa-bai-dee-mai khrup/kah.
I'm fine.	Sa-bai-dee khrup/kah.
I'm very well.	Dee-mark khrup/kah.
I'm so so.	Sa-bai sa-bai.
What's your name?	Khun-chue-ar-rai khrup/kah?
My name is Joe.	Phom-chue Joe khrup.
My name is Alice.	Deeshan chue Alice kah.
It's nice to meet you.	Yin-dee-tee dai ruu jak khun khrup/kah.
Excuse me.	Khor thod khrup/kah.
I'm sorry.	Phom sia jai khrup (M)/Deeshan sia chy kah (F).
It's okay/It doesn't matter.	Mai pen rai khrup/kah.
Yes.	Chai khrup/kah
No.	Mai chai khrup/kah
Please.	Karoona
Thank you.	Khop-khun-khrup/kah.
You're welcome.	Mai pen rai khrup/kah.

GETTING AROUND

How do I get to . . .	Phom/chan ja pai . . . (name of the place) . . . dai yang-ngai khrup/kah?
. . . the train station?	sa-ta-nee rod-fai
. . . the post office?	pai-sa-nee
. . . the tourist office?	sam-nak-ngan tong-teow

. . . the hospital?	rong-pha-ya-barn
Does this bus go to?	Rod-khan-nee bpai-nai khrup/ka?
Where is . . .	Yoo tee-nai khrup/ka?
. . . the bathroom?	hong nam
. . . the subway?	sa-ta-nee rot-fai-tai-din
. . . the bank?	ta-na-kahn
. . . the hotel?	rong ram
. . . the store?	Rarn
. . . the market?	Talaat
Left	Sai
Right	Kwah
Straight ahead	trong-pai
Is it far?	Klai mai khrup/kah?

USEFUL PHRASES

Do you speak English?	Khun pood pa-sa ung-grid dai mai khrup/kah?
I don't speak Thai.	Phom/chan pood pa-sa Thai mai dai khrup/kah.
I don't understand.	Phom/chan mai cao jai khrup/kah.
I don't know.	Phom/chan mai roo khrup/kah.
I'm American/British.	Phom/chan pen American/Ung-grid khrup/kah.
I'm sick.	Phom/chan mai sa-bai khrup/kah.
Please call a doctor.	Choo-ay re-ak mor doo-ay khrup/kah.
Do you have any rooms?	Khun-mee hawng-mai khrup/kah?
How much does it cost?	Tao rai khrup/kah?
Too expensive.	pa-eng gern-pai
It's beautiful.	soo-ay.
When?	Muah-rai khrup/kah?
Where?	Tee-nai khrup/kah?
Help!	Choo-ay doo-ay!
Stop!	Yoot!

NUMBERS

1	nueng
2	song
3	sam
4	see
5	hah
6	hok
7	jet
8	bpaet
9	gao
10	sib
11	sib-et
12	sib-song
13	sib-sam
14	sib-see
15	sib-hah
16	sib-hok
17	sib-jet
18	sib-bpaet
19	sib-gao
20	yee-sib
21	yee-sib-et
30	sam-sib
40	see-sib
50	hah-sib
60	hok-sib
70	jet-sib
80	bpaet-sib
90	gao-sib
100	nueng-roy
101	nueng-roy-nung
200	Song-roy

DAYS AND TIME

Today	wannee
Tomorrow	proong nee
Yesterday	Muah-waan-nee
Morning	thawn-chao
Afternoon	thawn bai
Night	thorn muet
What time is it?	gee-mong-laew khrup/kah?
It's 2	song mong.
It's 4	see mong.
It's 2:30	song mong sarm-sip na-tee.
It's 2:45	song mong see-sip hah na-tee.
Monday	wan-jun
Tuesday	wan-ung-kan
Wednesday	wan-poot
Thursday	wan-phra-roo-hud
Friday	wan-sook
Saturday	an-sao
Sunday	an-ar-teet
January	ok-ka-ra-kom
February	oom-pha-parn
March	ee-na-kom
April	ay-sar-yon
May	rus-sa-pa-kom
June	e-tu-na-yon
July	a-rak-ga-da-kom
August	ing-ha-kom
September	un-ya-yon
October	hu-la-kom
November	rus-sa-ji-ga-yon
December	an-wa-kom

MENU GUIDE

The first term you should file away is "aroi," which means delicious. You'll no doubt use that one again and again, whether you're dining at food stalls or upscale restaurants. When someone asks "Aroi mai?" that's your cue to practice your Thai—most likely your answer will be a resounding "aroi mak" (It's very delicious).

Another useful word is "Kaw," which simply means "Could I have . . .?" However, the most important phrase to remember may be "Gin ped dai mai?" or "Can you eat spicy food?" Answer this one wrong and you might have a five-alarm fire in your mouth. You can answer with a basic "dai" (can), "mai dai" (cannot), or "dai nit noi" (a little). Most restaurants will tone down dishes for foreigners, but if you're visiting a food stall or if you're nervous, you can ask your server "Ped mai?" ("Is it spicy?") or specify that you would like your food "mai ped" (not spicy), "ped nit noi khrup/kah" (a little spicy), or if you have very resilient taste buds, "ped ped" (very spicy). Don't be surprised if the latter request is met with some laughter—and if all Thai eyes are on you when you take your first bite. Remember, water won't put out the fire; you'll need to eat something sweet or oily, or drink beer or milk.

food	a-harn
breakfast	a-harn chao
lunch	a-harn klang wan
dinner	a-harn yen
eat here	gin tee nee khrup/kah
take away	kaw glub baan khrup/kah
The check, please.	Check bin khrup/kah
More, please.	Kaw eek noi khrup/kah
Another please.	Kaw eek an khrup/kah
A table for two, please.	Kaw toh song tee khrup/kah
vegetarian	gin jay
spicy	ped
Is it spicy?	Ped mai?
not spicy	mai ped
a little spicy	ped nit noi khrup/kah
very spicy	ped ped
steamed	nueng
stir-fried	pad
stir-fried with ginger	pad king

stir-fried hot and spicy	pad ped
grilled (use phao instead when referring to seafood)	ping
deep-fried	tawd
boiled	thom

BASIC INGREDIENTS

rice	khao
steamed rice	khao suay
fried rice	khao pad
sticky rice	khao niao
rice with curry sauce	khao gaeng
rice porridge (usually for breakfast)	joke
noodles	kuay theow
egg noodles	ba mee
egg	kai
vegetables	pak
meat	nua
pork	moo
chicken	gai
roast duck	bped
beef	nua (same as meat)
fish	pla
prawns	gung
squid	pla muek
crab	bpu
vegetarian	jay
galanga (herb)	ka
ginger	king
lemongrass	ta krai
garlic	kratiam
fish sauce	nam pla

soy sauce	see-ew
chili paste (spicy dips usually accompanied by various vegetables)	nam prik
satay sauce (peanut base sauce made of crushed peanuts, coconut milk, chili, and curry)	satay

BEVERAGES

Thai iced tea (*cha yen*) is Thai black tea mixed with cinnamon, vanilla, star anise, often food coloring, and sometimes other spices. It's usually served cold, but you might see a hot version being enjoyed at the end of a meal. It's very sweet. Use caution when buying from food stalls that are working off a block of ice—though made with purified water, the ice is not always kept clean in transportation and storage.

ice	nam kang
iced coffee	ga-fare-yen
coffee with milk	ga-fare sai noom
whisky	wis-gee
tea	nam charr
plain water	nam plao
soda water	nam soda
a sweet drink brewed from lemongrass	nam takrai
vodka	what gaa
gin	gin

APPETIZERS

spring rolls	por pia tawd
panfried rice noodles	mee krob
spicy raw papaya salad	som tam
spicy beef salad	yum nua

MEAT AND SEAFOOD

chicken fried with cashew nuts	gai pad med mamuang himmapan
spicy chicken with basil	gai ka-prao
grilled chicken	gai yang

curry soup	gaeng ga-ree
green curry soup	gaeng keow wan
mild yellow curry soup	gaeng massaman
red curry soup	gaeng ped
hot and sour curry	kaeng som
minced meat with chilies and lime juice	larb
spicy salad	yum
panfried rice noodles	pad tai
"soup made with coconut cream, chicken, lemongrass, and chilies"	tom ka gai
lemongrass soup with shrimp and mushrooms	tom yum kung

FRUIT

banana	gluay
tamarind	ma karm
papaya	ma la gore
mango	ma muang
coconut	ma prao
mangosteen	mung kood
mandarin orange	som
pomegranate	tub tim

DESSERTS

dessert	ka nom
mango with sticky rice	kao niao ma muang
grilled bananas	gluay bping
coconut pudding	ka nom krog
rice based dessert cooked in coconut milk	kao larm
spicy raw papaya salad	som tam
spicy beef salad	yum nua

TRAVEL SMART THAILAND

GETTING HERE AND AROUND

Thailand is a long country, stretching some 1,100 miles north to south. Bangkok is a major Asian travel hub, so you'll likely begin your trip by flying into the capital. Relatively affordable flights are available from Bangkok to every major city in the country, and if you're strapped for time, flying is a great way to get around. But train travel, where available, can be an enjoyable sightseeing experience if you're not in a rush, and Thailand also has a comprehensive bus system.

I AIR TRAVEL

Bangkok is 17 hours from San Francisco, 18 hours from Seattle and Vancouver, 20 hours from Chicago, 22 hours from New York, and 10 hours from Sydney. Add more time for stopovers and connections, especially if you're using more than one carrier. Be sure to check your itinerary carefully if you are transferring in Bangkok—most low-cost carriers and domestic flights now operate out of Don Muang airport, while Suvarnabhumi airport remains the international hub. On popular tourist routes during peak holiday times, domestic flights in Thailand are often fully booked. Make sure you have reservations, and make them well in advance of your travel date. Be sure to reconfirm your return flight when you arrive in Thailand.

Airline Security Issues Transportation Security Administration. The TSA has answers for almost every question that might come up. ⊕ www.tsa.gov.

AIRPORTS

Bangkok remains Thailand's gateway to the world. The look of that gateway changed a couple of years ago with the opening of the new international Suvarnabhumi (pronounced *soo-wanna-poom*) Airport, 30 km (18 miles) southeast of town. The new airport quickly exceeded capacity, however, and Don Muang is

back in service: almost all budget airlines and domestic flights now operate out of Don Muang. Shuttle service is available between the two airports. Neither airport is close to the city, but both offer shuttle links and/or bus and taxi service throughout Bangkok. The smoothest ride to Suvarnabhumi is the BTS Skytrain, which now links the international airport with key areas in the city. Chiang Mai International Airport, which lies on the edge of that town, has a large new terminal to handle the recent sharp increases in national and regional air traffic. Taxi service to most hotels costs about B120 (about $4).

Perhaps Thailand's third-busiest airport (especially in high season) is the one at Phuket, a major link to the southern beaches region, particularly the islands of the Andaman Coast.

Bangkok Airways owns and runs the airports in Sukhothai, Trat, and Koh Samui. They have the only flights to these destinations, which can be expensive in high season. You also have to use the airport transport options they offer unless your hotel picks you up.

Airport Information Airports of Thailand. This website has information on the country's major airports, though much of it is in Thai. ⊕ www.airportthai.co.th. **Don Muang Airport** ⊕ www.donmuangairportonline.com. **Suvarnabhumi Airport** ⊕ www.suvarnabhumiairport.com.

GROUND TRANSPORTATION

At Suvarnabhumi, free shuttle buses run from the airport to a public bus stand, where you can catch a bus into the city. Many public buses stop near Don Muang; there's also a train stop across the highway from the airport, accessible by footbridge.

Meter taxis run between both airports and town and charge a B50 airport fee on top of the meter charge. Be sure to find the public taxi stand upon leaving either airport. Touts are notorious for approaching travelers in the airport and offering rides at rates that far exceed the norm. Taxis in town will often try to set a high flat fee to take you to the airport, though this is technically illegal. If you do talk a taxi driver into charging by the meter, expect a long, scenic trip to the airport.

Suvarnabhumi Airport offers six types of limousines for hire—visit the limo counter on Level 2 in the baggage claim hall.

If possible, plan your flights to arrive and depart outside of rush hours. A trip to Suvarnabhumi from the main hotel strip along Sukhumvit Road can take as little as 25 minutes if traffic is moving, but hours during traffic jams—the same goes for the Khao San Road area.

■TIP→ It helps to have a hotel brochure or an address in Thai for the driver. Also, stop at one of the ATMs in the arrival hall and get some baht before leaving the airport so you can pay your taxi driver.

INTERNATIONAL FLIGHTS

Bangkok is one of Asia's—and the world's—largest air hubs, with flights to most corners of the globe and service from nearly all of the world's major carriers, plus dozens of minor carriers. Most flights from the United States stop in Hong Kong, Tokyo, or Taipei on the way to Bangkok.

Delta and Japan Airlines (JAL) are both major carriers with hubs in the United States and offer daily flights between the United States and Thailand. JAL is one of the best options, with a flight time of 17 hours from Dallas including a stopover at Tokyo's Narita airport. East Coast travelers departing from New York or Washington, D.C., could also consider using British Airways or Virgin Atlantic/Thai Airways via London or Singapore Airlines from Newark via Amsterdam. From the West Coast, Thai Airways has connections from Los Angeles. Cathay Pacific often has good fares from San Francisco. Often the best prices can be found on

sites such as Kayak (⊕ *www.kayak.com*) or Vayama (⊕ *www.vayama.com*).

■TIP→ Many Asian airlines (Thai Airways, Singapore Airlines, Cathay Pacific, Malaysia Airlines) are rated among the best in the world for their service. They often have more comfortable seats, better food selections (still without extra charge), and more entertainment options than do most U.S.-based carriers. Many Asian airlines also allow you to change your bookings for free (or for a nominal charge) if done a week in advance. Lastly, tickets purchased from these carriers are generally no more expensive than those offered by U.S. carriers. And the extra creature comforts these airlines provide can leave you a little less frazzled when you reach your destination, ensuring that you don't spend half your vacation recovering from the trip over.

For years, Bangkok Airways offered the only direct flights between Bangkok and Siem Reap, Cambodia (home of Angkor Wat), with exorbitant prices. A cheaper alternative exists now: Cambodia Angkor Air. The airline flies throughout the region, as do several budget airlines, making short country-hopping excursions far more feasible than before.

Chiang Mai, Thailand's second-biggest city, is slowly becoming an important regional destination, and direct flights between here and Hong Kong, Singapore, Tokyo, Taipei, various points in China, Luang Prabang in Laos, and other Asian destinations may be available. However, these routes seem to change with the wind, so check before your trip. As Myanmar opens up, more travelers are adding that country to their regional itineraries. Several carriers—Thai, Bangkok Airways, Myanmar International—offer regular nonstop flights between Bangkok and Yangon, as does budget AirAsia.

Airline Contacts Asiana Airlines
☎ *800/227–4262* ⊕ *us.flyasiana.com*. **British Airways** ☎ *800/247–9297* ⊕ *www.britishairways.com*. **Cathay Pacific** ☎ *800/233–2742* ⊕ *www.cathaypacific.com*.

China Airlines ☎ 800/227–5118 ⊕ www.
china-airlines.com. **Delta Airlines** ☎ 888/750–
3284 for U.S. reservations, 800/658-228 for
international reservations ⊕ www.delta.com.
EVA Air ☎ 800/695–1188 ⊕ www.evaair.com.
Japan Airlines ☎ 800/525–3663 ⊕ www.jal.
com. **Korean Air** ☎ 800/438–5000 ⊕ www.
koreanair.com. **Lao Airlines** ☎ 21/212051
in Laos ⊕ www.laoairlines.com. **Malaysia Airlines** ☎ 800/552–9264 ⊕ www.
malaysiaairlines.com. **Royal Khmer Airlines**
☎ 855/23994888 ⊕ www.royalkhmerairlines.
com. **Singapore Airlines** ☎ 800/742–3333
⊕ www.singaporeair.com. **Thai Airways**
☎ 800/426–5204 ⊕ www.thaiairwaysusa.com.
United Airlines ☎ 800/864–8331 for U.S.
reservations, 800/538–2929 for international
reservations ⊕ www.united.com.

AIR TRAVEL WITHIN THAILAND

Thai Airways has by far the largest network of any airline in Thailand, and
connects all major and many minor destinations across the country. Bangkok
Airways, which bills itself as a luxury
boutique airline with comfy seats and
good food, covers many routes and is the
only airline to service Koh Samui, Trat,
and Sukhothai. Both Thai and Bangkok
Airways fly a mix of larger jet aircraft
and smaller turbo-props. For the last few
years, buying tickets on the Thai Airways
website was an act reserved for masoch-
ists; it can be easier and cheaper to go to
a travel agent to get Thai Airways tickets.
The websites of other Thai airlines generally work well for online bookings.

Budget airlines now cover Thailand's skies
and have dramatically lowered the cost
of travel. Best known are Nok Air (a sub-
sidiary of Thai Airways), Thai AirAsia,
and Orient Thai (parent company of the
now-defunct One-Two-Go, which was
grounded temporarily by the Thai government following a fatal crash in Phuket).

With budget carriers, you'll save the most
by booking online and as far in advance
as you can. There's a small fee for booking over the phone, and you may not get
an English-speaking operator. The airlines

keep their prices low by charging extra
for services like food—or not offering it
at all. They charge less for flights at odd
hours (often late in the day), and change
their schedules based on the availability of cheap landing and takeoff times.
AirAsia, generally the cheapest of the
budget carriers, seems to change its flight
times and routes every couple of months.
■**TIP→** Delays are more common the
later in the day you're flying, so if you
need to make an international connection, morning flights are a safer bet.

Regional Carriers AirAsia ☎ 02/515–9999
in Thailand ⊕ www.airasia.com. **Bangkok
Airways** ☎ 02/134–3960 in Thailand ⊕ www.
bangkokair.com. **JetStar Asia** ☎ 02/267–5125
in Thailand, 866/397–8170 from other countries ⊕ www.jetstar.com. **Nok Air** ☎ 02/900–
9955 ⊕ www.nokair.com. **Myanmar Airways
International** ⊕ maiair.com. **Orient Thai
Airlines** ☎ 1126 in Thailand, 662/229–4100
in other countries ⊕ www.orient-thai.com. **Silk
Airlines** ☎ 053/904985 in Thailand ⊕ www.
silkair.com. **Thai Airways** ☎ 02/288–7000
in Thailand ⊕ www.thaiairways.com. **Tiger
Airways** ☎ 800/852–7146 in Thailand ⊕ www.
tigerairways.com.

■ BUS TRAVEL

Thai buses are cheap and faster than
trains, and reach every corner of the
country. There are usually two to three
buses a day on most routes and several
(or even hourly) daily buses on popular routes between major towns. Most
buses leave in the morning, with a few
other runs spaced out in the afternoon
and evening. Buses leave in the evening
for long overnight trips. Overnight buses
are very popular with Thais, and they're
a more efficient use of time, but they do
crash with disturbing regularity and many
expats avoid them.

■**TIP→** Avoid taking private bus company
trips from the Khao San Road area. The
buses are not as comfortable as public
buses, they take longer, and they usually
try to trap you at an affiliated hotel once

you reach your destination. This is particularly the case for cross-border travel into Cambodia. There have also been many reports of rip-offs, scams, and luggage thefts on these buses over the years.

There are, generally speaking, three classes of bus service: cheap, no-frills locals on short routes that stop at every road crossing and for anyone who waves them down; second- and first-class buses on specific routes that have air-conditioning, toilets (sometimes), and loud chopsocky movies (too often); and VIP buses that provide nonstop service between major bus stations and have comfortable seats, drinks, snacks, air-conditioning, and movies (often starring Steven Seagal or Jean-Claude Van Damme). If you're setting out on a long bus journey, it's worth inquiring about the onboard entertainment—14 hours on a bus with continuous karaoke VCDs blasting out old pop hits can be torturous. Air-conditioned buses are usually so cold that you'll want an extra sweater. On local buses, space at the back soon fills up with all kinds of oversize luggage, so it's best to sit toward the middle or the front.

Bangkok has three main bus stations, serving routes to the north (Mo Chit), south (Southern Terminal), and east (Ekamai). Chiang Mai has one major terminal. All have telephone information lines, but the operators rarely speak English. It's best to buy tickets at the bus station, where the bigger bus companies have ticket windows. Thais usually just head to the station an hour before they'd like to leave; you may want to go a day early to be sure you get a ticket if your plans aren't flexible—especially if you hope to get VIP tickets. Travel agents can sometimes get tickets for you, but often the fee is more than half the cost of the ticket. All fares are paid in cash.

Many small towns don't have formal bus terminals, but rather a spot along a main road where buses stop. Information concerning schedules can be obtained from TAT offices and the bus stations.

▌CAR TRAVEL

Car travel in Thailand has its ups and downs. Major thoroughfares tend to be congested, but the limited number of roads and the straightforward layout of cities combine to make navigation relatively easy. The exception, of course, is Bangkok. Don't even think about negotiating that tangled mass of traffic-clogged streets. Hire a driver instead.

Cars are available for rent in Bangkok and in major tourist destinations. However, even outside Bangkok the additional cost of hiring a driver is a small price to pay for peace of mind. If a foreigner is involved in an automobile accident, he or she—not the Thai—is likely to be judged at fault, no matter who hit whom.

That said, car rental can be the most pleasant, affordable way to tour the country's rural areas.

If you do decide to rent a car, know that traffic laws are routinely disregarded. Bigger vehicles have the unspoken right of way, motorcyclists seem to think they are invincible, and bicyclists often don't look around them. Few Thai drivers go anywhere anymore without a cell phone stuck to one ear. ▌TIP➔ Drive very carefully, as those around you generally won't.

Police checkpoints are common, especially near international borders and in the restive south. You must stop for them, but will most likely be waved through.

Rental-company rates in Thailand begin at about $40 a day for a jeep or $50 for an economy car with unlimited mileage. It's better to make your car-rental reservations when you arrive in Thailand, as you can usually secure a discount.

Jeeps and other vehicles are widely available for rent from private owners in tourist spots—particularly beach areas—and prices generally begin at about $25 a day. But be wary of the renter and any contract you sign (which might be in Thai). Often these vehicles come with no insurance that covers you, so you are liable for any damage incurred.

You must have an International Driving Permit (IDP) to drive or rent a car in Thailand. IDP's are not difficult to obtain, and having one in your wallet may save you from unwanted headaches if you do have to deal with local authorities. Check the AAA website for more info as well as for IDPs ($15) themselves.

GASOLINE

A liter of gasoline costs close to B40. Many gas stations stay open 24 hours and have clean toilet facilities and minimarts. As you get farther away from developed areas, roadside stalls sell gasoline from bottles or tanks.

PARKING

You can park on most streets; no-parking areas are marked either with red-and-white bars on the curb or with circular blue signs with a red "don't" stroke through the middle. The less urban the area, the more likely locals will double- and triple-park to be as close as possible to their destination. Thai traffic police do "boot" cars and motorcycles that are improperly parked, though only when they feel like it. The ticketing officer usually leaves a sheet of paper with a contact number to call; once you call, he returns, you pay your fine (often subject to negotiation), and he removes the boot.

In cities the larger hotels, restaurants, and department stores have garages or parking lots. Rates vary, but count on B10 or more an hour. If you purchase something, parking is often free, but you must have your ticket validated.

ROAD CONDITIONS

Thai highways and town roads are generally quite good. Byways and rural roads range from good to indescribably bad. In rainy season expect rural dirt roads to be impassable bogs.

■ TIP→ Leafy twigs and branches lying on a road are not decorations but warnings that something is amiss ahead. Slow down and proceed with caution.

Thai traffic signs will be familiar to all international drivers, though most roads are marked in Thai. Fortunately, larger roads, highways, and tourist attractions often have English signs, too. Signs aren't always clear, so you may find yourself asking for directions quite often.

If you have a choice, don't drive at night. Motorists out after dark often drive like maniacs, and may be drunk. Likewise, if you have a choice, avoid driving during key holidays such as Songkran. The Bangkok newspapers keep tallies of road deaths during each big holiday, and the numbers are enough to frighten anyone off the highway. When you are driving anywhere in the country, at all times beware of oxcarts, cows, dogs, small children, and people on bikes suddenly joining the traffic fray.

ROADSIDE EMERGENCIES

Should you run into any problems, you can contact the Tourist Police at their hotline, 1155.

RULES OF THE ROAD

As in the United Kingdom, drive on the left side of the road, even if the locals don't. Speed limits are 60 kph (37 mph) in cities, 90 kph (56 mph) outside, and 130 kph (81 mph) on expressways, not that anyone pays much heed. If you're caught breaking traffic laws, you officially have to report to the police station to pay a large fine. In reality, an on-the-spot fine of B100 or B200 can usually be paid. Never presume to have the right of way in Thailand, and always expect the other driver to do exactly what you think they should not.

■ MOTORCYCLE TRAVEL

Many people rent small motorcycles to get around the countryside or the islands. ⚠ A Thai city is not the place to learn how to drive a motorcycle. Phuket in particular is unforgiving to novices—don't think of driving one around there unless you are experienced. Motorcycles skid easily on wet or gravel roads. On Koh Samui a sign posts the year's count of foreigners who never made it home from their vacations because of such accidents. In the past people often did not bother to wear a helmet in the evening, but government crackdowns have made it common practice to drive as safely at night as during the day. Shoes, a shirt, and long pants will also offer some protection in wrecks, which are common. When driving a motorbike, make sure your vehicle has a rectangular sticker showing up-to-date insurance and registration. The sticker should be pasted somewhere toward the front of the bike, with the Buddhist year in big, bold numbers. You can rent smaller 100cc to 125cc motorcycles for only a few dollars a day. Dirt bikes and bigger road bikes, 250cc and above, start at $20 per day.

Two-wheeled vacations are a growing segment of Thai tourism, especially in the north. With Thailand's crazy traffic, this is not a good option for first-time tourists to the area. That said, Golden Triangle Rider has a fantastic website (⊕ *www. gt-rider.com*) on biking in the area, with information on rentals and routes.

TAXI TRAVEL

Most Thai taxis now have meters installed, and these are the ones tourists should take. (However, the drivers of Chiang Mai's small fleet of "meter" taxis often demand flat fees instead. Bargain.) Taxis waiting at hotels are more likely to demand a high flat fare than those flagged down on the street. ■TIP➔ **Never enter any taxi until the price has been established or the driver agrees to use the meter.** Most taxi drivers do not speak English, but all understand the finger count. One finger means B10, two is for B20, and so on. Whenever possible, ask at your hotel front desk what the approximate fare should be. If you flag down a meter taxi and the driver refuses to use the meter, you can try to negotiate a better fare or simply get another taxi. If you negotiate too much, he will simply take you on a long route to jack the meter price up.

TRAIN TRAVEL

Trains are a great way to get around Thailand. Though they're a bit slower and generally more expensive than buses, they're more comfortable and safer. They go to (or close to) most major tourist destinations, and many go through areas where major roads don't venture. The State Railway of Thailand has four lines, all of which terminate in Bangkok. Hualamphong is Bangkok's main terminal; you can book tickets for any route in the country there. (Chiang Mai's station is another major hub, where you can also buy tickets for any route.)

TRAIN ROUTES

The Northern Line connects Bangkok with Chiang Mai, passing through Ayutthaya, Phitsanulok, and Sukhothai. The Northeastern Line travels up to Nong Khai, on the Laotian border (across from Vientiane), and has a branch that goes east to Ubon Ratchathani. The Southern Line goes all the way south through Surat Thani (get off here for Koh Samui) to the Malaysian border and on to Kuala Lumpur and Singapore, a journey that takes 37 hours. The Eastern Line splits and goes to both Pattaya and Aranyaprathet on the Cambodian border. A short line also connects Bangkok with Nam Tok to the west, passing through Kanchanaburi and the bridge over the River Kwai along the way. (There's no train to Phuket; you have to go to the Phun Phin station, about 14 km [9 miles] from Surat Thani and change to a bus.) ⚠ **The Southern Line has been attacked in insurgency-related violence. Check the security situation before booking a trip to the south.**

TICKETS AND RAIL PASSES

The State Railway of Thailand offers two types of rail passes. Both are valid for 20 days of unlimited travel on all trains in either second or third class. The cheaper of the two does not include supplementary charges such as air-conditioning and berths. Ask at Bangkok's Hualamphong Station for up-to-date prices and purchasing; if the train is your primary mode of transportation, it may be worth it. If you don't plan to cover many miles by train, individual tickets are probably the way to go.

Even if you purchase a rail pass, you're not guaranteed seats on any particular train; you'll need to book these ahead of time through a travel agent or by visiting the advance booking office of the nearest train station. Seat reservations are required on some trains and are strongly advised on long-distance routes, especially if you want a sleeper on the Bangkok to Chiang Mai trip. Bangkok to Chiang Mai and other popular routes need to be booked several days in advance, especially during the popular tourist season between November and January, as well as during the Thai New Year in April. Tickets for shorter, less frequented routes can be bought a day in advance or, sometimes, right at the station before departure. Most travel agencies have information on train schedules, and many will book seats for you for a small fee, saving you a trip to the station.

The State Railway of Thailand's rather basic website has timetables, routes, available seats, and other information, but no way to book tickets. The British-based website Seat 61 also has lots of helpful information about train travel in Thailand. Train schedules in English are available from travel agents and from major railway stations.

CLASSES OF SERVICE

Local trains are generally pretty slow and can get crowded, but you'll never be lonely! On some local trains there's a choice between second and third class.

Most long-distance trains offer second- or third-class tickets, and some overnight trains to the north (Chiang Mai) and to the south offer first-class sleeping cabins. First-class sleepers have nice individual rooms for two to four people, but they are increasingly rare. If you have the chance, splurging on a first-class overnight cabin can be a unique, almost romantic experience. You'd be hard-pressed to find a first-class sleeper cabin this cheap anywhere else in the world (B1,453 for a Bangkok to Chiang Mai ticket).

Second-class cars have comfy padded bench seats or sleeper bunks with sheets and curtains. Tickets are about half the price of first-class (B881, Bangkok to Chiang Mai), and since the couchettes are quite comfortable, most westerners choose these. Second class is generally air-conditioned, but on overnight journeys you have a choice of air-conditioning or fan-cooled cars. The air-conditioning tends to be freezing (bring a sweater and socks) and leave you dehydrated. Sleeping next to an open train window can leave you deaf and covered in soot. It's your choice. Third-class cars have hard benches and no air-conditioning, but are wildly cheap (B271, Bangkok to Chiang Mai).

Meals are served at your seat in first and second classes.

Information **Chiang Mai Railway Station** ☎ *053/244795.* **Hualamphong Railway Station** ☎ *1690 Railway call center.* **Seat 61** ⊕ *www.seat61.com/Thailand.htm.* **The State of the Railways of Thailand** ⊕ *www.railway. co.th/home/Default.asp?lenguage=Eng.*

▌ TUK-TUK TRAVEL

So-called because of their flatulent sound, these three-wheel cabs can be slightly less expensive than taxis, and are, because of their maneuverability, sometimes a more rapid form of travel through congested traffic. All tuk-tuk operators drive as if chased by hellhounds. Tuk-tuks are not very comfortable, require hard bargaining skills, are noisy, are very polluting, are very difficult to see out of if you are more than 4 feet tall, and subject you to the polluted air they create—so they're best used for short journeys, if at all. They are fun to take once, mildly amusing the second time, and fully unpleasant by the third.

If a tuk-tuk driver rolls up and offers to drive you to the other side of Bangkok for B20, think twice before accepting, because you will definitely be getting more than you bargained for. By dragging you along to his friend's gem store, tailor's shop, or handicraft showroom, he'll usually get a petrol voucher as commission. He'll tell you that all you need to do to help him put rice on his family's table is take a five-minute look around. Sometimes that's accurate, but sometimes you'll find it difficult to leave without buying something. It can be fun at times to go along with it all and watch everybody play out their little roles, but other times you really just want a ride to your chosen destination. Either way you end up paying for it.

ESSENTIALS

■ ACCOMMODATIONS

Nearly every town offers accommodation. In smaller towns hotels may be fairly simple, but they will usually be clean and inexpensive. In major cities or resort areas there are hotels to fit all price categories. The least-expensive places may have Asian toilets (squat type with no seat) and a fan rather than air-conditioning. Breakfast is sometimes included in the room rate at hotels and guesthouses.

During the peak tourist season hotels are often fully booked and rates are at their highest. During holidays, such as between December 30 and January 2, Chinese New Year (in January or February, depending on the year), and Songkran (the Thai New Year in April), rates climb even higher, and reservations are difficult to obtain on short notice. Weekday rates at some resorts are often lower, and virtually all hotels will discount their rooms if they are not fully booked. You often can get a deal by booking mid- to upper-range hotel rooms through Thai travel agents. They get a deeply discounted rate, part of which they then pass on to you.

Don't be reticent about asking for a special rate. Though it may feel awkward to haggle, because western hotel prices aren't negotiable, this practice is perfectly normal in Thailand. Often it will get you nothing, but occasionally it can save you up to 50% if you catch a manager in the right mood with a bunch of empty rooms. Give it a whirl. The worst they can say is "no."

The lodgings we list are the cream of the crop in each price category. We always list the facilities that are available, but we don't specify whether they cost extra; when pricing accommodations, always ask what's included and what costs extra. Hotels have private bath unless otherwise noted.

APARTMENT AND HOUSE RENTALS

It is possible to rent apartments or houses for longer stays in most places in Thailand. Bangkok, Chiang Mai, Phuket, and Pattaya in particular have large expat and long-term tourist communities. Also, many hotels and guesthouses are willing to offer greatly reduced rates for long-term guests. Agents are available in all big cities, and are used to helping foreigners. Often they will be the only way to find an affordable place quickly in a city like Bangkok. The *Bangkok Post, Chiang Mai CityLife* magazine, *Chiang Mai Mail, Phuket Gazette,* and *Pattaya Mail* are all good places to begin looking for agents or places for rent.

GUESTHOUSES

Though the "guesthouse" label is tacked onto accommodations of all sizes and prices, guesthouses are generally smaller, cheaper, and more casual than hotels. They are often family-run, with small restaurants. The least-expensive rooms often have shared baths, and linens may not be included. At the other end of the spectrum, $25 will get you a room with all the amenities—air-conditioning, cable TV, en-suite bathrooms, even Internet access—in just about every corner of the country. ■TIP➔ Even if you're traveling on a strict budget, make sure your room has window screens or a mosquito net.

HOTELS

Thai luxury hotels are among the best in the world. Service is generally superb—polite and efficient—and most of the staff speak English. At the other end of the scale, budget lodgings are simple and basic—a room with little more than a bed. Expect any room costing more than the equivalent of $25 a night to come with hot water, air-conditioning, and a TV. Southeast Asian hotels traditionally have two twin beds. Make sure to ask for one big bed if that is your preference, though this is often two twins pushed together.

Many hotels have restaurants and offer room service throughout most of the day and night. Many will also be happy to make travel arrangements for you—for which they receive commissions. Use hotel safe-deposit boxes if they are offered.

■ COMMUNICATIONS

INTERNET

Many hotels and guesthouses now offer Wi-Fi connections, though they can be slow and/or expensive. This is slowly starting to improve, and reliable Wi-Fi connections are becoming more common. Many hotels also have business centers that provide Internet access.

Outside of large hotels and business centers, the electrical supply can be temperamental. Surging and dipping power supplies are normal, and power outages are not unheard-of.

Even the smallest towns have Internet shops, and many have cafés that offer Wi-Fi (with purchase). Shops used to dealing with foreigners often will allow you to connect a laptop. Typical Internet prices in tourist areas range from about B20 to B60 per hour, sometimes more in coffee shops. Larger hotels and resorts usually charge a lot more, so make sure to ask in advance.

Contacts Cybercafes. This website lists more than 4,000 Internet cafés worldwide, though it is far from complete. ⊕ www.cybercafes.com.

PHONES

The country code for Thailand is 66. When dialing a Thailand number from abroad, drop the initial 0 from the local area code.

To call Cambodia from overseas, dial the country code (855) and then the area code, omitting the first 0. The code for Phnom Penh is 023; for Siem Reap it's 063. Unfortunately, Cambodia's international lines are sometimes jammed; booking and requesting information through

websites is consequently the best option. Almost all Internet shops offer overseas calling, which runs up to 50¢ a minute, depending on the location. Skype and other Internet calling options are often the easiest, cheapest methods for international calls—especially if you're in a place with free Wi-Fi.

To call Laos from overseas, dial the country code (856) and then the area code, omitting the first 0. The outgoing international code is 00, but IDD phones are rare. In cities, Wi-Fi is becoming more readily available and so, too, is the option of Skype.

CALLING WITHIN THAILAND

There are three major phone companies and at least four cell-phone operators. Payphones are available throughout the country, and they generally work, though long-distance calls can only be made on phones that accept both B1 and B5 coins.

Many hotels and guesthouses use cruddy third-party pay phones, which rarely work well but make extra money for the hotel. Avoid them if you can.

CALLING OUTSIDE THAILAND

The country code for the United States is 1.

To make overseas calls, you can use either your hotel switchboard—Chiang Mai and Bangkok have direct dialing—or the overseas telephone facilities at the central post office and telecommunications building. You'll find one in all towns.

MOBILE PHONES

If you have a GSM cell phone and your operator allows it, your phone may work in Thailand (but it's best to check with your provider before leaving home). However, the roaming charges can be deadly. Many travelers use their cell phones to send and receive text messages, a cheap way to stay in touch.

Alternatively, if you have a dual-, tri- or quad-band GSM phone (and it has not been locked to one number by your phone company), you can buy a SIM card (the chip that keeps your phone number and account) in Thailand. These are becoming more widely available, and often offered for free on arrival at Thai airports. Pop the SIM card into your phone, and have a local number while visiting. Then buy phone cards (available at all minimarts) in B100 to B500 denominations and pay for calls as you go, generally B3 to B10 a minute depending on the time of day and number you are calling. International calls will run about B5 to B40 a minute.

If your phone will not work in Thailand, you can buy a used phone at any cell phone shop, which are ubiquitous (all malls in Thailand have them). If for some reason you prefer to rent a cell phone, some options are:

Contacts Cellular Abroad. This company rents and sells GMS phones and sells SIM cards that work in many countries. ☎ 800/287–5072 ⊕ www.cellularabroad.com. **Mobal.** This outfit rents mobiles and sells GSM phones (starting at $7 a day) that will operate in 190 countries. Per-call rates vary throughout the world. ☎ 888/888–9162 ⊕ www.mobalrental.com. **Planet Fone.** Rent cell phones starting at $2.95 a day, or $21 a week. ☎ 888/988–4777 ⊕ www.planetfone.com.

▮ CUSTOMS AND DUTIES

THAILAND

Most people pass through customs at Suvarnabhumi without even so much as a glance from a customs officer. Officers worry more about people smuggling opium across borders than they do about an extra bottle of wine or your new camera. That said, if you're bringing any foreign-made equipment from home, such as cameras, it's wise to carry the original receipt with you or register it with U.S. Customs before you leave (Form 4457). Otherwise, you may end up paying duty on your return.

One liter of wine or liquor, 200 cigarettes or 250 grams of smoking tobacco, and all personal effects may be brought into Thailand duty-free. Visitors may bring in and leave with any amount of foreign currency; you cannot leave with more than B50,000 without obtaining a permit. Narcotics, pornographic materials, protected wild animals and wild animal parts, and firearms are strictly prohibited.

Some tourists dream of Thailand as a tropical paradise floating on a cloud of marijuana smoke—not so. Narcotics are strictly illegal, and jail terms for the transporting or possession of even the smallest amounts are extremely harsh.

If you purchase any Buddha images (originals or reproductions), artifacts, or true antiques and want to take them home, you need to get a certificate from the Fine Arts Department. Taking unregistered or unauthorized antiques out of the country is a major offense to the culture-conscious Thais. If you get a particularly good reproduction of an antique, get a letter or certificate from the seller saying it is a reproduction, or risk losing it on your way out of the country. Art or antiques requiring export permits must be taken to one of the museums listed here at least a week before the departure date. You will have to fill out an application and provide two photographs—front and side views—of the object as well as a photocopy of your passport information page.

Antiques Permits Chiang Mai National Museum ☎ 053/221308. **National Museum—Bangkok** ☎ 02/224–1333.

CAMBODIA AND LAOS

You are allowed to bring 200 cigarettes or the equivalent in cigars or tobacco and one bottle of liquor into Cambodia. You are not allowed to bring in or take out local currency, nor are you allowed to remove Angkor antiquities (even though, sadly, they can be found for sale in shops across Thailand). The export of other antiques or religious objects requires a permit. Contact your embassy for assistance in obtaining one before laying out money on an expensive purchase.

Tourists are allowed to bring up to one liter of spirits and two liters of wine into Laos, as well as 200 cigarettes, 50 cigars,

LOCAL DO'S AND TABOOS

THE KING

King Bhumibol Adulyadej has ruled Thailand for more than 60 years, and is revered by his people. Any insult against him is an insult against the national religion and patrimony. Lighthearted remarks or comparisons to any other person living or dead are also taboo. If you don't have something nice to say about the king, don't say anything at all.

GOOD MANNERS

Thais aim to live with a "cool heart" or *jai yen*—free from emotional extremes. Since being in a hurry shows an obvious lack of calm, they don't rush and aren't always punctual. Try to leave space in your itinerary for this relaxed attitude, since something will invariably happen to slow your progress.

Always remove your shoes when you enter a home. Do not step over a seated person's legs. Don't point your feet at anyone; keep them on the floor, and take care not to show the soles of your feet (as the lowest part of the body, they are seen by Buddhists as the least holy). Never touch a person's head, even a child's (the head is the most sacred part of the body in Buddhist cultures), and avoid touching a monk if you're a woman.

When possible do not give or receive anything with your left hand; use your right hand and support it lightly at the elbow with your left hand to show greater respect. Don't be touchy-feely in public. Speak softly and politely—a calm demeanor always accomplishes more than a hot-headed attitude. Displays of anger, raised voices, or even very direct speech are considered bad form.

Thais don't like anything done in twos, a number associated with death. Hence, you should buy three mangoes, not two; stairways have odd numbers of stairs; and people rarely want to have their photo taken if there are only two people.

OUT ON THE TOWN

Many Thais drink and smoke, but smoking is banned in many public buildings (including restaurants and bars). While you might spot a few drunken Thais stumbling about on a Saturday night, public drunkenness is not any more welcome here than it would be at home. Backpackers who flock to Thailand for cheap beer and beach parties rarely leave a favorable impression on the locals.

DOING BUSINESS

Thais are polite and formal in their business doings, employing the same sense of propriety as in everyday life. In professional settings, it is always best to address people with the courtesy title, *khun* (for males and females). As anywhere, greet a business associate with a Buddhist *wai* (hands clasped, head bowed.)

Business cards are hugely popular in Southeast Asia and it's a good idea to have some on hand. You can have them made quickly and cheaply in Thailand if necessary.

Local copy shops and business centers are about as common as Internet shops—ask around. In the cities, the nearest business-service center is likely a block or two away. Department stores such as Central (⊕ *www.central.co.th/index_en.html*) usually dedicate the majority of a floor to school supplies and business services.

or 250 grams of tobacco. Bringing in or taking out local currency is prohibited, as is the export of antiques and religious artifacts without a permit.

Note that the dissemination of foreign religious and political materials is forbidden, and you should refrain from bringing such materials into the country.

MYANMAR (BURMA)
Visitors to Myanmar are allowed to bring two bottles of liquor, 400 cigarettes, 100 cigars, 250 grams of tobacco and half a liter of perfume per person.

Thailand Contacts Thai Customs Department ⊕ *www.customs.go.th/wps/wcm/ connect/custen/home/homewelcome.*

U.S. Information U.S. Customs and Border Protection ⊕ *www.cbp.gov.*

▌ EATING OUT

Thai food is eaten with a fork and spoon; the spoon held in the right hand and the fork is used like a plow to push food into the spoon. Chopsticks are used only for Chinese food, such as noodle dishes. After you have finished eating, place your fork and spoon on the plate at the 5:25 position; otherwise the server will assume you would like another helping.

If you want to catch a waiter's attention, use the all-purpose polite word, *krup* if you are a man and *ka* if you are a woman. Beckoning with a hand and fingers pointed upward is considered rude; point your fingers downward instead.

MEALS AND MEALTIMES
Thai cuisine's distinctive flavor comes particularly from the use of fresh Thai basil, lemongrass, tamarind, lime, and citrus leaves. And though some Thai food is fiery hot from garlic and chilies, an equal number of dishes serve the spices on the side, so that you can adjust the incendiary level. Thais use *nam pla,* a fish sauce, instead of salt.

Restaurant hours vary, but Thais eat at all times of day, and in cities you will find eateries open through the night. In Thailand breakfast outside the hotel often means noodle soup or curry on the street (or banana pancakes in backpacker areas). Street vendors also sell coffee, although die-hard caffeine addicts may not get enough of a fix; Thai coffee isn't simply coffee, but a combination of ground beans with nuts and spices. If you're desperate, look for a western-style espresso machine or a Chinese coffee shop.

The lunch hour is long—roughly 11:30 to 2—in smaller towns and rural areas, a holdover from when Thailand was primarily a country of rice farmers and everyone napped during the hottest hours of the day.

Unless otherwise noted, the restaurants listed in this guide are open daily for lunch and dinner.

PAYING
Expect to pay for most meals in cash. Larger hotels and fancy restaurants in metropolitan areas accept some major credit cards, but they will often charge an extra 2% to 4% for the convenience. If you are at the restaurant of the hotel where you are staying, you can generally just add the bill to your room and leave a cash tip if you desire. Street vendors and small, local restaurants only accept cash. (⇨ *Tipping, below.)*

RESERVATIONS AND DRESS
Generally, reservations are not necessary at Thai restaurants, and even then are only accepted at the most expensive and popular ones.

Because Thailand has a hot climate, jackets and ties are rarely worn at dinner except in expensive hotel restaurants. Attire tends to fit the setting: People dress casually at simple restaurants and in small towns, but the Bangkok and Chiang Mai elite love dressing to the hilt for a posh night on the town. We mention dress only when men are required to wear a jacket or tie.

WINES, BEER, AND SPIRITS

Singha, Tiger, and Heineken are at the top end of Thailand's beer market, while Chang, Leo, and a host of other brands fight it out for the budget drinkers. It's also becoming more common to find imports such as Guinness, Corona, Budweiser, and the ever-popular Beerlao lining the shelves of cosmopolitan bars.

If you want to drink like the hip locals, don't bother with beer. Grab a bottle of whisky (Chivas Regal, Johnnie Walker, or the very affordable 100 Pipers) to mix with soda.

Rice whisky, which tastes sweet and has a whopping 35% alcohol content, is another favorite throughout Thailand. It tastes and mixes more like rum than whisky. Mekong and Sam Song are by far the most popular rice whiskies, but you will also see labels such as Kwangthong, Hong Thong, Hong Ngoen, Hong Yok, and Hong Tho. Thais mix their rice whisky with soda water, though it goes great with Coke, too.

Many Thais are just beginning to develop a taste for wine, and the foreign tipples on offer are expensive and generally mediocre. Thirty years ago the king first brought up the idea of growing grapes for wine and fruit through his Royal Projects Foundation. Now both fruit- and grape-based wines are made in various places upcountry. Their quality generally does not match international offerings (they tend to taste better if you don't think of them as wines, as such), but some are quite pleasant. International markets often carry them, and they can occasionally be found on the menus of larger restaurants.

▌ ELECTRICITY

The electrical current in Thailand is 220 volts, 50 cycles alternating current (AC); wall outlets take either two flat prongs, like outlets in the United States, or Continental-type plugs, with two round prongs, or sometimes both. Plug adapters are cheap and can be found without

WORD OF MOUTH

Was the service stellar or not up to snuff? Did the food give you shivers of delight or leave you cold? Did the prices and portions make you happy or sad? Rate restaurants and write your own reviews in Travel Ratings or start a discussion about your favorite places in Travel Talk on ⊕ *www. fodors.com.* Your comments might even appear in our books. Yes, you, too, can be a correspondent!

great difficulty in tourist areas and electrical shops. Outlets outside expensive international hotels are rarely grounded, so use caution when plugging in delicate electronic equipment like laptops.

In Cambodia, Laos, and Myanmar the electrical current is 220 volts AC, 50 Hz. In Laos, outside Vientiane and Luang Prabang, electricity is spotty, and even in Luang Prabang there are frequent late-afternoon outages in hot weather. In Myanmar, locals joke that Yangon (Rangoon) is so advanced, the city has power six times a day. Actually, many cities throughout the region suffer power outages as development and demand exceed supply.

Consider making a small investment in a universal adapter, which has several types of plugs in one lightweight, compact unit. Most laptops and mobile phone chargers are dual voltage (i.e., they operate equally well on 110 and 220 volts), so require only an adapter. These days the same is true of small appliances such as hair dryers. Always check labels and manufacturer instructions to be sure. Don't use 110-volt outlets marked "For shavers only" for high-wattage appliances such as hair dryers.

Contacts Steve Kropla's Help for World Traveler's. This website has information on electrical and telephone plugs around the world. ⊕ *www.kropla.com.* **Walkabout Travel Gear.** Walkabout Travel Gear has a good coverage of electricity under "adapters." ⊕ *www. walkabouttravelgear.com.*

▌ EMERGENCIES

Thais are generally quite helpful, so you should get assistance from locals if you need it. The Tourist Police will help you in case of a robbery or rip-off. The Tourist Police hotline is ☎ *1155.*

Many hotels can refer you to an English-speaking doctor. Major cities in Thailand have some of Southeast Asia's best hospitals, and the country is quickly becoming a "medical holiday" destination (i.e., a cost-effective place to have plastic surgery, dental work). However, if you are still wary about treating serious health problems in Thailand, you can fly cheaply to Singapore for the best medical care in the region.

Most nations maintain diplomatic relations with Thailand and have embassies in Bangkok; a few have consulates also in Chiang Mai.

In Bangkok U.S. Embassy ⊠ *95 Wireless Rd.* ☎ *800/13–202–2457* ⊕ *www.bangkok. usembassy.gov.*

In Chiang Mai U.S. Consulate ⊠ *387 Wichaynond Rd.* ☎ *053/107700* ⊕ *www. chiangmai.usconsulate.gov.*

In Phnom Penh, Cambodia U.S. Embassy ⊠ *No. 1 St. 96, behind Wat Phnom, Cambodia* ☎ *023/728–000* ⊕ *cambodia.usembassy.gov.*

In Vientiane, Laos U.S. Embassy ⊠ *BP 114, Rue Bartholonié, Laos* ☎ *21/267–000* ⊕ *www. laos.usembassy.gov.*

In Yangon, Myanmar U.S. Embassy Rangoon ⊠ *110 University Ave., Kamayut Township, Yangon (Rangoon), Myanmar* ☎ *536–509* ⊕ *burma. usembassy.gov.*

General Emergency Contacts Police ☎ *191.* **Tourist Police** ☎ *1155.*

▌ HEALTH

The most common vacation sickness in Thailand is traveler's diarrhea. You can take some solace in knowing that it is also the most common affliction of the locals. It generally comes from eating contaminated food, be it fruit, veggies, unclean water, or badly prepared or stored foods—really anything. It can also be triggered by a change in diet. Avoid ice unless you know it comes from clean water, uncooked or undercooked foods (particularly seafood, sometimes served raw in salads), and unpasteurized dairy products. ▮TIP➔ **Drink only bottled water or water that has been boiled for at least 20 minutes, even when brushing your teeth.** The water served in pitchers at small restaurants or in hotel rooms is generally safe, as it is either boiled or from a larger bottle of purified water, though if you have any suspicions about its origins, it's best to go with your gut feeling.

The best way to treat "Bangkok belly" is to wait for it to pass. Take Pepto-Bismol to help ease your discomfort and if you must travel, take Imodium (known generically as loperamide), which will immobilize your lower gut and everything in it. It doesn't cure the problem, but simply postpones it until a more convenient time. Note that if you have a serious stomach sickness, taking Imodium can occasionally intensify the problem, leading to a debilitating fever and sickness. If at any time you get a high fever with stomach sickness, find a doctor.

If you have frequent, watery diarrhea for more than two days, see a doctor for diagnosis and treatment. Days of sickness can leave you seriously dehydrated and weak in the tropics.

In any case, drink plenty of purified water or tea—chamomile, lemongrass, and ginger are good choices. In severe cases, rehydrate yourself with a salt-sugar solution (½ teaspoon salt and 4 tablespoons sugar per quart of water) or rehydration salts, available at any pharmacy.

SHOTS AND MEDICATIONS

■TIP➔ No vaccinations are required to enter Thailand, but we strongly recommend the hepatitis A vaccination, and you should make sure your tetanus and polio vaccinations are up-to-date, as well as measles, mumps, and rubella.

Malaria and dengue fever are also possible (though remote) risks as you move out of the main tourist areas. There is much debate about whether travelers headed to Thailand should take malarial prophylactics. Though many western doctors recommend that you take antimalarials, many health-care workers in Thailand believe they can do more harm than good: They can have side effects, they are not 100% effective, they can mask the symptoms of the disease if you do contract it, and they can make treatment more complicated. Consult your physician, see what medications your insurance will cover, and do what makes you feel most comfortable.

There are no prophylactics available for dengue fever. The best way to prevent mosquito-borne illness is to protect yourself against mosquitoes as much as possible (⬧ Specific Issues in Thailand, below).

According to the U.S. government's National Centers for Disease Control (CDC) there's also a risk of hepatitis B, rabies, and Japanese encephalitis in rural areas of Thailand, as well as drug-resistant malaria near the Myanmar border and in parts of Cambodia. In most urban or easily accessible areas you need not worry. However, if you plan to visit remote regions or stay for more than six weeks, check with the CDC's International Travelers Hotline.

Health Warnings National Centers for Disease Control & Prevention (CDC). ☎ 800/311–3435 international travelers' health line ⊕ www.cdc.gov/travel. **World Health Organization** (WHO). ⊕ www.who.int/en.

SPECIFIC ISSUES IN THAILAND

The avian flu crisis that ripped through Southeast Asia at the start of the 21st century had a devastating impact on Thailand. Poultry farmers went out of business, tourists stayed away, and each week brought news of a new species found to be infected (including isolated cases of humans contracting the virus). At this writing, the worry has died down as human cases continue to be exceedingly rare. That doesn't mean it won't flare up again, but note that all cases have occurred in rural areas outside the tourist track, and most infected people dealt with large numbers of dead birds.

Malaria and dengue fever, though more common than bird flu, are still quite rare in well-traveled areas. Malarial mosquitoes generally fly from dusk to dawn, while dengue carriers do the opposite; both are most numerous during the rainy season, as they breed in stagnant water.

The best policy is to avoid being bitten. To that end, wear light-color clothing and some form of insect repellent (preferably containing DEET) on any exposed skin when out and about in the mornings and evenings, especially during the rainy season. Make sure that hotel rooms have air-conditioning, mosquito nets over the bed, good screens over windows, or some combination thereof. You can also use a bug spray (available everywhere) in your room before heading out to dinner, and return to a bug-free room. ■TIP➔ The ubiquitous bottles of menthol-scented Siang Pure Oil both ward off mosquitoes and stop the incessant itching of bites.

Dengue fever tends to appear with a sudden high fever, sweating, headache, joint and muscle pain (where it got the name "breakbone fever"), and nausea. A rash of red spots on the chest or legs is a telltale sign. Malaria offers a raft of symptoms, including fever, chills, headache, sweating, diarrhea, and abdominal pain. A key sign is the recurrent nature of the symptoms, coming in waves every day or two.

Find a doctor immediately if you think you may have either disease. In Thailand, the test for both is quick and accurate and the doctors are much more accustomed to treating these diseases than are doctors in the United States. Left untreated, both diseases can quickly become serious, possibly fatal. Even when properly treated, dengue has a long recovery period, leaving the victim debilitated for weeks, sometimes months.

Reliable condoms in a variety of brands and styles are available at most 7-Elevens (yes, they have come to Thailand), supermarket, and minimart, usually near the checkout counter. ⚠ Be aware that a high percentage of sex workers in Thailand are HIV positive, and unprotected sex is extremely risky.

Do not fly within 24 hours of scuba diving, as you may risk decompression sickness, which is caused by tiny bubbles forming in the body if you move from deep water (higher pressure) to the surface (lower pressure) too quickly. The low pressure encountered while flying can trigger the sickness.

OVER-THE-COUNTER REMEDIES

Thailand has nearly every drug known to the western world, and many that aren't. All are readily available at pharmacies throughout the country. They are also often cheaper than in the United States and many drugs don't require the prescriptions and doctor visits needed at home. Be wary, however, of fake medications. It's best to visit larger, well-established pharmacies that locals vouch for.

▊ HOURS OF OPERATION

Thai business hours generally follow the 9 to 5 model, though the smaller the business, the more eclectic the hours. Nearly all businesses either close or slow to a halt during lunch hour—don't expect to accomplish anything important at this time. Many tourist businesses in the north and on the beaches and islands in the south often shut down outside the main tourist seasons of November through January and June through August.

Thai and foreign banks are open weekdays 8:30 to 3:30 (sometimes longer), except for public holidays. Most commercial concerns in Bangkok operate on a five-day week and are open 8 to 5. Government offices are generally open weekdays 8:30 to 4:30, with a noon to 1 lunch break. Generally speaking, avoid visiting any sort of office during the Thai lunch hour—or bring a book to pass the time.

Gas stations in Thailand are usually open at least 8 to 8 daily; many, particularly those on the highways, are open 24 hours a day. Twenty-four hour minimart-style gas stations are growing in popularity. Many also have fast-food restaurants and convenience stores.

Each museum keeps its own hours and may select a different day of the week to close (though it's usually Monday); it's best to call before visiting.

Temples are generally open to visitors from 7 or 8 in the morning to 5 or 6 pm, but in truth they don't really have set hours. If a compound has gates, they open at dawn to allow the monks to do their rounds. Outside of major tourist sights like Wat Po in Bangkok, few temples appear to have fixed closing times.

Most pharmacies are open daily 9 to 9. You'll find a few 24-hour pharmacies in tourist areas.

Most small stores are open daily 8 to 8, whereas department and chain stores are usually open from 10 until 10.

HOLIDAYS

Thailand: New Year's Day (January 1); Chinese New Year (January 23, 2012); Makha Bhucha Day (on the full moon of the third lunar month); Chakri Day (April 6); Songkran (mid-April); Labor Day (May 1); Coronation Day (May 5); Ploughing Day (May 9); Visakha Bucha (May, on the full moon of the sixth lunar month); Buddhist Lent day (July); Queen's Birthday (August 12); Chulalongkorn Memorial Day (October 23); King's

Birthday (December 5); Constitution Day (December 10). Government offices, banks, commercial concerns, and department stores are usually closed on these days, but smaller shops stay open.

Cambodia: New Year's Day (January 1); Victory Day (January 7); Meak Bochea Day (February); International Women's Day (March 8); Cambodian New Year (mid-April, depending on the lunar cycle); Labor Day (May 1); Visak Bochea (the Buddha's Birthday, early May); King Sihamoni's birthday (May 13–15); Visaka Bochea (May 19); Royal Ploughing Ceremony (May); International Children's Day (June 1); Queen Mother's birthday (June 18); Pchum Ben (September); Constitution Day (September 24); Anniversary of Paris Peace Agreement (October 23); Coronation Day (October 29); Sihanouk's birthday (October 31); Independence Day (November 9); Water Festival (November); Human Rights Day (December 10).

Laos: New Year's Day (January 1); Pathet Lao Day (January 6); Army Day (late January); International Women Day (March 8); Day of the People's Party (March 22); Lao New Year (Water Festival, April 13–15); Labor Day (May 1); Buddha Day (May 2); Children's Day (June 1); Lao Issara (August 13); Day of Liberation (October 12); National Day (December 2).

Myanmar: Independence Day (January 4); Union Day (February 12); Peasants' Day (March 2); Full Moon of Tabaung (March); Armed Forces Day (March 27); Thingyan (April); Burmese New Year (April); Labor Day (May 1); Buddha's Birthday (May 25); Martyr's Day (July 19); Buddhist Lent (July); Thadingyut, End of Lent (October); Full Moon of Thauzangmone (November): National Day (December 8); Christmas Day (December 25).

LANGUAGE

Thai is the country's national language. It has five tones, which makes it confusing to most foreigners. Thankfully, Thais tend to be patient with people trying to speak their language, and will often guess what you are trying to say, even if it's badly mispronounced. In polite conversation, a male speaker will use the word "krup" to end a sentence or to acknowledge what someone has said. Female speakers use "ka." It's easy to speak a few words, such as "sawahdee krup" or "sawahdee ka" (good day) and "khop khun krup" or "khop khun ka" (thank you).

With the exception of taxi drivers, Thais working with travelers in the resort and tourist areas of Thailand generally speak sufficient English to permit basic communication. If you find yourself truly unable to communicate something important to a Thai, he or she will often start grabbing people from the street at random to see if they speak English to help you out.

MAIL

Thailand's mail service is generally reliable and efficient. It is a good idea—and cheap—to send all packages registered mail. Major hotels provide basic postal services.

If something must get to its destination quickly, send it via FedEx, UPS, or DHL, which have branches in the major tourist centers. "Overnight" shipping time from Thailand to the United States via these international carriers is actually at least two working days. Expect to pay at least B800 to B1,000 for an "overnight" letter. Major offices of the Thailand Post also offer overseas express mail service (EMS), though it usually takes longer than an international carrier and costs nearly as much.

Letter, packet, and parcel rates through the Thailand Post are low—B30 for a letter to the United States, B25 for a letter to Europe. Allow at least 10 days for your mail to arrive. A sea, air, and land service (SAL) is available for less urgent mail at a much cheaper rate. Note it can take up to three months for packages to reach their destination by this method. Bangkok's central general post office on Charoen Krung (New Road) is open weekdays 8 to 8, weekends and public holidays 8 to 1. Upcountry post offices close at 4:30 pm.

Post offices in major towns are often quite crowded. Never go to a post office during lunch hour unless you bring a book and a mountain of patience.

If you need to receive mail in Bangkok, have it sent to you "poste restante" at the following address: Poste Restante, General Post Office, Bangkok, Thailand. There's a small charge for each piece collected. Thais write their last name first, so be sure to have your last name written in capital letters and underlined.

SHIPPING PACKAGES

Parcels are easy to send from Thailand via Thai Post. Rates vary according to weight, destination, and shipping style (air or surface). Expect to pay between B700 and B1,100 for a kilo package shipped by sea, which will take up to three months to arrive in the United States and another additional B300 to B350 per additional kilo. Most shops catering to tourists will offer to pack and ship your purchases anywhere in the world, usually at very reasonable rates. If you want to ship a larger piece, most furniture and antiques stores can help with freight shipping.

Although thousands of travelers have had no problems with the Thai Post, there has been at least one major incident of postal larceny in Chiang Mai, so if you're shipping something precious, consider paying the extra money to send it by an international courier like DHL, Federal Express, or UPS.

Express Services DHL Worldwide ⊠ *Asok BTS station, 236/7–8 Sukhumvit Rd., Between Sukhumvit 12–14, Bangkok* ☎ *02/345-5000.* **Federal Express** ⊠ *8th fl., Green Tower, Rama IV, Bangkok* ☎ *1782 Bangkok hotline,* *800/236–236 outside Bangkok.* **UPS** ⊠ *16/1 Sukhumvit Soi 44/1, Bangkok* ☎ *02/728-9000.*

∎ MONEY

It's possible to live and travel quite inexpensively if you do as Thais do—eat in small, neighborhood restaurants, use buses, and stay at non-air-conditioned hotels. Traveling this way, two people could easily get by on $50 a day or less. Once you start enjoying a little luxury, prices can jump as much as you let them. Imported items are heavily taxed.

Resort areas and Bangkok are much pricier than other parts of the country.

Prices throughout this guide are given for adults. Substantially reduced fees are almost always available for children, students, and senior citizens.

ATMS AND BANKS

Your own bank will probably charge a fee for using ATMs abroad, as will the foreign bank you use. Nevertheless, you'll usually get a better rate of exchange at an ATM than you will at a currency-exchange office or even when changing money in a bank.

∎TIP→ **PIN numbers with more than four digits are not recognized at ATMs in many countries. If yours has five or more, remember to change it before you leave.**

Thankfully, over the last few years, ATMs have sprouted like mushrooms around the country. Only smaller towns don't yet have them, and even that is changing. Most ATMs accept foreign bank cards; all pay in baht. As of this writing, most Thai ATMs charge extra B150 ($5) fee per transaction, plus your home bank may well add extra fees for using a foreign bank and/or converting foreign currency. Do contact your bank and ask about this before leaving to avoid any nasty billing surprises. Some Thai ATMs take Cirrus, some take Plus, some take both.

CREDIT CARDS

It's a good idea to inform your credit-card company and the bank that issues your ATM card before you travel, especially if you don't travel internationally very often. Otherwise, the credit-card company might put a hold on your card owing to unusual activity—not a good thing halfway through your trip. Record all your credit-card numbers—as well as the phone numbers to call if your cards are lost or stolen—in a safe place, so you're prepared should something go wrong. Both MasterCard and Visa have general numbers you can call (collect if you're abroad) if your card is lost, but you're better off calling the number of your issuing bank, since MasterCard and Visa usually just transfer you to your bank; your bank's number is usually printed on your card.

If you plan to use your credit card for cash advances, you'll need to apply for a PIN at least two weeks before your trip. Although it's usually cheaper (and safer) to use a credit card abroad for large purchases (so you can cancel payments or be reimbursed if there's a problem), note that some credit-card companies *and* the banks that issue them add substantial percentages to all foreign transactions, whether they're in a foreign currency or not. Check on these fees before leaving home, so there won't be any surprises when you get the bill.

■TIP➔ Before you charge something at shops, restaurants or hotels that cater to tourists, ask the merchant whether or not he or she plans to do a dynamic currency conversion (DCC). In such a transaction the credit-card processor (shop, restaurant, or hotel, not Visa or MasterCard) converts the currency and charges you in dollars. In most cases you'll pay the merchant a 3% fee for this service in addition to any credit-card company and issuing-bank foreign-transaction surcharges.

Dynamic currency conversion programs are becoming increasingly widespread. Merchants who participate in them are

> ### WORST-CASE SCENARIO
>
> Your money and credit cards have just been stolen. These days, this shouldn't destroy your vacation. First, report the theft of the credit cards. Then get any traveler's checks you were carrying replaced.
>
> **Overseas Citizens Services.** The U.S. State Department's Overseas Citizens Services can wire money to any U.S. consulate or embassy abroad for a fee of $30. Just have someone back home wire money or send a money order or cashier's check to the state department, which will then disburse the funds. ☎ 888/407-4747. **Western Union.** Western Union sends money almost anywhere. Have someone back home order a transfer online, over the phone, or at one of the company's offices. ☎ 800/325-6000 ⊕ www.westernunion.com.

supposed to ask whether you want to be charged in dollars or the local currency, but they don't always do so. And even if they do offer you a choice, they may well avoid mentioning the additional surcharges. The good news is that you *do* have a choice. And if this practice really gets your goat, you can avoid it entirely thanks to American Express; with its cards, DCC simply isn't an option.

Credit cards are almost always accepted at upper-end hotels, resorts, boutique stores, and shopping malls, and that list is slowly expanding. Expect to pay a 2% to 4% service charge. It is often illegal, but that's what everyone does.

Reporting Lost Cards American Express ☎ 800/528-4800 ⊕ www.americanexpress. com. **Diners Club** ☎ 800/2-DINERS ⊕ www. dinersclub.com. **MasterCard** ☎ 800/627-8372 in U.S., 800/11-887-0663 Thailand ⊕ www. mastercard.com. **Visa** ☎ 800/847-2911 in U.S., 800/11-535-0660 Thailand ⊕ www.visa.com.

CURRENCY AND EXCHANGE

The basic unit of currency is the baht. There are 100 satang to one baht. Baht come in six different bills, each a different color: B10, brown; B20, green; B50, blue; B100, red; B500, purple; and B1,000, beige. Coins in use are 25 satang, 50 satang, B1, B2, B5, and B10. The B10 coin has a gold-color center surrounded by silver.

Major hotels will convert traveler's checks and major currencies into baht, though exchange rates are better at banks and authorized money changers. The rate tends to be better in any larger city than up-country, and is better in Thailand than in the United States.

At this writing, B30 = US$1.

CURRENCY CONVERSION

Google. Google does currency conversion. Just type in the amount you want to convert and an explanation of how you want it converted (e.g., "14 Swiss francs in dollars"), and then voilà. ⊕ *www. google.com.*

Oanda.com. This website allows you to print out a handy table with the current day's conversion rates. ⊕ *www.oanda.com.*

XE.com. This website is a good currency conversion Web site. ⊕ *www.xe.com.*

∎TIP➔ Even if a currency-exchange booth has a sign promising no commission, rest assured that there's some kind of huge, hidden fee. (Oh, that's right. The sign didn't say no fee.) And as for rates, you're almost always better off getting foreign currency at an ATM or exchanging money at a bank.

∎ PACKING

Light cotton or other natural-fiber clothing is appropriate for Thailand; drip-dry is an especially good idea, because the tropical sun and high humidity encourage frequent changes of clothing. Avoid delicate fabrics, because you may have difficulty getting them laundered. A sweater is welcome on cool evenings or in overly air-conditioned restaurants, buses, and trains.

The paths leading to temples can be rough, so bring a sturdy pair of walking shoes. Slip-ons are preferable to lace-up shoes, as they must be removed before you enter shrines and temples.

Bring a hat and UV-protection sunglasses and use them. The tropical sun is powerful, and its effects long-lasting and painful.

Thailand has a huge range of clothing options at good prices, though it may be difficult to find the right sizes if you're not petite.

∎ PASSPORTS AND VISAS

U.S. citizens arriving by air need only a valid passport, not a prearranged visa, to visit Thailand for less than 30 days. Technically, travelers need an outgoing ticket and "adequate finances" for the duration of their Thailand stay to receive a 30-day stamp upon entry, but authorities in Bangkok rarely check your finances, unless you look like the sort who might sponge off Thai society. They do occasionally ask to see an outbound ticket. Scrutiny is inconsistent; authorities periodically crack down on long-term tourists who try to hang out in Thailand indefinitely by making monthly "visa runs" across international borders. ⚠ Tourists who arrive in Thailand by land from a neighboring country are now granted only a 14-day visa. As of this writing, tourists are not allowed to spend more than 90 days of any six-month period in Thailand, and immigration officials sometimes opt to count days and stamps in your passport.

If for whatever reason you are traveling to Thailand on a one-way ticket, airline officials might ask you to sign a waiver before allowing you to board, relieving them of responsibility should you be turned away at immigration.

If you want to stay longer than one month, you can apply for a 60-day tourist visa through a Royal Thai embassy. The embassy in Washington, D.C., charges about $40 for this visa, and you'll need to show them a round-trip ticket and a current bank statement to prove you can afford the trip. Be sure to apply for the correct number of entries; for example, if you're going to Laos for a few days in the middle of your stay, you'll need to apply for two Thailand entries.

Tourist visas can also be extended one month at a time once you're in Thailand. You must apply in person at a Thai immigration office; expect the process to take a day. You application will be granted at the discretion of the immigration office where you apply.

If you overstay your visa by a day or two, you'll have to pay a B500 fine for each day overstayed when you leave the country. Recently, immigration officials have reportedly started jailing foreigners who overstay by more than six weeks.

U.S. Passport Information U.S. Department of State ☎ 877/487-2778 ⊕ travel.state.gov/passport.

Visa Extensions Bangkok Immigration ✉ Soi Suan Phlu, South Sathorn Rd., Bangkok ☎ 02/141-9889. **Chiang Mai Immigration** ✉ 71 Airport Road, Chiang Mai ☎ 053/201-755. **Royal Thai Embassy in Washington, D.C.** ☎ 202/944-3600 ⊕ www.thaiembdc.org.

▮ RESTROOMS

Western-style facilities are usually available, although you still may find squat toilets in older buildings. For the uninitiated, squat toilets can be something of a puzzle. You will doubtless find a method that works best for you, but here's a general guide: squat down with feet on either side of the basin and use one hand to keep your clothes out of the way and the other for balance or, if you're really good, holding your newspaper. The Thai version of a bidet is either a hose or a big tank of water with a bowl. If you've had the foresight to bring tissues with you, throw the used paper into the basket alongside the basin. Finally, pour bowls of water into the toilet to flush it—and after thoroughly washing your hands, give yourself a pat on the back. Except at plusher hotels and restaurants, plumbing in most buildings is archaic, so resist the temptation to flush your paper unless you want to be remembered as the foreigner who ruined the toilet.

Find a Loo The Bathroom Diaries. This website is flush with unsanitized info on restrooms the world over—each one located, reviewed, and rated. ⊕ www.thebathroomdiaries.com.

▮ SAFETY

You should not travel in the four southern provinces closest to the Malaysian border: Yala, Pattani, Songkhla, and Narathiwat. A low-grade and seemingly endless insurgency there, which began in 2004, has led to the deaths of more than 5,000, with thousands more injured. Although the insurgents originally targeted government institutions and officials, they have also bombed tourist centers, shopping malls, restaurants, trains, and the airport at Hat Yai. Fear permeates both Buddhist and Muslim communities in these southern provinces; often locals have no idea who is attacking or why. Witnesses to drive-bys and bombings are afraid to speak. Residents avoid driving at night, shops close early, and southern towns turn eerily quiet by sundown.

In spring 2010 political demonstrations in Bangkok resulted in the worst outbreaks of violence in decades. At this writing, the political situation remains tenuous, though day-to-day life in Thailand is generally not affected. Stay informed about local developments as best you can, and determine whether the possible dangers make you too uneasy to travel or stay in Thailand. The *Bangkok Post* (⊕ www.bangkokpost.com) and the *Nation* (⊕ www.nationmultimedia.com) are the best sources of local news.

Thailand is generally a safe country, and millions of foreigners visit each year without incident. That said, every year a few tourists are attacked or raped and murdered, generally either in Bangkok or in the southern beaches regions. Be careful at night, particularly in poorly lighted areas or on lonely beaches. Follow other normal precautions: watch your valuables in crowded areas and lock your hotel rooms securely. Thai crooks generally try to relieve you of cash through crimes of convenience or negligence, not violence.

Credit-card scams—from stealing your card to swiping it several times when you use it at stores—are a frequent problem. Don't leave your wallet behind when you go trekking, and make sure you keep an eye on the card when you give it to a salesperson.

■ TIP➔ A great little invention is the metal doorknob cup that can be found at Thai hardware shops. It covers your doorknob and locks it in place with a padlock, keeping anyone from using a spare key or even twisting the knob to get into your room. A good B300 investment, it's usable anywhere.

Guesthouses also offer commission for customers brought in by drivers, so be wary of anyone telling you that the place where you booked a room has burned down overnight or is suddenly full. Smile and be courteous, but be firm about where you want to go. If the driver doesn't immediately take you where you want to go, get out and get another taxi.

Watch out for scams while shopping. Bait and switch is common, as is trying to pass off reproductions as authentic antiques. True antiques and artifact vendors will gladly help you finish the necessary government paperwork to take your purchase home. Keep in mind that authentic Thai or other Southeast Asian antiques in Thailand are usually stunningly expensive. Thais, Chinese, Malaysians, and Singaporeans are all fanatical collectors themselves, and pay as much as any western buyer. If you think you're getting a super deal on a Thai antique, think twice.

Thailand offers many adventurous ways to spend your days, few of which include the safety provisions demanded in western countries. Motorcycle wrecks are a common way to cut a vacation tragically short.

Thailand's most famous danger comes from the ocean. The Asian tsunami hit the Andaman coast in December 2004 and killed more than 5,300 people in Thailand. Reports from the areas hit show that many people could have been saved if they had known how to recognize the signs of an impending tsunami, or if an evacuation plan had been in place. Tsunamis are rare and very unpredictable. It's highly unlikely you'll experience one, but it pays to be prepared. If you plan to stay in a beach resort, ask if they have a tsunami plan in place, and ask what it is. If you feel an earthquake, leave any waterside area. ⚠ Pay attention to the ocean: if you see all of the water race off the beach, evacuate immediately and head for high ground. A tsunami could be only minutes away. Remember, a tsunami is a series of waves that could go on for hours. Do not assume it is over after the first wave.

⚠ Thai beaches almost never have lifeguards, but that doesn't mean they don't have undertows or other dangers.

FEMALE TRAVELERS

Foreign women in Thailand get quite a few stares, and Thai women as often as Thai men will be eager to chat and become your friend. Although there's no doubt that attitudes are changing, traditional Thai women dress and act modestly, so loud or overly confident behavior from a foreign woman can be a shock to both men and women alike. It's also worth noting that Thai men often see foreign women as something exotic. If you're being subjected to unwelcome attention, be firm, but try to stay calm—"losing face" is a big concern among Thai men, and embarrassing them (even if it's deserved) can have ugly repercussions.

General Information U.S. Department of State ⊕ www.travel.state.gov.

Safety Transportation Security Administration (TSA). ⊕ www.tsa.gov.

▋ TAXES

A 7% (and sometimes more) Value Added Tax (V.A.T.) is built into the price of all goods and services, including restaurant meals. You can reclaim some of this tax on souvenirs and other high-price items purchased at stores that are part of the V.A.T. refund program at the airport upon leaving the country. You cannot claim the V.A.T. refund when leaving Thailand by land at a border crossing. Shops that offer this refund will have a sign displayed; ask shopkeepers to fill out the necessary forms and make sure you keep your receipts. You'll have to fill out additional forms at the airport.

V.A.T. refund guidelines are particular. The goods must be purchased from stores displaying the "V.A.T. Refund for Tourists" sign. Purchases at each shop you visit must total more than B2,000 before they can fill out the necessary forms. The total amount claimed for refund upon leaving the country cannot be less than B5,000. You must depart the country from an international airport, where you finish claiming your refund at the V.A.T. Refund Counter—allow an extra hour at the airport for this process. You cannot claim V.A.T. refunds for gemstones.

For refunds less than B30,000 you can receive the money in cash at the airport, or have it wired to a bank account or to a credit card for a B100 fee. Refunds over B30,000 are paid either to a bank account or credit card for a B100 fee.

▋ TIME

Thailand is 7 hours ahead of Greenwich Mean Time. It's 12 hours ahead of New York, 15 hours ahead of Los Angeles, 7 hours ahead of London, and 3 hours behind Sydney.

Time Zones Timeanddate.com. Timeanddate.com can help you figure out the correct time anywhere. ⊕ www.timeanddate.com/worldclock.

▋ TIPPING

Tipping is not a local custom, but it is expected of foreigners, especially at larger hotels and restaurants and for taxi rides. If you feel the service has been less than stellar, you are under no obligation to leave a tip, especially with crabby cabbies.

In Thailand tips are generally given for good service, except when a price has been negotiated in advance. If you hire a private driver for an excursion, do tip him. With metered taxis in Bangkok, however, the custom is to round the fare up to the nearest B5. Hotel porters expect at least a B20 tip, and hotel staff who have given good personal service are usually tipped. A 10% tip is appreciated at a restaurant when no service charge has been added to the bill.

▋ VISITOR INFO

ONLINE TRAVEL TOOLS

All About Thailand Sites worth checking out are: ⊕ www.discoverythailand.com and ⊕ www.sawadee.com.

Visitor Information Tourism Authority of Thailand (TAT). Tourism Authority of Thailand (TAT) is a great place to begin research. ☎ 1672 Thailand contact center, 323/461–9814 in Los Angeles, 212/432–0433 in New York ⊕ www.tourismthailand.org.

INDEX

PHOTO CREDITS

Front cover: Chederros/Nomad/age fotostock [Description: Floating market, Thailand]. Back cover (from left to right): Dudareu Mikhail/Shutterstock; Olives Jean-Michel/Shutterstock; Andy Lim/Shutterstock. Spine: Chaloemphan/Shutterstock. 1, Michael Yamashita/Aurora Photos. 2, Steven Allan/iStockphoto. 5. José Fuste Raga/age fotostock. Chapter 1: Experience Thailand: 10-11, Ingolf Pompe 17 / Alamy. 12 and 13 (left), SuperStock/age fotostock. 13 (right), Sylvain Grandadam/age fotostock. 16, Travelscape Images / Alamy. 17 (left), SuperStock/age fotostock. 17 (right), Kevin O'Hara/age fotostock. 18 and 19, Dave Stamboulis. 20 (left), iNNOCENt/Shutterstock. 20 (center), Christine Gonsalves/Shutterstock. 20 (top right), John Hemmings/Shutterstock. 20 (bottom right), Shenval / Alamy. 21 (top left), sippakorn/Shutterstock. 21 (center), Frank van den Bergh/iStockphoto. 21 (right), Bartlomiej K. Kwieciszewski/Shutterstock. 21 (bottom left), siambizkit/Shutterstock. 22 and 23 (left), Tourism Authority of Thailand. 23 (right), Phil Date/Shutterstock. 24, Bruno Morandi/age fotostock. 25 (left), Ben Heys/Shutterstock. 25 (right), Cris Haigh / Alamy. 26, Hemis / Alamy. 28, Dave Stamboulis. 30, Cojocaru Emanuela/Shutterstock. 31(left), pambrick, fodors.com member. 31 (right), Dave Stamboulis. 32, Muellek/Shutterstock. 33, North Wind Picture Archives/Alamy. 34 (left), Alvaro Leiva/age fotostock. 34 (top right), Thomas Cockrem/Alamy. 34 (bottom right), Genevieve Dietrich/Shutterstock. 35 (left), Juha Sompinmäki/Shutterstock. 35 (top right), Thomas Cockrem/Alamy. 35 (bottom right), Bryan Busovicki/Shutterstock. 36 (left), Mary Evans Picture Library/Alamy. 36 (top right), Content Mine International/Alamy. 37 (left), Sam DCruz/Shutterstock. 37 (top right), Newscom. 37 (bottom right), Ivan Vdovin/age fotostock. 38 (left and top right), Thor Jorgen Udvang/Shutterstock. 38 (bottom right), AFP/Getty Images/Newscom. Chapter 2: Bangkok: 39, Angelo Cavalli/age fotostock. 40, Marco Simoni/age fotostock. 41 (top), Steve Silver/age fotostock. 41 (bottom), Peter Hooree/Alamy. 42, jaume/Shutterstock. 54-55, Chris L Jones/ Photolibrary.com. 56 (top), Gina Smith/Shutterstock. 56 (bottom left), PCL/Alamy. 56 (bottom right), John Hemmings/Shutterstock. 58, Andy Lim/Shutterstock. 59 (top left), do_ok/Shutterstock. 59 (center left), Heinrich Damm. 59 (bottom left), Steve Vidler/eStockphoto. 59 (right), Plotnikoff/Shutterstock. 60 (top), P. Narayan/age fotostock. 60 (bottom), Dave Stamboulis. 61, Wayne Planz/Shutterstock. 77, Travel Pix Collection/age fotostock. 78 (top), Juha Sompinmäki/Shutterstock. 78 (bottom), SuperStock/age fotostock. 79 (top), BlueMoon Stock/Alamy. 79 (2nd from top), John Lander/Alamy. 79 (3rd from top), kd2/Shutterstock. 79 (bottom), Mireille Vautier/Alamy. 80 (top), David Kay/Shutterstock. 80 (center), ARCO/I Schulz/age fotostock. 80 (bottom), jamalludin/Shutterstock. 86, Songchai W/Shutterstock. 103 (top), The Peninsula Bangkok. 103(middle left), Tibor Bognar / Alamy. 103 (middle right), LOOK Die Bildagentur der Fotografen GmbH / Alamy. 103 (bottom left), 2007 Shangri-La Hotels and resorts. 103(bottom right), Hilton Hotels Corporation. 111, Ingolf Pompe 6 / Alamy. 116, Luca Invernizzi Tettoni/Tips Italia/ photolibrary.com. 118, Dave Stamboulis. 127, Tourism Authority of Thailand. Chapter 3: Around Bangkok: 129, Jon Arnold Images / Alamy. 130 (top), Steve Raymer/age fotostock. 130(center), Richard Wainscoat / Alamy. 130 (bottom), Can Sengunes / Alamy. 131, Jeremy Horner / Alamy. 132, Olympus/Shutterstock. 139, Juriah Mosin/Shutterstock. 140 (top right), Ian Trower/Alamy. 140 (top left), Andy Lim/Shutterstock. 140 (bottom left), Elena Elisseeva/Shutterstock. 140 (bottom right), Robert Fried/Alamy. 141 (top), Juriah Mosin/Shutterstock. 141 (bottom), Chris Howey/Shutterstock. 142 (top), Asia/Alamy. 142 (bottom), Ronald Sumners/Shutterstock. 143, dbimages/Alamy. 153, Denis Babenko/Shutterstock. 162, Tourism Authority of Thailand. Chapter 4: The Gulf Coast Beaches: 169, travelstock44 / Alamy. 171 (left), Angelo Cavalli/age fotostock. 171 (right), Craig Lovell/Alamy. 172, Ozerov Alexander/Shutterstock. 184-85, José Fuste Raga/age fotostock. 187 (left), Gonzalo Azumendi/age fotostock. 187 (right), LOOK Die Bildagentur der Fotografen GmbH/Alamy. 189 (left), Gavriel Jecan/age fotostock. 189 (right), Dave Stamboulis. 197, Dave Stamboulis. 205, Chiva-Som International. 210, dave smurthwaite/iStockphoto. 214, GUIZIOU Franck/age fotostock. 225, aragami12345s/Shutterstock. 230, Ozerov Alexander/Shutterstock. Chapter 5: Phuket And The Andaman Coast: 233, Efired/Shutterstock. 234, Phaitoon Sutunyawatchai/Shutterstock. 235 (top), Ozerov Alexander/Shutterstock. 235 (bottom left), anekoho/Shutterstock. 235 (bottom right), Banana Republic images/Shutterstock. 236, Chie Ushio. 237 (top), Dave Stamboulis. 237 (bottom), William Berry/Shutterstock. 238, Stephane Bidouze/Shutterstock. 257, Abigail Silver/TAT. 261, Dave Stamboulis. 267, Dave Stamboulis. 275, Pichugin Dmitry/Shutterstock. 283, OM3/age fotostock. 296, Andy Lim/Shutterstock. Chapter 6: Chang Mai: 301, Gonzalo Azumendi/age fotostock. 302 (top), Blanscape/Shutterstock. 302 (bottom), hanging pixels/Shutterstock. 303 (top), stoykovic/Shutterstock. 303 (bottom), Brukenkam/Shutterstock. 304, 501room/Shutterstock. 312, Muellek/Shutterstock. 317, Jean Du Boisberranger / Hemis.fr /Aurora Photos. 332, Four Seasons Hotels and Resorts. 342-43, Dave Stamboulis. 344 (top and 2nd from top), wikipedia.org. 344 (3rd from top), mediacolor's/Alamy. 344 (4th from top), Dave Stamboulis. 344 (bottom), Hemis/Alamy. 345 (top), Dave Stamboulis. 345 (center), Bryan Busovicki/Shutterstock. 345 (bottom), David Bleeker

Photography.com/Alamy. 352, TC, fodors.com member. Chapter 7: Northern Thailand: 357, Gonzalo Azumendi/age fotostock. 358, MERVYN REES / Alamy. 359, Angelo Cavalli/age fotostock. 360, Dave Stamboulis / Alamy. 361(top), kentoh/Shutterstock. 361 (bottom), Andrea Skjold/Shutterstock. 362, Vitaly Maksimchuk/Shutterstock. 374, David South / Alamy. 394, Raffaele Meucci/age fotostock. 395, Stuart Pearce/age fotostock. 396 (top and bottom), SuperStock/age fotostock. 397 (top), John Arnold Images Ltd/Alamy. 397 (bottom), KLJ Photographic Ltd/iStockphoto. 398 (top), SuperStock/age fotostock. 398 (bottom), Anders Ryman/Alamy. 399 (top), Val Duncan/Kenebec Images/Alamy. 399 (bottom), Simon Podgorsek/iStockphoto. 400, Robert Fried/Alamy. 407, Valery Shanin/Shutterstock. 418, Luciano Mortula/Shutterstock. 420, Juha Sompinmäki/Shutterstock. 421 (top), ChieUshio. 421 (center), Khoo Si Lin/Shutterstock. 421 (bottom), N. Frey Photography/Shutterstock. 422,Idealink Photography/Alamy. 423, Joel Blit/Shutterstock. 424 (top), David Halbakken/Alamy. 424 (bottom), SteveSPF/Shutterstock. 425 (left), javarman/Shutterstock. 425 (top right), qingqing/Shutterstock. 425 (bottom right), Michele Falzone/Alamy. 426 (left), J Marshall - Tribaleye Images/Alamy. 426 (top right), Julien Grondin/Shutterstock. 426 (bottom right), Juha Sompinmäki/Shutterstock. 427 (left), Julien Grondin/Shutterstock. 427 (top right), Jon Arnold Images Ltd/Alamy. 427 (bottom right), hfng/Shutterstock. Chapter 8: Cambodia: 435, Atlantide S.N.C./age fotostock. 436 (top), Roger Hutchings / Alamy. 436 (bottom), Gavin Hellier/age fotostock. 437, f1 online / Alamy. 438, isaxar/Shutterstock. 449, Luciano Mortula/Shutterstock. 461, Ryan Fox/age fotostock. 470, Evan Wong/Shutterstock. 479, Ben Heys/Shutterstock. 481, Linga Bar. 484-85, Roy Garnier/Alamy. 486, José Fuste Raga/age fotostock. 487 (top), Luciano Mortula/iStockphoto. 487 (bottom), Bruno Morandi/age fotostock. 488 (top right), Tito Wong/Shutterstock. 488 (left), Danita Delimont/Alamy. 488 (bottom right) and 489, Craig Lovell/Eagle Visions Photography/Alamy. 490 (top), Jordí Camí/age fotostock. 490 (bottom), 491, Brianna May/iStockphoto. 492 (top), R. Matina/age fotostock. 492 (bottom), Vladimir Renard/wikipedia.org. 493 (top), Paul Panayiotou/Alamy. 493 (bottom), Bernard O'Kane/Alamy. 494, Joris Van Ostaeyen/iStockphoto. 495 (top), Robert Preston Photography/Alamy. 495 (bottom), Jie Xu/iStockphoto. 503, Vladimir Korostyshevskiy/Shutterstock. Chapter 9: Laos: 509, MOB IMAGES / Alamy. 510 (top), Henry Westheim Photography / Alamy. 510 (bottom), Ron Yue / Alamy. 511, Travel Ink/ Alamy. 512, Galyna Andrushko/Shutterstock. 522, luha sompinmaki/Shutterstock. 530, Lucid Images/age fotostock. 533, WitthayaP/Shutterstock. 547, Angelo Cavalli/age fotostock. 555, Dave Stamboulis. 563, Dave Stamboulis. 568, Gautier Willaume/iStockphoto. Chapter 10: Myanmar: 573, tacud/Shutterstock. 574 (top), Matej Hudovernik/Shutterstock. 574 (middle left), gnomeandi/Shutterstock. 574 (middle right), JM Travel Photography/Shutterstock. 574 (bottom), GunnerL/Shutterstock. 576, Bule Sky Studio/Shutterstock. 581, Juriah Mosin/Shutterstock. 585, Ko.Yo/Shutterstock. 596, Chantal de Bruijne/Shutterstock. 604, Chantal de Bruijne/Shutterstock. 607, lunapiena/Shutterstock. 613, Masterlu I Dreamstime.com.

NOTES

NOTES